Sarah J. B. Hale, Eliza Acton

Modern Cookery in All Its Branches

embracing a series of plain and simple instructions to private families and others

Sarah J. B. Hale, Eliza Acton

Modern Cookery in All Its Branches
embracing a series of plain and simple instructions to private families and others

ISBN/EAN: 9783337091576

Printed in Europe, USA, Canada, Australia, Japan

Cover: Foto ©Andreas Hilbeck / pixelio.de

More available books at **www.hansebooks.com**

MODERN COOKERY

IN ALL ITS BRANCHES.

MODERN COOKERY

IN ALL ITS BRANCHES:

EMBRACING A SERIES OF PLAIN AND SIMPLE INSTRUCTIONS
TO PRIVATE FAMILIES AND OTHERS, FOR THE CAREFUL
AND JUDICIOUS PREPARATION OF EVERY VARIETY
OF FOOD AS DRAWN FROM PRACTICAL
OBSERVATION AND EXPERIENCE.

BY MISS ELIZA ACTON.

WITH DIRECTIONS FOR SETTING OUT AND ORNAMENTING THE TABLE,
CARVING, RELATIVE DUTIES OF MISTRESS AND MAID, TO., &c.

THE WHOLE CAREFULLY REVISED

By MRS. S. J. HALE.

Illustrated with numerous Engravings.

PHILADELPHIA:
JOHN E. POTTER & CO.,
Nos. 614 & 617 SANSOM STREET.

PREFACE.

In history we find frequent mention of those who have attained high position in the State, through no other virtue than superior attainments in the Art of Cookery. No title seemed too noble, or emoluments too vast, to mark the bestower's sense of the value of a favorite and successful cook. Laying aside his ladle, he has ruffled it with the noblest of the land. Royal dames have delighted to do him honor; while in the conclave of statesmen, or in the cabinet of sovereigns, he has been alike the accepted and well-approved confidant and adviser. In these more modern days, although we do not go to such extreme lengths in rewarding the professors of the culinary art, yet are we by no means insensible to its importance, or backward in our appreciation of its results.

To be an able and successful cook should be the aim of every prudent housekeeper, for we know of no surer mark of sloth or negligence than an ill-served table. For if incapacity and indifference be allowed to exist in the kitchen, need we be surprised to find it in the parlor. Nor need we remind our fair readers how often an ill-cooked dish is the source, not only of bitter mortification, but of domestic discord and unhappiness. And is it not also equally true that many of the mental and physical derangements of both mind and body are frequently to be traced directly to the careless and imperfect preparation of our daily food.

A would-be frugal housekeeper, actuated by the best motives, and really striving to "make both ends meet," is perplexed at her want of success, and is anxiously looking abroad for causes that she would find much nearer home. And what else is the

(xxi)

reason but that, notwithstanding an expensive outlay in provisions, bad cooking spoils and renders uneatable a large
proportion; and that which should have graced her table, and
delighted the palates of her household, becomes fit for naught
else than food for pigs, and is therefore consigned to the already overgorged swill tub. In how many of our households
is not this notoriously the case? If thus the art of Cooking ex-
ercises so great an influence upon the health and happiness of
the community, we are sure we need no longer dwell upon the
importance, nor urge upon our readers the necessity of a closer
study of this truly important branch of our domestic economy.

This volume is offered to the experienced housekeeper as
well as to the young beginner, as a faithful and intelligent
counsellor and guide, in whom they can place the fullest confidence, and whose directions they can unhesitatingly follow.
Every recipe having been fully tested, is now presented to
them as the result of actual individual experience. They will
be found to be practical, clear and simple, readily understood
and as easily followed. So precise are the directions on every
page, that no novice, however unsophisticated, need be mis-
led. Appended to each recipe is a summary of the different
ingredients which it contains, with the exact proportions of
each and the precise time necessary to dress the whole: thus
showing at a glance its various requirements.

The directions for boning poultry and game are entirely
new, and also very exact; while those pages devoted to explain-
ing the somewhat rare accomplishment of carving, and how to
set out a table, will, we trust, be found equally acceptable and
instructive to our readers.

To our country-women, then, throughout the land we dedi-
cate this work in the fullest assurance that, in many households,
it will become a valued and honored servant, always ready
when needed, ever willing to advise; and whose counsels when
faithfully followed will tend to add to the gratifications of
many an American home.

CONTENTS.

CHAPTER 1.

SOUPS.

CHAPTER II.

FISH.

(23)

CHAPTER III.

GRAVIES.

CHAPTER IV.

SAUCES.

CHAPTER V.

STORE SAUCES.

CHAPTER VI.

FORCEMEATS.

CHAPTER VII.

BOILING, ROASTING, ETC.

CHAPTER VIII.

BEEF.

CHAPTER IX.

VEAL.

CHAPTER X.

MUTTON AND LAMB.

CHAPTER XI.

PORK.

CHAPTER XII.

POULTRY.

CHAPTER XIII.

GAME.

CHAPTER XIV.

CURRIES, POTTED MEATS, &c.

CHAPTER XV.

VEGETABLES.

CHAPTER XVI.

PASTRY.

CHAPTER XVII.

BOILED PUDDINGS.

3 *

CHAPTER XVIII.

BAKED PUDDINGS.

CHAPTER XIX.

SOUFFLES, OMLETS, &c.

CHAPTER XX.

SWEET DISHES, OR ENTREMETS.

CHAPTER XXI.

PRESERVES.

CHAPTER XXII.

PICKLES.

CHAPTER XXIII.

CAKES.

CHAPTER XXIV.

CONFECTIONARY.

CHAPTER XXV.

DESSERT-DISHES.

CONTENTS.

CHAPTER XXVI.

SYRUPS, LIQUEURS, ETC.

Strawberry Vinegar of delicious flavour 374
Strawberry Acid Royal 375
Very fine Raspberry Vinegar ib.
Oxford Punch 376
Oxford receipt for Bishop ib.
To Mull Wine, (an excellent French receipt) 377
A birth-day Syllabub ib.
Cuirasseau, or Curaçoa; (an excellent and wholesome Liqueur) ib.
Mint Julep; (an American receipt) 378
Delicious Milk Lemonade 378
Excellent Portable Lemonade ib.
Excellent Barley Water; (poor Xury's receipt) ib.
Raisin Wine; (which, if long kept, really resembles foreign) ib.
Excellent Elderberry Wine 379
Very good Ginger Wine ib.
Excellent Orange Wine ib.
Currant Wine 380
To clean Bottles in large numbers ib.

CHAPTER XXVII.

COFFEE, CHOCOLATE, ETC.

To roast Coffee 381
To make Coffee 382
To make French breakfast Coffee ib.
To boil Coffee and refine it ib.
Burnt Coffee; (in France vulgarly called Gloria) 383
To make Chocolate; (French receipt). ib.
To make Tea ib.

CHAPTER XXVIII.

BREAD.

To purify Yeast for Bread or Cakes 384
The Oven ib.
To make Bread ib.
Bordyke Bread; (Author's receipt) 385
Brown Bread 386
Potato Bread ib.
Dyspepsia Bread ib.
Rye and Indian Bread 387
Geneva Rolls ib.
Rusks 388
Crusts to serve with Cheese ib.
Good Captains' Biscuits ib.
Breakfast Batter Cakes ib.
Tea Cakes 388
Muffins 389
Wheat Muffins ib.
Rice Muffins ib.
Rice Cakes ib.
Buckwheat Cakes ib.
Flannel Cakes ib.
Yeast 390
Milk Yeast ib.
Hard Yeast ib.
Potato Yeast 391
Prepared Yeast, (Dr. Lettsom's) ib.

CHAPTER XXIX.

AMERICAN MODE OF COOKING INDIAN CORN, PUMPKINS, ETC.

Indian Cake, or Bannock 391
Indian Corn, or Maize Pudding baked 392
Boiled Maize Pudding ib.
Pumpkin and Squash Pie ib.
Currot Pies 393
American Custard Pudding ib.
American Plum Pudding ib.
American Apple Pudding ib.
Bird's Nest Pudding 393
Hasty Pudding ib.
Dry-bread ib.
Another sort of Brewis 394
To preserve Cheese ib.
American Mince-meat ib.
American Souse ib.
Pork and Beans ib.

CHAPTER XXX.

DIRECTIONS FOR CARVING.

Garnishing and setting out a Table 395
Fish ib.
Turbot, &c. ib.
A Cod's Head and Shoulders ib.
Salmon ib.
Soles 396
Mackerel ib.
Eels, Whiting Jack, &c. ib.
Aitch bone or Beef ib.
A Round, or Buttock, and flank of Beef ib.

2

CONTENTS.

APPENDIX.

TABLE OF

WEIGHTS AND MEASURES,

By which persons not having scales and weights at hand may readily measure the articles wanted to form any receipt, without the trouble of weighing. Allowance to be made for an extraordinary dryness or moisture of the article weighed or measured.

~~~~~~~~~~~~~~~~~~~~~~~~~~~~

WEIGHT AND MEASURE.

Wheat flour...............one pound is ....one quart.

Indian meal...............one pound, two ounces, is......one quart.

Butter, when soft ....one pound is ....one quart.

Loaf sugar, broken.........one pound is ....one quart.

White sugar, powdered.......one pound, one ounce is ....one quart.

Best brown sugar ....one pound, two ounces, is......one quart.

Eggs ....ten eggs are ....one pound.

Flour.....................eight quarts are ....one peck.

Flour.....................four pecks are ....one bushel.

LIQUIDS.

Sixteen large table-spoonfuls are ....half a pint.

Eight large table-spoonfuls are...........................one gill.

Four large table-spoonfuls are ....half a gill.

Two gills are..half a pint

Two pints are..one quart.

Four quarts are..one gallon.

A common-sized tumbler holds ....half a pint

A common-sized wine-glass ....half a gill.

Twenty-five drops are equal to one tea-spoonful.

MODERN COOKERY.

CHAPTER I.

SOUPS.

INTRODUCTORY REMARKS.

THE art of preparing good, wholesome, palatable soups, *without great expense,* which is so well understood in France, and in other countries where they form part of the daily food of all classes of the people, has hitherto been very much neglected in England and America: it is one, therefore, to which we would particularly direct the attention of the cook, who will find, we think, on a careful perusal of the present chapter, that it presents no difficulties which a common degree of care and skill will not easily overcome. The reader, who may be desirous to excel in it, should study the instructions given under the article *Bouillon,* where the principles of this branch of cookery are fully explained.

The spices and other condiments used to give flavour to soups and gravies should be so nicely proportioned that none predominate nor overpower the rest; and this delicate *blending of savours* is perhaps the most difficult part of a cook's task: it is an art, moreover, not easily acquired, except by long experience, unless great attention be combined with some natural refinement of the palate.

A zealous servant will take all possible pains on her first entrance into a family, to ascertain the particular tastes of the individuals she serves; and will be guided entirely by them in the preparation of her dishes, however much they may be opposed to her own ideas, or to her previous practice.

Exceeding cleanliness, both in her personal habits and appearance, and in every department of her work, is so essential in a cook, that no degree of skill, nor any other good qualities which she may possess, can ever atone for the want of it. The very idea of a *dirty cook* is so revolting, that few people will be induced to tolerate the reality; and we would therefore most strongly urge all* employed in the culinary department of a household, who may be anxious for their own success

---

* An active, cleanly, and attentive kitchen-maid will generally become an admirable cook

(37)

in life, or solicitous to obtain the respect and approbation of their employers, to strive to the utmost against any tendency to slovenliness of
which they may be conscious, or which may be pointed out to them by
others.

Modern Copper Soup or Stock-Pot.

A FEW DIRECTIONS TO THE COOK.

In whatever vessel soup is boiled, see that it be perfectly clean, and
let the inside of the cover and the rim be equally so.   Wash the meat,
and prepare the vegetables with great nicety before they are laid into
it; and be careful to keep it always closely shut when it is on the fire.
Never, on any account, set the soup by in it, but strain it off at once
into a clean pan; and fill the stock-pot immediately with water: pursue
the same plan with all stewpans and saucepans directly they are
emptied.

Skim the soup thoroughly when it *first* begins to boil, or it can never
afterwards be rendered clear; throw in some salt, which will assist to
bring the scum to the surface, and when it has all been taken off, add
the herbs and vegetables; for if not long stewed in the soup, their
flavour will prevail too strongly.   Remember, that the trimmings, and
especially the *bones* of fresh meat, the necks of poultry, the liquor in
which a joint has been boiled, and the shank-bones of mutton, are all
excellent additions to the stock-pot, and should be carefully reserved
for it.

Let the soup heat gradually over a moderate fire, and after it has
been well skimmed, draw it to the side of the stove and keep it *simmering softly*, but without ceasing, until it is done; for on this, as will
hereafter be shown, its excellence principally depends.   Every good
cook understands perfectly the difference produced by the fast boiling,
or the *gentle stewing* of soups and gravies, and will adhere strictly to
the latter method.

Pour boiling water, in small quantities at first, to the meat and
vegetables of which the soup is to be made when they have been fried
or browned; but otherwise, add *cold* water to the meat.

Unless precise orders to the contrary have been given, onions, eschalots, and garlic, should be used for seasoning with great moderation
always; for not only are they very offensive to many eaters, but to persons of delicate habit their effects are sometimes extremely prejudi-
cial; and it is only in coarse cookery that their flavour is allowed ever
strongly to prevail.

A small proportion of sugar, about an ounce to the gallon, will very much improve the flavour of gravy-stock, and of all rich brown soups; it may be added also to some others with advantage; and for this, directions will be given in the proper places.

Two ounces of salt may be allowed for each gallon of soup or broth in which large quantities of vegetables are stewed; but an ounce and a half will be sufficient for such as contain few or none; it is always easy to add more if needful, but oversalting in the first instance is a fault for which there is no remedy but that of increasing the proportions of all the other ingredients, and stewing the whole afresh, which occasions needless trouble and expense, even when time will admit of its being done.

As no particle of fat should be seen floating on your soups when they are sent to table, it is desirable that the stock should be made the day before it is wanted, that it may become quite cold, when the fat may be entirely cleared off without difficulty.

When cayenne pepper is not mixed with rice-flour, or with any other thickening, grind it down with the back of a spoon, and stir a little liquid to it before it is thrown into the stewpan, as it is apt to remain in lumps, and to occasion great irritation of the throat when swallowed so.

Serve. not only soups and sauces, but all your dishes, *as hot as possible.*

TO THICKEN SOUPS.

Except for white soups, to which arrow-root is, we think, more appropriate, we prefer, to all other ingredients generally used for this purpose, the finest and freshest rice-flour, which after being passed through a lawn-sieve, should be thoroughly blended with the salt, pounded spices, catsup, or wine, required to finish the flavouring of the soup. Sufficient liquid should be added to it very gradually to render it of the consistency of batter, and it should also be perfectly smooth; to keep it so, it should be moistened sparingly at first, and beaten with the back of a spoon until every lump has disappeared. The soup should boil quickly when the thickening is stirred into it, and be simmered for ten minutes afterwards. From an ounce and a half to two ounces of rice-flour will thicken sufficiently a quart of soup.

Instead of this, arrow-root or the condiment known by the name of *tous les mois*, which greatly resembles it, or potato-flour, or the French thickening called *roux* (see page 92) may be used in the following proportions:—Two and a half ounces of either of the first three, to four pints and a half of soup; to be mixed gradually with a little cold stock or water, stirred into the boiling soup, and simmered for a minute.

Six ounces of flour with seven of butter,* will be required to thicken a tureen of soup; as much as half a pound is sometimes used; these must be added by degrees and carefully stirred round in the soup until smoothly blended with it, or they will remain in lumps.

All the ingredients used for soups should be fresh, and of good quality, particularly Italian pastes of every kind (maccaroni, vermicelli, &c.),

* We would recommend any other thickening in preference to this unwholesome mixture

as they contract, by long keeping, a peculiarly unpleasant, musty, flavour.

Onions, freed from the outer skin, dried gradually to a deep brown, in a slow oven, and flattened, will keep for almost any length of time, and are extremely useful for heightening the colour and flavour of broths and gravies.*

TO FRY BREAD TO SERVE WITH SOUP.

Cut some slices a quarter-inch thick, from a stale loaf; pare off the crust, and divide the bread into dice, or cut it with a deep paste-cutter into any other form. For half a pound of bread put two ounces of the best butter into a frying-pan, and when it is quite melted, add the bread; keep it turned, over a gentle fire, until it is equally coloured to a very pale brown, then drain it from the butter, and dry it on a soft cloth, or a sheet of paper placed before a clear fire, upon a dish, or on a sieve reversed.

SIPPETS A LA REINE.

Having cut the bread as for common sippets, spread it on a dish, and pour over it a few spoonsful of thin cream, or of good milk; let it soak for an hour, then fry it in fresh butter of a delicate brown, drain, and serve the sippets hot.

TO MAKE NOUILLES; (an elegant substitute for Vermicelli.)

Wet, with the yolks of four eggs, as much fine, dry, sifted flour as will make them into a firm, but very smooth paste. Roll it out as thin as possible, and cut it into bands of about an inch and a quarter in width. Dust them lightly with flour, and place four of them one upon the other. Cut them obliquely in the finest possible strips; separate them with the point of a knife, and spread them on writing paper, so that they may dry a little before they are used. Drop them gradually into the boiling soup, and in ten minutes they will be done.

Various other forms may be given to this paste at will. It may be divided into a sort of riband maccaroni; or stamped with small confectionary cutters into different shapes.

VEGETABLE VERMICELLI; (vegetables cut very fine for Soups.)

Cut the carrots into inch lengths, then pare them round and round in ribbons of equal thickness, till the inside is reached; next cut these ribands into straws, or very small strips; celery is prepared in the same way; and turnips also are first pared into ribands, then sliced into strips: these last require less boiling than the carrots, and attention must be paid to this, for if broken, the whole would have a bad appearance in soup. The safer plan is to boil each vegetable separately, till tolerably tender, in a little pale broth (in water, if this be not at hand), to drain them well, and put them into the soup, which should be clear, only a few minutes before it is dished. For cutting them small, in other forms, the proper instruments will be found at the hardware-shops.

* The fourth part of one of these dried onions (des oignons brûlés), of moderate size is sufficient for a tureen of a. 1p.

BOUILLON, (*the Common Soup of France ; Cheap, and very Wholesome.*)

This soup, or *broth*, as we should perhaps designate it in England, is made once or twice in the week, in every family of respectability in France; and by the poorer classes as often as their means will enable them to substitute it for the vegetable or *maigre* soups, on which they are more commonly obliged to subsist. It is served usually on the first day, with slices of untoasted bread soaked in it; on the second, it is generally varied with vermicelli, rice, or semoulina. The ingredients are, of course, often otherwise proportioned than as we have given them, and more or less meat is allowed, according to the taste or circumstances of the persons for whom the bouillon is prepared; but the process of making it is always the same, and is thus described (rather learnedly) by one of the most skilful cooks in Europe: " The stock or soup-pot of the French artizan," says Monsieur Carême, " supplies his principal nourishment; and it is thus managed by his wife, who, without the slightest knowledge of chemistry, conducts the process in a truly scientific manner. She first lays the meat into her earthen stock-pot, and pours cold water to it in the proportion of about two quarts to three pounds of the beef;* she then places it by the side of the fire, where it slowly becomes hot; and as it does so, the heat enlarges the fibre of the meat, dissolves the gelatinous substances which it contains, allows the albumen (or the muscular part which produces the scum) to disengage itself, and rise to the surface, and the OZMAZOME (*which is the most savoury part of the meat*) to be diffused through the broth. Thus, from the simple circumstance of boiling it in the gentlest manner, a relishing and nutritious soup will be obtained, and a dish of tender and palatable meat, but if the pot be placed and kept over a quick fire, the *albumen* will coagulate, harden the meat, prevent the water from penetrating it, and the *osmazome* from disengaging itself; the result will be a broth without flavour or goodness, and a tough, dry bit of meat."

Caption under illustration:

French *Pot-au-Feu;* or, Earthen Soup-Pot.

It must be observed in addition, that as the meat of which the *bouillon* is made, is almost invariably sent to table, a part of the rump, the mouse-buttock, or the leg-of-mutton piece of beef, should be selected for it; and the simmering should be continued only until this is perfectly tender. When the object is simply to make good, pure-flavoured beef broth, part of the shin, or leg, with a pound or two of the neck, will best answer the purpose. When the *bouilli* (that is to say, the beef which is boiled in the soup) is to be served, bind it into a good shape, add to it a calf's foot, if easily procurable, as this much improves the quality of the *bouillon;* pour cold water to it in the proportion mentioned above, and proceed as Monsieur Carême directs, to heat the soup *slowly* by the side of the fire; remove carefully the head of scum,

* This is a large proportion of meat for the family of a French artizan ; a pound to the quart would be nearer the reality : but it is not the refuse-meat which would be purchased by persons of the same rank in England for making broth.

which will gather on the surface, before the boiling commences, and continue the skimming at intervals, for about twenty minutes longer, pouring in once or twice a little cold water. Next, add salt in the proportion of two ounces to the gallon; this will cause a little more scum to rise,—clear it quite off, and throw in three or four turnips, as many carrots, half a head of celery, four or five young leeks, an onion stuck with six or eight cloves, a large half tea-spoonful of pepper-corns, and a bunch of savoury herbs. Let the whole stew VERY softly, without ceasing, from four hours and a half to six hours, according to the quantity: the beef in that time will be extremely tender, but not over done. It will be excellent eating, if properly managed, and might often, we think, be substituted with great advantage for the hard, half-boiled, salted beef, so often seen at an English table. It should be served with a couple of cabbages, which have been first boiled in the usual way, then pressed very dry, and stewed for about ten minutes in a little of the broth, and seasoned with pepper and salt. The other vegetables from the bouillon may be laid round it or not, at choice. The soup, if served on the same day, must be strained, well cleared from fat, and sent to table with fried or toasted bread, unless the continental mode of putting slices or crusts of *untoasted* bread into the tureen, and soaking them for ten minutes in a ladleful or two of the bouillon, be, from custom, preferred.

Beef, 8 to 9 lbs.; water, 6 quarts; salt, 3 ozs. (more if needed); carrots, 4 to 6; turnips, 4 or 5; celery, one small head; leeks, 4 to 6; one onion, stuck with 6 cloves; pepper-corns, one small tea-spoonful; large bunch of savoury herbs: (calf's foot, if convenient) to *simmer* five to six hours.

Obs. 1.—This broth forms in France the foundation of all richer soups and gravies. Poured on fresh meat (a portion of which should be veal), instead of water, it makes at once an excellent *consommée*, or strong jellied stock. If properly managed, it is very clear and pale and with an additional weight of beef, and some spoonsful of glaze, may easily be converted into an amber-coloured gravy-soup, suited to modern taste.

Obs. 2.—It is a common practice abroad to boil poultry, pigeons, and even game in the *pot-au-feu*, or soup-pot. They should be properly trussed, stewed in the broth just long enough to render them tender, and served immediately, when ready, with a *good* sauce. A small ham, if well soaked, washed exceedingly clean, and freed entirely from any rusty, or blackened parts, laid with the beef when the water is first added to it, and boiled from three hours and a half to four hours, in the bouillon, is very superior in flavour to those cooked in water only, and infinitely improves the soup, which cannot, however, so well be eaten, until the following day, when all the fat can easily be taken from it: it would, of course, require no salt.

CLEAR, PALE, GRAVY-SOUP OR STOCK.

Rub a deep stewpan or soup-pot with butter, and lay into it three quarters of a pound of ham freed entirely from fat, skin, and rust, four pounds of leg or neck of veal, and the same weight of lean beef, all cut into thick slices; set it over a clear and rather brisk fire, until the meat is of a fine amber-colour: it must be often moved, and closely

watched, that it may not stick to the pan, nor burn. When it is equally
browned, lay the bones upon it, and pour in gradually four quarts of
boiling water. Take off the scum carefully as it rises, and throw in a
pint of cold water at intervals, to bring it quickly to the surface. When
no more appears, add two ounces of salt, two onions, two large carrots,
two turnips, one head of celery, a two-ounce faggot of savoury herbs, a
dozen cloves, half a tea-spoonful of whole white pepper, and two large
blades of mace. Let the soup boil gently from five hours and a half, to
six hours and a half; then strain it through a very clean, fine cloth, laid
in a hair sieve. When it is perfectly cold, remove every particle of fat
from the top; and, in taking out the soup, leave the sediment untouched; heat in a clean pan the quantity required for table, add salt to
it if needed, and a few drops of Chili or of cayenne vinegar. Harvey's
sauce, or very fine mushroom catsup, may be substituted for these.
When thus prepared, the soup is ready to serve: it should be accompanied by pale sippets of fried bread, or sippets à la reine. Rice, maccaroni in lengths or rings, vermicelli, or nouilles, may in turn be used,
to vary it; but they must always be boiled apart till tender, in broth, or
water, and well drained before they are slipped into it. The addition
of young vegetables, too, and especially of asparagus, will convert it
into an elegant spring-soup; but they, likewise, must be separately
cooked.

ANOTHER RECEIPT FOR GRAVY-SOUP.

Instead of browning the meat in its own juices, put it with the onions
and carrots, into a deep stewpan, with a quarter-pint of bouillon; set it
over a brisk fire at first, and when the broth is somewhat reduced, let
it boil gently until it has taken a fine colour and forms a glaze (or jelly)
at the bottom of the stewpan; then pour to it the proper quantity of
water, and finish the soup by the preceding receipt.*

Obs.—A rich, old-fashioned English brown gravy-soup may be made
with beef only. It should be cut from the bones, dredged with flour, seasoned with pepper and salt, and fried a clear brown; then stewed for
six hours, if the quantity be large, with a pint of water to each pound
of meat, and vegetables as above, except onions, of which four moderate-sized ones, also fried, are to be added to every three quarts of the
soup, which, after it has been strained, and cleared from fat, may be
thickened with six ounces of fresh butter, worked up very smoothly
with five of flour. In twenty minutes afterwards, a table-spoonful of
the best soy, half a pint of sherry, and a little cayenne, may be added
to the soup, which will then be ready to serve.

* The juices of meat, drawn out with a small portion of liquid, as directed here, may
easily be reduced to the consistency in which they form what is called glaze; for par-
ticulars of this, see Chapter III. The best method, though perhaps not the easiest, of
making the clear, amber-coloured stock, is to pour a ladleful or two of pale, but strong
beef-broth to the veal, and to boil it briskly until well reduced, thrusting a knife, when
this is done, into the meat, to let the juices escape; then to proceed more slowly and
cautiously as the liquid approaches the state in which it would burn. It must be
allowed to take a dark amber-colour only, and the meat must be turned, and often
moved in it. When the desired point is reached, pour in more boiling broth, and let
the pan remain off the fire for a few minutes, to detach and melt the glaze; then shake
it well round before the boiling is continued. A certain quantity of deeply coloured
glaze, made apart, and stirred into strong, clear, pale stock would produce the desired
effect of this, with much less trouble.

VERMICELLI SOUP; (*Potage au Vermicelle.*)

Drop very lightly, and by degrees, six ounces of vermicelli, broken rather small, into three quarts of boiling bouillon, or clear gravy soup; let it simmer half an hour* over a gentle fire, and stir it often. This is the common French mode of making vermicelli soup, and we can recommend it as a particularly good one for family use. In England it is customary to soak, or to blanch the vermicelli, then to drain it well, and to stew it for a shorter time in the soup: the quantity, also, must be reduced quite two ounces, to suit modern taste.

Bouillon, or gravy-soup, 3 quarts; vermicelli, 6 ozs.; 30 minutes. Or, soup, 3 quarts; vermicelli, 4 ozs.; blanched in boiling water, 5 minutes; stewed in soup, 10 to 15 minutes.

SEMOULINA SOUP; (*Soupe à la Sémoule.*)

Semoulina is used in the same way as the vermicelli. It should be dropped very lightly and by degrees into the boiling soup, which should be stirred all the time it is being added, and very frequently afterwards; indeed, it should scarcely be quitted for a moment until it is ready for table. Skim it carefully, and let it simmer from twenty to five and twenty minutes. This, when the semoulina can be procured good and fresh, is, to our taste, an excellent soup.

Soup, 3 quarts; semoulina, 6 ozs.: nearly, or quite 25 minutes.

MACCARONI SOUP.

Throw four ounces of fine fresh†. mellow maccaroni into a pan of fast-boiling water, with about an ounce of fresh butter, and a small onion stuck with three or four cloves.‡ When it has swelled to its full size, and become tender, drain it well, and slip it into a couple of quarts of clear gravy-soup; let it simmer for a few minutes, when it will be ready for table. Observe, that the maccaroni should be boiled quite tender; but it should by no means be allowed to burst, nor to become pulpy. Serve grated Parmesan cheese with it.

Maccaroni, 4 ozs.; butter, 1 oz.; 1 small onion; 5 cloves; three-quarters of an hour or more. In soup, 5 to 10 minutes.

Obs.—The maccaroni for soups should always be either broken into short lengths before it is boiled, or sliced quickly afterwards into small rings not more than the sixth of an inch thick, unless the *cut* maccaroni be used; this requires but ten minutes boiling, and should be dropped into the soup in the same way as vermicelli. Four ounces of it will be sufficient for two quarts of stock. It may be added to white soup after having been previously boiled in water or veal-broth, and well drained from it: it has a rather elegant appearance in clear gravy-soup, but should have a boil in water before it is thrown into it.

---

* When of very fine quality, the vermicelli will usually require less boiling than this.

† We must here repeat our warning against the use of long-kept maccaroni, vermicelli, or semoulina; as when stale, they will render any dish into which they are introduced, quite unfit for table.

‡ For White Soups, omit the onion

POTAGE AUX NOUILLES, OR TAILLERINE SOUP.

Make into nouille paste the yolks of four fresh eggs, and when ready cut, drop it gradually into five pints of boiling soup; keep this gently stirred for ten minutes, skim it well, and serve it quickly. This is a less common, and a more delicately flavoured soup than the vermicelli, provided always that the nouilles be made with really fresh eggs. The same paste may be cut into very small diamond squares, stars, or any other form, then left to dry a little, and boiled in the soup until swelled to its full size, and tender.

Nouille paste of four eggs; soup, 5 pints: 10 minutes.

SAGO SOUP.

Wash in several waters, and float off the dirt from six ounces of sago; put it into three quarts of good cold gravy-stock, and let it stew gently from half to three quarters of an hour; stir it occasionally, that it may not burn nor stick to the stew-pan. A quarter-ounce more of sago to each pint of liquid, will thicken it to the consistency of peas-soup. It may be flavoured with half a wineglassful of Harvey's sauce, as much cayenne as it may need, the juice of half a lemon, an ounce of sugar, and two glasses of sherry; or these may be omitted, and good beef-broth may be substituted for the gravy-soup, for a simple family dinner, or for an invalid.

Sago, 6 ozs.; soup, 3 quarts: 30 to 45 minutes.

TAPIOCA SOUP.

This is made in the same manner, and with the same proportions as the preceding soup, but it must be simmered from fifty to sixty minutes.

RICE SOUP.

In France this soup is served well thickened with the rice, which is stewed in it for upwards of an hour and a half, and makes thus, even with the common bouillon of the country, an excellent winter potage. Pick, and wipe in a dry cloth, eight ounces of the best rice; add it, in small portions, to four quarts of hot soup, of which the boiling should not be checked as it is thrown in. When a clear soup is wanted, wash the rice, give it five minutes' boil in water, drain it well, throw it into as much boiling stock or well-flavoured broth as will keep it covered till done, and simmer it very softly until the grains are tender, but still separate; drain it, slip it into the soup, and let it remain in it a few minutes before it is served, but without simmering. When stewed in the stock, it may be put at once, after being drained, into the tureen, and the clear gravy-soup may be poured to it.

An easy English mode of making rice-soup is this: put the rice into plenty of cold water; when it boils, throw in a small quantity of salt let it simmer ten minutes, drain it well; throw it into the boiling soup and simmer it gently from ten to fifteen minutes longer; some rice will be tender in half that time. An extra quantity of stock must be allowed for the reduction of this soup, which is always considerable.

WHITE RICE SOUP.

Throw four ounces of well-washed rice into boiling water, and in five minutes after pour it into a sieve, drain it well, and put it into a couple of quarts of good white, boiling stock; let it stew till tender, season the soup with salt, cayenne, and pounded mace; stir to it three-quarters of a pint of very rich cream, give it one boil, and serve it quickly.

Rice, 4 ozs.: boiled 5 minutes. Soup, 2 quarts: three-quarters of an hour or more. Seasoning of salt, mace, and cayenne; cream, three-quarters of a pint: 1 minute.

RICE-FLOUR SOUP.

Mix with a little cold broth, eight ounces of fine rice-flour, and pour it into a couple of quarts of fast-boiling broth, or gravy-soup. Add to it mace, and cayenne, with a little salt, if needful. It will require but ten minutes' boiling.

Soup, 2 quarts; rice-flour, 8 ozs.: 10 minutes.

Obs.—Two dessert-spoonsful of currie-powder, and the strained juice of half a moderate-sized lemon, will greatly improve this soup: it may also be converted into a good common white soup (if it be made of veal stock), by the addition of three-quarters of a pint of thick cream to the rice.

STOCK FOR WHITE SOUP.

Though a knuckle of veal is usually preferred for this stock, part of the neck will, on an emergency, answer very well. Whichever joint be chosen, let it be thoroughly washed, once or twice divided, and laid into a delicately clean soup-pot, or well-tinned large stout iron sauce-pan, upon a pound of lean ham, freed entirely from skin and fat, and cut into thick slices. Should *very* rich soup be wished for, pour in a pint only of cold water for each pound of meat, but otherwise a pint and a half may be allowed. When the soup has been thoroughly cleared from scum, which should be carefully taken off, from the time of its first beginning to boil, throw in an ounce of salt to the gallon (more can be added afterwards, if needed), two mild onions, a moderate-sized head of celery, two carrots, a small tea-spoonful of whole white pepper, and two blades of mace; and let the soup stew very softly from five to six hours, if the quantity be large: it should simmer until the meat falls from the bones. The skin of a calf's-head, a calf's-foot, or an old fowl, may always be added to this stock, with good effect. Strain it into a clean deep pan, and keep it in a cool place till wanted for use.

Lean ham, 1 lb.; veal, 7 lbs.; water, 4 to 6 quarts; salt, 1½ oz. (more, if needed); onions, 2; celery, 1 head; carrots, 2; pepper-corns, 1 tea-spoonful; mace, 2 blades: five to six hours.

MUTTON-STOCK FOR SOUPS.

Equal parts of beef and mutton, with the addition of a small portion of ham, or of very lean bacon, make excellent stock, especially for winter-soups. The necks of fowls, the bones of an undressed calf's-head, or of any uncooked joint, may be added to it with advantage. According to the quality of soup desired, pour from a pint to a pint and a half of cold water to each pound of meat; and after the liquor has been well-skimmed on its beginning to boil, throw in an ounce and a half of salt to the gallon, two small heads of celery, three mild, middling-sized onions, three well-flavoured turnips, as many carrots, a faggot of thyme and parsley, half a tea-spoonful of white pepper-corns, twelve cloves, and a large blade of mace.   Draw the soup-pot to the side of the fire, and boil the stock as gently as possible for about six hours; then strain, and set it by for use.   Be particularly careful to clear it *entirely* from fat before it is prepared for table.   One-third of beef or *veal*, with two of mutton, will make very good soup; or mutton only will answer the purpose quite well upon occasion.

Beef, 4 lbs.; mutton, 4 lbs. (or, beef or veal, from 2 to 3 lbs.; mutton, from 5 to 6 lbs.); water, 1 gallon, to 1½; salt, 1½ oz.; mild turnips, 1 lb.; onions, 6 ozs.; carrots, ¾ lb.; celery, 6 to 8 ozs.; 1 bunch of herbs; pepper-corns, ½ tea-spoonful; cloves, 12; mace, 1 large blade: six hours.

Obs. — Salt should be used sparingly at first for stock in which any portion of ham is boiled; allowance should also be made for its reduction, in case of its being required for gravy.

COMMON CARROT SOUP.

The easiest way of making this soup is to boil some carrots very tender in water slightly salted; then to pound them extremely fine, and to mix gradually with them boiling gravy-soup (or bouillon), in the proportion of a quart to twelve ounces of the carrot.   The soup should then be passed through a strainer, seasoned with salt and cayenne, and served *very* hot, with fried bread in a separate dish.   If only the red outsides of the carrot be used, the colour of the soup will be very bright: they should be weighed after they are pounded.   Turnip-soup may also be made in the same manner.

Soup, 2 quarts; pounded carrot, 1½ lb.; salt, cayenne: 5 minutes.

COMMON TURNIP SOUP.

Wash and wipe the turnips, pare and weigh them; allow a pound and a half for every quart of soup.   Cut them in slices about a quarter of an inch thick.   Melt four ounces of butter in a clean stew-pan, and put in the turnips before it begins to boil; stew them gently for three quarters of an hour, taking care that they shall not brown.   Then have the proper quantity of soup ready boiling, pour it to them, and let them simmer in it for three quarters of an hour.   Pulp the whole through a coarse sieve or soup-strainer, put it again on the fire, keep it stirred until it has boiled three minutes, take off the scum, add salt and pepper, if required, and serve it very hot.

Turnips, 3 lbs.; butter, 4 ozs.: ¾ hour.   Soup, 2 quarts: ¾ hour. Last time: 3 minutes.

A QUICKLY MADE TURNIP SOUP.

Pare and slice into three pints of veal or mutton-stock, or of good broth, three pounds of young mild turnips; stew them gently from twenty-five to thirty minutes, or until they can be reduced quite to pulp; press the whole through a sieve, add to it another quart of stock, a seasoning of salt, white pepper, and one lump of sugar; simmer it a minute or two, skim, and serve it.   A large white onion, when the flavour is liked, may be sliced and stewed with the turnips.   A little cream improves much the colour of this soup.

Turnips, 3 lbs.; soup, 5 pints: 25 to 30 minutes.

POTATO SOUP.

Mash to a smooth paste three pounds of good mealy potatoes, that have been steamed, or boiled very dry; mix with them by degrees, two quarts of boiling broth, pass the soup through a strainer, set it again on the fire, add pepper and salt, and let it boil five minutes. Take off entirely the black scum that will rise upon it, and serve it very hot with fried or toasted bread. Where the flavour is approved, two ounces of onions, minced and fried a light brown, may be added to the soup, and stewed in it for ten minutes before it is sent to table.

Potatoes, 3 lbs.; broth, 2 quarts: 5 minutes. (With onions, 2 ozs.:) 10 minutes.

APPLE SOUP; (*Soupe à la Bourguignon.*)

Clear the fat from five pints of good mutton-broth, *bouillon*, or shin of beef stock, and strain it through a fine sieve; add to it, when it boils, a pound and a half of good pudding apples, and stew them down in it very softly, to a smooth pulp; press the whole through a strainer, add a small teaspoonful of powdered ginger, and plenty of pepper, simmer the soup for a couple of minutes, skim, and serve it very hot, accompanied by a dish of rice, boiled as for curries.

Broth, 5 pints; apples, 1½ lb.: 25 to 40 minutes. Ginger, 1 teaspoonful; pepper, ½ teaspoonful: 2 minutes.

VEAL SOUP.

Take four pounds of a knuckle of veal, break, and cut it small, put it into a stew-pan with two gallons of water; when it boils, skim it, and let it simmer till reduced to two quarts; strain, and season it with white pepper, salt, a little mace, a dessertspoonful of lemon juice, and return it to the pot, adding two onions finely minced, a head of celery, and a turnip cut in small pieces. Let it simmer about half an hour longer, thicken it with a large tablespoonful of flour kneaded with an ounce of butter.

WESTERFIELD WHITE SOUP.

Break the bone of a knuckle of veal in one or two places, and put it on to stew, with three quarts of cold water to five pounds of meat; when it has been quite cleared from scum, add to it an ounce and a half of salt, two ounces and a half of onions, twenty corns of white pepper, and two or three blades of mace, with a *little* cayenne pepper. When the soup is reduced one-third by slow simmering, strain it off, and set it by till cold; then free it carefully from the fat and sediment, and heat it again in a very clean stew-pan. Mix with it when it boils, a pint of thick cream smoothly blended with an ounce of good arrow root, two ounces of very fresh vermicelli previously boiled tender in water slightly salted and *well drained* from it, and an ounce and a half of almonds blanched, and cut in strips;* give it one minute's simmer, and serve it immediately, with a French roll in the tureen.

---

* We have given this receipt without any variation from the original, as the soup made exactly by it was much approved by the guests of the hospitable country gentleman, at whose elegant table it was served often for many years; but we would rather recommend that the almonds should be pounded, or merely blanched, cut in spikes, stuck into the crumb of a French roll, and put into the tureen, simply to give flavour to the soup.

Veal, 5 lbs. ; water, 3 quarts ; salt, 1½ oz. ; onions, 2½ ozs. ; 20 corns white pepper ; 2 large blades of mace : 5 hours or *more*. Cream, 1 pint ; almonds, 1½ oz. ; vermicelli, 1 oz : 1 minute. Little thickening, if needed.

Obs.—Cream should always be boiled for a few minutes before it is added to any soup. The yolks of two or three very fresh eggs beaten well, and mixed with half a pint of the boiling soup, may be stirred into the whole, after it is taken from the fire. Some persons put the eggs into the tureen, and add the soup to them by degrees ; but this is not so well. If a superior white soup to this be wanted, put three quarts of water to seven pounds of veal, and half a pound of the lean part of a ham ; or, instead of water, use very clear, weak, veal broth. Grated Parmesan cheese should be handed round the table when white or maccaroni soup is served.

MOCK TURTLE, OR CALF'S HEAD SOUP.

After having taken out the brain and washed and soaked the head well, pour to it nine quarts of cold water, bring it gently to boil, skim it very clean, boil it, if large, an hour and a half, lift it out, and put into the liquor eight pounds of neck of beef, lightly browned in a little fresh butter, with three or four thick slices, or a knuckle of lean ham, four large onions sliced, three heads of celery, three large carrots, a large bunch of sweet herbs, the rind of a lemon pared very thin, a desertspoonful of pepper-corns, two ounces of salt, and after the meat has been taken from the head, all the bones and fragments. Stew these gently from seven to eight hours, then strain off the stock, and set it into a very cool place, that the fat may become firm enough on the top to be cleared off easily. The skin and fat of the head should be taken off together and divided into strips of two or three inches in length, and one in width ; the tongue may be cut in the same manner, or into dice. Put the stock, of which there ought to be between four and five quarts, into a large soup or stew pot ; thicken it when it boils with four ounces of fresh butter* mixed with an equal weight of fine dry flour, a half-teaspoonful of pounded mace, and a third as much of cayenne (it is better to use these sparingly at first, and to add more should the soup require it, after it has boiled some little time) ; pour in half a pint of sherry, stir the whole together until it has simmered for a minute or two, then put in the head, and let it stew gently from an hour and a quarter to an hour and a half ; stir it often, and clear it perfectly from scum. Slip into it, just before it is ready for table, three dozens of small forcemeat-balls ; the brain cut into dice (after having been well soaked, scalded,† and freed from the film), dipped into beaten yolk of egg, then into the finest crumbs mixed with salt, white pepper, a little grated nutmeg, fine lemon-rind, and chopped parsley fried a fine brown, well drained and dried ; and as many egg-balls, the size of a small marble, as the yolks of four eggs will supply. (See Chapter VI.) This quantity will be sufficient for two large tureens of soup ; when the whole is not wanted for table

---

* When the butter is considered unobjectionable, the flour, without it, may be mixed to the smoothest batter possible, with a little cold stock or water, and stirred briskly into the boiling soup: the spices should be blended with it.

† The brain should be blanched, that is, thrown into boiling water with a little salt in it, and boiled from five to eight minutes ; then lifted out, and laid into cold water for a quarter of an hour ; it must be wiped very dry before it is fried.

at the same time. it is better to add wine only ti so much as will be required for immediate consumption, or if it cannot conveniently be divided, to heat the wine in a small saucepan with a little of the soup, tc turn it into the tureen, and then to mix it with the remainder by stirring the whole gently after the tureen is filled. Some persons simply put in the cold wine just before the soup is dished, but this is not so well.

Whole calf's head with skin on, boiled 1½ hour. Stock: neck of veef, browned in butter, 8 lbs.; lean of ham, ½ to ¾ lb. (or a knuckle); onions, 4; large carrots, 3; heads of celery, 3; large bunch sweet herbs; salt, 2 ozs. (as much more to be added when the soup is made as will season it sufficiently); thin rind, 1 lemon; peppercorns, 1 dessertspoonful; bones and trimmings of head: 8 hours. Soup: stock, 4 to 5 quarts; flour and butter for thickening, of each 4 ozs.; pounded mace, half-teaspoonful; cayenne, third as much (more of each as needed); sherry, half pint: 2 to 3 minutes. Flesh of head and tongue, nearly or quite, 2 lbs.: 1¼ to 1½ hour. Forcemeat-balls, 36; the brain cut and fried; egg-balls, 16 to 24.

Obs.—When the brain is not blanched it must be cut thinner in the form of small cakes, or it will not be done through by the time it has taken enough colour: it may be altogether omitted without much detriment to the soup, and will make an excellent corner dish, if gently stewed in white gravy for half an hour, and served with it thickened with cream and arrow-root, to the consistency of good white sauce, then rather highly seasoned, and mixed with plenty of chopped parsley, and some lemon-juice.

GOOD CALF'S HEAD SOUP; (*not expensive.*)

Boil down from six to seven pounds of the thick part of a shin of neef with a little lean ham, or a slice of hung beef trimmed free from the smoky edges, should either of these last be at hand, in five quarts of water, till reduced nearly half, with the addition, when it first begins to stew, of an ounce of salt, a large bunch of savoury herbs, one large onion, a head of celery, three carrots, two or three turnips, two small blades of mace, eight or ten cloves, and a few white or black peppercorns. Let it boil gently, that it may not be too much reduced, for six or seven hours, then strain it into a clean pan and set it by for use. Take out the bone from half a calf's head with the skin on (the butcher will do this if desired,) wash, roll and bind it with a bit of tape or twine, and lay it into a stewpot, with the bones and tongue; cover the whole with the beef stock, and stew it for an hour and a half; then lift it into a deep earthen pan and let it cool in the liquor, as this will prevent the edges from being dry or discoloured. Take it out before it is quite cold; strain, and skim all the fat carefully from the stock: heat five pints in a large clean saucepan, with the head cut into small thick slices or into inch-squares. As quite the whole will not be needed, leave a portion of the fat, but add every morsel of the skin to the soup, and of the tongue also. Should the first of these not be perfectly tender, it must be simmered gently till it is so; then stir into the soup from six to eight ounces of fine rice-flour mixed with a quarter-teaspoonful of cayenne, twice as much freshly pounded mace, half a wineglassful of mushroom catsup, and sufficient cold broth or water to render it of the consistency of batter; boil the whole from eight to ten minutes;

take off the scum, and throw in two glasses of sherry; dish the soup and slip into the tureen some delicately fried, and well dried forcemeat-balls made by the receipt No. 1, 2, or 3 of Chapter VI. A small quantity of lemon-juice or other acid can be added at pleasure. The wine and forcemeat-balls may be omitted, and the other seasonings of the soup a little heightened. As much salt as may be required should be added to the stock when the head first begins to boil in it: the cook must regulate also by the taste the exact proportion of cayenne, mace, and catsup, which will flavour the soup agreeably. The fragments of the head, with the bones and the residue of the beef used for stock, if stewed down together with some water and a few fresh vegetables, will afford some excellent broth, such as would be highly acceptable, especially if well thickened with rice, to many a poor family during the winter months.

Stock: shin of beef, 6 to 7 lbs.; water, 5 quarts: stewed down (with vegetables, &c.) till reduced nearly half. Boned half-head with skin on stewed in stock, 1½ hour. Soup: stock, 5 pints; tongue, skin of head, and part of flesh: 15 to 40 minutes, or more if not quite tender. Rice-flour, 6 to 8 ozs.; cayenne, quarter-teaspoonful; mace, twice as much; mushroom catsup, ½ wineglassful: 10 minutes. Sherry, 2 wineglasses-ful, forcemeat-balls, 20 to 30.

WHITE OYSTER SOUP; (*or, Oyster Soup a la Reine.*)

When the oysters are small, from two to three dozens for each pint of soup should be prepared, but this number can, of course, be diminished or increased at pleasure. Let the fish (which should be finely conditioned natives) be opened carefully; pour the liquor from them, and strain it; rinse them in it well, and beard them; strain the liquor a second time through a lawn-sieve or folded muslin, and pour it again over the oysters. Take a portion from two quarts of the palest veal stock, and simmer the beards in it from twenty to thirty minutes. Heat the soup, flavour it well with mace and cayenne, and strain the stock from the oyster-beards into it. Plump the fish in their own liquor, but do not let them boil; pour the liquor to the soup, and add to it a pint of boiling cream; put the oysters into the tureen, dish the soup, and send it to table quickly. Should any thickening be required, stir briskly to the stock an ounce and a half of arrow-root, ground very smooth in a mortar, and carefully mixed with a little milk or cream; or, in lieu of this, when a *rich* soup is liked, thicken it with four ounces of fresh butter well blended with three of flour.

Oysters, 8 to 12 dozens; pale veal stock, 2 quarts; cream, 1 pint; thickening, 1½ oz. arrow-root, or butter, 4 ozs., flour, 3 ozs.

BROWN RABBIT SOUP.

Cut down into joints, flour, and fry lightly, two full grown, or three young rabbits; add to them three onions of moderate size, also fried to a clear brown; on these pour gradually seven pints of boiling water, throw in a large teaspoonful of salt, clear off all the scum with care as it rises, and then put to the soup a faggot of parsley, four not very large carrots, and a small teaspoonful of peppercorns; boil the whole very softly from five hours to five and a half; add more salt if needed, strain off the soup, let it cool sufficiently for the fat to be skimmed clean from it, heat it afresh, and send it to table with sippets of fried bread. Spice, with a thickening of rice-flour, or of wheaten flour browned in the oven, and mixed with a spoonful or two of very good mushroom catsup, or of Harvey's sauce, can be added at pleasure to the above, with a few drops of eschalot-wine, or vinegar; but the simple receipt will be found extremely good without them.

Rabbits, 2 full grown, or 3 small; onions fried, 3, middling-sized; water, 7 pints; salt, 1 large teaspoonful or more; carrots, 4; faggot of parsley; peppercorns, 1 small teaspoonful; 5 to 5½ hours.

PIGEON SOUP.

Take eight pigeons, cut down two of the oldest, and put them with the necks, pinions, livers, and gizzards of the others, into four quarts of water; let it boil till the substance is extracted, and strain it; season the pigeons with mixed spices and salt, and truss them as for stewing; pick and wash clean a handful of parsley, chives or young onions, and a good deal of spinach, chop them; put in a frying-pan a quarter of a pound of butter, and when it boils, mix in a handful of bread crumbs, keep stirring them with a knife till of a fine brown; boil the whole pigeons till they become tender in the soup, with the herbs, and fried bread. If the soup be not sufficiently high seasoned, add more mixed spices and salt.

PHEASANT OR CHICKEN SOUP.

Half roast a brace of well-kept pheasants, and flour them rather thickly when they are first laid to the fire. As soon as they are nearly cold take all the flesh from the breasts, put it aside, and keep it covered from the air; carve down the remainder of the birds into joints, bruise the bodies thoroughly, and stew the whole gently from two to three hours in five pints of strong beef broth; then strain off the soup, and press as much of it as possible from the pheasants. Let it cool, and in the mean time strip the skin from the breasts, mince them small, and pound them to the finest paste, with half as much fresh butter, and half of dry crumbs of bread; season these well with cayenne, sufficiently with salt, and moderately with pounded mace, and grated nutmeg, and add, when their flavour is liked, three or four eschalots, previously boiled tender in a little of the soup, left till cold, and minced before they are put into the mortar; moisten the mixture with the yolks of two or three eggs, roll it into small balls of equal size, dust a little flour upon them, skim all the fat from the soup, heat it in a clean stewpan, and when it boils throw them in and poach them from ten to twelve minutes, but first ascertain that the soup is properly seasoned with salt and cayenne. Minced savoury herbs, and even grated lemon-rind, would, perhaps, improve the forcemeat, as well as a small portion of lean ham, a thick slice of which might be stewed in the soup for the purpose. We have recommended that the birds should be partially roasted before they are put into the soup-pot, because their flavour is much finer when this is done than when they are simply stewed; they should be placed rather near to a brisk fire that they be quickly browned on the surface, without losing any of their juices, and the basting should be constant. A slight thickening of rice-flour or arrow-root can be added to the soup at pleasure, and the forcemeat-balls may be fried and slipped into the tureen when they are preferred so. Half a dozen eschalots lightly browned in butter, and a small head of celery may also be thrown

in after the birds begin to stew, but nothing should be allowed to prevail over the natural flavour of the game itself; and this should be
observed equally with other kinds, as partridges, grouse, and venison.

Pheasants 2: roasted 20 to 30 minutes. Strong beef broth, or stock,
5 pints: 2 to 3 hours. Forcemeat-balls: breasts of pheasants, half as
much of dry bread-crumbs and of butter, salt, mace, cayenne; yolks of
2 or 3 eggs (and at choice 3 or 4 boiled eschalots).

Obs.—The stock may be made of six pounds of shin of beef, and four
quarts of water reduced to within a pint of half. An onion, a large car
rot, a bunch of savoury herbs, and some salt and spice should be added
to it: one pound of neck of veal or of beef will improve it.

PARTRIDGE SOUP.

This is, we think, superior in flavour to the pheasant soup. It should
be made in precisely the same manner, but three birds allowed for it
instead of two. Grouse and partridges together will make a still finer
one: the remains of roast grouse even, added to a brace of partridges,
will produce a very good effect.

MULLAGATAWNY SOUP.

Slice, and fry gently in some good butter three or four large onions,
and when they are of a fine equal amber-colour, lift them out with a
slice, and put them into a deep stewpot, or large thick saucepan; throw
a little more butter into the pan, and then brown lightly in it a young
rabbit, or the prime joints of two, or a fowl cut down small, and floured.
When the meat is sufficiently browned, lay it upon the onions, pour
gradually to them a quart of good boiling stock, and stew it gently from
three quarters of an hour to an hour; then take it out, and press the
stock and onions through a fine sieve or strainer. Add to them two
pints and a half more of stock, pour the whole into a clean pan, and
when it boils stir to it two heaped tablespoonsful of currie-powder mixed
with nearly as much of browned flour, and a little cold water or broth;
put it in the meat, and simmer it for twenty minutes or longer should it
not be perfectly tender, add the juice of a small lemon just before it is
dished, serve it very hot, and send boiled rice to table with it. Part of
a pickled mango is sometimes stewed in this soup, and is much recommended by persons who have been long resident in India. We have
given here the sort of receipt commonly used in England for mullagatawny, but a much finer soup may be made by departing from it in
some respects. The onions, of which the proportion may be increased
or diminished to the taste, after being fried slowly, and with care, that
no part should be overdone, may be stewed for an hour in the first quart
of stock with three or four ounces of grated cocoa-nut, which will impart a rich mellow flavour to the whole. After all of this that can be
rubbed through the sieve has been added to as much stock as will be
required for the soup, and the currie-powder and thickening have boiled
in it for twenty minutes, the flesh of part of a calf's head previously
stewed almost sufficiently, and cut as for mock turtle, with a sweetbread also stewed or boiled in broth tolerably tender, and divided into
inch-squares, will make an admirable mullagatawny, if simmered in the
stock until they have taken the flavour of the currie-seasoning. The
flesh of a couple of calves' feet, with a sweetbread or two, may, when
more convenient, be substituted for the head. A large cupful of thick

cream, first mixed and boiled with a teaspoonful of flour or arrow-root to prevent its curdling, and stirred into the soup before the lemon-juice, will enrich and improve it much.

Rabbit, 1, or the best joints of two, or foul, 1; large onions, 4 to 6 . stock, 1 quart: ¾ to 1 hour.   2½ pints more of stock; currie-powder, 2 heaped tablespoonsful, with 2 of browned flour; meat and all simmered together 20 minutes or more; juice of lemon, 1 small; or part of pickled mango stewed in the soup.

Or,—onions, 3 to 6; cocoa-nut, 3 to 4 ozs.; stock, 1 quart: stewed, 1 hour.   Stock, 3 pints, (in addition to the first quart); currie-powder and thickening each, 2 large tablespoonsful: 20 minutes.   Flesh of part of calf's head and sweetbread, 15 minutes, or more.   Thick cream, 1 cupful; flour, or arrow-root, 1 teaspoonful: boiled two minutes, and stirred to the soup.   Chili vinegar, 1 tablespoonful, or lemon-juice, 2 tablespoonsful.

Obs. 1.—The brain of the calf's head stewed for twenty minutes in a little of the stock, then rubbed through a sieve, diluted gradually with more of the stock, and added as thickening to the soup, will be found an admirable substitute for part of the flour.

Obs. 2.—Three or four pounds of a breast of veal, or an equal weight of mutton, free from bone and fat, may take the place of rabbits or fowls in this soup, for a plain dinner.   The veal should be cut into squares of an inch and a half, or into strips of an inch in width, and two in length; and the mutton should be trimmed down in the same way, or into very small cutlets.

Obs. 3.—For an elegant table, the joints of rabbit or of fowl should always be boned before they are added to the soup, for which, in this case, a couple of each will be needed for a single tureen, as all the inferior joints must be rejected.

TO BOIL RICE FOR MULLAGATAWNY SOUPS, OR FOR CURRIES.

The Patna, or small-grained rice, which is not so good as the Carolina for the general purposes of cookery, is the sort which ought to be served with currie.   First take out the unhusked grains, then wash the rice in two or three different waters, and put it into a large quantity of cold; bring it gently to boil, keeping it uncovered, and boil it softly for fifteen minutes, when it will be perfectly tender, and every grain will remain distinct.   Throw it into a *large* cullender, and let it drain for ten minutes near the fire; should it not then appear *quite* dry, turn it into a dish, and set it for a short time into a gentle oven, or let it steam in a clean saucepan near the fire.   It should neither be stirred, except just at first, to prevent its lumping while it is still quite hard, nor touched with either fork or spoon; the stewpan may be shaken occasionally, should the rice seem to require it, and it should be thrown lightly from the cullender upon the dish.   A couple of minutes before it is done, throw in some salt, and from the time of its beginning to boil, remove the scum as it rises.

Patna rice, ½ lb.; cold water, 2 quarts: boiled slowly, 15 minutes. Salt, 1 large teaspoonful.

Obs.—This, of all the modes of boiling rice, which we have tried, and they have been very numerous, is indisputably the best.   The Carolina rice even answers, well dressed, in this way.   One or two minutes, more or less, will, sometimes, from the varying quality of the grain, be requisite to render it tender.

ANOTHER RECEIPT FOR BOILING RICE; *(not so good as the preceding one.)*

Wash the rice thoroughly in several waters, and soak it for an hour; drain and throw it into a large quantity of fast-boiling water. Leave it uncovered, take off the scum, and add salt when it is nearly done. When it has boiled from fifteen to eighteen minutes, drain it well, heap it lightly in a dish, and place it in a gentle oven to dry.

Obs.—Rice is of far better flavour when cooked in so much water only as it will absorb; but it cannot then so easily be rendered dry enough to serve with currie, or with curried soups. One pint of rice, washed and soaked for a few minutes, then wiped very dry, and dropped by degrees into five half pints of water, which should boil quickly, and continue to do so, while the rice is being added, and for a minute afterwards, and then placed over the fire, that it may stew very softly for half an hour, or until it is tender, and as dry as it will become without being burned, will be found very good. The addition of a couple of ounces of fresh butter, when it is nearly done, will convert it into a very palatable dish of itself.

AN EXCELLENT GREEN PEAS SOUP.

Take at their fullest size, but before they are of bad colour or worm-eaten, three pints of fine large peas, and boil them as for table (see Chapter XV.) with half a teaspoonful of carbonate of soda in the water, that they may be very green. When they are quite tender, drain them well, and put them into a couple of quarts of boiling, pale, but *good* beef or veal stock, and stew them in it gently for half an hour, then work the whole through a fine hair-sieve; put it into a clean pan and bring it to the point of boiling; add salt, should it be needed, and a small teaspoonful of pounded sugar, clear off the scum entirely, and serve the soup as hot as possible, with small pale sippets of fried bread. An elegant variety of it is made by adding a half pint more of stock to the peas, and about three quarters of a pint of asparagus points, boiled apart, and well drained before they are thrown into it, which should be done only the instant before it is sent to table: the fried bread will not then be needed.

Green peas, 3 pints: boiled 25 to 30 minutes, or more. Veal or beef stock, 2 quarts (with peas:) ½ an hour. Sugar, one small teaspoonful; salt, if needed.

Obs.—When there is no stock at hand, four or five pounds of shin of beef, boiled slowly down with three quarts of water to two, and well seasoned with savoury herbs, young carrots, and onions, will serve instead quite well. A thick slice of lean, undressed ham would improve it.

Should a common English peas soup be wished for, make it somewhat thinner than the one above, and add to it, just before it is dished, from half to three quarters of a pint of young peas boiled tender, and well drained.

GREEN PEAS SOUP, WITHOUT MEAT.

Boil tender, in three quarts of water, with the proportions of salt and soda directed for them in Chapter XV., one quart of large, full grown peas; drain and pound them in a mortar, mix with them gradually five pints of the liquor in which they were boiled, put the whole again over the fire, and stew it gently for a quarter of an hour; then press it through a hair-sieve. In the mean time, simmer, in from three to four ounces of butter,* three large, or four small cucumbers, pared and sliced, the hearts of three or four lettuces shred small, from one to four onions, according to the taste, cut thin, a few small sprigs of parsley, and, when the flavour is liked, a dozen leaves or more of mint, roughly chopped: keep these stirred over a gentle fire for nearly or quite an hour, and strew over them a half-teaspoonful of salt, and a good season- ing of white pepper or cayenne. When they are partially done, drain them from the butter, put them into the strained stock, and let the whole boil gently until all the butter has been thrown to the surface, and been entirely cleared from it; then throw in from half to three- quarters of a pint of young peas, boiled as for eating, and serve the soup immediately.

When more convenient, the peas, with a portion of the liquor, may be pressed through a sieve, instead of being crushed in a mortar; and when the colour of the soup is not so much a consideration as the fla- vour, they may be slowly stewed until perfectly tender in four ounces of good butter, instead of being boiled: a few green onions, and some branches of parsley may then be added to them.

Green peas, 1 quart; water, 5 pints; cucumbers, 3 to 6; lettuces, 3 or 4; onions, 1 to 4; little parsley; mint (if liked), 12 to 20 leaves; butter, 3 to 4 ozs.; salt, half-teaspoonful; seasoning of white pepper or cayenne: 50 to 60 minutes. Young peas, $\frac{1}{2}$ to $\frac{3}{4}$ of a pint.

Obs.—We must repeat that the peas for these soups must not be *old*, as when they are so, their fine sweet flavour is entirely lost, and the dried ones would have almost as good an effect; nor should they be of inferior kinds. Freshly gathered marrowfats, taken at nearly, or quite their full growth, will give the best quality of soup. We are credibly informed, but canoot assert it on our own authority, that it is often made for expensive tables in early spring, with the young tender plants or halms of the peas, when they are about a foot in height. They are cut off close to the ground, like small salad, then boiled and pressed through a strainer, and mixed with the stock. The flavour is affirmed to be ex- cellent.

.A CHEAP GREEN PEAS SOUP.

Wash very clean, and throw into an equal quantity of boiling water, salted as for peas, three quarts of the shells, and in from twenty to thirty minutes, when they will be quite tender, turn the whole into a large strainer, and press the pods strongly with a wooden spoon. Mea- sure the liquor, put two quarts of it into a clean, deep saucepan, and when it boils add to it a quart of full grown peas, two, or even three large cucumbers, as many moderate-sized lettuces freed from the coarser leaves, and cut small, one large onion (or more if liked,) sliced ex- tremely thin and stewed for half an hour in a morsel of butter before it is added to the soup, or gently fried without being allowed to brown; a branch or two of parsley, and, when the flavour is liked, a dozen leaves of mint. Stew these softly for an hour, with the addition of a small teaspoonful, or a larger quantity if required, of salt, and a good seasoning of fine white pepper, or of cayenne; then press the whole of the vegetables with the soup through a hair-sieve, beat it afresh, and

---

* Some persons prefer the vegetables slowly fried to a fine brown, then drained on a sieve, and well dried before the fire; but though more savoury so, they do not improve the colour of the soup.

send it to table with a dish of small fried sippets. The colour will not
he so bright as that of the more expensive soups which precede it, but
it will be excellent in flavour.

Pea-shells, 3 quarts ; water, 3 quarts : 20 to 30 minutes. Liquor
from these, 2 quarts ; full-sized green peas, 1 quart ; large cucumbers,
2 or 3 ; lettuces, 3 ; onion, 1 (or more) ; little parsley ; mint, 12 leaves ;
seasoning of salt and pepper or cayenne : stewed 1 hour.

Obs.—The cucumbers should be pared, quartered, and freed from the
seeds before they are added to the soup. The peas, as we have said already more than once, should not be *old*, but taken at their full growth,
before they lose their colour : the youngest of the shells ought to be selected for the liquor.

RICH PEAS SOUP.

Soak a quart of fine yellow split peas for a night, drain them well,
and put them into a large soup-pot with five quarts of good brown gravy
stock ; and when they have boiled gently for half an hour, add to the soup
three onions, as many carrots, and a turnip or two, all sliced and fried
carefully in butter ; stew the whole softly till the peas are reduced to
pulp, then add as much salt and cayenne as may be needed to season it
well, give it two or three minutes' boil, and pass it through a sieve,
pressing the vegetables with it. Put into a clean saucepan as much as
may be required for table, add a little fresh stock to it should it be too
thick, and reduce it by quick boiling if too thin ; throw in the white
part of some fresh celery sliced a quarter of an inch thick, and when
this is tender send the soup quickly to table with a dish of small fried
sippets. A dessertspoonful or more of currie-powder greatly improves
peas soup : it should be smoothly mixed with a few spoonsful of it, and
poured to the remainder when this first begins to boil after having been
strained.

Split peas, 1 quart : soaked one night. Good brown gravy soup 5
quarts : 30 minutes. Onions and carrots browned in butter, 3 of each ;
turnips, 2 : 2½ to 3½ hours. Cayenne and salt as needed. Soup, 5
pints ; celery sliced, 1 large or 2 small heads : 20 minutes.

Obs.—When more convenient, six pounds of neck of beef well scored
and equally, but carefully browned, may be boiled gently with the peas
and fried vegetables in a gallon of water (which should be poured to
them boiling) for four or five hours.

COMMON PEAS SOUP.

Wash well a quart of good split peas, and float off such as remain on
the surface of the water ; soak them for one night, and boil them with
a bit of soda the size of a filbert in just sufficient water to allow them
to break to a mash. Put them into from three to four quarts of good
beef broth, and stew them in it gently for an hour ; then work the whole
through a sieve, heat afresh as much as may be required for table, season
it with salt and cayenne or common pepper, clear it perfectly from scum,
and send it to table with fried or toasted bread. Celery sliced and
stewed in it as directed for the rich peas soup, will be found a great improvement to this.

Peas, 1 quart : soaked 1 night ; boiled in two quarts or rather more
of water, 2 to 2½ hours. Beef broth, 3 to 4 quarts : 1 hour. Salt and
cayenne or pepper as needed : 3 minutes.

PEAS SOUP WITHOUT MEAT.

To a pint of peas, freed from all that are worm-eaten, and well washed, put five pints of cold water, and boil them tolerably tender; then add a couple of onions (more or less according to the taste), a couple of fine carrots grated, one large or two moderate-sized turnips sliced, all gently fried brown in butter; half a teaspoonful of black pepper, and three times as much of salt. Stew these softly, keeping them often stirred, until the vegetables are sufficiently tender to press through a sieve; then rub the whole through one, put it into a clean pan, and when it boils throw in a sliced head of celery, heighten the seasoning if needful, and in twenty minutes serve the soup as hot as possible, with a dish of fried or toasted bread cut into dice. A little Chili vinegar can be added when liked: a larger proportion of vegetables also may be boiled down with the peas at pleasure. Weak broth, or the liquor in which a joint has been boiled, can, when at hand, be substituted for water, but the soup is very palatable as we have given the receipt for it. Some persons like it flavoured with a little mushroom catsup.

Split peas, 1 pint; water, 5 pints: 2 hours or more. Onions, 2; carrots, 2; large turnip, 1; pepper, ½ teaspoonful; salt, 1½ teaspoonful: 1 to 1½ hour. Celery, 1 head: 20 minutes.

OX-TAIL SOUP.

An inexpensive and very nutritious soup may be made of ox-tails, but it will be insipid in flavour without the addition of a little ham, knuckle of bacon, or a pound or two of other meat. Wash and soak three tails, pour on them a gallon of cold water, let them be brought gradually to boil, throw in an ounce and a half of salt, and clear off the scum carefully as soon as it forms upon the surface; when it ceases to rise, add four moderate-sized carrots, from two to four onions, according to the taste, a large faggot of savoury herbs, a head of celery, a couple of turnips, six or eight cloves, and a half-teaspoonful of peppercorns. Stew these gently from three hours to three and a half, if the tails be very large; lift them out, strain the liquor, and skim off all the fat; cut the meat from the tails (or serve them, if preferred, divided into joints), and put it into a couple of quarts or rather more of the stock; stir in, when these begin to boil, a thickening of arrow-root or of rice-flour (see page 39), mixed with as much cayenne and salt as may be required to flavour the soup well, and serve it very hot. If stewed down until the flesh falls away from the bones, the ox-tails will make stock which will be quite a firm jelly when cold; and this, strained, thickened, and well flavoured with spices, catsup, or a little wine, would, to many tastes, be a superior soup to the above. A richer one still may be made by pouring good beef broth instead of water to the meat in the first instance.

Ox-tails, 3; water, 1 gallon; salt, 1½ oz.; carrots, 4; onions, 2 to 4; turnips, 2; celery, 1 head; cloves, 8; peppercorns, ½ teaspoonful; faggot of savoury herbs: 3 hours to 3½. For a richer soup, 5 to 6 hours. (Ham or gammon of bacon at pleasure, with other flavourings.)

Obs.—To increase the savour of this soup when the meat is not served in it, the onions, turnips, and carrots may be gently fried until of a fine light brown, before they are added to it.

A CHEAP AND GOOD STEW SOUP.

Put from four to five pounds of the gristly part of the shin of beef into three quarts of cold water, and stew it very softly indeed, with the addition of the salt and vegetables directed for bouillon (see page 41), until the whole is very tender; lift out the meat, strain the liquor, and put it into a large clean saucepan, add a thickening of rice-flour or arrow-root, pepper and salt if needed, and a tablespoonful of mushroom catsup. In the mean time, cut all the meat into small, thick slices, add it to the soup, and serve it as soon as it is very hot. The thickening and catsup may be omitted, and all the vegetables, pressed through a strainer, may be stirred into the soup instead, before the meat is put back into it.

SOUP IN HASTE.

Chop tolerably fine a pound of lean beef, mutton, or veal, and when it is partly done, add to it a small carrot and one small turnip, cut in slices, half an ounce of celery, the white part of a moderate-sized leek, or a quarter-ounce of onion. Mince all these together, and put the whole into a deep saucepan with three pints of cold water. When the soup boils, take off the scum, and add a little salt and pepper. In half an hour it will be ready to serve with or without straining: it may be flavoured at will, with cayenne, catsup, or aught else that is preferred. It may be converted into French spring broth, by passing it through a sieve, and boiling it again for five or six minutes with a handful of young and nicely-picked sorrel.

Meat, 1 lb.; carrot, 2 ozs.; turnip, 1½ oz.; celery, ½ oz.; onion, ¼ oz.; water, 3 pints: half an hour. Little pepper and salt.

Obs.—Three pounds of beef or mutton, with two or three slices of ham, and vegetables in proportion to the above receipt, all chopped fine, and boiled in three quarts of water for an hour and a half, will make an excellent family soup on an emergency; additional boiling will of course improve it, and a little spice should be added after it has been skimmed, and salted. It may easily be converted into carrot, turnip, or ground-rice soup after it is strained.

VEAL OR MUTTON BROTH.

To each pound of meat add a quart of cold water, bring it gently to boil, skim it very clean, add salt in the same proportion as for bouillon (see page 41), with spices and vegetables also, unless *unflavoured* broth be required, when a few peppercorns, a blade or two of mace, and a bunch of savoury herbs will be sufficient; though for some purposes even these, with the exception of the salt, are better omitted. Simmer the broth for about four hours, unless the quantity be very small, when from two and a half to three will be sufficient. A little rice boiled down with the meat will both thicken the broth and render it more nutritious. Strain it off when done, and let it stand till quite cold, that the fat may be entirely cleared from it: this is especially needful when it is to be served to an invalid.

Veal or mutton, 4 lbs.; water, 4 quarts; salt. For vegetables, &c. see page 39; rice (if used), 4 ozs.: 4 hours or more.

MILK SOUP WITH VERMICELLI.

Throw into five pints of boiling milk a small quantity of salt, and then drop lightly into it five ounces of good fresh vermicelli; keep the milk stirred as this is added, to prevent its gathering into lumps, and continue to stir it very frequently from fifteen to twenty minutes, or until it is perfectly tender. The addition of a little pounded sugar and powdered cinnamon, renders this a very agreeable dish. In Catholic countries, milk soups of various kinds constantly supply the place of those made with meat, on *maigre* days; and with us they are sometimes very acceptable, as giving a change of diet for the nursery or sick room. Rice, semoulina, sago, cocoa nut, and maccaroni may all in turn be used for them as directed for other soups in this chapter, but they will be required in rather smaller proportions with the milk.

Milk, 5 pints; vermicelli, 5 ozs.: 15 to 20 minutes.

CHAPTER II.

FISH.

TO CHOOSE FISH.

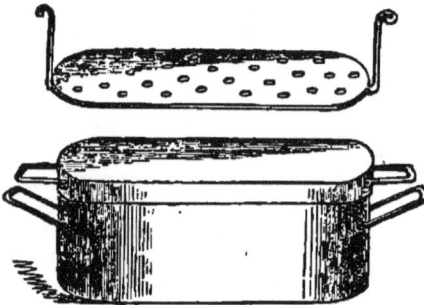
Copper Fish or Ham Kettle.

THE cook should be well acquainted with the signs of freshness and good condition in fish, as many of them are most unwholesome articles of food when stale, or out of season. The eyes should be bright, the gills of a fine clear red, the body stiff, the flesh firm, yet elastic to the touch, and the smell not disagreeable. When all these marks are reversed, and the eyes are sunken, the gills very dark in hue, the fish itself flabby and of offensive odour, it is bad, and should be avoided. The chloride of soda, will, it is true, restore it to a tolerably eatable state,* if it be not very much over-kept, but it will never resemble in quality fish that is fresh from the water.

Small Fish Kettle, called a Mackerel Kettle.

A good turbot is thick, and full fleshed, and the under side is of a pale cream colour or yellowish white; when this is of a bluish tint, and the fish is thin and soft, it should be rejected. The same observations apply equally to soles.

The best salmon and cod fish are known by a small head, very thick shoulders, and a small tail; the scales of the former should be bright, and its flesh of a fine red colour: to be eaten in perfection it should be dressed as soon as it is caught, before the curd (or white substance which lies between the flakes of flesh) has melted

---

* We have known this applied very successfully to salmon which from some hours keeping in sultry weather had acquired a slight degree of taint, of which no trace remained after it was dressed.

and rendered the fish oily. In that state it is really *crimp*, but continues so only for a very few hours; and it bears therefore a much higher price in the London market then, than when mellowed by having been kept a day or two.

The flesh of cod fish should be white and clear before it is boiled, whiter still after it is boiled, and firm though tender, sweet and mild in flavour, and separated easily into large flakes. Many persons consider it rather improved than otherwise by having a little salt rubbed along the inside of of the back-bone and letting it lie from twenty-four to forty-eight hours before it is dressed. It is sometimes served crimp like salmon, and must then be sliced as soon as it is dead, or within the shortest possible time afterwards.

Herrings, mackerel, and whitings, lose their freshness so rapidly, that unless newly caught they are quite uneatable. The herring may, it is said, be deprived of the strong rank smell which it emits when broiled or fried, by stripping off the skin, under which lies the oil that causes the disagreeable odour. The whiting is a peculiarly pure flavoured and delicate fish, and acceptable generally to invalids from being very light of digestion.

Eels should be alive and brisk in movement when they are purchased, but the "horrid barbarity," as it is truly designated, of skinning and dividing them while they are so, is without excuse as they are easily destroyed "by piercing the spinal marrow close to the back part of the skull with a sharp pointed knife, or skewer. If this be done in the right place all motion will instantly cease." We quote Doctor Kitchener's assertion on this subject; but we know that the mode of destruction which he recommends is commonly practised by the London fishmongers. Boiling water also will immediately cause vitality to cease, and is perhaps the most humane and ready method of destroying the fish.

Lobsters, prawns, and shrimps are very stiff when freshly boiled, and the tails turn strongly inwards; when these relax, and the fish are soft and watery, they are stale; and the smell will detect their being so instantly even if no other symptoms of it be remarked. If bought alive, lobsters should be chosen by their weight and "liveliness." The hen lobster is preferred for sauce and soups, on account of the coral; but the flesh of the male is generally considered of finer flavour for eating. The vivacity of their leaps will show when prawns and shrimps are fresh from the sea.

Oysters should close forcibly on the knife when they are opened: if the shells are apart ever so little they are losing their condition, and when they remain far open the fish are dead, and fit only to be thrown away. Small plump natives are very preferable to the larger and coarser kinds.

TO CLEAN FISH.

Let this be done always with the most scrupulous nicety, for nothing can more effectually destroy the appetite, or *disgrace the cook*, than fish sent to table imperfectly cleaned. Handle it lightly, and never throw it roughly about, so as to bruise it; wash it well, but do not leave it longer in the water than is necessary, for fish, like meat, loses its flavour from being soaked. When the scales are to be removed, lay the fish flat upon its side, and hold it firmly with the left hand, while they are scraped off with the right; turn it, and when both sides are done, pour or pump sufficient water over to float off all the loose scales;

then proceed to open and empty it. Be sure that not the slightest particle of offensive matter be left in the inside; wash out the blood entirely, and scrape or brush it away, if needful, from the back-bone. This may easily be accomplished, without opening the fish so much as to render it unsightly when it is sent to table. The red mullet is dressed without being emptied, and smelts are drawn at the gills. When the scales are left on, the outside of the fish should be wel washed and wiped with a coarse cloth, drawn gently from the head to the tail. Eels, to be wholesome, should be skinned, but they are sometimes dressed without; boiling water should then be poured upon them, and they should be left in it from five to ten minutes, before they are cut up. The dark skin of the sole must be stripped off when it is fried, but it must be left on, like that of a turbot, when the fish is boiled, and it should be dished with the white side upwards. Whitings are skinned, and dipped usually into egg and bread-crumbs, when they are to be fried; but for boiling or broiling, the skin must be left on.

TO KEEP FISH.

We find that all the smaller kinds of fish keep best if emptied and cleaned as soon as they are brought in, then wiped gently as dry as they can be, and hung separately by the head on the hooks in the ceiling of a cool larder, or in the open air when the weather will allow. When there is danger of their being attacked by flies, a wire safe, placed in a strong draught of air, is better adapted to the purpose. Soles in winter will remain good a couple of days when thus prepared; and even whitings and mackerel may be kept so without losing any of their excellence. Salt may be rubbed slightly over cod fish, and well along the back-bone, but it injures the flavour of salmon, the inside of which may be rubbed with vinegar, and peppered instead. When excessive sultriness renders all of these modes unavailing, the fish must at once be partially cooked to preserve it, but this should be avoided if possible, as it is very rarely so good when this method is resorted to.

TO SWEETEN TAINTED FISH.

The application of the pyroligneous acid will effect this when the taint is but slight. A wineglassful, mixed with two of water, may be poured over the fish, and rubbed upon the parts more particularly requiring it; it must then be left for some minutes untouched, and afterwards washed in several waters, and soaked until the smell of the acid is no longer perceptible. The chloride of soda, from its powerful antiputrescent properties, will have more effect when the fish is in a worse state. It should be applied in the same manner, and will not at all injure the flavour of the fish, which is not fit for food when it cannot be perfectly purified by either of these means. The chloride may be diluted more or less, as occasion may require.

BRINE FOR BOILING FISH

Fish is exceedingly insipid if sufficient salt be not mixed with the water in which it is boiled, but the precise quantity required for it will depend, in some measure, upon the kind of salt which is used. Fine common salt is that for which our directions are given; but when the Maldon salt, which is very superior in strength, as well as in its other qualities, is substituted for it, a smaller quantity must be allowed.

About four ounces to the gallon of water will be sufficient for small fish in general; an additional ounce, or rather more, will not be too much for cod fish, lobsters, crabs, prawns, and shrimps; and salmon will require eight ounces, as the brine for this fish should be strong: the water should always be perfectly well skimmed from the moment the scum begins to form upon the surface.

Mackerel, whiting, and other small fish, 4 ozs. of salt to a gallon of water. Cod fish, lobsters, crabs, prawns, shrimps, 5 to 6 ozs. Salmon, 8 ozs.

TO RENDER BOILED FISH FIRM.

Put a small bit of saltpetre with the salt into the water in which it is boiled: a quarter-ounce will be sufficient for a gallon.

TO KEEP FISH HOT FOR TABLE.

Never leave it in the water after it is done; but if it cannot be sent to table as soon as it is ready to serve, lift it out, lay the fish-plate into a large and very hot dish, and set it across the fish-kettle; just dip a clean cloth into the boiling water, and spread it upon the fish; place a tin cover over it, and let it remain so until two or three minutes before it is wanted, then remove the cloth, and put the fish back into the kettle for an instant that it may be as hot as possible; drain, dish, and serve it immediately: the water should be kept boiling the whole time.

TO BOIL A TURBOT.
In season all the year.

A fine turbot, in full season, and well served, is one of the most delicate and delicious fish that can be sent to table; but it is generally an expensive dish, and its excellence so much depends on the manner in which it is dressed, that great care should be taken to prepare it properly. After it is emptied, wash the inside until it is perfectly cleansed, and rub *lightly* a little fine salt over the outside, as this will render less washing and handling necessary, by at once taking off the slime; change the water several times, and when the fish is as clean as it is possible to render it, draw a sharp knife through the thickest part of the middle of the back nearly through to the bone. *Never cut off the fins* of a turbot when preparing it for table, and remember that it is the dark side of the fish in which the incision is to be made, to prevent the skin of the white side from cracking. Dissolve in a well-cleaned turbot, or common fish-kettle, in as much cold spring water as will cover the fish abundantly, salt, in the proportion of four ounces to the gallon, and a *morsel* of saltpetre; wipe the fish-plate with a clean cloth, lay the turbot upon it with the white side upwards, place it in the kettle, bring it slowly to boil, and clear off the scum *thoroughly* as it rises. Let the water only just simmer until the fish is done, then lift it out, drain, and slide it gently on to a very hot dish, with a hot napkin neatly arranged over the drainer. Send it immediately to table with rich lobster sauce, good plain melted butter, and a dish of dressed cucumber. For a simple dinner, anchovy, or shrimp-sauce is sometimes served with a small turbot. Should there be any cracks in the skin of the fish, branches of curled parsley may be laid lightly over them, or part of the inside coral of the lobster, rubbed through a fine hair-sieve, may be sprinkled over the fish; but it is better without either, when it is very white, and unbroken. When garnishings are in favour, a slice of lemon and a tuft of curled parsley may be placed alternately round the edge of the dish. A border of fried smelts, or of fillets of soles, was formerly served, in general, round a turbot, and is always a very admissible addition, though no longer so fashionable as it was. From fifteen to twenty minutes will boil a moderate-sized fish, and from twenty to thirty a large one; but as the same time will not always be sufficient for a fish of the same weight, the cook must watch it attentively, and lift it out as soon as its appearance denotes its being done.

Moderate sized-turbot, 15 to 20 minutes. Large, 20 to 30 minutes. Longer, if of unusual size.

Obs.—A lemon gently squeezed, and rubbed over the fish, is thought to preserve its whiteness. Some good cooks still put turbot into *boiling* water, and to prevent its breaking, tie it with a cloth tightly to the fish-plate; but cold water seems better adapted to it, as it is desirable that it should be gradually heated through before it begins to boil.

TURBOT A LA CREME.

Raise carefully from the bones the flesh of a cold turbot, and clear it from the dark skin; cut it into small squares, and put it into an exceedingly clean stewpan or saucepan; then make and pour upon it the cream-sauce of Chapter IV., or make as much as may be required for the fish by the same receipt, with equal proportions of milk and cream, and a little additional flour. Heat the turbot slowly in the sauce, but do not allow it to boil, and send it very hot to table. The white skin of the fish is not usually added to this dish, and it is of better appearance without it; but for a family dinner, it may be left on the flesh, when it is much liked. No acid must be stirred to the sauce until the whole is ready for table.

TO BROIL SALMON.

This is a good method of dressing a small quantity of salmon for one or two persons. It may be cut in slices the whole round of the fish, each taking in two divisions of the bone; or the fish may be split, and the bone removed, and the sides of the fish divided into cutlets of three or four inches each: the former method is preferable, if done neatly with a sharp knife. Rub it thoroughly dry with a clean rough cloth; then do each piece over with salad oil or butter. Have a nice clean gridiron over a very clear fire, and at some distance from it. When the bars are hot through wipe them, and rub with lard or suet to prevent sticking; lay on the salmon, and sprinkle with salt. When one side is brown, carefully turn and brown the other. They do equally well or better in a tin or flat dish, in an oven, with a little bit of butter, or sweet oil; or they may be done in buttered paper on the gridiron. Sauce, lobster or shrimp.

TO BAKE SALMON.

If a small fish, turn the tail to the mouth, and skewer it; forcemeat may be put in the belly, or, if part of a large fish is to be baked, cut it in slices, egg it over, and dip it in the forcemeat. Stick bits of butter about the salmon (a few oysters laid round are an improvement.) It will require occasional basting with the butter. When one side becomes brown, let it be carefully turned, and when the second side is brown, it is done. Take it up carefully, with all that lies about it in the baking dish. For sauce, melted butter, with two tablespoonful of port wine, one of catsup, and the juice of a lemon, poured over the fish, or anchovy sauce in a boat.

PICKLE SALMON.

Do not scrape off the scales, but clean the fish carefully, and cut into pieces about eight inches long. Make a strong brine of salt and water; to two quarts, put two pounds of salt, and a quarter of a pint of vinegar; in all, make just enough to cover the fish; boil it slowly, and barely as much as you would for eating hot. Drain off all the liquor; and, when cold, lay the pieces in a kit or small tub. Pack it as close as possible, and fill up with equal parts of best vinegar and the liquor in which the fish was boiled. Let it remain so a day or two, then again fill up. Serve with a garnish of fresh fennel. The same method of pickling will apply to sturgeon, mackerel, herrings, and sprats. The three latter are sometimes baked in vinegar, flavoured with allspice and bay leaves, and eat very well; but will not keep more than a few days.

TO BOIL SALMON.

In full season from May to August: may be had much earlier, but is scarce and dear.

To preserve the fine colour of this fish, and to *set the curd* when it is quite freshly caught, it is usual to put it into *boiling*, instead of cold water. Scale, empty, and wash it with the greatest nicety, and be especially careful to cleanse all the blood from the inside. Stir into the fish-kettle eight ounces of common salt to the gallon of water, let it boil quickly for a minute or two, take off all the scum, put in the salmon and boil it moderately fast, if it be small, but more gently should it be very thick; and assure yourself that it is quite sufficiently done, before it is sent to table, for nothing can be more distasteful, even to the eye, than fish which is under dressed.

From two to three pounds of the thick part of a fine salmon will require half an hour to boil it, but eight or ten pounds will be done enough in little more than double that time; less, in proportion to its weight, should be allowed for a small fish, or for the thin end of a large one. Do not allow the salmon to remain in the water after it is ready to serve, or both its flavour and appearance will be injured. Dish it on a hot napkin, and send dressed cucumber, and anchovy, shrimp, or lobster sauce, and a tureen of plain melted butter to table with it.

To each gallon of water, 8 ozs. salt. Salmon, 2 to 3 lbs. (thick) ½ hour: 8 to 10 lbs., 1¼ hour: small, or thin fish, less time.

Obs.—A fashionable mode of serving salmon at the present day is to divide the larger portion of the body into three equal parts; to boil them in water, or in a marinade; and to serve them dished in a line, but not close together, and covered with a rich Genevese sauce; it appears to us that the skin should be stripped from any fish over which the sauce is poured, but in this case it is not customary.

CRIMPED SALMON.

Cut into slices an inch and a half, or two inches thick, the body of a salmon *quite newly caught;* throw them into strong salt and water as they are done, but do not let them soak in it; wash them well, lay them on a fish-plate, and put them into fast-boiling water, salted, and well skimmed. In from ten to fifteen minutes they will be done. Dish them on a napkin, and send them very hot to table with lobster sauce, and plain melted butter; or with the caper fish sauce of Chapter IV

4

The water should be salted as for salmon boiled in the ordinary way and the scum should be cleared off with great care after the fish is in.

In boiling water, 10 to 15 minutes.

SALMON A LA ST. MARCEL.

Separate some cold boiled salmon into flakes, and free them entirely from the skin; break the bones, and boil them in a pint of water for half an hour. Strain off the liquor, put it into a clean saucepan and stir into it by degrees when it begins to boil quickly, two ounces of butter mixed with a large teaspoonful of flour, and when the whole has boiled for two or three minutes add a teaspoonful of essence of anchovies, one of good mushroom catsup, half as much lemon-juice or Chili vinegar, a half teaspoonful of pounded mace, some cayenne, and a very little salt. Heat the fish very slowly in the sauce by the side of the fire, but do not allow it to boil. When it is very hot, dish, and send it quickly to table. French cooks, when they re-dress fish or meat of any kind, prepare the flesh with great nicety, and then put it into a stewpan, and pour the sauce upon it, which is, we think, better than the more usual English mode of laying it into the boiling sauce. The cold salmon may also be re-heated in the cream sauce of Chapter IV. or in the Maître d'Hotel sauce which follows it; and will be found excellent with either. This receipt is for a moderate sized dish.

Obs.—We regret that we cannot give insertion to a larger number of receipts for dressing this truly excellent fish, which answers for almost every mode of cookery. It may be fried in cutlets, broiled, baked, roasted, or stewed; served in a common, or in a raised pie, or in a potato-pasty; in a salad, in jelly; collared, smoked, or pickled; and will be found good prepared by any of these processes. A rather full seasoning of savoury herbs is thought to correct the effect of the natural richness of the salmon. For directions to broil, bake, or roast it, the reader is referred to Chapter VII.

TO BOIL COD FISH.

In highest season from October to the beginning of February; in perfection about Christmas.

When this fish is large, the head and shoulders are sufficient for a handsome dish, and they contain all the choicer portion of it, though not so much substantial eating, as the middle of the body, which, in consequence, is generally preferred to them by the frugal housekeeper. Wash the fish, and cleanse the inside, and the back-bone in particular, with the most scrupulous care; lay it into the fish kettle and cover it well with cold water mixed with five ounces of salt to the gallon, and about a quarter ounce of saltpetre to the whole. Place it over a moderate fire, clear off the scum perfectly, and let the fish boil gently until it is done. Drain it well* and dish it carefully upon a very hot napkin with the liver and the roe as a garnish. To these are usually added tufts of lightly scraped horse-raddish round the edge. Serve well made oyster sauce and plain melted butter with it; or anchovy sauce when oysters cannot be procured. The cream sauce of Chapter IV. is also an appropriate one for this fish.

Moderate sized, 20 to 30 minutes. Large, ½ to ¾ hour.

---

* This should be done by setting the fish-plate across the kettle for a minute or two.

SLICES OF COD FISH FRIED.

Cut the middle or tail of the fish into slices nearly an inch thick, season them with salt and white pepper or cayenne, flour them well, and fry them of a clear equal brown on both sides; drain them on a sieve before the fire, and serve them on a well-heated napkin, with plenty of crisped parsley round them. Or, dip them into beaten egg, and then into fine crumbs mixed with a seasoning of salt and pepper (some cooks add one of minced herbs also,) before they are fried. Send melted butter and anchovy sauce to table with them.

8 to 12 minutes.

Obs.—This is a much better way of dressing the thin part of the fish than boiling it, and as it is generally cheap, it makes thus an economical, as well as a very good dish : if the slices are lifted from the frying-pan into a good curried gravy, and left in it by the side of the fire for a few minutes before they are sent to table, they will be found excellent.

STEWED COD.

Put into boiling water, salted as usual, about three pounds of fresh cod fish cut into slices an inch and a half thick, and boil them gently for five minutes; lift them out, and let them drain. Have ready-heated in a wide stewpan nearly a pint of veal gravy or of very good broth, lay in the fish, and stew it for five minutes, then add four tablespoonsful of extremely fine bread-crumbs, and simmer it for three minutes longer. Stir well into the sauce a large teaspoonful of arrow-root, quite free from lumps, a fourth part as much of mace, something less of cayenne, and a tablespoonful of essence of anchovies, mixed with a glass of white wine and a dessertspoonful of lemon juice. Boil the whole for a couple of minutes, lift out the fish carefully with a slice, pour the sauce over, and serve it quickly.

Cod fish, 3 lbs.: boiled 5 minutes. Gravy, or strong broth, nearly 1 pint: 5 minutes. Bread-crumbs, 4 tablespoonsful: 3 minutes. Arrow-root, 1 large teaspoonful; mace, ¼ teaspoonful; less of cayenne; essence of anchovies, 1 tablespoonful; lemon-juice, 1 dessertspoonful; sherry or Madeira, 1 wineglassful: 2 minutes.

Obs.—A dozen or two of oysters, bearded, and added with their strained liquor to this dish two or three minutes before it is served, will, to many tastes, vary it very agreeably.

STEWED COD FISH, IN BROWN SAUCE.

Slice the fish, take off the skin, flour it well, and fry it quickly a fine brown; lift it out and drain it on the back of a sieve, arrange it in a clean stewpan, and pour in as much good brown gravy, boiling, as will nearly cover it; add from one to two glasses of port wine, or rather more of claret, a dessertspoonful of Chili vinegar, or the juice of half a lemon, and some cayenne, with as much salt as may be needed. Stew the fish very softly until it just begins to break, lift it carefully with a slice into a very hot dish, stir into the gravy an ounce and a half of butter, smoothly kneaded with a large teaspoonful of flour, and a little pounded mace, give the sauce a minute's boil, pour it over the fish, and serve it immediately. The wine may be omitted, good shin of beef stock substituted for the gravy, and a teaspoonful of soy, one of essence of anchovies, and two tablespoonsful of Harvey's sauce added to flavour it.

TO BOIL SALT FISH.

When very salt and dry, this must be long-soaked before it is boiled, but it is generally supplied by the fishmongers nearly or quite ready to dress. When it is not so, lay it for a night into a large quantity of cold water, then let it lie exposed to the air for some time, then again put it into water, and continue thus until it is well softened. Brush it very clean, wash it thoroughly, and put it with abundance of cold water into the fish kettle, place it near the fire and let it heat very slowly indeed. Keep it just on the point of simmering, without allowing it ever to *boil* (which would render it hard), from three quarters of an hour to a full hour, according to its weight; should it be quite small and thin, less time will be sufficient for it; but by following these directions, the fish will be almost as good as if it were fresh. The scum should be cleared off with great care from the beginning. Egg sauce and boiled parsneps are the usual accompaniments to salt fish, which should be dished upon a hot napkin, and which is sometimes also thickly strewed with chopped eggs.

SALT FISH; (*a la Maître d'Hotel.*)

Boil the fish by the foregoing receipt, or take the remains of that which has been served at table, flake it off clear from the bones, and strip away every morsel of the skin; then lay it into a very clean saucepan or stewpan, and pour upon it the sharp Maître d'Hotel sauce of Chapter IV.; or, dissolve gently two or three ounces of butter with four or five spoonsful of water, and a half-teaspoonful of flour; add some pepper or cayenne, very little salt, and a dessertspoonful or more of minced parsley. Heat the fish slowly quite through in either of these sauces, and toss or stir it until the whole is well mixed; if the second be used, add the juice of half a lemon, or a small quantity of Chili vinegar, just before it is taken from the fire. The fish thus prepared may be served in a deep dish, with a border of mashed parsneps or potatoes.

TO BOIL CODS SOUNDS.

Should they be highly salted, soak them for a night, and on the following day, rub off entirely the discoloured skin; wash them well, lay them into plenty of cold milk and water, and boil them gently from thirty to forty minutes, or longer, should they not be quite tender. Clear off the scum as it rises with great care, or it will sink, and adhere to the sounds, of which the appearance will then be spoiled. Drain them well, dish them on a napkin, and send egg sauce and plain melted butter to table with them.

TO FRY CODS' SOUNDS IN BATTER.

Boil them as directed above, until they are nearly done, then lift them out, lay them on to a drainer, and let them remain till they are cold; cut them across in strips of an inch deep, curl them round, dip them into a good French or English batter, fry them of a fine pale brown, drain and dry them well, dish them on a hot napkin, and garnish them with crisped parsley.

TO MAKE CHOWDER.

Lay some slices cut from the fat part of pork in a deep stew-pan, mix sliced onions with a variety of sweet herbs, and lay them on the pork; bone and cut a fresh cod into thin slices, and place them on the pork, then put a layer of pork, on that a layer of biscuit, then alternately the other materials until the pan is nearly full, season with pepper and salt, put in about a quart of water, cover the stew-pan very close, and let it stand, with fire above as well as below, for four hours; then skim it well, and it is done.

TO BOIL ROCK-FISH, BLACK-FISH, AND SEA-BASS.

Clean the fish with scrupulous care, particularly the back-bone, then lay the fish into the fish-kettle and cover it with cold water, strewing in a handful of salt (and a small pinch of saltpetre, if you have it), and place it over a moderate fire. Clean off the scum carefully, and let it boil very gently till it is done; then drain it, as directed for cod-fish, and dish it nicely — garnished with hard-boiled eggs, cut in halves. Celery sauce, or anchovy sauce, is the proper kind for these fish, or plain melted butter.

TO BOIL HALIBUT.

Take a small halibut, or what you require from a large fish. Put it into the fish-kettle, with the back of the fish undermost, cover it with cold water, in which a handful of salt and a bit of saltpetre, the size of a hazle-nut, have been dissolved. When it begins to boil skim it carefully, and then let it just simmer till it is done. Four pounds of fish will require half an hour, nearly, to boil it. Drain it, garnish with horse-radish or parsley—egg sauce, or plain melted butter, are served with it.

FILLETS OF HALIBUT, BLACK-FISH, &c.

The word *fillet*, whether applied to fish, poultry, game, or butcher's meat, means simply the flesh of either (or of certain portions of it), raised clear from the bones in a handsome form, and divided or not, as the manner in which it is to be served may require. It is an elegant mode of dressing various kinds of fish, and even those which are not the most highly esteemed, afford an excellent dish when thus prepared. The fish, to be filletted with advantage, should be large; the flesh may then be divided down the middle of the back, next, separated from the fins, and with a very sharp knife raised clean from the bones.* When thus prepared, the fillets may be divided, trimmed into a good form, egged, covered with fine crumbs, fried in the usual way, and served with the same sauces as the whole fish; or each fillet may be rolled up, in its entire length, if very small, or after being once divided, if large, and fastened with a slight twine, or a short thin skewer; then egged, crumbed, and fried in plenty of boiling lard; or merely well floured and fried from eight to ten minutes. When the fish are not very large, they are sometimes boned without being parted in the middle, and each side is rolled from the tail to the head, after being first spread with butter, a few bread-crumbs, and a high seasoning of mace and cayenne; or with pounded lobster mixed with a large portion of the coral, and the same seasoning, and proportion of butter; then laid into a dish, well covered with crumbs of bread and clarified butter, and baked from twelve to sixteen minutes, or until the crumbs are coloured to a fine brown in a moderate oven.

---

* A celebrated French cook gives the following instructions for raising these fillets: —" Take them up by running your knife first between the bones and the flesh, then between the skin and the fillet; by leaning pretty hard on the table they will come off very neatly."

The fillets may likewise be cut into small strips or squares of uniform size, lightly dredged with pepper or cayenne, salt and flour, and fried in butter over a brisk fire; then well drained, and sauced with a good bechamel, flavoured with a teaspoonful of minced parsley.

BAKED SOLES, HALIBUT AND CARP.

Clarify from two to three ounces of fresh butter, and pour it into the dish in which the fish are to be served; add to it a little salt, some cayenne, a teaspoonful of essence of anchovies, and from one to two glasses of sherry, or of any other dry white wine; lay in a couple of fine soles which have been well cleaned and wiped very dry, strew over them a thick layer of fine bread-crumbs, moisten them with clarified butter, set the dish into a moderate oven, and bake the fish a quarter of an hour; we would recommend a little lemon-juice to be mixed with the sauce.

Baked 15 minutes.

Obs.—The fish are, we think, better without the wine in this receipt. They require but a small portion of liquid, which might be supplied by a little additional butter, a spoonful of water or pale gravy, the lemon-juice, and store-sauce. Minced parsley may be mixed with the bread-crumbs when it is liked.

SOLES OR CARP STEWED IN CREAM.

Prepare some very fresh middling sized fish with exceeding nicety, put them into boiling water slightly salted, and simmer them for two minutes only; lift them out, and let them drain; lay them into a wide stewpan with as much sweet rich cream as will nearly cover them; add a good seasoning of pounded mace, cayenne and salt; stew the fish softly from six to ten minutes, or until the flesh parts readily from the bones; dish them, stir the juice of half a lemon to the sauce, pour it over the soles, and send them immediately to table. Some lemon-rind may be boiled in the cream, if approved; and a small teaspoonful of arrow-root, very smoothly mixed with a little milk, may be stirred to the sauce (should it require thickening) before the lemon-juice is added. Turbot and brill also may be dressed by this receipt, time, proportioned to their size, being of course allowed for them.

Soles, 3 or 4: boiled in water 2 minutes. Cream, ½ to whole pint, salt, mace, cayenne: fish stewed, 6 to 10 minutes. Juice of half a lemon.

TO BOIL STURGEON.

Take off the skin, which is very rich and oily; cut in slices; season with pepper and salt; broil over a clear fire; rub over each slice a bit of butter, and serve with no other accompaniment than lemon; or the slices may be dipped in seasoning or forcemeat, twisted in buttered white paper, and so broiled. For sauce, serve melted butter with catsup. Garnish with sliced lemon, as the juice is generally used with the fish.

TO ROAST STURGEON.

A piece of sturgeon may be tied securely on a spit, and roasted. Keep it constantly basted with butter, and when nearly done dredge with bread crumbs. When the flakes begin to separate, it is done. It will take about half an hour before a brisk fire. Serve with good gravy, thickened with butter and flour, and enriched with an anchovy, a glass of sherry wine, and the juice of half a Seville orange or lemon.

TO STEW STURGEON.

Take enough gravy to cover the fish; set it on with a tablespoonful of salt, a few corns of black pepper, a bunch of sweet herbs, an onion or two, scraped horse-radish, and a glass of vinegar. Let this boil a few minutes; then set it aside to become pretty cool; then add the fish; let it come gradually to boil; and then stew gently till the fish begins to break. Take it off immediately; keep the fish warm; strain the gravy, and thicken with a good piece of butter; add a glass of port or sherry wine, a grate of nutmeg, and a little lemon juice. Simmer till it thickens, and then pour over the fish. Sauce, anchovy.

TO FRY STURGEON.

Cut the fish into rather thin slices; sprinkle it well with salt on both sides; when the salt has drawn out all the moisture of the fish, roll it in bread crumbs and egg, and fry it in hot lard. When done, take it out and put a glass of water, a spoonful of vinegar, and a little lemon-peel into the pan, give it a boil, cup and strain it over the fish.

TO BOIL WHITINGS; (*French Receipt.*)

Having scraped, cleaned, and wiped them, lay them on a fish-plate, and put them into water at the point of boiling; throw in a handful of salt, two bay leaves, and plenty of parsley, well washed, and tied together; let the fish *just simmer* from five to ten minutes, and watch them closely that they may not be over-done. Serve parsley and butter with them, and use in making it the liquor in which the whitings have been boiled.

Just simmered from 5 to 10 minutes.

BAKED WHITINGS A LA FRANCAISE.

Proceed with these exactly as with baked soles, page 70, or, pour a little clarified butter into a deep dish, and strew it rather thickly with finely-minced mushrooms, mixed with a teaspoonful of parsley, and (when the flavour is liked, and considered appropriate) with an eschalot or two, or the white part of a few green onions, also chopped very small. On these place the fish, after they have been scaled, emptied, thoroughly washed, and wiped dry: season them well with salt, and white pepper, or cayenne; sprinkle more of the herbs upon them; pour gently from one to two glasses of light white wine into the dish, cover the whitings with a thick layer of fine crumbs of bread, sprinkle these plentifully with clarified butter, and bake the fish from fifteen to twenty minutes. Send a cut lemon only to table with them. When the wine is not liked, a few spoonsful of pale veal gravy can be used instead; or a larger quantity of clarified butter, with a tablespoonful of water, a teaspoonful of lemon-pickle and of mushroom catsup, and a few drops of soy.

15 to 20 minutes.

TO BOIL MACKEREL.

In full season in May, June, and July; may be had also in early spring.

Open the fish sufficiently to admit of the insides being *perfectly cleansed*, but not more than is necessary for this purpose; empty them with care, lay the roes apart, and wash both them and the mackerel delicately clean. It is customary now to lay these, and the greater number of other fish as well, into cold water when they are to be boiled, formerly all were plunged at once into fast-boiling water. For such as are small and delicate, it should be warm, but not scalding; they should be brought gently to a soft boil, and simmered until they are done; the scum should be cleared off as it rises, and the usual proportion of salt stirred into the water before the mackerel are put in. The roes are commonly replaced in the fish, but as they sometimes require more boiling than the mackerel themselves, it is better, when they are very large, to lay them upon the drainer by their sides. From fifteen to twenty minutes will generally be sufficient to boil a full-sized mackerel: some will be done in less time, but they must be watched, and lifted out as soon as the tails split, and the eyes are starting.

Dish them on a napkin, and send fennel or gooseberry sauce to table with them, and plain melted butter also.

Small mackerel, 10 to 15 minutes; large, 15 to 20 minutes.

TO BAKE MACKEREL.

After they have been cleaned and well washed, wipe them very dry, fill the insides with the forcemeat, No. 1 of Chapter VI., sew them up, arrange them, with the roes, closely together in a coarse baking-dish, flour them lightly, strew a little fine salt over, and stick bits of butter upon them; or pour some equally over them, after having just dissolved it in a small saucepan. Half an hour in a moderate oven will bake them. Oyster forcemeat is always appropriate for any kind of fish which is in season, while the oysters are so, but the mackerel are commonly served, and are very good with that which we have named. Lift them carefully into a hot dish after they are taken from the oven, and send melted butter, and the sauce cruets to table with them.

½ hour.

Obs.—The dish in which they are baked should be buttered before they are laid in.

FRIED MACKEREL; (*common French receipt.*)

After the fish have been emptied and washed extremely clean, cut off the heads and tails, split the bodies quite open, and take out the backbones;* wipe the mackerel very dry, dust fine salt, and pepper (or cayenne), over them, flour them well, fry them a fine brown in boiling lard, drain them thoroughly, and serve them with the following sauce: Dissolve in a small saucepan an ounce and a half of butter smoothly mixed with a teaspoonful of flour, some salt, pepper, and cayenne, shake these over a gentle fire until they are lightly coloured, then add by slow degrees nearly half a pint of good broth, or gravy, and the juice of one large lemon: boil the sauce for a couple of minutes, and serve it very hot. Or, instead of this, add a large teaspoonful of strong-made mustard, and a dessertspoonful of Chili vinegar, to some thick melted butter, and serve it with the fish. A spoonful of Harvey's sauce, or of mushroom catsup, can be mixed with this last, at pleasure.

FILLETS OF MACKEREL; (*fried or broiled.*)

Take off the flesh quite whole on either side, from three fine mackerel, which have been opened and properly cleaned; let it be entirely free from bone, dry it well in a cloth, then divide each part in two, and dip them into the beaten yolks of a couple of eggs, seasoned with salt

---

* We recommend in preference that the flesh of the fish should be taken off the bones as in the following receipt

and white pepper or cayenne; cover them equally with fine dry crumbs of bread, and fry them like soles; or dip them into clarified butter, and then again into the crumbs, and broil them over a very clear fire of a fine brown. Dish them in a circle one over the other, and send them to table with the Màitre d'Hotel sauce of Chapter IV., or with the one which follows it. The French pour the sauce into the centre of the dish, but for broiled fillets this is not so well, we think, as serving it in a turcen. The roes of the fish, after being well washed and soaked, may be dressed with them, or they may be made into patties. Minced parsley can be mixed with the bread-crumbs when it is liked.

BOILED FILLETS OF MACKEREL.

After having taken off and divided the flesh of the fish, as above, place it flat in one layer in a wide stewpan or saucepan, and just cover the fillets with cold water; throw in a teaspoonful of salt, and two or three small sprigs of parsley. Bring the mackerel slowly to a boil, clear off the scum with care, and after two or three minutes of slow simmering, try the fillets with a fork; if the thick part divides with a touch, they are done. Lift them out cautiously with a slice; drain, and serve them very hot with good parsley and butter; or strip off the skin quickly, and pour a Màitre d'Hotel sauce over them.

MACKEREL BROILED WHOLE; (*an excellent receipt.*)

Empty, and cleanse perfectly a fine and very fresh mackerel, but without opening it more than is needful; dry it well, either in a cloth, or by hanging it in a cool air until it is stiff; make, with a sharp knife, a deep incision the whole length of the fish, on either side of the back-bone, and about half an inch from it, and with a feather put in a little cayenne and fine salt, mixed with a few drops of good salad oil or cla-rified butter. Lay the mackerel over a moderate fire upon a well heated gridiron, which has been rubbed with suet; loosen it gently should it stick, which it will do unless often moved; and when it is equally done on both sides, turn the back to the fire. About half an hour will broil it well. If a sheet of thickly-buttered writing-paper be folded round it, and just twisted at the ends before it is laid on the grid-iron, it will be finer eating than if exposed to the fire; but sometimes when this is done, the skin will adhere to the paper, and be drawn off with it, which injures its appearance. A cold Màitre d'Hotel sauce (see Chapter IV.), may be put into the back before it is sent to table. This is one of the very best modes of dressing a mackerel, which in flavour is quite a different fish when thus prepared to one which is simply boiled. A drop of oil is sometimes passed over the skin to pre-vent its sticking to the iron. It may be laid to the fire after having been merely cut as we have directed, when it is preferred so.

30 minutes; 25 if *small.*

MACKEREL STEWED WITH WINE; (*very good.*)

Work very smoothly together a large teaspoonful of flour with two ounces of butter, put them into a stewpan, and stir or shake them round over the fire until the butter is dissolved; add a quarter-teaspoonful of mace, twice as much salt, and some cayenne; pour in by slow degrees three glasses of claret, and when the sauce boils, lay in a couple of fine mackerel, well cleaned, and wiped quite dry; stew them very softly from fifteen to twenty minutes, and turn them when half done; lift them out, and dish them carefully; stir a teaspoonful of made-mustard to the sauce, give it a boil, and pour it over the fish. When more convenient, substitute port wine and a little lemon-juice, for the claret.

Mackerel, 2; flour, 1 teaspoonful; butter, 2 ozs.; seasoning of salt, mace, and cayenne; claret, 3 glassesful; made-mustard, 1 teaspoonful: 15 to 20 minutes.

FILLETS OF MACKEREL STEWED IN WINE; (*excellent.*)

Raise the flesh entire from the bones on either side of the mackerel, and divide it once, if the fish be small, but cut the whole into six parts of equal size should they be large. Mix with flour, and dissolve the butter as in the preceding receipt, and when it has simmered for a minute throw in the spice, a little salt, and the thinly pared rind of half a small fresh lemon; lay in the fillets of fish, shake them over a gentle fire from four to five minutes, and turn them once in the time; then pour to them in small portions a couple of large glassesful of port wine, a tablespoonful of Harvey's sauce, should it be at hand, a teaspoonful of soy, and one of lemon-juice; stew the mackerel very softly until the thinner parts begin to break, lift them out with care, dish and serve them in their sauce as hot as possible. We can recommend the dish to our readers as a very excellent one. A garnish of fried sippets can be placed round the fish at will. A teaspoonful of made-mustard should be stirred to the sauce before it is poured over the fish.

Mackerel, 2; butter, 2 ozs.; flour, 1 teaspoonful; rind of ½ lemon; salt, cayenne, pounded mace: 2 minutes. Fish, 4 to 5 minutes. Port wine, 2 large glassesful; Harvey's sauce, 1 tablespoonful; soy and lemon-juice each, 1 teaspoonful: 4 to 6 minutes. Mustard, 1 teaspoonful.

Obs.—Trout may be dressed by this receipt.

TO BOIL HADDOCKS.
In the best season in October, November, and December.

Scrape the outsides very clean, open the fish, empty them, wash the insides thoroughly, take out the gills, curl the haddocks round, fasten the tails to the mouths, arrange them on a fish-plate, and lay them into warm water salted as for mackerel, with a very small bit of saltpetre to render them firm. Skim the water, and simmer them from seven to ten minutes, according to their size. Send them very hot to table, with a tureen of melted butter, and one of anchovy sauce.

7 to 10 minutes.

BAKED HADDOCKS.

After they have been cleaned, dry them thoroughly, then bake them, as directed in the common receipt for pike, or fill them with oyster-forcemeat, or with No. 1 of Chapter IV., if more convenient, and proceed as for baked mackerel.

20 to 30 minutes; longer if very large.

TO BOIL PLAICE OR FLOUNDERS.
Plaice in season from May to January; flounders in September, October, and November.

After having emptied and well cleaned the fish, make an incision in the back as directed for turbot; lay them into cold spring water; add salt, and saltpetre in the same proportion as for cod fish, and let them just simmer for four or five minutes after the water first begins to boil, or longer, should their size require it, but guard against their being broken.   Serve them with plain melted butter.

4 to 5 minutes: longer if needful.

TO FRY PLAICE OR FLOUNDERS.

Sprinkle them with salt, and let them lie for two or three hours before they are dressed.   Wash and clean them thoroughly, wipe them very dry, flour them well, and wipe them again with a clean cloth; dip them into egg, and fine bread-crumbs, and fry them in plenty of lard. If the fish be large, raise the flesh in .handsome fillets from the bones, and finish them as directed for fillets of soles.

Obs.—Plaice is said to be rendered less watery by beating it gently with a paste-roller before it is cooked.   It is very sweet and pleasant in flavour while it is in the best season, which is from the end of May to about September.

TO ROAST, BAKE, OR BROIL RED MULLET.

In best season through the summer: may be had all the year.

First wash, and then dry the fish thoroughly in a cloth, but neither scale nor open it; wrap it closely in a sheet of thickly-buttered paper, tie this securely at the ends, and over the mullet with packthread, and roast it in a Dutch oven, or broil it over a clear and gentle fire, or bake it in a moderate oven: from twenty to thirty minutes will be sufficient generally. to dress it in either way, if it be only of moderate size.   For sauce, put into a little good melted butter the liquor which has flowed from fish, a small dessertspoonful of essence of anchovies, some cayenne, a glass of port wine, or claret, and a little lemon-juice.   Remove the packthread, and send the mullet to table in the paper case.   This is the usual mode of serving it; but it is dished without the paper, for dinners of high taste.

20 to 30 minutes.

TO BOIL GREY MULLET.

This fish varies so much in size and quality, that it is difficult to give exact directions for the time of cooking it.   When quite young and small, it may be boiled by the receipt for whitings, haddocks, and other fish of about their size; but at its finest growth it must be laid into cold water, and managed like larger fish.   We have ourselves partaken of one which was caught upon our eastern coast, that weighed ten pounds, of which the flesh was quite equal to that of salmon, but its weight was, we believe, an unusual one.   Anchovy, or caper fish sauce, with melted butter, may be sent to table with grey mullet.

TO FRY SMELTS AND OTHER SMALL FISH.

In season from beginning of November to May.

Smelts when quite fresh have a perfume resembling that of a cucumber, and a peculiarly delicate and agreeable flavour when dressed. Draw them at the gills, as they must not be opened; wash and dry them thoroughly in a cloth; dip them into beaten egg-yolk, and then into the finest bread-crumbs, mixed with a small quantity of flour; fry them of a clear golden brown, and serve them very crisp and dry, with good melted butter in a tureen.   They are sometimes dipped into batter and then fried; when this is done, we would recommend for them the French batter of Chapter IV.

3 to 4 minutes.

TO BAKE A SHAD.

Empty and wash the fish with care, but do not open it more than is necessary, and keep on the head and fins. Then stuff it with forcemeat No. 2, of Chapter VI. Sew it up, or fasten it with fine skewers, and rub the fish over with the yolk of egg and a little of the stuffing.

Put into the pan in which the fish is to be baked about a gill of wine, or the same quantity of water mixed with a tablespoonful of cayenne vinegar, or common vinegar will do. Baked in a moderate oven 1½ or 2 hours, according to its size.

TO BROIL SHAD.

This delicate and delicious fish is excellent broiled. Clean, wash, and split the shad, wipe it dry, and sprinkle it with pepper and salt— broil it like mackerel.

SHAD, TOURAINE FASHION; (*Alose à la mode de Touraine.*)
In season in April, May, and early part of June.

Empty and wash the fish with care, but do not open it more than is needful; fill it either with the forcemeat No. 1, or No. 2 of Chapter VI., and its own roe; then sew it up, or fasten it securely with very fine skewers, wrap it in a thickly-buttered paper, and broil it gently for an hour over a charcoal fire. Serve it with caper sauce, or with cayenne vinegar and melted butter.

We are indebted for this receipt to a friend who has been long resident in Touraine, at whose table the fish is constantly served, thus dressed, and is considered excellent. It is likewise often gently stewed in the light white wine of the country, and served covered with a rich bechamel. Many fish more common with us than the shad might be advantageously prepared in the same manner. The charcoal fire is not indispensable: any that is entirely free from smoke will answer. We would suggest as an improvement, that oyster-forcemeat should be substituted for that which we have indicated, until the oyster season ends.

Broiled gently, 1 hour, more or less, according to its size.

STEWED TROUT; (*good common receipt.*)
In season from May to August.

Melt three ounces of butter in a broad stewpan, or well tinned iron saucepan, stir to it a tablespoonful of flour, some mace, cayenne, and nutmeg; lay in the fish after it has been emptied, washed very clean, and wiped perfectly dry; shake it in the pan, that it may not stick, and when lightly browned on both sides, pour in three quarters of a pint of good veal stock, add a small bunch of parsley, one bay leaf, a roll of lemon-peel, and a little salt: stew the fish *very gently* from half to three quarters of an hour, or more, should it be unusually fine. Dish the trout, skim the fat from the gravy, and pass it through a hot strainer over the fish, which should be served immediately. A little acid can be added to the sauce at pleasure, and a glass of wine when it is considered an improvement. This receipt is for one large, or for two middling-sized fish. We can recommend it as a good one, from our own experience.

Butter, 3 ozs.; flour, 1 tablespoonful; seasoning of mace, cayenne, and nutmeg; trout, 1 large, or 2 moderate sized; veal stock, ¾ pint; parsley, *small* faggot; 1 bay-leaf; roll of lemon-rind; little salt: ½ to ¾ hour.

Obs.—Trout may be stewed in equal parts of strong veal gravy, and of red or white wine, without having been previously browned; the sauce should then be thickened, and agreeably flavoured with lemon juice, and the usual store-sauces, before it is poured over the fish. They are also good when wrapped in buttered paper and baked or broiled: if very small, the better mode of cooking them is to fry them whole. They should never be plain boiled, as, though a naturally delicious fish, they are then very insipid.

TO FRY TROUT.

Clean and dry them thoroughly in a cloth, fry them plain in hot butter, or beat the white of egg on a plate, dip the trout in the egg and then in very fine bread-crumbs, which have been rubbed through a sieve—biscuit powder is better. Fry them till of a delicate brown; it takes but a few minutes, if the trout be small—serve with crisp parsley and plain melted butter.

TO BAKE PIKE, OR TROUT; (*common receipt.*)

Pour warm water over the outside of the fish, and wipe it very clean with a coarse cloth drawn from the head downwards, that the scales may not be disturbed; then wash it well in cold water, empty, and clean the inside with the greatest nicety, fill it either with the common forcemeat, No. 1, or with No. 4, of Chapter VI., sew it up, fasten the tail to the mouth, give it a slight dredging of flour, stick small bits of butter thickly over it, and bake it from half to three quarters of an hour, should it be of moderate size, and upwards of an hour, if it be large. Should there not be sufficient sauce with it in the dish, plain melted butter, and a lemon, or anchovy sauce may be sent to table with it. When more convenient, the forcemeat may be omitted, and a little fine salt and cayenne, with some bits of butter, put into the inside of the fish, which will then require rather less baking. A buttered paper should always be laid over it in the oven, should the outside appear likely to become too highly coloured, or too dry, before the fish is done; and it is better to wrap quite small pike in buttered paper at once, before they are sent to the oven.

Moderate-sized pike, 30 to 45 minutes; large pike, 1 to 1¼ hour.

TO BOIL PERCH.

First wipe or wash off the slime, then scrape off the scales, which adheres rather tenaciously to this fish; empty and clean the insides perfectly, take out the gills, cut off the fins, and lay the perch into equal parts of cold and of boiling water, salted as for mackerel: from eight to ten minutes will boil them unless they are very large. Dish them on a napkin, garnish them with curled parsley, and serve melted butter with them, or *Maître d'Hotel sauce maigre.*

Very good French cooks put them at once into boiling water, and keep them over a brisk fire for about fifteen minutes. They dress them also without taking off the scales or fins until they are ready to serve, when they strip the whole of the skin off carefully, and stick the red fins into the middle of the backs; the fish are then covered with the Steward's sauce, thickened with eggs.

In warm water, 8 to 10 minutes, in boiling, 12 to 15.

TO FRY PERCH OR TENCH.

Scale, and clean them perfectly; dry them well, flour and fry them in boiling lard. Serve plenty of fried parsley round them.

TO FRY EELS.

In season all the year, but not so well-conditinned in April and May as in otner months.

First kill, then skin, empty, and wash them as clean as possible; cut them into four-inch lengths, and dry them well in a soft cloth. Season them with fine salt, and white pepper, or cayenne, flour them thickly, and fry them a fine brown in boiling lard; drain and dry them as directed for soles, and send them to table with plain melted butter and a lemon, or the sauce-cruets. Eels are sometimes dipped into batter and then fried; or into egg and fine bread-crumbs (mixed with minced parsley or not, at pleasure), and served with plenty of crisped parsley round, and on them.

It is an improvement for these modes of dressing the fish to open them entirely and remove the bones: the smaller parts should be thrown into the pan a minute or two later than the thicker portions of the bodies, or they will not be equally done.

BOILED EELS; (*German receipt.*)

Pare a fine lemon, and strip from it entirely the white inner rind, slice it, and remove the pips with care, put it with a blade of mace, a small half-teaspoonful of white pepper-corns, nearly twice as much of salt, and a moderate-sized bunch of parsley, into three pints of cold water, bring them gently to boil, and simmer them for twenty minutes; let them become quite cold, then put in three pounds of eels skinned, and cleaned with great nicety, and cut into lengths of three or four inches; simmer them very softly from ten to fifteen minutes, lift them with a slice into a very hot dish, and serve them with a good Dutch sauce, or with parsley and butter acidulated with lemon-juice, or with vinegar.

EELS; (*Cornish receipt.*)

Skin, empty, and wash as clean as possible, two or three fine eels, cut them into short lengths, and just cover them with cold water; add sufficient salt and cayenne to season them, and stew them very softly indeed from fifteen to twenty minutes, or longer should they require it. When they are nearly done, strew over them a tablespoonful of minced parsley, thicken the sauce with a teaspoonful of flour mixed with a slice of butter, and add a quarter-pint or more of clotted cream. Give the whole a boil, lift the fish into a hot dish, and stir briskly the juice of half a lemon into the sauce; pour it upon the eels, and serve them immediately. Very sweet thick cream is, we think, preferable to clotted cream for this dish. The sauce should be of a good consistence, and a dessertspoonful of flour will be needed for a large dish of the stew, and from one and a half to two ounces of butter. The size of the fish must determine the precise quantity of liquid and of seasoning which they will require.

By substituting pale veal gravy for water, and thin strips of lemon-rind for the parsley, this may be converted into a white fricasse of eels: a flavouring of mace must then be added to it, and the beaten yolks of two or three eggs, mixed with a couple of spoonsful of cream, must be

stirred into the sauce before the lemon-juice, but it must on no account
be allowed to boil afterwards. Rich brown gravy and port wine highly
spiced, with acid as above, will give another variety of stewed eels.
For this dish the fish are sometimes fried before they are laid into the
sauce.

TO BOIL LOBSTERS.
In season from April to October.

Choose them by the directions which we have already given at the
commencement of this chapter, and throw them into plenty of *fast-
boiling* salt and water, that life may be destroyed in an instant. A
moderate-sized lobster will be done in from fifteen to twenty-five minutes: a large one in from half an hour to forty minutes; before they
are sent to table, the large claws should be taken off, and the shells
cracked across the joints without disfiguring them; the tail should be
separated from the body and split quite through the middle; the whole
neatly dished upon a napkin, and garnished with curled parsley or not,
at choice. A good remoulade, or any other sauce of the kind that may
be preferred, should be sent to table with it; or oil and vinegar, when
better liked.

To 1 gallon water 5 ozs. salt. Moderate-sized lobster, 15 to 25 minutes. Large lobster, 30 to 40 minutes.

LOBSTER FRICASSEED, OR AU BÉCHAMEL. (ENTRÉE.)

Take the flesh from the claws and tails of two moderate-sized lobsters, cut it into small thick slices or dice; heat it slowly quite through
in about three quarters of a pint of good white sauce or béchamel; and
serve it when it is at the point of boiling, after having stirred briskly
to it a little lemon-juice, just as it is taken from the fire. The coral,
pounded and mixed gradually with a few spoonsful of the sauce, should
be added previously. Good shin of beef stock, made without vegetables (see page 53), and somewhat reduced by quick boiling, if mixed
with an equal proportion of cream, and thickened with arrow-root, will
answer extremely well, in a general way, for this dish, which is most
excellent, if well made. The sauce should never be thin; nor more
than sufficient in quantity to just cover the fish. For a second course
dish only as much must be used as will adhere to the fish, which after
being heated should be laid evenly into the shells after they have been
split quite through the centre of the backs in their entire length, without being broken or divided at the joint, and nicely cleaned. When
thus arranged, the lobster may be thickly covered with well-dried, fine,
pale, fried crumbs of bread; or with unfried ones, which must then be
equally moistened with clarified butter, and browned with a salamander.
A small quantity of salt, mace, and cayenne, may be required to finish
the flavouring of either of these preparations.

BUTTERED CRAB, OR LOBSTER.
In season during the same time as Lobsters.

Slice quite small, or pull into light flakes with a couple of forks, the
flesh of either fish; put it into a saucepan with a few bits of good butter lightly rolled in flour, and heat it slowly over a gentle fire; then
pour over and mix thoroughly with it, from one to two teaspoonsful of
made-mustard smoothly blended with a tablespoonful or more of common vinegar: add to it a tolerable seasoning of cayenne. Grate in a

little nutmeg, and when the whole is well heated serve it immediately either in the shell of the crab or lobster, or in scollop-shells, and serve it plain, or with bread-crumbs over, as in the preceding receipt. A spoonful or so of good meat jelly is, we think, a great improvement to this dish, for which an ounce and a half of butter will be quite sufficient.

Crabs are boiled like lobsters.

TO STEW LOBSTERS.

A middling sized lobster is best: pick all the meat from the shells and mince it fine; season with a little salt, pepper, and grated nutmeg; add three or four spoons of rich gravy and a small bit of butter. If you have no gravy, use more butter, and two spoonsful of vinegar; stew about twenty minutes.

LOBSTER COLD.

It is frequently eaten in this way, with a dressing of vinegar, mustard, sweet oil, and a little salt and cayenne.

The meat of the lobster must be minced very fine.

TO COOK TERRAPINS.

This is a favourite dish for suppers and parties; and, when well cooked, they are certainly very delicious. Many persons in Philadelphia have made themselves famous for cooking this article alone. Mrs. Rubicam, who during her lifetime always stood first in that way, prepared them as follows:—Put the terrapins alive in a pot of boiling water, where they must remain until they are quite dead. You then divest them of their outer skin and toe-nails; and, after washing them in warm water, boil them again until they become quite tender, adding a handful of salt to the water. Having satisfied yourself of their being perfectly tender, take off the shells and clean the terrapins very carefully, removing the sand-bag and gall without breaking them. Then cut the meat and entrails into small pieces, and put into a saucepan, adding the juice which has been given out in cutting them up, but *no water*, and season with salt, cayenne, and black pepper, to your taste; adding a quarter of a pound of good butter to each terrapin, and a handful of flour for thickening. After stirring a short time, add four or five tablespoonsful of cream, and a half pint of good Madeira to every four terrapins, and serve hot in a deep dish. Our own cook has been in the habit of putting in a very little mace, a large tablespoonful of mustard, and *ten drops of the gall*; and, just before serving, adding the yolks of four hard boiled eggs. During the stewing, particular attention must be paid to stirring the preparation frequently; and it must be borne in mind, that terrapins cannot possibly be too hot.—*Sanderson.*]

OYSTERS.

In season from September to April.

The old-fashioned plan of *feeding* oysters with a sprinkling of oatmeal or flour, in addition to the salt and water to which they were committed, has long been rejected by all genuine amateurs of these nutritious and excellent fish, who consider the plumpness which the oysters are supposed to gain from the process but poor compensation for the flavour which they are sure to lose. To cleanse them when they first come up from the beds, and to keep them in good condition for four or

five days, they only require to be covered with cold water, with five
ounces of salt to the gallon dissolved in it before it is poured on them:
this should be changed with regularity every twenty-four hours. By
following this plan with exactness they may be kept alive from a week
to ten days, but will remain in perfect condition scarcely more than
half that time. Oysters should be eaten always the instant they are
opened. They are served often before the soup, in the first course of a
dinner, left upon their shells, and arranged usually in as many plates as
there are guests at table.

TO STEW OYSTERS.

A pint of small plump oysters will be sufficient for quite a moderate-
sized dish, but twice as many will be required for a large one. Let
them be very carefully opened, and not mangled in the slightest degree;
wash them free from grit in their own *strained* liquor, lay them into a
very clean stewpan or well-tinned saucepan, strain the liquor a second
time, pour it on them, and beat them slowly in it. When they are just
beginning to simmer, lift them out with a slice or a bored wooden spoon,
and take off the beards; add to the liquor a quarter-pint of good cream,
a seasoning of pounded mace and cayenne, and a little salt, and when it
boils, stir in from one to two ounces of good butter, smoothly mixed with
a large teaspoonful of flour; continue to stir the sauce until these are
perfectly blended with it, then put in the oysters and let them remain
by the side of the fire until they are very hot: they require so little
cooking, that if kept for four or five minutes nearly simmering, they
will be ready for table, and they are quickly hardened by being allowed
o boil, or by too much stewing. Serve them garnished with pale fried
ippets. Fried bread, see Chapter IV.

Small plump oysters, 1 pint: their own liquor: brought slowly to the
point of simmering. Cream, ¼ pint; seasoning of pounded mace and
cayenne; salt as needed; butter, 1 to 2 ounces; flour, 1 large teaspoonful.

Obs.—A little lemon-juice should be stirred quickly into the stew
just as it is taken from the fire. Another mode of preparing this dish
is to add the strained liquor of the oysters to about an equal quantity of
rich bechamel, with a little additional thickening; then to heat them
in it, after having prepared and plumped them properly. Or, the beards
of the fish may be stewed for half an hour in a little pale veal gravy,
and this, when strained and mixed with the oyster-liquor, may be brought
to the consistency of cream with the French thickening of Chapter VI.,
or, with flour and butter, then seasoned with spice as above: the process should be quite the same in all of these receipts, though the composition of the sauce is varied. Essence of anchovies, or yolks of eggs
can be added to the taste.

TO SCALLOP OYSTERS.

Large coarse oysters should never be dressed in this way. Select
small plump ones for the purpose, let them be opened carefully, give
them a scald in their own liquor, wash them in it free from grit, and
beard them neatly. Butter the scallop shells and shake some fine bread-
crumbs over them; fill them with alternate layers of oysters, crumbs
of bread, and fresh butter cut into small bits; pour in the oyster-liquor,
after it has been strained, put a thick, smooth layer of bread-crumbs on

the top, moisten them with clarified butter, place tl e shells in a Dutch oven before a clear fire, and turn them often till the tops are equally and lightly browned: send them immediately to table.

Some persons like a little white pepper or cayenne, and a flavouring of nutmeg added to the oysters; others prefer pounded mace.   I rench cooks recommend with them a mixture of minced mushrooms stewed in butter till quite tender, and sweet herbs finely chopped.   The fish is sometimes laid into the shells after having been bearded only.

SCALLOPED OYSTERS A LA REINE.

Plump and beard the oysters, after having rinsed them well in their own strained liquor; add to this about an equal quantity of very rich white sauce, and thicken it, if needful, with a half-teaspoonful of flour, mixed with a small slice of butter, or with as much arrow-root only; put in the oysters, and keep them at the point of simmering for three or four minutes; lay them into the shells, and cover the tops thickly with crumbs fried a delicate brown and well dried; or heap over them instead, a layer of fine crumbs; pour clarified butter on them, and brown them with a salamander.

OYSTER SAUSAGES.

Beard, rinse well in their strained liquor, and mince, but not finely, three dozens and a half of plump oysters, and mix them with ten ounces of fine bread-crumbs, and ten of beef-suet chopped extremely small; add a saltspoonful of salt, and one of pepper, or less than half the quantity of cayenne, twice as much pounded mace, and the third of a small nutmeg grated; moisten the whole with two unbeaten eggs, or with the yolks only of three, and a dessertspoonful of the whites.   When these ingredients have been well worked together, and are perfectly blended, set the mixture in a cool place for two or three hours before it is used; make it into the form of small sausages or sausage-cakes, flour and fry them in butter of a fine light brown; or throw them into boiling water for three minutes, drain, and let them become cold, dip them into egg and bread-crumbs, and broil them gently until they are lightly coloured.   A small bit should be cooked and tasted before the whole is put aside, that the seasoning may be heightened if required.   The sausages thus made are very good.

Small plump oysters, 3½ dozens; bread-crumbs, 10 ozs.; beef-suet, 10 ozs.; seasoning of salt, cayenne, pounded mace, and nutmeg; unbeaten eggs 2, or yolks of 3.

Obs.—The fingers should be well floured for making up these sausages.

TO FRY OYSTERS.

They should be large for this purpose.   Simmer them for a couple of minutes in their own liquor, beard and dry them in a cloth, dredge them lightly with flour, dip them in egg and fine bread-crumbs, and fry them a delicate brown in boiling lard; or make a thick batter with eggs and flour, season it with plenty of mace and white pepper, dip the oysters in and then fry them.

OYSTERS AU GRATIN.

Take the best oysters you can find, and dry them on a napkin; you then place them on a silver shell, made expressly for the purpose, or fine, large, deep oyster shells, which should be well cleaned, placing in them four or six oysters, according to their size; season with salt, pepper, nutmeg, parsley, mushrooms hashed very fine, a small quantity of bread-crumbs, with which the surface of the oysters must be covered, placing on top of all a small piece of the best butter. Then put them in a hot oven, and let them remain until they acquire a golden colour Serve them hot.

BROILED OYSTERS.

The oysters should be the largest and finest you can get. Prepare your gridiron, which should be a double one made of wire, by rubbing with butter, and having placed your oysters so that they will all receive the heat equally, set them over a brisk fire, and broil both sides without burning them. Let them be served hot, with a small lump of fresh butter, pepper and salt, added to them.

ANCHOVIES FRIED IN BATTER.

Scrape very clean a dozen or more of fine anchovies, and soak them in plenty of spring water from two to six hours; then wipe them dry, open them, and take out the back-bones, without dividing the fish. Season the insides highly with cayenne, close the anchovies, dip them into the French batter of Chapter VI., or into a light English batter, and fry them a pale amber-colour: in from four to five minutes they will be quite sufficiently done.

CHAPTER III.

GRAVIES.

INTRODUCTORY REMARKS.

GRAVIES are not often required either in great variety, or in abundant quantities, when only a moderate table is kept, and a clever cook will manage to supply, at a trifling cost, all that is generally needed for plain family dinners; while an

Gravy Kettle.

unskilful or extravagant one will render them sources of unbounded expense.* But however small the proportions in which they are made, their *quality* should be particularly attended to, and they should be well adapted in flavour to the dishes they are to accompany. For some, a high degree of savour is desirable; but for fricassees, and other preparations of delicate white meats, this should be avoided, and a soft, smooth sauce of refined flavour should be used in preference to any of more piquant relish.

Instead of frying the ingredients for brown gravies, which is usually done in common English kitchens, French cooks pour to them at first a

* We know of an instance of a cook who stewed down two or three pounds of beef to make gravy for a single brace of partridges; and who complained of the *meanness* of her employers (who were by no means affluent) because this was objected to.

small quantity of liquid, which is reduced by rapid boiling to what is technically called *glaze :* particular directions for which will be found in the next receipt to this, and also at pages 43 and 90. When the glaze has acquired the proper colour, boiling broth should be added in small portions, and well shaken round the stewpan to detach it entirely ; the meat may then be stewed gently for three or four hours with a few mushrooms, should they be at hand, a bunch of parsley, and some green onions.

A thick slice or two of an unboiled ham is an almost indispensable addition to rich soup or gravy ; and to supply it in the most economical manner, a large, highly cured one, or more, not over fatted, should be kept for the purpose, and cut as required. The bones of undressed meat will supply almost, or quite as good gravy-stock as the meat itself, if well boiled down, particularly those of the loin, or neck of veal: and as the flesh of these may be dressed in many ways advantageously without them, the whole joint may be turned to excellent account by so dividing it.

The necks of poultry, with the feet properly skinned, a few herbs, a morsel or two of ham or of lean bacon, and such slight flavourings beside as the spice-box can supply, with a few drops of good mushroom catsup, will of themselves, if well managed, produce sufficient gravy to serve with the birds from which they are taken ; and if not wanted for the purpose, they should always be stewed down, or thrown into the stock-pot, for which the shank-bones of legs of mutton, and all trimmings of meat should likewise be reserved. Excellent broth for the sick or for the needy, may also be made of them at little cost, when they are not required for other uses.

To deepen the colour of gravies, the thick mushroom *pressings* of Chapter V., or a little soy (when its flavour is admissible), or cavice, or Harvey's sauce* may be added to it ; and for some dishes, a glass of claret, or of port wine.

Vermicelli, or rasped cocoa-nut, lightly, and *very* gently browned in a small quantity of butter, will both thicken and enrich them, if about an ounce of either to the pint of gravy be stewed gently in it from half an hour to an hour, and then strained out.

All the ingredients indicated at page 39, for giving consistency to soups, will answer equally for gravies, which should not, however, be too much thickened, particularly with the unwholesome mixture of flour and butter, so commonly used for the purpose. Arrow-root, or rice-flour, or common flour gradually browned in a slow oven, are much better suited to a delicate stomach. No particle of fat should ever be perceptible upon them when they are sent to table ; and when it cannot be removed by skimming, they should be allowed to become sufficiently cold for it to congeal, and be taken off at once without trouble. It may be cleared from such as have not been thickened, by passing them through a closely woven cloth, which has previously been laid into, and well wrung from, some cold water.

TO HEIGHTEN THE COLOUR AND THE FLAVOUR OF GRAVIES.

This is best done by the directions given for making Espagnole. An

* *Harvey's sauce, cavice, and soy* are very little known in America ; these flavourings, when named, may be dispensed with, or pepper sauce or tomato sauce substituted instead.

ounce or two of the lean of unboiled ham, cut into dice and coloured slowly in a small stewpan, or smoothly tinned iron saucepan, with less than an ounce of butter, a blade of mace, two or three cloves, a bay-leaf, a few small sprigs of savoury herbs, and an eschalot or two, or about a teaspoonful of minced onion, and a little young parsley root, when it can be had, will convert common shin of beef stock, or even strong broth, into an excellent gravy, if it be gradually added to them after they have stewed slowly for quite half an hour, and then boiled with them for twenty minutes or more.   The liquid should not be mixed with the other ingredients until the side of the stewpan is coloured of a reddish brown; and should any thickening be required, a teaspoonful of flour should be stirred in well, and simmered for three or four minutes before the stock is added : the pan should be strongly shaken round afterwards to detach the browning from it, and this must be done often while the ham is stewing.

Obs.—The cook who is not acquainted with this mode of preparing or enriching gravies, will do well to make herself acquainted with it; as it presents no difficulties, and is exceedingly convenient and advantageous when they are wanted in small quantities, very highly flavoured and well coloured.   An unboiled ham, kept in cut, will be found, as we have already said, a great economy for this, and other purposes, saving much of the expense commonly incurred for gravy-meats.   As eschalots, when sparingly used, impart a much finer savour than onions, though they are not commonly so much used in England, we would recommend that a small store of them should always be kept.

SHIN OF BEEF STOCK, (*for Gravies.*)

There is no better foundation for strong gravies than shin of beef stewed down to a jelly (which it easily becomes), with the addition only of some spice, a bunch of savoury herbs, and a moderate proportion of salt; this, if kept in a cool larder, boiled softly for two or three minutes every second or third day, and each time put into a clean, well-scalded pan, will remain good for many days, and may easily be converted into excellent soup or gravy.   Let the bone be broken in one or two places, take out the marrow, which, if not wanted for immediate use, should be clarified, and stored for future occasions; put a pint and a half of cold water to the pound of beef, and stew it very gently indeed for six or seven hours, or even longer should the meat not then be quite in fragments.   The bones of calf's feet which have been boiled down for jelly, the liquor in which the head has been cooked, and any remains of ham quite freed from the smoky parts, from rust and fat, will be serviceable additions to this stock.   A couple of pounds of the neck of beef may be added to six of the shin with very good effect; but for white soup or sauces this is better avoided.

Shin of beef, 6 lbs.; water, 9 pints; salt, 1 oz.; large bunch savoury herbs; peppercorns, 1 teaspoonful; mace, 2 blades.

RICH PALE VEAL GRAVY, OR, CONSOMMÉE.

The French, who have always at hand their stock-pot of good *bouillon* (beef soup or broth), make great use of it in preparing their gravies.   It is added instead of water to the fresh meat, and when this, in somewhat large proportions, is boiled down in it, with the addition only of a bunch of parsley, a few green onions, and a moderate seasoning of salt, a strong and very pure-flavoured pale gravy is produced. When the best joints of fowls, or of partridges have been taken for fricassees or cutlets, the remainder may be stewed with a pound or two of veal into a consommée, which then takes the name of chicken or of game gravy. For a large dinner it is always desirable to have in readiness such stock as can easily and quickly be converted into white and other sauces. To make this, arrange a slice or two of lean ham in a stew-pan or saucepan with three pounds of the neck of veal once or twice divided (unless the thick fleshy part of the knuckle can be had), and pour to them three full pints of strong beef or veal broth; or if this cannot conveniently be done, increase the proportion of meat or dimin-ish that of the liquid, substituting water for the broth, throw in some salt after the boiling has commenced, and the gravy has been well skim-med, with one mild onion, a bunch of savoury herbs, a little celery, if in season, a carrot, a blade of mace, and a half-saltspoonful of pepper-corns; stew these very gently for four hours; then, should the meat be quite in fragments, strain off the gravy, and let it become sufficiently cold to allow the fat to be entirely cleared from it. A handful of nicely prepared mushroom-buttons will much improve its flavour; and the bones of boiled calf's feet, or the fresh ones of fowls will be found ex-cellent additions to it. A better method of making it, when time and trouble are not regarded, is to heat the meat, which ought then to be free of bones, quite through, with from a quarter to half a pint of broth only, and when on probing it with the point of a knife no blood issues from it, and it has been turned and equally done, to moisten it with the remainder of the broth, which should be boiling.

Lean of ham, 6 to 8 ozs.; neck or knuckle of veal, 3 lbs.; strong broth, 3 pints, (or veal, 4 lbs., and water, 3 pints); salt; bunch of sa-voury herbs; mild onion, 1; carrot, 1 large or 2 small; celery, ½ small head; mace, 1 large blade; peppercorns, ½ saltspoonful: 4 hours or more. Or: ham, ½ lb.; veal, 4 lbs.; broth, third of a pint: nearly 1 hour. Additional broth, 3 pints: 3½ to 4½ hours.

RICH DEEP-COLOURED VEAL GRAVY.

Lay into a large thick stewpan or saucepan, from half to three quar-ters of a pound of undressed ham, freed entirely from fat, and from the smoked edges, and sliced half an inch thick; on this place about four pounds of lean veal, cut from the best part of the knuckle or from the neck (part of the fillet, which in France is often used for it instead, not being generally purchasable here, the butchers seldom dividing the joint); pour to them about half a pint of good broth,* and place the pan over a brisk fire until it is well reduced, then thrust a knife into the meat, and continue the stewing more gently until a glaze is formed as we have described at page 90. The latter part of the process must be *very slow;* the stewpan must be frequently shaken, and the gravy close-ly watched that it may not burn; when it is of a fine *deep* amber co-lour, pour in sufficient boiling broth to cover the meat, add a bunch of parsley, and a few mushrooms and green onions. A blade or two of mace, a few white peppercorns, and a head of celery, would, we think,

* When there is no provision of this in the house, the quantity required may be made with a small quantity of beef, and the trimmings of the veal, by the directions for Bouillon, page 41.

be very admissible additions to this gravy, but it is extremely good without. Half the quantity can be made, but it will then be rather more troublesome to manage.

Undressed ham, 8 to 12 ozs.; lean veal, 4 lbs.; broth, ½ pint: 1 to 2 hours. Broth, 3 to 4 pints; bunch of parsley and green onions; mushrooms, ¼ to ½ pint: 1½ to 2 hours.

GOOD BEEF OR VEAL GRAVY; (*English receipt.*)

Flour and fry lightly in a bit of good butter a couple of pounds of either beef or veal; drain the meat well from the fat, and lay it into a small thick stewpan or iron saucepan; pour to it a quart of boiling water; add, after it has been well skimmed and salted, a large mild onion sliced, very delicately fried, and laid on a sieve to drain, a carrot also sliced, a small bunch of thyme and parsley, a blade of mace and a few peppercorns; stew these gently for three hours or more, pass the gravy through a sieve into a clean pan, and when it is quite cold clear it entirely from fat, heat as much as is wanted for table, and if not sufficiently thick stir into it from half to a whole teaspoonful of arrow-root mixed with a little mushroom catsup.

Beef or veal, 2 lbs.; water, 2 pints; fried onion, 1 large; carrot, 1; small bunch of herbs; salt, 1 small teaspoonful or more; mace, 1 blade; peppercorns, 20: 3 to 3½ hours.

A RICH ENGLISH BROWN GRAVY.

Brown lightly and carefully from four to six ounces of lean ham, thickly sliced and cut into large dice; lift these out, and put them into the pan in which the gravy is to be made; next, fry lightly also, a couple of pounds of neck of beef, dredged moderately with flour, and slightly with pepper; put this when it is done over the ham; and then brown gently, and add to them one *not* large common onion. Pour over these ingredients a quart of boiling water, or of weak but well-flavoured broth, bring the whole slowly to a boil, clear off the scum with great care, throw in a saltspoonful of salt, four cloves, a blade of mace, twenty corns of pepper, a bunch of savoury herbs, a carrot, and a few slices of celery: these last two may be fried or not, as is most convenient. Boil the gravy very softly until it is reduced to little more than a pint; strain, and set it by until the fat can be taken from it. Heat it anew, add more salt if needed, and a little mushroom catsup, cayenne-vinegar, or whatever flavouring it may require for the dish with which it is to be served: it will seldom need any thickening. A dozen small mushrooms prepared as for pickling, may be added to it at first with advantage. Half this quantity of gravy will be sufficient for a single tureen, and the economist can diminish a little the proportion of meat when it is thought too much.

GRAVY FOR VENISON.

If possible, let this be made with a little of the neck, or of any odd trimmings of the venison itself. Cut down the meat small, and let it stand over a slow fire until the juices are well drawn out; then to each pound of it add a pint and a quarter of boiling water; throw in a small half-teaspoonful of salt, and eight or ten corns of pepper; skim it thoroughly, and let it boil two hours and a half; then strain it, let it cool, take off every particle of fat, give it a minute's simmer, and send it very hot to table.

Neck, or other trimmings of venison, 1 lb.; water, 1¼ pint; salt, small ½ teaspoonful; peppercorns, 8 or 10: 2½ hours.

SWEET SAUCE, OR GRAVY FOR VENISON.

Add to a quarter pint of common venison gravy a couple of glasses of port wine or claret, and half an ounce of sugar in lumps.

ESPAGNOLE (SPANISH SAUCE); *(a highly flavoured gravy.)*

Dissolve a couple of ounces of good butter in a thick stewpan or saucepan, throw in from four to six sliced eschalots, four ounces of the lean of an undressed ham, three ounces of carrot, cut in small dice, one bay leaf, two or three branches of parsley, and one or two of thyme, but these last must be small; three cloves, a blade of mace, and a dozen corns of pepper; add part of a root of parsley, if it be at hand, and keep the whole stirred or shaken over a moderate fire for twenty minutes, then add by degrees one pint of very strong veal stock or gravy, and stew the whole gently from thirty to forty minutes: strain it, skim off the fat, and it will be ready to serve.

Butter, 2 ozs.; eschalots, 4 to 6; lean of undressed ham, 4 ozs.; carrots, 3 ozs.; bay leaf, 1; little thyme and parsley, in branches; cloves, 3; mace, 1 blade; peppercorns, 12; little parsley root: fried gently, 20 minutes. Strong veal stock, or gravy, 1 pint: stewed very softly, 30 to 40 minutes.

GRAVY IN HASTE.

Chop fine a few bits of lean meat, a small onion, a few slices of carrot and turnip, and a little thyme and parsley; put these with half an ounce of butter into a thick saucepan, and keep them stirred until they are slightly browned; add a little spice, and water in the proportion of a pint to a pound of meat; clear the gravy from scum, let it boil half an hour, then strain it for use.

Meat, 1 lb.; 1 small onion; little carrot, turnip, thyme, and parsley; butter, ½ oz.; cloves, 6; corns of pepper, 12; water, 1 pint: ½ hour.

CHEAP GRAVY FOR A ROAST FOWL.

When there is neither broth nor gravy to be had, nor meat of which either can be made, boil the neck of the fowl after having cut it small, in half a pint of water with any slight seasonings of spice or herbs, or with a little salt and pepper only; it should stew very softly for an hour or more, or the quantity will be too much reduced. When the bird is just ready for table, take the gravy from the dripping-pan, and drain off the fat from it as closely as possible; strain the liquor from the neck to it, mixing them smoothly, pass the gravy again through the strainer, heat it, add salt and pepper or cayenne, if needed, and serve it extremely hot. When this is done, the fowl should be basted with good butter only, and well floured when it is first laid to the fire. Many cooks always mix the gravy from the pan when game is roasted with that which they send to table with it, as they think that this enriches the flavour; but it is not always considered an improvement by the eaters.

Neck of fowl; water, ½ pint; pepper, salt (little vegetable and spice at choice): stewed gently, 1 hour; strained, stirred to the gravy of the roast, well cleared from fat.

ANOTHER CHEAP GRAVY FOR A FOWL.

A little good broth added to half a dozen dice of lean ham, lightly browned in a morsel of butter, with half a dozen corns of pepper and a small branch or two of parsley, and stewed for half an hour, will make excellent gravy of a common kind. When there is no broth, the neck of the chicken must be stewed down to supply its place.

QUITE COMMON BROWN GRAVY.

Cut a sheep's melt into slices half an inch thick, flour them lightly, and either fry them a pale brown, or dissolve a small slice of butter in a thick saucepan, lay them in and shake them over a moderate fire until they have taken sufficient colour; then pour gradually to them between half and three quarters of a pint of boiling water; add a not very full seasoning of salt and pepper, and stew the gravy very gently for upwards of an hour and a half. Strain, and skim off the fat, and it will be ready for table. When it is to accompany ducks or geese, brown a minced onion with the melt, and add a sprig of lemon thyme. This, though a very cheap, is a rich gravy in flavour; but it would be infinitely improved by using for it equal parts of neck of beef (or of beef steak) and sheep's melt; or the bone and the lean only of a thick mutton cutlet. A little catsup, or a very small quantity of spice, will likewise be good additions to it; and a slice or two of a root of celery, and of a carrot, might be boiled down with the meat. A bit or two of lean ham will heighten greatly the flavour of *all* brown gravies.

1 sheep's melt; butter, $\frac{1}{2}$ to 1 oz.; parsley, 1 or 2 small branches: gently browned. Boiling water, $\frac{1}{2}$ to $\frac{3}{4}$ pint; pepper, salt: $1\frac{1}{2}$ hour, or more. *Slowly* stewed. (Onion, carrot, celery, mushroom catsup, little spice, or bit or two of lean ham at choice.)

Obs.—Part of an ox's melt is sometimes used for gravy in common cookery, but it is, we should say, too coarse for the purpose, and the flavour is peculiarly, and we think disagreeably, sweet; but a skilful cook, may perhaps, by artificial means, render it more palatable.

Obs. 2.—The best gravies possible, may be made with the bones of all *uncooked* meat except pork.

GRAVY OR SAUCE FOR A GOOSE.

Mince, and brown in a small saucepan, with a slice of butter, two ounces of mild onion. When it begins to brown, stir to it a teaspoonful of flour, and in five or six minutes afterwards, pour in by degrees the third of a pint of good brown gravy; let this simmer fifteen minutes; strain it; bring it again to the point of boiling, and add to it a teaspoonful of made-mustard mixed well with a glass of port wine. Season it with cayenne pepper, and salt, if this last be needed. Do not let the sauce *boil* after the wine is added, but serve it *very* hot.

Onions, 2 ozs.; butter, $1\frac{1}{2}$ oz.: 10 to 15 minutes. Flour, 1 teaspoonful: 5 to 6 minutes. Gravy, $\frac{1}{3}$ pint: 15 minutes. Mustard, 1 teaspoonful; port wine, 1 glassful; cayenne pepper; salt. See also Christopher North's own sauce.

ORANGE GRAVY, FOR WILD FOWL.

Boil for about ten minutes, in half a pint of rich and highly-flavoured brown gravy, or espagnole, half the rind of an orange, pared as thin as possible, and a small strip of lemon-rind, with a bit of sugar the size of a hazel-nut. Strain it off, add to it a quarter pint of port or claret, the juice of half a lemon, and a tablespoonful of orange-juice; season it with cayenne, and serve it as hot as possible.

Gravy, ½ pint; ⅓ the rind of an orange; lemon-peel, 1 small strip; sugar, size of hazel-nut: 10 minutes. Juice of ½ a lemon: orange-juice, 1 tablespoonful; cayenne. See also Christopher North's own sauce.

MEAT JELLIES FOR PIES AND SAUCES.

A very firm meat jelly is easily made by stewing slowly down equal parts of shin of beef, and knuckle or neck of veal, with a pint of cold water to each pound of meat; but to give it flavour, some thick slices of lean unboiled ham should be added to it, two or three carrots, some spice, a bunch of parsley, one mild onion, or more, and a moderate quantity of salt; or part of the meat may be omitted, and a calf's-head, or the scalp of one, very advantageously substituted for it, though the flavouring must then be heightened, because, though very gelatinous, these are in themselves exceedingly insipid to the taste. If rapidly boiled, the jelly will not be clear, and it will be difficult to render it so without clarifying it with the whites of eggs, which it ought never to require; if very gently stewed, on the contrary, it will only need to be passed through a fine sieve, or cloth. The fat must be carefully removed, after it is quite cold. The shin of beef recommended for this and other receipts, should be from the middle of the leg of young heifer beef, not of that which is large and coarse.

Middle of small shin of beef, 3 lbs.; knuckle or neck of veal, 3 lbs.; lean of ham, ½ lb.; water, 3 quarts; carrots, 3 large, or 2 small; bunch of parsley; 1 mild onion, stuck with 8 cloves; 2 small bay-leaves; 1 large blade of mace; small saltspoonful of peppercorns; salt, ¾ oz. (more if needed): 5 to 6 hours' very gentle stewing.

Obs.—A finer jelly may be made by using a larger proportion of veal than of beef, and by adding clear beef or veal broth to it instead of water, in a small proportion at first, as directed in the receipt for consommée, see page 85, and by pouring in the remainder when the meat is heated through. The necks of poultry, any inferior joints of them omitted from a fricassee, or other dish, or an old fowl, will further improve it much; an eschalot or two may at choice be boiled down in it, instead of the onion, but the flavour should be scarcely perceptible.

A CHEAPER MEAT JELLY.

One calf's foot, a pound and a half or two pounds of neck of veal or beef, a small onion, a carrot, a bunch of parsley, a little spice, a bit or two of quite lean ham, dressed or undressed, and five half pints of water, boiled *very* slowly for five or six hours will give a strong, though not a highly flavoured jelly. More ham, any bones of unboiled meat, poultry, or game will, in this respect, improve it; and the liquor in which fowls or veal have been boiled for table should, when at hand, be used for it instead of water. These jellies keep much better and longer when no vegetables are stewed down in them.

GLAZE.

This is merely *strong*, clear gravy or jelly boiled quickly down to the consistency of thin cream; but this reduction must be carefully managed that the glaze may be brought to the proper point without being burned; it must be attentively watched, and stirred without being quitted for a moment from the time of its beginning to thicken; when it has reached the proper degree of boiling, it will jelly in dropping from the spoon, like preserve, and should then be poured out immediately, or it will burn. When wanted for use, melt it gently by placing the vessel which contains it (see article *Glazing*, Chapter VII.) in a pan of ooiling water, and with a paste-brush lay it on to the meat, upon which it will form a sort of clear varnish. In consequence of the very great reduction which it undergoes, salt should be added to it sparingly when it is made. Any kind of stock may be boiled down to glaze; but unless it be strong, a pint will afford but a spoonful or two; a small quantity of it, however, is generally sufficient, unless a large repast is to be served. Two or three layers must be given to each joint. The jellies which precede this will answer for it extremely well; and it may be made also with shin of beef stock, for common occasions, when no other is at hand.

ASPIC, OR CLEAR SAVOURY-JELLY.

Boil a couple of calf's feet, with three or four pounds of knuckle of veal, three-quarters of a pound of lean ham, two large onions, three whole carrots, and a large bunch of herbs, in a gallon of water, till it is reduced more than half. Strain it off; when perfectly cold, remove every particle of fat and sediment, and put the jelly into a very clean stewpan, with four whites of eggs well beaten; keep it stirred until it is nearly boiling; then place it by the side of the fire to simmer for a quarter of an hour. Let it settle, and pour it through a jelly-bag until it is quite clear. Add, when it first begins to boil, three blades of mace, a teaspoonful of white peppercorns, and sufficient salt to flavour it properly, allowing for the ham, and the reduction. French cooks flavour this jelly with taragon vinegar when it is clarified: cold poultry, game, and fish are served in, or garnished with it; when it is to be moulded, with slices of boiled tongue laid in the middle in a chain, or carved fowl, or aught else, it will be well to throw in a pinch of isinglass; and hams are often placed on a thick layer of it *roughed*, and then covered entirely with more for large breakfasts, or cold repasts. It is also used as gravy for meat pies.

Calf's feet, 2; veal, 4 lbs.; ham, ¾ lb.; onions, 2; carrots, 3; herbs, large bunch; mace, 3 blades; white whole pepper, 1 teaspoonful; water, 1 gallon: 5 to 6 hours. Whites of eggs, 4: 15 minutes.

CHAPTER IV.

SAUCES.

INTRODUCTORY REMARKS.

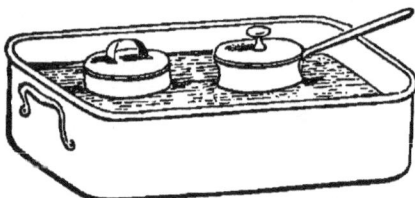

Bain Marie, or Water Bath.

THE difference between good and bad cookery can scarcely be more strikingly shown than in the manner in which sauces are prepared and served. If well made, appropriate to the dishes they accompany, and sent to table with them as hot as possible, they not only give a heightened relish to a dinner, but they prove that both skill and taste have have been exerted in its arrangements. When coarsely or carelessly prepared, on the contrary, as they too often are, they greatly discredit the cook, and are anything but acceptable to the eaters. Melted butter, the most common of all—the "*one sauce*" of England and America, which excites the raillery of foreigners—is frequently found to be such an intolerable compound, either oiled or lumpy, or composed principally of flour and water, that it says but little for the state of cookery amongst us. We trust that the receipts in the present chapter are so clearly given, that if strictly followed they will materially assist the learner in preparing tolerably palatable sauces at the least. The cut at the commencement of the chapter exhibits the vessel called a *bain marie*, in which saucepans are placed when it is necessary to keep their contents hot without allowing them to boil: it is extremely useful when dinners are delayed after they are ready to serve.

TO THICKEN SAUCES.

When this is done with the yolks of eggs, they should first be well beaten, and then mixed with a spoonful of cold stock, should it be at hand, and with one or two of the boiling sauce, which should be stirred very quickly to them, and they must in turn be stirred briskly to the sauce, which may be held over the fire, and well shaken for an instant afterwards, but never placed upon it, nor allowed to boil.

To the *roux* or French thickening (which follows,) the gravy or other liquid which is to be mixed with it should be poured boiling, and in small quantities, the saucepan being often well shaken round, and the sauce made to boil up after each portion is added. If this precaution be observed, the butter will never float upon the surface, but the whole will be well and smoothly blended: it will otherwise be difficult to clear the sauce from it perfectly.

For invalids, or persons who object to butter in their soups or sauces, flour only, mixed to a smooth batter and stirred into the boiling liquid, may be substituted for other thickening: arrow-root also, used in the same way, will answer even better than flour.

FRENCH THICKENING; OR, BROWN ROUX.

For ordinary purposes this may be made as it is wanted for use; but when it is required for various dishes at the same time, or for cookery upon a large scale, it can be prepared at once in sufficient quantity to last for several days, and it will remain good for some time. Dissolve with a very gentle degree of heat, half a pound of good butter, then draw it from the fire, skim it well, give time for it to settle, pour it gently from the sediment into a very clean frying-pan, and place it over a slow but clear fire. Put into a dredging box about seven ounces of fine dry flour; add it gradually to the butter, shake the pan often as it is thrown in, and keep the thickening constantly stirred until it has acquired a clear light brown colour. It should be very slowly and equally done, or its flavour will be unpleasant. Pour it into a jar, and stir a spoonful or two as it is needed into boiling soup or gravy. When the butter is not clarified it will absorb an additional ounce of flour, the whole of which ought to be fine and dry. This thickening may be made in a well-tinned stewpan even better than in a frying-pan, and if simmered over a coal fire it should be placed high above it, and well guarded from smoke.

WHITE ROUX, OR FRENCH THICKENING.

Proceed exactly as for the preceding receipt, but dredge in the flour as soon as the butter is in full simmer, and be careful not to allow the thickening to take the slightest colour: this is used for white gravies or sauces.

SAUCE TOURNÉE, OR, PALE THICKENED GRAVY.

Sauce tournée is nothing more than rich pale gravy made with veal or poultry (see consommée, page 85) and thickened with delicate white roux. The French give it a flavouring of mushrooms and green onions, by boiling some of each in it for about half an hour before the sauce is served; it must then be strained previously to being dished. Either first dissolve an ounce of butter, and then dredge gradually to it three quarters of an ounce of flour, and proceed as for the preceding receipt: or blend the flour and butter perfectly with a knife, before they are thrown into the stewpan, and keep them stirred without ceasing over a clear and gentle fire until they have simmered for some minutes, then place the stewpan high over the fire, and shake it constantly until the roux has lost the raw taste of the flour; next, stir very gradually to it a pint of the gravy, which should be boiling: set it by the side of the stove for a few minutes and skim it thoroughly.

Butter, 1 oz.; flour, ¾ oz.; strong, pale gravy, seasoned with mushrooms and green onions, 1 pint.

Obs. 3.—With the addition of three or four yolks of very fresh eggs, mixed with a seasoning of mace, cayenne, and lemon-juice, this becomes *German sauce*, now much used for fricassees, and other dishes; and minced parsley (boiled) and cayenne vinegar, each in sufficient quantity to flavour it agreeably, convert it into a good fish sauce.

BÉCHAMEL.

This is a fine French white sauce, now very much served at good English tables. It may be made in various ways, and more or less expensively; but it should always be thick, smooth, and rich, though delicate in flavour. The most ready mode of preparing it, is to take an equal proportion of very strong, pale veal gravy, and of good cream

(a pint of each, for example), and then by rapid boiling over a very
clear fire, to reduce the gravy nearly half; next, to mix with part of
the cream a tablespoonful of fine dry flour, to pour it to the remainder,
when it boils, and to keep the whole stirred for five minutes or more
over a slow fire, for if placed upon a fierce one, it would be liable to
burn; then to add the gravy, to stir and mix the sauce perfectly, and
to simmer it for a few minutes longer. All the flavour should be given
by the gravy, in which French cooks boil a handful of mushrooms, a
few green onions, and some branches of parsley before it is reduced:
but a good béchamel may be made without them, with a strong consommée. (See pale veal gravy, page 85) well reduced.

Strong pale veal gravy (flavoured with mushrooms or not), 1 pint:
reduced half. Rich cream, 1 pint; flour, 1 tablespoonful: 5 minutes.
With gravy, 4 or 5 minutes.

Obs.— Velouté, which is a rather thinner sauce or gravy, is made by
simply well reducing the cream and stock separately, and then mixing
them together without any thickening.

COMMON BÉCHAMEL.

Cut half a pound of veal, and a slice of lean ham into small dice, and
stew them in butter, with vegetables, as directed in the foregoing receipt: stir in the same proportion of flour, then add the milk, and let
the sauce boil very gently for an hour. It should not be allowed to
thicken too much before it is strained.

Obs.—Common béchamel, with the addition of a spoonful of made-
mustard, is an excellent sauce for boiled mutton.

RICH MELTED BUTTER.

This is more particularly required in general for lobster sauce, when
it is to be served with turbot or brill, and for good oyster sauce as well.
Salmon is itself so rich, that less butter is needed for it than for sauce
which is to accompany a drier fish. Mix to a very smooth batter a
dessertspoonful of flour, a half-saltspoonful of salt, and half a pint of
cold water; put these into a delicately clean saucepan, with from four
to six ounces of well-flavoured butter, cut into small bits, and shake the
sauce strongly round, almost without cessation, until the ingredients
are perfectly blended, and it is on the point of boiling; let it simmer
for two or three minutes, and it will be ready for use. The best French
cooks recommend its not being allowed to *boil,* as they say it tastes less
of flour if served when it is just at the point of simmering.

Cold water, ½ pint; salt, ½ spoonful; flour, 1 dessertspoonful: 3 to 4
minutes. Butter; 4 to 6 ozs.

MELTED BUTTER; (*a good common receipt.*)

Put into a basin a large teaspoonful of flour, and a little salt, then
mix with them very gradually and very smoothly a quarter-pint of cold
water; turn these into a small clean saucepan, and shake or stir them
constantly over a clear fire until they have boiled a couple of minutes,
then add an ounce and a half of butter cut small, keep the sauce stirred
until this is entirely dissolved, give the whole a minute's boil, and serve
it quickly. The more usual mode is to put the butter in at first with
the flour and water; but for inexperienced or unskilful cooks the safer
plan is to follow the present receipt.

Water, ¼ pint; flour, 1 teaspoonful: 2 minutes. Butter, 1½ oz: 1 minute.

Obs.—To render this a *rich* sauce, increase or even *double* the proportion of butter.

FRENCH MELTED BUTTER.

Pour half a pint of good, but not very thick, boiling melted butter, to the well-beaten yolks of two very fresh eggs, and stir them briskly as it is added; put the sauce again into the saucepan, and shake it high over the fire for an instant, but do not allow it to boil, or it will curdle. Add a little lemon-juice or vinegar, and serve it immediately.

NORFOLK SAUCE, OR, RICH MELTED BUTTER WITHOUT FLOUR.

Put three tablespoonsful of water into a small saucepan, and when it boils add four ounces of fresh butter; as soon as this is quite dissolved, take the saucepan from the fire and shake it round until the sauce looks thick and smooth. It must not be allowed to boil after the butter is added.

Water, 3 tablespoonsful; butter, 4 ozs.

WHITE MELTED BUTTER.

Thicken half a pint of new milk with rather less flour than is directed for the common melted butter, or with a little arrowroot, and stir into it by degrees, after it has boiled, a couple of ounces of fresh butter cut small; do not cease to stir the sauce until this is entirely dissolved, or it may become oiled, and float upon the top. Thin cream, substituted for the milk, and flavoured with a few strips of lemon-rind cut extremely thin, some salt, and a small quantity of pounded mace, if mixed with rather less flour, and the same proportion of butter, will make an excellent sauce to serve with fowls or other dishes, when no gravy is at hand to make white sauce in the usual way.

BURNT BUTTER.

Melt in a frying-pan three ounces of fresh butter, and keep it stirred slowly over a gentle fire until it is of a dark brown colour; then pour to it a couple of tablespoonsful of good *hot* vinegar, and season it with black pepper, and a little salt. In France, this is a favourite sauce with boiled skate, which is served with plenty of crisped parsley, in addition, strewed over it.

Butter, 3 ozs.; vinegar, 2 tablespoonsful; pepper; salt.

CLARIFIED BUTTER.

Put the butter into a very clean and well-tinned saucepan or enamelled stewpan, and melt it gently over a clear fire; when it just begins to simmer, skim it thoroughly, draw it from the fire, and let it stand a few minutes that the butter-milk may sink to the bottom; then pour it clear of the sediment through a muslin strainer or a fine hair-sieve; put it into jars, and store them in a cool place. Butter, thus prepared, will answer for all the ordinary purposes of cookery, and remain good for a great length of time. In France, large quantities are melted down in autumn for winter use. The clarified butter ordered for the various receipts in this volume is merely dissolved with a gentle degree of heat in a small saucepan, skimmed, and poured out for use, leaving the thick sediment behind.

VERY GOOD EGG SAUCE.

Boil four fresh eggs for quite fifteen minutes, then lay them into plenty of fresh water, and let them remain until they are perfectly cold Break the shells by rolling them on a table, take them off, separate the whites from the yolks, and divide all of the latter into quarter-inch dice; mince two of the whites only, tolerably small, mix them lightly and stir them into the third of a pint of rich melted butter, or of white sauce. serve the whole as hot as possible.

Eggs, 4: boiled 15 minutes, left till cold. The yolks of all, whites of 2; third of pint of good melted butter or white sauce. Salt as needed.

COMMON EGG SAUCE.

Boil a couple of eggs hard, and when they are quite cold cut the whites and yolks separately; mix them well, put them into a very hot tureen, and pour boiling to them a quarter-pint of melted butter: stir, and serve the sauce immediately.

Whole eggs, 2; melted butter, ¼ pint.

EGG SAUCE FOR CALF'S HEAD.

This is a provincial sauce, served sometimes with fish, and with calf's head also. Thicken to the proper consistency with flour and butter some good pale veal gravy, throw into it when it boils from one to two large teaspoonsful of minced parsley, add a slight squeeze of lemon-juice, a little cayenne, and then the eggs.

Veal gravy, ½ pint; flour, 1½ oz.; butter, 2 ozs.; minced parsley, 1 dessertspoonful; lemon-juice, 1 teaspoonful; little cayenne; eggs, 3 to 4.

ENGLISH WHITE SAUCE.

Boil softly in half a pint of well-flavoured pale veal gravy a few very thin strips of fresh lemon-rind, for just sufficient time to give their flavour to it; stir in a thickening of arrow-root, or of flour and butter; add salt if needed, and mix with the gravy a quarter-pint of boiling cream.

Good pale veal gravy, ½ pint; third of rind of 1 lemon: 15 to 20 minutes. Freshly pounded mace, third of saltspoonful; butter, 1 to 2 ozs.; flour, 1 teaspoonful (or arrow-root an equal quantity); cream, ¼ pint.

Obs.—For the best kind of white sauce, see *béchamel.*

VERY COMMON WHITE SAUCE.

The neck and the feet of a fowl, nicely cleaned, and stewed down in half a pint of water, until it is reduced to less than a quarter-pint, with a thin strip or two of lemon-rind, a small blade of mace, a small branch or two of parsley, a little salt, and half a dozen corns of pepper, then strained, thickened, and flavoured by the preceding receipt, and mixed with something more than half the quantity of cream, will answer for this sauce extremely well; and if it be added, when made, to the liver of the chicken, previously boiled for six minutes in the gravy, then bruised to a smooth paste, and passed through a sieve, it will become an excellent liver sauce. A little strained lemon-juice is generally added to it when it is ready to serve: it should be stirred very briskly in.

DUTCH SAUCE.

Put into a small saucepan the yolks of three fresh eggs, the juice of a large lemon, three ounces of butter, a little salt and nutmeg, and a wineglassful of water. Hold the saucepan over a clear fire, and keep the sauce stirred until it *nearly* boils: a little cayenne may be added. The safest way of making all sauces that will curdle by being allowed to boil, is to put them into a jar, and to set the jar over the fire, in a saucepan of boiling water, and then to stir the ingredients constantly until the sauce is thickened sufficiently to serve.

Yolks of eggs, 3; juice, 1 lemon; butter, 3 ozs.; little salt and nutmeg; water, 1 wineglassful; cayenne at pleasure.

Obs.—A small cupful of veal gravy, mixed with plenty of blanched and chopped parsley, may be used instead of water for this sauce, when it is to be served with boiled veal, or with calf's head.

FRICASSEE SAUCE.

Stir briskly, but by degrees, to the well beaten yolks of two large, or of three small fresh eggs, half a pint of common English white sauce; put it again into the saucepan, give it a shake over the fire, but be extremely careful not to allow it to boil, and just before it is served stir in a dessertspoonful of strained lemon-juice. When meat or chickens are fricasseed, they should be lifted from the saucepan with a slice, drained on it from the sauce, and laid into a very hot dish before the eggs are added, and when these are just set, the sauce should be poured on them.

BREAD SAUCE.

Pour quite boiling on half a pint of the finest bread-crumbs, an equal measure of new milk; cover them closely with a plate, and let the sauce remain for twenty or thirty minutes; put it then into a delicately clean saucepan, with a small saltspoonful of salt, half as much pounded mace, a little cayenne, and about an ounce of fresh butter; keep it stirred constantly over a clear fire for a few minutes, then mix with it a couple of spoonsful of good cream, give it a boil, and serve it immediately. When cream is not to be had, an additional spoonful or two of milk must be used; and as the sauce ought to be perfectly smooth, it is better to shake the crumbs through a cullender before the milk is poured to them; they should be of stale bread, and very lightly grated. As some will absorb more liquid than others, the cook must increase a little the above proportion, should it be needed. Equal parts of milk and of thin cream make an excellent bread sauce: more butter can be used to enrich it when it is liked.

Bread-crumbs and new milk, each ½ pint (or any other measure)· soaked 20 to 30 minutes, or more. Salt, small saltspoonful; mace, half as much; little cayenne; butter, 1 oz.: boiled 4 to 5 minutes. 2 to 4 spoonsful of good cream (or milk): 1 minute. Or: bread-crumbs, ½ pint; milk and cream, each ¼ pint; and from 2 to 4 spoonsful of either in addition.

Obs.—Very pale, strong veal gravy is sometimes poured on the bread-crumbs, instead of milk; and these, after being soaked, are boiled extremely dry, and then brought to the proper consistency with rich cream. The gravy may be highly flavoured with mushrooms when this is done.

BREAD SAUCE WITH ONION.

Put into a very clean saucepan nearly half a pint of fine bread crumbs, and the white part of a large *mild* onion, cut into quarters.

6

pour to these three quarters of a pint of new milk, and boil them very
gently, keeping them often stirred, until the onion is perfectly tender,
which will be in from forty minutes to an hour.   Press the whole
through a hair-sieve, which should be as clean as possible; reduce the
sauce by quick boiling, should it be too thin; add a seasoning of salt
and grated nutmeg, an ounce of butter, and four spoonsful of cream,
and when it is of the proper thickness, dish, and send it quickly to
table.

Bread-crumbs, nearly ½ pint; white part of 1 large mild onion; new
milk, ¾ pint: 40 to 60 minutes.   Seasoning of salt and grated nutmeg;
butter, 1 oz.; cream, 4 tablespoonsful : to be boiled till of a proper consistency.

Obs.—This is an excellent sauce for those who like a *subdued* flavour of onion in it; but as many persons object to any, the cook should
ascertain whether it be liked before she follows this receipt.

COMMON LOBSTER SAUCE.

Add to half a pint of good melted butter, a tablespoonful of essence
of anchovies, a small half-saltspoonful of freshly pounded mace, and
less than a quarter one of cayenne.   If a couple of spoonsful of cream
are at hand, stir them to the sauce when it boils; then put in the flesh
of the tail and claws of a small lobster cut into dice (or any other form)
of equal size.   Keep the saucepan by the side of the fire until the fish
is quite heated through, but do not let the sauce boil again: serve it
very hot.   A small quantity can be made on occasion with the remains
of a lobster which has been served at table.

Melted butter, ½ pint; essence of anchovies,* 1 tablespoonful; pound
ed mace, small ½ saltspoonful; less than ¼ one of cayenne; cream (if
added), 2 tablespoonsful; flesh of small lobster.

GOOD LOBSTER SAUCE.

Select for this a perfectly fresh hen lobster; split the tail carefully,
and take out the inside coral; pound half of it in a mortar very smoothly
with less than an ounce of butter, rub it through a hair-sieve, and put
it aside.   Cut the firm flesh of the fish into dice of not less than half
an inch in size; and when these are ready, make as much *good* melted
butter as will supply the quantity of sauce required for table, and if to
be served with a turbot, or other large fish, to a numerous company, let
it be plentifully provided.   Season it well with cayenne, mace, and
salt; add to it a few spoonsful of rich cream, and then mix a small por
tion of it very gradually with the pounded coral; when this is sufficiently liquefied, pour it into the sauce, and stir the whole well together; put in immediately the flesh of the fish, and heat the sauce
thoroughly by the side of the fire, without allowing it to boil, for if it
should do so its fine colour would be destroyed.   The whole of the
coral may be used for the sauce when no portion of it is required for
other purposes.

GOOD OYSTER SAUCE.

At the moment they are wanted for use, open three dozens of fine
plump native oysters; save carefully and strain their liquor, rinse them

* Anchovies, from which this essence is made, are small sea-fish, not known in
America   The flavouring must therefore be dispensed with.

separately in it, put them into a very clean saucepan, strain the liquor again, and pour it to them; heat them slowly, and keep them from one to two minutes at the simmering point, without allowing them to *boil*, as that will render them hard.   Lift them out and beard them neatly; add to the liquor three ounces of butter, smoothly mixed with a large dessertspoonful of flour; stir these without ceasing until they boil, and are perfectly mixed; then add to them gradually a quarter-pint, or rather more, of new milk, or of thin cream (or equal parts of both), and continue the stirring until the sauce boils again; add a little salt, should it be needed, and a small quantity of cayenne in the finest powder; put in the oysters, and keep the saucepan by the side of the fire, until the whole is thoroughly hot, and begins to simmer, then turn the sauce into a well-heated tureen, and send it immediately to table.

Small plump oysters, 3 dozens; butter, 3 ozs; flour, 1 large dessertspoonful; the oyster-liquor; milk or cream, full ¼ pint · little salt and cayenne.

COMMON OYSTER SAUCE.

Prepare and plump two dozens of oysters as directed in the receipt above; add their strained liquor to a quarter-pint of *thick* melted butter made with milk, or with half milk and half water; stir the whole until it boils, put in the oysters, and when they are quite heated through, send the sauce to table without delay.   Some persons like a little cayenne and essence of anchovies added to it when it is served with fish; others prefer the unmixed flavour of the oysters.

Oysters, 2 dozens; their liquor; melted butter, ¼ pint.   (Little cayenne and 1 dessertspoonful of essence of anchovies when liked.)

CREAM SAUCE FOR FISH.

Knead very smoothly together with a strong bladed knife, a *large* teaspoonful of flour with three ounces of good butter; stir them in a very clean saucepan or stewpan, over a gentle fire until the butter is dissolved, then throw in a little salt, and some cayenne, give the whole one minute's simmer, and add, very gradually, half a pint of good cream; keep the sauce constantly stirred until it boils, then mix with it a dessertspoonful of essence of anchovies, and half as much vinegar or lemon-juice.   The addition of shelled shrimps, or lobster cut in dice, will convert this at once into a most excellent sauce of either.   Pounded mace may be added to it with the cayenne; and it may be thinned with a few spoonsful of milk should it be too thick.   Omit the essence of anchovies, and mix with it some parsley boiled very green, and minced, and it becomes a good sauce for boiled poultry.

Butter, 3 ozs.; flour, 1 *large* teaspoonful: 2 to 3 minutes.   Cream, ½ pint; essence of anchovies, 1 large dessertspoonful (more if liked); vinegar or lemon-juice, 1 teaspoonful; salt, ¼ saltspoonful.

SHARP MAITRE D'HOTEL SAUCE; (*English Receipt.*)

For a rich sauce of this kind, mix a dessertspoonful of flour with four ounces of good butter, but with from two to three ounces only for common occasions; knead them together until they resemble a smooth paste, then proceed exactly as for the sauce above, but substitute good pale veal gravy, or strong, pure-flavoured veal broth, or shin of beef stock (which, if well made, has little colour), for the cream; and when these have boiled for two or three minutes, stir in a tablespoonful of common vinegar, and one of Chili vinegar, with as much cayenne as will flavour the sauce well, and salt, should it be needed; throw in from two to three dessertspoonsful of finely-minced parsley, give the whole a boil, and it will be ready to serve.   A tablespoonful of mushroom catsup or of Harvey's sauce may be added with the vinegar, when the colour of the sauce is immaterial.   It may be served with boiled calf's head, or with boiled eels with good effect; and, as we have directed in another part of this volume, various kinds of cold meat and fish may be re-warmed for table in it.   With a little more flour, and a flavouring of essence of anchovies, it will make, without parsley, an excellent sauce for these last, when they are first dressed.

Butter, 2 to 4 ozs.; flour, one dessertspoonful; pale veal gravy or strong broth, or shin of beef stock, ½ pint; cayenne; salt, if needed, common vinegar, 1 tablespoonful; Chili vinegar, 1 tablespoonful. (Cat sup or Harvey's sauce, according to circumstances.)

FRENCH MAITRE D'HOTEL,* OR STEWARD'S SAUCE.

Add to half a pint of rich, pale veal gravy, well thickened with the white *roux* of page 93, a good seasoning of pepper, salt, minced parsley, and lemon-juice; or make the thickening with a small tablespoonful of flour, and a couple of ounces of butter; keep these stirred constantly over a very gentle fire from ten to fifteen minutes, then pour to them the gravy, boiling, in small portions, mixing the whole well as it is added, and letting it boil up between each, for unless this be done, the butter will be likely to float upon the surface.   Simmer the sauce for a few minutes, and skim it well, then add salt should it be needed, a tolerable seasoning of pepper or of cayenne, in fine powder, from two to three teaspoonsful of minced parsley, and the strained juice of a small lemon.   For some dishes, this sauce is thickened with the yolks of eggs, about four to the pint.   The French work into their sauces generally a small bit of fresh butter, just before they are taken from the fire, to give them mellowness: this is done usually for the Mâitre d'Hotel.

THE LADY'S SAUCE; (*for fish.*)

Pound to a very smooth paste the inside coral of a lobster with a small slice of butter, and some cayenne; rub it through a hair-sieve, gather it together, and mix it very smoothly with from half to three-quarters of a pint of *sauce tournée*, or of cream fish-sauce, previously well seasoned with cayenne and salt, and moderately with pounded mace; bring it to the *point* of boiling only, stir in quickly, but gradually, a tablespoonful of strained lemon-juice, and serve it very hot.   When neither cream nor gravy is at hand, substitute *rich* melted butter, mixed with a dessertspoonful or two of essence of anchovies, and well seasoned.   The fine colour of the coral will be destroyed by boiling.   This sauce, which the French call *Sauce à l'Aurore*, may be served with brill, boiled soles, grey mullet, and some few other kinds of fish: it is quickly made when the lobster butter of Chapter XIV. is in the house.

Coral of lobster, pounded; cream-sauce, or *sauce tournée* (thickened pale veal gravy), ½ to ¾ pint; lemon-juice, 1 tablespoonful; salt. cayenne, and mace, as needed.   Or: *rich* melted butter, instead of other sauce; essence of anchovies, 2 dessertspoonsful; other seasoning, as above.

---

* The Mâitre d'Hotel is, properly, the *House Steward.*

Obs.—The proportion of spices here must, of course, depend on the flavouring which the gravy or sauce may have already received.

GENEVEVE SAUCE, OR SAUCE GENEVOISE.

Cut into dice three ounces of the lean of a well-flavoured ham, and put them with half a small carrot, four cloves, a blade of mace, two or three very small sprigs of lemon-thyme, and of parsley, and rather more than an ounce of butter into a stewpan, just simmer them from three-quarters of an hour to a whole hour, then stir in a teaspoonful of flour; continue the slow stewing for about five minutes, and pour in by degrees a pint of good boiling veal gravy, and let the sauce again simmer softly for nearly an hour. Strain it off, heat it in a clean saucepan, and when it boils, stir in a wineglassful and a half of good sherry or Madeira, two tablespoonsful of lemon-juice, some cayenne, a little salt if needed, and a small tablespoonful of flour, very smoothly mixed with two ounces of butter. Give the whole a boil after the thickening is added, pour a portion of the sauce over the fish (it is served principally with salmon and trout), and send the remainder very hot to table in a tureen.

Lean of ham, 3 ozs.; ½ small carrot; 4 to 6 cloves; mace, 1 large blade; thyme and parsley, 3 or 4 *small* sprigs of each; butter, 1 to 1½ oz.: 50 to 60 minutes. Veal gravy, 1 pint: ¾ to 1 hour. Sherry or Madeira, 1½ glassful; lemon-juice, 2 tablespoonsful; seasoning of cayenne and salt; flour, 1 tablespoonful; butter, 2 ozs.: 1 minute.

Obs.—A teaspoonful or more of essence of anchovies is usually added to the sauce, though it is scarcely required.

SAUCE ROBERT.

Cut into small dice four or five large onions, and brown them in a stewpan with three ounces of butter, and a dessertspoonful of flour. When of a deep yellow brown, pour to them half a pint of beef or of veal gravy, and let them simmer for fifteen minutes; skim the sauce, add a seasoning of salt and pepper, and, at the moment of serving, mix in a dessertspoonful of made-mustard.

Large onions, 4 or 5; butter, 3 ozs.; flour, dessertspoonful: 10 to 15 minutes. Gravy, ½ pint: 15 minutes. Mustard, dessertspoonful.

SAUCE PIQUANTE.

Brown lightly, in an ounce and a half of butter, a tablespoonful of minced eschalots, or three of onions; add a teaspoonful of flour when they are partially done; pour to them half a pint of gravy or of *good* broth, and when it boils, add three chilies, a bay-leaf, and a very small bunch of thyme. Let these simmer for twenty minutes; take out the thyme and bay-leaf, add a high seasoning of black pepper, and half a wineglassful of the best vinegar. A quarter-teaspoonful of cayenne may be substituted for the chilies.

Eschalots, 1 tablespoonful, or three of onions; flour, 1 teaspoonful; butter, 1½ oz.: 10 to 15 minutes. Gravy or broth, ½ pint; chilies 3; bay-leaf; thyme, small bunch: 20 minutes. Pepper, plenty; vinegar, ¼ wineglassful.

EXCELLENT HORSERADISH SAUCE; (*to serve hot or cold with roast beef.*)

Wash and wipe a stick of *young* horseradish, grate it as small as

possible on a fine grater, then with two ounces (or a couple of large
tablespoonsful) of it, mix a small teaspoonful of salt, and four tablespoonsful of good cream; stir in briskly and by degrees, three dessertspoonsful of vinegar. To heat the sauce, put it into a small and delicately clean saucepan, hold it over, but do not place it *upon* the fire,
and stir it without intermission until it is near the point of simmering,
but do not allow it to boil, or it will curdle instantly.

Horseradish pulp, 2 ozs. (or, 2 *large* tablespoonsful); salt, 1 teaspoonful; good cream, 4 tablespoonsful; vinegar, 3 dessertspoonsful.

Obs.—Common English salad-mixture is often added to the grated
horseradish when the sauce is to be served cold.

HOT HORSERADISH SAUCE; (*to serve with boiled or stewed meat, or fish.*)

Mix three ounces of young, tender, grated horseradish with half a
pint of good brown gravy, and let it stand by the side of the fire until it
is on the point of boiling; add salt if required, a teaspoonful of made-
mustard, and a dessertspoonful of garlic or of eschalot vinegar, if at
hand; if not, twice as much common vinegar for it.

Some cooks stew the horseradish in vinegar for ten minutes, and
after having drained it from this, mix it with nearly half a pint of thick
melted butter.

Horseradish, grated, 3 ozs.; brown gravy, ½ pint; made-mustard, 1
teaspoonful; eschalot or garlic vinegar, 1 dessertspoonful (or common
vinegar, twice as much).

CHRISTOPHER NORTH'S OWN SAUCE FOR MANY MEATS.

Throw into a small basin a heaped saltspoonful of *good* cayenne pepper, in very fine powder, and half the quantity of salt;* add a small
dessertspoonful of well-refined, pounded and sifted sugar; mix these
thoroughly; then pour in a tablespoonful of the strained juice of a fresh
lemon, two of Harvey's sauce, a teaspoonful of the very best mushroom
catsup (or of cavice), and three tablespoonsful, or a small wineglassful,
of port wine. Heat the sauce by placing the basin in a saucepan of
boiling water, or turn it into a jar, and place this in the water. Serve
it directly it is ready with geese or ducks, tame or wild; roast pork,
venison, fawn, a grilled blade-bone, or any other broil. A slight flavour
of garlic or eschalot vinegar may be given to it at pleasure. Many
persons use it with fish. It is good cold; and, if bottled directly it is
made, may be stored for several days. It is the better for being mixed
some hours before it is served. *The proportion of cayenne may be
doubled when a very pungent sauce is desired.*

Good cayenne pepper in fine powder, 1 *heaped* saltspoonful; salt,
half as much; pounded sugar, 1 small dessertspoonful; strained lemon-
juice, 1 tablespoonful; Harvey's sauce, 2 tablespoonsful; best mushroom catsup, 1 teaspoonful; port wine, 3 tablespoonsful, or small wine
glassful. (Little eschalot, or garlic-vinegar at pleasure.)

Obs.—This sauce is exceedingly good when mixed with the brown
gravy of a hash or stew, or with that which is served with game or
other dishes.

POOR MAN'S SAUCE; (*served with Turkey Poults.*)

Mix with four tablespoonsful of minced onions, half a teaspoonful of

---

* *Characteristically, the salt* of this sauce ought, perhaps, to prevail more strongly
over the *sugar*, but it will be found for most tastes sufficiently *piquant* as it is.

salt, nearly as much pepper, two tablespoonsful of water, and three of good sharp vinegar. Boil the sauce for a few minutes, and serve it hot; or send it to table cold, when it is liked so. Vinegar may entirely supply the place of the water in this case, and a spoonful or two of oil may be mixed with it. A small desertspoonful of minced parsley is likewise sometimes mixed with the onions. Their strong flavour may be in some measure weakened by steeping them for an hour or more in a pint of cold water after they are minced.

SALLAD DRESSING.

For a salad of moderate size pound very smoothly the yolks of two hard-boiled eggs with a small teaspoonful of unmade mustard, half as much sugar in fine powder, and a saltspoonful of salt. Mix gradually with these a small cup of cream, or the same quantity of very pure oil, and two tablespoonsful of vinegar. More salt and acid can be added at pleasure; but the latter usually predominates too much in English salads. A few drops of cayenne vinegar will improve this receipt.

Hard yolks of eggs, 2; unmade mustard, 1 small teaspoonful; sugar, half as much; salt, 1 saltspoonful; cream or oil, small cupful; vinegar, 2 tablespoonsful.

Obs. 1.—To some tastes a teaspoonful or more of eschalot vinegar would be an acceptable addition to this sauce, which may be otherwise varied in numberless ways. Cucumber-vinegar may be substituted for other, and small quantities of soy, cavice, essence of anchovies, or catsup may in turn be used to flavour the compound. The salad-bowl too may be rubbed with a cut clove of garlic, to give the whole composition a very slight flavour of it. The eggs should be boiled for fifteen minutes, and allowed to become quite cold always before they are pounded, or the mixture will not be smooth: if it should curdle, which it will sometimes do, if not carefully made, add to it the yolk of a very fresh unboiled egg.

Obs. 2.—As we have before had occasion to remark, garlic, when very sparingly and judiciously used, imparts a remarkably fine savour to a sauce or gravy, and neither a strong nor a coarse one, as it does when used in larger quantities. The veriest morsel (or, as the French call it, a mere *soupçon*) of the root is sufficient to give this agreeable piquancy, but unless the proportion be extremely small, the effect will be quite different. The Italians dress their salads upon a round of delicately toasted bread, which is rubbed with garlic, saturated with oil, and sprinkled with cayenne, before it is laid into the bowl: they also eat the bread thus prepared, but with less of oil, and untoasted often before their meals, as a digestor.

FRENCH SALAD DRESSING.

Stir a saltspoonful of salt and half as much pepper into a large spoonful of oil, and when the salt is dissolved, mix with them four additional spoonsful of oil, and pour the whole over the salad; let it be *well* turned, and then add a couple of spoonsful of vinegar; mix the whole thoroughly and serve it without delay. The salad should not be dressed in this way until the instant before it is wanted for table: the proportions of salt and pepper can be increased at pleasure, and common, or cucumber vinegar may be substituted for the tarragon, which, however is more frequently used in France than any other

Salt, 1 spoonful; pepper, ½ as much; oil, 5 salad-spoonsful; tarragon, or other vinegar, 2 spoonsful.

OUR OWN SAUCE FOR SALAD OR COLD MEAT.

Mix with the yolks of two very fresh unboiled eggs a half-saltspoonful of salt, a third as much of cayenne, and a slight grating of nutmeg; then stir very gradually to them three tablespoonsful of oil of the finest quality working the sauce like the Mayonnaise; and when it is perfectly smooth, add three spoonsful of good meat-jelly, and two of cucumber-vinegar. The shin of beef stock for gravies, which will be strongly jellied when cold, will answer very well for this sauce when no richer is at hand.

MAYONNAISE; (*a very fine sauce for cold meat, poultry, fish, or salad.*)

Put into a large basin the yolks only of two fine and very fresh eggs, carefully freed from the germs, with a little salt and cayenne; stir these well together, then add about a teaspoonful of the purest salad oil, and work the mixture round with a wooden spoon until it appears like cream. Pour in by slow degrees nearly half a pint of oil, continuing at each interval to work the sauce as at first until it resumes the smoothness of a custard, and not a particle of the oil remains visible; then add a couple of tablespoonsful of plain or of tarragon vinegar, and one of cold water to whiten the sauce. A bit of clear veal jelly the size of an egg will improve it greatly; and a morsel of garlic not larger than a pea, bruised as fine as possible, will give it a very agreeable relish, even to persons to whom garlic generally is distasteful. In lieu of this, a few drops of eschalot vinegar may be stirred in; and the flavour may be varied with lemon-juice, and cucumber, or Chili vinegar at choice. The reader who may have a prejudice against the unboiled eggs which enter into the composition of the Mayonnaise, will find that the most fastidious taste would not detect their being raw, if the sauce be well made; and persons who dislike oil may partake of it in this form, without being aware of its presence, provided always that it be perfectly fresh. and pure in flavour, for otherwise it is easily perceptible.

Yolks of fresh unboiled eggs, 2; salt, ½ saltspoonful or rather more; cayenne; oil, full third of pint; common, or tarragon vinegar, 2 tablespoonsful; cold water, 1 tablespoonful; garlic, morsel size of pea (or few drops of eschalot vinegar). Meat jelly (if at hand), size of an egg.

Obs.—When a much larger proportion of vinegar is liked, a third yolk of egg should be used, or the sauce will be too thin. It is sometimes coloured green with the juice of parsley, and other herbs. A spoonful or two of cold béchamel, or of good white sauce, is always an improvement to it.

FENNEL SAUCE.

Strip from the stems, wash very clean, and boil quickly in salt and water until it is quite tender, a handful of young fennel; press the water well from it, mince it very small, and mix it gradually with the quantity of melted butter required for table.

Fennel, small handful: 10 minutes, or until quite tender. Melted butter, ¼ to ½ pint; little salt.

Obs.—The French use good pale veal gravy thickened with flour and butter for this sauce.

PARSLEY AND BUTTER.

Proceed exactly as for the fennel, but boil the parsley four or five minutes less; and be careful to press the water from it thoroughly. For an improved sauce, substitute béchamel or white melted butter for the common melted butter.

Melted butter, or thickened veal gravy, third of pint; parsley, boiled and minced, 1 dessertspoonful.

GOOSEBERRY SAUCE FOR MACKEREL.

Cut the stalks and tops from half to a whole pint of quite young gooseberries, wash them well, just cover them with cold water and boil them very gently indeed until they are tender; drain them well, and mix with them a small quantity of melted butter made with rather less flour than usual. Some eaters prefer the mashed gooseberries without any addition; others like that of a little ginger. The best way of making this sauce is to turn the gooseberries into a hair-sieve to drain, then to press them through it with a wooden spoon, and to stir them in a clean stewpan or saucepan over the fire with from half to a whole teaspoonful of sugar, just to soften their extreme acidity, and a bit of fresh butter about the size of a walnut. When the fruit is not passed through the sieve it is an improvement to seed it.

COMMON SORREL SAUCE.

Strip from the stalks and the large fibres, from one to a couple of quarts of freshly-gathered sorrel; wash it very clean, and put it into a well-tinned stewpan or saucepan (or into a German enamelled one, which would be far better), without any water; add to it a small slice of good butter, some pepper and salt, and stew it gently, keeping it well stirred, until it is exceedingly tender, that it may not burn; then drain it on a sieve, or press the liquid well from it; chop it as fine as possible; and boil it again for a few minutes with a spoonful or two of gravy, or the same quantity of cream or milk, mixed with a half-teaspoonful of flour, or with only a fresh slice of good butter. The beaten yolk of an egg or two stirred in just as the sorrel is taken from the fire will soften the sauce greatly, and a saltspoonful of pounded sugar will also be an improvement.

ASPARAGUS SAUCE, FOR LAMB CHOPS.

Cut the green tender points of some young asparagus into half-inch lengths, wash them well, drain and throw them into plenty of boiling salt and water. When they are quite tender, which may be in from ten to fifteen minutes, turn them into a hot strainer and drain the water thoroughly from them; put them, at the instant of serving, into half a pint of thickened veal gravy (see Sauce Tournée), mixed with the yolks of a couple of eggs, and well seasoned with salt and cayenne, or white pepper; or, into an equal quantity of good melted butter: add to this last a squeeze of lemon-juice. The asparagus will become yellow if reboiled, or if left long in the sauce before it is served.

Asparagus points, ½ pint: boiled 10 to 15 minutes, longer if not quite tender. Thickened veal gravy, ½ pint; yolks of eggs, 2. Or: good melted butter, ½ pint; lemon-juice, small dessertspoonful, seasoning of salt and white pepper.

GREEN MINT SAUCE, FOR ROAST LAMB.

The mint for this sauce should be fresh and young, for the leaves when old are tough. Strip them from the stems, wash them with great nicety, and drain them on a sieve or dry them in a cloth. Chop them very fine, put them into a sauce-tureen, and to three heaped table-spoonsful of the mint add two of pounded sugar; mix them well, and then add gradually six tablespoonsful of good vinegar. The sauce made thus is excellent, but Lisbon sugar can be used for it when preferred, and all the proportions can be varied to the taste. It is commonly served too liquid, and not sufficiently sweetened; and it will be found much more wholesome, and generally far more palatable made by this receipt.

Young mint minced, 3 heaped tablespoonsful; pounded sugar, 2 tablespoonsful; vinegar, 6 tablespoonsful.

CAPER SAUCE.

Stir into the third of a pint of good melted butter from three to four dessertspoonsful of capers; add a little of the vinegar, and dish the sauce as soon as it boils. Keep it stirred after the berries are added: part of them may be minced, and a little Chili vinegar substituted for their own. Pickled nasturtiums make a very good sauce, and their flavour is sometimes preferred to that of the capers. For a large joint, increase the quantity of butter to half a pint.

Melted butter, third of pint; capers, 3 to 4 dessertspoonsful.

BROWN CAPER SAUCE.

Thicken half a pint of good veal or beef gravy as directed for Sauce Tournée, and add to it two tablespoonsful of capers, and a dessertspoonful of the pickle liquor, or of Chili vinegar, with some cayenne if the former be used, and a proper seasoning of salt.

Thickened veal, or beef gravy, ½ pint; capers, 2 tablespoonsful; caper-liquor or Chili vinegar, 1 dessertspoonful.

CAPER SAUCE FOR FISH.

To nearly half a pint of very rich melted butter add six spoonsful of *strong* veal gravy or jelly, a tablespoonful of essence of anchovies, and some Chili vinegar or cayenne. When there is no gravy at hand substitute a half wineglassful of mushroom catsup, or of Harvey's sauce; though these deepen the colour more than is desirable.

COMMON CUCUMBER SAUCE.

Pare, slice, dust slightly with pepper, and with flour, two or three young cucumbers, and fry them a fine brown, in a little butter, or dissolve an ounce and a half in a small stewpan, or iron saucepan, and shake them in it over a brisk fire from twelve to fifteen minutes; pour to them, by degrees, nearly half a pint of strong beef broth, or of brown gravy; add salt, and more pepper if required; stew the whole for five minutes, and send the sauce very hot to table. A minced onion may be browned with the cucumbers when it is liked, and a spoonful of vinegar added to them before they are served.

Cucumbers, 2 or 3; butter, 1½ oz.; broth or gravy, nearly ½ pint, salt, pepper.

ANOTHER COMMON SAUCE OF CUCUMBERS.

Cucumbers which have the fewest seeds are best for this sauce. Pare and slice a couple, or three, should they be small, and put them into a saucepan, in which two ounces, or rather more, of butter have been dissolved, and are beginning to boil; place them high over the fire, that they may stew as softly as possible without taking colour, for three-quarters of an hour, or longer should they require it; add to them a good seasoning of white pepper, and some salt, when they are half done, and just before they are served stir to them half a teaspoonful of flour, mixed with a morsel of butter; stew in some minced parsley, give it a boil, and finish with a spoonful of good vinegar.

WHITE CUCUMBER SAUCE.

Quarter some young quickly grown cucumbers, without many seeds in them; empty them of these, and take off the rinds. Cut them into inch lengths, and boil them from fifteen to eighteen minutes in salt and water; squeeze, and work them through a sieve; mix them with a few spoonsful of béchamel, or thick white sauce; do not let them *boil* again, but serve them very hot. A sauce of better flavour is made by boiling the cucumbers in veal gravy well seasoned, and stirring in the beaten yolks of two or three eggs, and a little vinegar or lemon-juice, at the instant of serving. Another also of cucumbers sliced, and stewed in butter, but without being at all browned, and then boiled in pale veal gravy, which must be thickened with rich cream, is excellent. A *morsel* of sugar improves this sauce.

Cucumbers, 3: 15 to 18 minutes. White sauce, ¼ pint.

WHITE MUSHROOM SAUCE.

Cut off the stems closely from half a pint of small button mushrooms; clean them with a little salt and a bit of flannel, and throw them into cold water, slightly salted, as they are done; drain them well, or dry them in a soft cloth, and throw them into half a pint of boiling béchamel (see page 93), or of white sauce made with very fresh milk, or thin cream, thickened with a tablespoonful of flour, and two ounces of butter. Simmer the mushrooms from ten to twenty minutes, or until they are quite tender, and dish the sauce, which should be properly seasoned with salt, mace, and cayenne.

Mushrooms, ½ pint; white sauce, ½ pint; seasoning of salt, mace, and cayenne: 10 minutes.

ANOTHER MUSHROOM SAUCE.

Prepare from half to a whole pint of very small mushroom-buttons with great nicety, and throw them into as much sauce tournée; when they are tender add a few spoonsful of rich cream, give the whole a boil, and serve it. Either of these sauces may be sent to table with boiled poultry, breast of veal, or veal-cutlets: the sauce tournée should be thickened rather more than usual when it is to be used in this receipt.

Mushrooms and sauce tournée each, ½ to whole pint: stewed till tender. Cream, 4 to 8 tablespoonsful.

BROWN MUSHROOM SAUCE.

Very small flaps, peeled and freed entirely from the fur, will answer for this sauce. Leave them whole, or quarter them, and stew them tender in some rich brown gravy; give a full seasoning of mace and cayenne, add thickening, and salt if needed, and a tablespoonful of good mushroom catsup.

COMMON TOMATA SAUCE.

Tomatas are so juicy when ripe, that they require but little liquid to reduce them to a proper consistency for sauce; and they vary so exceedingly in size and quality that it is difficult to give precise directions for the exact quantity which is needed for them. Take off the stalks, halve the tomatas, and gently squeeze out the seeds and watery pulp; then stew them softly with a few spoonsful of gravy or of strong broth until they are quite melted. Press the whole through a hair-sieve, and heat it afresh with a little additional gravy should it be too thick, and some cayenne, and salt. Serve it very hot.

Fine ripe tomatas, 6 or 8; gravy or strong broth, 4 tablespoonsful: ½ to ¾ hour, or longer if needed. Salt and cayenne sufficient to season the sauce, and two or three spoonsful more of gravy if required.

Obs.—For a large tureen of this sauce, increase the proportions; and should it be at first too liquid, reduce it by quick boiling. When neither gravy nor broth is at hand, the tomatas may be stewed perfectly tender, but very gently, in a couple of ounces of butter, with some cayenne and salt only, or with the addition of a very little finely minced onion; then rubbed through a sieve, and heated, and served without any addition, or with only that of a teaspoonful of vinegar; or, when the colour is not a principal consideration, with a few spoonsful of rich cream, smoothly mixed with a little flour to prevent its curdling. The sauce must be stirred without ceasing should the last be added, and boiled for four or five minutes.

A FINER TOMATA SAUCE.

Stew very gently a dozen fine red tomatas, prepared as for the preceding receipt, with two or three sliced eschalots, four or five chilies, or a capsicum or two, or in lieu of either, with a quarter-teaspoonful of cayenne pepper, a few small dice of lean ham, and half a cupful of rich gravy. Stir these often, and when the tomatas are reduced quite to a smooth pulp, press them through a sieve; put them into a clean saucepan, with a few spoonsful more of rich gravy, or Espagnole, add salt, if needed, boil the sauce, stirring it well, for ten minutes, and serve it very hot. When the gravy is exceedingly good, and highly flavoured, the ham may be omitted: a dozen small mushrooms, nicely cleaned, may also be sliced, and stewed with the tomatas, instead of the eschalots, when their flavour is preferred, or they may be added with them. The exact proportion of liquid used is immaterial, for should the sauce be too thin, it may be reduced by rapid boiling, and diluted with more gravy if too thick.

BOILED APPLE SAUCE.

Apples of a fine cooking sort require but a very small portion of liquid to boil down well and smoothly for sauce, if placed over a gentle fire in a close-shutting saucepan, and simmered as softly as possible, until they are well broken; and their flavour is injured by the common mode of adding so much to them, that the greater part must be drained off again before they are sent to table. Pare the fruit quickly, quarter it, and be careful entirely to remove the cores; put one tablespoonful of water into a saucepan before the apples are thrown in; and proceed, as we have directed, to simmer them until they are nearly ready to serve: finish the sauce by the receipt which follows.

Apples, ½ lb.; water, 1 tablespoonful; stewed very softly: 30 to 60 minutes.

Obs.—These proportions are sufficient only for a small tureen of the sauce, and should be doubled for a large one.

BAKED APPLE SAUCE; (*good*.)

Put a tablespoonful of water into a quart basin, and fill it with good boiling apples, pared, quartered, and *carefully* cored: put a plate over, and set them into a moderate oven for about an hour, or until they are reduced quite to a pulp; beat them smooth with a clean wooden spoon, adding to them a little sugar, and a morsel of fresh butter, when these are liked, though they will scarcely be required.

The sauce made thus is far superior to that which is boiled. When no other oven is at hand, a Dutch or an American one would answer for it.

Good boiling apples, 1 quart: baked, 1 hour (more or less according to the quality of the fruit, and temperature of the oven); sugar, 1 oz.; butter, ½ oz.

BROWN APPLE SAUCE.

Stew gently down to a thick and perfectly smooth marmalade, a pound of pearmains, or of any other well-flavoured boiling apples, in about the third of a pint of rich brown gravy: season the sauce rather highly with black pepper or cayenne, and serve it very hot. Currie sauce will make an excellent substitute for the gravy when a very piquante accompaniment is wanted for pork or other rich meats.

Apples pared and cored, 1 lb.; good brown gravy, third of pint: ¾ to 1¼ hour. Pepper or cayenne as needed.

WHITE ONION SAUCE.

Strip the skin from some large white onions, and after having taken off the tops and roots, cut them in two, throw them into cold water as they are done, cover them plentifully with more, and boil them very tender; lift them out, drain, and then press the water thoroughly from them; chop them small, rub them through a sieve or strainer, put them into a little rich melted butter, mixed with a spoonful or two of cream or milk, add a seasoning of salt, give the sauce a boil, and serve it very hot. Portugal onions, when they can be obtained, are superior to any others, both for this and for most other purposes of cookery.

For the finest kind of onion sauce, see *Soubise*, below.

BROWN ONION SAUCE.

Cut off both ends of the onions, and slice them into a saucepan in which two ounces of butter have been dissolved; keep them stewing over a clear fire until they are lightly coloured; then pour to them half a pint of brown gravy. and when they have boiled until they are per-

fectly tender, work the sauce altogether through a strainer, season it
with a little cayenne, and serve it very hot.

ANOTHER BROWN ONION SAUCE

Mince the onions, stew them in butter until well coloured, stir in a
dessertspoonful of flour, shake the stewpan over the fire for three or four
minutes, pour in only as much broth or gravy as will leave the sauce
tolerably thick, season, and serve it.

SOUBISE; (*French Receipt.*)

Peel some fine white onions, and trim away all tough and discoloured
parts; mince them small, and throw them into plenty of boiling water;
when they have boiled quickly for five minutes, drain them well in a
sieve, then stew them very softly indeed in an ounce or two of fresh
butter, until they are dry and perfectly tender; stir to them as much
béchamel as will bring them to the consistency of very thick peas soup,
pass the whole through a strainer, pressing the onion strongly that none
may remain behind, and heat the sauce afresh, without allowing it to
boil. A small half-teaspoonful of pounded sugar is sometimes added to
this soubise.

White part of onions, 2 lbs.: blanched 5 minutes. Butter, 2 ozs.:
30 to 50 minutes. Béchamel, ¾ to 1 pint, or more.

Obs.—These sauces are served more particularly with lamb or mutton cutlets, than with any other meats; but they would probably find
many approvers if sent to table with roast mutton, or boiled veal. Half
the quantity given above will be sufficient for a moderate-sized dish.

A FINE SAUCE, OR PURÉE OF VEGETABLE MARROW.

Pare one or two half grown marrows and cut all the seeds; take r.
pound of the vegetable, and slice it with one ounce of mild onion, into a
pint of strong veal broth or of pale gravy; stew them very softly for
nearly or quite an hour; add salt and cayenne, or white pepper, when
they are nearly done; press the whole through a fine and delicately
clean hair-sieve, heat it afresh, and stir to it when it boils about the
third of a pint of rich cream. Serve it with boiled chickens, stewed or
boiled veal, lamb cutlets, or any other delicate meat. When to be
served as a purée, an additional half pound of the vegetable must be used;
and it should be dished with small fried sippets round it. For a maigre
dish, stew the marrow and onion quite tender in butter, and dilute them
with half boiling water and half cream.

Vegetable marrow, 1 lb; mild onion, 1 oz.; strong broth or pale
gravy, 1 pint: nearly or quite 1 hour. Pepper or cayenne, and salt as
needed; good cream from ¼ to ½ of pint. For purée, ½ lb. more o
marrow.

EXCELLENT TURNIP, OR ARTICHOKE SAUCE FOR BOILED MEAT.

Pare, slice, and boil quite tender, some finely-grained mild turnips,
press the water from them thoroughly, and pass them through a sieve.
Dissolve a slice of butter in a clean saucepan, and stir to it a large teaspoonful of flour, or mix them smoothly together before they are put in,
and shake the saucepan round until they boil; pour to them very gradually, nearly a pint of thin cream (or of good milk mixed with a portion of cream,) add the turnips with a half-teaspoonful or more of salt,

and when the whole is well mixed and very hot, pour it over boiled mutton, veal, lamb, or poultry. There should be sufficient of the sauce to cover the meat entirely, and when properly made it improves greatly the appearance of a joint. A little cayenne tied in a muslin may be boiled in the milk before it is mixed with the turnips. Jerusalem artichokes make a more delicate sauce of this kind even than turnips; the weight of both vegetables must be taken after they are pared.

Pared turnips or artichokes, 1 lb.; fresh butter, 1½ oz.; flour, 1 large teaspoonful (twice as much if all milk be used); salt, ½ teaspoonful or more; cream, or cream and milk mixed, from ¾ to 1 pint.

CELERY SAUCE.

Slice the white part of from three to five heads of young tender celery; peel it if not very young, and boil it in salt and water for twenty minutes. If for white sauce, put the celery, after it has been well drained, into half a pint of veal broth or gravy, and let it stew until it is quite soft; then add an ounce and a half of butter, mixed with a dessertspoonful of flour, and a quarter-pint of thick cream, or the yolks of three eggs. The French, after boiling the celery, which they cut very small, for about twenty minutes, drain, and chop it; then put it with a slice of butter into a stewpan, and season it with pepper, salt, and nutmeg; they keep these stirred over the fire for two or three minutes, and then dredge in a dessertspoonful of flour; when this has lost its raw taste, they pour in a sufficiency of white gravy to moisten the celery, and to allow for twenty minutes' longer boiling. A very good common celery sauce is made by simply stewing the celery, cut into inch-lengths, in butter, until it begins to be tender; and then adding a spoonful of flour, which must be allowed to brown a little, and half a pint of good broth or beef gravy, with a seasoning of pepper or cayenne.

Celery, 3 to 5 heads: 20 minutes. Veal broth, or gravy, ½ pint: 20 to 40 minutes. Butter, 1½ oz.; flour, 1 dessertspoonful; cream, ¼ pint, or three yolks of eggs.

SWEET PUDDING SAUCE.

Boil together for fifteen minutes the thin rind of half a small lemon, an ounce and a half of fine sugar, and a wineglassful of water; then take out the lemon-peel, and mix very smoothly an ounce of butter with rather more than a half-teaspoonful of flour, stir them round in the sauce until it has boiled one minute; next add a wineglassful and a half of sherry or Madeira, or two thirds of that quantity and a quarter-glass of brandy: when quite hot, serve the sauce.

Port-wine sauce is made in the same way, with the addition of a dessertspoonful of lemon-juice, some grated nutmeg, and a little more sugar: orange rind and juice may be used to give it flavour when preferred to lemon.

Rind ½ lemon; sugar, 1½ oz.; water, 1 wineglassful: 15 minutes. Butter, 1 oz.; flour, large ½ teaspoonful: 1 minute. Wine, 1½ wineglassful; or, 1 of wine, and ¼ glass of brandy.

PUNCH SAUCE FOR SWEET PUDDINGS

This is a favourite sauce with custard, plain bread, and plum-puddings. With two ounces of sugar and a quarter-pint of water, boil very gently the rind of half a small lemon, and somewhat less of orange-peel, from fifteen to twenty minutes; strain out the rinds, thicken the sauce with an ounce and a half of butter and nearly a teaspoonful of flour, add a half-glass of brandy, the same of white wine, two thirds of a glass of rum, with the juice of half an orange, and rather less of lemon-juice: serve the sauce very hot, but do not allow it to boil after the spirit is stirred in.

Sugar, 2 ozs.; water, ¼ pint; lemon and orange rind: 14 to 20 minutes. Butter, 1½ oz.; flour, 1 teaspoonful; brandy and white wine each ½ wineglassful; rum, two thirds of glassful; orange and lemon juice.

COMMON PUDDING SAUCE.

Sweeten a quarter-pint of good melted butter with an ounce and a half of sugar, and add to it gradually a couple of glasses of wine; stir it until it is at the point of boiling, and serve it immediately. Lemon-grate, or nutmeg, can be added at pleasure.

A DELICIOUS GERMAN PUDDING SAUCE.

Dissolve in half a pint of sherry or of Madeira, from three to four ounces of fine sugar, but do not allow the wine to boil; stir it hot to the well-beaten yolks of six fresh eggs, and mill the sauce over a gentle fire until it is well thickened and highly frothed; pour it over a plum, or any other kind of sweet boiled pudding, of which it much improves the appearance. Half the quantity will be sufficient for one of moderate size. A small machine, resembling a chocolate mill, is used in Germany for frothing this sauce; but a couple of silver forks, fastened together at the handles, will serve for the purpose, on an emergency. We recommend the addition of a dessertspoonful of strained lemon-juice to the wine.

For large pudding, sherry or Madeira, ½ pint; fine sugar, 3 to 4 ozs.; yolks of eggs, 6; lemon-juice (if added), 1 dessertspoonful.

Obs.—The safer plan with sauces liable to curdle is to thicken them always in a jar or jug, placed in a saucepan of water; when this is not done, they should be held over the fire, but never placed *upon* it.

PARSLEY-GREEN, FOR COLOURING SAUCES.

Gather a quantity of young parsley, strip it from the stalks, wash it very clean, shake it as dry as possible in a cloth, pound it in a mortar, press all the juice closely from it through a hair-sieve reversed, and put it into a clean jar; set it into a pan of boiling water, and in about three minutes, if *gently* simmered, the juice will be poached sufficiently; lay it then upon a clean sieve to drain, and it will be ready for use.

TO CRISP PARSLEY.

Pick some branches of young parsley, wash them well, drain them from the water, and swing them in a clean cloth until they are quite dry; place them on a sheet of writing paper in a Dutch oven, before a brisk fire, and keep them frequently turned until they are quite crisp. They will be done in from six to eight minutes.

FRIED PARSLEY.

When the parsley has been prepared as for crisping, and is *quite* dry, throw it into plenty of lard or butter, which is on the point of boil ing; take it up with a skimmer the instant it is crisp, and drain it on a cloth spread upon a sieve reversed, and placed before the fire.

TARTAR MUSTARD.

Rub four ounces of the best mustard very smooth with a full teaspoonful of salt, and wet it by degrees with strong horseradish vinegar, a dessertspoonful of cayenne or of Chili vinegar, and one or two of tarragon vinegar, when its flavour is not disliked. A quarter-pint of vinegar poured boiling upon an ounce of scraped horseradish, and left for one night, closely covered, will be ready to use for this mustard, but it will be better for standing two or three days.

Mustard, 4 ozs.; salt, large teaspoonful; cayenne, or Chili vinegar, 1 dessertspoonful; horseradish vinegar, third of pint.

Obs.—This is an exceedingly pungent compound, but has many admirers.

ANOTHER TARTAR MUSTARD.

Mix the salt and mustard smoothly, with equal parts of horseradish vinegar and of common vinegar. Mustard made by these receipts will keep long, if put into jars or bottles, and closely stopped. Cucumber, eschalot, or any other of the flavoured vinegars for which we have given receipts, may in turn be used for it, and mushroom, gherkin, or India pickle-liquor, likewise.

MILD MUSTARD.

Mustard for instant use should be mixed with milk, to which a spoonful or two of very thin cream may be added.

MUSTARD THE COMMON WAY.

The great art of mixing mustard, is to have it perfectly smooth, and of a proper consistency. The liquid with which it is moistened should be added to it in small quantities, and the mustard should be well rubbed, and beaten with a spoon. Mix a half-teaspoonful of salt with two ounces of the flour of mustard, and stir to them by degrees, sufficient boiling water to reduce it to the appearance of a thick batter; do not put it into the mustard-glass until cold. Some persons like a half-teaspoonful of sugar, in the finest powder, mixed with it. It ought to be sufficiently diluted always to drop easily from the spoon.

FRENCH BATTER; (*for frying vegetables, and for apple, peach, or orange fritters.*)

Cut a couple of ounces of good butter into small bits, pour on it less than a quarter-pint of boiling water, and when it is dissolved, add three quarters of a pint of cold water, so that the whole shall not be quite milk warm; mix it then by degrees, and very smoothly, with twelve ounces of fine dry flour, and a *small* pinch of salt, if the batter be for fruit fritters, but with more if for meat or vegetables. Just before it is used, stir into it the whites of two eggs beaten to a solid froth; but previously to this, add a little water should it appear too thick, as some flour requires more liquid than other, to bring it to the proper consistency.

Butter, 2 ozs.; water, from ¾ to nearly 1 pint; little salt; flour, ¾ lb.; whites of 2 eggs, beaten to snow.

7

TO PREPARE BREAD FOR FRYING FISH.

Cut thick slices from the middle of a loaf of light bread, pare the crust entirely from them, and dry them gradually in a cool oven until they are crisp quite through; let them become cold, then roll or beat them into fine crumbs, and keep them in a dry place for use. To strew over hams or cheeks of bacon, the bread should be left all night in the oven, which should be sufficiently heated to brown, as well as to harden it: it ought indeed to be entirely converted into equally-coloured crust. It may be sifted through a dredging-box on to the hams, after it has been reduced almost to powder.

BROWNED FLOUR FOR THICKENING SOUPS AND GRAVIES.

Spread it on a tin or dish, and colour it without burning, in a gentle oven, or before the fire in a Dutch or American oven: turn it often, or the edges will be too much browned before the middle is enough so. This, blended with butter, makes a convenient thickening for soups or gravies, of which it is desirable to deepen the colour; and it requires less time and attention than the French *roux* of page 92.

FRIED BREAD-CRUMBS.

Grate lightly into very fine crumbs four ounces of stale bread, and *shake* them through a cullender, without rubbing or touching them with the hands. Dissolve two ounces of fresh butter in a frying-pan, throw in the crumbs, and stir them constantly over a moderate fire, until they are all of a clear gold colour; lift them out with a skimmer, spread them on a soft cloth laid upon a sieve reversed, and dry them before the fire. They may be more delicately prepared by browning them in a gentle oven without the addition of butter.

Bread, 4 ozs.; butter, 2 ozs.

FRIED BREAD, OR SIPPETS OF BREAD FOR GARNISHING.

Cut the crumb of a stale loaf in slices a quarter-inch thick: form them into diamonds, or half diamonds, or shape them with a paste-cutter in any other way; fry them in fresh butter, some of a very pale brown, and others a deeper colour: dry them well, and place them alternately round the dish that is to be garnished. They may be made to adhere to the edge of the dish, when they are required for *ornament* only, by means of a little flour and white of egg brushed over the side which is placed on it: this must be allowed to dry before they are served.

THE RAJAH'S SAUCE.

Strain, very clear, the juice of six fine lemons; add to it a *small* teaspoonful of salt, a drachm of good cayenne-pepper, and a slight strip or two of the lemon-rind cut extremely thin. Give the sauce three or four minutes simmering: turn it into a China jug or basin; and when it is quite cold, strain it again, put it into small dry bottles, cork them well, and store them in a cool place which is free from damp. The sauce is good without being boiled, but is apt to ferment after a time: it is, we think, of much finer flavour than Chili vinegar.

Lemon-juice ½ pint; salt 1 *small* teaspoonful; cayenne 1 drachm simmered 5 minutes.

CHAPTER V.

STORE SAUCES.

OBSERVATIONS.

A WELL-selected stock of these will always prove a convenient re-source for giving colour and flavour to soups, gravies, and made dishes; but unless the consumption be considerable, they should not be over-abundantly provided, as few of them are improved by age, and many are altogether spoiled by long keeping, especially if they be not perfectly secured from the air by sound corking, or if stored where there is the slightest degree of damp. To prevent loss, they should be examined at short intervals, and at the first appearance of mould or fermentation, such as will bear the process should be reboiled, and put, when again quite cold, into clean bottles; a precaution often especially needful for mushroom catsup when it has been made in a wet season. This, with walnut catsup, Harvey's sauce, cavice, lemon-pickle, Chili, cucumber, and eschalot vinegar, will be all that is commonly needed for family use, but there is at the present day an extensive choice of these stores on sale, in London, and should there be a demand for them in America, they could easily be procured.

MUSHROOM CATSUP.

Cut the ends of the stalks from two gallons of freshly-gathered mush-rooms (the large flaps are best for this purpose, but they should not be worm-eaten); break them into a deep earthen pan, and strew amongst them three-quarters of a pound of salt, reserving the larger portion of it for the top. Let them stand for three, or even four days, and stir them gently once every four and twenty hours; then drain off the liquor with-out pressing the mushrooms; strain and measure it; put it into a very clean stewpan, and boil it quickly until reduced nearly or quite half. For every quart, allow half an ounce of whole black pepper, and a drachm of mace; or, instead of the pepper, a quarter-teaspoonful (ten grains) of *good* cayenne; pour the catsup into a clean jug or jar, lay a folded cloth over it, and keep it in a cool place until the following day; pour it gently from the sediment, put it into small bottles, cork them well, and rosin them down. A teaspoonful of salad-oil may be poured into each bottle before it is corked, the better to exclude the air from the catsup: it must be kept in a dry cool place.

Mushrooms, 2 gallons; salt, ¾ lb.; to macerate three or four days. To each quart of liquor, ½ oz. black pepper, or quarter-teaspoonful cay-enne; and 1 drachm mace: to be reduced half.

Obs. 1.—Catsup made thus will not be too salt, nor will the flavour of the mushrooms be overpowered by that of the spices; of which a larger quantity, and a greater variety, can be used at will.

Obs. 2.—After the mushrooms have stood for three or four days, as we have directed, the whole may be turned into a large stewpan, brought slowly to a boil, and simmered for a few minutes before the liquor is strained off. We think the catsup keeps rather better when this is done, but we recommend only just sufficient simmering to preserve it

well.   When the mushrooms are crushed, or mashed, as some authors
direct, the liquor will necessarily be very thick; it is better to proceed
as above, and then to boil the *squeezings* of the mushrooms with the
sediment of the catsup, and sufficient cloves, pepper, allspice, and ginger,
to flavour it highly: this *second* catsup will be found very useful to mix
with common thickened sauces, hashes, and stews.   In some seasons it
is necessary to boil the catsup with the spice a second time after it has
been kept for three or four months: this, by way of precaution, can
always be done, but it had better then be put into large bottles in the
first instance, and stored in the small ones afterwards.

DOUBLE MUSHROOM CATSUP.

On a gallon of fresh mushrooms strew three ounces of salt, and pour
to them a quart of ready-made catsup (that which is a year old will do
if it be perfectly good); keep these stirred occasionally for four days,
then drain the liquor very dry from the mushrooms, and boil it for fifteen
minutes, with an ounce of whole black pepper, a drachm and a half of
mace, an ounce of ginger, and three or four grains only of cayenne.

Mushrooms, 1 gallon; salt, 3 ozs.; mushroom catsup, 1 quart; peppercorns, 1 oz.; mace, 1½ drachm; ginger, 1 oz.; cayenne, 3 to 4 grains:
15 minutes.

COMPOUND, OR COOK'S CATSUP.

Take a pint and a half of mushroom catsup when it is first made, and
ready boiled (the double is best for the purpose), simmer in it for five
minutes, an ounce of small eschalots or onions, nicely peeled; add to
these half a pint of walnut catsup, and a wineglassful of cayenne vinegar,* or of Chili vinegar; give the whole one boil, pour it out, and when
cold, bottle it with the eschalots.

Mushroom catsup, 1½ pint; eschalots or onions, 1 oz.; walnut catsup
or pickle, ½ pint; cayenne or Chili vinegar, 1 wineglassful.

WALNUT CATSUP.

The vinegar in which walnuts have been pickled, when they have
remained in it a year, will generally answer all the purposes for which
this catsup is required, particularly if it be drained from them and boiled
for a few minutes, with a little additional spice, and a few eschalots;
but where the vinegar is objected to, it may be made by boiling either
the expressed juice of young walnuts for an hour, with six ounces of
fine anchovies, four ounces of eschalots, half an ounce of black pepper,
a quarter ounce of cloves, and a drachm of mace, to every quart; or as
follows :—

Pound in a mortar a hundred young walnuts, strewing amongst them
as they are done half a pound of salt; then pour to them a quart of
strong vinegar, and let them stand until they have become quite black,
keeping them stirred three or four times a day; next add a quart of
strong old beer, and boil the whole together for ten minutes; strain it,
and let it remain until the next day; then pour it off clear from the
sediment, add to it one large head of garlic bruised, half an ounce of
nutmegs bruised, the same quantity of cloves and black pepper, and two
drachms of mace: boil these together for half an hour, and the following

* We have always had the cayenne-vinegar used in this receipt, but the Chili would,
without doubt, answer as well, or better.

day bottle and cork the catsup well. It will keep for a dozen years. Many persons add to it, before it is boiled, a bottle of port wine; and others recommend a large bunch of sweet herbs to be put in with the spice.

1st Recipe. Expressed juice of walnuts, 1 quart; eschalots, 4 ozs.; black pepper, ½ oz.; cloves, ¼ oz.; mace, 1 drachm: 1 hour.

2d. Walnuts, 100; salt, ¼ lb.; vinegar, 1 quart: to stand till black. Strong beer, 1 quart; anchovies, ½ lb.; 1 head garlic; nutmegs, ½ oz.; cloves, ½ oz.; black pepper, ½ oz.; mace, 2 drachms: ½ hour.

ANOTHER GOOD RECEIPT FOR WALNUT CATSUP.

Beat a hundred green walnuts in a large marble mortar until they are thoroughly bruised and broken, and then put them into a stone jar, with half a pound of eschalots, cut in slices, one head of garlic, half a pound of salt, and two quarts of vinegar; let them stand for ten days, and stir them night and morning. Strain off the liquor, and boil it for half an hour with the addition of two ounces of anchovies, two of whole pepper, half an ounce of cloves, and two drachms of mace; skim it well, strain it off, and when it is quite cold pour it gently from the sediment (which may be reserved for flavouring common sauces) into small dry bottles; secure it from the air by sound corking, and store it in a dry place.

Walnuts, 100; eschalots, ½ lb.; garlic, 1 head; salt, ½ lb.; vinegar, 2 quarts: 10 days. Anchovies, 2 ozs.; black pepper, 2 ozs.; mace, ¼ oz.; cloves, ½ oz.: ½ hour.

LEMON PICKLE OR CATSUP.

Either divide six small lemons into quarters, remove all the pips that are in sight, and strew three ounces of salt upon them, and keep them turned in it for a week, or, merely make deep incisions in them, and proceed as directed for pickled lemons. When they have stood in a warm place for eight days, put into a stone jar two ounces and a half of finely scraped horseradish, and two ounces of eschalots, or one and a half of garlic; to these add the lemons with all their liquor, and pour on them a pint and a half of boiling vinegar in which half an ounce of bruised ginger, a quarter ounce of whole white pepper, and two blades of mace have been simmered for two or three minutes. The pickle will be fit for use in two or three months, but may stand four or five before it is strained off.

Small lemons, 6; salt, 3 ozs.: 8 days. Horseradish, 2½ ozs.; eschalots, 2 ozs., or garlic 1½ oz.; vinegar, 1½ pint; ginger, ½ oz.; whole white pepper, ¼ oz.; mace, 2 blades: 3 to 6 months.

PONTAC CATSUP FOR FISH.

On one pint of ripe elderberries stripped from the stalks, pour three-quarters of a pint of boiling vinegar, and let it stand in a cool oven all night; the next day strain off the liquid without pressure, and boil it for five minutes with a half-teaspoonful salt, a small race of ginger, a blade of mace, forty corns of pepper, twelve cloves, and four eschalots. Bottle it with the spice when it is quite cold.

BOTTLED TOMATAS, OR TOMATA CATSUP.

Cut half a peck of ripe tomatas into quarters; lay them on dishes, and sprinkle over them half a pound of salt. The next day drain the juice from them through a hair-sieve into a stewpan, and boil it half an hour with three dozens of small capsicums, and half a pound of eschalots; then add the tomatas, which should be ready pulped through a strainer. Boil the whole for thirty minutes longer; have some clean bottles, kept warm by the fire, fill them with the catsup while it is quite hot; cork, and rosin them down directly.

Tomatas, ½ peck; salt, ½ lb.; capsicums, 3 doz.; eschalots, ½ lb.: ½ hour. After pulp is added, ½ hour.

Obs. — This receipt has been kindly contributed by a person who makes by it every year large quantities of the catsup, which is considered excellent: for sauce, it must be mixed with gravy or melted butter. We have not ourselves been able to make trial of it.

EPICUREAN SAUCE.

Mix well, by shaking them in a bottle a quarter pint of Indian soy, half a pint of Chili vinegar, half a pint of walnut catsup, and a pint and a half of the best mushroom catsup. These proportions make an excellent sauce, either to mix with melted butter, and to serve with fish, or to add to different kinds of gravy; but they can be varied, or added to, at pleasure.

Indian soy, ¼ pint; Chili vinegar, ½ pint; walnut catsup, ½ pint; mushroom catsup, 1½ pint.

Obs. — A pint of port wine, a few eschalots, and some thin strips of lemon-rind will convert this into an admirable store-sauce. Less soy would adapt it better to many tastes.

TARRAGON VINEGAR.

Gather the tarragon just before it blossoms, which will be late in July, or early in August; strip it from the larger stalks, and put it into small stone jars or wide-necked bottles, and in doing this twist some of the branches so as to bruise the leaves and wring them asunder; then pour in sufficient distilled or very pale vinegar to cover the tarragon; let it infuse for two months, or more: it will take no harm even by standing all the winter. When it is poured off, strain it very clear, put it into small dry bottles, and cork them well. Sweet basil vinegar is made in exactly the same way, but it should not be left on the leaves more than three weeks. The jars or bottles should be filled to the neck with the tarragon before the vinegar is added: its flavour is strong and peculiar, but to many tastes very agreeable. It imparts quite a foreign character to the dishes for which it is used.

GREEN MINT VINEGAR.

Pick and slightly chop, or bruise, freshly-gathered mint, and put it into bottles; fill them nearly to the necks, and add vinegar as for tarragon: in forty days, strain it off, and bottle it for use.

The mint itself, ready minced for sauce, will keep well in vinegar though the colour will not be very good.

CUCUMBER VINEGAR.

First wipe, and then, without paring, slice into a jar some young and quickly-grown cucumbers; pour on them as much boiling vinegar as will cover them well, with a teaspoonfu of salt and two-thirds as much of peppercorns to the pint and a half of vinegar: it may remain on them for a month, or even for two, if well defended from the air. A mild onion can be intermixed with the cucumbers, when its flavour is considered an improvement.

CELERY VINEGAR.

Put into a wide-necked bottle or pickle-jar eight ounces of the white part of the root and stalks of fine fresh celery cut into slices, and pour on it a pint of boiling vinegar; when a little cool, cork it down, and in three weeks it will be ready to strain, and to bottle for keeping. Half an ounce of bruised celery-seed will answer the same purpose, when the root cannot be obtained. This is an agreeable addition to a salad, when its flavour is much liked: a half-teaspoonful of salt should be boiled in it.

ESCHALOT, OR GARLIC VINEGAR.

On from four to six ounces of eschalots, or on two of garlic, peeled and bruised, pour a quart of the best vinegar; stop the jar or bottle close, and in a fortnight or three weeks the vinegar may be strained off for use: a few drops will give a sufficient flavour to a sauce, or to a tureen of gravy.

Eschalots, 4 to 6 ozs.; or, garlic, 2 to 4 ozs.; vinegar, 1 quart: 15 to 21 days.

Obs.—These roots may be used in smaller or in larger proportion, as a slighter or a stronger flavour of them is desired, and may remain longer in the vinegar without any detriment to it.

ESCHALOT WINE.

This is a far more useful preparation even than the preceding one, since it can be used to impart the flavour of the eschalot to dishes for which acid is not required. Peel and slice, or bruise, four ounces of eschalots, put them into a bottle, and add to them a pint of sherry; in a fortnight pour off the wine, and should it not be strongly flavoured with the eschalots, steep in it two ounces more, for another fortnight; a half-teaspoonful of cayenne may be added at first. The bottle should be shaken occasionally, while the eschalots are infusing, but should remain undisturbed for the last two or three days, that the wine may be clear when it is poured off to bottle for keeping. Sweet-basil wine is made by steeping the fresh leaves of the herb in wine, from ten to fifteen days. Eschalots, 4 ozs.; sherry 1 pint: 15 days, or more.

HORSERADISH VINEGAR.

On four ounces of young and freshly-scraped horseradish pour a quart of boiling vinegar, and cover it down closely: it will be ready for use in three or four days, but may remain for weeks, or months, before the vinegar is poured off. An ounce of minced eschalot may be substituted for one of the horseradish, if the flavour be liked.

CAYENNE VINEGAR.

Put from a quarter to half an ounce of the best cayenne pepper into a bottle, and pour on it a pint of pale vinegar. Cork it closely, and shake it well every two or three days. It may remain any length of time before it is poured off, but will very soon be ready for use. From being so extremely pungent, it is, for some purposes, preferable to Chili vinegar, as the cayenne seasoning can be given with less of acid. It may be made of any degree of strength. We warn the young house-keeper against using *essence of cayenne* (or cayenne steeped in brandy) for flavouring any dishes, as the brandy is very perceptible always, and gives an exceedingly coarse taste.

Good cayenne pepper, ¼ to ½ oz.; vinegar, 1 pint: infuse from 2 weeks to 12 months.

LEMON BRANDY; (*for flavouring sweet dishes.*)

Fill any sized wide-necked bottle lightly with the very thin rinds of fresh lemons, and cover them with good brandy; let them remain three weeks, then strain off the spirit and keep it well corked for use: a few apricot-kernels blanched and infused with the lemon-rind will give an agreeable flavour.

ANOTHER STORE-FLAVOURING FOR PUDDINGS OR CAKES.

Rasp on from two to four ounces of sugar the rinds of a couple of fine lemons, reduce the lumps to powder, and add it gradually to, and pound it with, an ounce of bitter almonds, blanched and wiped very dry. When these have been beaten to a fine paste, and the whole is well blended, press the mixture into a small pan, tie a paper over, and keep it for use. The proportions can be varied at pleasure, and the quantities increased: from a teaspoonful to three times as much can be mixed with the ingredients for a pudding. Cakes require more in proportion to their size.

Rinds large lemons, 2; sugar, 2 to 4 ozs.; bitter almonds, 1 oz.

DRIED MUSHROOMS.

Peel small, sound, freshly-gathered flaps, cut off the stems, and scrape out the fur entirely; then arrange the mushrooms singly on tins or dishes, and dry them as gradually as possible in a gentle oven. Put them, when they are done, into tin canisters, and store them where they will be secure from damp. French cooks give them a single boil in water, from which they then are well drained, and dried, as usual. When wanted for table, they should be put into cold gravy, slowly heated, and gently simmered, until they are tender.

MUSHROOM POWDER.

When the mushrooms have been prepared with great nicety, and dried, as in the foregoing receipt, pound them to a very fine powder; sift it, and put it immediately into small and perfectly dry bottles; cork and seal them without delay, for if the powder be long exposed to the air, so as to imbibe any humidity, or if it be not well secured from it in the bottles, it will be likely to become putrid: much of that which is purchased, even at the best Italian warehouses, is found to be so, and, as it is sold at a very high price, it is a great economy, as well as a surer plan, to have it carefully prepared at home. It is an exceedingly useful store, and an elegant addition to many dishes and sauces. To insure its being good, the mushrooms should be gathered in dry weather, and if any addition of spices be made to the powder (some persons mix with it a seasoning of mace and cayenne), they should be put into the oven for awhile before they are used: but even these precautions will not be sufficient, unless the powder be stored in a very dry place after it is bottled. A teaspoonful of it, with a quarter-pint of strong veal gravy, as much cream, and a small dessertspoonful of flour, will make an excellent béchamel or white sauce.

POTATO FLOUR ; (*Fecule de Pommes de terre.*)

Grate into a large vessel full of cold water, six pounds of sound mealy potatoes, and stir them well together. In six hours pour off the water, and add fresh, stirring the mixture well; repeat this process every three or four hours during the day, change the water at night, and the next morning pour it off; put two or three quarts more to the potatoes, and turn them directly into a hair-sieve, set over a pan to receive the flour, which may then be washed through the sieve, by pouring water to it. Let it settle in the pan, drain off the water, spread the potato-sediment on dishes, dry it in a slow oven, sift it, and put it into bottles or jars, and cork or cover them closely. The flour thus made will be beautifully white, and perfectly tasteless. It will remain good for years.

TO MAKE FLOUR OF RICE.

Take any quantity of whole rice, wash it thoroughly, changing the water several times; drain and press it in a cloth, then spread it on a dish, and dry it perfectly; beat it in a mortar to a smooth powder, and sift it through a fine sieve. When used to thicken soup or sauces, mix it with a small quantity of cold water or of broth, and pour it to them while they are boiling.

This flour, when newly made, is of much purer flavour than any usually prepared for sale.

POWDER OF SAVOURY HERBS.

All herbs which are to be dried for storing should be gathered in fine weather; cleared from dirt and decayed leaves; and dried quickly, but without scorching, in a Dutch oven before the fire, or in any other that is not too much heated. The leaves should then be stripped from the stalks, pounded, sifted, and closely corked in separate bottles; or several kinds may be mixed and pounded together for the convenience of seasoning in an instant gravies, soups, forcemeats, and made dishes: appropriate spices, celery-seed, and dried lemon-peel, all in fine powder, can be added to the herbs.

THE DOCTOR'S ZEST.

Pound to the finest powder, separately, eight ounces of basket salt, a quarter-ounce of cayenne, a drachm of mace, and of nutmeg; of cloves and pimento, a drachm and a half each; then add the other ingredients, one by one, to the salt, and pound them together until they are perfectly well blended. Put the zest into wide-mouthed phials, and cork them tightly. Half an ounce of mushroom-powder, and a drachm of dried lemon-peel, will greatly improve this mixture.

CHAPTER VI.

FORCEMEATS.

GENERAL REMARKS.

THE coarse and unpalatable compounds so constantly met with under the denomination of forcemeat, even at tables otherwise tolerably well served, show with how little attention they are commonly prepared.

Many very indifferent cooks pique themselves on never doing any thing by rule, and the consequence of their throwing together at random (or "by guess" as they call it) the ingredients which ought to be proportioned with exceeding delicacy and exactness is, repeated failure in all they attempt to do. Long experience and a very correct eye may, it is true, enable a person to dispense occasionally with weights and measures, without hazarding the success of their operations; but it is an experiment which the learner will do better to avoid.

A large marble or Wedgwood mortar is indispensable in making all the finer kinds of forcemeat; and equally so indeed for many other purposes in cookery; no kitchen, therefore, should be without one; and for whatever preparation it may be used, the pounding should be continued with patience and perseverance until not a single lump nor fibre be perceptible in the mass of the articles beaten together. This particularly applies to potted meats, which should resemble the smoothest paste; as well as to several varieties of forcemeat. Of these last it should be observed, that such as are made by the French method (see *quenelles*) are the most appropriate for an elegant dinner, either to serve in soups or to fill boned poultry of any kind; but when their exceeding lightness, which to foreigners constitutes one of their greatest excellencies, is objected to, it may be remedied by substituting dry crumbs of bread for the panada, and pounding a small quantity of the lean of a boiled ham, with the other ingredients: however, this should be done only for the balls.

No particular herb or spice should be allowed to predominate powerfully in these compositions; but the whole of the seasonings should be taken in such quantity only as will produce an agreeable savour when they are blended together.

NO. 1.   GOOD COMMON FORCEMEAT, FOR ROAST VEAL, TURKEYS, &C.

Grate very lightly into exceedingly fine crumbs, four ounces of the inside of a stale loaf, and mix thoroughly with it, a quarter of an ounce of lemon-rind pared as thin as possible, and minced extremely small; the same quantity of savoury herbs, of which two-thirds should be parsley, and one-third thyme, likewise finely minced, a little grated nutmeg, a half-teaspoonful of salt, and as much common pepper or cayenne as will season the forcemeat sufficiently. Break into these, two ounces of good butter in very small bits, add the unbeaten yolk of one egg, and with the fingers work the whole well together until it is smoothly mixed. It is usual to chop the lemon-rind, but we prefer it lightly grated on a fine grater. It should always be *fresh* for the purpose, or it will be likely to impart a very unpleasant flavour to the forcemeat.

Half the rind of a moderate-sized lemon will be sufficient for this quantity; which for a large turkey must be increased one-half.

Bread-crumbs, 4 ozs.; lemon-rind, ¼ oz. (or grated rind of ½ lemon); mixed savoury herbs, minced, ¼ oz.; salt, ½ teaspoonful; pepper ¼ to ⅓ of teaspoonful; butter, 2 ozs.; yolk, 1 egg.

Obs.—This, to our taste, is a much nicer and more delicate forcemeat than that which is made with chopped suet, and we would recommend it for trial in preference. Any variety of herb or spice may be used to give it flavour, and a little minced onion or eschalot can be added to it also; but these last do not appear to us suited to the meats for which the forcemeat is more particularly intended. Half an ounce of the butter may be omitted on ordinary occasions: and a portion of marjoram or of sweet basil may take the place of part of the thyme and parsley when preferred to them.

NO. 2.   ANOTHER GOOD COMMON FORCEMEAT.

Add to four ounces of bread-crumbs two of the lean of a boiled ham, quite free from sinew, and *very* finely minced; two of good butter, a dessertspoonful of herbs, chopped small, some lemon-grate, nutmeg, a little salt, a good seasoning of pepper or cayenne, and one whole egg, or the yolks of two. This may be fried in balls of moderate size, for five minutes, to serve with roast veal, or it may be put into the joint in the usual way.

Bread-crumbs, 4 ozs.; lean of ham, 2 ozs.; butter, 2 ozs.; minced herbs, 1 dessertspoonful; lemon-grate, 1 teaspoonful; nutmeg, mace, and cayenne, together, 1 small teaspoonful; little salt; 1 whole egg, or yolks of 2.

NO. 3.   SUPERIOR SUET FORCEMEAT, FOR VEAL, TURKEYS, &C.

Mix well together six ounces of fine stale crumbs, with an equal weight of beef-kidney suet, chopped extremely small, a large dessertspoonful of parsley, mixed with a little lemon-thyme, a teaspoonful of salt, a quarter one of cayenne, and a saltspoonful or rather more of mace and nutmeg together; work these up with three unbeaten egg-yolks, and three teaspoonsful of milk; then put the forcemeat into a large mortar, and pound it perfectly smooth. Take it out, and let it remain in a cool place for half an hour at least before it is used: then roll it into balls, if it be wanted to serve in that form; flour and fry them gently from seven to eight minutes, and dry them well before they are dished.

Beef suet finely minced, 6 ozs.; bread-crumbs, 6 ozs.; parsley, mixed with little thyme, 1 large dessertspoonful; salt, 1 teaspoonful; mace, large saltspoonful, and one-fourth as much cayenne; unbeaten egg-yolks, 3; milk, 3 teaspoonsful: well pounded. Fried in balls, 7 to 8 minutes, or poached, 6 to 7.

Obs.—The finely grated rind of half a lemon can be added to this forcemeat at pleasure; and for some purposes a *morsel* of garlic, or three or four minced eschalots, may be mixed with it before it is put into the mortar.

NO. 4.   COMMON SUET FORCEMEAT.

Beef suet is commonly used in the composition of this kind of forcemeat, but we think that veal-kidney suet, when it could be obtained, would have a better effect; though the reader will easily comprehend that it is scarcely possible for us to have every variety of every receipt which we insert put to the test: in some cases we are compelled merely to suggest what appear to us likely to be improvements. Strip carefully every morsel of skin from the suet, and mince it small; to six ounces add eight of bread-crumbs, with the same proportion of herbs, spice, salt, and lemon-peel, as in the foregoing receipt, and a couple of whole eggs, which should be very slightly beaten, after the specks have been taken out with the point of a small fork. Should more liquid be required, the yolk of another egg, or a spoonful or two of milk, may be used. Half this quantity will be sufficient for a small joint of veal, or for a dozen balls, which, when it is more convenient to serve it in that form, may be fried or browned beneath the roast, and then dished round it, though this last is not a very refined mode of dressing them. From eight to ten minutes will dry them well.

NO. 5.   OYSTER FORCEMEAT.

Open carefully a dozen fine plump natives, take off the beards, strain their liquor, and rinse the oysters in it. Grate four ounces of the crumb of a stale loaf into fine light crumbs, mince the oysters, but not too small, and mix them with the bread; add an ounce and a half of good butter, broken into minute bits, the grated rind of half a small lemon, a small saltspoonful of pounded mace, some cayenne, a little salt, and a large teaspoonful of parsley: mix these ingredients well, and work them together with the unbeaten yolk of one egg, and a little of the oyster liquor, the remainder of which can be added to the sauce which usually accompanies this forcemeat.

Oysters, 1 dozen; bread-crumbs, 4 ozs.; butter, 1½ oz.; rind ½ small lemon; mace, 1 saltspoonful; some cayenne and salt; minced parsley, 1 large teaspoonful; yolk 1 egg; oyster-liquor, 1 dessertspoonful: rolled into balls, and fried from 7 to 10 minutes, or poached from 5 to 6 minutes.

Obs.—In this forcemeat the flavour of the oysters should prevail entirely over that of all the other ingredients which are mixed with them.

NO. 6.   A FINER OYSTER FORCEMEAT.

Pound the preceding forcemeat to the smoothest paste, with the addition only of half an ounce of fresh butter, should it be sufficiently dry to allow of it. It is remarkably good when thus prepared, and may be poached or fried in balls for soups or made dishes, or used to fill boned fowls, or the breasts of boiled turkeys with equally good effect.

NO. 7.   MUSHROOM FORCEMEAT.

Cut closely off the stems of some small, just-opened mushrooms, peel them, and take out the fur. Dissolve an ounce and a half of good butter in a saucepan, throw them into it with a little cayenne, and a slight sprinkling of mace, and stew them softly, keeping them well shaken, from five to seven minutes; then turn them into a dish, spread them over it, and raise one end, that the liquid may drain from them. When they are quite cold, mince, and then mix them with four ounces of fine bread-crumbs, an ounce and a half of good butter, and part of that in which they were stewed, should the forcemeat appear too moist to admit of the whole, as the yolk of one egg, at the least, must be added, to bind the ingredients together; strew in a saltspoonful of salt, a third as much of cayenne, and about the same quantity of mace and nutmeg, with a teaspoonful of grated lemon-rind. The seasonings must be rather sparingly used, that the flavour of the mushrooms may not be over-powered by them. Mix the whole thoroughly with the unbeaten yolk of one egg, or of two, and use the forcemeat poached in small balls for soup, or fried and served in the dish with roast fowls, or round minced veal; or to fill boiled fowls, partridges, or turkeys.

Small mushrooms, peeled and trimmed, 4 ozs.; butter, 1½ oz.; slight sprinkling mace and cayenne: 5 to 7 minutes. Mushrooms minced; bread-crumbs, 4 ozs.; butter, 1½ oz. (with part of that used in the stewing); salt, 1 saltspoonful; third as much of cayenne, of mace, and of nutmeg; grated lemon-rind, 1 teaspoonful; yolk of 1 or 2 eggs. In balls, poached, 5 to 6 minutes; fried, 6 to 8 minutes.

Obs.—This, like most other forcemeats, is improved by being well beaten in a large mortar after it is entirely mixed.

NO. 8.   ONION AND SAGE STUFFING, FOR PORK, GEESE, OR DUCKS.

Boil three large onions from ten to fifteen minutes, chop them small, and mix with them an equal quantity of bread-crumbs, a heaped table-spoonful of minced sage, an ounce of butter, a half saltspoonful of pepper, and twice as much of salt, and put them into the body of the goose; part of the liver boiled for two or three minutes, and shred fine, is sometimes added to these, and the whole is bound together with an egg-yolk or two; but they are quite as frequently served without. The onions can be used raw, when their very strong flavour is not objected to, but the odour of the whole dish will then be somewhat overpowering.

Large onions, 3: boiled 20 to 30 minutes. Sage, 2 to 3 dessertspoons-ful (or ½ to ¾ oz.); butter, 1 oz.; pepper, ½ teaspoonful; salt, 1 teaspoonful.

NO. 9.   MR. COOKE'S FORCEMEAT FOR DUCKS OR GEESE.

Two parts of chopped onion, two parts of bread-crumbs, three of butter, one of pounded sage, and a seasoning of pepper and salt.

This receipt we have not proved.

NO. 10.   FORCEMEAT BALLS FOR MOCK TURTLE SOUPS.

The French forcemeat, No. 15 of the present Chapter, is the most elegant and appropriate forcemeat to serve in mock turtle, but a more solid and highly seasoned one is usually added to it in this country. In very common cookery the ingredients are merely chopped small and mixed together with a moistening of eggs; but when the trouble of pounding and blending them properly is objected to, we would recommend the common veal forcemeat, No. 1, in preference, as the undressed veal and suet, when merely minced, do not produce a good effect. Four ounces each of these, with an ounce or so of the lean of a boiled ham, and three ounces of bread-crumbs, a large dessertspoonful of minced parsley, a small portion of thyme, or marjoram, a saltspoonful of white pepper, twice as much salt, or more, a little cayenne, half a small nutmeg, and a couple of eggs, well mixed with a fork first, to separate the meat, and after the moistening is added, with the fingers, then rolled into balls, and boiled in a little soup for twelve minutes, is the manner in which it is prepared; but the reader will find the following receipt very superior to it:— Rasp, that is to say, scrape with a knife, clear from the fibre, four ounces of veal, which should be cut into thick slices, and taken quite free from skin and fat; chop it fine, and then pound it as smoothly as possible in a large mortar, with three ounces of the rasped fat of an unboiled ham, of good flavour, or of the finest bacon, and one of butter, two ounces of bread-crumbs, a tablespoonful of the lean of a boiled ham, should it be at hand, a good seasoning of cayenne, nutmeg, and mace, mixed together, a heaped dessertspoonful of minced herbs, and the yolks of two eggs; poach a small bit when it is mixed, and add any further seasoning it may require; and when it is of good flavour, roll it into balls of moderate size, and boil them twelve minutes; then drain and slip them into the soup. No forcemeat should be boiled in the soup itself, on account of the fat which would escape from it in the process : a little stock should be reserved for the purpose.

Very common : — Lean of neck of veal, 4 ozs.; beef-kidney suet, 4 ozs., both finely chopped; bread-crumbs, 3 ozs.; minced parsley, large dessertspoonful; thyme or marjoram, *small* teaspoonful; lean of boiled ham, 1 to 2 ozs.; white pepper, 1 saltspoonful; salt, twice as much; ½ small nutmeg; eggs, 2 : in balls, 12 minutes.

Better forcemeat :—Lean veal rasped, 4 ozs.; fat of unboiled ham, or finest bacon, 3 ozs.; butter, 1 oz.; bread-crumbs, 2 ozs.; lean of boiled ham, minced, 1 large tablespoonful; minced herbs, 1 heaped dessert-spoonful; full seasoning of mace, nutmeg, and cayenne, mixed; yolks of eggs, 2: 12 minutes.

NO. 11.   EGG BALLS.

Boil four or five new-laid eggs for ten or twelve minutes, and lay them into fresh water until they are cold. Take out the yolks, and pound them smoothly with the beaten yolk of one raw egg, or more, if required; add a little salt and cayenne, roll the mixture into very small balls, and boil them for two minutes. Half a teaspoonful of flour is sometimes worked up with the eggs.

Hard yolks of eggs, 4; 1 raw; little salt, cayenne : 2 minutes.

NO. 12.   BRAIN CAKES.

Wash and soak the brains well in cold water, and afterwards in hot; then remove the skin and large fibres, and boil them in water, slightly salted, from two to three minutes; beat them up with a teaspoonful of sage, very finely chopped, or with equal parts of sage and parsley, half a teaspoonful or rather more of salt, half as much mace, a little white pepper or cayenne, and one egg; drop them in small cakes, and fry them a fine light brown: two yolks of eggs will make the cakes more deli-cate than the white and yolk of one. A teaspoonful of flour and a little lemon-grate are sometimes added.

NO. 13.   ANOTHER RECEIPT FOR BRAIN CAKES.

Boil the brains in a little good veal-gravy very gently for ten minutes, drain them on a sieve, and when cold, cut them into thick dice; dip them into beaten yolk of egg, and then into very fine bread-crumbs, mixed with salt, pounded spices, and fine herbs, minced extremely small; fry them of a light brown, drain and dry them well, and slip them into the soup or hash after it is dished. When broth or gravy is not at hand, the brains may be boiled in water.

NO. 14.   AN EXCELLENT FRENCH FORCEMEAT.

Take six ounces of veal free from fat and skin, cut it into dice and put it into a saucepan with two ounces of butter, a large teaspoonful of parsley finely minced, half as much thyme, salt, and grated lemon-rind, and a sufficient seasoning of nutmeg, cayenne, and mace, to flavour it pleasantly. Stew these *very* gently from twelve to fifteen minutes, then lift out the veal and put into the saucepan two ounces of bread-crumbs; let them simmer until they have absorbed the gravy yielded by the meat; keep them stirred until they are as dry as possible; beat the yolk of an egg to them while they are hot, and set them aside to cool. Chop and pound the veal, add the bread to it as soon as it is cold, beat them well together, with an ounce and a half of fresh butter, and two of the finest bacon, scraped quite clear from rust, skin, and fibre; put to them the yolks of two small eggs, and mix them well; then take the forcemeat from the mortar, and set it in a very cool place until it is wanted for use.

Veal, 6 ozs.; butter, 2 ozs.; minced parsley, 1 teaspoonful; thyme, salt, and lemon-peel, each ¼ teaspoonful; little nutmeg, cayenne, and mace: 12 to 15 minutes. Bread-crumbs, 2 ozs.; butter, 1½ oz.; rasped bacon, 2 ozs.; yolks of eggs, 2 to 3.

Obs. 1.—When this forcemeat is intended to fill boned fowls, the livers of two or three, boiled for four minutes, or stewed with the veal for the same length of time, then minced and pounded with the other ingredients, will be found a great improvement; and, if mushrooms can be procured, two tablespoonsful of them chopped small, should be stewed and beaten with it also. A small portion of the best end of the neck will afford the quantity of lean required for this receipt, and the remains of it will make excellent gravy.

NO. 15.   FRENCH FORCEMEAT CALLED QUENELLES.

This is a peculiarly light and delicate kind of forcemeat, which, by good French cooks, is compounded with exceeding care. It is served abroad in a variety of forms, and is made of very finely-grained white veal, or of the undressed flesh of poultry, or of rabbits, rasped quite free from sinew, then chopped and pounded to the finest paste, first by itself, and afterwards with an equal quantity of boiled calf's udder or of butter, and of *panada*, which is but another name for bread soaked in cream or gravy and then dried over the fire until it forms a sort of paste. As the three ingredients should be equal in *volume*, not in weight, they are each rolled into a separate ball before they are mixed, that their size may be determined by the eye. When the fat of the fillet of veal (which in England is not often divided for sale, as it is in France) is not to be procured, a rather less proportion of butter will serve in its stead. The following will be found a very good, and not a troublesome receipt for veal forcemeat of this kind.

Rasp quite clear from sinew, after the fat and skin have been entirely cleared from it, four ounces of the finest veal; chop, and pound it well: if it be carefully prepared there will be no necessity for passing it through a sieve, but this should otherwise be done. Soak in a small saucepan two ounces of the crumb of a stale loaf in a little rich but pale veal gravy, or white sauce; then press and drain as much as possible of the moisture from it, and stir it over a gentle fire until it is as dry as it will become without burning: it will adhere in a ball to the spoon, and leave the saucepan quite dry when it is sufficiently done. Mix with it, while it is still hot, the yolk of one egg, and when it is quite cold, add it to the veal with three ounces of very fresh butter, a quarter-teaspoonful of mace, half as much cayenne, a little nutmeg, and a saltspoonful of salt. When these are perfectly beaten, and well blended together, add another whole egg after having merely taken out the germs; the mixture will then be ready for use, and may be moulded into balls, or small thick oval shapes, a little flattened, and poached in soup or gravy from ten to fifteen minutes. These *quenelles* may be served by themselves in a rich sauce, as a corner dish, or in conjunction with other things. They may likewise be first poached for three or four minutes, and left on a drainer to become cold; then dipped into egg and the finest bread-crumbs, and fried, and served as croquettes.

NO. 16.   FORCEMEAT FOR RAISED AND OTHER COLD PIES.

The very finest sausage-meat, highly seasoned, and made with an equal proportion of fat and lean, is an exceedingly good forcemeat for veal, chicken, rabbit, and some few other pies; savoury herbs minced small, may be added to heighten its flavour, if it be intended for immediate eating; but it will not then remain good quite so long, unless they should have been previously dried. To prevent its being too dry, two or three spoonsful of cold water should be mixed with it before it is put into the pie. One pound of lean veal to one and a quarter of the pork-fat is sometimes used, and smoothly pounded with a high seasoning of spices, herbs, and eschalots, or garlic, but we cannot recommend the introduction of these last into pies unless they are especially ordered: mushrooms may be mixed with any kind of forcemeat with far better effect. Equal parts of veal and fat bacon will also make a good forcemeat for pies, if chopped finely and well spiced.

Sausage-meat, well seasoned. Or: veal, 1 lb.; pork-fat, 1½ lb.; salt, 1 oz.; pepper, ¼ to ½ oz.; fine herbs, spice, &c., as in forcemeat No. 1, or sausage-meat. Or: veal and bacon, equal weight, seasoned in the same way.

PANADA.

This is the name given to the soaked bread which is mixed with the French forcemeats, and which renders them so peculiarly delicate. Pour on the crumb of two or three rolls, or on that of any other very light bread, as much good boiling broth, milk, or cream as will cover and moisten it well; put a plate over to keep in the steam, and let it remain for half an hour, or more; then drain off the superfluous liquid, and squeeze the panada dry by wringing it round in a thin cloth into a ball; put it into a small stewpan, or well tinned saucepan, and pour to it as much only of rich white sauce, or of gravy, as it can easily absorb, and stir it constantly with a wooden spoon, over a clear and gentle fire, until it forms a very dry paste, and adheres in a mass to the spoon; when it is in this state, mix with it, thoroughly, the unbeaten yolk of two fresh eggs, which will give it firmness, and set it aside to become quite cold before it is put into the mortar. The best French cooks give the highest degree of savour that they can to this panada, and add no other seasoning to the forcemeats of which it forms a part: it is used in an equal proportion with the meat, and calf's udder or butter of which they are composed, as we have shown in the preceding receipt for quenelles. They stew slowly, for the purpose, a small bit of lean ham, two or three minced eschalots, a bayleaf, a few mushrooms, a little parsley, a clove or two, and a small blade of mace, in a little good butter, and when they are sufficiently browned, pour to them as much broth or gravy as will be needed for the panada; and when this has simmered from twenty to thirty minutes, so as to have acquired the proper flavour, without being much reduced, they strain it over, and boil it into the bread. The common course of cookery in an English kitchen does not often require the practice of the greater niceties and refinements of the art: and *trouble* (of which the French appear to be perfectly regardless when the excellence of their preparations is concerned) is there in general so much thought of, and exclaimed against, that a more summary process would probably meet with a better chance of success.

A quicker and rougher mode of making the panada, and indeed the forcemeat altogether, is to pour strong veal broth or gravy upon it, and after it has soaked, to boil it dry, without any addition except that of a little fine spice, lemon-grate, or any other favourite seasoning. Minced herbs, salt, cayenne, and mace may be beaten with the meat, to which a small portion of well-pounded ham may likewise be added at pleasure.

CHAPTER VII.

BOILING, ROASTING, &c.

TO BOIL MEAT.

LARGE joints of meat should be neatly trimmed, washed extremely clean, and skewered or bound firmly into good shape, when they are of a nature to require it; then well covered with *cold* water, brought to boil over a moderate fire, and simmered until they are done. the scum being carefully and entirely cleaned from the surface of the water, as it gathers there, which will be principally from within a few minutes of its beginning to boil, and during a few minutes afterwards. If not thoroughly skimmed off at the proper time, it will sink, and adhere to the joint, giving it a very uninviting appearance.

We cannot too strongly again impress upon the cook the advantages of *gentle simmering* over the usual fast-boiling of meat, by which, as has been already forcibly shown (see article *Bouillon*, Chapter I.), the outside is hardened and deprived of its juices before the inside is half done, while the starting of the flesh from the bones which it occasions, and the altogether ragged aspect which it gives, are most unsightly.

8

Picked or salted meat requires longer boiling than fresh; and that which is smoked and dried longer still. This last should always be slowly heated, and if, from any circumstances, time cannot have been allowed for soaking it properly, and there is a probability of its being too salt when served, it should be brought very softly to boil in a large quantity of water, which should in part be changed as soon as it becomes quite briny, for as much more that is ready boiling.

It is customary to lay large joints upon a fish-plate, or to throw some wooden skewers under them, to prevent their sticking to the vessel in which they are cooked; and it is as well to take the precaution, though, unless they be placed over a very fierce fire, they cannot be in danger of this. The time allowed for them is about the same as for roasting, from fifteen to twenty minutes to the pound. For cooking rounds of beef, and other ponderous joints, a pan of this form is very convenient.

By means of two almost equally expensive preparations, called a *poêlée*, and a *blanc*, the insipidity which results from boiling meat or vegetables in water only, may be removed, and the whiteness of either will be better preserved. Turkeys, fowls, sweetbreads, calf's brains, cauliflowers, and artichoke bottoms, are the articles for which the *poêlée* and the *blanc* are more especially used for refined foreign cookery: the reader will judge by the following receipts how far they are admissible into that of the economist.

POELÉE.

Cut into large dice two pounds of lean veal, and two pounds of fat bacon, cured without saltpetre, two large carrots, and two onions; to these add half a pound of fresh butter, put the whole into a stewpan, and stir it with a wooden spoon over a gentle fire, until the veal is very white, and the bacon is partially melted; then pour to them three pints of clear boiling broth or water, throw in four cloves, a small bunch or two of thyme and parsley, a bay-leaf, and a few corns of white pepper; boil these gently for an hour and a half, then strain the *poêlée* through a fine sieve, and set it by in a cool place. Use it instead of water for boiling the various articles we have already named: it will answer for several in succession, and will remain good for many days. Some cooks order a *pound* of butter in addition to the bacon, and others substitute beef-suet in part for this last.

A BLANC.

Put into a stewpan one pound of fat bacon rasped, one pound of beef suet cut small, and one pound of butter, the strained juice of two lemons, a couple of bay-leaves, three cloves, three carrots, and three onions divided into dice, and less than half a pint of water. Simmer these gently, keeping them often stirred, until the fat is well melted, and the water has evaporated; then pour in rather more than will be required for the dish which is to be cooked in the blanc; boil it softly until all the ingredients have given out their full flavour, skim it well, and salt if needed, and strain it off for use. A calf's head is often boiled in this.

ROASTING.

Roasting, which is quite the favourite mode of dressing meat in the United States, and one, of consequence, most familiar to us, requires unremitting attention on the part of the cook, rather than any great exertion of skill.   Large kitchens are usually fitted with a smoke-jack, by means of which several spits, if needful, can be kept turning at the same time; but in small establishments, a roaster which allows of some economy in point of fuel is more commonly used.   That shown in the print is of very advantageous construction in this respect, as a joint may be cooked in it with a comparatively small fire, the heat being strongly reflected from the screen upon the meat; in consequence of this, it should never be placed very close to the grate, as the surface of the joint would then become dry and hard.

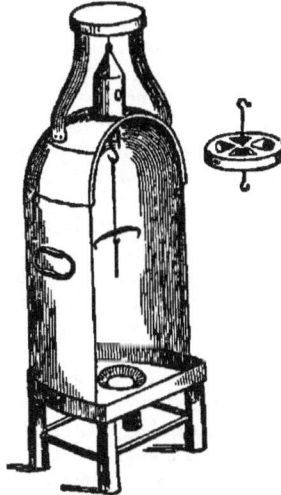

Bottle-jack and Niche Screen.*

A more convenient form of roaster, with a spit placed horizontally, and turned by means of a wheel and chain, of which the movement is regulated by a spring contained in a box at the top, is of the same economical order as the one above.

For roasting without either of these, make up a fire proportioned in width and height to the joint which is to be roasted, and which it should surpass in dimensions every way, by two or three inches. · Place some moderate-sized lumps of coal on the top; let it be free from smoke and ashes in front; and so compactly arranged that it will neither require to be disturbed, nor supplied with fresh fuel, for some considerable time after the meat is laid down. Spit the joint and place it very far from the fire at first; keep it constantly basted,

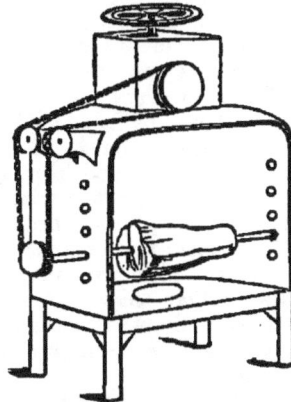

Improved Spring-jack and Roaster.

and when it is two parts done, move it nearer to the fire that it may be properly browned; but guard carefully against it being burned.   A few minutes before it is taken from the spit, sprinkle a little fine salt over it, baste it thoroughly with its own dripping, or with butter, and dredge it with flour: as soon as the froth is well risen, dish, and serve the meat. Or, to avoid the necessity of the frothing, which is often greatly objected to on account of the raw taste retained by the flour dredge the roast liberally soon after it is first laid to the fire; the flour

* The bottle-jack, without the screen, is used in many families very successfully; it is wound up like a watch, by means of a key, and turns very regularly until it has run down.

will then form a savoury incrustation upon it, and assist to prevent the escape of its juices. When meat or poultry is wrapped in buttered paper it must not be floured until this is removed, which should be fifteen or twenty minutes before either is served.

Remember always to draw back the dripping-pan when the fire has to be stirred, or when fresh coals are thrown on, that the cinders and ashes may not fall into it.

When meat is very lean, a slice of butter, or a small quantity of clarified dripping should be melted in the pan to baste it with at first; though the use of the latter should be scrupulously avoided for poultry, or any delicate meats, as the flavour it imparts is to many persons peculiarly objectionable. Let the spit be kept bright and clean, and wipe it before the meat is put on; balance the joint well upon it, that it may turn steadily, and if needful secure it with screw-skewers. A cradle spit, which is so constructed that it contains the meat in a sort of framework, instead of passing through it, may be often very advantageously used instead of an ordinary one, as the perforation of the meat by this last must always occasion some escape of the juices; and it is, moreover, particularly to be objected to in roasting joints or poultry which have been boned and filled with forcemeat. The cradle spit (for which see "Turkey Boned and Forced," Chapter XII.) is much better suited to these, as well as to a sucking pig, sturgeon, salmon, and other large fish; but it is not very commonly to be found in our kitchens, many of which exhibit a singular scantiness of the conveniences which facilitate the labours of the cook.

For heavy and substantial joints, a quarter of an hour is generally allowed for every pound of meat; and, with a sound fire and frequent basting, will be found sufficient when the process is conducted in the usual manner; but by the *slow method*, as we shall designate it, almost double the time will be required. Pork, veal, and lamb, should always be well roasted; but many eaters prefer mutton and beef rather underdressed, though some persons have a strong objection to the sight even of any meat that is not thoroughly cooked.

Joints which are thin in proportion to their weight, require less of the fire than thick and solid ones. Ribs of beef, for example, will be sooner ready to serve than an equal weight of the rump, round or sirloin; and the neck or shoulder of mutton, or spare rib of pork, than the leg.

When to preserve the succulence of the meat is more an object than to economize fuel, beef and mutton should be laid at twice the usual distance from the fire, and allowed to remain so until they are perfectly heated through; the roasting, so managed, will of course be *slow*; and from three hours and a half to four hours will be necessary to cook by this method a leg of mutton of ordinary size, for which two hours would amply suffice in a common way; but the flesh will be remarkably tender, and the flow of gravy from it most abundant. It should not be drawn near the fire until within the last hour, and should then be placed only so close as to brown it properly. No kind of roast indeed should at any time be allowed to take colour too quickly; it should be heated gradually, and kept at least at a moderate distance from the fire until it is nearly done, or the outside will be dry and hard, if not burned, while the inside will be only half-cooked.

STEAMING.

The application of steam to culinary purposes is becoming very general in our kitchens at the present day, especially in those of large establishments, many of which are furnished with apparatus for its use, so admirably constructed, and so complete, that the process may be conducted on an extensive scale, with very slight trouble to the cook; and with the further advantage of being *at a distance from the fire*, the steam being conveyed by pipes to the

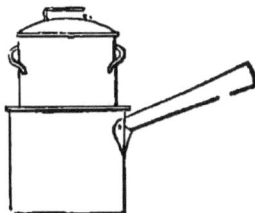

Saucepan, with Steamer.

vessels intended to receive it. Fish, butcher's meat, poultry, vegetables, puddings, maccaroni, and rice, are all subjected to its action, instead of being immersed in water, as in simple boiling; and the result is to many persons perfectly satisfactory; though, as there is a difference of opinion amongst first-rate cooks, with regard to the comparative merits of the two modes of dressing *meat* and *fish*, a trial should be given to the steaming, on a small scale, before any great expenses are incurred for it, which may be done easily with a common saucepan or boiler, fitted like the one shown above, with a simple tin steamer. Servants not accustomed to the use of these, should be warned against boiling in the vessel itself any thing of coarse or strong flavour, when the article steamed is of a delicate nature. The vapour from soup containing onions, for example, would have a very bad effect on a sweet pudding especially, and on many other dishes. Care and discretion, therefore, must be exercised on this point. By means of a kettle fixed over it, the steam of the boiler in the kitchen range, may be made available for cooking, in the way shown by the engraving, which exhibits fish, potatoes, and their sauces, all in progress of steaming at the same time. The limits of our work do not permit us to enter at much length upon this subject, but the reader who may wish to understand the nature of steam, and the various modes in which its agency may be applied to domestic purposes, will do well to consult Mr. Webster's excellent work, (Encyclopædia of Domestic Economy,) of which we have more particularly spoken in another chapter. The quite inexperienced cook may require to be told, that any article of food which is to be cooked by steam in a saucepan of the form exhibited in the first of the engravings of this section, must be prepared exactly as for boiling, and laid into the sort of strainer affixed to the top of the saucepan; and that water, or some other kind of liquid, must be put into the saucepan itself, and kept boiling in it, the lid being first closely fixed into the steamer.

STEWING.

This very wholesome, convenient, and *economical* mode of cookery is by no means so well understood nor profited by in England or America as on the continent, where its advantages are fully appreciated. So very small a quantity of fuel is necessary to sustain the gentle degree of ebullition which it requires, that this alone would recommend it to the careful housekeeper; but if the process be skilfully conducted, meat

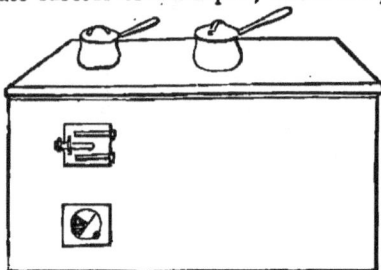

Hot Plate, or Hearth.

softly stoved or stewed, in close-shutting, or luted vessels, is in every respect equal, if not superior, to that which is roasted; but it must be *simmered* only, and in the gentlest possible manner, or, instead of being tender, nutritious, and highly palatable, it will be dry, hard, and indigestible. The common cooking stoves in this country, as they have hitherto been constructed, have rendered the ex-act regulation of heat which stewing requires rather difficult; and the smoke and blaze of a large coal fire are very unfavourable to many other modes of cookery as well. The American as well as the French have generally the advantage of the embers and ashes of the wood which is their ordinary fuel; and they have always, in addition, a stove of this construction in which charcoal or *braise* (for explanation of this word, see remarks on preserving, Chapter XXI.) only is burned; and

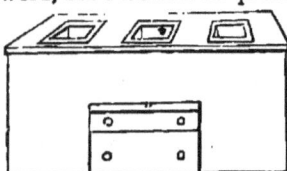

upon which their stewpans can, when there is occasion, be left uncovered, without the danger of their contents being spoiled, which there generally is with us. It is true that of late great improvements have been made in our own stoves;* and the hot plates, or *hearths* with which the kitchens of good houses are always furnished, are admirably adapted to the sim-mering system; but when the cook has not the convenience of one, the stewpans must be placed on trevets high *above* the fire, and be constantly watched, and moved, as occasion may require, nearer to, or further from the flame.

No copper vessels from which the inner tinning is in the slightest degree worn away should ever be used for this or for any other kind of cookery; for not health only, but life itself, may be endangered by them.† We have ourselves seen a dish of acid fruit which had been boiled without sugar, in a copper pan from which the tin lining was half worn away, *coated with verdigris* after it had become cold; and from the careless habits of the person who had prepared it, the chances were greatly in favour of its being served to a family afterwards, if it had not been accidentally discovered. Salt acts upon the copper in the same manner as acids: vegetables, too, from the portion of the latter which they contain, have the same injurious effect; and the greatest danger results from allowing preparations containing any of these to become cold (or cool) in the stewpan, in contact with the exposed part of the copper in the inside. Thick, well-tinned iron saucepans will

[* This remark will apply well to this country: an intelligent housekeeper can readily adapt the various improvements that are constantly making in stoves and ranges for cooking.]

† Sugar, being an antidote to the poisonous effects of verdigris, should be plentifully taken, dissolved in water, so as to form quite a syrup, by persons who may unfortu-nately have partaken of any dish into which this dangerous ingredient has entered.

answer for all the ordinary purposes of common English cookery, even for stewing, provided they have tightly-fitting lids to prevent the escape of the steam; but the copper ones are of more convenient form, and better adapted to a superior order of cookery.

We shall have occasion to speak more particularly in another part of this work, of the German enamelled stewpans, so safe, and so well suited, from the extreme nicety of the composition, resembling earthenware or china, with which they are lined, to all delicate compounds. The cook should be warned, however, that they retain the heat so long that the contents will boil for several minutes after they are removed from the fire, and this must be guarded against when they have reached the exact point at which further boiling would have a bad effect; as would be the case with some preserves, and other sweets.

BROILING.

Broiling is the best possible mode of cooking and of preserving the flavour of several kinds of fish, amongst which we may specify mackerel and whitings;* it is also incomparably superior to frying for steaks and cutlets, especially of beef and mutton; and it is far better adapted, also, to the preparation of food for invalids; but it should be carefully done, for if the heat be too fierce, the outside of the meat will be scorched and hardened so as to render it uneatable; and if, on the contrary, it be too gentle, the gravy will be drawn out, and yet the flesh will remain so entirely without firmness,

A Conjurer.

as to be unpleasant eating. A brisk fire *perfectly free from smoke*, a very clean gridiron, tender meat, a dish and plates as hot as they can be, and great despatch in sending it to table when done, are all essential to the serving of a good broil. The gridiron should be well heated, and rubbed with mutton suet before the meat is laid on, and it should be placed slopingly over the fire, that the fat may run off to the back of the grate, instead of falling on the live coals and smoking the meat: if this precaution should not prevent its making an occasional blaze, lift the gridiron quickly beyond the reach of the smoke, and hold it away until the fire is clear again. Steaks and chops should be turned often, that the juices may be kept in, and that they may be equally done in every part. If, for this purpose, it should be necessary, for want of steak-tongs, to use a fork, it should be passed through the outer skin, or fat of the steak, but never stuck into the lean, as by that means much of the gravy will escape. Most eaters prefer broiled beef or mutton, rather under-dressed; but pork chops should always be tho-

---

* Salmon broiled in slices is a favourite dish with eaters who like the full rich flavour of the fish preserved, as it is much more luscious (but less delicate) dressed thus than when it is boiled. The slices should be cut from an inch to an inch and a half thick and taken from the middle of a *very fresh* salmon; they may be seasoned with cayenne only, and slowly broiled over a very clear fire; or, folded in buttered paper before they are laid on the gridiron; or, lightly brushed with oil, and highly seasoned; or, dipped into egg-yolks and then into the finest crumbs mixed with salt, spice, and plenty of minced herbs, then sprinkled with clarified butter; but in whichever way they are prepared they will require to be gently broiled, with every precaution against their being smoked. From half to three quarters of an hour will cook them. Dried salmon cut into thin slices is merely warmed through over a slow fire.

roughly cooked.   When a fowl or any other bird is cut asunder before
it is broiled, the inside should first be laid to the fire: this should be
done with kidneys also.   Fish is less dry, and of better flavour, as well
as less liable to be smoked, if it be wrapped in a thickly buttered sheet
of writing paper before it is placed on the gridiron.   For the more deli-
cate-skinned kinds, the bars should be rubbed with chalk instead of
suet, when the paper is omitted.   Cutlets, or meat in any other form,
when egged and crumbed for broiling, should afterwards be dipped into
clarified butter, or sprinkled with it plentifully, as the egg-yolk and
bread will otherwise form too dry a crust upon it.   French cooks season
their cutlets both with salt and pepper, and brush a little oil or butter
over them to keep them moist; but unless this be done, no seasoning
of salt should be given them until they are just ready to be dished: the
French method is a very good one.

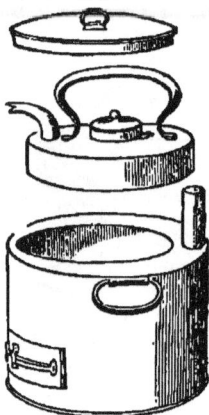

Steaks or cutlets may be quickly cooked with a
sheet or two of lighted paper only, in the apparatus
shown in the preceding page, and called a conjurer.
Lift off the cover and lay in the meat properly seasoned, with a small slice of butter under it, and insert the lighted paper in the aperture shown in the
plate; in from eight to ten minutes the meat will
be done, and found to be remarkably tender, and
very palatable: it must be turned and moved occasionally during the process.   This is an especially
convenient mode of cooking for persons whose
hours of dining are rendered uncertain by the nature of their avocations.   For medical men en-
gaged in extensive country practice it has been
often proved so.   The conjurer costs but a few
shillings.   Another form of this economical apparatus, with which a pint of water may be made to
boil by means of only a sheet of paper wrapped round a cone, in the
inside, is shown in the second plate.

FRYING.

This is an operation, which, though apparently
very simple, requires to be more carefully and
skilfully conducted than it commonly is.   Its success depends principally on allowing the fat to
attain the exact degree of heat which shall give
firmness, without too quick browning or scorching,

Sauté Pan.

before anything is laid into the pan; for if this be neglected the article
fried will be saturated with the fat, and remain pale and flaccid.   When
the requisite degree of colour is acquired before the cooking is complete,
the pan should be placed high above the fire, that it may be continued
slowly to the proper point.   Steaks and cutlets should be seasoned with
salt and pepper, and dredged on both sides lightly with flour before they
are laid into the pan, in which they should be often moved and turned,
that they may be equally done, and that they may not stick nor burn to
it.   From ten to fifteen minutes will fry them.   They should be evenly
sliced, about the same thickness as for broiling, and neatly trimmed and
divided in the first instance.   Lift them into a hot dish when done,

pour the fat from the pan, and throw in a small slice of butter; stir to this a large teaspoonful of flour, brown it gently, and pour in by degrees a quarter pint of hot broth or water; shake the pan well round, add pepper, salt, and a little good catsup, or any other store sauce which may be preferred to it, and pour the gravy over the steaks: this is the most common mode of saucing and serving them.

Minute directions for fish, and others for omlets, and for different preparations of batter, are given in their proper places; but we must again observe, that a very small fryingpan (scarcely larger than a dinner-plate) is necessary for many of these; and, indeed, the large and *thick* one suited to meat and fish, and used commonly for them, is altogether unfit for nicer purposes.

The *sauté-pan*, shown in the preceding page, is much used by French cooks instead of a frying-pan; it is more particularly convenient for tossing quickly over the fire small collops, or aught else which requires but little cooking.

All fried dishes, which are not sauced, should be served extremely dry, upon a neatly-folded damask cloth: they are best drained, upon a sieve reversed, placed before the fire.

A wire basket of this form is convenient for frying parsley and other herbs. It must be placed in a pan well filled with fat, and lifted out quickly when the herbs are done: they may likewise be crisped in it over a clear fire, without being fried.

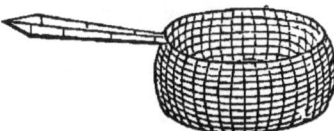

Wire Basket for Frying

BAKING.

The oven may be used with advantage for many purposes of cookery, for which it is not commonly put into requisition. Calves' feet, covered with a proper proportion of water, may be reduced to a strong-jelly if left in it for some hours; the half-head, boned and rolled, will be found excellent eating, if laid, with the bones, into a deep pan and baked quite tender in sufficient broth, or water, to keep it covered in every part until done; good soup also may be made in the same way, the usual ingredients being at once

American Oven.*

added to the meat, with the exception of the vegetables, which will not become tender if put into cold liquor, and should therefore be thrown in after it begins to simmer. Baking is likewise one of the best modes of dressing various kinds of fish: pike and red mullet amongst others. Salmon cut into thick slices, freed from the skin, well seasoned with spice, mixed with salt (and with minced herbs, at pleasure), then arranged evenly in a dish, and covered thickly with crumbs of bread,

* By means of this oven, which, from its construction, reflects the heat very strongly, bread, cakes, and pies, can be perfectly well baked before a large clear fire : but, as we have stated in another part of our work, the consumption of fuel necessary to the process renders it far from economical. A spit has lately been introduced into some of the American ovens, converting them at once into portable and convenient roasters.

moistened with clarified butter, as directed in Chapter II., for baked
soles, and placed in the oven for about half an hour, will be found very
rich and highly flavoured. Part of the middle of the salmon left entire,
well cleaned, and thoroughly dried, then seasoned, and securely wrapped
in two or three folds of thickly buttered paper, will also prove excellent
eating, if gently baked. (This may likewise be roasted in a Dutch
oven, either folded in the paper, or left without it, and basted with
butter.)

Hams, when freshly cured, and not over salted, if neatly trimmed,
and closely wrapped in a coarse paste, are both more juicy, and of finer
flavour baked than boiled. Savoury or pickled beef, too, put into a deep
pan, with a little gravy, and plenty of butter, or chopped suet on the
top, to prevent the outside from becoming dry; then covered with paste,
or with several folds of thick paper, and set into a moderate oven for
four or five hours, or even longer, if it be of large weight, is an excellent dish. A goose, a leg of pork, and a sucking pig, if properly attended
to while in the oven, are said to be nearly, or quite as good as if roasted;
but baking is both an unpalatable and an unprofitable mode of cooking
joints of meat in general, though its great convenience to many persons
renders it a very common one.

It is usual to raise meat from the dish in which it is sent to the oven
by placing it, properly skewered, on a stand, so as to allow potatoes or
a batter pudding to be baked under it. A few button onions, freed from
the outer skin, or three or four large ones, cut in halves, are sometimes
put beneath a shoulder of mutton. Two sheets of paper spread separately with a thick layer of butter, clarified marrow, or any other fat,
and fastened securely over the outside of a joint, will prevent its being
too much dried by the fierce heat of the oven. A few spoonsful of water
or gravy should be poured into the dish with potatoes, and a little salt
sprinkled over them.

A celebrated French cook recommends *braising in the oven:* that is
to say, after the meat has been arranged in the usual manner, and just
brought to boil over the fire, that the braising pan, closely stopped,
should be put into a moderate oven, for the same length of time as
would be required to stew the meat perfectly tender.

BRAISING.

English Braising-pan.

Braising is but a more expensive mode
of stewing meat. The following French
recipe will explain the process. We
would observe, however, that the layers
of beef or veal, in which the joint to be
braised is imbedded, can afterwards be converted into excellent soup, gravy, or glaze;
and that there need, in consequence, be no
waste, nor any unreasonable degree of ex-
pense attending it; but it is a troublesome process, and quite as good a
result may be obtained by simmering the meat in very strong gravy.
Should the flavour of the bacon be considered an advantage, slices of it
can be laid over the article braised, and secured to it with a fillet of
tape.

"*To braise the inside* (or *small fillet*, as it is called in France) *of a sirloin of beef:* Raise the fillet clean from the joint; and with a sharp knife strip off all the skin, leaving the surface of the meat as smooth as possible; have ready some strips of unsmoked bacon, half as thick as your little finger, roll them in a mixture of thyme finely minced, spices in powder, and a little pepper and salt. Lard the fillet quite through with these, and tie it round with tape in any shape you choose. Line the bottom of a stewpan (or braising-pan) with slices of bacon; next put in a layer of beef, or veal, four onions, two bay-leaves, two carrots, and a bunch of sweet herbs, and place the fillet on them. Cover it with slices of bacon, put some trimmings of meat all round it, and pour on to it half a pint of good bouillon or gravy. Let it stew as gently as possible for two hours and a half; take it up, and keep it very hot; strain, and reduce the gravy by quick boiling until it is thick enough to glaze with; brush the meat over with it; put the rest in the dish with the fillet, after the tape has been removed from it, and send it directly to table."

Equal parts of Madeira and gravy are sometimes used to moisten the meat.

No attempt should be made to braise a joint in any vessel that is not very nearly of its own size.

A round of buttered paper is generally put over the more delicate kinds of braised meat, to prevent their being browned by the fire, which in France is put round the lid of the braising-pan, in a groove made on purpose to contain it. The embers of a wood fire mixed with the hot ashes are best adapted to sustain the regular, but gentle degree of heat required for this mode of cooking.

The pan shown at the head of this section, with a closely fitting copper tray, serving for the cover, is used commonly in England for braising; but a stewpan of modern form, or any other vessel which will admit of embers being placed upon the lid, will answer for the purpose as well.

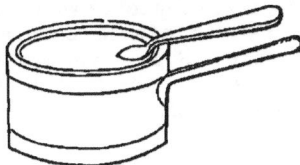

Common cooks sometimes stew meat in a mixture of butter and water, and *call it braising.*

Copper Stewpan.

LARDING.

Larding Pins.

Cut into slices, of the same length and thickness, some bacon of the finest quality; trim away the outsides, place the slices evenly upon each other, and with a sharp knife divide them obliquely into small strips of equal size. For pheasants, partridges, hares, fowls, and fricandeaux, the bacon should be about the eighth of an inch square, and two inches in length; but for meat which is to be larded quite through, instead of on the outside merely, the bits of bacon (properly called lardoons) must be at least the third of an inch square.

In general, the breasts only of birds are larded, the backs and thighs of rabbits, and the whole of the upper surface of a fricandeau: these should be thickly covered with small lardoons, placed at regular intervals, and in lines which intersect each other, so as to form rather minute diamonds.

The following directions for larding a partridge will serve equally for poultry, or for other kinds of game:—

Secure one end of the bacon in a slight larding-pin, and on the point of this take up sufficient of the flesh of the bird to hold the lardoon firmly; draw the pin through it, and part of the bacon, of which the two ends should be left of equal length. Proceed thus, until the breast of the pheasant is entirely garnished with lardoons, when it ought to resemble in appearance a cake thickly stuck with slips of almonds.

The larger strips of bacon, after being rolled in a high seasoning of minced herbs and spices, are used to lard the *inside* of meat, and they should be proportioned to its thickness, as they must be passed quite through it. For example: a four inch slice from a rump of beef will require lardoons of very nearly that length, which must be drawn through with a large larding-pin, and left in it, with the ends just out of sight on either side.

In France, truffles, anchovies, slices of tongue, and of fat, all trimmed into proper shape, are occasionally used for larding. The bacon employed there for the purpose is cured without any saltpetre (as this would redden the white meats), and it is never smoked: the receipt for it will be found in Chapter XI.

A turkey is sometimes larded with alternate lardoons of fat bacon and of bullock's tongue, which has been pickled but not dried: we apprehend that the lean of a half-boiled ham, of good colour, could answer the purpose quite as well, or better.

Larding the surface of meat, poultry, or game, gives it a good appearance, but it is a more positive improvement to meat of a dry nature to interlard the inside with large lardoons of well-seasoned, delicate, striped bacon.

BONING.

Very minute directions being given in other parts of our volume for this, we confine ourselves here to the following rules:—in disengaging the flesh from it, work the knife always *close to the bone*, and take every care not to pierce the outer skin.

TO BLANCH MEAT OR VEGETABLES.

This is merely to throw either into a pan of boiling water for a few minutes, which gives firmness to the first, and is necessary for some modes of preparing vegetables.

The breast only of a bird is sometimes held in the water while it boils, to render it firm for larding. To preserve the whiteness of meat, and the bright green of vegetables, they are lifted from the water after they have boiled a few minutes, and are thrown immediately into spring water, and left till cold.

5 to 10 minutes.

GLAZING.

This process we have explained at the article *Glaze*, Chapter III. The surface of the meat should be covered, evenly, with two or three separate layers of the glaze, which, if properly made, soon becomes firm. A ham should be well dried in the oven before it is laid on. Cutlets of all kinds may be glazed before they are sent to table, with very good effect. The figure above represents a glaze-pot and brush, used for heating and applying the preparation: a jar placed in a pan of boiling water may be substituted for the first, when it is not at hand.

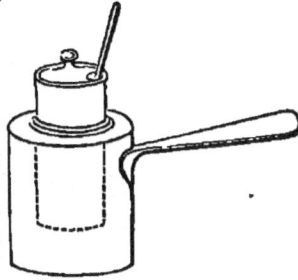

TOASTING.

A very cheap apparatus, by which chops can be dressed before a clear fire, is shown by the first of these figures; and the second is peculiarly convenient when bread or muffins are required to be toasted expeditiously and in large quantities, without much time and attention being bestowed upon them.

To brown the surface of a dish without baking or placing it at the fire.

This is done with a salamander, as it is called, formed like the engraving below; it is heated in the fire, and held over the dish sufficiently near to give it colour. It is very much used in a superior order of cookery. A kitchen shovel is sometimes substituted for it on an emergency.

CHAPTER VIII.

BEEF.

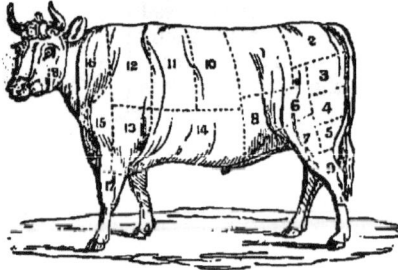

<table>
<tr><td>No.</td><td>No.</td></tr>
<tr><td>1. Sirloin.</td><td>10. Fore Rib.   (Five Ribs.)</td></tr>
<tr><td>2. Rump.</td><td>11. Middle Rib   (Four Ribs.)</td></tr>
<tr><td>3. Edge-bone.</td><td>12. Chuck Rib.   (Three Ribs.)</td></tr>
<tr><td>4. Buttock, or Round.</td><td>13. Shoulder, or Leg of Mutton Piece.</td></tr>
<tr><td>5. Mouse Buttock.</td><td>14. Brisket.</td></tr>
<tr><td>6. Veiny Piece.</td><td>15. Clod.</td></tr>
<tr><td>7. Thick Flank.</td><td>16. Neck.</td></tr>
<tr><td>8. Thin Flank.</td><td>17. Shin.</td></tr>
<tr><td>9. Leg.</td><td>18. Cheek.</td></tr>
</table>

TO CHOOSE BEEF.

If young and freshly killed, the lean of ox-beef will be smoothly grained, and of a fine, healthy, carnation-red, the fat rather white than yellow, and the suet white and firm.   Heifer-beef is more closely grained, and rather less bright of colour, the bones are considerably smaller, and the fat of a purer white.

Of bull-beef we only speak to warn our readers, that it is of all meat the coarsest and the most rank in flavour.   It may be known by its dark hue, its close tough fibre, and the scanty proportion, bad appearance, and strong odour of its fat.

In choice and well-fed beef, the lean will be found intergrained with fat : very lean meat is always of an inferior quality.

The ribs, the sirloin, and the rump, are the proper joints for roasting. The round, or buttock, the edge-bone, the second round, or mouse-buttock, the shin, the brisket, the shoulder, or leg of mutton piece, and the clod may be boiled or stewed.   The neck is generally used for soup or gravy ; and the thin flank for collaring.   The best steaks are cut from the middle of the rump ; the next best from the veiny piece, or from the chuck-rib.   The inside of the sirloin, commonly used for the purpose in France, makes by far the most delicate steaks ; but though *exceedingly* tender, they are considered by English epicures to be wanting in flavour.

The finest part of the sirloin is the chump-end, which contains the larger portion of the fillet : of the ribs, the middle ones are those generally preferred by experienced housekeepers.

TO ROAST SIRLOIN, OR RIBS OF BEEF.

Let the joint hang as long as it can possibly be kept perfectly sweet. When it is first brought in, remove the pipe of marrow which runs along the backbone, and cut out the kernels from the fat. Be very careful in summer to guard it from flies; examine it frequently in warm or damp weather; and scrape off with a knife, or wipe away with a dry cloth, any moisture which may appear on the surface: when this has been done, dust some powdered ginger or pepper over it. Unless the joint should be very large, its appearance will be improved by taking off the ends of the bones, which may then be laid in salt for a few days, and afterwards boiled. Spit the beef firmly; keep it far back from the fire until it is well heated through; baste it constantly; and proceed as directed in the general rules for roasting (see page 131). Persons who object to meat being *frothed* for table, have it dredged with flour when it is first placed at the fire, and sprinkled with fine salt when it is nearly done. It is not necessary to paper the fat of beef, as many cooks direct, if proper attention be given to it while roasting.

As a general rule, it may be observed,·that when the steam from the meat draws strongly towards the fire, it is nearly or quite ready to serve. The time required to roast it will depend on the state of the weather,[*] the size and strength of the fire, the thickness of the joint, the use or non-use of a meat-screen or reflector, the general temperature of the kitchen and other contingencies. A quarter of an hour for each pound of meat is commonly allowed for solid, heavy joints, and, if the directions we have given be attended to, this will not be found too much even for persons who prefer beef somewhat rare: it must be left longer at the fire if wished very thoroughly roasted, and quite double the usual time when the plan we have noticed at page 132, is adopted. When likely to be sent to table hashed, minced, or dressed a second time in any way, the juices of the meat should be dried up as little as possible when it is first cooked.

ROAST RUMP OF BEEF.

As this joint is generally too large to serve whole, as much of it as will form a handsome dish should be cut from the chump end to roast. It must be managed as the sirloin, to which it is commonly preferred by · connoisseurs. When boned and rolled into the form of a fillet of veal, as it sometimes is, nearly or quite an additional hour should be allowed to dress it.

TO ROAST PART OF A ROUND OF BEEF.

The natural division of the meat will show where the silver side of the round is to be separated from the upper or tongue side, which is the proper part for roasting, and which will be found equally good and profitable for the purpose, if allowed to hang as long as it can be kept sweet before it is dressed. Care should be taken in dividing the meat, not to pierce the inner skin. The silver side, with the udder, if there should be one to the joint, may be pickled, spiced, or simply salted, and will be excellent either way. The outside fat should be drawn tightly round

---

[*] The meat will be much sooner done in hot weather than in cold. If frozen, it must be thawed *very gradually* before it is put to the fire, or no length of time will roast it; this will be effected better by laying it into cold water for some hours before it is wanted, than by any other means.

the remainder of the beef, which must be firmly skewered, or bound with tape, to keep it in form. It will require long roasting at a strong, steady fire, and should be kept constantly basted.

Beef, 14 lbs.: 4½ to 5 hours.

Obs.—We think that larding the beef quite through with large lardoons of firm fat, of udder, or of bacon, would be an improvement; and we ought also to observe, that unless it be young and of fine quality, it will not answer well for roasting.

TO ROAST A FILLET OF BEEF.

Raise the fillet from the inside of the sirloin, or from part of it, with a sharp knife; leave the fat on, trim off the skin, lard it through, or all over, or roast it, quite plain; baste it with butter, and send it very hot to table, with tomata sauce, or sauce piquante, or eschalot sauce, in a tureen. It is sometimes served with brown gravy or currant jelly: it should then be garnished with forcemeat-balls, made as for hare. If not very large, an hour and a quarter will roast it well with a brisk fire.

Obs.—The remainder of the joint may be boned, rolled, and roasted, or braised; or made into meat cakes; or served as a miniature round of beef.

1 hour, 15 minutes.

ROAST BEEF STEAK.

If extremely tender, a large slice from the middle of the rump will make an excellent small dish of roast meat, when a joint is not easily to be procured. Let it be smoothly cut, from an inch to an inch and a half thick, flattened on a table, and the inside sprinkled with a little fine salt and cayenne, or common pepper. Make a roll of forcemeat, as No. 1 (page 122), adding, at pleasure, a flavouring of minced onion or eschalot, and increasing the quantity of spices; place this on one end of the steak, and roll it up tightly in it; skewer and bind the meat so that the forcemeat cannot escape, fasten a buttered paper over it, and roast it an hour and a half, or more, according to its size. Twenty minutes before it is served, take off the paper, and flour the meat, which should be kept well basted with butter all the time it is roasting. Send brown gravy to table with it, and pour a little over the beef.

1½ hour, or more.

TO BROIL BEEF STEAKS.

The steaks should be from half to three-quarters of an inch thick, equally sliced, and freshly cut from the middle of a well-kept, finely grained, and tender rump of beef. They should be neatly trimmed, and once or twice divided, if very large. The fire, as we have already said in the general directions for broiling (page 135), must be strong and clear. The bars of the gridiron should be thin, and not very close together. When they are thoroughly heated, without being sufficiently burning to scorch the meat, wipe and rub them with fresh mutton suet; next pepper the steaks slightly, but never season them with salt before they are dressed; lay them on the gridiron, and when done on one side, turn them on the other, being careful to catch, in the dish in which they are to be sent to table, any gravy which may threaten to drain from hem when they are moved. Let them be served the *instant* they are taken from the fire; and have ready at the moment, dish, cover, and

plates, as hot as they can be. From eight to ten minutes will be sufficient to broil steaks for the generality of eaters, and more than enough
for those who like them but partially done.

Genuine amateurs seldom take prepared sauce or gravy with their
steaks, as they consider the natural juices of the meat sufficient. When
any accompaniment to them is desired, a small quantity of choice mushroom catsup may be warmed in the dish that is heated to receive them;
and which, when the not very refined flavour of a raw eschalot is liked,
as it is by some eaters, may previously be rubbed with one, of which
the large end has been cut off. A thin slice or two of fresh butter is
sometimes laid under the steaks, where it soon melts and mingles with
the gravy which flows from them. The appropriate tureen sauces for
broiled beef steaks are onion, tomata, oyster, eschalot, hot horseradish,
and brown cucumber, or mushroom sauce.

Obs. 1.—We have departed a little in this receipt from our previous
instructions for broiling, by recommending that the steaks should be
turned but *once,* instead of " often," as all great authorities on the subject direct. By trying each method, our readers will be able to decide
for themselves upon the preferable one: we can only say, that we have
never eaten steaks so excellent as those which have been dressed *exactly*
in accordance with the receipt we have just given, and we have taken
infinite pains to ascertain the really best mode of preparing this very
favourite English dish, which so constantly makes its appearance both
carelessly cooked and ill served, especially at private tables.

Obs. 2.—It is a good plan to throw a few bits of charcoal on the fire
some minutes before the steaks are laid down, as they give forth
strong heat without any smoke.

The upright gridirons, by which meat is rather *toasted* than broiled
though used in many kitchens and generally pronounced exceedingly
convenient, where they have been tried, do not appear to us so well
adapted for dressing steaks as those of less modern fashion, which are
placed *over,* instead of before the fire.

BEEF STEAKS A LA FRANÇAISE.

The inside of the sirloin freed from skin, and cut evenly into round
quarter-inch slices, should properly be used for these; but when it cannot be obtained, part of the rump must be substituted for it. Season
the steaks with fine salt and pepper, brush them with a little clarified
butter, and boil them over a clear, brisk fire. Mix a teaspoonful of
parsley, minced extremely fine, with a large slice of fresh butter, a
little cayenne, and a small quantity of salt. When the steaks are done,
put the mixture into the dish intended for them, and lay them upon it;
garnish them plentifully with fried potatoes. It is an improvement to
squeeze the juice of half a lemon on the butter, before the meat is
heaped over it. The potatoes should be sliced rather thin, coloured of
a fine brown, and placed evenly round the meat.

BEEF STEAKS A LA FRANÇAISE (ENTRÉE); (*another receipt.*

Cut the beef into small thin steaks as above, season them with fine
salt and pepper, dredge them lightly with flour, and fry them in butter
over a brisk fire; arrange them in a chain round a very hot dish, and
pour into the centre a little olive sauce.

9

STEWED BEEF STEAK (ENTRÉE).

This may be cut from one to two inches thick, and the time of stewing it must be proportioned to its size. Dissolve a slice of butter in a large saucepan or stewpan, and brown the steak on both sides, moving it often that it may not burn; then shake in a little flour, and when it is coloured pour in by degrees rather more than sufficient broth or water to cover the meat. When it boils, season it with salt, take off the scum, slice in one onion, a carrot or two, and half a turnip; add a small bunch of sweet herbs, and stew the steak very softly from two hours and a half to three hours. A quarter of an hour before it is served, stir well into the gravy three teaspoonsful of rice flour smoothly mixed with a little cayenne, half a wineglassful of mushroom catsup, and a slight seasoning of spice. A teaspoonful of currie powder, in addition, will improve both the flavour and the appearance of the sauce. The onion is sometimes browned with the meat; and the quantity is considerably increased. Eschalots may be used instead, where their strong flavour is approved. A few button-mushrooms, stewed from twenty to thirty minutes with the meat, will render the catsup unnecessary. Wine, or any favourite store sauce, can be added at will.

2½ to 3 hours.

FRIED BEEF STEAK.

We have little to add here to the directions of page 136, which are sufficient to enable the cook to send a dish of fried steaks to table properly dressed. Currie sauce, highly *onioned*, is frequently served with them.

BEEF STEAK STEWED IN ITS OWN GRAVY; (*Good and wholesome.*)

Trim all the fat and skin from a rump steak of nearly an inch thick, and divide it once or twice; just dip it into cold water, let it drain for an instant, sprinkle it on both sides with pepper, and then flour it rather thickly; lay it quite flat into a well-tinned iron saucepan or stewpan, which has been rinsed with cold water, of which a tablespoonful should be left in it. Place it over (not upon) a *very* gentle fire, and keep it just simmering from an hour and a half to an hour and three quarters, when, if the meat be good, it will have become perfectly tender. Add salt to it when it first begins to boil, and turn it when rather more than half done. A couple of spoonsful of gravy, half as much catsup, and a slight seasoning of spice, would, to many tastes, improve this dish, of which, however, the great recommendation is its wholesome simplicity, which renders it suitable to the most delicate stomach. A thick mutton cutlet from the middle of the leg is excellent dressed thus.

1½ to 1¾ hour.

BEEF OR MUTTON CAKE; (*Very good.*)

Chop two pounds of lean and very tender beef or mutton, with three quarters of a pound of beef suet; mix them well, and season them with a dessertspoonful of salt, nearly as much pounded cloves, a teaspoonful of pounded mace, and half a teaspoonful of cayenne. Line a round baking dish with thin slices of fat bacon, press the meat closely into it, smooth the top, and cover it with bacon, set a plate on it with a weight, and bake it two hours and a quarter. Take off the bacon, and serve the meat hot, with a little rich brown gravy, or set it by until cold, when it will be equally good. The fat of the meat which is used for this dish can be chopped up with it instead of suet, where it is liked as well ; and onion, or eschalot, shred fine, minced savoury herbs, grated lemon-peel, rasped bacon, or mushrooms cut small, may in turn be added to vary it in flavour.

Lean beef or mutton, 2 lbs ; suet, ¾ lb. ; salt and cloves in powder, each a dessertspoonful ; mace, 1 teaspoonful ; half as much cayenne : baked 2¼ hours.

Obs.—A larger portion of suet, or of fat will render these cakes lighter, but will not otherwise improve them : they may be made of veal or of venison, but one-third of mutton suet or of fat bacon should be mixed with this last.

GERMAN STEW.

Cut into about three-inch squares, two pounds and a half of the leaner part of the veiny piece of beef, or of any joint which is likely to be tender, and set it on to stew, with a pint and three quarters of cold broth, or water, and one large onion sliced. When these begin to boil, add a teaspoonful of salt, and a third as much of pepper, and let them simmer gently for an hour and a half. Have ready some young white cabbages, parboiled ; press the water well from them, lay them in with the beef, and let the whole stew for another hour. More onions, and a seasoning of mixed spices, or a few bits of lean bacon, or of ham, can be added to this stew when a higher flavour is desired ; but it is very good without.

Beef, 2½ lbs. ; water, or broth, 1¾ pint ; onion, 1 ; salt, 1 teaspoonful ; third as much pepper : 1½ hour. Parboiled cabbages, 3 or 4: 1 hour.

WELSH STEW.

Take the same proportions of beef, and of broth or water, as for the German stew. When they have simmered gently for an hour, add the white part of from twenty to thirty leeks, or two dozens of button onions, and five or six young mild turnips, cut in slices, a small lump of white sugar, nearly half a teaspoonful of white pepper, and more than twice as much salt. Stew the whole softly from an hour and a quarter to an hour and a half, after the vegetables are added.

Beef and water as above : 1 hour. Leeks, 20 to 30 ; or small onions, 24 ; young turnips, 6 ; small lump of sugar ; white pepper, nearly ½ teaspoonful ; salt, twice as much : 1¼ to 1½ hour.

A GOOD ENGLISH STEW.

On three pounds of tender rump of beef, freed from skin and fat, and cut down into two-inch squares, pour rather more than a quart of cold broth or gravy. When it boils add salt if required, and a little cayenne, and keep it just simmering for a couple of hours ; then put to it the grated rind of a large lemon, or of two small ones, and half an hour after stir to it a tablespoonful of rice-flour, smoothly mixed with a wine glassful of mushroom catsup, a dessertspoonful of lemon-juice, and a teaspoonful of soy : in fifteen minutes it will be ready to serve. A glass and a half of port, or of white wine, will greatly improve this stew, which may likewise be flavoured with the store-sauce of page 117, or with another, which we find excellent for the purpose, made with half a pint of port wine, the same of mushroom-catsup, a quarter-pint of walnut-pickle, a tablespoonful of the best soy, and a dessert-spoonful of cayenne-vinegar, all well shaken together and poured into a bottle containing the thin rind of a lemon and two fine mellow ancho-vies, of moderate size. A few delicately fried forcemeat-balls may be slipped into it after it is dished.

Obs.—The limits of our work will not permit us to devote a further space to this class of dishes, but an intelligent cook will find it easy to vary them in numberless ways. Mushrooms, celery, carrots, sweet herbs, parboiled new potatoes, green peas, rice, and currie-powder may be advantageously used for that purpose. Oxtails, just blanched and cut into joints, will be found excellent substitutes for the beef: mutton and veal also may be dressed in the same way. The meat and vege-tables can be browned before broth or water is poured to them; but, though perhaps more savoury, the stew will then be much less delicate. Each ..nd of vegetable should be allowed something more than suffi-cient time to render it perfectly tender, but not so much as would reduce it to pulp.

TO STEW SHIN OF BEEF.

.Wash, and set it on to stew in sufficient cold water to keep it just covered until it is done. When it boils, take off the scum, and put an ounce and a quarter of salt to the gallon of water. It is usual to add a few cloves and some black pepper, slightly bruised and tied up loosely in a fold of muslin, two or more onions, a root of celery, a bunch of savoury herbs, four or five carrots, and as many turnips, either whole or sliced: if to be served with the meat, the last two will require a little more than the ordinary time of boiling, but otherwise they may be sim-mered with the meat from the beginning. Give the beef from four to five hours' gentle stewing; and serve it with part of its own liquor thickened and flavoured, or quite plain. An excellent dish for a family may be made by stewing the thick fleshy part of the shin or leg in stock made of the knuckle, with a few bits of lean ham, or a slice of hung beef from which the smoked edges have been carefully pared away, and some spice, salt, and vegetables: by frying these last before they are thrown into the soup-pot the savour of the stew will be greatly heightened; and a tureen of good soup may be made of its remains, after it has been served at table.

Ox-cheek, after having been soaked for four or five hours, and washed with great nicety, may be dressed like the shin; but as it has little fla-vour, the gravy should be strained, and quite cleared from fat, then put into a clean saucepan, and thickened as soon as it boils, with the fol-lowing mixture:—three dessertspoonsful of rice-flour, nearly a wine-glassful of catsup, a teaspoonful of currie-powder, or a little powdered ginger and cayenne. When these have stewed for ten minutes, dish the head, pour the sauce over, and serve it.

Shin of beef, 4 to 5 hours. Ox-cheek, 2 to 3 hours.

FRENCH BEEF A LA MODE; (*a common receipt.*)

Take seven or eight pounds of a rump of beef (or of any other tender joint), free from bone, and skewer it firmly into a good shape. Put two ounces of butter into a thick saucepan or stewpan, and when it boils stir to it a tablespoonful of flour; keep these well shaken over a gentle fire until they are of a fine amber colour; then lay in the beef, and brown it on both sides, taking care that it shall not stick to the pan. Pour to it by slow degrees, letting each portion boil before the next is added, or the butter will float upon the surface and be difficult to clear off afterwards, three quarters of a pint of hot water, or gravy ; add a bunch of savoury herbs, one large or two small carrots cut in thick slices, two or three moderate-sized onions, two bay-leaves, and sufficient pepper and salt to season the gravy. Let the meat simmer gently from four to five hours, and turn it when it is half done. When ready to serve, lift the beef into a hot dish, lay the vegetables round, and pour the gravy over it, after having taken out the herbs and skimmed away the fat. In France, half or the whole of a calf's foot is stewed with the beef, which is there generally larded through with thick strips of fat bacon. (For larding, see page 139.) Veal dressed in this way is even better than beef. The stewpan used for either would be as nearly of the size of the meat as possible.

Beef, 7 to 8 lbs. : 4 to 5 hours.

STEWED SIRLOIN OF BEEF.

As a matter of convenience we have occasionally had this joint stewed instead of roasted, and have found it excellent. Cut out the inside or fillet as entire as possible, and reserve it for a separate dish ; then remove the bones with care, or let the butcher do this for you ; spread the meat flat on a table and cover the inside with thin slices of striped bacon, after having first strewed over it a mixed seasoning of a small teaspoonful of salt, half as much mace or nutmeg, and a moderate quantity of pepper or cayenne. Roll and bind the meat firmly, lay it into a stewpan or thick iron saucepan nearly of its size, and add the bones and as much good beef broth as will nearly cover the joint. Should this not be at hand, put a few slices of lean ham or bacon under the beef, and lay round it three pounds of neck or knuckle of veal, or of stewing beef, divided into several parts ; then pour to it cold water instead of broth. In either case, so soon as it has boiled a few minutes and been well cleaned from scum, throw in a large faggot of savoury herbs, three or four carrots, as many leeks, or a large onion, stuck with a dozen cloves ; and, an hour later, two blades of mace, and half a teaspoonful of peppercorns. Stew the beef *very* gently indeed from four to five hours, and longer, should the joint be large : serve it with a good Espagnole, sauce piquante, or brown caper sauce. Add what salt may be needed before the vegetables are thrown in ; and, after the meat is lifted out, boil down to soup or gravy the liquor in which it has been stewed. To many tastes it would be an improvement to flour and brown the outside of the beef in butter before the broth or water is poured to it : it may also be stewed (but somewhat longer) half-covered with rich gravy, and turned when partially done. Minced eschalots may be strewed over the inside before it is rolled, when their strong savour is relished, or veal forcemeat may supply their place.

TO STEW A RUMP OF BEEF.

This joint is more easily carved, and is of better appearance when the bones are removed before it is dressed. Roll and bind it firmly cover it with strong cold beef broth or gravy, and stew it very gently indeed from six hours to between seven and eight ; add to it, after the scum has been well cleared off, one large or two moderate-sized onions stuck with thirty cloves, a head of celery, two carrots, two turnips, and a large faggot of savoury herbs. When the beef is perfectly tender quite through, which may be known by probing it with a sharp thin skewer, remove the fillets of tape, dish it neatly, and serve it with a rich Espagnole, and a garnish of forced tomatas, or with a highly flavoured brown English gravy, and stewed carrots in the dish: for these last the mild preparation of garlic or eschalots, of page 110, may be substituted with good effect; they should be well drained, laid round the meat, and a little brown gravy poured over the whole.

This is the most simple and economical manner of stewing the beef; but should a richer one be desired, half roast the joint, and stew it afterwards in strong gravy, to which a pint of mushrooms, and a pint of sherry or Madeira, should be added an hour before it is ready for table. Keep it hot while a portion of the gravy is thickened with a well-made brown roux (see Chapter IV., page 96), and seasoned with salt, cayenne, and any other spice it may require. Garnish it with large balls of forcemeat, highly seasoned with minced eschalots, rolled in egg and bread-crumbs, and fried a fine golden brown.

Plainly stewed from 6 to 7 or 8 hours. Or: half roasted, then stewed from 4 to 5 hours.

Obs.—Grated horse-radish, mixed with some well-thickened brown gravy, a teaspoonful of mustard, and a little lemon-juice or vinegar, is a good sauce for stewed beef.

BEEF PALATES. (ENTRÉE.)

First rub them well with salt, to take off the slime; then wash them thoroughly in several waters, and leave them to soak for half an hour before they are dressed. Set them over the fire in cold water, and boil them gently until the skin will peel off, and the palates are tolerably tender. It is difficult to state the exact time required for this. as some will be done enough in two hours and a half, and others in not less than from four to five hours. When thus prepared, the palates may be cut into various forms, and simmered until fit to serve, in rich brown gravy, highly flavoured with ham, cayenne, wine, and lemon-peel; or they will make an excellent currie. As they are very insipid of themselves, they require a sauce of some piquancy, in which, after they have been peeled and trimmed, they should be stewed from twenty to thirty minutes, or until they are perfectly tender. The black parts of them must be cut away, when the skin is taken off. An onion, stuck with a few cloves, a carrot sliced, a teaspoonful of whole white pepper, a slice of butter, and a teaspoonful of salt, may be boiled with the palates in the first instance; and they will be found very good, if sent to table in the curried gravy of Chapter XIV., or in the Soubise of Chapter IV., made thinner than the receipts direct.

Boiled from 2½ to 4 or 5 hours. Stewed from 20 to 30 minutes.

Obs.—A French cook of some celebrity, orders the palates to be laid on the gridiron until the skin will peel or scrape off: the plan seems a good one, but we have not tried it.

BEEF PALATES; (*Neapolitan mode.*)

Boil the palates until the skin can be easily removed, then stew them very tender in good veal broth, lay them on a drainer and let them cool; cut them across obliquely into strips of about a quarter inch in width, and finish them by either of the receipts for dressing maccaroni, which will be found in Chapters XIV. and XVIII.

STEWED OX-TAILS.

They should be sent from the butcher ready jointed. Soak and wash them well, cut them into joints, or into lengths of two or three joints, and cover them with cold broth or water. As soon as they boil, remove the scum, and add a half-teaspoonful of salt, or as much more as may be needed, and a little common pepper, or cayenne, an onion stuck with half a dozen cloves, two or three small carrots, and a bunch or two of parsley. When these have simmered for two hours and a quarter, try the meat with a fork, and should it not be perfectly tender, let it remain over the fire until it is so. Ox-tails sometimes require nearly or quite three hours' stewing: they may be served with the vegetables, or with the gravy strained from them, and thickened like the English stew, of page 147.

Ox-tails, 2; water or broth to cover them; salt, ½ teaspoonful, or more; little pepper or cayenne; onion, 1; cloves, 6; carrots, 2 or 3; parsley, 2 or 3 branches: 2¼ to 3 hours.

TO SALT AND PICKLE BEEF, IN VARIOUS WAYS.

Let the meat hang a couple of days in mild weather, and four or five in winter, before it is salted or pickled. During the heat of summer it is better to immerse it entirely in brine, that it may be secured alike from the flies, and from the danger of becoming putrid. Trim it, and take out the kernels from the fat; then rub a little fine dry salt over it, and leave it until the following day; drain it well from the blood, which will be found to have flowed from it, and it will be ready for any of the following modes of curing, which are all excellent of their kind, and have been well proved.

In very cold weather, the salt may be applied quite warm to the meat: it should always be perfectly dry, and reduced to powder.

Saltpetre hardens and renders meat indigestible; sugar, on the contrary, mellows and improves it much; and it is more tender when cured with bay salt than when common salt is used for it.

TO SALT AND BOIL A ROUND OF BEEF.

Mix an ounce of saltpetre, finely powdered, with half a pound of very coarse sugar, and rub the beef thoroughly with them; in two days add three-quarters of a pound of common salt, well dried and beaten; turn and rub the meat well in every part with the pickle for three weeks, when it will be fit to dress. Just wash off the salt, and skewer the beef as round and as even as possible; bind it tightly with broad tape, cover it with cold water, and let it simmer gently for at least five hours. Carrots, mashed turnips, or cabbages, are usually served with boiled beef; and horseradish stewed for ten minutes in equal parts of vinegar and water, then pressed well from them, and mixed with some rich melted butter, is a good sauce for it.

Beef, 20 lbs.; coarse sugar, ½ lb.; saltpetre, 1 oz.: 2 days. Salt, ¾ lb.: 21 days. Boil 5 hours, or more.

Obs.—-Beef cured by this receipt, if properly boiled, is tender, of good colour and flavour, and not over salt. The rump, edge-bone, and brisket may be salted, or pickled in the same way as the round.

HAMBURGH PICKLE FOR BEEF, HAMS, AND TONGUE.

Boil together, for twenty minutes, two gallons of water, three pounds of bay salt, two pounds of coarse sugar, two ounces of saltpetre, and two of black pepper, bruised, and tied in a fold of muslin; clear off the scum thoroughly, as it rises, pour the pickle into a deep earthen-pan, and when it is quite cold lay in the meat, of which every part must be perfectly covered with it. A moderate-sized round of beef will be ready for table in a fortnight; it should be turned occasionally in the brine. Five pounds of common salt may be substituted for the quantity of bay salt given above; but the meat will not be so finely flavoured.

Water, 2 gallons; bay salt, 3 lbs.; saltpetre, 2 ozs.; black pepper, 2 ozs.; sugar, 2 lbs.: 20 minutes.

ANOTHER PICKLE FOR TONGUES, BEEF, AND HAMS.

To three gallons of spring water add six pounds of common salt, two pounds of bay salt, two pounds of common loaf sugar, and two ounces of saltpetre. Boil these over a gentle fire, and be careful to take off all the scum as it rises: when quite cold it will be fit for use. Rub the meat to be cured with fine salt, and let it drain for a day or two, in order to free it from the blood; then immerse it in the brine, taking care that every part of it shall be covered. Young pork should not remain more than from three to five days in the pickle; but hams for drying may be left in it for a fortnight at least: tongues will be ready in rather less time. Beef may remain from one week to two, according to its size, and the degree of saltness desired for it. A little experience will soon teach the exact time required for the different kinds of meat. When the pickle has been in use for about three months, boil it up again gently, and take the scum carefully off. Add to it three pounds of common salt, four ounces of sugar, and one of saltpetre: it will remain good for a year or more.

Water, 3 gallons; common salt, 6 lbs.; bay salt, 2 lbs.; loaf sugar, 2 lbs.; saltpetre, 2 ozs.: boil 20 to 30 minutes.

DUTCH, OR HUNG BEEF.

For fourteen pounds weight of the round, the rump, or the thick flank of beef, mix two ounces of saltpetre with the same quantity of coarse sugar; rub the meat with them in every part, and let it remain for two days, then add one pound of bay salt, four ounces of common salt, and one ounce of ground black pepper. Rub these ingredients thoroughly into the beef, and in four days pour over it a pound of treacle; rub and turn it daily for a fortnight; drain, and send it to be smoked. When wanted for table, lay it into plenty of cold water, boil it very slowly, and press it under a heavy weight while hot. A slice of this beef, from which the edges have been carefully trimmed, will serve to flavour soups or gravies as well as ham.

Beef, 14 lbs.; saltpetre and coarse sugar, each 2 ozs.: 2 days. Bay salt, 1 lb.; common salt, 4 ozs.; pepper, 1 oz.: 4 days. Treacle, 1 lb.: 14 days.

Obs.—Three quarters of a pound of coarse sugar may be rubbed into the meat at first, and the treacle may be altogether omitted; cloves and mace, too, may be added in the same proportion as for spiced beef.

COLLARED BEEF.

Only the thinnest part of the flank, or the ribs, which are not so generally used for it, will serve conveniently for collaring. The first of these should be hung in a damp place for a day or two, to soften the outer skin; then rubbed with coarse sugar, and left for a couple of days; when, for eight pounds of the meat, one ounce of saltpetre and half a pound of salt should be added. In ten days it will be fit to dress. The bones and tough inner skin must be removed, and the beef sprinkled thickly on the under side with parsley and other savoury herbs shred small, before it is rolled, which should be done very tightly: it must then be secured with a cloth, and bound as closely as possible with broad tape. It will require nearly or quite five hours of gentle boiling, and should be placed while hot under a weight, or in a press, without having the tape and cloth removed.

Beef, 8 lbs.; sugar, 3 ozs.; salt, 8 ozs.: 10 days. Boil 5 hours.

COLLARED BEEF; *(another way.)*

Mix half an ounce of saltpetre with the same quantity of pepper, four ounces of bay salt, and four of common salt; with these rub well from six to seven pounds of the thin flank, and in four days add seven ounces of treacle; turn the beef daily in the pickle for a week or more; dip it into water, bone it and skin the inside, roll and bind it up very tightly lay it into cold water, and boil it for three hours and a half. We have found beef dressed by this receipt extremely good: herbs can, of course, be added to it as usual. Spices and juniper berries would to many tastes improve it, but we give the receipt simply as we have been accustomed to have it used.

Thin flank, 6 to 7 lbs.; bay-salt, and common salt, each 4 ozs.; saltpetre, ½ oz.; pepper, ½ oz.: 4 days. Treacle, 7 ozs.: 8 to 10 days. Boiled 3½ hours.

A COMMON RECEIPT FOR SALTING BEEF.

One ounce of saltpetre, and a pound of common salt, will be sufficient for sixteen pounds of beef. Both should be well dried, and finely powdered; the saltpetre rubbed first equally over the meat, and the salt next applied in every part. It should be rubbed thoroughly with the pickle and turned daily, from a week to ten days. An ounce or two of sugar mixed with the saltpetre will render the beef more tender and palatable.

Beef, 16 lbs.; saltpetre, 1 oz.; salt, 1 lb.: 7 to 10 days.

SPICED ROUND OF BEEF; *(very highly flavoured.)*

Rub the beef well in every part with half a pound of coarse brown sugar, and let it remain two days; then reduce to powder, and mix thoroughly before they are applied to the meat, two ounces of saltpetre three quarters of a pound of common salt, a quarter-pound of black pepper, three ounces of allspice, and four of bruised juniper-berries. Rub these ingredients strongly and equally over the joint, and do so daily for three weeks, turning it at the same time. Just wash off the spice, and put the beef into a tin, or covered earthen pan as nearly of its size as possible, with a cup of water or gravy; cover the top thickly with chopped beef-suet, and lay a coarse thick crust over the pan; place the cover on it, and bake the meat from five to six hours in a well-heated oven, which should not, however, be sufficiently fierce to harden the outside of the joint, which, if properly managed, will be exceedingly tender. Let it cool in the pan; and clear off the suet before it is dished. It is to be served cold, and will remain good for a fortnight.

Beef, 20 to 25 lbs. weight; sugar, 3 ozs.: 2 days. Saltpetre, 2 ozs.; common salt, ¾ lb.; black pepper, 4 ozs.; allspice, 3 ozs.; juniper-berries, 4 ozs.: 21 days. Baked 5 to 6 hours.

Obs.—We have not ourselves tested this receipt, but the meat cured by it has received such high commendations from several of our friends who have partaken of it frequently, that we think we may safely insert it without. The proportion of allspice appears to us more than would be agreeable to many tastes, and we would rather recommend that part of it should be omitted, and that a portion of nutmeg, mace, and cloves should be substituted for it; as we have found these spices to answer well in the following receipt.

SPICED BEEF; (*good and wholesome.*)

For twelve pounds of the round, rump, or thick flank of beef, take a large teaspoonful of freshly-pounded mace, and of ground black pepper, twice as much of cloves, one small nutmeg, and a quarter teaspoonful of cayenne, all in the finest powder. Mix them *well* with seven ounces of brown sugar, rub the beef with them and let it lie three days; add to it then half a pound of fine salt, and rub and turn it once in twenty-four hours for twelve days. Just wash, but do not soak it; skewer, or bind it into good form, put it into a stewpan or saucepan nearly of its size, pour to it a pint and a half of good beef broth, and when it begins to boil, take off the scum, and throw in one small onion, a moderate-sized faggot of thyme and parsley, and two large, or four small carrots. Let it simmer quite softly for four hours and a half, and if not wanted to serve hot, leave it in its own liquor until it is nearly cold. This is an excellent and far more wholesome dish than the hard, bright-coloured beef which is cured with large quantities of salt and saltpetre: two or three ounces of juniper-berries may be added to it with the spice, to heighten its flavour.

Beef, 12 lbs.; sugar, 7 ozs.; mace and black pepper, each, 1 large teaspoonful; cloves, in powder, 1 large dessertspoonful; nutmeg, 1; cayenne, ¼ teaspoonful: 3 days. Fine salt, ½ lb.: 12 days. Beef broth (or bouillon), 1½ pint; onion, 1 small; bunch of herbs; carrots, 2 large, or 4 small: stewed 4½ hours.

Obs.—We give this receipt *exactly* as we have often had it used, but celery and turnips might be added to the gravy; and when the appearance of the meat is much considered, three-quarters of an ounce of salt-petre may be mixed with the spices; the beef may also be plainly boiled in water only, with a few vegetables, or baked in a deep pan with a little gravy. No meat must ever be left to cool in the stewpan or saucepan in which it is cooked; it must be lifted into a pan of its own depth, and the liquor poured upon it.

A MINIATURE ROUND OF BEEF.

"Select a fine rib of beef, and have it cut small or large in width, according to your taste; it may thus be made to weigh from five to twelve pounds, or more. Take out the bone, and wrap the meat round like a fillet of veal, securing it with two or three wooden skewers; place it in a strong pickle for four or five days, and then cook it, taking care that it does not boil, but only simmers from forty minutes, or more, according to its size. It is best to put it on in hot water, as it will not draw the gravy so much as cold. Many persons adjust a rib of beef in this way for roasting: let them try it salted, and they need not envy the possessor of the finest round of beef." We give the receipt to our readers in its original form, and we can assure them, from our own experience, that it is a good one; but we would recommend that, in dressing the meat, quite the usual time for each pound of it should be allowed. When boned and rolled at the butcher's, the skewers should be removed when it is first brought in; it should be well wiped with a dry cloth, or washed with a little fresh brine, and a small quantity of salt and salt-petre should be rubbed over the inside; it may then be firmly bound with tape, and will be quite ready to boil when taken from the pickle. The sirloin, after the inside fillet is removed, may be cured and dressed in the same way, and will be found super-excellent, if the beef be well fatted and properly kept. The Hamburg pickle (see page 152,) is perhaps the best for these joints. Part of the rump, taken clear of bone, answers admirably when prepared by this receipt.

BEEF ROLL, OR, CANELLON DE BŒUF. (ENTRÉE.)

Chop and mix thoroughly two pounds of lean and very tender beef, with one pound of slightly striped bacon; season them with a large teaspoonful of pepper, a little salt, a small nutmeg, or two-thirds as much of mace, the grated rind of a lemon, or a teaspoonful of thyme and parsley finely minced. Form the whole into a thick rouleau, wrap a buttered paper round it, enclose it in a paste made of flour and water, and send it to a moderate oven for a couple of hours. Remove the paper and the crust, and serve the meat with a little brown gravy. Lamb and veal are excellent dressed in this way, particularly when mixed with plenty of mushrooms. Brown cucumber sauce should be served with the lamb; and currie, or oyster sauce, when there are no mushrooms, with the veal. A flavouring of onion or of eschalot, where it is liked, can be added at pleasure to the beef; suet, or the fat of the meat, may be substituted for the bacon.

Beef, 2 lbs.; bacon, 1 lb.; pepper, ¼ oz.; little salt; small nutmeg, rind of 1 lemon, or fine herbs, 1 tablespoonful: baked 2 hours.

MINCED COLLOPS AU NATUREL.

Mince finely a pound of very tender undressed beef, free from fat or skin; season it with a moderate quantity of pepper and salt, set it over a gentle fire, and keep it stirred with a fork until it is quite hot, that it may not gather into lumps. Simmer it very slowly in its own gravy from ten to twelve minutes, and then, should it be too dry, add a little boiling water, broth, or gravy; stew it two minutes longer, and serve it directly.

These collops are particularly suited to persons in delicate health, or of weak digestion; and when an extra dish is required at a short notice, from the expedition with which they may be dressed, they are a convenient resource.

10 to 12 minutes.

SAVOURY MINCED COLLOPS.

Make a little brown thickening (see page 92) with about an ounce and a half of butter, and a dessertspoonful of flour; when it begins to be coloured, shake lightly into it a large teaspoonful of finely-shred parsley or mixed savoury herbs, two-thirds as much of salt, and half the quantity of pepper. Keep these stirred over a gentle fire until the thickening is of a deep yellow brown; then add a pound of rump-steak, finely minced, and keep it well separated with a fork until it is quite hot; next pour to it gradually half a cupful of boiling water, and stew the collops very gently for ten minutes. Before they are served, stir to them a little catsup, Chili vinegar, or lemon-juice: a small quantity of minced onion, eschalot, or a *particle* of garlic, may be added at first to the thickening when the flavour is not objected to.

SCOTCH MINCED COLLOPS.

"Chop the beef small, season it with salt and pepper, put it, in its raw state, into small jars, and pour on the top some clarified butter. When wanted for use, put the clarified butter into a frying-pan, and slice some onions into the pan and fry them. Add a little water to them, and then put in the minced meat. Stew it well, and in a few minutes it will be fit to serve."

BEEF TONGUES.

These may be cured by any of the receipts which we have already given for pickling beef, or for those which will be found further on for hams and 'bacon. Some persons prefer them cured with salt and saltpetre only, and dried naturally in a cool and airy room. For such of our readers as like them highly and richly flavoured we give our own method of having them prepared, which is this:—" Rub over the tongue a handful of fine salt, and let it drain until the following day.; then, should it weigh from seven to eight pounds, mix thoroughly an ounce of saltpetre, two ounces of the coarsest sugar, and half an ounce of black pepper; when the tongue has been well rubbed with these, add three ounces of bruised juniper-berries; and when it has laid two days, eight ounces of bay salt, dried and pounded; at the end of three days more, pour on it half a pound of treacle, and let it remain in the pickle a fortnight after this; then hang it to drain, fold it in brown paper, and send it to be smoked over a wood fire for two or three weeks. Should the peculiar flavour of the juniper-berries prevail too much, or be disapproved, they may be in part, or altogether, omitted; and six ounces of sugar may be rubbed into the tongue in the first instance when it is liked better than treacle.

Tongue, 7 to 8 lbs.; saltpetre, 1 oz.; black pepper, ½ oz.; sugar, 2 ozs.; juniper-berries, 3 ozs.: 2 days. Bay salt, 8 ozs.: 3 days. Treacle, ½ lb.: 14 days.

Obs.—Before the tongue is salted, the gullet, which has an unsightly appearance, should be trimmed away: it is indeed usual to take the root off entirely, but some families prefer   left on for the sake of the fat.

BEEF TONGUES; (*a Suffolk receipt.*)

For each very large tongue, mix with half a pound of salt two ounces of saltpetre and three-quarters of a pound of the coarsest sugar; rub the tongues daily, and turn them in the pickle for five weeks, when they will be fit to be dressed, or to be smoked.

1 large tongue; salt, ½ lb.; sugar, ¾ lb.; saltpetre, 2 ozs.: 5 weeks

TO DRESS BEEF TONGUES.

When taken fresh from the pickle they require no soaking unless they should have remained in it much beyond the usual time, or have been cured with a more than common proportion of salt; but when they have been smoked and hung for some time, they should be laid for two or three hours in cold, and as much longer in tepid water, before they are dressed: if extremely dry, ten or twelve hours must be allowed to soften them, and they should always be brought very slowly to boil. Two or three carrots and a large bunch of savoury herbs, added after the scum is cleared off, will improve them. They should be simmered until they are extremely tender, when the skin will peel from them easily. A highly dried tongue will usually require from three and a half to four hours' boiling; an unsmoked one, about an hour less; and for one which has not been salted at all, a shorter time will suffice.

TO ROAST A BEEF HEART.

Wash and soak the heart very thoroughly, cut away the lobes, fill the cavities with a veal forcemeat (No. 1, page 126), secure it well with a needle and twine, or very coarse thread, and roast it at a good fire for an hour and a half, keeping it basted plentifully with butter. Pour melted butter over it, after it is dished, and send it to table as hot as possible. Many persons boil the heart for three quarters of an hour before it is put to the fire, and this is said to render it more delicate eating; the time of roasting must of course be proportionately diminished. Good brown gravy may be substituted for the melted butter, and currant jelly also may be served with it.

1½ hour, or more.

BEEF KIDNEY.

Trim, and cut the kidney into slices; season them with salt and pepper, and dredge them well with flour; fry them on both sides, and when they are done through, lift them out, empty the pan, and make a gravy for them with a small slice of butter, a dessertspoonful of flour, pepper and salt, and a cup of boiling water; shake these round and give them a minute's simmering: add a little mushroom catsup, lemon-juice, eschalot vinegar, or any store sauce that will give a good flavour. Minced herbs are to many tastes an improvement to this dish, to which a small quantity of onion shred fine can be added when it is liked.

6 to 9 minutes.

AN EXCELLENT HASH OF COLD BEEF.

Put a slice of butter into a thick saucepan, and when it boils throw in a dessertspoonful of minced herbs, and an onion (or two or three eschalots) shred small: shake them over the fire until lightly browned, then stir in a tablespoonful of flour, a little cayenne, some mace or nutmeg, and half a teaspoonful of salt. When the whole is well coloured, pour to it three quarters of a pint or more of broth or gravy, according to the quantity of meat to be served in it. Let this boil gently for fifteen minutes; then strain it; add half a wineglassful of mushroom or of compound catsup; lay in the meat, and keep it by the side of the fire until it is heated through and is on the point of simmering, but be sure not to let it boil. Put some fried or toasted sippets into a very hot dish, and serve the hash directly.

A COMMON HASH OF COLD BEEF OR MUTTON.

Take the meat from the bones, slice it small, trim off the brown edges, and stew down the trimmings with the bones well broken, an onion, a bunch of thyme and parsley, a carrot cut into thick slices, a few peppercorns, four cloves, some salt, and a pint and a half of water. When this is reduced to little more than three-quarters of a pint, strain it, clear it from the fat, thicken it with a large dessertspoonful of rice flour, or rather less of arrow-root; add salt and pepper if needed, boil the whole for a few minutes, then lay in the meat and heat it well. Boiled potatoes are sometimes sliced hot into a very common hash.

Obs.—The cook should be reminded that if the meat in a hash or mince be allowed to boil, it will immediately become hard, and can then only be rendered eatable by very *long stewing*, which is by no means desirable for meat which is already sufficiently done.

BRESLAW OF BEEF; (*good.*)

Trim the brown edges from half a pound of underdressed roast beef, shred it small, and mix it with four ounces of fine bread-crumbs, a teaspoonful of minced parsley, and two-thirds as much of thyme, two ounces of butter broken small, half a cupful of gravy or cream, a high seasoning of pepper and cayenne, and mace, or nutmeg, a small teaspoonful of salt, and three large eggs, well beaten. Melt a little butter in a pie dish, pour in the beef, and bake it half an hour; turn it out, and send it to table with brown gravy in a tureen. When cream or gravy is not at hand, an additional egg or two, and rather more butter, must be used. We think that grated lemon-rind improves the breslaw. A portion of fat from the joint can be added where it is liked. The mixture is sometimes baked in buttered cups.

Beef, ½ lb.; bread-crumbs, 4 ozs.; butter, 2 ozs.; gravy or cream, ½ cupful; parsley, 1 teaspoonful; thyme, two-thirds of teaspoonful; eggs, 3, or 4, if small; salt, 1 teaspoonful; pepper and nutmeg, ½ teaspoonful each: bake ½ hour.

NORMAN HASH.

Peel and fry two dozens of button onions in butter until they are lightly browned, then stir to them a tablespoonful of flour, and when the whole is of a deep amber shade, pour in a glass and a half of red wine, and a large cup of boiling broth or water; add a seasoning of salt and common pepper, or cayenne, and a little lemon-pickle, catsup, or lemon-juice, and boil the whole until the onions are quite tender; cut and trim into small handsome slices the remains of either a roast or boiled joint of beef, and arrange them in a clean saucepan; pour the gravy and onions on them, and let them stand for awhile to imbibe the flavour of the sauce; then place the hash near the fire, and when it is thoroughly hot serve it immediately, without allowing it to boil.

FRENCH RECEIPT FOR HASHED BOUILLI.

Shake over a slow fire a bit of butter the size of an egg, and a table-spoonful of flour; when they have simmered for a minute, stir to them a little finely-chopped onion, and a dessertspoonful of minced parsley; so soon as the whole is equally browned, add sufficient pepper, salt, and nutmeg to season the hash properly, and from half to three-quarters of a pint of boiling water or of bouillon. Put in the beef cut into small but thick slices; let it stand by the fire and heat gradually; and when near the point of boiling thicken the sauce with the yolks of three eggs, mixed with a tablespoonful of lemon-juice. For change, omit the eggs, and substitute a tablespoonful of catsup, and another of pickled gher-kins [small cucumbers], minced or sliced.

BAKED MINCED BEEF.

Mince tolerably fine, with a moderate proportion of its own fat, as much of the inside of a cold roast joint as will suffice for a dish: that which is least done is best for the purpose. Season it rather highly with cayenne and mace, or nutmeg, and moderately with salt; add, when they are liked, one or two eschalots, minced small, with a few chopped mushrooms, either fresh or pickled, or two tablespoonsful of mushroom catsup. Moisten the whole, mixing it well, with a cupful of *good* gravy, and put it into a deep dish. Place on the top an inch-thick layer of bread-crumbs; moisten these plentifully with clarified butter, passed through a small strainer over them, and send the mince to a slow oven for twenty minutes, or brown it in a Dutch oven.

TO BOIL MARROW BONES.

Let the large ends of the bones be sawed by the butcher, so that when they are dished they may stand upright; and if it can be done conveniently, let them be placed in the same manner in the vessel in which they are boiled. Put a bit of paste, made with flour and water, over the ends where the marrow is visible, and tie a cloth tightly over them; take the paste off before the bones are sent to table, and serve them, placed upright in a napkin, with slices of dry toasted bread, apart. When not wanted for immediate use, they may be partially boiled, and set into a cool place, where they will remain good for many days.

Large marrow bones, 2 hours; moderate sized, 1½ hour. To keep: boil them 1½ hour, and from ½ to ¾ hour more when wanted for table.

BAKED MARROW BONES.

When the bones have been sawed to the length of a deep pie dish, wash and wipe them dry, lay them into it, and cover them entirely with a good batter. Send them to a moderate oven for an hour or more, and serve them in the batter.

CLARIFIED MARROW FOR KEEPING.

Take the marrow from the bones while it is as fresh as possible; cut it small, put it into a very clean jar, and melt it with a gentle heat, either in a pan of water placed over the fire, or at the mouth of a cool oven; strain it through a muslin, let it settle for a minute or two, and pour it, clear of sediment, into small jars. Tie skins, or double folds of thick paper, over them as soon as the marrow is cold, and store it in a cool place. It will remain good for months.

CHAPTER IX.

VEAL.

No.
1. Loin, Best End.
2. Loin, Chump End.
3. Fillet.
4. Hind Knuckle.
5. Fore Knuckle.

No.
6. Neck, Best End.
7. Neck, Scrag End
8. Blade Bone.
9. Breast, Best End.
10. Breast, Brisket End

TO CHOOSE VEAL.

Veal should be fat, finely grained, white, firm, and not overgrown: for when very large it is apt to be coarse and tough. It is more difficult to keep than any other meat except pork, and should never be allowed to acquire the slightest taint before it is dressed, as any approach to putridity renders it equally unwholesome and offensive to the taste. The fillet, the loin, the shoulder, and the best end of the neck, are the parts generally selected for roasting; the breast and knuckle are more usually stewed or boiled. The udder, or firm white fat of the fillet, is much used by French cooks instead of butter, especially in the composition of their forcemeats: for these, it is first well boiled, then left until quite cold, and afterwards thoroughly pounded before it is mixed with the other ingredients. The head and feet of the calf are valuable articles of food, both for the nutriment which the gelatinous parts of them afford, and for the great variety of modes in which they may be dressed. The kidneys, with the rich fat that surrounds them, and the sweetbreads especially, are well known delicacies; the liver and the heart also are very good eating; and no meat is so generally useful for rich soups and gravies as veal.

TO TAKE THE HAIR FROM A CALF'S HEAD WITH THE SKIN ON.

It is better to do this before the head is divided; but if only the half of one with the skin on can be procured, it must be managed in the same way. Put it into plenty of water which is on the point of simmering, but which does not positively boil, and let it remain in until it does so, and for five or six minutes afterwards, but at the first full bubble draw it from the fire and let it merely scald; then lift it out, and with a knife that is *not* sharp scrape off the hair as closely and as quickly as possible. The butchers have an instrument on purpose for the operation; but we have had the head look quite as well when done in the manner we have just described, as when it has been sent in ready prepared by them. After the hair is off, the head should be well washed, and if it cannot be cooked the same day, it must be wiped extremely dry before it is hung up; and when it has not been divided, it should be left whole until the time approaches for dressing it. The brain must then be taken out, and both that and the head well soaked and washed with the greatest nicety. When the half head only is scalded, the brain should first be removed. Calves' feet are freed from the hair easily in the same manner; indeed, we find it a better mode of having it cleared from them·than the one we have given in Chapte⁻ XX., though that is practised by many good butchers.

BOILED CALF'S HEAD.

When the head is dressed with the skin on, which many persons prefer, the ear must be cut off quite close to it; it will require three quarters of an hour or upwards of additional boiling, and should be served covered with fried crumbs: the more usual mode, however, is to boil it without the skin. In either case, first remove the brain, wash the head delicately clean, and soak it for a quarter of an hour; cover it plentifully with cold water, remove the scum as it rises with great care, throw in a little salt, and boil the head gently until it is perfectly tender. In the mean time, wash and soak the brains first in cold and then in warm water, remove the skin or film, boil them in a small saucepan from fourteen to sixteen minutes, according to their size, and when they are done, chop and mix them with eight or ten sage leaves boiled tender, and finely minced, or, if preferred, with parsley boiled instead; warm them in a spoonful or two of melted butter, or white sauce; skin the tongue, trim off the root, and serve it in a small dish with the brains laid round it. Send the head to table very hot, with parsley and butter poured over it, and some more in a tureen. A cheek of bacon, or very delicate pickled pork, and greens, are the usual accompaniments to boiled calf's head.

We have given here the common English mode of serving this dish, by some epicures considered the best, and by others, as exceedingly insipid. On the Continent, tomata sauce takes the place of the parsley and butter; and rich oyster or Dutch sauce are varieties often substituted for it in this country.

With the skin on, from 2¼ to 2¾ hours; without the skin, from 1¼ to 1¾ hour.

CALF'S HEAD, THE WARDER'S WAY; (*an excellent receipt.*)

Boil the half-head until tolerably tender; let it cool, and bone it entirely; replace the brain, lay the head into a stewpan, and simmer it gently for an hour in rich gravy. From five and twenty to thirty minutes before it is dished, add, if procurable, half a pint of mushroom-buttons. Thicken the gravy, if needful, with rice-flour, or with flour and butter, and serve plenty of forcemeat-balls round the head. For dishes of this kind, a little sweet-basil wine, or a few sprigs of the herb itself, impart a very agreeable flavour. When neither these nor mushrooms are within reach, the very thin rind of a small but fresh lemon nay be boiled in the gravy, and the strained juice added at the instant if serving.

Boiled from 1 to 2 hours; stewed 1 hour.

Obs.—The skin, *with the ear,* may be left on the head for this receipt, and the latter slit into narrow strips from the tip to within an

10

Inch and a half of the base; which will give it a feathery and ornamental appearance: the head may then be glazed or not at pleasure.

PREPARED CALF'S HEAD; (*the Cook's receipt.*)

Take away the brains and tongue from the half of a calf's head, an
then remove the bones, being careful in doing so to keep the knife at
close to them as possible, and to avoid piercing the outer skin: in this
consists the whole art of boning, in which an attentive cook may easily
render herself expert. Next wash the head and dry it in a clean cloth;
sprinkle over the inside a little pounded mace and cayenne, or white
pepper; roll it up tightly, and bind it round with tape or twine. Lay
into a small stewpot three or four pounds of neck of veal or of beef,
twice or thrice divided, and place the head upon it with the bones well
oroken; pour in half a gallon of cold water, or as much as will suffice
to keep the head covered until it is done, and simmer it very gently
from an hour and a quarter to an hour and three quarters. When it is
extremely tender, lift it out, and if wanted for table, remove the bind-
ing, and serve it very hot, with currie sauce, rich oyster sauce, or egg
sauce and brown gravy; but should the remains, or the whole of it be
required for the following receipts, pour no gravy over it: in the latter
case do not take off the tape for several hours. The tongue may be
stewed with the head, but will require rather less time. We do not
think it needful to repeat in every receipt our directions for adding salt
to, and removing carefully the scum from, meats that are stewed or
ooiled, but the cook must not neglect either. When the trouble of
boning is objected to, it can be dispensed with for some of the dishes
which follow, but not for all. After the head is taken out, boil the
gravy until it is well reduced, and rich: it should be strongly jellied
when cold. A bone of ham, or a slice of hung beef will much improve
its flavour; but vegetables must be avoided if it be wanted to keep: a
little spice and a faggot of parsley may be added to it, and a calf's foot
will be sure to give it the requisite degree of firmness. This receipt
is for a head without the skin.

HASHED CALF'S HEAD.

When the whole of this dish has to be prepared, make for it a quart
of stock, and proceed in all else as in making mock turtle soup;
but after the head has been parboiled, cut down a full pound and
a half of it for the hash, and slice it small and thick, instead of dividing
it into dice. Make the brains into cakes (see page 126), and garnish the dish with forcemeat balls, rolled in egg, and in the finest
bread-crumbs, then fried a delicate brown, and well drained, and dried
upon a warm sieve reversed. The wine and other seasonings should
be the same as for the soup.

Rich gravy, 1 quart; flesh of calf's head, full 1½ lb.; wine, and
other seasonings, as for mock turtle soup.

Obs.—The gravy for this hash should be stewed with ham, eschalots,
&c., exactly as for the soup.

CHEAP HASH OF CALF'S HEAD.

Take the flesh from the bone of a cold boiled head, and put it aside
until wanted; take about three pints of the liquor in which it was

cooked; break the bones, and stew them down with a small bunch of
savoury herbs, a carrot, or two should they be small, a little carefully
fried onion, four cloves, a dozen corns of pepper, and either a slice or
two of lean unboiled ham, or the bone of a boiled one, quite cleared of
flesh, well bruised and broken, and freed carefully from any of the
smoked outsides. If neither of these can be had, from half to a whole
pound of neck of beef should be stewed with the bones, or the whole
will be insipid in flavour. When the liquid is reduced nearly half,
strain it, take off the fat, thicken it with a little well-made roux, or, if
more convenient, with flour and butter, stirred into it when it boils, or
with rice flour or arrow-root, mixed with a little spice, mushroom catsup, or Harvey's sauce, and a small quantity of lemon pickle or Chili
vinegar. Heat the meat slowly in the sauce when it is ready, but do
not allow it to boil. The forcemeat, No. 1. of Chapter VI., may be
rolled into balls, fried, and served round it. The gravy should be *well*
seasoned.

TO DRESS COLD CALF'S HEAD OR VEAL A LA MAITRE D'HOTEL.   (GOOD.)

(English receipt.)

Cut into small delicate slices, or into scollops of equal size, sufficient
cold calf's head or veal for a dish. Next knead very smoothly together
with a knife two ounces of butter, and a small dessertspoonful of flour;
put these into a stewpan or well-tinned saucepan, and keep them stirred
or shaken over a gentle fire until they have simmered for a minute or
two, but do not let them take the slightest colour; then add to them in
very small portions (letting the sauce boil up after each is poured in)
half a pint of pale veal gravy, or of good shin-of-beef stock, and when
the whole is very smoothly blended, and has boiled for a couple of minutes, mix together and stir to it a tablespoonful of common vinegar, a
dessertspoonful of Chili vinegar, a little cayenne, a tablespoonful of
good mushroom catsup, and a *very small* bit of sugar; and when the
sauce again boils, strew a tablespoonful of minced parsley over the
meat, lay it in, and let it stand by the fire until it is quite heated
through, but do not allow it to boil: if kept just at the simmering point
for ten or twelve minutes, it may be served perfectly hot without. The
addition of the mushroom catsup converts this into an English sauce,
and renders it in colour, as well as in flavour, unlike the French one
which bears the same name, and which is acidulated generally with
lemon-juice instead of vinegar. Pickled mushrooms are sometimes
added to the dish: the parsley when it is objected to may be omitted,
and the yolks of two or three eggs mixed with a little cream may be
stirred in, but not allowed to boil, just before the meat is served. When
veal is used for this hash instead of calf's head, it should be cut into
slices not much larger than a twenty-five cent piece, and freed entirely
from fat, sinew, and the brown edges. When neither broth nor gravy
is at hand, a morsel or two of lean ham, and a few of the trimmings or
bones of the head or joint, may be boiled down to supply its place.

Sufficient cold calf's head, or meat, for a dish; butter, 2 ozs.; flour,
1 small dessertspoonful; gravy, or strong broth, ½ pint; vinegar, and
mushroom catsup, of each 1 tablespoonful; Chili vinegar, 1 dessertspoonful; *small* bit of sugar; little cayenne, and salt if needed;
parsley, 1 tablespoonful (pickled mushrooms or not at pleasure).

Obs.—Soles or codfish are very good, if raised neatly from the bones, or *flaked*, and heated in this Mâitre d'Hotel sauce.

CALF'S HEAD BRAWN; (*author's receipt.*)

The half of a fine large calf's head, with the skin on, will best answer for this brawn. Take out the brains, and bone it entirely, or get the butcher to do this; rub a little fine salt over, and let it drain for ten or twelve hours; next wipe it dry, and rub it well in every part with three-quarters of an ounce of saltpetre finely powdered (or with an ounce should the head be *very* large) and mixed with four ounces of common salt, and three of bay salt, also beaten fine; turn the head daily in this pickle for four or five days, rubbing it a little each time; and then pour over it four ounces of treacle, and continue to turn it every day, and baste it with the brine very frequently for a month. Hang it up for a night to drain, fold it in brown paper, and send it to be smoked where wood only is burned, from three to four weeks. When wanted for table, wash and scrape it very clean, but do not soak it; lay it, with the rind downwards, into a saucepan or stewpan, which will hold it easily; cover it *well* with cold water, as it will swell considerably in the cooking; let it heat rather slowly, skim it thoroughly when it first begins to simmer, and boil it as gently as possible from an hour and three-quarters to a couple of hours, or more, should it not then be *perfectly* tender quite through; for unless sufficiently boiled, the skin, which greatly resembles brawn, will be unpleasantly tough when cold. When the fleshy side of the head is done, which will be twenty minutes or half an hour sooner than the outside, pour the water from it, leaving so much only in the stewpan as will just cover the gelatinous part, and simmer it until this is thoroughly tender. The head thus cured is very highly flavoured, and most excellent eating. The receipt for it is entirely new, having originated with ourselves. We give the reader, in addition, the result of our first experiment with it, which was exceedingly successful:—"A half calf's head, not very large, without the skin, pickled with three ounces of common salt, two of bay salt, half an ounce of saltpetre, one ounce of brown sugar, and *half an ounce of pepper*, left four days; then three ounces of treacle added, and the pickling continued for a month; smoked nearly as long, and boiled between one hour and a half, and two hours." The pepper was omitted in our second trial, because it did not improve the appearance of the dish, although it was an advantage in point of flavour. Juniper-berries might, we think, be added with advantage, when they are liked; and cayenne tied in a muslin might supply the place of the pepper. It is an infinite improvement to have the skin of the head left on.

TO ROAST A FILLET OF VEAL.

Take out the bone and put a good roll of forcemeat (No. 1, page 122) under the flap, dividing first, with a sharp knife, the skin from the meat sufficiently to admit the quantity required; secure it well, truss the veal firmly into good shape, place it at a distance from the fire at first, and baste it with butter. The outside will have a richer crust of browning if the meat be washed, wiped tolerably dry, and well floured before it is laid to the fire. It should be carefully watched, and basted often, that the fat may not burn. Pour melted butter over it after it is dished, and serve with it a boiled cheek of bacon and a lemon. Roast it from three hours and a half, to four hours and a half, according to its size.

BOILED FILLET OF VEAL.

A small and delicately white fillet should be selected for this purpose. Bind it round with tape, after having washed it thoroughly; cover it well with cold water, and bring it gently to boil; watch, and clear off carefully, the scum as it rises, and be, at the same time, very cautious not to allow the water to become smoked. Let the meat be *gently simmered* from three hours and a half to four and a half, according to its weight. Send it to table with rich white sauce, and a boiled tongue; or make for it in the first instance the oyster forcemeat of Chapter VI., and serve with the veal a tureen of well-made oyster sauce.

3½ to 4½ hours.

ROAST LOIN OF VEAL.

It is not usual to stuff a loin of veal, but we greatly recommend the practice, as an infinite improvement to the joint. Make the same forcemeat as for the fillet; and insert it between the skin and the flesh just over the ends of the bones. Skewer down the flap, place the joint at a moderate distance from a sound fire, keep it constantly basted, and be especially careful not to allow the kidney fat to burn: to prevent this, and to ensure the good appearance of the joint, a buttered paper is often fastened round the loin, and removed about half an hour before it is taken from the fire. It is the fashion in some counties to serve *egg-sauce* and brown gravy with roast loin, or breast of veal.

The cook will scarcely need to be told that she must separate the skin from the flank, with a sharp knife, quite from the end, to the place where the forcemeat is to be put, and then skewer the whole very securely. When the veal is not papered, dredge it well with flour soon after it is laid to the fire.

2 to 2½ hours.

BOILED LOIN OF VEAL.

If dressed with care and served with good sauces, this, when the meat is small and white, is an excellent dish, and often more acceptable to persons of delicate habit than roast veal. Take from eight to ten pounds of the best end of the loin, leave the kidney in with all its fat, skewer or bind down the flap, lay the meat into cold water, and boil it as *gently as possible* from two hours and a quarter to two and a half, clearing off the scum perfectly, as in dressing the fillet. Send it to table with well-made oyster sauce, or béchamel, or with white sauce well flavoured with lemon-juice, and with parsley, boiled, pressed dry, and finely chopped.

2¼ to 2½ hours.

STEWED LOIN OF VEAL.

Take part of a loin of veal, the chump end will do; put into a large, thick, well-tinned iron saucepan, or into a stewpan, about a couple of ounces of butter, and shake it over a moderate fire until it begins to brown; flour the veal well all over, lay it into the saucepan, and when it is of a fine, equal light-brown, pour gradually in veal broth, gravy, or boiling water to nearly half its depth; add a little salt, one or two sliced carrots, a small onion, or more when the flavour is much liked, and a bunch of parsley; stew the veal very softly for an hour or rather more; then turn it, and let it stew for nearly or quite another hour, or longer should it not appear perfectly done. As none of our receipts have been tried with large, coarse veal, the cooking must be regulated by that circumstance, and longer time allowed should the meat be of more than middling size. Dish the joint; skim all the fat from the gravy, and strain it over the meat; or keep the joint hot while it is rapidly reduced to a richer consistency. This is merely a plain family stew.

BOILED BREAST OF VEAL.

Let both the veal and the sweetbread be washed with exceeding nicety, cover them with cold water, clear off the scum as it rises, throw in a *little* salt, add a bunch of parsley, a large blade of mace, and twenty white peppercorns; simmer the meat from an hour to an hour and a quarter, and serve it covered with rich onion sauce. Send it to table very hot. The sweetbread may be taken up when half done, and curried, or made into cutlets, or stewed in brown gravy. When onions are objected to, substitute white sauce and a cheek of bacon for them, or parsley and butter, if preferred to it.

1 to 1¼ hour.

TO ROAST A BREAST OF VEAL.

Let the caul remain skewered over the joint till within half an hour of its being ready for table; place it at a moderate distance from a brisk fire, baste it constantly, and in about an hour and a half remove the caul, flour the joint, and let it brown. Dish and pour melted butter over it, and serve it with a cut lemon, and any other of the usual accompaniments to veal. It may be garnished with fried balls of the forcemeat (No. 1, Chapter VI.), about the size of a walnut.

2 to 2½ hours.

TO BONE A SHOULDER OF VEAL, MUTTON OR LAMB.

Spread a clean cloth upon a table or dresser, and lay the joint flat upon it, with the skin downwards; with a sharp knife cut off the flesh from the inner side, nearly down to the blade bone, of which detach the edges first, then work the knife *under* it, keeping it always *close to the bone*, and using all possible precaution not to pierce the outer skin; when it is in every part separated from the flesh, loosen it from the socket with the point of

Shoulder of Veal or Mutton, the knife, and remove it; or, without dividing the two bones, cut round the joint until it is freed entirely from the meat, and proceed to detach the second bone. That of the knuckle is frequently left in, but for some dishes it is necessary to take it out; in doing this, be careful not to tear the skin. A most excellent grill may be made by leaving sufficient meat for it upon the bones of a shoulder of mutton, when they are removed from the joint: it will be found very superior to the broiled blade-bone of a *roast* shoulder, which is so much esteemed by many people.

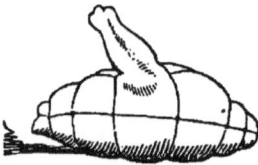

STEWED SHOULDER OF VEAL; (*English receipt.*)

Bone a shoulder of veal, and strew the inside thickly with savoury herbs, minced small; season it well with salt, cayenne, and pounded mace; and place on these a layer of ham cut in thin slices, and freed from rind and rust. Roll the veal, and bind it tightly with a fillet; roast it for an hour and a half, then simmer it gently in good brown gravy for five hours; add forcemeat balls before it is dished; skim the fat from the gravy, and serve it with the meat. This receipt, for which we are indebted to a correspondent on whom we can depend, and which we have not, therefore, proved ourselves, is for a joint which weighs ten pounds before it is boned.

ROAST NECK OF VEAL.

The best end of the neck will make an excellent roast. A forcemeat may be inserted between the skin and the flesh, by first separating them with a sharp knife; or the dish may be garnished with the forcemeat in balls. From an hour and three-quarters to a couple of hours will roast it. Pour melted butter over it when it is dished, and serve it like other joints. Let it be floured when first laid to the fire, kept constantly basted, and always at a sufficient distance to prevent its being scorched.

1¾ to 2 hours.

For the forcemeat, see No. 1, Chapter VI. From 8 to 10 minutes will fry the balls.

KNUCKLE OF VEAL; (en *Ragout.*)

Cut in small thick slices the flesh of a knuckle of veal, season it with a little fine salt and white pepper, flour it lightly, and fry it in butter to a pale brown, lay it into a very clean stewpan or saucepan, and just cover it with boiling water; skim it clean, and add to it a faggot of thyme and parsley, the white part of a head of celery, a small quantity of cayenne, and a blade or two of mace. Stew it very softly from an hour and three-quarters, to two hours and a half. Thicken and enrich the gravy if needful with rice-flour and mushroom catsup or Harvey's sauce, or with a large teaspoonful of flour, mixed with a slice of butter, a little good store-sauce and a glass of sherry or Madeira. Fried forcemeat balls of No. 1, page 122, may be added at pleasure. With an additional quantity of water, or of broth (made with the bones of the joint), a pint and a half of young green peas stewed with the veal for an hour will give an agreeable variety of this dish.

BOILED KNUCKLE OF VEAL.

After the joint has been trimmed and well washed, put it into a vessel well adapted to it in size, for if it be very large, so much water will be required that the veal will be deprived of its flavour; it should be well covered with it, and *very gently* boiled until it is perfectly tender in every part, but not so much done as to separate from the bone. Clear off the scum with scrupulous care when the simmering first commences, and throw in a small portion of salt; as this, if sparingly used, will not redden the meat, and will otherwise much improve it. Parsley and butter is usually both poured over, and sent to table with a knuckle of veal, and boiled bacon also should accompany it. From the sinewy nature of this joint, it requires more than the usual time of cooking, a quarter of an hour to the pound not being sufficient for it.

Veal, 6 to 7 lbs.: 2 hours or more.

KNUCKLE OF VEAL WITH RICE OR GREEN PEAS.

Pour over a small knuckle of veal rather more than sufficient water to cover it; bring it slowly to a boil; take off all the scum with great care, throw in a teaspoonful of salt, and when the joint has simmered for about half an hour, throw in from eight to twelve ounces of well-washed rice, and stew the veal gently for an hour and a half longer, or until both the meat and rice are perfectly tender. A seasoning of cayenne and mace in fine powder with more salt, should it be required, must be added twenty or thirty minutes before they are served. For a superior stew, good veal broth may be substituted for the water.

Veal, 6 lbs.; water, 3 to 4 pints; salt, 1 teaspoonful: 30 to 40 minutes. Rice, 8 to 12 ozs.: 1½ hour. Seasoning of cayenne, mace, and more salt if needed. A quart or even more of full-grown green peas added to the veal as soon as the scum has been cleared off will make a most excellent stew. It should be well seasoned with white pepper, and the mace should be omitted. Two or three cucumbers, pared and freed from the seeds, may be sliced into it when it boils, or four or five young lettuces shred small may be used to give it flavour.

BORDYKE VEAL CAKE; (good.)

Take a pound and a half of veal perfectly clear of fat and skin, and eight ounces of the nicest striped bacon; chop them separately, then mix them well together with the grated rind of a small lemon, half a teaspoonful of salt, a fourth as much of cayenne, the third part of a nutmeg, grated, and a half-teaspoonful of freshly pounded mace. When it is pressed into the dish, let it be somewhat higher in the centre than at the edge; and whether to be served hot or cold, lift it out as soon as it comes from the oven, and place it on a strainer that the fat may drain from it: it will keep many days if the under side be dry. The bacon should be weighed after the rind, and any rust it may exhibit, have been trimmed from it: that cured by the East Farleigh receipt, (see Chapter XI.) is best for the purpose. This cake is excellent cold, better indeed than the preceding one; but slices of either if preferred hot, may be warmed through in a Dutch oven, or on the gridiron, or in a few spoonsful of gravy. The same ingredients made into small cakes, well floured, and slowly fried from twelve to fifteen minutes, then served with gravy made in the pan as for cutlets, will be found extremely good.

Veal, 1½ lb.; striped bacon, 8 ozs.; salt and mace, 1 teaspoonful each; rind of lemon, 1; third of 1 nutmeg; cayenne, 4 grains: baked 1¼ to 1½ hour.

FRICANDEAU OF VEAL. (ENTRÉE.)

French cooks always prefer for this dish, which is a common one in their own country, that part of the fillet to which the fat or udder is attached;* but the flesh of the finer part of the neck, or loin, raised clear from the bones, may be made to answer the purpose nearly, or quite as well, and often much more conveniently, as the meat with us is not divided for sale as in France; and to purchase the entire fillet, for the sake of the fricandeau, would render it exceedingly expensive Lay the veal flat upon a table, or dresser, with the skin uppermost, and

---

* Called by them the noix.

endeavour, with one stroke of an exceedingly sharp knife, to clear this off, and to leave the surface of the meat extremely smooth; next lard it thickly with small *lardoons*, as directed for a partridge (page 140,) and make one or two incisions in the under side with the point of a knife, that it may the better imbibe the flavour of the seasonings. Take a stewpan, of sufficient size to hold the fricandeau, and the proper quantity of vegetables compactly arranged, without much room being left round the meat. Put into it a couple of large carrots, cut in thick slices, two onions of moderate size, two or three roots of parsley, three bay-leaves, two small blades of mace, a branch or two of lemon thyme, and a little cayenne, or a saltspoonful of white peppercorns. Raise these high in the centre of the stewpan, so as to support the meat, and prevent its touching the gravy. Cover them with slices of very fat bacon, and place the fricandeau gently on them ; then pour in as much good veal broth, or stock, as will nearly cover the vegetables without reaching to the veal. A calf's foot, split in two, may with advantage be laid under them in the first instance. Stew the fricandeau *very* gently for upwards of three hours, or until it is found to be extremely tender when probed with a fine skewer or a larding-pin. Plenty of live embers must then be put on the lid of the stewpan for ten minutes, or a quarter of an hour, to render the lardoons firm. Lift out the fricandeau, and keep it hot; strain and reduce the gravy very quickly, after having skimmed off every particle of fat; glaze the veal, and serve it on a ragout of sorrel, cucumbers, or spinach. This, though rather an elaborate receipt, is the best we can offer to the reader for a dish, which is now almost as fashionable with us as it is common on the Continent. Some English cooks have a very summary method of preparing it; they merely lard and boil the veal until they can "cut it with a spoon," then glaze and serve it with "brown gravy in the dish." This may be very tolerable eating, but it will bear small resemblance to the French fricandeau.

3½ to 4 hours.

SPRING-STEW OF VEAL.

Cut two pounds of veal, free from fat, into small half-inch thick cutlets; flour them well, and fry them in butter with two small cucumbers sliced, sprinkled with pepper, and floured, one moderate sized lettuce, and twenty-four green gooseberries cut open lengthwise and seeded. When the whole is nicely browned, lift it into a thick saucepan, and pour gradually into the pan half a pint, or rather more, of boiling water, broth, or gravy. Add as much salt and pepper as it requires. Give it a minute's simmer, and pour it over the meat, shaking it well round the pan as this is done. Let the veal stew gently from three quarters of an hour to an hour. A bunch of green onions cut small may be added to the other vegetables if liked ; and the veal will eat better if slightly seasoned with salt and pepper before it is floured ; a portion of fat can be left on it if preferred.

Veal, 2 lbs.; cucumbers, 2; lettuce, 1; green gooseberries, 24; water or broth, ½ pint or more: ¾ to 1 hour.

NORMAN HARRICO.

Brown in a stewpan, or fry lightly, after having sprinkled them with pepper, salt and flour, from two to three pounds of veal cutlets. If taken from the neck, chop the bones very short, and trim away the greater part of the fat. Arrange them as flat as they can be in a saucepan; give a pint of hot water a boil in the pan in which they have been browned, and pour it on them; add a small faggot of parsley, and, should the flavour be liked, one of green onions also. Let the meat simmer softly for half an hour; then cover it with small new potatoes which have had a single boil in water, give the saucepan a shake, and let the harrico stew very gently for another half hour, or until the potatoes are quite done, and the veal is tender. When the cutlets are thick and the potatoes approaching their full size, more time will be required for the meat, and the vegetables may be at once divided: if extremely young they will not need the previous boil. Before the harrico is served, skim the fat from it, and add salt and pepper should it not be sufficiently seasoned. A few bits of lean ham, or shoulder of bacon browned with the veal, will much improve this dish, and for some tastes, a little acid will render it more agreeable. Very delicate pork chops may be dressed in the same way.

Veal, 2 to 3 lbs.; water (or gravy), 1 pint; new potatoes, 1½ to 2 lbs.; faggot, parsley and green onions: 1 hour or more.

VEAL CUTLETS.

Take them, if possible, free from bone, and after having trimmed them into proper shape, beat them with a paste roller until the fibre of the meat is thoroughly broken; flour them well to prevent the escape of the gravy, and fry them from twelve to fifteen minutes over a fire which is not sufficiently fierce to burn them before they are quite cooked through: they should be of a fine amber brown, and *perfectly done*. Lift them into a hot dish, pour the fat from the pan, throw in a slice of fresh butter, and when it is melted, stir or dredge in a dessertspoonful of flour; keep these shaken until they are well coloured, then pour gradually to them a cup of gravy or boiling water; add pepper, salt, a little lemon pickle or juice, give the whole a boil, and pour it over the cutlets: a few forcemeat-balls, fried, and served with them, is usually a very acceptable addition to this dish, even when it is garnished or accompanied with rashers of ham or bacon. A morsel of *glaze*, or of the jelly of roast meat, should, when at hand, be added to the sauce, which a little mushroom powder would further improve: mushroom sauce, indeed, is considered by many epicures as indispensable with veal cutlets. We have recommended, in this one instance, that the meat should be thoroughly *beaten*, because we find that the veal is wonderfully improved by the process, which, however, we still deprecate for other meat.

12 to 15 minutes.

VEAL CUTLETS, OR COLLOPS. (ENTRÉE.) (*A la Française.*)

Cut the veal into small, thin, round collops of equal size, arrange them evenly in a sauté-pan, or in a small frying-pan, and sprinkle a little fine salt, white pepper, and grated nutmeg on them. Clarify, or merely dissolve in a clean saucepan, with a gentle degree of heat, an ounce or two of good butter, and pour it equally over the meat. Set the pan aside until the dinner-hour, then fry the collops over a clear fire, and when they are lightly browned, which will be in from four to five minutes, lift them into a hot dish, and sauce them with a little *Espagnole*, or with a gravy made quickly in the pan, and flavoured with lemon-juice and cayenne. They are excellent even without any sauce.

3 to 4 minutes.

SCOTCH COLLOPS. (ENTRÉE.)

Prepare the veal as for the preceding receipt, but dip the collops into beaten egg and seasoned bread-crumbs, and fry them directly in good butter, over a moderate fire, of a light golden brown; drain them well in lifting them from the pan, and sauce them like the collops *à la Française*.

VEAL CUTLETS, A LA MODE DE LONDRES; OR, LONDON FASHION. (ENTRÉE.)

Raise the flesh entire from the upper side of the best end of a neck of veal, free it from the skin, and from the greater portion of the fat, slice it equally into cutlets little more than a quarter of an inch thick, brush them with egg, strew them with fine bread-crumbs, and fry them of a light brown. Toast, or fry apart as many small slices of bacon as there are cutlets, and let them be trimmed nearly to the same shape; place them alternately on their edges round the inside of a hot dish (so as to form a sort of chain), and pour into the middle some rich gravy made in the pan, and very slightly flavoured with eschalot; or substitute for this some good brown mushroom sauce. Savoury herbs, grated lemon-rind, nutmeg, or mace, salt, and white pepper, or cayenne, should be mixed with the bread-crumbs, in the proper proportions, for cutlets of calf's head; or they may be varied at pleasure. A cheek of bacon is best adapted to this dish.

SWEETBREADS. (ENTRÉE.) *(Simply dressed.)*

In whatéver way sweetbreads are dressed, they should first be well soaked in lukewarm water, then thrown into boiling water to *blanch* them, as it is called, and to render them firm. If lifted out after they have boiled from five to ten minutes, according to their size, and laid immediately into fresh spring water to cool, their colour will be the better preserved. They may then be gently stewed for three quarters of an hour in veal gravy, which, with the usual additions of cream, lemon, and egg-yolks, may be converted into a fricassee sauce for them when they are done; or they may be lifted from it, *glazed*, and served with good Spanish gravy; or, the glazing being omitted, they may be sauced with the sharp *Maître d'Hôtel* sauce of page 99. They may also be simply floured, and roasted in a Dutch oven, being often basted with butter, and frequently turned. A full sized sweetbread, after having been blanched, will require quite three quarters of an hour to dress it.

Blanched 5 to 10 minutes. Stewed ¾ hour or more.

SWEETBREAD CUTLETS. (ENTRÉE.)

Boil the sweetbreads for half an hour in water, or veal broth, and when they are perfectly cold, cut them into slices of equal thickness, brush them with yolks of egg, and dip them into very fine bread-crumbs, seasoned with salt, cayenne, grated lemon-rind, and mace; fry them in butter of a fine light brown, arrange them in a dish, placing them high in the centre, and pour *under* them a gravy made in the pan, thickened with mushroom powder, and flavoured with lemon-juice; or, in lieu of this, sauce them with some rich brown gravy, to which a glass of sherry or Madeira has been added. When it can be done conveniently, take as many slices of a cold boiled tongue as there are sweetbread cutlets; pare the rind from them, trim them into good shape, and dress them with the sweetbreads, after they have been egged and seasoned in the same way; place each cutlet upon a slice of tongue when they are dished. For variety, substitute *croutons* of fried bread, stamped out to the size of the cutlets, with a round or fluted paste or cake cutter. The crumb of a stale loaf, very evenly sliced, is best for the purpose.

STEWED CALF'S FEET; (*cheap and good.*)

This is an excellent family dish, highly nutritious, and often very inexpensive, as the feet, during the summer, are usually sold at a low rate. Wash them with nicety, divide them at the joint, and split the claws; arrange them closely in a thick stewpan or saucepan, and pour in as much cold water as will cover them about half an inch: three pints will be sufficient for a couple of large feet. When broth or stock is at hand it is good economy to substitute it for the water, as, by this means, a portion of strong and well-flavoured jellied gravy will be obtained for general use, the full quantity not being needed as sauce for the feet. The whole preparation will be much improved by laying a thick slice of the lean of an unboiled ham, knuckle of bacon, hung beef, or the end of a dried tongue, at the bottom of the pan, before the other ingredients are added; or, when none of these are at hand, by supplying the deficiency with a few bits of stewing-beef or veal: the feet being of themselves insipid, will be much more palatable with one or the other of these additions. Throw in from half to three quarters of a teaspoonful of salt when they begin to boil, and, after the scum has been all cleared off, add a few branches of parsley, a little celery, one small onion or more, stuck with half a dozen cloves, a carrot or two, a large blade of mace, and twenty corns of whole pepper; stew them softly until the flesh will part entirely from the bones; take it from them; strain part of the gravy, and skim off all the fat, flavour it with catsup, or any other store sauce, and thicken it, when it boils, with arrow-root, or flour and butter; put in the flesh of the feet, and serve the dish as soon as the whole is very hot. A glass of wine, a little lemon-juice, and a few forcemeat-balls, will convert this into a very superior stew; a handful of mushroom-buttons also simmered in it for half an hour before it is dished will vary it agreeably.

Calf's feet (large), 2; water, 3 pints; salt, $\frac{1}{2}$ to $\frac{3}{4}$ teaspoonful; onions, 1 to 3; cloves, 6; peppercorns, 20; mace, large blade; little celery and parsley; carrots, 1 or 2: stewed softly, $2\frac{1}{2}$ to $3\frac{1}{4}$ hours. Mushroom catsup, 1 tablespoonful; flour, or arrow-root, 1 large teaspoonful· butter, 1 to 2 ozs. Cayenne, to taste.

CALF'S LIVER FRIED.

To render the liver firm when dressed, lay it into a deep dish, and pour over it half a pint of vinegar; turn it often in this, and let it lie for four and twenty hours, or longer even, if more convenient. Sliced onions, or eschalots, and branches of parsley, may be steeped with it in the vinegar, when their flavour is relished; but, in general, they would not, we think, be considered an improvement. Wash and wipe the liver very dry, slice it evenly, season it with pepper, salt, and savoury herbs shred extremely small, then flour and fry it in butter quickly of a fine light brown; lift it out and keep it very hot, while a gravy is made for it in the pan. Pour out the fat, throw in a small slice of fresh butter, and when it boils stir to it a half-teaspoonful of flour; add a seasoning of pepper and salt; about a quarter-pint of boiling water, and a little lemon-juice, Chili vinegar, or lemon-pickle; shake the pan well round, give the whole a boil; sauce the liver with it, and send it to table with or without a garnish of curled bacon.

TO ROAST CALF'S LIVER.

Take the whole or part of a fine white sound liver, and either lard it as a fricandeau upon the surface, or with large strips of highly-seasoned bacon in the inside (see Larding, page 139); or should either of these modes be objected to, merely wrap it in a well-buttered paper, and roast it from an hour to an hour and a quarter, at a moderate distance from a clear fire, keeping it constantly basted. Remove the paper, and froth the liver well from ten to fifteen minutes before it is done. It should be served with a sauce of some piquancy, such as a poivrade, or brown eschalot, in addition to some good gravy. French cooks steep the liver over-night in vinegar, with a sliced onion and branches of savoury herbs laid over it; this whitens and renders it firm. As an economical mode, some small bits of the liver may be trimmed off, floured, and lightly fried with a sliced onion, and stewed down for gravy in three quarters of a pint of water which has been poured into the pan, with the addition of a few peppercorns, and a small bunch of herbs. A seasoning of salt must not be forgotten, and a little lemon-pickle, or juice, would generally be considered an improvement.

1 to 1¼ hour.

BLANQUETTE OF VEAL OR LAMB, WITH MUSHROOMS. (ENTRÉE.)

Slice very thin the white part of some cold veal, divide and trim it into scallops not larger than a shilling, and lay it into a clean saucepan or stewpan. Wipe with a bit of new flannel and a few grains of salt, from a quarter to half a pint of mushroom-buttons, and slice them into a little butter which just begins to simmer; stew them to it from twelve to fifteen minutes, without allowing them to take the slightest colour; then lift them out and lay them on the veal. Pour boiling to them a pint of sauce tournée (see page 93); let the blanquette remain near but not close to the fire for awhile; bring it nearer, heat it slowly, and when it is on the point of boiling mix a spoonful or two of the sauce from it with the well-beaten yolks of four fresh eggs; stir them to the remainder; add the strained juice of half a small lemon; shake the saucepan above the fire until the sauce is just set, and serve the blanquette instantly.

Cold veal, ¾ lb.; mushrooms, ¼ to ½ pint: stewed in 1½ oz. butter, 12 to 15 minutes. Sauce tournée, or thickened veal gravy, 1 pint; yolks of eggs, 4; lemon-juice, 1 tablespoonful.

Obs.—Any white meat may be served *en blanquette*. The mushrooms are not indispensable for it, but they are always a great improvement. White sauce substituted for the thickened veal gravy will at once convert this dish into an inexpensive fricassée. Mace, salt, and cayenne, must be added to either preparation, should it require seasoning.

MINCED VEAL.

When there is neither gravy nor broth at hand, the bones and trimmings of the meat must be boiled down to furnish what is required for the mince. As cold meat is very light in weight, a pound of the white part of the veal will be sufficient for a dish, and for this quantity a pint of gravy will be needed. Break down the bones of the joint well, add the trimmings of the meat, a small bunch of savoury herbs, a slice or two of carrot or of celery, a blade of mace, a few white peppercorns, and a bit or two of lean ham, boiled, or unboiled if it can be had, as either will improve the flavour of the mince. Pour to these a pint and a half of water, and stew them gently for a couple of hours; then strain off the gravy, let it cool and clear it entirely from the fat. Cut the white part of the veal small with a very sharp knife, after all the gristle and brown edges have been trimmed away. Some persons like a portion of fat minced with it, others object to the addition altogether. Thicken the gravy with a teaspoonful and a half of flour smoothly mixed with a small slice of butter, season the veal with a saltspoonful or more of salt, and half as much white pepper and grated nutmeg, or pounded mace; add the lightly-grated rind of half a small lemon; mix the whole well, put it into the gravy, and heat it thoroughly by the side of the fire without allowing it to boil; serve it with pale-toasted sippets in and round the dish. A spoonful or two of cream is always an improvement to this mince.

MINCED VEAL AND OYSTERS.

The most elegant mode of preparing this dish is to mince about a pound of the whitest part of the inside of a cold roast fillet or loin of veal, to heat it without allowing it to boil, in a pint of rich white sauce, or béchamel, and to mix with it at the moment of serving three dozens of small oysters ready bearded, and plumped in their own strained liquor, which is also to be added to the mince; the requisite quantity of salt, cayenne, and mace should be sprinkled over the veal before it is put into the sauce. Garnish the dish with pale fried sippets of bread, or with *fleurons** of brioche, or of puff-paste. Nearly half a pint of mushrooms minced, and stewed white in a little butter, may be mixed with the veal instead of the oysters; or should they be very small they may be added to it whole: from ten to twelve minutes will be sufficient to make them tender. Balls of delicately fried oyster-forcemeat laid round the dish will give another good variety of it.

Veal minced, 1 lb.; white sauce, 1 pint; oysters, 3 dozens, with their liquor; or mushrooms, ½ pint, stewed in butter 10 to 12 minutes.

VEAL-SYDNEY. (GOOD.)

Pour boiling on an ounce and a half of fine bread-crumbs nearly half a pint of good veal stock or gravy, and let them stand till cool; mix with them then, two ounces of beef-suet shred very small, half a

* *Fleurons,* flowers, or flower-like figures, cut out with tin shapes.

pound of cold roast veal carefully trimmed from the brown edges, skin, and fat, and finely minced; the grated rind of half a lemon, nearly a teaspoonful of salt, a little cayenne, the third of a teaspoonful of mace or nutmeg, and four well-beaten eggs. Whisk up the whole well together, put it into a buttered dish, and bake it from three quarters of an hour to an hour. Cream may be used instead of gravy when more convenient, but this last will give the better flavour. A little clarified butter put into the dish before the other ingredients are poured in will be an improvement.

Bread-crumbs, 1½ oz.; gravy or cream, nearly ½ pint; beef-suet, 2 ozs.; cold veal, ½ lb.; rind of ½ lemon; salt, small teaspoonful; third as much mace and nutmeg; little cayenne; eggs, 4 large or 5 small: ¾ to 1 hour.

FRICASSEED VEAL.

Divide into small, thick, handsome slices of equal size, about a couple of pounds of veal, quite free from fat, bone, and skin; dissolve a couple of ounces of butter in a wide stewpan, and just as it begins to boil lay in the veal, and shake it over the fire until it is quite firm on both sides; but do not allow it to take the slightest colour. Stir in a tablespoonful of flour, and when it is well mixed with the cutlets, pour gradually to them, shaking the pan often, sufficient boiling veal gravy to almost cover them. Stew them gently from fifty to sixty minutes, or longer should they not be perfectly tender. Add a flavouring of mace, some salt, a quarter-pint of rich cream, a couple of egg-yolks, and a little lemon-juice, observing, when the last are added, the directions given for a blanquette of veal, page 173. Strips of lemon-rind can be stewed in the gravy at pleasure. Two or three dozens of mushroom-buttons, added twenty minutes before it is served, will much improve this fricassee.

CHAPTER X.
MUTTON.

No.
1. Leg.
2. Best End of Loin.
3. Chump End of Loin.
4. Neck, Best End.
5. Neck, Scrag End.

No.
6. Shoulder.
7. Breast.
A Saddle is the Two Loins.
A Chine, the Two Necks.

TO CHOOSE MUTTON.

THE best mutton is small-boned, plump, finely-grained, and short legged: the lean of a dark, rather than of a bright hue, and the fat white and clear: when this is yellow, the meat is rank, and of bad quality. Mutton is not considered by experienced judges to be in perfection until it is nearly or quite five years old; but to avoid the additional expense of feeding the animal so long, it is commonly brought into the market at three years old. The leg and the loin are the superior joints; and the preference would probably be given more frequently to the latter, but for the superabundance of its fat, which renders it a not very economical dish. The haunch consists of the leg and the part of the loin adjoining it; the saddle, of the two loins together, or of the undivided *back* of the sheep: these last are always roasted, and are served usually at good tables, or for company-dinners, instead of the smaller joints. The shoulder, dressed in the ordinary way, is not very highly esteemed; but when boned, rolled, and filled with forcemeat, it is of more presentable appearance, and to many tastes, far better eating; though some persons prefer it in its natural form, accompanied by stewed onions. It is occasionally boiled or stewed, and covered with rich onion sauce. The neck is sometimes roasted, but it is more generally boiled; the scrag, or that part of it which joins the head, is seldom used for any other purpose than making broth, and should be taken off before the joint is dressed. Cutlets from the thick end of the loin are commonly preferred to any others, but they are frequently taken likewise from the best end of the neck (sometimes called the *back-ribs*) and from the middle of the leg. Mutton kidneys are dressed in various ways, and are excellent in many. The trotters and the head of a sheep may be converted into very good dishes, but they are scarcely worth the trouble which is required to render them palatable. The loin and the leg are occasionally cured and smoked like hams or bacon.

TO ROAST A HAUNCH OF MUTTON.

This joint should be well kept, and when the larder-accommodations of a house are not good, the butcher should be requested to hang it the the proper time. Roast it carefully at a large sound fire, and let it remain at a considerable distance for at least a couple of hours; then draw it nearer, but never sufficiently so to burn or injure the fat. Keep it constantly basted; flour it soon after it is laid to the fire, instead of frothing it, as this latter mode is not generally relished, though fashion is in its favour. In from three and a half to four hours, the haunch will be done, and it will require something less of time when not kept back at first, as we have advised; but if roasted entirely on the plan mentioned at page 132, it will be much finer than in the usual way. Serve it with a good Espagnole, or with plain mutton-gravy and currant-jelly. This joint, when the meat is of very fine quality, may be dressed and served exactly like venison.

3½ to 4 hours. 5 hours or more by the *slow* method.

ROAST SADDLE OF MUTTON.

This is an excellent joint, though not considered a very economical one. It is usual for the butcher to raise the skin from it before it is sent in, and to skewer it on again, that in the roasting the juices of the meat may be better preserved, and the fat prevented from taking too much colour, as this should be only slightly browned. In something less than half an hour before the mutton is done, remove the skin, and flour the joint lightly after having basted it well. Our own great objection to frothed meat would lead us to recommend that the skin should be taken off half an hour earlier, and that the joint should be kept at sufficient distance from the fire to prevent the possibility of the fat being burned; and that something more of time should be allowed for the roasting. With constant basting, great care, and good management, the cook may always ensure the proper appearance of this, or of any other joint (except, perhaps, of a haunch of venison) without having recourse to papering or pasting, or even to replacing the skin; but when unremitted attention cannot be given to this one part of the dinner, it is advisable to take all precautions that can secure it from being spoiled.

2½ to 2¾ hours. More if *very* large.

TO ROAST A LEG OF MUTTON.

In a cool and airy larder, a leg of mutton will hang many days with advantage, if the kernel be taken out, and the flap wiped very dry when it is first brought in; and it is never tender when freshly killed: in warm weather it should be well dredged with pepper to preserve it from the flies. If washed before it is put upon the spit, it should be wiped as dry as possible afterwards, and well floured soon after it is laid to the fire. When the excellence of the joint is more regarded than the expense of fuel, it should be roasted by what we have denominated the *slow method*; that is to say, it should be kept at a considerable distance from the fire, and remain at it four hours instead of two: it may be drawn nearer for the last twenty or thirty minutes, to give it colour. The gravy will flow from it in great abundance when it is cut, and the meat will be very superior to that roasted in the usual way. When this plan is not pursued, the mutton should still be kept quite a foot from the fire until it is heated through, and never brought sufficiently near to scorch or to harden any part. It should be *constantly basted* with its own fat, for if this be neglected, all other precautions will fail to ensure a good roast; and after it is dished, a little fine salt should be sprinkled lightly on it, and a spoonful or two of boiling water ladled over. This is the most palatable mode of serving it, but it may be frothed when it is preferred so, though we would rather recommend that the flour should be dredged on in the first instance, as it then prevents the juices of the meat from escaping, and forms a savoury coating to it; while the raw taste which it so often retains with mere frothing is to many eaters especially objectionable.

Leg of mutton, 7 to 8 lbs.; slow method 4 hours, common method 1¾ to 2 hours.

SUPERIOR RECEIPT FOR ROAST LEG OF MUTTON.

Cover the joint well with cold water, bring it gradually to boil, and let it simmer gently for half an hour; then lift it out, put it immediately on to the spit, and roast it from an hour and a quarter to an hour and a half, according to its weight. This mode of dressing the joint renders it remarkably juicy and tender; but there must be no delay in putting it on the spit after it is lifted from the water; it may be garnished with roast tomatas.

Boiled, ½ hour; roast, 1¼ to 1½ hour.

LEG OF MUTTON BONED AND FORCED.

Turn the under-side of the mutton upwards, and with a sharp knife

I I

cut through the middle of the skin from the knuckle to the first joint, and raise it from the flesh on the side along which the bone runs, until the knife is just above it, then cut through the flesh down to the bone; work the knife round it in every part till you reach the socket; next remove the flat bone from the large end of the joint, and pass the knife freely round the remaining one, as it is not needful to take it out clear of the meat; when you again reach the middle joint, loosen the skin round it with great care, and the two bones can then be drawn out without being divided. This being done, fill the cavities with the force-meat, No. 1. (page 122), adding to it a somewhat high seasoning of eschalot, garlic, or onion; or cut out with the bone, nearly a pound of the inside of the mutton, chop it fine with six ounces of delicate striped bacon, and mix with it thoroughly three-quarters of an ounce of parsley, and half as much of thyme and winter savory, all minced extremely small; a half teaspoonful of pepper (or a third as much of cayenne); the same of mace, salt, and nutmeg, and either the grated rind of a small lemon, or four eschalots finely shred. When the lower part of the leg is filled, sew the skin neatly together where it has been cut open, and tie the knuckle round tightly, to prevent the escape of the gravy. Replace the flat bone at the large end, and with a long needle and twine, draw the edges of the meat together over it. If it can be done conveniently, it is better to roast the mutton thus prepared in a cradle spit or upon a hanging or bottle-jack, with the knuckle downwards. Place it at first far from the fire, and keep it constantly basted. It will require nearly or quite three hours roasting. Remove the twine before it is served, and send it very hot to table with some rich brown gravy; or it may be put into a braising-pan and stewed gently four or five hours.

MOCK VENISON.

Hang a plump and finely-grained leg of mutton in a cool place, for as many days as it can possibly be kept without becoming altogether uneatable. Lay it on a dish, pour over, and rub well into it, about half a small cupful of pyroligneous acid, and let it remain ten minutes. Wash it very thoroughly, cut off the knuckle, and trim away the flap, and any part that may continue very offensive, or take a few inches from either end of the joint; then lay it into a close-shutting stewpot, or thick iron saucepan of its own size, with no other liquid than the drops of water which adhere to it, and simmer it over a *very* slow fire, from four and a half to five hours, turning it several times, that it may be equally done. Give it no seasoning beyond pepper and salt. Should the gravy be too much reduced, add two spoonsful of boiling water, or of mutton gravy. Send the meat to table in its own juices, with currant jelly, or sharp venison sauce apart. We owe this receipt entirely to accident; for, wishing to have proof of the anti-putrescent qualities of the pyroligneous acid, we had it applied to a leg of mutton which, had been kept too long, and which was dressed in the way we have described. When brought to table, its resemblance to venison, both in appearance and flavour, was remarkable; and several persons partook of it hashed on the following day, and were all perfectly unconscious that they were not really eating venison; in the latter instance, it was served in rich gravy made in part of hare; a glass of port wine, a little compound catsup, and a thickening of rice flour were added. The meat, of course, was only heated through, and not allowed to boil.   On a second trial we found it an improvement to touch the mutton in every part with a feather dipped in the acid, as soon as it gave evidence of having been sufficiently kept, and then to let it hang three or four days longer: it was again washed with the acid, and afterwards with cold water before it was dressed.

TO BOIL A LEG OF MUTTON; (an excellent receipt.)

Trim into handsome form a well-kept, but perfectly sweet leg of mutton, of middling weight; wash, but do not soak it; lay it into a vessel as nearly of its size as convenient, and pour in rather more than sufficient cold water to cover it; set it over a good fire, and when it begins to boil, take off the scum, and continue to do so until no more appears; throw in a tablespoonful of salt (after the first skimming), which will assist to bring it to the surface, and as soon as the liquor is clear, add two moderate-sized onions, stuck with a dozen cloves, a large faggot of parsley, thyme, and savory, and four or five large carrots, and half an hour afterwards, as many turnips.   Draw the pan to the side of the fire, and let the mutton be simmered *gently* for two hours and a half, from the time of its first beginning to boil.   Serve it with caper, brown cucumber, or oyster sauce.   If stewed *softly*, as we have directed, the mutton will be found excellent dressed thus; otherwise, it will but resemble the unpalatable and ragged-looking joints of fast-boiled meat, so constantly sent to table by common English cooks. Any undressed bones of veal, mutton, or beef, boiled with the joint, will improve it much, and the liquor will then make excellent soup or bouillon.

2 to 2½ hours.

COLD ROAST LEG OF MUTTON.

When only a few slices have been cut from the middle of the joint, it will still afford a fillet of tolerable size, which, dressed in the following manner, will make a dish of better appearance and savour than a common hash or mince.   Take off as much of the large end of the leg, quite through, as will render that side of the fillet perfectly flat; cut also evenly through the joint, where it has been carved; then remove the bone from the fillet, and replace it with veal forcemeat (No. 1, page 122); put the meat, with the bones, knuckle, and trimmings, into a stewpot, or stout saucepan adapted to its size, and just cover it with water, or with broth in preference, when any stock is at hand; as soon as it boils, add a couple of onions, a bunch of parsley, two or even three bay-leaves, four or five carrots, and as many turnips (*plenty of vegetables*, in fact), and simmer the whole gently for nearly, or quite a couple of hours.   Thickening, spice, or store-sauce, can be added to the gravy at will, before the meat is served, which it should be with the vegetables round it.

A FILLET OF MUTTON.

Cut some inches from either end of a large and well-kept leg of mutton, and leave the fillet shaped like one of veal.   Remove the bone, and fill the cavity with forcemeat (No. 1, page 122), which may be flavoured with a little minced onion, when its flavour is liked: more forcemeat may be added by detaching the skin sufficiently on the flap side to admit it.   When thus prepared, the fillet may be floured, and

roasted, served with currant-jelly and brown gravy, or with only melted
butter poured over it; or it may be stewed gently for nearly or quite
four hours, in a pint of gravy or water, after having been floured and
browned all over in a couple of ounces of butter; it must then be turned
every hour, that it may be equally done.   Two or three small onions, a
faggot of herbs, a couple of carrots sliced, four or five cloves, and twenty
whole peppercorns can be added at will.

Roasted 2 hours, or stewed 4 hours.

TO ROAST A LOIN OF MUTTON.

The flesh of the loin of mutton is superior to that of the leg, when
roasted; but to the frugal housekeeper this consideration is usually
overbalanced by the great weight of fat attached to it; this, however,
when economy is more considered than appearance, may be pared off
and melted down for various kitchen uses, or finely chopped, and substituted for suet in making hot pie or pudding crust.   When thus reduced in size, the mutton will be soon roasted.   If it is to be dressed in
the usual way, the butcher should be desired to take off the skin; care
should be taken to preserve the fat from being ever so slightly burned;
it should be managed, indeed, in the same manner as the saddle, in
every respect, and carved also in the same way, that is to say, the meat
should be cut out in slices the whole length of the back-bone, and close
to it.

Without the fat, 1 to 1½ hour; with, 1¼ to 1¾ hour.

TO DRESS A LOIN OF MUTTON LIKE VENISON.

Skin and bone a loin of mutton, and lay it into a stewpan, or braising-
pan, with a pint of water, a large onion stuck with a dozen cloves, half
a pint of port wine and a spoonful of vinegar; add, when it boils, a small
faggot of thyme and parsley, and some pepper and salt: let it stew
three hours, and turn it often.   Make some gravy of the bones, and add
it at intervals to the mutton when required.

This receipt comes to us so strongly recommended by persons who
have partaken frequently of the dish, that we have not thought it needful to prove it ourselves.

3 hours.

TO ROAST A SHOULDER OF MUTTON.

Flour it well, and baste it constantly with its own dripping; do not
place it close enough to the fire for the fat to be in the slightest degree
burned, or even too deeply browned.   An hour and a half will roast it,
if it be of moderate size.   Stewed onions are often sent to table with it.
A shoulder of mutton is sometimes boiled, and smothered with onion
sauce.

1½ hour.

SPICED SHOULDER OF MUTTON.

Bone the joint, and rub it, if large, with four ounces of the coarsest
sugar (or with three, if it be small), well mixed with a dessertspoonful
of pounded cloves, half that quantity of pepper and of mace, and a fourth
part as much of ginger: the following day add four ounces of salt.   Keep
the mutton turned, and rubbed occasionally with the pickle from eight
to ten days; then roll it up tight, bind it with a fillet, and stew it gently,
for four hours in a pint and a half of beef broth, or put into the stewpan

with it a pound and a half of neck of beef, three half pints of water, one large mild onion, two carrots, two turnips, and a large faggot of herbs. When the mutton is perfectly tender, serve it with some of its own gravy, thickened and highly flavoured with lemon-pickle, or with any other acid sauce; or send it to table with a good sauce piquante.

Mutton, 8 to 9 lbs.; sugar, 4 ozs.; cloves, in powder, 1 dessertspoonful; mace, and pepper, 1 teaspoonful each; ginger, $\frac{1}{2}$ teaspoonful; salt, 4 ozs.: 8 to 10 days.   Beef broth, 1$\frac{1}{2}$ pint: 4 hours.

Obs.—For variety, the inside of the mutton may be thickly strewed with minced herbs before it is rolled.

FORCED SHOULDER OF MUTTON.

Cut off all the flesh from the inside of the joint down to the blade-bone, and reserve it for a separate dish. It may be lightly browned with some turnips or carrots, or both, and made into a small harrico, or stewed simply in its own gravy, or it will make in part, a pudding or a pie.   Bone the mutton (see page 140), flatten it on a table, lay over the inside some thin and neatly-trimmed slices of striped bacon, and spread over them some good veal forcemeat (No. 1, page 122) to within an inch of the outer edge; roll the joint up tightly towards the knuckle (of which the bone may be left in or not, at pleasure), secure it well with tape or twine, and stew it gently in good gravy, from four hours to four and a half.

4 to 4$\frac{1}{2}$ hours.

Obs.—In France it is usual to substitute *sausage-meat* for the bacon and veal stuffing in this dish.

MUTTON CUTLETS STEWED IN THEIR OWN GRAVY; (*good.*)

Trim the fat entirely from some cutlets taken from the loin; just dip them into cold water, dredge them moderately with pepper, and plentifully on both sides with flour; rinse a thick iron saucepan with spring-water, and leave a couple of tablespoonsful in it; arrange the cutlets in one flat layer, if it can be done conveniently, and place them over a very gentle fire; throw in a little salt when they begin to stew, and let them simmer as *softly as possible*, but without ceasing, from an hour and a quarter to an hour and a half. If dressed with great care, which they require, they will be equally tender, easy of digestion, and nutritious; and being at the same time free from everything which can disagree with the most delicate stomach, the receipt will be found a valuable one for invalids.   The mutton should be of good quality, but the excellence of the dish mainly depends on its being *most gently stewed;* for if allowed to boil quickly all the gravy will be dried up, and the meat will be unfit for table.   The cutlets must be turned when they are half done: a couple of spoonsful of water or gravy may be added to them should they not yield sufficient moisture, but this is rarely needful.

1$\frac{1}{4}$ to 1$\frac{3}{4}$ hour.

TO BROIL MUTTON CUTLETS.   (ENTRÉE.)

These may be taken from the loin, or the best end of the neck, but the former are generally preferred.   Trim off a portion of the fat, or the whole of it, unless it be liked; pepper the cutlets, heat the gridiron, rub it with a bit of the mutton suet, broil them over a brisk fire, and turn them often until they are done; this, for the generality of eaters, will be in about eight minutes if they are not more than half an inch thick, which they should not be. French cooks season them with pepper and salt, and give them a light coating of dissolved butter or of oil, before they are laid to the fire, and we have found the cutlets so managed extremely good.

Lightly broiled, 7 to 8 minutes. Well done, 10 minutes.

Obs. — A cold Maître d'Hotel sauce may be laid under the cutlets when they are dished ; or they may be served quite dry, or with brown gravy ; or when none is at hand, with good melted butter seasoned with mushroom catsup, cayenne, and Chili vinegar, or lemon-juice.

CHINA CHILO.

Mince a pound of an undressed loin or leg of mutton, with or without a portion of its fat, mix with it two or three young lettuces shred small, a pint of young peas, a teaspoonful of salt, half as much pepper, four tablespoonsful of water, from two to three ounces of good butter, and, if the flavour be liked, a few green onions minced. Keep the whole well stirred with a fork, over a clear and gentle fire until it is quite hot, then place it closely covered by the side of the stove, or on a high trevet, that it may stew as softly as possible for a couple of hours. One or even two half-grown cucumbers, cut small by scoring the ends deeply as they are sliced, or a quarter-pint of minced mushrooms may be added with good effect; or a dessertspoonful of curric-powder and a large chopped onion. A dish of boiled rice should be sent to table with it.

Mutton, 1 pint; green peas, 1 pint; young lettuces, 2; salt, 1 teaspoonful ; pepper, ½ teaspoonful ; water, 4 tablespoonsful ; butter, 2 to 3 ozs.: 2 hours. Varieties: cucumbers, 2; or mushrooms minced, ¼ pint; or currie-powder, 1 dessertspoonful, and 1 large onion.

A GOOD FAMILY STEW OF MUTTON.

Put into a broad stewpan or saucepan a flat layer of mutton chops, freed entirely from fat and from the greater portion of the bone, then just dipped into cold water, seasoned with pepper, and lightly dredged with flour; on these put a layer of mild turnips sliced half an inch thick, and divided into squares; then some carrots of the same thickness, with a seasoning of salt and black pepper between them; next, another layer of chops, then plenty of vegetables, and as much weak broth or cold water as will barely cover the whole; bring them slowly to a boil, and let them just simmer from two to three hours, according to the quantity. One or two minced onions may be strewed between the other vegetables when their flavour is liked. The savour of the dish will be increased by browning the chops in a little butter before they are stewed, and still more so by frying the vegetables lightly as well, before they are added to it. A head or two of celery would to many tastes improve the flavour of the whole. In summer, cucumber, green onions, shred lettuces, and green peas may be substituted for the winter vegetables.

Mutton, free from fat, 2½ lbs.; turnips, 3 lbs.; carrots, 3 lbs.; celery (if added), 2 small heads: 2 to 3 hours.

Obs.—The fat and trimmings of the mutton used for this and for other dishes into which only the lean is admissible may be turned to advantage by cutting the whole up rather small, and then boiling it in a quart of water to the pound, with a little spice, a bunch of herbs and some salt, until the fat is nearly dissolved: the liquid will then, if strained off and left until cold, make tolerable broth, and the cake of fat which is on the top, if again just melted and poured free of sediment into small pans, will serve excellently for common pies and for frying kitchen dinners. Less water will of course produce broth of better quality, and the addition of a small quantity of fresh meat or bones will render it very good.

AN IRISH STEW.

Take a couple of pounds of small thick mutton cutlets with or without fat according to the taste of the persons to whom the stew is to be served; take also four pounds of good potatoes, weighed after they are pared, slice them thick, and put a portion of them, in a flat layer, into a large thick saucepan or stewpan; season the mutton well with pepper, and place some of it on the potatoes, cover it with another layer, and proceed in the same manner with all, reserving plenty of the vegetable for the top; pour in three quarters of a pint of cold water, and add, when the stew begins to boil, an ounce of salt; let it simmer gently for two hours, and serve it very hot. When the addition of onion is liked, strew in two or three minced ones with the potatoes.

Mutton cutlets, 2 lbs.; potatoes, 4 lbs.; pepper, ½ oz.; salt, 1 oz.; water, ¾ pint: 2 hours.

Obs.—For a real Irish stew the potatoes should be boiled to a mash: an additional quarter-hour may be necessary for the full quantity here, but for half of it two hours are quite sufficient.

CUTLETS OF COLD MUTTON.

Trim into well-shaped cutlets, which should not be very thin, the remains of a roast loin or neck of mutton, or of a quite under-dressed stewed or boiled joint; dip them into egg and well-seasoned breadcrumbs, and broil or fry them over a quick fire that they may be browned and heated through without being too much done. This is a very good mode of serving a half-roasted loin or neck. When the cutlets are broiled they should be dipped into, or sprinkled thickly with butter just dissolved, or they will be exceedingly dry; a few additional crumbs should be made to adhere to them after they are moistened with this.

MUTTON KIDNEYS A LA FRANÇAISE. (ENTRÉE.)

Skin six or eight fine fresh mutton kidneys, and, without opening them, remove the fat; slice them rather thin, strew over them a large dessertspoonful of minced herbs, of which two-thirds should be parsley and the remainder thyme, with a tolerable seasoning of pepper or cayenne, and some fine salt. Melt two ounces of butter in a frying-pan, put in the kidneys and brown them quickly on both sides; when nearly done, stir amongst them a dessertspoonful of flour, and shake them well in the pan; pour in the third of a pint of gravy (or of hot water in default of this), the juice of half a lemon, and as much of Harvey's sauce, or of mushroom catsup, as will flavour the whole pleasantly; bring these to the point of boiling, and pour them into a dish garnished with fried sippets, or lift out the kidneys first, give the sauce a boil and pour it on them. We generally have the store-sauce of page 147 (see English stew) used to flavour this dish in preference to simple catsup.

In France, a couple of glasses of champagne, or, for variety, of claret, are frequently added to the gravy; one of port wine can be substituted for either of these. A dessertspoonful of minced eschalots may be strewed over the kidneys with the herbs; or two dozens of very small ones, previously stewed till tender in fresh butter over a gentle fire, may be added after they are dished. This is a very excellent and approved receipt.

Fried 6 minutes.

BROILED MUTTON KIDNEYS.

Split them open lengthwise without dividing them; strip off the skin and fat; run a fine skewer through the points and across the back of the kidneys to keep them flat while broiling; season them with pepper or cayenne; lay them over a clear brisk fire, with the cut sides towards it; turn them in from four to five minutes; and in as many more dish, and serve them quickly, with or without a cold Maître d'Hotel sauce under them. French cooks season them with pepper and fine salt, and brush a very small quantity of oil, or clarified butter over them before they are broiled: we think this an improvement.

8 to 10 minutes.

OXFORD RECEIPT FOR MUTTON KIDNEYS. (BREAKFAST DISH, OR ENTRÉE.)

Fry gently, in a little good butter, a dozen croûtons (slices of bread, of uniform shape and size, trimmed free from crust,) cut half an inch thick, about two inches and a half wide, and from three to four in length: lift them out and keep them hot. Split quite asunder six fine fresh kidneys, after having freed them from the skin and fat; season them with fine salt and cayenne; arrange them evenly in a clean frying-pan, and pour some clarified butter over them. Fry them over a somewhat brisk fire; dish each half upon a croûton; make a sauce in the pan as for veal cutlets, but use gravy for it instead of water, should it be at hand; add a little wine or catsup; pour it round the croûtons, and serve the kidneys instantly.

10 minutes.

TO ROAST A FORE QUARTER OF LAMB.

This should be laid to a clear brisk fire, and carefully and plentifully basted from the time of its becoming warm until it is ready for table; but though it requires quick roasting, it must never be placed sufficiently near the fire to endanger the fat, which is very liable to *catch* or burn. When the joint is served, the shoulder should be separated from the ribs with a sharp knife, and a small slice of fresh butter, a little cayenne, and a squeeze of lemon-juice should be laid between them; if the cook be an expert carver, this had better be done before the lamb is sent to table. The cold Maître d'Hotel sauce of page 100, may be substituted for the usual ingredients, the parsley being omitted or not, according to the taste. Serve good mint sauce, and a fresh salad with this roast.

A leg, shoulder, or loin of lamb should be cooked by the same directions as the quarter, a difference only being made in the time allowed for each.

Fore-quarter of lamb, 1¾ to 2 hours. Leg, 1½ hour (less if *very* small); loin, 1 to 1¼ hour.

Obs.—The time will vary a little, of course, from the difference in the weather, and in the strength of the fire. Lamb should always be *well* roasted.

SADDLE OF LAMB.

This is an exceedingly nice joint for a small party. It should be roasted at a brisk fire, and kept constantly basted with its own dripping: it will require from an hour and three quarters to two hours roasting. Send it to table with mint sauce, and if convenient, with brown cucumber sauce also, and a salad.

1¾ to 2 hours.

Obs.—The following will be found an excellent receipt for mint sauce :—With three heaped tablespoonsful of finely-chopped young mir.t, mix two of pounded and sifted sugar, and six of the best vinegar: stir it until the sugar is dissolved.

ROAST LOIN OF LAMB.

Place it at a moderate distance from a clear fire, baste it frequently, froth it when nearly done, and serve it with the same sauces as the preceding joints. A loin of lamb may be boiled and sent to table with white cucumber, mushroom, common white sauce, or parsley and butter.

1 to 1¼ hour.

STEWED LEG OF LAMB WITH WHITE SAUCE. (ENTRÉE.)

Choose a small plump leg of lamb, not much exceeding five pounds in weight; put it into a vessel nearly of its size, with a few trimmings, or a bone or two of undressed veal if at hand; cover it with cold water, bring it slowly to a boil, clear off the scum with great care when it is first thrown to the surface, and when it has all been skimmed off, add a bunch of thyme and parsley, and two carrots of moderate size. Let the lamb *simmer* only, but without ceasing, for an hour and a quarter; serve it covered with béchamel, or rich English white sauce, and send a boiled tongue to table with it, and some of the sauce in a tureen.

1¼ hour.

LOIN OF LAMB STEWED IN BUTTER. (ENTRÉE.)

Wash the joint, and wipe it very dry; skewer down the flap, and lay it into a close-shutting and thick stewpan, or saucepan, in which three ounces of good butter have been just dissolved, but not allowed to boil; let it simmer slowly over a very gentle fire for two hours and a quarter, and turn it when it is rather more than half done. Lift it out, skim and pour the gravy over it; send brown asparagus, cucumber, or soubise sauce to table with it; or brown gravy, mint sauce, and a salad.

2¼ hours.

LAMB OR MUTTON CUTLETS, WITH SOUBISE SAUCE. (ENTRÉE.)

The best end of two necks of either will be required for a handsome dish. Cut them thin with one bone to each; trim off the fat and all the skin, scrape the bones very clean that they may look white, and season the cutlets with salt and white pepper; brush them with egg, dip them into very fine bread-crumbs, then into clarified butter, and again into the bread-crumbs, which should be flattened evenly upon them, and broil them over a very clear and brisk fire, or fry them in a little good butter of a fine clear brown; press them in two sheets of white blotting-paper to extract the grease, and dish them on end. with the points meeting at the top; or place them one over the other in a chain, and pour into the centre a soubise, or a purée of cucumbers. Brown cucumber sauce, or a rich gravy, may be substituted for either of these in serving a quite simple dinner.   Cutlets of the loin may be dressed in the same way, after being dipped into crumbs of bread mixed with a full seasoning of minced herbs, and a small quantity of eschalot, when its flavour is liked.   The small flat bone at the end of the cutlets should be taken off, to give them a very good appearance.

LAMB CUTLETS IN THEIR OWN GRAVY.

Follow exactly the receipt for mutton cutlets dressed in the same way, but allow for those of lamb fifteen or twenty minutes less of time, and an additional spoonful of liquid.

CUTLETS OF COLD LAMB.

See the receipt for Cutlets of Cold Mutton, page 183.

CHAPTER XI.

PORK.

No.		No.	
1. The Spare Rib.		4. Fore Loin.	
2. Hand.		5. Hind Loin.	
3. Belly, or Spring.		6. Leg.	

TO CHOOSE PORK.

This meat is so proverbially, and we believe even *dangerously* un wholesome when ill fed, or in any degree diseased, that its quality should be closely examined before it is purchased. When not home-fatted, it should be bought if possible of some respectable farmer, or miller, unless the butcher who supplies it can be perfectly relied on. Both the fat and lean should be very white, and the latter finely grained; the rind should be thin, smooth, and cool to the touch; if it be clammy, the pork is stale, and should be at once rejected; it ought also to be scrupulously avoided when the fat, instead of being quite clear of all blemish, is full of small kernels, which are indicative of disease. The manner of cutting up the pork varies in different counties, and also according to the purposes for which it is intended. The legs are either made into hams, or slightly salted for a few days and boiled; they are also sometimes roasted when the pork is not large nor coarse, with a savoury forcemeat inserted between the skin and flesh of the knuckle. The part of the shoulder called the hand is also occasionally pickled in the same way as hams and bacon, or it may be salted and boiled, but it is too sinewy for roasting. After these and the head have been taken off, the remainder, without further division than being split down the back, may be converted into whole sides, or *flitches*, as they are usually called, of bacon; but when the meat is large, and required in part for various other purposes, a chine may be taken out, and the fat pared off the bones of the ribs and loins for bacon; the thin part of the body converted into pickled pork, and the ribs and other bones roasted, or made into pies or sausages. The feet, which are generally salted down for immediate use, are excellent if laid for two or three weeks into the same pickle as the hams, then well covered with cold water, and slowly boiled until tender.

The loins of young and delicate pork are roasted with the skin on; and this is scored in regular stripes of about a quarter-inch wide with the point of a sharp knife, before the joints are laid to the fire. The skin of the leg also is just cut through in the same manner. This is done to prevent its blistering, and to render it more easy to carve, as the skin (*or crackling*) becomes so crisp and hard in the cooking, that it is otherwise sometimes difficult to divide it.

To be at any time fit for table, pork must be *perfectly sweet*, and thoroughly cooked; great attention also should be given to it when it is in pickle, for if any part of it be long exposed to the air, without being turned into, or well and frequently basted with the brine, it will often become tainted during the process of curing it.

TO MELT LARD.

Strip the skin from the inside fat of a freshly killed and well-fed pig; slice it small and thin; put it into a new or well-scalded jar, set it into a pan of boiling water, and let it simmer over a clear fire. As it dissolves, strain it into small stone jars, or deep earthen pans, and when perfectly cold, tie over it the skin that was cleared from the lard, or bladders which have been thoroughly washed and wiped very dry. Lard thus prepared is extremely pure in flavour, and keeps perfectly well, if stored in a cool place; it may be used with advantage in making pastry, as well as for frying fish, and for various other purposes. It is better to keep the last drainings of the fat apart from that which is first poured off, as it will not be quite so fine in quality.

TO PRESERVE UNMELTED LARD FOR MANY MONTHS.

For the particular uses to which the leaf-fat, or fleed, can be advantageously applied, see fleed-crust, Chapter XVI. It may be kept well during the summer months by rubbing fine salt rather plentifully upon it when it is first taken from the pig, and leaving it for a couple of days; it should then be well drained, and covered with a strong brine: this, in warmer weather, should be changed occasionally. When wanted for use, lay it into cold water for two or three hours, then wipe it dry, and it will have quite the effect of the fresh leaf when made into paste.

Inner fat of pig, 6 lbs.; fine salt, $\frac{1}{2}$ to $\frac{3}{4}$ lb.: 2 days. Brine; to each quart of water, 6 ozs. salt.

TO ROAST A SUCKING PIG.

After the pig has been scalded and prepared for the spit, wipe it as dry as possible, and put into the body about half a pint of fine bread-crumbs, mixed with three heaped teaspoonsful of sage, minced very small, three ounces of good butter, a large saltspoonful of salt, and two thirds as much of pepper, or some cayenne. Sew it up with soft, but strong cotton, truss it as a hare, with the fore legs skewered back, and the hind ones forward; lay it to a strong, clear fire, but keep it at a moderate distance, as it would quickly blister or scorch if placed too near. So soon as it has become warm, rub it with a bit of butter, tie it in a fold of muslin, or of thin cloth, and repeat this process constantly while it is roasting. When the gravy begins to drop from it, put basins, or small deep tureens under, to catch it in. As soon as the pig is of a fine light amber brown, and the steam draws strongly towards the fire, wipe it quite dry with a clean cloth, and rub a bit of cold butter over it. When it is half done, a pig iron, or, in lieu of this, a large flat iron should be hung in the centre of the grate, or the middle of the pig will be done long before the ends. When it is ready for table, lay it into a very hot dish, and before the spit is withdrawn, take off and open the head, and split the body in two; chop together quickly the stuffing and the brains, put them into half a pint of good veal gravy, ready thickened, add a glass of Madeira or of sherry, and the gravy which has dropped from the pig; pour a small portion of this under the meat, and serve the remainder as hot as possible in a tureen; a little pounded mace and cayenne, with a squeeze of lemon-juice, may be added, should the flavour require heightening. Fine bread sauce, and plain gravy should likewise be served with it. Some persons still prefer the old-fashioned currant sauce to any other; and many have the brains and stuffing stirred into rich melted butter, instead of gravy; but the receipt which we have given has usually been so much approved, that we can recommend it with some confidence, as it stands. Modern taste would perhaps be rather in favour of rich brown gravy and thick tomata sauce, or sauce Poivrade.

In dishing the pig, lay the body flat in the middle, and the head and ears at the ends and sides. When very pure oil can be obtained, it is preferable to butter for the basting: it should be laid on with a bunch of feathers. A suckling of three weeks old is considered as best suited to the spit; and it should always be dressed, if possible, the day it is killed.

1¼ to 1¾ hour.

BAKED PIG.

Prepare the pig exactly as for roasting, truss, and place it in the dish in which it is to be sent to the oven, and anoint it thickly in every part with white of egg which has been slightly beaten: it will require no basting, nor furthei attention of any kind, and will be well crisped by this process.

PIG A LA TARTARE.

When the shoulders of a cold roast pig are left entire, take them off with care, remove the skin, trim them into good form, dip them into clarified butter or very pure salad oil, then into fine crumbs highly seasoned with cayenne and mixed with about a half-teaspoonful of salt. Broil them over a clear brisk fire, and send them quickly to table, as soon as they are heated through and equally browned, with tomata sauce, or sauce Robert. Curried crumbs and a currie-sauce will give an excellent variety of this dish; and savoury herbs, with two or three eschalots chopped small together and mixed with the bread-crumbs, and brown eschalot sauce to accompany the broil, will likewise be an acceptable one to many tastes.

SUCKING PIG EN BLANQUETTE. (ENTRÉE.)

Raise the flesh from the bones of a cold roast pig, free it from the crisp outer skin or crackling, and cut it down into small handsome slices. Dissolve a bit of butter the size of an egg, and, if they can be easily procured, throw in a handful of button-mushrooms, cleaned and sliced; shake these over the fire for three or four minutes, then stir to them a dessertspoonful of flour, and continue to shake or toss them gently, but do not allow them to brown. Add a small bunch of parsley, a bay-leaf, a middling-sized blade of mace, some salt, a small quantity of cayenne or white pepper, half a pint of good veal or beef broth, and from two to three glasses of light white wine. Let these boil gently until reduced nearly one third; take out the parsley and mace, lay in the meat and bring it slowly to the point of simmering; stir to it the beaten yolks of three fresh eggs, and the strained juice of half a lemon. Serve the blanquette very hot.   •

TO ROAST PORK.

When the skin is left on the joint which is to be roasted, it must be scored in narrow strips of equal width, before it is put to the fire, and laid at a considerable distance from it at first, that the meat may be heated through before the skin hardens or begins to brown; it must never stand still for an instant, and the basting should be constant. Pork is not at the present day much served at very good tables, particularly in this form; and it is so still less with the old savoury stuffing of sage and onions, though some eaters like it always with the leg: when it is ordered for this joint, therefore, prepare it as directed for a goose, at page 125, and after having loosened the skin from the knuckle, insert as much as can well be secured in it. A little clarified butter, or salad oil may be brushed over the skin quite at first, particularly should the meat not be very fat, but unless remarkably lean, it will speedily yield sufficient dripping to baste it with. Joints from which the fat has been pared will require, of course, far less roasting than those on which the crackling is retained. Brown gravy and apple or tomata sauce are the usual accompaniments to all roasts of pork, except a sucking pig; they should always be thoroughly cooked.

Leg of pork of 8 lbs., 3 hours; loin of from 5 to 6 lbs., with the skin on, 2 to 2¼ hours; spare-rib of 6 to 7 lbs.. 1¼ hour.

TO ROAST A SADDLE OF PORK.

The skin of this joint may be removed entirely, but if left on it must be scored lengthwise, or in the direction in which it will be carved. The pork should be young, of fine quality, and of moderate size. Roast it very carefully, either by the directions given in the preceding receipt, or when the skin is taken off, by those for a saddle of mutton, allowing in the latter case from three quarters of an hour to a full hour more of the fire for it in proportion to its weight. Serve it with good brown gravy and tomata sauce, or sauce Robert; or with apple sauce should it be preferred. 20 minutes to the pound, quite.

TO ROAST SPARE-RIB.

Spare-rib should be rubbed with powdered sage mixed with salt and pepper, before it is roasted. It will require, if large and thick, two or three hours to roast it; a very thin one may be roasted in an hour. Lay the thick end to the fire. When you put it down, dust on some flour, and baste with a little butter.

The shoulder, loin, and chine are roasted in the same manner. A shoulder is the most economical part to buy, and is excellent boiled. Pork is always salted before it is boiled.

Apple-sauce is always proper to accompany roasted pork; this, with potatoes, mashed or plain, mashed turnips, and pickles, is good.

TO BROIL OR FRY PORK CUTLETS.

Cut them about half an inch thick from a delicate loin of pork, trim them into neat form, and take off part of the fat, or the whole of it when it is not liked; dredge a little pepper or cayenne upon them, and broil them over a clear and moderate fire from fifteen to eighteen minutes, sprinkle a little fine salt upon them just before they are dished. They may be dipped into egg and then into bread-crumbs mixed with minced sage, then finished in the usual way. When fried, flour them well, and season them with salt and pepper first. Serve them with gravy made in the pan, or with sauce Robert.

COBBETT'S RECEIPT FOR CURING BACON; (*extracted from his "Cottage Economy."*)

" All other parts being taken away, the two sides that remain, and which are called *flitches*, are to be cured for bacon. They are first rubbed with salt on their inside, or flesh sides, then placed one on the other, the flesh sides uppermost, in a salting trough, which has a gutter round its edges to drain away the brine; for to have sweet and fine bacon, the flitches must not be sopping in brine, which gives it the sort of taste that barrel-pork and sea-junk have, and than which nothing is more villanous. Every one knows how different is the taste of fresh dry salt from that of salt in a dissolved state. Therefore, *change the salt often;* once in four or five days. Let it melt and sink in, but let it not lie too long. Change the flitches, put that at bottom which was first on the top. Do this a couple of times. This mode will cost you a great deal more in salt than the *sopping mode;* but without it your bacon will not be so sweet and fine, nor keep so well. As to the time required for making the flitches sufficiently salt, it depends on circum-stances; the thickness of the flitch, the state of the weather, the place wherein the salting is going on. It takes a longer time for a thick than for a thin flitch; it takes longer in dry than in damp weather; it takes longer in a dry than in a damp place. But for the flitches of a hog of five score, in weather not very dry or very damp, about six weeks may do; and as yours is to be *fat*, which receives little injury from over-salting, give time enough; for you are to have bacon until Christmas comes again. The place for salting should, like a dairy, always be cool, but always admit of a free circulation of air; confined air, though cool, will taint meat sooner than the mid-day sun accompanied with a breeze. With regard to smoking the bacon, two precautions are neces-sary: first, to hang the flitches where no rain comes down upon them, and next, that the smoke must proceed from wood, not peat, turf nor coal. As to the time that it requires to smoke a flitch, it must depend a good deal upon whether there be a constant fire beneath, and whether the fire be large or small. A month will do if the fire be pretty con-stant, and such as a farm-house fire usually is. But over-smoking, or rather, too long hanging in the air, makes the bacon *rust*. Great atten-tion should, therefore, be paid to this matter. The flitch ought not to be dried up to the hardness of a board, and yet it ought to be perfectly dry. Before you hang it up, lay it on the floor, scatter the flesh-side pretty thickly over with bran or with some fine saw-dust, *not of deal or fir*. Rub it on the flesh, or pat it well down upon it. This keeps the smoke from getting into the little openings, and makes a sort of crust to be dried on.

" To keep the bacon sweet and good, and free from *hoppers*, sift fine some clean and dry *wood-ashes*. Put some at the bottom of a box or chest long enough to hold a flitch of bacon. Lay in one flitch; and then put in more ashes, then another flitch, and cover this with six or eight inches of the ashes. The place where the box or chest is kept ought to be *dry*, and should the ashes become damp they should be put in the fire-place to dry, and when cold, put back again. With these precautions the bacon will be as good at the end of the year as on the first day."

Obs.—Although the preceding directions for curing the bacon are a little vague as regards the proportions of salt and pork, we think those for its after-management will be acceptable to many of our readers, as in our damp climate it is often a matter of great difficulty to preserve hams and bacon through the year from rust.

A GENUINE YORKSHIRE RECEIPT FOR CURING HAMS AND BACON.

" Let the swine be put up to fast for twenty-four hours before they are killed (and observe that neither a time of severe frost nor very damp weather is favourable for curing bacon). After a pig has been killed and scalded, let it hang twelve hours before it is cut up, then for every stone, or fourteen pounds weight of the meat, take one pound of salt, an ounce and a quarter of saltpetre, and half an ounce of coarse sugar. Rub the sugar and saltpetre first into the fleshy parts of the pork, and remove carefully with a fork any extravasated blood that may appear on it, together with the broken vessels adjoining; apply the salt espe-cially to those parts, as well as to the shank-ends of the hams, and any other portions of the flesh that are more particularly exposed. Before the salt is added to the meat, warm it a little before the fire, and use only a part of it in the first instance; then, as it dissolves, or is absorbed

by the meat, add the remainder at several different times. Let the
meat in the mean while lie either on clean straw, or on a cold brick or
stone floor: it will require from a fortnight to three weeks' curing
according to the state of the atmosphere. When done, hang it in a
cool dry place, where there is a thorough current of air, and let it
remain there until it is perfectly dry, when the salt will be found to
have crystallized upon the surface. The meat may then be removed
to your store, and kept in a close chest, surrounded with clean *outer
straw.* If very large, the hams will not be in perfection in less than
twelve months from the time of their being stored."

Pork, 20 stone ; salt, 20 lbs. ; saltpetre, 20 ozs. ; sugar 10 ozs. : 14 to
21 days.

KENTISH MODE OF CUTTING UP AND CURING A PIG.

To a porker of sixteen stone Kentish weight, (that is to say, eight
pounds to the stone, or nine stone two pounds of common weight,) allow
two gallons of salt, two pounds of saltpetre, one pound of coarse sugar,
and two pounds of bay-salt, well dried and reduced to powder. Put
aside the hams and cheeks to be cured by themselves ; let the feet, ears,
tail, and eye-parts of the head be salted for immediate eating. The
blade-bones, and ends of the loins and ribs reserved for sausage-meat
should it be wanted, and the loin and spare-ribs for roasting. Divide
and salt the remainder thus: Mix well together the saltpetre, sugar,
and bay-salt, and rub the pork gently with them in every part; cover
the bottom of the pickling tub with salt, and pack in the pork as closely
as possible, with a portion of the remaining salt between each layer. A
very little water is sometimes sprinkled in to facilitate the dissolving of
the salt into a brine, but this is better avoided, if possible, and in damp
weather will not be needed. If in a fortnight it should not have risen,
so as almost entirely to cover the meat, boil a strong brine of salt, saltpetre, sugar, and bay-salt; let it remain till perfectly cold, and then
pour it over the pork. A board, with a heavy stone weight upon it,
should be kept upon the meat, to force it down under the brine. In
from three to four months it will be fit for table, and will be delicate
and excellent pickled pork.

The pickling parts of a porker of sixteen stone (Kentish weight, or
nine stone two pounds of common weight, or fourteen pounds to the
stone); common salt, 2 gallons; saltpetre, 2 lbs. ; coarse sugar, 1 lb. ;
bay-salt, 2 lbs.

FRENCH BACON FOR LARDING.

Cut the bacon from the pig with as little lean to it as possible. Rub
it well in every part, with salt which has been dried, reduced to powder,
and sifted ; put the layers of bacon close against and upon each other,
in a shallow wooden trough, and set in a cool, but not a damp cellar;
add more salt all round the bacon, and lay a board, with a very heavy
weight upon it. Let it remain for six weeks, then hang it up in a dry
and airy place.

Pork, 14 lbs. ; salt, 14 ozs. : 6 weeks.

TO PICKLE CHEEKS OF BACON AND HAMS.

One pound of common salt, one pound of the coarsest sugar, and one
ounce of saltpetre, in fine powder, to each stone (fourteen pounds) of
the meat will answer this purpose extremely well. An ounce of black

pepper can be added, if liked, and when less sugar is preferred, the proportion can be diminished one-half, and the quantity of salt as much increased. Bacon also may be cured by this receipt, or by the Bordyke one for hams. A month is sufficient time for the salting, unless the pork be very large, when five weeks must be allowed for a ham. The ingredients may be well mixed, and all applied at the same time.

To each 14 lbs. of pork, salt, 1 lb.; coarse sugar, 1 lb.; saltpetre, 1 oz.; pepper (if used), 1 oz.: 4 to 5 weeks.

HAMS SUPERIOR TO WESTPHALIA.

Take the hams as soon as the pig is sufficiently cold to be cut up, rub them well with common salt, and leave them for three days to drain; throw away the brine, and for a couple of hams of from fifteen to eighteen pounds weight, mix together two ounces of saltpetre, a pound of coarse sugar, and a pound of common salt; rub the hams in every part with these, lay them into deep pickling-pans with the rind downwards, and keep them for three days well covered with the salt and sugar; then pour over them a bottle of good vinegar, and turn them in the brine, and baste them with it daily for a month; drain them well, rub them with bran, and let them be hung for a month high in a chimney over a wood-fire to be smoked.

Hams, of from 15 to 18 lbs. each, 2; to drain 3 days. Common salt, and coarse sugar, each 1 lb.; saltpetre, 2 ozs.: 3 days. Vinegar, 1 bottle: 1 month. To be smoked 1 month.

Obs.—Such of our readers as shall make trial of this admirable receipt, will acknowledge, we doubt not, that the hams thus cured are in reality superior to those of Westphalia. It was originally given to the public by the celebrated French cook, Monsieur Ude, to whom, after having proved it, we are happy to acknowledge *our* obligation for it. He directs that the hams when smoked should be hung as high as possible from the fire, that the fat may not be melted; a very necessary precaution, as the mode of their being cured renders it peculiarly liable to do so. This, indeed, is somewhat perceptible in the cooking, which ought, therefore, to be conducted with especial care. The hams should be very softly simmered,* and not *over*-done. They should be large, and of finely-fed pork, or the receipt will not answer. We give the result of our first trial of it, which was perfectly successful.

Leg of farm-house pork, 14 to 15 lbs.; saltpetre, 1½ oz.; *strong* coarse salt, 6 ozs.; coarse sugar, 8 ozs.: 3 days. Fine white-wine vinegar, 1 pint. In pickle, turned daily, 1 month. Smoked over wood, 1 month.

Obs.—When two hams are pickled together a smaller proportion of the ingredients is required for each, than for one which is cured by itself.

HAMS; (*Bordyke Receipt.*)

After the hams have been rubbed with salt, and well drained from the brine, according to our previous directions, take, for each fourteen pounds weight of the pork, one ounce of saltpetre in fine powder, mixed with three ounces of the coarsest sugar; rub the meat in every part with these, and let it remain some hours, then cover it well with eight ounces of bay-salt, dried and pounded, and mixed with four ounces of

---

* We have not been able to make the trial ourselves, but we think they would be even finer baked than boiled.

common salt : in four days add one pound of treacle, and keep the hams
turned daily, and well basted with the pickle for a month. Hang them
up to drain for a night, fold them in brown paper, and send them to be
smoked for a month. An ounce of ground black pepper is often mixed
with the saltpetre in this receipt, and three ounces of bruised juniper-
berries are rubbed on to the meat before the salt is added, when hams
of a very high flavour are desired.

Ham, 14 lbs. ; saltpetre, 1 oz. ; coarse sugar, 3 ozs. : 8 to 12 hours.
Bay-salt, ½ lb. ; common salt, 4 ozs. : 4 days. Treacle, 1 lb. : 1 month.
To heighten flavour, black pepper, 1 oz. ; juniper-berries, 3 ozs.

TO BOIL A HAM.

The degree of soaking which must be given to a ham before it is
boiled, must depend both on the manner in which it has been cured,
and on its age. If highly salted, hard, and old, a day and night, or even
longer, may be requisite to dilate the pores sufficiently, and to extract a
portion of the salt. To do either effectually the water must be several
times changed during the steeping. We generally find hams cured by
any of the receipts which we have given in this chapter quite enough
soaked in twelve hours ; and they are more frequently laid into water
only early in the morning of the day on which they are boiled. Those
pickled by Monsieur Ude's receipt need much less steeping than any
others. After the ham has been scraped, or brushed, as clean as possible, pare away lightly any part which, from being blackened or rusty,
would disfigure it ; though it is better *not* to cut the flesh at all unless
it be really requisite for the good appearance of the joint. Lay it into
a ham-kettle, or into any other vessel of a similar form, and cover it
plentifully with cold water ; bring it *very slowly indeed* to boil, and
clear off carefully the scum which will be thrown up in great abundance.
So soon as the water has been cleared from this, draw back the pan
quite to the edge of the stove, that the ham may be simmered softly,
but steadily, until it is tender. On no account allow it to boil fast. A
bunch of herbs and three or four carrots, thrown in directly after the
water has been skimmed, will improve it. When it can be probed very
easily with a sharp skewer, or larding-pin, lift it out, strip off the skin,
which may be kept to cover the ham when cold, and should there be
an oven at hand, set it in for a few minutes, after having laid it on a
drainer ; strew fine raspings over it, or grate a hard-toasted crust, or sift
upon it the prepared bread of page 114, unless it is to be glazed, when
neither of these must be used.

Small ham, 3½ to 4 hours ; moderate sized, 4 to 4½ hours ; very large,
5 to 5½ hours.

Obs.—We have seen the following manner of boiling a ham recommended, but we have not tried it :—" Put into the water in which it is
to be boiled, a quart of old cider and a pint of vinegar, a large bunch of
sweet herbs, and a bay-leaf. When it is two thirds done, skin, cover it
with raspings, and set it in an oven until it is done enough : it will
prove incomparably superior to a ham boiled in the usual way."

FRENCH RECEIPT FOR BOILING A HAM.

After having soaked, thoroughly cleaned, and trimmed the ham, put
over it a little very sweet clean hay, and tie it up in a thin cloth : place

it in a ham kettle, a braising pan, or any other vessel as nearly of its size as can be, and cover it with two parts of cold water, and one of light white wine (we think the reader will perhaps find *cider* a good substitute for this); add, when it boils and has been skimmed, four or five carrots, two or three onions, a large bunch of savoury herbs, and the smallest bit of garlic. Let the whole simmer gently from four to five hours, or longer should the ham be very large. When perfectly tender, lift it out, take off the rind, and sprinkle over it some fine crumbs, or some raspings of bread mixed with a little finely minced parsley.

TO BAKE A HAM.

Unless when too salt, from not being sufficiently soaked, a ham (particularly a young and fresh one) eats much better baked than boiled, and remains longer good. The safer plan is to lay it into plenty of cold water over night. The following day soak it for an hour or more in warm water, wash it delicately clean, trim smoothly off all rusty parts, and lay it with the rind downwards into a coarse paste rolled to about an inch thick; moisten the edges, draw, pinch them together, and fold them over on the upper side of the ham, taking care to close them so that no gravy can escape. Send it to a well-heated, but not a fierce oven. A very small ham will require quite three hours baking, and a large one five. The crust and the skin must be removed while it is hot. When part only of a ham is dressed, this mode is better far than boiling it.

TO BOIL BACON.

When very highly salted and dried, it should be soaked for an hour before it is dressed. Scrape and wash it well, cover it plentifully with cold water, let it both heat and boil slowly, remove all the scum with care, and when a fork or skewer will penetrate the bacon easily lift it out, strip off the skin, and strew raspings of bread over the top, or grate upon it a hard crust which has been toasted until it is crisp quite through; or should it be at hand, use for the purpose the bread recommended at page 114, then dry it a little before the fire, or set it for a few minutes into a gentle oven. Bacon requires long boiling, but the precise time depends upon its quality, the flesh of young porkers becoming tender much sooner than that of older ones; sometimes, too, the manner in which the animal has been fed renders the meat hard, and it will then, unless thoroughly cooked, prove very indigestible. From ten to fifteen minutes less for the pound must be allowed for unsmoked bacon, or for pickled pork.

Smoked bacon (striped), 2 lbs., from 1¼ to 1½ hour; unsmoked bacon, or pork, 1 to 1¼ hour.

Obs.—The thickest part of a large gammon of bacon will require from twenty to thirty minutes longer boiling than the thinner side.

BACON BROILED OR FRIED.

Cut it evenly in thin slices, or *rashers*, as they are generally called, pare from them all rind and rust, curl them round, fasten them with small slight skewers, then fry, broil, or toast them in a Dutch oven; draw out the skewers before they are sent to table A few minutes will dress them either way. They may also be cooked without being curled. The rind should always be taken off, and the bacon gently toasted, grilled, or fried, that it may be well done without being too much dried, or hardened : it should be cut *thin*. Fry what eggs you want in butter, and when dished lay an egg on each slice of ham, and serve.

DRESSED RASHERS OF BACON.

Slice rather thicker than for frying, some cold boiled bacon, and strew it lightly on both sides with fine raspings of bread, or with a grated crust which has been very slowly and gradually toasted until brown quite through. Toast or warm the rashers in a Dutch oven, and serve them with veal cutlets, or any other delicate meat. The bacon thus dressed is much nicer than when broiled or fried without the previous boiling.

4 to 5 minutes.

TONBRIDGE BRAWN.

Split open the head of a middling-sized porker, remove the brain and all the bones, strew the inside rather thickly with fine salt, and let it drain until the following day. Cleanse the ears and feet in the same manner; wipe them all from the brine, lay them into a large pan, and rub them well with an ounce and a half of saltpetre mixed with six ounces of sugar; in twelve hours, add six ounces of salt; the next day pour a quarter-pint of good vinegar over them, and keep them turned in the pickle every twenty-four hours, for a week, then wash it off the ears and feet, and boil them for about an hour and a half; bone the feet while they are warm, and trim the gristle from the large ends of the ears. When these are ready, mix a large grated nutmeg with a tea-spoonful and a half of mace, half a teaspoonful of cayenne, and as much of cloves. Wash, but do not soak the head; wipe and flatten it on a board; cut some of the flesh from the thickest parts, and (when the whole of the meat has been seasoned equally with the spices) lay it on the thinnest; intermix it with that of the ears and feet, roll it up very tight, and bind it firmly with broad tape; fold a thin pudding-cloth quite closely round it, and tie it securely at both ends. A braising-pan, from its form, is best adapted for boiling it, but if there be not one at hand, place the head in a vessel adapted to its size, with the bones and trim-mings of the feet and ears, a large bunch of savoury herbs, two mode-rate-sized onions, a small head of celery, three or four carrots, a tea-spoonful of peppercorns, and sufficient cold water to cover it well; boil it very gently for four hours, and leave it until two parts cold in the liquor in which it was boiled. Take off the cloth, and put the brawn between two dishes or trenchers, with a heavy weight on the upper one. The next day take off the fillets of tape, and serve the head whole or · sliced.

ITALIAN PORK CHEESE.

Chop, not very fine, one pound of lean pork with two pounds of the inside fat; strew over and mix thoroughly with them three teaspoonsful of salt, nearly half as much pepper, a half-teaspoonful of mixed parsley, thyme, and sage (and sweet-basil, if it can be procured), all minced ex-tremely small. Press the meat closely and evenly into a shallow tin,— such as are used for Yorkshire puddings will answer well,—and bake it in a very gentle oven from an hour to an hour and a half: it is served cold, in slices. Should the proportion of fat be considered too much, it can be diminished on a second trial.

Minced mushrooms or truffles may be added with very good effect to all meat-cakes, or compositions of this kind.

Lean of pork, 1 lb.; fat, 2 lbs.; salt, 3 teaspoonsful; pepper, 1½ teaspoonful; mace, ½ teaspoonful; nutmeg, 1 small; mixed herbs, 1 large tablespoonful: 1 to 1½ hour.

[Pickled pork takes more time than other meat. If you buy your pork ready salted, ask how many days it has been in salt; if many, it will require to be soaked in water before you dress it. When you cook it, wash and scrape it as clean as possible; when delicately dressed, it is a favourite dish with almost every body. Take care it does not boil fast; if it does, the knuckle will break to pieces before the thick part of the meat is warm through; a leg of seven pounds takes three hours and a half very slow simmering. Skim your pot very carefully, and when you take the meat out of the boiler, scrape it clean.

The proper vegetables are parsnips, potatoes, turnips, or carrots. Some like cabbage, but it is a strong, rank vegetable, and does not agree with a delicate stomach.]

SAUSAGE-MEAT CAKE, OR, PAIN DE PORC FRAIS.

Season very highly from two to three pounds of good sausage-meat, both with spices and with sage, or with thyme and parsley, if these be preferred; press the mixture into a pan, and proceed exactly as for the veal-cake of page 168. A few minced eschalots can be mixed with the meat for those who like their flavour.

SAUSAGES.

Common farm-house sausages are made with nearly equal parts of fat and lean pork, coarsely chopped, and seasoned with salt and pepper only. They are put into skins (which have previously been turned inside out, scraped very thin, washed with exceeding nicety, and wiped very dry), then twisted into links, and should be hung in a cool airy larder, when they will remain good for some length of time. Odd scraps and trimmings of pork are usually taken for sausage-meat when the pig is killed and cut up at home; but the chine and blade-bone are preferred in general for the purpose. The pork rinds, as we have already stated, will make a strong and almost flavourless jelly, which may be used with excellent effect for stock, and which, with the addition of some pork-bones, plenty of vegetables, and some dried peas, will make a very nutritious soup for those who do not object to the pork-flavour which the bones will give. Half an ounce of salt, and nearly or quite a quarter-ounce of pepper will sufficiently season each pound of the sausage-meat.

KENTISH SAUSAGE-MEAT.

To three pounds of lean pork add two of fat, and let both be taken clear of skin. As sausages are lighter, though not so delicate when the meat is somewhat coarsely chopped, this difference should be attended to in making them. When the fat and lean are partially mixed, strew over them two ounces and a half of dry salt, beaten to powder, and mixed with one ounce of ground black pepper, and three large tablespoonsful of sage, very finely minced. Turn the meat with the chopping-knife, until the ingredients are well blended. Test it before it is taken off the block, by frying a small portion that if more season

ing be desired, it may at once be added. A full-sized nutmeg, and a small dessertspoonful of pounded mace would, to many tastes, improve it. This sausage-meat is usually formed into cakes, which, after being well floured, are roasted in a Dutch oven. They must be watched, and often turned, that no part may be scorched. The meat may also be put into skins, and dressed in any other way.

Lean of pork, 3 lbs.; fat, 2 lbs.; salt, 2½ ozs.; pepper, 1 oz.; minced sage, 3 large tablespoonsful.

EXCELLENT SAUSAGES.

Chop, first separately, and then together, one pound and a quarter of veal, perfectly free from fat, skin, and sinew, an equal weight of lean pork, and of the inside fat of the pig. Mix well, and strew over the meat an ounce and a quarter of salt, half an ounce of pepper, one nutmeg grated, and a *large* teaspoonful of pounded mace. Turn, and chop the sausages until they are equally seasoned throughout, and tolerably fine; press them into a clean pan, and keep them in a very cool place. Form them, when wanted for table, into cakes something less than an inch thick, flour and fry them then for about ten minutes in a little butter.

Lean of veal and pork, of each, 1 lb. 4 ozs.; fat of pork, 1 lb. 4 ozs.; salt, 1¼ oz.; pepper, ½ oz.; nutmeg, 1; mace, 1 *large* teaspoonful: fried in cakes, 10 minutes.

POUNDED SAUSAGE-MEAT; (*very good.*)

Take from the best end of a neck of veal, or from the fillet or loin, a couple or more pounds of flesh without any intermixture of fat or skin; chop it small, and pound it thoroughly in a large mortar, with half its weight of the inside, or leaf-fat, of a pig; proportion salt and spice to it by the preceding receipt, form it into cakes, and fry it as above.

BOILED SAUSAGES.

Sausages are sometimes boiled in the skins, and served upon a toast, as a corner dish. They should be put into boiling water, and simmered from seven to ten minutes, according to their size.

SAUSAGES AND CHESTNUTS. (ENTRÉE.) *An excellent dish.* (*French.*)

Roast, and take the husk and skin from forty fine Spanish chestnuts; fry gently, in a morsel of butter, six small flat oval cakes of fine sausage-meat, and when they are well browned, lift them out and pour into a saucepan, which should be bright in the inside, the greater part of the fat in which they have been fried; mix with it a large teaspoonful of flour, and stir these over the fire till they are well and equally browned; then pour in by degrees nearly half a pint of strong beef or veal broth, or gravy, and two glasses of good white wine; add a *small* bunch of savoury herbs, and as much salt and pepper, or cayenne, as will season the whole properly; give it a boil, lay in the sausages round the pan, and the chestnuts in the centre; stew them *very* softly for nearly an hour; take out the herbs, dish the sausages neatly, and heap the chestnuts in the centre, strain the sauce over them and serve them very hot. This is a corner dish. There should be no sage mixed with the pork to dress thus.

Chestnuts, roasted, 40; sausages, 6; gravy, nearly ½ pint; sherry or Madeira, 2 wineglassesful: stewed together from 50 to 60 minutes.

TRUFFLED SAUSAGES; (*Saucisses aux Truffles.*)

With two pounds of the lean of young tender pork, mix one pound of fat, a quarter of a pound of truffles, minced very small, an ounce and a half of salt, a seasoning of cayenne, or quite half an ounce of white pepper, a nutmeg, a teaspoonful of freshly pounded mace, and a dessertspoonful or more of savoury herbs dried and reduced to powder. Test a morsel of the mixture; heighten any of the seasonings to the taste; and put the meat into delicately clean skins: if it be for immediate use, and the addition is liked, moisten it, before it is dressed, with one or two glassesful of Madeira. The substitution of a clove of garlic for the truffles will convert these into *Saucisses à l'Ail*, or garlic sausages.

CHAPTER XII.

POULTRY.

Boiled Fowl.

TO CHOOSE POULTRY.

YOUNG, plump, well-fed, but not over-fatted poultry is the best. The skin of fowls and turkeys should be clear, white, and finely grained, the breasts broad and full-fleshed, the legs smooth, the toes pliable and easily broken when bent back; the birds should also be heavy in proportion to their size. This applies equally to geese and ducks, of which the breasts likewise should be very plump, and the feet yellow and flexible: when these are red and hard, the bills of the same colour, and the skin full of hairs, and extremely coarse, the birds are old.

White-legged fowls and chickens should be chosen for boiling, because their appearance is the most delicate when dressed; but the dark-legged ones often prove more juicy and of better flavour when roasted, and their colour then is immaterial.

Every precaution should be taken to prevent poultry from becoming ever so slightly tainted before it is cooked, but unless the weather be exceedingly sultry, it should not be quite freshly killed:* pigeons only

---

*If from accidental circumstances it should become apparently unfit for table, it may be restored to an eatable state by the same means as fish; it should not, however, be purchased, at any time, when it exhibits a greenish tint on any part of the skin, as this indicates its being already stale.

are the better for being so, and are thought to lose their flavour by hanging even a day or two. Turkeys, as we have stated in our receipts for them, are very tough and poor eating if not sufficiently long kept. A goose, also, in winter, should hang some days before it is dressed, and fowls, likewise, will be improved by it.

All kinds of poultry should be *thoroughly cooked*, though without being over-done, for nothing in general can more effectually destroy the appetite than the taste and appearance of their flesh when brought to table half roasted or boiled.

TO BONE A FOWL OR TURKEY WITHOUT OPENING IT.

After the fowl has been drawn and singed, wipe it inside and out with a clean cloth, but do not wash it. Take off the head, cut through the skin all round the first joint of the legs, and pull them from the fowl, to draw out the large tendons. Raise the flesh first from the lower part of the back-bone, and a little also from the end of the breast-bone, if necessary; work the knife gradually to the socket of the thigh; with the point of the knife detach the joint from it, take the end of the bone firmly in the fingers, and cut the flesh clean from it down to the next joint, round which pass the point of the knife carefully, and when the skin is loosened from it in every part, cut round the next bone, keeping the edge of the knife close to it, until the whole of the leg is done. Remove the bones of the other leg in the same manner; then detach the flesh from the back and breast-bone sufficiently to enable you to reach the upper joints of the wings; proceed with these as with the legs, but be especially careful not to pierce the skin of the second joint: it is usual to leave the pinions unboned, in order to give more easily its natural form to the fowl when it is dressed. The merry-thought and neck-bones may now easily be cut away, the back and side-bones taken out without being divided, and the breast-bone separated carefully from the flesh (which, as the work progresses, must be turned back from the bones upon the fowl, until it is completely inside out). After the one remaining bone is removed, draw the wings and legs back to their proper form, and turn the fowl the right side outwards.

A turkey is boned exactly in the same manner, but as it requires a very large proportion of forcemeat to fill it entirely, the legs and wings are sometimes drawn into the body, to diminish the expense of this. If very securely trussed, and sewn, the bird may be either boiled, or stewed in rich gravy, as well as roasted, after being boned and forced.

ANOTHER MODE OF BONING A FOWL OR TURKEY.

Cut through the skin down the centre of the back, and raise the flesh carefully on either side with the point of a sharp knife, until the sockets of the wings and thighs are reached. Till a little practice has been gained, it will perhaps be better to bone these joints before proceeding further; but after they are once detached from it, the whole of the body may easily be separated from the flesh and taken out entire: only the neck-bones and merrythought will then remain to be removed. The bird thus prepared may either be restored to its original form, by filling the legs and wings with forcemeat, and the body with the livers of two or three fowls, if they can be procured, mixed with alternate layers of parboiled tongue, freed from the rind, fine sausage meat, or veal

forcemeat, or thin slices of the nicest bacon, or aught e.se of good flavour, which will give a marbled appearance to the fowl when it is
carved; and then be sewn up and trussed as usual; or the legs and
wings may be drawn inside the body, and the bird being first flattened
on a table may be covered with sausage meat, and the various other
ingredients we have named, so placed that it shall be of equal thickness
in every part; then tightly rolled, bound firmly together with a fillet of
broad tape, wrapped in a thin pudding-cloth, closely tied at both ends,
and dressed as follows:—Put it into a braising-pan, stewpan, or thick
iron saucepan, bright in the inside, and fitted as nearly as may be to its
size; add all the chicken-bones, a bunch of sweet herbs, two carrots,
two bay-leaves, a large blade of mace, twenty-four white peppercorns,
and any trimmings or bones of undressed veal which may be at hand;
cover the whole with good veal-broth, add salt, if needed, and stew it
very softly, from an hour and a quarter to an hour and a half; let it cool
in the liquor in which it was stewed; and after it is lifted out, boil down
the gravy to a jelly and strain it; let it become cold, clear off the fat,
and serve it cut into large dice or roughed, and laid round the fowl,
which is to be served cold. If restored to its form, instead of being
rolled, it must be stewed gently for an hour, and may then be sent to
table hot, covered with mushroom, or any other good sauce that may be
preferred; or it may be left until the following day, and served garnished with the jelly, which should be firm, and very clear and well-
flavoured: the liquor in which the calf's foot has been boiled down,
added to the broth, will give it the necessary degree of consistency.
French cooks add three or four onions to these preparations of poultry
(the last of which is called a *galantine*); but these our own taste would
lead us to reject.

Rolled, 1¼ to 1½ hour; galantine, 1 hour.

Obs.—A couple of fowls, boned and rolled, make an excellent pie.

TO BONE FOWLS FOR FRICASSEES, CURRIES, AND PIES.

First carve them entirely into joints, then remove the bones, beginning with the legs and wings, at the head of the largest bone; hold this
with the fingers, and work the knife as directed in the receipt above.
The remainder of the birds is too easily done to require any instructions.

TO ROAST A TURKEY.

In very cold weather a turkey in
its feathers will hang (in an airy larder) quite a fortnight with advantage;
and, however fine a quality of bird it
may be, unless sufficiently long kept,
it will prove not worth the dressing,
though it should always be *perfectly
sweet* when prepared for table. Pluck,
draw, and singe it with exceeding

Turkey trussed for Roasting.

care; wash, and then dry it thoroughly with clean cloths, or merely
wipe the outside well, without wetting it, and pour water plentifully
through the inside. Fill the breast with forcemeat (No. 1, page 122),
or with the finest sausage meat, highly seasoned with minced herbs,
lemon-rind mace, and cayenne. Truss the bird firmly, lay it to a clear

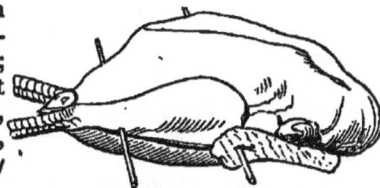

sound fire, baste it constantly and bountifully with butter, and serve it when done with good brown gravy, and well-made bread sauce. An entire chain of delicate fried sausages is still often placed in the dish, round a turkey, as a garnish.

It is usual to fold and fasten a sheet of buttered writing-paper over the breast to prevent its being too much coloured: this should be removed twenty minutes before the bird is done. The forcemeat of chestnuts (No. 15, Chapter VI.) may be very advantageously substituted for the commoner kinds in stuffing it, and the body may then be filled with chestnuts, previously stewed until tender in rich gravy, or simmered over a slow fire in plenty of rasped bacon, with a high seasoning of mace, nutmeg, and cayenne, until they are so; or, instead of this, well-made chestnut sauce, or a dish of stewed chestnuts, may be sent to table with the turkey.

1½ to 2½ hours.

Obs.—A turkey should be laid at first far from the fire, and drawn nearer when half done, though never sufficiently so to scorch it; it should be *well* roasted, for even the most inveterate advocates of underdressed meats will seldom tolerate the taste or *sight* of partially-raw poultry.

TO BOIL A TURKEY.

A delicate but plump hen-turkey of moderate size should be selected for boiling. Pick and draw it, using the greatest precaution not to break the gall bladder; singe it with writing paper, take off the head and neck, cut through the skin round the first joint of the legs, and draw them off: this is best accomplished by fastening the

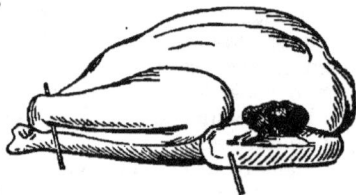
Turkey for Boiling.

feet to a strong hook, and then pulling the bird away from it. Wash it exceedingly clean, and then wipe it dry; fill the breast with the forcemeat No. 1 or 2 of Chapter VI., or with the oyster, chestnut, or French forcemeat, of which the receipts are given in the same chapter. In trussing it draw the legs into the body, break the breast-bone, and give the turkey as round and plump an appearance as can be. Put it into plenty of *warm* water, clear off the scum with the greatest care as it is thrown to the surface, and boil the bird *very gently* from an hour and a half to two hours and a quarter. A very large turkey would require a longer time, but it is unsuited to this mode of cooking. When the oyster-forcemeat is used, a large tureen of rich oyster sauce should accompany the dish; but celery sauce, or good white sauce, may otherwise be sent to table with it; and a boiled tongue or a small ham is usually served in addition. For a plain family dinner, a delicate cheek of bacon is sometimes substituted for either of these, and parsley and butter for a more expensive sauce. *Fast boiling* will cause the skin of the bird to break, and must therefore be especially avoided: it should hang for some days before it is dressed, for if quite freshly killed it will not be tender, but it must be *perfectly* sweet to be fit for table.

Moderate-sized turkey, 1½ to 2 hours; large turkey, longer; very small one, less time.

TURKEY BONED AND FORCED; (*an excellent dish.*)

Take a small, well-kept, but quite sweet hen-turkey, of from seven to eight pounds weight, and remove, by the receipt for a fowl (page 200), all the bones except those of the pinions, without opening the bird; draw it into shape, and fill it entirely with exceedingly fine sausage-meat, beginning with the legs and wings; plump the breast well in preparing it, and when its original form is quite restored, tie it securely at both ends, and at the extremities of the legs; pass a slight iron skewer through these and the body, and another through the wings and body; then lay a twine over the back of the turkey, and pass it under the ends of the first skewer, cross it in the centre of the back, and pass it under the ends of the second skewer; then carry it over the pinions to keep them firmly in their place, and fasten it at the neck. When a cradle spit, of which the engraving below shows the form, and which opens

Cradle Spit.

with a joint to receive the roast, is not at hand, a bottle-jack will be found more convenient than any other for holding the turkey; and after the hook of this is passed through the neck, it must be further supported by a string running across the back and under the points of the skewer which confines the pinions to the hook; for, otherwise, its weight would most probably cause it to fall. Flour it well, place it far from the fire until it is heated through, and baste it plentifully and incessantly with butter. An hour and three quarters will roast it well. Break and boil down the bones for gravy in a pint and a half of water, with a little salt, a few slices of celery, a dozen corns of pepper, and a branch or two of parsley. Brown gently in a morsel of good butter, a couple of ounces of lean ham, add to them a slight dredge of flour, and a little cayenne, and pour to them the broth from the bones, after it has boiled an hour, and been strained and skimmed; shake the stewpan well round, and stew the gravy until it is wanted for table; clear it entirely from fat; strain, and serve it very hot.

The turkey may be partially filled with the forcemeat No. 1 or 3, of Chapter VI., and the sausage-meat may then be placed on either side of it.

Hen turkey between 7 and 8 lbs. weight, boned, filled with sausage-meat, 3 to 4 lbs.; or with forcemeat No. 1, or with No. 3, Chapter VI., 1 lb. (that is to say, 1 lb. of bread-crumbs, and the other ingredients in proportion.) Sausage-meat, 2 to 3 lbs. roasted 1¾ hour.

Obs.—When a common spit is used for the turkey, it must be fastened *to*, and not put *upon* it.

Bread sauce can be served with the bird, or not, at pleasure.

It will be found an improvement to moisten the sausage-meat with one or two spoonsful of water: it should be finely minced, well spiced, and mixed with herbs, when the common forcemeat is not used in addition. In preparing it a pound and a quarter of fat should be mixed with each pound of the lean.

To give the turkey a very good appearance, the breast may be larded by the directions of page 139.

TURKEY À LA FLAMANDE, OR, DINDE POUDRÉE.

Prepare as for boiling a fine well-kept hen turkey; wipe the inside thoroughly with a dry cloth, but do not wash it; throw in a little salt to draw out the blood, let it remain a couple of hours or more, then drain and wipe it again; next, rub the outside in every part with about four ounces of fine dry salt, mixed with a large tablespoonful of pounded sugar; rub the turkey well with these, and turn it every day for four days; then fill it entirely with equal parts of choice sausage-meat, and of the crumb of bread soaked in boiling milk or cream, and wrung dry in a cloth; season these with the grated rind of a large lemon, a small nutmeg, some mace, cayenne, and fine herbs, in the same proportion as for veal forcemeat (No. 1, page 122.) Sew the turkey up very securely, and when trussed, roll it in a cloth, tie it closely at both ends, and boil it very gently between three and four hours. When taken up, sprinkle it thickly with fine crumbs of bread, mixed with plenty of parsley, shred extremely small. Serve it cold, with a sauce made of the strained juice and grated rind of two lemons, a teaspoonful of made-mustard, and one of pounded sugar, with as much oil as will prevent its being more than pleasantly acid, and a little salt, if needed; work these together until perfectly mixed, and send them to table in a tureen.

This receipt was given to us abroad, by a Flemish lady, who had had the dish often served with great success in Paris. We have inserted it on her authority, not on our own experience; but we think it may be quite depended on.

TO ROAST A GOOSE.

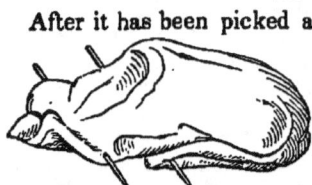

After it has been picked and singed with care, put into the body of the goose two parboiled onions of moderate size, finely chopped, and mixed with half an ounce of minced sage-leaves, a saltspoonful of salt, and half as much black pepper, or a proportionate quantity of cayenne; to these add a small slice of fresh butter. Truss the goose, and after it is on the spit, tie it firmly at both ends that it may turn steadily, and that the seasoning may not escape; roast it at a brisk fire, and keep it constantly basted. Serve it with brown gravy, and apple or tomata sauce. When the taste is in favour of a stronger seasoning than the above, which occurs, we apprehend, but seldom, use raw onions for it, and increase the quantity; but should one still milder be preferred, mix a handful of fine bread-crumbs with the other ingredients, or two or three minced apples. The body of a goose is sometimes filled entirely with mashed potatoes, which, for this purpose, ought to be boiled very dry, and well blended with two or three ounces of butter, or with some *thick cream*, some salt, and white pepper or cayenne: to these minced sage and parboiled onions can also be added at pleasure. A teaspoonful of made-mustard, half as much of salt, and a small portion of cayenne, smoothly mixed with a glass o. port wine, are sometimes poured into the goose just before it is served, through a cut made in the apron.

1¼ to 1¾ hour.

Goose ready for the Spit.

Obs.—We extract, for the benefit of our readers, from a work in our possession, the following passage, of which we have had no opportunity of testing the correctness. "Geese, with sage and onions, may be deprived of power to breathe forth any incense, thus:—Pare from a lemon all the yellow rind, taking care not to bruise the fruit nor to cut so deeply as to let out the juice. Place this lemon in the centre of the seasoning within the bird. When or before it is brought to table, let the flap be gently opened, remove the lemon with a tablespoon; avoid breaking, and let it instantly be thrown away, as its white pithy skin will have absorbed all the gross particles which else would have escaped."

TO ROAST A GREEN GOOSE.

Season the inside with a little pepper and salt, and roast the goose at a brisk fire from forty to fifty minutes. Serve it with good brown gravy only, and sorrel sauce.

TO ROAST A FOWL.

Strip off the feathers, and carefully pick every stump or plug from the skin, as nothing can be more uninviting than the appearance of any kind of poultry where this has been neglected, nor more indicative of slovenliness on the part of the cook. Take off the head and neck close to the body, but leave sufficient of the skin to tie over the part that is cut. In drawing the bird, do not open it more than is needful, and use great

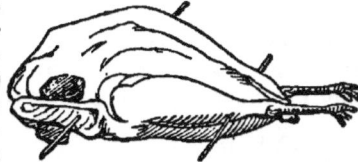

Fowl for Roasting.

precaution to avoid breaking the gall-bladder. Hold the legs in boiling water for two or three minutes, that the skin may be peeled from them easily; cut off the claws, and then, with a bit of lighted writing-paper, singe off the hairs without blackening the fowl. Wash, and wipe it afterwards very dry, and let the liver and gizzard be made delicately clean, and fastened into the pinions. Truss, and spit it firmly; flour it well when first laid to the fire, baste it frequently with butter, and when it is done, draw out the skewers, dish it, pour a little good gravy over, and send it to table with bread, mushroom, egg, chestnut, or olive sauce. A common mode of serving roast fowls in France is *aux cres-sons*, that is, laid upon young water-cresses, which have previously been freed from the outer leaves, thoroughly washed, shaken dry in a clean cloth, and sprinkled with a little fine salt, and a small quantity of vinegar: these should cover the dish, and after the fowls are placed on them, gravy should be poured over as usual.

The body of a fowl may be filled with very small mushrooms prepared as for partridges (see partridges with mushrooms), then sewn up, roasted, and served with mushroom-sauce: this is an excellent mode of dressing it. A slice of fresh butter mixed with some salt and cayenne or pepper; a little rasped bacon; or a bit or two of the lean of beef or veal minced, or cut into dice, may be put inside the bird when either is considered an improvement. An ounce or two of fresh butter smoothly mixed with a teaspoonful of *really good* mushroom-powder, a little pounded mace, salt, and cayenne, will impart much more of flavour to the fowl.

Full-sized fowl, 1 hour: young chicken, 25 to 35 minutes.

Obs.—As we have already observed in our general remarks on roast-ing, the time must be regulated by various circumstances, which we named, and which the cook should always take into consideration. A buttered paper should be fastened over the breast, and removed about fifteen minutes before the fowl is served: this will prevent its taking too much colour.

ROAST FOWL; (*a French Receipt.*)

Fill the breast of a fine fowl with good forcemeat, roast it as usual, and when it is very nearly ready to serve take it from the fire, pour lukewarm butter over it in every part, and strew it thickly with very fine bread-crumbs; sprinkle these again with butter, and dip the fowl into more crumbs. Put it down to the fire, and when it is of a clear, light brown all over, take it carefully from the spit, dish, and serve it with lemon-sauce, and with gravy thickened and mixed with plenty of minced parsley, or with brown-gravy and any other sauce usually served with fowls. Savoury herbs shred small, spice, and lemon-grate, may be mixed with the crumbs at pleasure. Do not pour gravy over the fowl when it is thus prepared.

TO ROAST A GUINEA FOWL.

Let the bird hang for as many days as the weather will allow; then stuff, truss, roast, and serve it like a turkey, or leave the head on and lard the breast. Send gravy and bread-sauce to table with it in either case: it will be found excellent eating.

¾ to 1 hour.

FOWL A LA CARLSFORT. (ENTRÉE.)

Bone a fowl without opening the back, and restore it to its original form by filling the vacant spaces in the legs and wings with forcemeat; put a roll of it also into the body, and a large sausage on either side; tie it very securely at both ends, truss it with fine skewers, and roast it for a full hour, keeping it basted plentifully with butter. When ap-pearance is not regarded, the pinions may be taken off, and the legs and wings drawn inside the fowl, which will then require a much smaller proportion of forcemeat:—that directed for veal (No. 1, page 122), will answer quite well in a general way, but for a dinner of ceremony, No. 17 or 18 of the same Chapter should be used in preference. The fowl must be *tied* securely to the spit, not put upon it. Bone chickens are excellent when entirely filled with well-made mushroom-forcemeat, or very delicate and nicely seasoned sausage-meat; and either roasted or stewed. Brown gravy, or mushroom sauce should then be sent to table with them.

BOILED FOWLS.

Fowls trussed for Boiling.

White-legged poultry should al-ways be selected for boiling, as they are of better colour when dressed than any others. Truss them firmly and neatly, with the legs drawn into the bodies, and the wings twisted over the backs; let them be well covered with water, which should be hot, but not boiling when they are put in. A full-sized fowl will require about three quarters of an hour from the time of its beginning to simmer; but young chickens not more than from twenty to twenty-five minutes: they should be *very gently* boiled, and the scum should be removed with great care as it gathers on the surface of the water. Either of the following sauces may be sent to table with them: parsley and butter, béchamel, English white sauce, oyster, celery, or white-mushroom sauce. The fowls are often dished with small tufts of delicately-boiled cauliflower placed round them; or with young vegetable marrow, scarcely larger than an egg, merely pared and halved after it is dressed: white sauce must be served with both of these. The livers and gizzards are not, at the present day, usually served in the wings of boiled fowls. When they are not so, the livers may be simmered for four or five minutes, then pressed to a smooth paste with a wooden spoon, and mixed very gradually with the sauce, which should not boil after they are added.

Full-sized fowl, ¾ hour: young chickens, 20 to 25 minutes.

Obs.—Half a gallon of cold added to an equal quantity of boiling water, will bring it to the proper degree of heat for putting in the fowls. For richer modes of boiling poultry, see *Blanc* and *Poêlée*, Chapter VII.

TO BROIL A CHICKEN OR FOWL.

Either of these, when merely split and broiled, is very dry and unsavoury eating; but will be greatly improved if first boiled gently from five to ten minutes and left to become cold, then divided, dipped into egg and well seasoned bread-crumbs, plentifully sprinkled with clarified butter, dipped again into the crumbs, and broiled over a clear and gentle fire from half to three quarters of an hour. It should be served very hot, with mushroom-sauce, or with a little good plain gravy, which may be thickened and flavoured with a teaspoonful of mushroom powder (should it be at hand), mixed with half as much flour and a little butter; or with some Espagnole. It should be opened at the back, and evenly divided quite through; the legs should be trussed like those of a boiled fowl; the breast-bone, or that of the back may be removed at pleasure, and both sides of the bird should be made as flat as they can, that the fire may penetrate every part equally; the inside should be first laid towards it. The neck, feet, and gizzard may be boiled down with a small quantity of onion and carrot previously browned in a morsel of butter, to make the gravy; and the liver, after having been simmered with them for five or six minutes, may be used to thicken it after it is strained. A teaspoonful of lemon-juice, some cayenne, and minced parsley should be added to it, and a little arrow-root, or flour and butter.

½ to ¾ hour.

FRICASSEED FOWLS OR CHICKENS. (ENTRÉE.)

To make a fricassee of good appearance without great expense, prepare, with exceeding nicety, a couple of plump chickens, strip off the skin, and carve them very neatly. Reserve the wings, breasts, merrythoughts, and thighs; and stew down the inferior joints with a couple of blades of mace, a small bunch of savoury herbs, a few white peppercorns, a pint and a half of water, and a small half-teaspoonful of salt. When something more than a third part reduced, strain the gravy, let it cool, and skim off every particle of fat. Arrange the joints which are to be fricasseed in one layer, if it can be done conveniently, and pour to them as much of the gravy as will nearly cover them; add the very thin rind of half a fine fresh lemon, and simmer the fowls gently from half to three quarters of an hour; throw in sufficient salt, pounded mace, and cayenne to give the sauce a good flavour, thicken it with a large teaspoonful of arrow-root, and stir to it the third of a pint of rich boiling cream; then lift the stewpan from the fire, and shake it briskly round while the beaten yolks of three fresh eggs, mixed with a spoonful or two of cream, are added; continue to shake the pan gently above the fire till the sauce is just set, but it must not be allowed to boil, or it will curdle in an instant.

½ to ¾ hour.

CHICKEN CUTLETS. (ENTRÉE.)

Skin, and cut into joints, one or two young chickens, and remove the bones with care from the breasts, merrythoughts, and thighs, which are to be separated from the legs. Mix well together a teaspoonful of salt, and nearly a fourth as much of mace, a little grated nutmeg, and cayenne; flatten, and form into good shape, the boned joints of chicken, and the flesh of the wings; rub a little of the seasoning over them in every part, dip them into beaten egg, and then into very fine bread-crumbs, and fry them gently in fresh butter until they are of a delicate brown. Some of the bones and trimmings may be boiled down in half a pint of water, with a roll of lemon-peel, a little salt, and eight or ten white peppercorns, to make the gravy, which, after being strained and cleared from fat, may be poured hot to some thickening made in the pan with a slice of fresh butter and a dessertspoonful of flour: a tea-spoonful of mushroom-powder would improve it greatly, and a small quantity of lemon-pickle or juice should be added before it is poured out, with salt and cayenne if required. Pile the cutlets high in the middle of the dish, and serve the sauce under them, or in a tureen.

CUTLETS OF FOWLS, PARTRIDGES, OR PIGEONS. (ENTRÉE.)
(French Receipt.)

Take closely off the flesh of the breast and wing together, on either side of the bone, and when you have thus raised the large *fillets*, as they are called, from three birds, which will give you but six cutlets, take the strips of flesh that lie under the wings, and that of the merry-thoughts, and flatten two or three of these together, that you may have nine cutlets at least, of equal size. When all are ready, fry to a pale brown as many diamond-shaped sippets of bread as there are fillets of fowl, and let them be quite as large; place these before the fire to dry, and wipe out the pan. Dip the cutlets into some yolks of eggs mixed with a little clarified butter, and strew them in every part with the finest bread-crumbs, moderately seasoned with salt, cayenne, and pounded mace. Dissolve as much good butter as will be required to dress them, and fry them in it of a light amber-colour: arrange them upon the sippets of bread, pile them high in the dish, and pour a rich brown gravy or Sauce Espagnole round, but not *over* them.

FRIED CHICKEN A LA MALABAR. (ENTRÉE.)

This is an Indian dish. Cut up the chicken, wipe it dry, and rub it well with currie-powder, mixed with a little salt; fry it in a bit of but-

ter, taking care that it is of a nice light brown. In the meantime cut
two or three onions into thin slices, draw them out into rings, and cut
the rings into little bits, about half an inch long; fry them for a long
time gently in a little bit of clarified butter, until they have gradually
dried up and are of a delicate yellow-brown. Be careful that they are
not burnt, as the burnt taste of a single bit would spoil the flavour of
the whole. When they are as dry as chips, without the least grease or
moisture upon them, mix a little salt with them, strew them over the
fried chicken, and serve up with lemon on a plate.

We have extracted this receipt from a clever little work called the
" Hand-Book of Cookery."

HASHED FOWL. (ENTRÉE.)

After having taken off, in joints, as much of a cold fowl or *fowls* as
will suffice for a dish, bruise the bodies with a paste roller, pour to them
a pint of water, and boil them for an hour and a half to two hours, with
the addition of a little pepper and salt only, or with a small quantity of
onion, carrot, and herbs. Strain, and skim the fat from the gravy, put
it into a clean saucepan, and, should it require thickening, stir to it
when it boils half a teaspoonful of flour, smoothly mixed with a small
bit of butter; add a little mushroom catsup, or store-sauce, with a slight
seasoning of mace or nutmeg. Lay in the fowl, and keep it near the
fire until it is heated quite through, and is at the point of boiling : serve
it with fried sippets round the dish. For a hash of higher relish, add
to the bones, when they are first stewed down, a large onion, minced
and browned in butter, and before the fowl is dished add some cayenne,
and the juice of half a lemon.

MINCED FOWL. (ENTRÉE.) (*French Receipt.*)

Raise from the bones all the more delicate parts of the flesh of either
cold roast, or cold boiled fowls, clear it from the skin, and keep it covered from the air until wanted for use. Boil the bones, well bruised,
and the skin, with three quarters or a pint of water, until reduced quite
half, then strain the gravy and let it cool; next, having first skimmed
off the fat, put it into a clean saucepan, with a quarter-pint of cream,
an ounce and a half of butter, well mixed with a dessertspoonful of
flour, a little pounded mace, and grated lemon-rind; keep these stirred
until they boil, then put in the fowl, finely minced, with three or four
hard-boiled eggs, chopped small, and sufficient salt, and white pepper,
or cayenne, to season it properly. Shake the mince over the fire until
it is just ready to boil, stir to it quickly a squeeze of lemon-juice, dish
it with pale sippets of fried bread, and serve it immediately. When
cream cannot easily be obtained, use milk, with a double quantity of
butter and flour. The eggs may be omitted; the mince may be warmed
in good white sauce, and a border formed round it of leaves of pastry,
fried or baked; or it may be served in a *vol-au-vent.* Poached eggs are
sometimes laid over it, and a garnish of curled bacon is placed round
the edge. Another excellent variety of the dish is also made by co-
vering the fowl thickly with very fine bread-crumbs, moistening them
with clarified butter, and giving them colour with a salamander, or in
a quick oven.*

---

* For minced fowl and oysters, follow the receipt for veal, page 174

I 9

COLD FOWLS, EN FRITURE.

Cut into joints, and take the skin from some cold fowls, lay them into
a deep dish, strew over them a little fine salt and cayenne, add the juice
of a lemon, and let them remain for an hour, moving them occasionally,
that they may all absorb a portion of the acid; then dip them one by
one into some French batter (see page 113), and fry them a pale brown
over a gentle fire. Serve them garnished with very green crisped
parsley. A few drops of eschalot vinegar may be mixed with the
lemon-juice which is poured to the fowls, or slices of raw onion or
eschalot, and small branches of sweet herbs may be laid amongst them,
and cleared off before they are dipped into the batter. Gravy made of
the trimmings, thickened, and well flavoured, may be sent to table with
them in a tureen, and dressed bacon (see page 196,) in a dish apart.

SCALLOPS OF FOWL, AU BÉCHAMEL. (ENTRÉE.)

Raise the flesh from a couple of fowls, as directed for cutlets in the
foregoing receipt, and take it as entire as possible from either side of
the breast; strip off the skin, lay the fillets flat, and slice them into
small thin scallops; dip them one by one into clarified butter, and
arrange them evenly in a delicately clean and not large frying-pan;
sprinkle a seasoning of fine salt over, and just before the dish is wanted
for table, fry them quickly without allowing them to brown; drain them
well from the butter, pile them in the centre of a hot dish, and sauce
them with some boiling béchamel. This dish may be quickly prepared
by taking a ready-dressed fowl from the spit or stewpan, and by raising
the fillets, and slicing the scallops into the boiling sauce before they
have had time to cool.

Fried, 3 to 4 minutes.

GRILLADE OF COLD FOWLS.

Carve and soak the remains of roast fowls as above, wipe them dry,
dip them into clarified butter, and then into fine bread-crumbs, and broil
them gently over a very clear fire. A little finely-minced lean of ham,
or grated lemon-peel, with a seasoning of cayenne, salt, and mace, mixed
with the crumbs, will vary this dish agreeably. When fried, instead
of broiled, the fowls may be dipped into yolk of egg, instead of butter,
but this renders them too dry for the gridiron.

COLD FOWLS; (the Housekeeper's Receipt; a Supper Dish.)

Cut very equally a sufficient number of slices from a cold ham, to
form two or even three layers round the rim of the dish which is to be
sent to table. Place the fowls, neatly carved and trimmed, in the
centre, with some branches of curled parsley, or other light foliage
amongst them. Cold tongue may be substituted for the ham with advantage. This dish has a handsome appearance, and is convenient for
the purpose of quick serving.

FOWLS A LA MAYONNAISE.

Carve with great nicety a couple of cold roast fowls; place the inferior joints, if they are served at all, close together in the middle of a
dish, and arrange the others round and over them, piling them as high
as you can in the centre. Border the dish with the hearts of young lettuces cut in two, and hard-boiled eggs, halved longthwise. At the mo-

ment of serving, pour over the fowls a well-made mayonnaise sauce (see page 104), or, if preferred, a salad mixture, compounded with thick cream, instead of oil.

TO ROAST DUCKS.

In preparing these for the spit, be careful to clear the skin entirely from the stumps of the feathers; take off the heads and necks, but leave the feet on, and hold them for a few minutes in boiling water to loosen the skin, which must be peeled off. Wash the insides of the birds by pouring water through them, but merely wipe the outsides with a dry cloth. Put into the bodies a seasoning of par-boiled onions mixed with minced sage, salt, pepper, and a slice of butter, when this mode of dressing them is

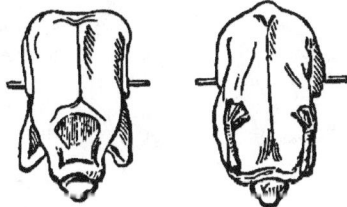

Ducks ready for the spit.

liked; but as the taste of a whole party is seldom in its favour, one, when a couple are roasted, is often served without the stuffing. Cut off the pinions at the first joint from the bodies, truss the feet behind the backs, spit the birds firmly, and roast them at a brisk fire, but do not place them sufficiently near to be scorched; baste them constantly, and when the breasts are well plumped, and the steam from them draws towards the fire, dish, and serve them quickly with a little good brown gravy poured round them, and some also in a tureen; or instead of this, with some which has been made with the necks, gizzards, and livers well stewed down, with a slight seasoning of browned onion, some herbs, and spice.

Young ducks, ½ hour: full sized, from ¾ to 1 hour.

Obs.—Olive-sauce may be served with roast as well as with stewed ducks.

STEWED DUCK. (ENTRÉE.)

A couple of quite young ducks, or a fine full-grown, but still tender one, will be required for this dish. Cut either down neatly into joints, and arrange them, in a single layer if possible, in a wide stewpan; pour in about three-quarters of a pint of strong, cold beef stock or gravy; let it be well cleared from scum when it begins to boil, then throw in a little salt, a rather full seasoning of cayenne, and a few thin strips of lemon-rind. Simmer the ducks very softly for three-quarters of an hour, or somewhat longer, should the joints be large; then stir into the gravy a tablespoonful of the finest rice-flour, mixed with a wineglassful or rather more of port wine, and a dessertspoonful of lemon-juice: in ten minutes after, dish the stew and send it to table instantly.

The ducks may be served with a small portion only of their sauce, laid in a circle, with green peas *à la Française*, heaped high in the centre; the lemon-rind and port wine should then be altogether omitted, and a small bunch of green onions and parsley, with two or three young carrots, may be stewed down with the birds; or three or four minced eschalots, delicately fried in butter, may be used to flavour the gravy. Turnips *au beurre*, prepared by the receipt of Chapter XV., may be substituted for the peas; and a well-made Espagnole may take the place of beef stock, when a dish of high savour is wished for. A duck is often stewed without being divided into joints. It should then be

firmly trussed, half roasted at a quick fire, and laid into the stewpan as
it is taken from the spit; or well browned in some French thickening,
then half covered with boiling gravy, and turned when partially done:
from an hour to an hour and a quarter will stew it well.

TO ROAST PIGEONS.

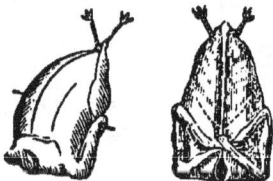

Pigeons for roasting.

These, as we have already said, should be
dressed while they are very fresh. If extremely young they will be ready in twelve
hours for the spit, otherwise, in twenty-four.
Take off the heads and necks, and cut off
the toes at the first joint; draw them carefully, that the gall-bladders may not be
broken, and pour plenty of water through
them; wipe them dry, and put into each
bird a small bit of butter lightly dipped into a little cayenne (formerly it
was rolled in minced parsley, but this is no longer the fashionable mode
of preparing them.) Truss the wings over the backs, and roast them
at a brisk fire, keeping them well and constantly basted with butter.
Serve them with brown gravy, and a tureen of parsley and butter. For
the second course, dish them upon young water-cresses, as directed for
roast fowl *aux cressons*, page 205. About twenty minutes will roast
them.

18 to 20 minutes; five minutes longer, if large; rather less, if *very*
young.

BOILED PIGEONS.

Truss them like boiled fowls, drop them into plenty of boiling water,
throw in a little salt, and in fifteen minutes lift them out, pour parsley
and butter over, and send a tureen of it to table with them.

TO STEW PIGEONS.

Wash and clean six pigeons, cut them into quarters, and put all their
giblets with them into a stewpan, a piece of butter, a little water, a bit
of lemon-peel, two blades of mace, some chopped parsley, salt, and pepper; cover the pan closely, and stew them till they are tender; thicken
the sauce with the yolk of an egg beaten up with three table-spoonsful
of cream and a bit of butter dusted with flour; let them stew ten
minutes longer before serving. This is an excellent and economical
way of cooking them.

CHAPTER XIII.

GAME.

TO CHOOSE GAME.

Buck venison, which is in season only from June to Michaelmas, is
considered finer than doe venison, which comes into the market in
October, and remains in season through November and December:
neither should be cooked at any other part of the year. The greater
the depth of fat upon the haunch the better the quality of the meat will

be, provided it be clear and white, and the lean of a dark hue. If tho cleft of the hoof, which is always left on the joint, be small and smooth, the animal is young; but it is old when the marks are the reverse of these.* Although the haunch is the prime and favourite joint of venison, the neck and shoulder are also excellent, stewed in various wayc, or made into pasties. If kept to the proper point, and well dressed, this is the most tender of all meat; but care is necessary to bring it into a fitting state for table without its becoming offensive. A free current of air in a larder is always a great advantage, as it assists materially in preserving the sweetness of every thing which is kept in it, while a close damp atmosphere, on the contrary, is more destructive of animal food of all kinds even than positive heat. The fumes of creosote are said to be an admirable preservative against putrescence, but we have not ourselves yet had experience of the fact. All moisture should be wiped daily, or even more frequently, from the venison, with soft cloths, when any appears upon the surface; and every precaution must be taken to keep off the flies, when the joint is not hung in a wire-safe. Black pepper thickly powdered on it will generally answer the purpose: with common care, indeed, meat may always be protected from their attacks, and to leave it exposed to them in warm weather is altogether inexcusable in the cook.

Hares and rabbits are stiff when freshly killed, and if young, the ears tear easily, and the claws are smooth and sharp. A hare in cold weather will remain good from ten to fourteen days; care only must be taken to prevent the inside from becoming musty, which it will do if it has been emptied in the field. Pigeons, partridges, and other game may be chosen by nearly the same tests as poultry: by opening the bill, the staleness will be detected easily if they have been too long kept. With few exceptions, game depends almost entirely for the fine flavour and the tenderness of its flesh, on the time which it is allowed to hang before it is cooked, and it is never good when very fresh; but it does not follow that it should be sent to table in a really offensive state, for this is agreeable to few eaters and disgusting to many, and nothing should at any time be served of which the appearance or the odour may destroy the appetite of any person present.

TO ROAST A HAUNCH OF VENISON.

To give venison the flavour and the tenderness so much prized by epicures, it must be well kept; and by taking the necessary precautions, it will hang a considerable time without detriment. Wipe it with soft dry cloths wherever the slightest moisture appears on the surface, and dust it plentifully with freshly-ground pepper or powdered ginger, to preserve it from the flies. The application of the pyroligneous or ascetic acid would effectually protect it from these, as well as from the effects of

* It must be observed that venison is not in perfect on when young: like mutton, it requires to be of a certain age before it is brought to table. The word cleft applies also to the thickest part of the haunch, and it is the depth of the fat on this which decides the quality of the joint.

the weather; but the joint must then be not only well washed, but *soaked* some considerable time, and this would be injurious to lt: the acid, therefore, should only be resorted to for the purpose of restoring to an eatable state that which would otherwise be lost, from having been kept beyond the point in which it is possible to serve it.

To prepare the venison for the spit, wash it slightly with tepid water, or merely wipe it thoroughly with damp cloths, and dry it afterwards with clean ones; then lay over the fat side a large sheet of thickly-buttered paper, and next a paste of flour and water about three quarters of an inch thick; cover this again with two or three sheets of stout paper, secure the whole well with .wine, and lay the haunch to a sound clear fire; baste the paper immediately with butter, or clarified dripping, and roast the joint from three hours and a half to four and a half, according to its weight and quality. Doe venison will require half an hour less time than buck venison. Twenty minutes before the joint is done remove the paste and paper, baste the meat in every part with butter, and dredge it very lightly with flour; let it take a pale brown colour, and send it to table as hot as possible with unflavoured gravy in a tureen, and good currant-jelly. It is not now customary to serve any other sauces with it; but should the old-fashioned sharp or sweet sauce be ordered, the receipt for it will be found at page 88.*

3½ to 4½ hours.

TO STEW A SHOULDER OF VENISON.

Bone the joint, by the directions given for a shoulder of veal or mutton (see page 166); flatten it on a table, season it well with cayenne, salt, and pounded mace, mixed with a very small proportion of allspice; lay over it thin slices of the fat of a loin of well-fed mutton, roll and bind it tightly, lay it into a vessel nearly of its size, and pour to it as much good stock made with equal parts of beef and mutton as will nearly cover it; stew it as slowly as possible from three hours to three and a half or longer, should it be very large, and turn it when it is half done. Dish and serve it with a good Espagnole, made with part of the gravy in which it has been stewed; or thicken this slightly with rice-flour, mixed with a glass or more of claret or of port wine, and as much salt and cayenne as will season the gravy properly.

Some cooks soak the slices of mutton-fat in wine before they are laid upon the joint; but no process of the sort will ever give to any kind of meat the true flavour of the venison, which to most eaters is far finer than that of the wine, and should always be allowed to prevail over all the condiments with which it is dressed. Those, however, who care for it less than for a dish of high artificial savour, can have eschalots, ham, and carrot, lightly browned in good butter, added to the stew when it first begins to boil.

3½ to 4 hours.

TO HASH VENISON.†

For a superior hash of venison, add to three quarters of a pint of strong thickened brown gravy, Christopher North's sauce, in the propor-

---

* Plates of minced eschalots are still sometimes handed round to the venison-eaters; but not at very refined tables, we believe.

† Minced collops of venison may be prepared exactly like those of beef; and venison-cutlets like those of mutton: the neck may be taken for both of these.

tion directed for in the receipt of page 102. Cut the venison in small thin slices of equal size, arrange them in a clean saucepan, pour the gravy on them, let them stand for ten minutes or more, then place them near the fire, and bring the whole very slowly to the *point* of boiling only : serve the hash immediately in a hot-water dish.

For a plain dinner, when no gravy is at hand, break down the bones of the venison small, after the flesh has been cleared from them, and boil them with those of three or four undressed mutton-cutlets, a slice or two of carrot, or a few savoury herbs, and about a pint and a half of water or broth, until the liquid is reduced quite one third   Strain it off, let it cool, skim off all the fat, heat the gravy, thicken it when it boils with a dessertspoonful or rather more of arrow-root, or with the brown *roux* of page 92, mix the same sauce with it, and finish it exactly as the richer hash above. It may be served on aippets of fried bread or not, at choice.

TO ROAST A HARE.

After the hare has been skinned, or cased, as it is called, wash it very thoroughly in cold water, and afterwards in warm. If in any degree overkept, or musty in the inside, which it will sometimes be when emp-

tied before it is hung up, and neglected afterwards, use vinegar, or the pyroligneous acid, well diluted, to render it sweet; then again throw it into abundance of water, that it may retain no taste of the acid. Pierce with the point of a knife any parts in which the blood appears to have settled,

Hare Dressed for Roasting.

and soak them in tepid water, that it may be well drawn out. Wipe the hare dry, fill it with the forcemeat No. 1, page 122, sew it up, truss and spit it firmly, baste it for ten minutes with lukewarm water, mixed with a very little salt, throw this away, and put into the pan a quart or more of new milk; keep it constantly laded over the hare, until it is nearly dried up, then add a large lump of butter, flour the hare, and continue the basting steadily until it is well browned ; for unless this be done, and the roast be kept at a proper distance from the fire, the outside will become so dry and hard as to be quite uneatable. Serve the hare when done, with good brown gravy (of which a little should be poured round it in the dish), and with fine red currant jelly. This is an approved English method of dressing it, but we would recommend in preference, that it should be basted plentifully with butter from the beginning (the strict economist may substitute clarified beef-dripping, and finish with a small quantity of butter only); and that the salt and water should be altogether omitted. Firstrate cooks merely wipe the hare inside and out, and rub it with its own blood before it is laid to the fire; but there is generally a rankness about it, especially after it has been many days killed, which, we should say, renders the washing indispensable, unless a coarse game-flavour be liked.

1¼ to 1¾ hour.

TO ROAST A RABBIT.

This, like a hare, is much improved by having the back-bone taken out, and the directions we have given will enable the cook, with very little practice, to remove it without difficulty. Line the inside, when this is done, with thin slices of bacon, fill it with forcemeat (No. 1, page 122), sew it up, truss, and roast it at a clear, brisk fire, and baste it constantly with butter. Flour it well soon after it is laid down. Serve it with good brown gravy, and with currant jelly, when this last is liked. For change, the back of the rabbit may be larded, and the bone left in, or not, at pleasure; or it can be plain roasted when more convenient.

¾ to 1 hour; less, if small.

TO BOIL RABBITS.

Rabbits that are three parts grown, or, at all events, which are still quite young, should be chosen for this mode of cooking. Wash and soak them well, truss them firmly, with the heads turned and skewered to the sides, drop them into plenty of boiling water, and simmer them gently from thirty to forty-five minutes: when

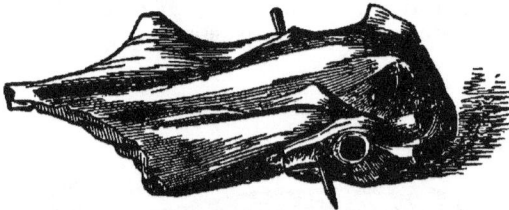

Rabbit Trussed for Boiling.

very young they will require even less time than this. Cover them with rich white sauce, mixed with the livers parboiled, and finely pounded, and well seasoned with cayenne and lemon-juice; or with white onion sauce, or with parsley and butter, made with milk or cream, instead of water, (the livers, minced, are often added to the last of these,) or with good mushroom sauce.

30 to 45 minutes.

FRIED RABBIT.

After the rabbit has been emptied, thoroughly washed, and well soaked, blanch it, that is to say, put it into boiling water, and let it boil from five to seven minutes; drain it, and when cold, or nearly so, cut it into joints, dip them into beaten egg, and then into fine bread-crumbs, seasoned with salt and pepper, and when all are ready, fry them in butter over a moderate fire, from twelve to fifteen minutes. Simmer two or three strips of lemon-rind in a little gravy, until it is well flavoured with it; boil the liver of the rabbit for five minutes, let it cool, and then mince it; thicken the gravy with an ounce of butter, and a small teaspoonful of flour, add the liver, give the sauce a minute's boil, stir in two tablespoonsful of cream, if at hand, and, last of all, a small quantity of lemon-juice. Dish the rabbit, pour the sauce *under* it, and serve it quickly. If preferred, a gravy can be made in the pan, as for veal cutlets, and the rabbit may be simply fried.

TO ROAST PARTRIDGES.

Let the birds hang as long as they can possibly be kept without becoming offensive; pick them carefully, draw, and singe them; wipe the insides thoroughly with a clean cloth; truss them with the head turned under the wing and the legs drawn close together or crossed. Flour them when first laid to the fire, and baste them plentifully with butter. Serve them with bread sauce, and good brown gravy: a little of this last should be poured over them. In some instances they are dished upon fried bread-crumbs, but these are better handed round the table by themselves. Where game is plenti-ful we recommend that the remains of a cold roasted partridge should be well bruised and boiled down with just so much water, or unfla-

A Partridge Trussed for Roasting.

voured broth, as will make gravy for a couple of other birds: this, sea-soned with salt and cayenne only, or flavoured with a few mushrooms, will be found a very superior accompaniment for roast partridges, to the best meat-gravy that can be made. A little eschalot, and a few herbs can be added to it at pleasure. It should be served also with boiled or with broiled partridges in preference to any other.

30 to 40 minutes.

Obs.—Rather less time must be allowed when the birds are liked underdressed. In preparing them for the spit, the crop must be re-moved through a slit cut in the back of the neck, the claws clipped close, and the legs held in boiling water for a minute, that they may be skinned the more easily.

BOILED PARTRIDGES.

This is a delicate mode of dressing young and tender birds. Strip off the feathers, clean, and wash them well; cut off the heads, truss them like boiled fowls, and when ready, drop them into a large pan of boiling water; throw a little salt on them, and in fifteen, or at the ut-most in eighteen minutes they will be ready to serve. Lift them out, dish them quickly, and send them to table with white mushroom-sauce, with bread sauce and game gravy (see preceding receipt), or with celery sauce. Our own mode of having them served is usually with a slice of fresh butter, about a tablespoonful of lemon-juice, and a good sprinkling of cayenne placed in a very hot dish, under them.

15 to 18 minutes.

PARTRIDGES WITH MUSHROOMS.

For a brace of young well-kept birds, prepare from half to three quar-ters of a pint of mushroom-buttons, or very small flaps, as for pickling Dissolve over a gentle fire an ounce and a half of butter, throw in the mushrooms with a slight sprinkling of salt and cayenne, simmer them from eight to ten minutes, and turn them, with the butter, on to a plate; when they are quite cold, put the whole into the bodies of the partridges, sew them up, truss them securely, and roast them on a vertical jack with the heads downwards; or should an ordinary spit be used, tie them firmly to it, instead of passing it through them. Roast them the usual time, and serve them with brown mushroom-sauce, or with gravy and bread sauce only. The birds may be trussed like boiled fowls, floured, and lightly browned in butter; half covered with *rich* brown gravy and stewed slowly for thirty minutes; then turned, and simmered for ano-ther half hour with the addition of some mushrooms to the gravy; or they may be covered with small mushrooms stewed apart, when they are sent to table. They can also be served with their sauce only, simply thickened with a small quantity of fresh butter, smoothly mixed with less than a teaspoonful of arrow-root and flavoured with cayenne and a little catsup, wine, or store-sauce.

Partridges, 2; mushrooms, ½ to ¾ pint; butter, 1½ oz.; little mace and cayenne: roasted 30 to 40 minutes, or stewed 1 hour.

Obs.—Nothing can be finer than the game flavour imbibed by the mushrooms with which the birds are filled, in this receipt.

BROILED PARTRIDGE; (*Breakfast dish.*)

" Split a young and well-kept partridge, and wipe it with a soft clean cloth inside and out, but do not wash it; broil it delicately over a very clear fire, sprinkling it with a little salt and cayenne; rub a bit of fresh butter over it the moment it is taken from the fire, and send it quickly to table with a sauce made of a good slice of butter browned with flour, a little water, cayenne, salt, and mushroom-catsup, poured over it." We give this receipt exactly as we received it from a house where we know it to have been greatly approved by various guests who have partaken of it there.

BROILED PARTRIDGE: (*French Receipt.*)

After having prepared the bird with great nicety, divided, and flattened it, season it with salt, and pepper, or cayenne, dip it into clarified butter, and then into very fine bread-crumbs, and take care that every part shall be equally covered: if wanted of particularly good appearance, dip it a second time into the butter and crumbs. Place it over a very clear fire, and broil it gently from twenty to thirty minutes. Send it to table with brown mushroom sauce, or some Espagnole.

[TO ROAST WILD PIGEONS.

Pigeons, when stuffed, require some green parsley to be chopped very fine with the liver and a bit of butter, seasoned with a little pepper and salt; or they may be stuffed with the same as a fillet of veal. Fill the belly of each bird with either of these compositions. They will roast in about twenty or thirty minutes. Serve with parsley and butter, with a dish under them, with some in a boat. Garnish with crisp parsley, fried bread crumbs, bread sauce or gravy.

TO ROAST SMALL BIRDS.

The most delicate of these are larks, which are in high season in November and December. When cleaned and prepared for roasting, brush them with the yolk of an egg, and roll in bread crumbs; spit them on a lark-spit, and tie that on a larger spit; ten or fifteen minutes at a quick fire will do them; baste them with fresh butter, and sprinkle them with bread crumbs, till they are quite covered, while roasting. Sauce, grated bread fried in butter, which set to drain before the fire that it may harden; serve the crumbs under the larks when you dish them, and garnish them with slices of lemon. *Wheatears* are dressed in the same way.

REED BIRDS.

Having carefully picked your birds, which should be very fat, draw them with the greatest care possible so as not to rob them of any fat, and truss them on a skewer, which you fasten to the spit, and cook them before a brisk fire; a very few minutes is requisite. In serving them, place them on buttered toast, and pour a small portion of gravy over them. Let them be hot. This is generally considered the best manner of serving reed-birds, although many persons prefer them breaded and fried, or barbacued. When they are very fat it is unnecessary to draw them. The season for this delicious bird is from tne middle of September to the first or second week in October.]

Obs.—There are few occasions, we think, in which the contents of the dripping-pan can be introduced at table with advantage; but in dressing moor game, we would strongly recommend the toast to be laid in it under the birds, as it will afford a superior relish even to the birds themselves.

A SALMI OF MOOR FOWL, PHEASANTS, OR PARTRIDGES. (ENTRÉE.)

This is an elegant mode of serving the remains of roasted game, but when a superlative salmi is desired, the birds must be scarcely more than half roasted for it. In either case, carve them very neatly, and strip every particle of skin and fat from the legs, wings, and breasts· bruise the bodies well, and put them with the skin, and other trimmings, into a very clean stew-pan. If for a simple and inexpensive dinner, merely add to them two or three sliced eschalots, a bay-leaf, a small blade of mace, and a few peppercorns; then pour in a pint, or rather more, of good veal gravy, or strong broth, and boil it briskly until reduced nearly half; strain the gravy, pressing the bones well, to obtain all the flavour, skim off the fat, add a little cayenne, and lemon-juice, heat the game very gradually, in it, but do not, on any account, allow it to boil; place sippets of fried bread round a dish, arrange the birds in good form in the centre, give the sauce a boil, and pour it on them. This is but a homely sort of salmi, though of excellent flavour if well made; it may require perhaps the addition of a little thickening, and two or three glasses of dry white wine poured to the bodies of the birds, with the broth, would bring it nearer to the French salmi in flavour. As the spongy substance in the inside of moor fowl and black game is apt to be extremely bitter, when they have been long kept, care should be taken to remove such parts as would endanger the preparation.

TO ROAST CANVASS-BACK DUCKS.

Let your duck be young and fat, if possible; having picked it well, draw it and singe carefully, without washing it, so as to preserve the blood, and consequently, all its flavour. You then truss it, leaving its head on for the purpose of distinguishing it from common game, and place it on the spit before a brisk fire, for at least fifteen minutes. Then serve it hot, in its own gravy, on a large chafing-dish. The best birds are found on the Potomac River; they have the head purple, and the breast silver colour, and it is considered superior in quality and flavour to any other species of wild duck. The season is only during the cold weather.

TO ROAST WILD DUCKS.

These are prepared for the spit exactly like the tame ones, with the exception of the stuffing, which is never used for wild fowl. A bit of soft bread soaked in port wine, or in claret, is sometimes put into them, but nothing more. Flour them well, lay them rather near to a very clear and brisk fire, that they may be quickly browned, and yet retain their juices. Baste them plentifully and constantly with butter, and, if it can be so regulated, let the spit turn with them rapidly. From fifteen to twenty minutes will roast them sufficiently for the generality of eaters; but for those who object to them much underdressed, a few additional minutes must be allowed. Something less of time will suffice when they are prepared for persons who like them scarcely more than heated through.

Teal, which is a more delicate kind of wild fowl, is roasted in the same way: in from ten to fifteen minutes it will be enough done for the fashionable mode of serving it, and twenty minutes will dress it well at a good fire.

TO ROAST WOODCOCKS OR SNIPES.

Woodcock.

Handle them as little and as lightly as possible, and pluck off the feathers gently; for if this be violently done the skin of the birds will be broken. *Do not draw them*, but after having wiped them with clean soft cloths, truss them with the head under the wing, and the bill laid close along the breast; pass a slight skewer through the thighs, catch the ends with a bit of twine, and tie it across to keep the legs straight. Suspend the birds with the feet downwards to a bird-spit, flour them well, and baste them with butter, which should be ready dissolved in the pan or ladle. Before the trail begins to drop, which it will do as soon as they are well heated, lay a thick round of bread, freed from the crust, toasted to a delicate brown, and buttered on both sides, into the pan under them to catch it, as this is considered finer eating even than the flesh of the birds; continue the basting, letting the butter fall from them into the basting-spoon or ladle, as it cannot be collected again from the dripping-pan should it drop there, in consequence of the toast or *toasts* being in it. There should be one of these for each woodcock, and the trail should be spread equally over it. When the birds are done, which they will be, at a brisk fire, in from twenty to twenty-five minutes, lay the toasts into a very hot dish, dress the birds upon them, pour a little gravy round the bread, and send more to table in a tureen.

Woodcock, 20 to 25 minutes; snipe, 5 minutes less.

TO ROAST THE PINTAIL, OR SEA PHEASANT.

This beautiful bird is by no means rare upon the coast, but we know not whether it be much seen in the markets generally. It is most excellent eating, and should be roasted at a clear quick fire, well floured when first laid down, turned briskly, and basted with butter almost without cessation. If drawn from the spit in from twenty-five to thirty minutes, then dished and laid before the fire for two or three more, it will give forth a singularly rich gravy. Score the breast when it is carved, sprinkle on it a little cayenne and fine salt, and let a cut lemon be handed round the table when the bird is served; or omit the scoring, and send round with it brown gravy, and Christopher North's sauce made hot.

20 to 30 minutes.

CHAPTER XIV.

CURRIES, POTTED MEATS, &c.

THE great superiority of the oriental curries over those generally prepared in Europe or America, is not, we believe, altogether the result of a want of skill or of experience on the part of our cooks, but is attributable, in some measure, to many of the ingredients, which in a *fresh and green state* add so much to their excellence, being here beyond our reach.

The natives of the East compound and vary this class of dishes, we are told, with infinite ingenuity, blending in them very agreeably many condiments of different flavour, until the highest degree of piquancy and savour is produced, the whole being tempered with fine vegetable acids. With us, turmeric and cayenne pepper prevail in them often far too powerfully: the prodigal use of the former should be especially avoided, as it injures both the quality and the *colour* of the currie which ought to be of a dark green, rather than of a red or yellow hue. The first is given by the genuine powder imported from India; the others, by the greater number of spurious ones, sold in England and America under its name. A couple of ounces of a sweet, sound cocoa-nut, lightly grated and stewed for nearly or quite an hour in the gravy of a currie, is a great improvement to its flavour: it will be found particularly agreeable with that of sweetbreads, and may be served in the currie, or strained from it at pleasure. Great care, however, should be taken not to use, for the purpose, a nut that is rancid. Spinage, cucumbers, vegetable marrow, tomatas, acid apples, green gooseberries (seeded), and tamarinds imported *in the shell*—not preserved—may all, in their season, be added with very good effect to curries of different kinds. Potatoes and celery are also occasionally boiled down in them.

The rice for a currie should always be sent to table in a separate dish from it, and, in serving them, it should be first helped, and the currie laid upon it.

MR. ARNOTT'S CURRIE-POWDER.

Turmeric, eight ounces.*
Coriander seed, four ounces.
Cummin seed, two ounces.
Fœnugreek seed, two ounces.
Cayenne, half an ounce. (More or less of this last to the taste.)

---

* We think it would be an improvement to diminish by two ounces the proportion of turmeric, and to increase that of the coriander seed; but we have not tried it.

Let the seeds be of the finest quality. Dry them well, pound, and sift them separately through a lawn sieve, then weigh, and mix them in the above proportions. This is an exceedingly agreeable and aromatic powder, when all the ingredients are perfectly fresh and good; but the preparing it is rather a troublesome process. Mr. Arnott recommends that when it is considered so, a "high-caste" chemist should be applied to for it.

MR. ARNOTT'S CURRIE.

"Take the heart of a cabbage, and nothing but the heart, that is to say, pull away all the outside leaves until it is about the size of an egg; chop it fine, add to it a couple of apples sliced thin, the juice of one lemon, half a teaspoonful of black pepper, with one large tablespoonful of *my* currie-powder, and mix the whole well together. Now take six onions that have been chopped fine and fried brown, a garlic head, the size of a nutmeg, also minced fine, two ounces of fresh butter, two tablespoonsful of flour, and one pint of strong mutton or beef gravy; and when these articles are boiling, add the former ingredients, and let the whole be well stewed up together: if not hot enough, add cayenne pepper. Next, put in a fowl that has been roasted and nicely cut up; or a rabbit; or some lean chops of pork or mutton; or a lobster, or the remains of yesterday's calf's head; or any thing else you may fancy, and you will have an excellent currie, fit for kings to partake of."

"Well! now for the rice! It should be put into water which should be frequently changed, and should remain in for half an hour at least; this both clears and soaks it. Have your saucepan full of water (the larger the better,) and when it boils rapidly, throw the rice into it: it will be done in fifteen minutes. Strain it into a dish, wipe the saucepan dry, return the drained rice into it, and put it over a gentle fire for a few minutes, with a cloth over it: every grain will be separate. When served, do not cover the dish."

Obs.—We have already given testimony to the excellence of Mr. Arnott's currie-powder, but we think the currie itself will be found somewhat too acid for English or American taste in general, and the proportion of onion and garlic by one half too much for any but well-seasoned Anglo-Indian palates. After having tried his method of boiling the rice, we still give the preference to that of page 54, Chapter I.

A BENGAL CURRIE.

Slice and fry three large onions in two ounces of butter, and lift them out of the pan when done. Put into a stewpan three other large onions and a small clove of garlic which have been pounded together, and smoothly mixed with a dessertspoonfu. of the best pale turmeric, a teaspoonful of powdered ginger, one of salt, and one of cayenne pepper; add to these the butter in which the onions were fried, and half a cupful of good gravy; let them stew for about ten minutes, taking care that they shall not burn. Next, stir to them the fried onions and half a pint more of gravy; add a pound and a half of mutton, or of any other meat, free from bone and fat, and simmer it gently for an hour, or more should it not then be perfectly tender.

Fried onions, 3 large; butter, 2 ozs.; onions, pounded, 3 large; garlic, 1 clove; turmeric, 1 dessertspoonful; powdered ginger, salt, cay-

enne, each 1 teaspoonful; gravy, ½ cupful: 10 minutes.   Gravy, ½ pint;
meat, 1½ lb. : 1 hour or more.

A COMMON INDIAN CURRIE.

For each pound of meat, whether veal, mutton, or beef, take a heaped
tablespoonful of good currie powder, a small teaspoonful of salt, and one
of flour; mix these well together, and after having cut down the meat
into thick small cutlets, or squares, rub half of the mixed powder equally
over it.   Next, fry gently from one to four or five large onions sliced,
with or without the addition of a small clove of garlic, or half a dozen
eschalots, according to the taste; and when they are of a fine golden
brown, lift them out with a slice and lay them upon a sieve to drain;
throw a little more butter into the pan and fry the meat lightly in it;
drain it well from the fat in taking it out, and lay it into a clean stewpan
or saucepan; strew the onion over it, and pour in as much boiling water
as will almost cover it.   Mix the remainder of the currie-powder
smoothly with a little broth or cold water, and after the currie has
stewed for a few minutes pour it in, shaking the pan well round that it
may be smoothly blended with the gravy.   Simmer the whole very
softly until the meat is perfectly tender: this will be in from an hour
and a quarter, to two hours and a half, according to the quantity and the
nature of the meat.   Mutton will be the soonest done; the brisket end
(gristles) of a breast of veal will require twice as much stewing, and
sometimes more.   A fowl will be ready to serve in an hour.   An acid
apple or two, or any of the vegetables which we have enumerated at
the commencement of this chapter, may be added to the currie, proper
time being allowed for cooking each variety.   Very young green peas
are liked by some people in it; and cucumbers pared, seeded, and cut
moderately small, are always a good addition.   A richer currie will of
course be produced if gravy or broth be substituted for the water: either
should be boiling when poured to the meat.   Lemon-juice should be
stirred in before it is served, when there is no other acid in the currie.
A dish of boiled rice must be sent to table with it.   A couple of pounds
of meat free from bone, is sufficient quite for a moderate-sized dish of
this kind, but those of the breast of veal are sometimes used for it,
when it is to be served to a large family-party of currie-eaters: from
half to a whole pound of rice should then accompany it.   For the proper mode of boiling it, see mullagatawny soup, Chapter I.   The small
grained, or Patna, is the kind which ought to be used for the purpose.
Six ounces is quite sufficient for a not large currie; and a pound, when
boiled, and heated lightly in a dish, appears an enormous quantity for a
modern table.

To each pound of meat, whether veal, mutton, or beef, 1 heaped
tablespoonful of good currie-powder, 1 small teaspoonful of salt, and a
large one of flour, to be well mixed, and half rubbed on to the meat
before it is fried, the rest added afterwards; onions fried, from 1 to 4 or
5 (with or without the addition of a clove of garlic, or half a dozen
eschalots); sufficient boiling water to nearly cover the meat; vegetables, as in receipt, at choice; stewed, 1¼ to 2½ hours· a fowl, 1 hour, or
rather less; beef, 2 lbs., 1½ hour, or more; veal gristles, 2½ to 3 hours.

Obs.—Rabbits make a very good currie when quite young.   Cayenne
pepper can always be added to heighten the pungency of a currie when
the proportion in the powder is not considered sufficient.

SELIM'S CURRIES. (*Captain White's.*)

These curries are made with a sort of paste, which is labelled with the above names, and as it has attracted some attention of late, and the curries made with it are very good, and quickly and easily prepared, we give the directions for them. "Cut a pound and a half of chicken, fowl, veal, rabbit, or mutton, into pieces an inch and a half square. Put from two to three ounces of fresh butter in a stewpan, and when it is melted put in the meat, and give it a good stir with a wooden spoon; add from two to three dessertspoonsful of the curry-paste; mix the whole up well together, and continue the stirring over a brisk fire from five to ten minutes, and the currie will be done. This is a dry currie. For a gravy currie, add two or three tablespoonsful of boiling water after the paste is well mixed in, and continue the stewing and stirring from ten to twelve minutes longer, keeping the sauce of the consistency of cream. Prepare salmon and lobster in the same way, but very quickly, that they may come up firm. The paste may be rubbed over steaks, or cutlets, when they are nearly broiled; three or four minutes will finish them."*

CURRIED EGGS.

Boil six or eight fresh eggs quite hard, as for salad, and put them aside until they are cold. Mix well together from two to three ounces of good butter, and from three to four dessertspoonsful of curry-powder; shake them in a stewpan, or thick saucepan, over a clear but moderate fire for some minutes, then throw in a couple of mild onions finely minced, and fry them gently until they are tolerably soft; pour to them by degrees from half to three quarters of a pint of broth or gravy, and stew them slowly until they are reduced to pulp; mix smoothly a small cup of thick cream with two teaspoonsful of wheaten or of rice-flour, stir them to the currie, and simmer the whole until the raw taste of the thickening is gone. Cut the eggs into half inch slices, heat them quite through in the sauce without boiling them, and serve them as hot as possible.

CURRIED SWEETBREADS.

Wash and soak them as usual, then throw them into boiling water with a little salt in it, and a whole onion, and let them simmer for ten minutes; or, if at hand, substitute weak veal broth for the water. Lift them out, place them on a drainer, and leave them until they are perfectly cold; then cut them into half-inch slices, and either flour and fry them lightly in butter, or put them, without this, into as much curried gravy as will just cover them; stew them in it very gently from twenty to thirty minutes; add as much lemon-juice or Chili vinegar as will acidulate the sauce agreeably,† and serve the currie very hot. As we have already stated in two or three previous receipts, an ounce or more of sweet freshly-grated cocoa-nut, stewed tender in the gravy, and strained from it before the sweetbreads are added, will give a peculiarly pleasant flavour to all curries.

---

* Unless the meat be *extremely* tender, and cut small, it will require from ten to fifteen minutes stewing: when no liquid is added, it must be stirred without intermission, or the paste will burn to the pan. It answers well for cutlets, and for mullagatawny soup also; but makes a very mild currie.

† We find that a small portion of Indian pickled mango, or of its liquor, is an agreeable addition to a currie, as well as to mullagatawny soup.

Blanched 10 minutes; sliced (fried or not); stewed from 20 to 30 minutes.

CURRIED OYSTERS.

" Let a hundred of large sea-oysters be opened into a basin, without losing one drop of their liquor. · Put a lump of fresh butter into a good-sized saucepan, and when it boils, add a large onion, cut into thin slices, and let it fry in the uncovered stewpan until it is of a rich brown : now add a bit more butter, and two or three tablespoonsful of currie-powder. When these ingredients are well mixed over the fire with a wooden spoon, add gradually either hot water, or broth from the stock-pot; cover the stewpan, and let the whole boil up.   Meanwhile, have ready the meat of a cocoa-nut, grated or rasped fine, put this into the stew-pan with a few sour tamarinds (if they are to be obtained, if not, a sour apple, chopped.)   Let the whole simmer over the fire until the apple is dissolved, and the cocoa-nut very tender; then add a cupful of strong thickening made of flour and water, and sufficient salt, as a currie will not bear being salted at table.   Let this boil up for five minutes. Have ready also, a vegetable marrow, or part of one, cut into bits, and sufficiently boiled to require little or no further cooking.   Put this in with a tomata or two; either of these vegetables may be omitted.   Now put into the stewpan the oysters with their liquor, and the milk of the cocoa-nut; stir them well with the former ingredients; let the currie stew gently for a few minutes, then throw in the strained juice of half a lemon.   Stir the currie from time to time with a wooden spoon, and as soon as the oysters are done enough serve it up with a corresponding dish of rice on the opposite side of the table.   The dish is considered at Madras the *ne plus ultra* of Indian cookery."*

We have extracted this receipt, as it stands, from the Magazine of Domestic Economy, the season in which we have met with it not permitting us to have it tested.   Such of our readers as may have partaken of the true Oriental preparation, will be able to judge of its correctness; and others may consider it worthy of a trial.   We should suppose it necessary to beard the oysters.

CURRIED GRAVY.

The quantity of onion, eschalot, or garlic used for a currie should be regulated by the taste of the persons for whom it is prepared; the very large proportions of them which are acceptable to some eaters, preventing others altogether from partaking of the dish.   Slice, and fry gently in a little good butter, from a couple to six large onions (with a bit of garlic, and four or five eschalots, or none of either), when they are coloured equally of a fine yellow-brown, lift them on to a sieve reversed to drain; put them into a clean saucepan, add a pint and a half of good gravy, with a couple of ounces of rasped cocoa-nut, or of any other of the condiments we have already specified, which may require as much stewing as the onions (an apple or two, for instance), and simmer them softly from half to three quarters of an hour, or until the onion is sufficiently tender to be pressed through a strainer.   We would recommend that for a delicate currie this should always be done; for a common one it is not necessary; and many persons prefer to have the whole of it

---

* Native oysters, prepared as for sauce, may be curried by the receipt for eggs or sweetbreads, with the addition of their liquor.

14

left in this last. After the gravy has been worked through the strainer, and again boils, add to it from three to four dessertspoonsful of currie-powder, and one of flour, with as much salt as the gravy may require, the whole mixed to a smooth batter with a small cupful of good cream.* Simmer it from fifteen to twenty minutes, and it will be ready for use. Lobster, prawns, shrimps, maccaroni, hard-boiled eggs, cold calf's head, and various other meats may be heated and served in it with advantage. For all these, and indeed for every kind of currie, acid of some sort should be added. Chili vinegar answers well when no fresh lemon-juice is at hand.

Onions, 2 to 6 (garlic, 1 clove, or eschalots, 4 to 5, *or neither*); fried a light brown. Gravy, 1½ pint; cocoa-nut, 2 ozs. (3, if very young): ⅓ to ¼ hour. Currie-powder, 3 to 4 dessertspoonsful; flour, 1 dessert-spoonful; salt, as needed; cream, 1 small cupful: 15 to 20 minutes.

Obs.—In India, curds are frequently added to curries, but that may possibly be from their abounding much more than sweet cream in so hot a climate.

POTTED MEATS.

Any tender and well-roasted meat, taken free of fat, skin, and gristle, as well as from the dry outsides, will answer for potting admirably, better, indeed, than that which is generally baked for the purpose, and which is usually quite deprived of its juices by the process. Spiced or *corned* beef also is excellent when thus prepared; and any of these will remain good a long time if mixed with cold fresh butter, instead of that which is clarified; but no addition that can be made to it will render the meat eatable, unless it be *thoroughly pounded;* reduced, in fact, to the smoothest possible paste, free from a single lump or a morsel of un-broken fibre. If *rent* into fragments, instead of being cut quite through the grain, in being minced, before it is put into the mortar, no beating will bring it to the proper state. Unless it be *very* dry, it is better to pound it for some time before any butter is added, and it must be long and patiently beaten after all the ingredients are mixed, that the whole may be equally blended and well mellowed in flavour.

The quantity of butter required will depend upon the nature of the meat; ham and salted beef will need a larger proportion than roast meat, or than the breasts of poultry and game; white fish, from being less dry, will require comparatively little. Salmon, lobsters, prawns, and shrimps are all extremely good, prepared in this way. They should, however, be perfectly fresh when they are pounded, and be set imme-diately afterwards into a very cool place. For these, and for white meats in general, mace, nutmeg, and cayenne or white pepper, are the appropriate spices. A small quantity of cloves may be added to hare and other brown meat, but allspice we would not recommend unless the taste is known to be in favour of it. The following receipt for pounding ham will serve as a general one for the particular manner of proceeding.

POTTED HAM; (*an excellent Receipt.*)

To be eaten in perfection this should be made with a freshly cured ham, which, after having been soaked for twelve hours, should be wiped

* This must be added only just before the currie is dished, when *any acid* fruit has been boiled in the gravy: it may then be first blended with a small portion of arrow root, or flour.

dry, nicely trimmed, closely wrapped in coarse paste, and baked very tender.* When it comes from the oven, remove the crust and rind, and when the ham is perfectly cold, take for each pound of the lean, which should be weighed after every morsel of skin and fibre has been carefully removed, six ounces of cold roast veal, prepared with equal nicety. Mince these quite fine with an exceedingly sharp knife, taking care to *cut* through the meat, and not to tear the fibre, as on this much of the excellence of the preparation depends. Next put it into a large stone or marble mortar, and pound it to the smoothest paste with eight ounces of fresh butter, which must be added by degrees. When three-parts beaten, strew over it a teaspoonful of freshly-pounded mace, half a large, or the whole of a *small* nutmeg grated, and the third of a tea-spoonful of cayenne well mixed together. It is better to limit the spice to this quantity in the first instance, and to increase afterwards either of the three kinds to the taste of the parties to whom the meat is to be served.† We do not find half a teaspoonful of cayenne and nearly two teaspoonsful of mace, more than is generally approved. After the spice is added, keep the meat often turned from the sides to the middle of the mortar, that it may be seasoned equally in every part. When perfectly pounded, press it into small potting-pans, and pour clarified butter‡ over the top. If kept in a cool and dry place, this meat will remain good for a fortnight, or more.

Lean of ham, 1 lb.; lean of roast veal, 6 ozs.; fresh butter, 8 ozs.; mace, from 1 to 2 teaspoonsful; ½ large nutmeg; cayenne, ¼ to ½ tea-spoonful.

Obs.—The roast veal is ordered in this receipt because the ham alone is generally too salt; for the same reason butter, fresh taken from the churn, or that which is but slightly salted and quite new, should be used for it in preference to its own fat. When there is no ready-dressed veal in the house, the best part of the neck, roasted or stewed, will supply the requisite quantity. The remains of a cold boiled ham will answer quite well for potting, even when a little dry.

POTTED CHICKEN, PARTRIDGE, OR PHEASANT.

Roast the birds as for table, but let them be thoroughly done, for if the gravy be left in, the meat will not keep half so well. Raise the flesh of the breast, wings, and merrythought quite clear from the bones, take off the skin, mince, and then pound it very smoothly with about one third of its weight of fresh butter, or something less, if the meat should appear of a proper consistence without the full quantity; season it with salt, mace, and cayenne only, and add these in small portions until the meat is rather highly flavoured with both the last: proceed with it as with other potted meats.

POTTED OX-TONGUE.

Boil tender an unsmoked tongue of good flavour, and the following day cut from it the quantity desired for potting, or take for this purpose

---

* See Baked Ham, Chapter XI., page 195.

† Spice, it must be observed, varies so very greatly in its quality that discretion is always necessary in using it.

‡ This should never be poured *hot* on the meat: it should be less than milk-warm when added to it.

the remains of one which has already been served at table. Trim off
the skin and rind, weigh the meat, mince it very small, then pound it
as fine as possible with four ounces of butter to each pound of tongue
small teaspoonful of mace, half as much of nutmeg and clove
tolerably high seasoning of cayenne. After the spices are well beaten
with the meat, taste it, and add more if required. A few ounces of any
well-roasted meat mixed with the tongue will give it firmness, in which
it is apt to be deficient. The breasts of turkeys, fowls, partridges, or
pheasants may be used for the purpose with good effect.

Tongue, 1 lb.; butter, 4 ozs.; mace, 1 teaspoonful; nutmeg and
cloves, each ½ teaspoonful; cayenne, 5 to 10 grains.

LOBSTER BUTTER.

Pound to the smoothest paste the coral of one or two fine lobsters,
mix with it about a third of its volume of fresh butter, and the same
proportion of spices as are given in the preceding receipt. Let the
whole be thoroughly blended; set it by for a while in a cool place and
pot it, or make it up into small pats and serve them with curled parsley
round the dish, or with any light foliage that will contrast well with
their brilliant colour. The flesh of the lobster may be cut fine with a
very sharp knife, and pounded with the coral.

POTTED MUSHROOMS.

The receipt for these, which we can recommend to the reader, will
be found in the next Chapter.

CHAPTER XV.

VEGETABLES.

THE quality of vegetables depends much both on the soil in which
they are grown, and on the degree of care bestowed upon their culture;
but if produced in ever so great perfection, their excellence will be entirely destroyed if they be badly cooked.

With the exception of artichokes, which are said to be improved by
two or three days' keeping, all the summer varieties should be dressed
before their first freshness has in any degree passed off (for their flavour
is never so fine as within a few hours of their being cut or gathered);
but when this cannot be done, precaution should be taken to prevent
their withering. The stalk-ends of asparagus, cucumbers, and vege
table-marrow should be placed in from one to two inches of cold water
and all other kinds should be spread on a cool brick floor. When th...
has been neglected, they must be thrown into cold water for some time
before they are boiled to recover them, though they will prove even
then but very inferior eating.

Vegetables, when not sufficiently cooked, are known to be so exceedingly unwholesome and indigestible, that the custom of serving them
crisp, which means, in reality, only half-boiled, should be altogether
disregarded when health is considered of more importance than fashion;
but they should not be allowed to remain in the water after they are

quite done, or both their nutritive properties and their flavour will be lost, and their good appearance destroyed. Care should be taken to *drain them thoroughly* in a warm strainer, and to serve them very hot, with well-made sauces, if with any.

Only dried peas or beans, Jerusalem artichokes, and potatoes, are put at first into cold water. All others require plenty of fast-boiling water, which should be ready salted and skimmed before they are thrown into it.

TO CLEAR VEGETABLES FROM INSECTS.

Lay them for half an hour or more into a pan of strong brine, with the stalk ends uppermost; this will destroy the small snails and other insects which cluster in the leaves, and they will fall out and sink to the bottom. A pound and a half of salt to the gallon of water will answer for this purpose, and if strained daily it will last for some time.

TO BOIL VEGETABLES GREEN.

After they have been properly prepared and washed, throw them into plenty of boiling water which has been salted and well skimmed; and keep them uncovered and boiling fast until they are done, taking every precaution against their being smoked. Should the water be very hard, a bit of soda the size of a hazel-nut, or a small half-teaspoonful of carbonate of soda, may be added with the salt, for every two quarts, and will greatly improve the colour of the vegetables; but if used in undue proportion, it will injure them; green peas especially will be quickly reduced to a mash if boiled with too large a quantity.

Water, 1 gallon; salt, 2 ozs.; soda, $\frac{1}{4}$ to $\frac{1}{2}$ oz.; or carbonate of soda, 1 teaspoonful.

TO BOIL POTATOES; (*a genuine Irish Receipt.*)

Potatoes, to boil well together, should be all of the same sort, and as nearly equal in size as may be. Wash off the mould, and scrub them very clean with a hard brush, but neither scoop nor apply a knife to them in any way, even to clear the eyes.* Rinse them well, and arrange them compactly in a saucepan, so that they may not lie loose in the water, and that a small quantity may suffice to cover them. Pour this in cold, and when it boils, throw in about a large teaspoonful of salt to the quart, and simmer the potatoes until they are nearly done, but for the last two or three minutes let them boil rapidly. When they are tender quite through, which may be known by probing them with a fork, pour all the water from them immediately, lift the lid of the saucepan to allow the steam to escape, and place them on a trevet, high over the fire, or by the side of it, until the moisture has entirely evaporated; then peel, and send them to table as quickly as possible, either in a hot napkin, or in a dish, of which the cover is so placed that the steam can pass off. There should be no delay in serving them after they are once taken from the fire: Irish families usually prefer them served in their skins. Some kinds will be done in twenty minutes, others in less than three quarters of an hour. We are informed that "the best potatoes are those which average from five to six to the pound, with few eyes,

---

* "Because," in the words of our clever Irish correspondent, "the water through these parts is then admitted into the very heart of the vegetable; and the latent heat, after cooking, is not sufficient to throw it off: this renders the potatoes very unwholesome."

but those pretty deep, and equally distributed over the surface." We cannot ourselves vouch for the correctness of the assertion, but we think it may be relied on.

20 minutes to ¾ hour or more.

Obs.—The water in which they are boiled should barely cover the potatoes.

ANOTHER WAY TO BOIL POTATOES.

Pare, wash and throw them into a pan of cold water; then put them on to boil in a clean pot with cold water sufficient to cover them, and sprinkle over a little salt; let them boil slowly *uncovered* till you can pass a fork through them; pour off the water, and set them where they will keep hot till wanted. When done in this way they are very mealy and dry.

Potatoes either boiled or roasted, should *never be covered* to keep them hot.

TO BOIL NEW POTATOES.

These are never good unless freshly dug. Take them of equal size, and rub off the skins with a brush, or a very coarse cloth, wash them clean, and put them, without salt, into boiling, or at least, quite hot water; boil them softly, and when they are tender enough to serve, pour off the water entirely, strew some fine salt over the potatoes, give them a shake, and let them stand by the fire in the saucepan for a minute, then dish and serve them immediately. Some cooks throw in a small slice of fresh butter, with the salt, and toss them gently in it after it is dissolved. This is a good mode, but the more usual one is to send melted butter to table with them, or to pour white sauce over them when they are very young, and served early in the season, as a side or corner dish.

Very small, 10 to 15 minutes: moderate sized, 15 to 20 minutes.

NEW POTATOES IN BUTTER.

Rub off the skins, wash the potatoes well, and wipe them dry; put them with three ounces of good butter, for a small dish, and with four ounces, or more, for a large one, into a well-tinned stewpan or saucepan, and simmer them over a gentle fire for about half an hour. Keep them well shaken or tossed, that they may be equally done, and throw in some salt when they begin to stew. This is a good mode of dressing them when they are very young and watery.

TO BOIL POTATOES; (*Captain Kater's Receipt.*)

Wash, wipe, and pare the potatoes, cover them with cold water, and boil them gently until they are done, pour off the water, and sprinkle a little fine salt over them; then take each potato separately with a spoon, and lay it into a clean *warm* cloth, twist this so as to press all the moisture from the vegetable, and render it quite round; turn it carefully into a dish placed before the fire, throw a cloth over, and when all are done, send them to table quickly. Potatoes dressed in this way are mashed without the slighest trouble; it is also by far the best method of preparing them for puddings or for cakes.

TO ROAST OR BAKE POTATOES.

Scrub, and wash exceedingly clean, some potatoes nearly assorted in size; wipe them very dry, and roast them in a Dutch oven before the

fire, placing them at a distance from it, and keeping them often turned;
arrange them in a coarse dish, and bake them in a moderate oven.
Dish them neatly in a napkin, and send them very hot to table; serve
cold butter with them.

1¾ to upwards of 2 hours.

SCOOPED POTATOES. (ENTREMETS); or *second course dish.*

Wash and wipe some large potatoes of a firm kind, and with a small
scoop adapted to the purpose, form as many diminutive ones as will fill
a dish; cover them with cold water, and when they have boiled gently
for five minutes, pour it off, and put more cold water to them; after they
have simmered a second time for five minutes, drain the water quite
away, and let them steam by the side of the fire from four to five min
utes longer. Dish them carefully, pour white sauce over them, and
serve them with the second course. Old potatoes thus prepared, have
often been made to pass for *new* ones, at the best tables, at the season in
which the fresh vegetable is dearest. The time required to boil them
will of course vary with their quality: we give the method which we
have found very successful.

FRIED POTATOES. (ENTREMETS.)

After having washed them, wipe and pare some raw potatoes, cut
them in slices of equal thickness, or into thin shavings, and throw them
into plenty of boiling butter, or very pure clarified dripping. Fry them
of a fine light brown, and very crisp; lift them out with a skimmer,
drain them on a soft warm cloth, dish them very hot, and sprinkle fine
salt over them. This is an admirable way of dressing potatoes, very
common on the Continent, but less so in England than it deserves to be.
When pared round and round to a corkscrew form, in ribbons or shavings
of equal width, and served dry and well fried, lightly piled in a dish,
they make a handsome appearance and are excellent eating. We have
known them served in this country with a slight sprinkling of cavenne.
If sliced, they should be something less than a quarter-inch thick.

MASHED POTATOES.

Boil them perfectly tender quite through, pour off the water and
steam them very dry by the directions already given in the receipt of
page 229; peel them quickly, take out every speck, and while they are
still hot press the potatoes through an earthen cullender, or bruise them
to a smooth mash with a strong wooden fork or spoon, but never pound
them in a mortar, as that will reduce them to a close heavy paste. *Let
them be entirely free from lumps,* for nothing can be more indicative of
carelessness or want of skill on the part of the cook, than mashed potatoes sent to table full of these. Melt in a clean saucepan a slice of
good butter with a few spoonsful of milk, or, better still, of cream; put
in the potatoes after having sprinkled some fine salt upon them, and stir
the whole over a gentle fire, with a *wooden* spoon, until the ingredients
are well mixed, and the whole is very hot. It may then be served
directly; or heaped high in a dish, left rough on the surface, and browned
before the fire; or it may be pressed into a well-buttered mould of
handsome form, which has been strewed with the finest bread-crumbs,
and shaken free of the loose ones, then turned out, and browned in a

Dutch or common oven.   More or less liquid will be required to moisten sufficiently potatoes of various kinds.

Potatoes mashed, 2 lbs.; salt, 1 teaspoonful; butter, 1 to 2 ozs.; milk or cream, ¼ pint.

Obs. — Mashed potatoes are often moulded with a cup, and then equally browned; any other shape will answer the purpose as well, and many are of better appearance.

ENGLISH POTATO-BALLS.

Boil some floury potatoes very dry, mash them as smoothly as possible, season them well with salt and white pepper; warm them with about an ounce of butter to the pound, or rather more if it will not render them too moist; a few spoonsful of good cream may be added, but they must be boiled very dry after it is stirred to them.   Let the mixture cool a little, roll it into balls, sprinkle over them vermicelli crushed slightly with the hand, and fry them a fine light brown.   They may be dished round a shape of plain mashed potatoes, or piled on a napkin by themselves.   They may likewise be rolled in egg and fine bread-crumbs instead of in the vermicelli, or in rice-flour, which answers very well for them.

POTATO BOULETTES.   (ENTREMETS); (*good.*)

Boil some good potatoes as dry as possible, or let them be prepared by Captain Kater's receipt; mash a pound of them very smoothly, and mix with them while they are still warm, two ounces of fresh butter, a teaspoonful of salt, a little nutmeg, the beaten and strained yolks of four eggs, and last of all the whites thoroughly whisked.   Mould with, and drop the mixture from a teaspoon, into a small pan of boiling butter, or of very pure lard, and fry the boulettes for five minutes over a moderate fire: they should be of a fine pale brown, and very light.   Drain them well and dish them on a hot napkin.

Potatoes, 1 lb.; butter, 2 ozs.; salt, 1 teaspoonful; eggs, 4: 5 minutes.

POTATO RISSOLES; (*French.*)

Mash and season the potatoes with salt, and white pepper, or cayenne, and mix with them plenty of minced parsley, and a small quantity of green onions, or eschalots; add sufficient yolks of egg to bind the mixture together, roll it into small balls, and fry them in plenty of lard or butter over a moderate fire, or they will be too much browned before they are done through.   Ham, or any other kind of meat finely minced, may be substituted for the herbs, or added to them.

POTATOES A LA MAÎTRE D'HOTEL.

Boil in the usual manner some potatoes of a firm kind, peel, and let them cool; then cut them equally into quarter-inch slices.   Dissolve in a very clean stewpan or saucepan from two to four ounces of good butter, stir to it a small dessertspoonful of flour, and shake the pan over the fire for two or three minutes; add by slow degrees a small cup of boiling water, some pepper, salt, and a tablespoonful of minced parsley; put in the potatoes, and toss them gently over a clear fire until they are quite hot, and the sauce adheres well to them; at the instant of serving add a dessertspoonful of strained lemon-juice.   Pale veal gravy may be substituted for the water; and the potatoes, after being thickly sliced, may be quickly cut of the same size with a small round cutter.

POTATOES A LA CREME.

Prepare the potatoes as above, and toss them gently in a quarterpint or more of thick white sauce or of common béchamel, with or without the addition of the minced parsley.

SPINACH. (ENTREMETS.) (*French Receipt.*)

Pick the spinach leaf by leaf from the stems, and wash it in abundance of spring water, changing it several times; then shake it in a dry cloth held by the four corners, or drain it on a large sieve. Throw it into sufficient well-salted boiling water to allow it to float freely, and keep it pressed down with a skimmer that it may be equally done. When quite young it will be tender in from eight to ten minutes, but to ascertain if it be so, take a leaf and squeeze it between the fingers. If to be dressed in the French mode, drain, and then throw it directly into plenty of fresh water, and when it is cool form it into balls and press the moisture thoroughly from it with the hands. Next, chop it extremely fine upon a clean trencher; put two ounces (for a large dish) of butter into a stewpan or bright thick saucepan, lay the spinach on it, and keep it stirred over a gentle fire for ten minutes, or until it appears dry; dredge in a spoonful of flour, and turn the spinach as it is added; pour to it gradually a few spoonsful of very rich veal gravy, or, if preferred, of *good* boiling cream, (with the last of these a dessertspoonful or more of pounded sugar may be added for a second-course dish, when the true French mode of dressing the vegetable is liked.) Stew the whole briskly until the whole is well absorbed; dish, and serve the spinach very hot, with small, pale fried sippets round it, or with leaves of puff paste fresh from the oven, or well dried after having been fried. For ornament, the sippets may be fancifully shaped with a tin cutter. A proper seasoning of salt must not be omitted in this or any other preparation of the spinach.

SPINACH; (*common English mode.*)

Boil the spinach very green in plenty of water, drain, and then press the moisture from it between two trenchers; chop it small, put it into a clean saucepan, with a slice of fresh butter, and stir the whole until well mixed and very hot. Smooth it in a dish, mark it in dice, and send it quickly to table.

ANOTHER COMMON ENGLISH RECEIPT FOR SPINACH.

Take it leaf by leaf from the stalks, and be very careful to clear it from any weeds that may be amongst it, and to free it by copious and repeated washings from every particle of grit. Put it into a large well-tinned stewpan or saucepan, with the water only which hangs about it; throw in a small spoonful of salt, and keep it constantly pressed down with a wooden spoon, and turned often for about a quarter of an hour, or until it is perfectly tender. Drain off the superfluous moisture, chop the spinach quickly on a hot trencher; dish and serve it immediately. Fried sippets of bread should always be served round this vegetable, unless it be prepared for an invalid.

BOILED TURNIP-RADISHES.

These should be freshly drawn, young and white. Wash and trim them neatly, leaving on two or three of the small inner leaves of the top. Boil them in plenty of salted water from twenty to thirty minutes, and as soon as they are tender send them to table well drained, with melted butter or white sauce. Common radishes, when young, tied in bunches, and boiled from eighteen to twenty-five minutes, then served on a toast like asparagus, are very good.

BOILED LEEKS.

Trim off the coarser leaves from some young leeks, cut them into equal lengths, tie them into small bunches, and boil them in plenty of water which has been previously salted and skimmed; serve them on a toast, and send melted butter to table with them.

20 to 25 minutes.

STEWED LETTUCES.

Strip off the outer leaves, and cut away the stalks; wash the lettuces with exceeding nicety, and throw them into water salted as for all green vegetables. When they are quite tender, which will be in from twenty to thirty minutes, according to their age, lift them out, and press the water thoroughly from them; chop them a little, and heat them in a clean saucepan with a seasoning of pepper and salt, and a small slice of butter; then dredge in a little flour and stir them well; add next a small cup of broth or gravy, boil them quickly until they are tolerably dry, then stir in a little pale vinegar or lemon-juice, and serve them as hot as possible, with fried sippets round them.

TO BOIL ASPARAGUS.

With a sharp knife scrape the stems of the asparagus lightly, but very clean, from within one to two inches of the green tender points, throw them into cold water as they are done, and when all are ready, tie them in bunches of equal size; cut the large ends evenly, that the asparagus may be all of the same length, and put it into plenty of boiling water prepared by the directions of page 229. Cut a round of bread quite half an inch thick, and after having pared off the crust, toast it a delicate brown on both sides. When the stalks of the asparagus are tender, lift it out directly, or it will lose both its colour and its flavour, and will also be liable to break; dip the toast quickly into the water in which it was boiled, and dish the vegetable upon it, with the points meeting in the centre. Send rich melted butter to table with it. In France, a small quantity of vinegar is stirred into the sauce before it is served; and many persons like the addition. Asparagus may be preserved for a day or two sufficiently fresh for use, by keeping the stalks immersed in an inch depth of cold water; but it is never so good as when dressed directly it is cut, or within a few hours after.

20 to 25 minutes.

Obs.—Abroad, boiled asparagus is very frequently served cold, and eaten with oil and vinegar, or a sauce Mayonnaise.

ASPARAGUS POINTS DRESSED LIKE PEAS. (ENTREMETS.)

This is a convenient mode of dressing asparagus, when it is too small and green to make a good appearance plainly boiled. Cut the points so far only as they are perfectly tender, in bits of equal size, not more than the third of an inch in length; wash them very clean, and throw them into plenty of boiling water, with the usual quantity of salt and a morsel of soda. When they are tolerably tender, which will be in from ten to twelve minutes, drain them well, and spread them on a clean cloth; fold it over them, wipe them gently, and when they are quite dry put them into a clean stewpan with a good slice of butter, which should be just dissolved before the asparagus is added; stew them in this over a brisk fire, shaking them often, for eight or ten minutes; dredge in about a small teaspoonful of flour, and add half that quantity of white sugar; then pour in boiling water to nearly cover the asparagus, and boil it rapidly until but little liquid remains: stir in the beaten yolks of two eggs, heap the asparagus high in a dish, and serve it very hot. The sauce should adhere entirely to the vegetable, as in green peas *à la Française*.

TO BOIL GREEN PEAS.

To be eaten in perfection these should be young, very freshly gathered, and shelled just before they are boiled; should there be great inequality in their size, the smaller ones may be separated from the others, and thrown into the saucepan four or five minutes later. Wash and drain the peas in a cullender, put them into plenty of fast-boiling water, salted by the directions of page 229, keep the pan uncovered, and let them boil rapidly until they are tender; drain them well, dish them quickly, and serve them very hot, with good melted butter in a tureen; or put a slice of fresh butter into the midst of the peas, heap them well over it in the centre of the dish, and let it dissolve before they are disturbed. Never, on any account, boil or mix mint with them unless it be expressly ordered, as it is particularly distasteful to many persons. It should be served in small heaps round them, if at all.

15 to 25 minutes, or more if *old*.

GREEN PEAS A LA FRANÇAISE; OR, FRENCH FASHION. (ENTREMETS.)

Throw a quart of young and freshly-shelled peas into plenty of spring water with a couple of ounces of butter, and with the hand work them together until the butter adheres well to the peas; lift them out, and drain them in a cullender; put them into a stewpan or thick saucepan without any water, and let them remain over a gentle fire, and be stirred occasionally for twenty minutes from the time of their first beginning to simmer; then pour to them as much boiling water as will just cover them; throw in a small quantity of salt, and keep them boiling quickly for forty minutes: stir well amongst them a small lump of sugar which has been dipped quickly into water, and a thickening of about half an ounce of butter very smoothly mixed with a teaspoonful of flour; shake them over the fire for a couple of minutes, and serve them directly, heaped high in a very hot dish: there will be no sauce except that which adheres to the peas if they be properly managed. We have found marrow-fats excellent, dressed by this receipt. Fresh and good butter should be used with them always.

Peas, 1 quart; butter, 2 ozs.: 20 minutes. Water to cover the peas; little salt: 40 minutes. Sugar, small lump; butter, ½ oz.; flour, 1 teaspoonful: 2 minutes.

GREEN PEAS WITH CREAM. (ENTREMETS.)

Boil a quart of young peas perfectly tender in salt and water, and drain them as dry as possible. Dissolve an ounce and a half of butter in a clean stewpan, stir smoothly to it when it boils a dessertspoonful of flour, and shake these over the fire for three or four minutes, but with-out allowing them to take the slightest colour; pour gradually to them a cup of rich cream, add a small lump of sugar pounded, let the sauce boil, then put in the peas and toss them gently in it until they are very hot: dish, and serve them quickly.

Peas, 1 quart: 18 to 25 minutes. Butter, 1½ oz.; flour, 1 dessert-spoonful: 3 to 5 minutes. Sugar, 1 saltspoonful; cream, 1 cupful.

TO BOIL FRENCH OR STRING BEANS.

When the beans are very small and young, merely take off the ends and stalks, and drop them into plenty of spring water as they are done; when all are ready wash and drain them well, throw them into a large saucepan of fast-boiling water, salted as usual (see page 229), and when they are quite tender, which will be in from twelve to eighteen minutes, pour them into a cullender, shake the water from them, dish, and send quickly to table with good melted butter in a tureen. When from half to two parts grown, cut the beans obliquely into a lozenge form, or, when a less modern fashion is preferred, split them lengthwise into delicate strips, and then cut them once across: the strings should be drawn off with the tops and stalks. No mode of dressing it can render this vegetable good when it is old, but if the sides be pared off, the beans cut thin, and boiled tender with rather more than the ordinary proportion of soda, they will be of excellent colour, and tolerably eatable.

FRENCH BEANS A LA FRANÇAISE. (ENTREMETS.)

Boil, and drain them thoroughly; put them into a clean stewpan, or well-tinned iron saucepan, and shake them over the fire until they are very dry and hot; add to them from two to four ounces of fresh butter cut into small bits, some white pepper, a little salt, and the juice of half a lemon; toss them gently for a few minutes over a clear fire, and serve them very hot. Should the butter turn to oil, a spoonful or two of veal gravy or boiling water must be added.

AN EXCELLENT RECEIPT FOR FRENCH BEANS A LA FRANÇAISE.

Prepare as many young and freshly-gathered beans as will serve for a large dish, boil them tender, and drain the water well from them Melt a couple of ounces of fresh butter, in a clean saucepan, and stir smoothly to it a small dessertspoonful of flour; keep these well shaken, and gently simmered until they are lightly browned, add salt and pepper, and pour to them by degrees a small cupful of good veal gravy (or, in lieu of this, of sweet rich cream), toss the beans in the sauce until they are as hot as possible; stir quickly in, as they are taken from the fire, the beaten yolks of two fresh eggs, and a little lemon-juice, and serve them without delay. The eggs and lemon are sometimes omitted, and a tablespoonful of minced parsley is added to the butter and flour; but this, we think, is scarcely an improvement.

Beans, 1 to 2 quarts: boiled 15 to 20 minutes. Butter, 2 ozs.; flour, 1 dessertspoonful; salt and pepper; veal gravy, *small* cupful; yolks of eggs, 2; lemon-juice, a dessertspoonful.

TO BOIL WINDSOR BEANS.

When young, freshly gathered, and well dressed, these beans, even with many persons accustomed to a luxurious table, are a favourite accompaniment to a dish of streaked bacon, or delicate pickled pork. Shell them only just before they are wanted, then wash, drain, and throw them into boiling water, salted as for peas. When they are quite tender, pour them into a hot cullender, drain them thoroughly, and send them to table quickly, with a tureen of parsley and butter, or with plain melted butter, when it is preferred. A boiled cheek of bacon, trimmed free of any blackened parts, may be dished *over* the beans, upon occasion.

20 to 30 minutes; less, when *very* young.

Obs.—When the skin of the beans appears wrinkled, they will generally be found sufficiently tender to serve, but they should be tasted to ascertain that they are so.

DRESSED CUCUMBERS.

Pare and slice them very thin, strew a little fine salt over them, and when they have stood a few minutes drain off the water, by raising one side of the dish, and letting it flow to the other; pour it away, strew more salt, and a moderate seasoning of pepper on them, add two or three tablespoonsful of the purest salad-oil, and turn the cucumbers well, that the whole may receive a portion of it; then pour over them from one to three dessertspoonsful of Chili vinegar, and a little common, should it be needed; turn them into a clean dish and serve them.

Obs.—If very young, cucumbers are usually dressed without being pared, but the tough rind of full-grown ones being extremely indigestible, should be avoided. The vegetable, though apt to disagree with persons of delicate habit, when sauced in the common mode, with salt, pepper, and vinegar only, may often be eaten by them with impunity when dressed with plenty of oil. It is difficult to obtain this perfectly fresh and pure here; and hence, perhaps, arises in part the prejudice, which amongst us, is so often found to exist against the use of this most wholesome condiment.

MANDRANG, OR MANDRAM; (*West Indian Receipt.*)

Chop together very small, two moderate-sized cucumbers, with half the quantity of mild onion; add the juice of a lemon, a saltspoonful or more of salt, a third as much of cayenne, and one or two glasses of Madeira, or of any other dry white wine. This preparation is to be served with any kind of roast meat.

ANOTHER RECEIPT FOR MANDRAM.

Take three or four cucumbers, so young as not to require paring; score the ends well, that when they are sliced they may fall into small bits; add plenty of young onions, cut fine, the juice of half a lemon, a glass of sherry or Madeira, and a dessertspoonful of vinegar.

STEWED CUCUMBERS. (*English mode.*)

Pare, and split into quarters, four or five full-grown but still young cucumbers; take out the seeds and cut each part in two; sprinkle them with white pepper or cayenne, flour and fry them lightly in a little butter, lift them from the pan, drain them on a sieve, then lay them into as much good brown gravy as will nearly cover them, and stew them gently from twenty-five to thirty minutes, or until they are quite tender. Should the gravy require to be thickened or flavoured, dish the cucumbers and keep them hot while a little flour and butter, or any other of the usual ingredients, is stirred into it. Some persons like a small portion of lemon-juice, or of vinegar added to the sauce; cucumber vinegar might be substited for these with very good effect, as the vegetable loses much of its fine and peculiar flavour when cooked.

25 to 30 minutes.

Obs.—The cucumbers may be left in entire lengths, thrown into well-salted boiling water, and simmered for ten minutes, then thoroughly drained upon the back of a sieve, and afterwards stewed very quickly till tender in some highly-flavoured brown gravy, or in the Spanish sauce of page 88.

CUCUMBERS A LA POULETTE.

The cucumbers for this dish may be pared and sliced very thin; or quartered, freed from the seeds, and cut into half-inch lengths; in either case they should be steeped in a little vinegar and sprinkled with salt for half an hour before they are dressed. Drain, and then press them dry in a soft cloth; flour them well, put a slice of butter into a stewpan or saucepan bright in the inside, and when it begins to boil throw in the cucumbers, and shake them over a gentle fire ten minutes, but be careful to prevent their taking the slightest colour; pour to them gradually as much strong, but very pale, veal stock or gravy as will nearly cover them; when it boils skim off the fat entirely, add salt and white pepper, if needed, and when the cucumbers are quite tender, strew in a large teaspoonful of finely-minced parsley, and thicken the sauce with the yolks of two or three eggs. French cooks add the flour when the vegetable has stewed in the butter, instead of dredging it upon them at first, and this is perhaps the better method.

CUCUMBERS A LA CREME.

Boil them tolerably tender in salt and water, drain them well, then stew them for a few minutes in a thick béchamel, and serve them in it.

FRIED CUCUMBERS TO SERVE IN COMMON HASHES AND MINCES.

If very young they need not be pared, but otherwise, take off the rind, slice, and dredge them lightly with pepper and flour, but put no salt at first; throw them into very hot butter or clarified dripping, or they will not brown; when they are nearly done sprinkle some salt amongst them, and as soon as they are quite tender, lift them out with a slice, drain them well, and place them lightly over the hash or mince. A small portion of onion may be fried with them when it is liked.

MELON.

This in France and in other parts of the Continent is served and eaten with the *bouilli* (or beef boiled tender in the soup-pot), with a seasoning of salt and pepper only; but the fruit is there far more abundant, and of infinitely finer growth than with us, and requires so little care, comparatively, that it is planted in many places in the open fields, where it flourishes admirably.

SALAD.

The herbs and vegetables for a salad cannot be too freshly gathered; they should be carefully cleared from insects and washed with scrupulous nicety; they are better when not prepared until near the time of sending them to table, and should not be sauced until the instant before they are served. Tender lettuces, of which the outer leaves should be stripped away, mustard and cress, young radishes, and occasionally chives or small green onions (when the taste of a party is in favour of these last) are the usual ingredients of summer salads. Half-grown cucumbers sliced thin, and mixed with them, are a favourite addition with many persons. In England it is customary to cut the lettuces extremely fine; the French, who object to the *flavour of the knife*, which they fancy this mode imparts, break them small instead. Young celery alone, sliced and dressed with a rich salad mixture (see page 103) is excellent: it is still in some families served thus always with roast pheasants.

Beet-root, baked or boiled, blanched endive, small salad-herbs which are easily raised at any time of the year, celery, and hardy lettuces, with any ready-dressed vegetable, will supply salads through the winter. Cucumber vinegar is an agreeable addition to these.

FRENCH SALAD.

In winter this is made principally of beautifully-blanched endive, washed delicately clean and broken into small branches with the fingers, then taken from the water and shaken dry in a basket kept for the purpose, or in a fine cloth; then arranged in the salad-bowl, and strewed with herbs (tarragon generally, when in season) minced small: the dressing is not added until just before the salad is eaten. In summer, young lettuces are substituted for the endive, and intermixed with a variety of herbs, some of which are not generally cultivated in England.

SUFFOLK SALAD.

Fill a salad-bowl from half to three parts full with very tender lettuces shred small, minced lean of ham, and hard-boiled eggs, or their yolks only, also minced, placed in alternate layers; dress the mixture with English salad-sauce, but do not pour it into the bowl until the instant of serving. A portion of cold chicken, cut in thin slices about the size of a shilling, may be added when convenient.

YORKSHIRE PLOUGHMAN'S SALAD.

Mix treacle and vinegar, in the proportion of one tablespoonful of the first to two of the latter; add a little black pepper, and eat the sauce with lettuces shred small (with an intermixture of young onions when they are liked.) This, though certainly not a very refined order of salad, is scarcely so unpalatable as such ingredients would seem to promise.

TO BOIL CAULIFLOWERS.

Trim off the outside leaves, and cut the stems quite close to the cauliflowers; let them lie for an hour in plenty of cold water, with a handful of salt in it, to draw out any insects that may be amongst them; then wash them very thoroughly, and examine them well, to be assured that no snail is left in any part of them, throw them into a large pan of boiling water, salted as for asparagus, and quite cleared from scum; for this, if not removed, will adhere to the cauliflowers and spoil their appearance. When the stalks are tender lift them out, dish them neatly, and send good melted butter to table with them.

20 to 30 minutes.

CAULIFLOWERS. (*French Receipt.*)

Cut the cauliflowers into small handsome tufts, and boil them until three parts done, drain them well, toss them for a moment in some *thick* melted butter or white sauce, and set them by to cool. When they are quite cold, dip them separately into the batter of page 130, fry them a light brown, arrange them neatly in a dish, and serve them very hot.

BROCCOLI.

This is boiled, and served in the same manner as cauliflowers when the heads are large; the stems of the branching broccoli are peeled, and the vegetable, tied in bunches, is dressed and served, like asparagus, upon a toast.

10 to 20 minutes.

TO BOIL ARTICHOKES.

After they have been soaked and *well* washed, cut off the stems quite close, trim away a few of the lower leaves, and clip the points of all; throw the artichokes into plenty of fast boiling water, ready salted and skimmed, with the addition, if it be at hand, of the proportion of soda directed in page 229, as this will greatly improve the colour of the vegetable. When extremely young, the artichokes will be tender in from half to three quarters of an hour, but they will require more than double that time when at their full growth: when the leaves can be drawn out easily, they are done. Send good melted butter to table with them. They should be boiled always with the stalk-ends uppermost.

Very young, ½ to ¾ hour; full grown, 1¼ to 2 hours.

Obs.—French cooks lift the tops from the artichokes before they are served, and replace them after having taken out the chokes: this must be expeditiously done to prevent the vegetable from cooling.

TO BOIL WINTER SQUASH.

Squash is a rich vegetable, particularly the yellow winter squash. This requires more boiling than the summer kind. Pare it, cut in pieces, take out the seeds and boil it in a very little water till it is quite soft. Then press out all the water, mash it and add a little butter, pepper and salt.

VEGETABLE MARROW.

It is customary to gather this when not larger than a turkey's egg, but we should say that the vegetable is not then in its perfection. The flesh is whiter and of better flavour when the gourd is about six inches long; at least we have found it so with the kinds which have fallen under our observation. It may either be boiled in the skin, then pared, halved, and served upon a toast; or quartered, freed from the seed, and left until cold, then dipped into egg and fine crumbs of bread, and fried; or it may be cut into dice, and reheated in a little good white sauce; or stewed tender in butter, and served in well-thickened veal gravy, flavoured with a little lemon-juice. It may likewise be mashed by the receipt which we have given for turnips, and in that form will be found excellent.   The French make a fanciful dish of the marrows thus: they boil them tender in water, and halve them lengthwise as is usual, they then slice a small bit off each to make them stand evenly in the dish, and after having hollowed the insides, so as to leave a more shell, about half an inch thick, they fill them with a thick rich mince of white meat, and pour white sauce round them; or they heap fried crumbs over the tops, place the dish in the oven for a few minutes, and serve them without sauce.

Size of turkey's egg, 10 to 15 minutes; moderate-sized, 20 to 30; large, ¾ to 1 hour.

TOMATAS EN SALADE.

These are now often served in England in the American fashion, merely sliced, and dressed like cucumbers, with salt, pepper, oil, and vinegar.   For various other American modes of preparing them for table, see tomata dumplings, Chapter XVII.

ROAST TOMATAS.   *To serve with roast leg, loin, or shoulder of mutton.*

Select them nearly of the same size, take off the stalks, and roast them gently in a Dutch oven, or if more convenient, place them at the edge of the dripping-pan, taking care that no fat from the joint shall fall upon them, and keeping them turned that they may be equally done. From ten to fourteen minutes will roast them.

STEWED TOMATAS.

Arrange them in a single layer, and pour to them as much gravy as will reach to half their height; stew them very softly until the under sides are done, then turn, and finish stewing them.   Thicken the gravy with a little arrow-root and cream, or with flour and butter, and serve it round them.

FORCED TOMATAS; (*English Receipt.*)

Cut the stems quite close, slice off the tops of eight fine tomatas, and scoop out the insides; press the pulp through a sieve, and mix with it one ounce of fine crumbs of bread, one of butter, broken very small, some pepper, or cayenne, and salt.   Fill the tomatas with the mixture, and bake them ten minutes in a moderate oven; serve them with brown gravy in the dish.   A few small mushrooms, stewed tender in a little butter, then minced and added to the tomata pulp, will very much improve this receipt.

Baked 10 minutes.

FORCED TOMATAS; (*French Receipt.*)

Let the tomatas be well shaped and of equal size; divide them nearly in the middle, leaving the blossom-side the largest, as this only is to be used; empty them carefully of their seeds and juice, and fill them with the following ingredients, which must previously be stewed tender in butter, but without being allowed to brown: minced mushrooms and shalots, with a moderate proportion of parsley, some lean of ham chopped small, a seasoning of cayenne, and a little fine salt, if needed; let them cool, then mix with them about a third as much of fine crumbs of bread, and two yolks of eggs; fill the tomatas, cover them with fine crumbs, moisten them with clarified butter, and bake them in a brisk oven until

15

they are well coloured.   Serve them as a garnish to stewed rump or
sirloin of beef, or to a boned and forced leg of mutton.

Minced lean of ham, 2 ozs.; mushrooms, 2 ozs.; bread-crumbs, 2
ozs.; shalots, 4 to 8; parsley, full teaspoonful; cayenne, quarter saltspoonful; little salt, if needed; butter, 2 ozs.; yolks of eggs, 2 to 3:
baked, 10 to 20 minutes.

Obs.—The French pound the whole of these ingredients with a bit
of garlic, before they fill the tomatas with them, but this is not absolutely necessary, and the garlic, if added at all, should be parboiled
first, as its strong flavour, combined with that of the eschalots, would
scarcely suit the general taste.   When the lean of a dressed ham is at
hand, only the herbs and vegetables will need to be stewed in the butter; this should be mixed with them into the forcemeat, which an
intelligent cook will vary in many ways.

PURÉE OF TOMATAS.

Divide a dozen fine ripe tomatas, squeeze out the seeds, and take off
the stalks; put them with one small mild onion (or more, if liked), and
about half a pint of very good gravy, into a well-tinned stewpan or
saucepan, and simmer them for nearly or quite an hour; a couple of
bay-leaves, some cayenne, and as much salt as the dish may require
should be added when they begin to boil.   Press them through a sieve,
heat them again, and stir to them a quarter-pint of good cream, previously mixed and boiled for five minutes with a teaspoonful of flour.
This purée is to be served with calf's head, veal cutlets, boiled knuckle
of veal, calf's brains, or beef palates.   For pork, beef, geese, and other
brown meats, the tomatas should be reduced to a proper consistency in
rich and highly-flavoured brown gravy, or Spanish sauce.

MUSHROOMS AU BEURRE; (*delicious.*)

Cut the stems from some fine meadow mushroom-buttons, and clean
them with a bit of new flannel and some fine salt, then either wipe them
dry with a soft cloth, or rinse them in fresh water, drain them quickly,
spread them in a clean cloth, fold it over them, and leave them ten
minutes, or more, to dry.   For every pint of them thus prepared, put an
ounce and a half of fresh butter into a thick iron saucepan, shake it over
the fire until it *just* begins to brown, throw in the mushrooms, continue
to shake the saucepan over a clear fire, that they may not stick to it,
nor burn, and when they have simmered three or four minutes, strew
over them a little salt, some cayenne, and pounded mace; stew them
until they are perfectly tender, heap them in a dish, and serve them
with their own sauce only, for breakfast, supper, or luncheon.   Nothing
can be finer than the flavour of the mushrooms thus prepared; and the
addition of any liquid is far from an improvement to it.   They are very
good when drained from the butter and served cold, and in a cool larder
may be kept for several days.   The butter in which they are stewed is
admirable for flavouring gravies, sauces, or potted meats.   Small flaps,
freed from the fur and skin, may be stewed in the same way; and either
these or the buttons, served under roast poultry or partridges, will give
a dish of very superior relish.

Meadow mushrooms, 3 pints, fresh butter, 4½ ozs.: 3 to 5 minutes.
Salt, 1 small teaspoonful; mace, half as much; cayenne, third of salt.

spoonful: 10 to 15 minutes. More spices to be added if required—much depending on their quality; but they should not overpower the flavour of the mushrooms.

Obs.—Persons inhabiting parts of the country where mushrooms are abundant, may send them easily, when thus prepared (or when potted by the following receipt), to their friends in cities, or in less productive counties. If poured into jars, with sufficient butter to cover them, they will travel any distance, and can be rewarmed for use.

POTTED MUSHROOMS.

Prepare either small flaps or buttons with great nicety, without wetting them, and wipe the former very dry, after the application of the salt and flannel. Stew them quite tender, with the same proportion of butter as the mushrooms au beurre, but increase a little the quantity of spice; when they are done turn them into a large dish, spread them over one end of it, and raise it two or three inches, that they may be well drained from the butter. As soon as they are quite cold, press them very closely into small potting-pans; pour lukewarm clarified butter thickly over them, and store them in a cool dry place. If intended for present use, merely turn them down upon a clean shelf; but for longer keeping, cover the tops first with very dry paper, and then with melted mutton-suet. We have ourselves had the mushrooms, after being simply spread upon a dish while hot, remain perfectly good in that state for seven or eight weeks: they were prepared late in the season, and the weather was consequently cool during the interval.

MUSHROOM-TOAST, OR CROUTE AUX CHAMPIGNONS; (*excellent.*)

Cut the stems closely from a quart, or more, of small just-opened mushrooms, peel them, and take out the fur. Dissolve from two to three ounces of fresh butter in a well-tinned saucepan or stewpan; put in the mushrooms, strew over them a quarter-teaspoonful of pounded mace mixed with a little cayenne, and let them stew over a gentle fire from ten to fifteen minutes; toss or stir them often during the time; then add a small dessertspoonful of flour, and shake the pan round until it is lightly browned. Next pour in, by slow degrees, half a pint of gravy or of good beef-broth; and when the mushrooms have stewed softly in this for a couple of minutes, throw in a little salt, and a squeeze of lemon-juice, and pour them on to a crust, cut about an inch and a quarter thick, from the under part of a moderate-sized loaf, and fried in good butter to a light brown, after having been first slightly hollowed in the inside. New milk, or thin cream, may be used with very good effect instead of the gravy; but a few strips of lemon-rind, and a small portion of nutmeg and mushroom-catsup should then be added to the sauce. The bread may be buttered and grilled over a gentle fire instead of being fried, and is better so.

Small mushrooms, 4 to 5 half pints; butter, 3 to 4 ozs.; mace, mixed with a little cayenne, ¼ teaspoonful: stewed softly 10 to 15 minutes. Flour, 1 small dessertspoonful: 3 to 5 minutes. Gravy or broth, ½ pint: 2 minutes. Little salt and lemon-juice.

TO BOIL SPROUTS, CABBAGES, SAVOYS, LETTUCES, OR ENDIVE.

All green vegetables should be thrown into abundance of fast-boiling water ready salted and skimmed, with the addition of the morsel of soda which we have recommended, in a previous page of this chapter, the pan should be left uncovered, and every precaution taken to prevent the smoke from reaching its contents.   Endive, sprouts, and spring greens, will only require copious washing before they are boiled; but savoys, large lettuces, and close-leaved cabbages should be thrown into salt and water for half an hour or more before they are dressed, with the tops downwards to draw out the insects.   The stems of these last should be cut off, the decayed leaves stripped away, and the vegetable halved or quartered, or split deeply across the stalk-end, and divided entirely before it is dished.

Very young greens, 15 to 20 minutes; lettuces, 20 to 30 minutes; large savoys, or cabbages, 1 to 1½ hour, or more.

Obs.—When the stalk of any kind of cabbage is tender, it is done. Turnip-greens should be well washed in several waters, and boiled in a very large quantity to deprive them of their bitterness.

STEWED CABBAGE.

Cut out the stalk entirely, and slice a fine firm cabbage or two in very thin strips; throw them after they have been well washed and drained, into a large pan of boiling water ready salted and skimmed, and when they are tender, which will be in from ten to fifteen minutes, pour them into a sieve or strainer, press the water thoroughly from them, and chop them slightly.   Put into a very clean saucepan about a couple of ounces of butter, and when it is dissolved add the cabbage, with sufficient pepper and salt to season it, and stir it over a clear fire until it appears tolerably dry; then shake lightly in a tablespoonful of flour, turn the whole well, and add by slow degrees a cup of thick cream: veal gravy or good white sauce may be substituted for this, when preferred to it.

TO BOIL TURNIPS.

Pare entirely from them the stringy rind, and either split the turnips once or leave them whole; throw them into boiling water slightly salted, and keep them closely covered from smoke and dust till they are tender. When small and young they will be done in from fifteen to twenty minutes; at their full growth they will require from three quarters to a full hour, or more, of gentle boiling.   After they become old and woolly, they are not worth dressing in any way.   When boiled in their skins and pared afterwards, they are said to be of better flavour and much less watery than when cooked in the usual way.

Young turnips, 15 to 20 minutes: full grown, ¾ to 1 hour, or more.

TO MASH TURNIPS.

Split them once or even twice should they be large; after they are pared, boil them very tender, and press the water thoroughly from them with a couple of trenchers, or with the back of a large plate and one trencher.   To ensure their being free from lumps, it is better to pass them through a cullender or coarse hair-sieve, with a wooden spoon; though, when quite young, they may be worked sufficiently smooth without this.   Put them into a clean saucepan, and stir them constantly for some minutes over a gentle fire, that they may be very dry; then add some salt, a bit of fresh butter, and a little cream, or in lieu of this new milk (we would also recommend a seasoning of white pepper or cayenne, when appearance and fashion are not particularly regarded), and con tinue to simmer and to stir them for five or six minutes longer, or until they have quite absorbed all the liquid which has been poured to them. Serve them always as hot as possible. This is an excellent receipt.

Turnips, weighed after they are pared, 3 lbs.: dried 5 to 8 minutes. Salt, 1 teaspoonful; butter, 1 oz. to 1½ oz.; cream or milk, nearly ½ pint: 5 or 6 minutes.

TURNIPS IN WHITE SAUCE. (ENTREMETS.)

When no scoop for the purpose is at hand, cut some small finely-grained turnips into quarters, and pare them into balls, or into the shape of plums or pears of equal size; arrange them evenly in a broad stew-pan or saucepan, and cover them nearly with good veal broth, throw in a little salt, and a morsel of sugar, and boil them rather quickly until they are quite tender, but unbroken; lift them out, draining them well from the broth; dish, and pour over them some thick white sauce. As an economy, a cup of cream, and a teaspoonful of arrowroot, may be added to the broth in which the turnips have stewed, to make the sauce; and when it boils, a small slice of butter may be stirred and well worked into it, should it not be sufficiently rich without.

TURNIPS STEWED IN BUTTER. (GOOD.)

This is an excellent way of dressing the vegetable when it is mild and finely grained; but its flavour otherwise is too strong to be agreeable. After they have been washed, wiped quite dry, and pared, slice the turnips nearly half an inch thick, and divide them into dice. Just dissolve an ounce of butter for each half-pound of the turnips, put them in as flat as they can be, and stew them very gently indeed, from three quarters of an hour to a full hour. Add a seasoning of salt and white pepper when they are half done. When thus prepared, they may be dished over fried or nicely broiled mutton cutlets, or served by themselves.

For a small dish: turnips, 1½ lb.; butter, 3 ozs.; seasoning of white pepper; salt, ½ teaspoonful, or more: ¾ to 1 hour. Large dish, turnips, 2 lbs.; butter, 4 ozs.

TURNIPS IN GRAVY.

To a pound of turnips sliced and cut into dice, pour a quarter-pint of boiling veal gravy, add a small lump of sugar, some salt and cayenne, or white pepper, and boil them quickly from fifty to sixty minutes. Serve them very hot.

TO BOIL CARROTS.

Wash the mould from them, and scrape the skin off lightly with the edge of a sharp knife, or, should this be objected to, pare them as thin and as equally as possible; in either case free them from all blemishes, and should they be very large, split them across the tops a few inches down; rinse them well, and throw them into plenty of boiling water with some salt in it. The skin of very young carrots may be rubbed off like that of new potatoes, and from twenty to thirty minutes will then be sufficient to boil them; but at their full growth they will require from an hour and a half to two hours. It was formerly the custom to tie them in a cloth, and to wipe the skin from them with it after they were dressed and old-fashioned cooks still use one to remove it; but all vegetables should, we think, be dished and served with the least possible delay after they are ready for table. Melted butter should accompany boiled carrots.

Very young carrots, 20 to 30 minutes. Full-grown ones, 1½ to 2 hours.

SWEET CARROTS. (ENTREMETS.)

Boil quite tender some fine highly-flavoured carrots, press the water from them, and rub them through the back of a fine hair-sieve; put them into a clean saucepan or stewpan, and dry them thoroughly over a gentle fire; then add a slice of fresh butter, and when this is dissolved and well mixed with them, strew in a dessertspoonful or more of powdered sugar, and a little salt; next, stir in by degrees some good cream, and when this is quite absorbed, and the carrots again appear dry, dish and serve them quickly with small sippets, *à la Reine* (see page 40), placed round them.

Carrots, 3 lbs., boiled quite tender: stirred over a gentle fire 5 to 10 minutes. Butter, 2 ozs.; salt, ½ teaspoonful; pounded sugar, 1 dessertspoonful; cream, ½ pint, stewed gently together until quite dry.

Obs.—For excellent *mashed carrots* omit the sugar, add a good seasoning of salt and white pepper, and half a pint of rich brown gravy; or for a plain dinner rather less than this of milk.

CARROTS AU BEURRE, OR BUTTERED CARROTS.

Either boil sufficient carrots for a dish quite tender, and then cut them into slices a quarter-inch thick, or first slice, and then boil them: the latter method is the most expeditious, but the other best preserves the flavour of the vegetable. Drain them well, and while this is being done just dissolve from two to four ounces of butter in a saucepan, and strew in some minced parsley, some salt, and white pepper or cayenne; then add the carrots, and toss them very gently until they are equally covered with the sauce, which should not be allowed to boil: the parsley may be omitted at pleasure. Cold carrots may be rewarmed in this way.

TO BOIL PARSNEPS.

These are dressed in precisely the same manner as carrots, but require much less boiling. According to their quality and the time of year, they will take from twenty minutes to nearly an hour. Every speck or blemish should be cut from them after they are scraped, and the water in which they are boiled should be well skimmed. They are a favourite accompaniment to salt-fish and boiled pork, and may be served either mashed or plain.

20 to 55 minutes.

FRIED PARSNEPS.

Boil them until they are about half done, lift them out, and let them cool; slice them rather thickly, sprinkle them with fine salt and white pepper, and fry them a pale brown in good butter. Serve them with roast meat, or dish them under it.

JERUSALEM ARTICHOKES.

Wash the artichokes, pare them quickly, and throw them as they are done into a saucepan of cold water, or of equal parts of milk and water; and when they are about half boiled add a little salt to them. Take

them up the instant they are perfectly tender: this will be n from
fifteen to twenty-five minutes, so much do they vary as to the time
necessary to dress them. If allowed to remain in the water after they
are done, they become black and flavourless. Melted butter should
always be sent to table with them.

15 to 25 minutes.

TO FRY JERUSALEM ARTICHOKES. (ENTREMETS.)

Boil them from eight to twelve minutes; lift them out, drain them
on a sieve, and let them cool; dip them into beaten eggs, and cover
them with fine bread-crumbs. Fry them a light brown, drain, pile them
in a hot dish, and serve them quickly.

HARICOTS BLANCS.

The haricot blanc is the seed of a particular kind of French bean, of
which we find some difficulty in ascertaining the English name, for
though we have tried several which resemble it in appearance, we have
found their flavour, after they were dressed, very different, and far from
agreeable. The large white Dutch runner is, we believe, the proper
variety for cooking; at least we have obtained a small quantity under
that name, which approached much more nearly than any others we
had tried to those which we had eaten abroad. The haricots, when
freshly harvested, may be thrown into plenty of boiling water, with
some salt and a small bit of butter; if old, they must be previously
soaked for an hour or two, put into cold water, brought to boil gently,
and simmered until they are tender, for if boiled fast the skins will burst
before the beans are done. Drain them thoroughly from the water when
they are ready, and lay them into a clean saucepan over two or three
ounces of fresh butter, a small dessertspoonful of chopped parsley, and
sufficient salt and pepper to season the whole; then gently shake or
toss the beans until they are quite hot and equally covered with the
sauce; add the strained juice of half a lemon, and serve them quickly.
The vegetable thus dressed is excellent; and it affords a convenient
resource in the season when the supply of other kinds is scantiest. In
some countries the dried beans are placed in water, over-night, upon a
stove, and by a very gentle degree of warmth are sufficiently softened
by the following day to be served as follows:—they are drained from
the water, spread on a clean cloth and wiped quite dry, then lightly
floured and fried in oil or butter, with a seasoning of pepper and salt,
lifted into a hot dish, and served under roast beef, or mutton.

TO BOIL BEET ROOT.

Wash the roots delicately clean, but neither scrape nor cut them, as
not a fibre even should be trimmed away, until after they are dressed.
Throw them into boiling water, and according to their size boil them
from one hour and a half to two hours and a half. Pare and serve them
whole, or thickly sliced, and send melted butter to table with them.
Beet-root is often mixed with winter salads; and it makes a pickle of
beautiful colour; but one of the most usual modes of serving it at the
present day is, with the cheese, cold and merely pared and sliced, after
having been boiled or baked.

1½ to 2½ hours.　Baked, 2½ to 3½ hours.

Obs.—This root must not be probed with a fork like other vegetables, to ascertain if it be done or not; but the cook must endeavour, by attention, to learn the time required for it. After it is lifted out, the thickest part may be pressed with the fingers, to which it will yield, if it be sufficiently boiled.

TO BAKE BEET ROOT.

Beet root, if slowly and carefully baked until it is tender quite through, is very rich and sweet in flavour, although less bright in colour than when it is boiled: it is also, we believe, remarkably nutritious and wholesome. Wash and wipe it very dry, but neither cut nor break any part of it; then lay it into a coarse dish, and bake it in a gentle oven for four or five hours: it will sometimes require even a longer me than this. Pare it quickly if to be served hot; but leave it to cool rst, when it is to be sent to table cold.

The white beet-root is dressed exactly like the red: the leaves of it re boiled and served like asparagus.

In slow oven from 4 to 6 hours.

STEWED BEET ROOT.

Bake or boil it tolerably tender, and let it remain until it is cold, then pare and cut it into slices; heat and stew it for a short time in some good pale veal gravy (or in strong veal broth for ordinary occasions), hicken this with a teaspoonful of arrow-root, and half a cupful or more f good cream, and stir in, as it is taken from the fire, from a tea to a ablespoonful of vinegar. The beet may be served likewise in thick white sauce, to which, just before it is dished, the mild eschalots of page 138 may be added.

TO STEW RED CABBAGE. (*Flemish Receipt.*)

Strip the outer leaves from a fine and fresh red cabbage; wash it well, and cut it into the thinnest possible slices, beginning at the top; put it into a thick saucepan in which two or three ounces of good butter have been just dissolved; add some pepper and salt, and stew it very slowly indeed for three or four hours in its own juice, keeping it often stirred, and well pressed down. When it is perfectly tender add a tablespoonful of vinegar; mix the whole up thoroughly, heap the cabbage in a hot dish, and serve broiled sausages round it; or omit these last, and substitute lemon-juice, cayenne pepper, and a half-cupful of good gravy.

The stalk of the cabbage should be split in quarters and taken entirely out in the first instance.

3 to 4 hours.

BOILED CELERY.

This vegetable is extremely good dressed like sea-kale, and served on a toast with rich melted butter. Let it be freshly dug, wash it with great nicety, trim the ends, take off the coarse outer-leaves, cut the roots of equal length, tie them in bunches, and boil them in plenty of water, with the usual proportion of salt, from twenty to thirty minutes.

20 to 30 minutes.

STEWED CELERY.

Cut five or six fine roots of celery to the length of the inside of the dish in which they are to be served; free them from all the coarser leaves, and from the green tops, trim the root ends neatly, and wash the vegetable in several waters till it is as clean as possible; then, either boil it tender with a little salt, and a bit of fresh butter the size of a walnut, in just sufficient water to cover it quite, drain it well, arrange it on a very hot dish, and pour a thick béchamel, or white sauce over it; or stew it in broth or common stock, and serve it with very rich, thickened, Espagnole or brown gravy. It has a higher flavour when partially stewed in the sauce, after being drained thoroughly from the broth. Unless very large and old, it will be done in from twenty-five to thirty minutes, but if not quite tender, longer time must be allowed for it. A cheap and expeditious method of preparing this dish is to slice the celery, to simmer it until soft in as much good broth as will only just cover it, and to add a thickening of flour and butter, or arrow-root, with some salt, pepper, and a small cupful of cream.

25 to 30 minutes, or more.

STEWED ONIONS.

Strip the outer skin from four or five fine Portugal onions, and trim the ends, but without cutting into the vegetable; arrange them in a saucepan of sufficient size to contain them all in one layer; just cover them with good beef, or veal gravy, and stew them very gently indeed for a couple of hours: they should be tender quite through, but should not be allowed to fall to pieces. When large, but not *mild* onions are used, they should be first boiled for half an hour in plenty of water, then drained from it, and put into boiling gravy: strong, well-flavoured broth of veal or beef, is sometimes substituted for this, and with the addition of a little catsup, spice, and thickening answers very well. The savour of this dish is heightened by flouring lightly and frying the onions of a pale brown before they are stewed.

Portugal onions, 4 or 5 (if fried, 15 to 20 minutes); broth or gravy, 1 to 1½ pint: nearly or quite 2 hours.

Obs.—When the quantity of gravy is considered too much, the onions may be only half covered, and turned when the under side is tender, but longer time must be allowed for stewing them.

TO FRY ONIONS.

Peel and slice them evenly, have ready a pan of hot butter, or salt-pork fat, and fry the onions till slightly browned.

TO BOIL ONIONS.

Take onions of the same size, peel and wash them, lay them in some pan or kettle with a broad bottom, so that the onions may not be piled one upon another. Cover them with water, or milk and water if you like them very mild and let them simmer slowly for 20 minutes, or till done.

CHAPTER XVI.

PASTRY.

INTRODUCTORY REMARKS.

THE greatest possible cleanliness and nicety should be observed in making pastry. The slab or board, paste-rollers, tins, cutters, stamps, everything, in fact, used for it, and especially the hands (for these last are not always so scrupulously attended to as they ought to be), should be equally free from the slightest soil or particle of dust. The more expeditiously the finer kinds of crust are made and despatched to the oven, and the less they are touched, the better. Much of their excellence depends upon the baking also; they should have a sufficient degree of heat to raise them quickly, but not so fierce a one as to colour them too much before they are done, and still less to burn them. The oven-door should remain closed after they are put in, and not be removed until the paste is *set*. Large raised pies require a steadily-sustained, or, what is technically called a soaking heat, and to ensure this the oven should be made very hot, then cleared, and closely shut from half to a whole hour before it is used, to concentrate the heat. It is an advantage in this case to have a large log or two of cord-wood burned in it, in addition to the usual firing.

In mixing paste, the water should be added gradually, and the whole gently drawn together with the fingers, until sufficient has been added, when it should be lightly kneaded until it is as smooth as possible. When carelessly made, the surface is often left covered with small dry crumbs or lumps; or the water *is* poured in heedlessly in so large a proportion that it becomes necessary to add more flour to render it *workable* in any way; and this ought particularly to be avoided when a certain weight of all the ingredients has been taken.

TO GLAZE OR ICE PASTRY.

The fine yellow glaze appropriate to meat pies is given with beaten yolk of egg, which should be laid on with a paste brush, or a small bunch of feathers: if a lighter colour be wished for, whisk the whole of the egg together, or mix a little milk with the yolk.

The best mode of icing fruit-tarts before they are sent to the oven is, to moisten the paste with cold water, to sift sugar thickly upon it, and to press it lightly on with the hand; but when a *whiter* icing is preferred, the pastry must be drawn from the oven when nearly baked, and brushed with white of egg, whisked to a froth; then well covered with the sifted sugar, and sprinkled with a few drops of water before it is put in again. this glazing answers also very well, though it takes a slight colour, if used before the pastry is baked.

FEUILLETAGE, OR FINE FRENCH PUFF PASTE.

This, when made by a good French cook, is the perfection of rich light crust, and will rise in the oven from one to six inches in height, but some practice is, without doubt, necessary to accomplish this. In summer it is a great advantage to have ice at hand, and to harden the butter over it before it is used; the paste also in the intervals of rolling is improved by being laid on an oven-leaf over a vessel containing it. Take an equal weight of good butter free from the coarse salt which is found in some, and which is disadvantageous for this paste, and of fine dry, sifted flour; to each pound of these allow the yolks of a couple of eggs, and a small teaspoonful of salt. Break a few small bits of the butter very lightly into the flour, put the salt into the centre, and pour on it sufficient water to dissolve it (we do not quite understand why the doing this should be better than mixing it with the flour, as in other pastes, but such is the method always pursued for it); add a little more water to the eggs, moisten the flour gradually, and make it into a *very* smooth paste, rather lithe in summer, and never *exceedingly* stiff, though the opposite fault, in an extreme, would render the crust unmanageable. Press, in a soft thin cloth, all the moisture from the remainder of the butter, and form it into a ball, but in doing this be careful not to soften it too much. Should it be in an unfit state for pastry, from the heat of the weather, put it into a basin, and set the basin in a pan of water mixed with plenty of salt and saltpetre, and let it remain in a cool place for an hour if possible, before it is used. When it is ready (and the paste should never be commenced until it be so), roll the crust out square,* and of sufficient size to enclose the butter, flatten this a little upon it in the centre, and then fold the crust well over it, and roll it out thin as lightly as possible, after having dredged the board and paste-roller with a little flour: this is called giving it *one turn*. Then fold it in three, give it another turn, and set it aside, where it will be very cool, for a few minutes; give it two more turns in the same way, rolling it each time very lightly, but of equal thickness, and to the full length that it will reach, taking always especial care that the butter shall not break through the paste. Let it again be set aside to become cold; and after it has been twice more rolled and folded in three, give it a half-turn, by folding it once only, and it will be ready for use.

Equal weight of the finest flour and good butter; to each pound of these, the yolks of two eggs, and a small saltspoonful of salt: 6½ turns to be given to the paste.

VERY GOOD LIGHT PASTE.

Mix with a pound of sifted flour six ounces of fresh, pure lard, and make them into a smooth paste with cold water; press the buttermilk from ten ounces of butter, and form it into a ball, by twisting it in a clean cloth. Roll out the paste, put the ball of butter in the middle, close it like an apple-dumpling, and roll it very lightly until it is less than an inch thick; fold the ends into the middle, dust a little flour over the board and paste-roller, and roll the paste thin a second time, then set it aside for three or four minutes in a very cool place; give it two more *turns*, and after it has again been left for a few minutes, roll it out twice more, folding it each time in three. This ought to render it fit for use. The sooner this paste is sent to the oven after it is made, the lighter it will be: if allowed to remain long before it is baked, it will be tough and heavy.

Flour, 1 lb.; lard, 6 ozs.; butter, 10 ozs.; little salt.

---

* The learner will perhaps find it easier to fold the paste securely round it in the form of a dumpling, until a little experience has been acquired.

ENGLISH PUFF-PASTE.

Break lightly into a couple of pounds of dried and sifted flour, eight ounces of butter; add a pinch of salt, and sufficient cold water to make the paste; work it as quickly and as lightly as possible, until it is smooth and pliable, then level it with the paste-roller until it is three-quarters of an inch thick, and place regularly upon it six ounces of butter in small bits; fold the paste like a blanket-pudding, roll it out again, lay on it six ounces more of butter, repeat the rolling, dusting each time a little flour over the board and paste, add again six ounces of butter, and roll the paste out thin three or four times, folding the ends into the middle.

Flour, 2 lbs.; little salt; butter, 1 lb. 10 ozs.

If very rich paste be required, equal portions of flour and butter must be used; and the latter may be divided into two, instead of three parts, when it is to be rolled in.

CREAM CRUST; (*very good.*)

Stir a little fine salt into a pound of dry flour, and mix gradually with it sufficient very thick, sweet cream to form a smooth paste; it will be found sufficiently good for common family dinners, without the addition of butter; but to make an excellent crust, roll in four ounces in the usual way, after having given the paste a couple of *turns*. Handle it as lightly as possible in making it, and send it to the oven as soon as it is ready; it may be used for fruit tarts, cannelons, puffs, and other varieties of small pastry, or for good meat-pies. Six ounces of butter to the pound of flour will give a *very rich* crust.

Flour, 1 lb.; salt, 1 small saltspoonful (more for meat pies); rich cream, ½ to ¾ pint; butter, 4 ozs.; for richest crust, 6 ozs.

PATE BRISÉE, OR FRENCH CRUST FOR HOT OR COLD MEAT-PIES.

Sift two pounds and a quarter of fine dry flour, and break into it one pound of butter, work them together with the fingers until they resemble fine crumbs of bread, then add a small teaspoonful of salt, and make them into a firm paste, with the yolks of four eggs, well beaten, mixed with half a pint of cold water, and strained: or for a somewhat richer crust of the same kind, take two pounds of flour, one of butter, the yolks of four eggs, half an ounce of salt, and less than the half-pint of water, and work the whole well until the paste is perfectly smooth.

Flour, 2¼ lbs.; butter, 1 lb.; salt, 1 small teaspoonful; yolks of eggs, 4; water, ½ pint. Or; flour, 2 lbs.; butter, 1 lb.; yolks of eggs, 4; water, less than ½ pint.

FLEAD CRUST.

Flead is the provincial name for the leaf, or inside fat of a pig, which makes excellent crust when fresh, much finer, indeed, than after it is melted into lard. Clear it quite from skin, and slice it very thin into the flour, add sufficient salt to give flavour to the paste, and make the whole up smooth and firm with cold water; lay it on a clean dresser, and beat it forcibly with a rolling-pin until the flead is blended perfectly with the flour. It may then be made into cakes with a paste-cutter, or used for pies, round the edges of which a knife should be passed, as the crust rises better when *cut* than if merely rolled to the proper size. With the addition of a small quantity of butter, which may either be

broken into the flour before the flead is mixed with it, or rolled into the
paste after it is beaten, it will be found equal to fine puff crust, with the
advantage of being more easy of digestion.

Quite common crust: flour, 1¼ lb.; flead, 8 ozs.; salt, 1 small teaspoonful.   Good common crust: flour, 1 lb.; flead, 6 ozs.; butter, 2 ozs.
Rich crust: flead, ¾ lb.; butter, 2 ozs.; flour, 1 lb.   The crust is very
good when made without any butter.

COMMON SUET-CRUST FOR PIES.

In many families this is preferred both for pies and tarts, to crust made
with butter, as being much more wholesome; but it should never be
served unless especially ordered, as it is to some persons peculiarly distasteful.   Chop the suet extremely small, and add from six to eight
ounces of it to a pound of flour, with a few grains of salt; mix these
with cold water into a firm paste, and work it very smooth.   Some
cooks beat it with a paste-roller, until the suet is perfectly blended with
the flour; but the crust is lighter without this.   In exceedingly sultry
weather the suet, not being firm enough to chop, may be sliced as thin
as possible, and well beaten into the paste after it is worked up.

Flour, 2 lbs.; beef or veal kidney-suet, 12 to 16 ozs.; salt (for fruit-
pies), ¼ teaspoonful; for meat-pies, 1 teaspoonful.

VERY SUPERIOR SUET-CRUST.

Strip the skin entirely from some fresh veal or beef kidney-suet; chop,
and then put it into the mortar, with a small quantity of pure-flavoured
lard, oil, or butter, and pound it perfectly smooth: it may then be used
for crust in the same way that butter is, in making puff-paste, and in
this form will be found a most excellent substitute for it, for *hot* pies or
tarts.   It is not quite so good for those which are to be served cold.
Eight ounces of suet pounded with two of butter, and worked with the
fingers into a pound of flour, will make an exceedingly good short crust;
but for a very rich one, the proportion must be increased.

Good short crust: flour, 1 lb.; suet, 8 ozs.; butter, 2 ozs.; salt, ½
teaspoonful.   Richer crust: suet, 16 ozs.; butter, 4 ozs.; flour, 1¼ lb.;
salt, 1 small teaspoonful.

VERY RICH SHORT CRUST FOR TARTS.

Break lightly, with the least possible handling, six ounces of butter
into eight of flour; add a dessertspoonful of pounded sugar, and two or
three of water; roll the paste for several minutes, to blend the ingredients well, folding it together like puff-crust, and touch it as little as
possible.

Flour, 8 ozs.; butter, 6 ozs.; pounded sugar, 1 dessertspoonful; water,
1 to 2 spoonsful.

BRIOCHE PASTE.

The brioche is a rich, light kind of unsweetened bun, or cake, very
commonly sold, and served to all classes of people in France, where it
is made in great perfection by good cooks and pastry-cooks.   It is
fashionable at some tables, though in a different form, serving principally as a crust to enclose *rissoles*, or to make *cannelons* and fritters.
We have seen it recommended for a *vol-au-vent*, for which we should
say it does not answer by any means so well as the fine puff-paste called
feuilletage.   The large proportion of butter and eggs which it contains

render it to many persons highly indigestible; and we mention this to warn invalids against it, as we have known it to cause great suffering to persons out of health.   To make it, take a couple of pounds* of fine dry flour, sifted as for cakes, and separate eight ounces of this from the remainder to make the leaven.   Put it into a small pan, and mix it lightly into a lithe paste, with half an ounce of yeast, and a spoonful or two of warm water; make two or three slight incisions across the top, throw a cloth over the pan, and place it near the fire for about twenty minutes, to rise.   In the interval make a hollow space in the centre of the remainder of the flour, and put into it half an ounce of salt, as much fine sifted sugar, and half a gill of cream, or a dessert-spoonful of water; add a pound of butter, as free from moisture as it can be, and quite so from large grains of salt; cut it into small bits, put it into the flour, and pour on it one by one six fresh eggs freed from the specks; then with the fingers work the flour gently into this mass until the whole forms a perfectly smooth, and not stiff paste: a seventh egg, or the yolk of one, or even of two, may be added with advantage if the flour will absorb them; but the brioche must always be *workable*, and not so moist as to adhere to the board and roller disagreeably.   When the leaven is well risen spread this paste out, and the leaven over it; mix them well together with the hands, then cut the whole into several portions, and change them about that the leaven may be incorporated perfectly and equally with the other ingredients: when this is done, and the brioche is perfectly smooth and pliable, dust some flour on a cloth, roll the brioche in it, and lay it into a pan; place it in summer in a cool place, in winter in a warm one.   It is usually made over-night, and baked in the early part of the following day.   It should then be kneaded up afresh the first thing in the morning.   To mould it in the usual form, make it into balls of uniform size, hollow these a little at the top by pressing the thumb round them, brush them over with yolk of egg, and put a second much smaller ball into the hollow part of each; glaze them entirely with yolk of egg, and send them to a quick oven for half an hour or more.   The paste may also be made into the form of a large cake, then placed on a tin, or copper oven-leaf, and supported with a pasteboard in the baking; for the form of which see introductory page of Chapter XXIII.

Flour, 2 lbs.; yeast, ½ oz.; salt and sugar, each ½ oz.; butter, 1 lb.; eggs, 6 to 8.

MODERN POTATO PASTY; (*an excellent family dish.*)

A tin mould of the construction shown in the plate, with a perforated moveable top, and a small valve to allow the escape of the steam, must be had for this pasty, which is an excellent family dish, and which may be varied in numberless ways.   Arrange at the bottom of the mould from two to three pounds of mutton cutlets, freed, according to the taste, from all, or from the greater portion of the fat, then washed, lightly dredged on both sides with flour, and seasoned with salt and pepper or cayenne.   Pour to them sufficient broth or water to make

* It should be remarked, that the directions for brioche-making are principally derived from the French, and that the pound in their country weighs two ounces more than with us: this difference will account for the difficulty of working in the number of eggs which they generally specify, and which render the paste too moist.

the gravy, and add to it at pleasure a tablespoonful of mushroom catsup or of Harvey's sauce. Have ready boiled, and *very* smoothly mashed, with about an ounce of butter, and a spoonful or two of milk or cream to each pound, as many good potatoes as will form a crust to the pasty of quite three inches thick; put the cover on the mould, and arrange

these equally upon it, leaving them a little rough on the surface. Bake the pastry in a moderate oven from three quarters of an hour to an hour and a quarter, according to its size and its contents. Pin a folded napkin neatly round the mould, before it is served, and have ready a hot dish to receive the cover, which must not be lifted off until after the pasty is on the table.

Chicken, or veal and oysters; delicate pork chops with a seasoning of sage and a little parboiled onion, or an eschalot or two finely minced; partridges or rabbits neatly carved, mixed with small mushrooms, and moistened with a little good stock, will all give excellent varieties of this dish, which may be made likewise with highly seasoned slices of salmon freed from the skin, sprinkled with fine herbs or intermixed with shrimps; clarified butter, rich veal stock, or good white wine, may be poured to them to form the gravy. To thicken this, a little flour should be dredged upon the fish before it is laid into the mould. Other kinds, such as cod, mackerel in fillets, salt fish (previously kept at the point of boiling until three parts done, then pulled into flakes, and put into the mould with hard eggs sliced, a little cream, flour, butter, cayenne, and anchovy-essence, and baked with mashed parsneps on the top), will all answer well for this pasty. Veal, when used for it, should be well beaten first: sweetbreads, sliced, may be laid in with it.

For a pasty of moderate size, two pounds, or two and a half of meat, and from three to four of potatoes will be sufficient: a quarter-pint of milk or cream, two small teaspoonsful of salt, and from one to two ounces of butter must be mixed up with these last.*

MODERN CHICKEN PIE.

Skin, and cut down into joints a couple of fowls, take out all the bones, and season the flesh highly with salt, cayenne, pounded mace, and nutmeg; line a dish with a thin paste, and spread over it a layer of the finest sausage-meat, which has previously been moistened with a spoonful or two of cold water; over this place closely together some of the boned chicken joints, then more sausage-meat, and continue thus

---

* A larger proportion of cream and butter well dried into the potatoes over a gentle fire, after they are mashed, will render the crust of the pasty richer and finer.

with alternate layers of each, until the dish is full; roll out, and fasten securely at the edges, a cover half an inch thick, trim off the superfluous paste, make an incision in the top, lay some paste leaves round it, glaze the whole with yolk of egg, and bake the pie from an hour and a half to two hours in a well-heated oven. Lay a sheet or two of writing-paper over the crust, should it brown too quickly. Minced herbs can be mixed with the sausage-meat at pleasure, and a small quantity of eschalot also, where the flavour is much liked: it should be well moistened with water, or the whole will be unpalatably dry. The pie may be served hot or cold, but we would rather recommend the latter.

A couple of very young tender rabbits will answer exceedingly well for it instead of fowls, and a border, or half paste in the dish will generally be preferred to an entire lining of the crust, which is now but rarely served, unless for pastry, which is to be taken out of the dish in which it is baked before it is sent to table.

A COMMON CHICKEN PIE.

Prepare the fowls as for boiling, cut them down into joints, and season them with salt, white pepper, and nutmeg, or pounded mace; arrange them neatly in a dish bordered with paste, lay amongst them three or four fresh eggs, boiled hard, and cut in halves, pour in some cold water, put on a thick cover, pare the edge, and ornament it, make a hole in the centre, lay a roll of paste, or a few leaves round it, and bake the pie in a moderate oven from an hour to an hour and a half. The back and neck bones may be boiled down with a bit or two of lean ham, to make a little additional gravy, which can be poured into the pie after it is baked.

PIGEON PIE.

Border a large dish with fine puff-paste, and cover the bottom with a veal cutlet, or tender rump steak, free from fat and bone, and seasoned with salt, cayenne, and nutmeg, or pounded mace; prepare with great nicety as many freshly-killed young pigeons as the dish will contain in one layer; put into each a slice or ball of butter, seasoned with a little cayenne and mace; lay them into the dish with the breasts downwards, and between and over them put the yolks of half a dozen or more of hard-boiled eggs; stick plenty of butter on them, season the whole well with salt and spice, pour in some cold water or veal broth for the gravy, roll out the cover three quarters of an inch thick, secure it well round the edge, ornament it highly, and bake it for an hour or more in a well-heated oven. It is a great improvement to fill the birds with small mushroom-buttons, prepared as for partridges (see Chapter XIII.): their livers also may be put into them.

BEEF-STEAK PIE.

From a couple to three pounds of rump-steak will be sufficient for a good family pie. It should be well kept though perfectly sweet, for in no form can tainted meat be more offensive than when it is enclosed in paste. Trim off the coarse skin, and part of the fat, should there be much of it (many eaters dislike it altogether in pies, and when this is the case every morsel should be carefully cut away). If the beef should not appear very tender, it may be gently beaten with a paste-roller until the fibre is broken, then divided into slices half as large as the hand,

and laid into a dish bordered with paste. It should be seasoned with
salt and pepper, or cayenne, and sufficient water poured in to make the
gravy and keep the meat moist. Lay on the cover, and be careful
always to brush the edge in every part with egg or cold water, then
join it securely to the paste which is round the rim, trim both off close
to the dish, pass the point of the knife through the middle of the cover,
lay some slight roll or ornament of paste round it, and decorate the
border of the pie in any of the usual modes, which are too common to
require description. Send the pie to a well-heated, but not fierce oven
for about an hour and twenty minutes. To make a richer beef-steak
pie put bearded oysters in alternate layers with the meat, add their
strained liquor to a little good gravy, in which the beards may be simmered for a few minutes, to give it further flavour, and make a light
puff paste for the crust. Some eaters like it seasoned with a small portion of minced onion or eschalot when the oysters are omitted. Mushrooms improve all meat-pies.

1 to 1½ hour.

MUTTON PIE.

A pound and a quarter of flour will make sufficient paste for a moderate-sized pie, and two pounds of mutton freed from the greater portion
of the fat will fill it. Butter a dish, and line it with about half the
paste rolled thin; lay in the mutton evenly, and sprinkle over three
quarters of an ounce of salt, and from half to a whole teaspoonful of
pepper according to the taste; pour in cold water to within an inch of
the brim. Roll the cover, which should be quite half an inch thick, to
the size of the dish; wet the edges of the paste with cold water or
white of egg, be careful to close them securely, cut them off close to
the rim of the dish, stick the point of the knife through the centre, and
bake the pie an hour and a quarter in a well-heated oven.

Flour, 1¼ lb.; dripping, ½ lb. (or suet, ⅓ lb. and butter, 2 ozs). Mutton, 2 lbs.; salt, ¾ oz.; pepper, half to whole teaspoonful; water, ¼ pint
1¼ hour.

RAISED PIES.

These may be made of any size,
and with any kind of meat, poultry,
or game, but the whole must be
entirely free from bone. When
the crust is not to be eaten, it is
made simply with a few ounces of
lard or butter dissolved in boiling
water, with which the flour is to be
mixed (with a spoon at first, as the
heat would be too great for the
hands, but afterwards with the fin-
gers) to a smooth and firm paste. The French, who excel greatly in
this form of pie,* use for it a good crust which they call a pâte brisée
(see page 252), and this is eaten usually with the meat which it con-

Raised Pie.

* We remember having partaken of one which was brought from Bordeaux, and
which contained a small boned ham of delicious flavour, surmounted by boned partridges, above which were placed fine larks likewise boned; all the interstices were
filled with superexcellent forcemeat; and the whole, being a solid mass of nourishing
viands, would have formed an admirable traveller's larder in itself.

16

tains. In either case the paste must be sufficiently stiff to retain its form perfectly after it is raised, as it will have no support to prevent its falling. The celebrated Monsieur Ude gives the following directions for moulding it to a proper shape without difficulty; and as inexperienced cooks generally find a little at first in giving a good appearance to these pies, we copy his instructions for them: "Take a lump of paste proportionate to the size of the pie you are to make, mould it in the shape of a sugar loaf, put it upright on the table, then with the palms of your hands flatten the sides of it; when you have equalized it all round and it is quite smooth, squeeze the middle of the point down to half the height of the paste," then hollow the inside by pressing it with the fingers, and in doing this be careful to keep it in every part of equal thickness. Fill it,* roll out the cover, egg the edges, press them securely together, make a hole in the centre, lay a roll of paste round it, and encircle this with a wreath of leaves, or ornament the pie in any other way, according to the taste; glaze it with well-beaten yolk of egg, and bake it from two to three hours in a well-heated oven if it be small, and from four to five hours if it be large, though the time must be regulated in some measure by the nature of the contents, as well as by the size of the dish.

Obs.—We know not if we have succeeued in making the reader comprehend that this sort of pie (with the exception of the cover, for which a portion must at first be taken off) is made from one solid lump of paste, which, after having been shaped into a cone, as Monsieur Ude directs, or into a high round, or oval form, is hollowed by pressing down the centre with the knuckles, and continuing to knead the inside equally round with the one hand, while the other is pressed close to the outside. It is desirable that the mode of doing this should be once *seen* by the learner, if possible, as mere verbal instructions are scarcely sufficient to enable the quite-inexperienced cook to comprehend at once the exact form and appearance which should be given to the paste.

A VOL-AU-VENT. (ENTRÉE.)

This dish can be successfully made only with the finest and lightest puff-paste (see feuilletage, page 250), as its height, which ought to be

from four to five inches, depends entirely on its rising in the oven. Roll it to something more than an inch in thickness, and cut it to the shape and size of the inside of the dish in which it is to be served, or stamp it out with a fluted tin of proper dimensions; then mark the cover evenly about an inch from the edge all round, and ornament it and the border also, with a knife, as fancy may direct; brush yolk of egg quickly over them, and put the vol-au-vent immediately into a brisk oven, that it may rise well, and be finely coloured, but do not allow it to be scorched. In from twenty to thirty minutes, should it

* For the mode of doing this, see observations, page 256, and note, page 257. A ham must be boiled or stewed tender, and freed from the skin and blackened parts before it is laid in; poultry and game, boned; and all meat highly seasoned.

appear baked through, as well as sufficiently browned, draw it out, and
with the point of a knife detach the cover carefully where it has been
marked, and scoop out all the soft unbaked crumb from the inside of the
vol-au-vent; then turn it gently on to a sheet of clean paper, to drain
the butter from it.   At the instant of serving, fill it with a rich fricassee of lobster, or of sweetbreads, or with *turbot à la crème*, or with the
white part of cold roast veal cut in thin collops not larger than a shilling, and heated in good white sauce with oysters (see minced veal and
oysters, page 174), or with any other of the preparations which we shall
indicate in their proper places, and send it immediately to table.   The
vol-au-vent, as the reader will perceive, is but the case, or crust, in
which various kinds of delicate ragouts are served in an elegant form.
As these are most frequently composed of fish, or of meats which have
been already dressed, it is an economical as well as an excellent mode
of employing such remains.   The sauces in which they are heated must
be quite thick, for they would otherwise soften, or even run through
the crust.   This, we ought to observe, should be examined before it is
filled, and should any part appear too thin, a portion of the crumb which
has been taken out should be fastened to it with some beaten egg, and
the whole of the inside brushed lightly with more egg, in order to make
the loose parts of the vol-au-vent stick well together.   This method is
recommended by an admirable and highly experienced cook, but it need
only be resorted to when the crust is not solid enough to hold the con
tents securely.

For moderate-sized vol-au-vent, flour, ½ lb.; butter, ½ lb.; salt, small
saltspoonful; yolk, 1 egg; little water.   Larger vol-au-vent, ¾ lb. flour;
other ingredients in proportion: baked 20 to 30 minutes.

Obs.—When the vol-au-vent is cut out with the fluted cutter, a second,
some sizes smaller, after being just dipped into hot water, should be
pressed nearly half through the paste, to mark the cover.   The border
ought to be from three quarters of an inch to an inch and a half wide.

A VAL-AU-VENT OF FRUIT.   (ENTREMETS.)

After the crust has been made and baked as above, fill it at the moment of serving with peaches, apricots, mogul, or any other richly
flavoured plums, which have been stewed tender in syrup; lift them
from this, and keep them hot while it is boiled rapidly almost to jelly,
then arrange the fruit in the vol-au-vent, and pour the syrup over it.
For the manner of preparing it, see compotes of fruit, Chapter XX.; but
increase the proportion of sugar nearly half, that the juice may be
reduced quickly to the proper consistency for the vol-au-vent.   Skin
and divide the apricots, and quarter the peaches, unless they should be
very small.

VOL-AU-VENT A LA CREME.   (ENTREMETS.)

After having raised the cover and emptied the vol-au-vent, lay it on a
sheet of paper, and let it become cold.   Fill it just before it is sent to
table with fruit, either boiled down to a rich marmalade, or stewed as
for the preceding vol-au-vent, and heap well-flavoured, but not too
highly sweetened, whipped cream over it.   The edge of the crust may
be glazed by sifting sugar over it, when it is drawn from the oven, and
holding a salamander or red-hot shovel above it; or it may be left
unglazed, and ornamented with bright-coloured fruit jelly.

OYSTER-PATTIES.* (ENTRÉE.)

Line some small patty-pans with fine puff-paste, rolled thin and to preserve their form when baked, put a bit of bread into each; lay on the covers, pinch and trim the edges, and send the patties to a brisk oven. Plump and beard from two to three dozens of small oysters; mix very smoothly a teaspoonful of flour with an ounce of butter, put them into a clean saucepan, shake them round over a gentle fire, and let them simmer for two or three minutes; throw in a little salt, pounded mace, and cayenne, then add, by slow degrees, two or three spoonsful of rich cream, give these a boil, and pour in the strained liquor of the oysters; next, lay in the fish, and keep at the point of boiling for a couple of minutes. Raise the covers from the patties, take out the bread, fill them with the oysters and their sauce, and replace the covers. We have found it, an improvement to stew the beards of the fish with a strip or two of lemon-peel, in a little good veal stock for a quarter of an hour, then to strain and add it to the sauce. The oysters, unless very small, should be once or twice divided.

GOOD CHICKEN PATTIES. (ENTRÉE.)

Raise the white flesh entirely from a young undressed fowl, divide it once or twice, and lay it into a small clean saucepan, in which about an ounce of butter has been dissolved, and just begins to simmer; strew in a slight seasoning of salt, mace, and cayenne, and stew the chicken very softly indeed for about ten minutes, taking every precaution against its browning: turn it into a dish with the butter, and its own gravy, and let it become cold. Mince it with a sharp knife; heat it, without allowing it to boil, in a little good white sauce (which may be made of some of the bones of the fowl), and fill ready-baked patty-crusts, or small *vol-au-vents* with it, just before they are sent to table; or stew the flesh only just sufficiently to render it firm, mix it after it is minced and seasoned with a spoonful or two of strong gravy, fill the patties, and bake them from fifteen to eighteen minutes. It is a great improvement to stew and mince a few mushrooms with the chicken.

The breasts of cold turkeys, fowls, partridges, or pheasants, or the white part of cold veal, minced, heated in a béchamel sauce, will serve at once for patties: they may also be made of cold game, heated in an *Espagnole*, or in a good brown gravy.

Obs. — A spoonful or two of jellied stock or gravy, or of good white sauce, converts these into admirable patties: the same ingredients make also very superior rolls or cannelons. For patties à la Cardinale, small mushroom-buttons stewed as for partridges, Chapter XIII., before they are minced, must be substituted for truffles; and the butter in which they are simmered should be added with them to the eggs.

EXCELLENT MEAT ROLLS.

Pound, as for potting (see page 227), and with the same proportion of butter and of seasonings, some half-roasted veal, chicken, or turkey. Make some forcemeat by the receipt No. 1, Chapter VI., and form it

---

These patties should be made small, with a thin crust, and be *well-filled* with the oysters and their sauce. The substitution of fried crumbs for the covers will vary them very agreeably. For lobster-patties prepare the fish as for a *vol-au-vent* but cut it smaller.

into small rolls, not larger than a finger; wrap twice or thrice as much
of the pounded meat equally round each of these, first moistening it with
a teaspoonful of water; fold them in good puff-paste, and bake them
from fifteen to twenty minutes, or until the crust is perfectly done.   A
small quantity of the lean of a boiled ham may be finely minced and
pounded with the veal, and very small mushrooms, prepared as for a
partridge (page 217), may be substituted for the forcemeat.

PATTIES, TARTLETS, OR SMALL VOLS-AU-VENTS.

These are quickly and easily made with two round paste-cutters, of
which one should be little more than half the size of the other: to give
the pastry a better appearance, they should be fluted.   Roll out some
of the lightest puff-paste to a half inch of thickness, and with the larger
of the tins cut the number of patties required; then dip the edge of the
small shape into hot water, and press it about half through them.   Bake
them in a moderately quick oven from ten to twelve minutes, and when
they are done, with the point of a sharp knife, take out the small rounds
of crust from the tops, and scoop all the crumb from the insides of the
patties, which may then be filled with oysters, lobster, chicken, or any
other of the ordinary varieties of patty meat, prepared with white sauce.
Fried crumbs may be laid over them instead of the covers, or these last
can be replaced.
For sweet dishes, glaze the pastry, and fill it with rich whipped
cream, preserve, or boiled custard; if with the last of these, put it back
into a very gentle oven until the custards are set.

ANOTHER RECEIPT FOR TARTLETS.

For a dozen tartlets, cut twenty-four rounds of paste of the usual size,
and form twelve of them into rings by pressing the small cutter quite
through them; moisten these with cold water, or white of egg, and lay
them on the remainder of the rounds of paste, so as to form the rims of
the tartlets.   Bake them from ten to twelve minutes, fill them with
preserve while they are still warm, and place over it a small ornament
of paste cut from the remnants, and baked gently of a light colour.
Serve the tartlets cold, or if wanted hot for table put them back into
the oven for one minute after they are filled.

A SEFTON, OR VEAL CUSTARD.

Pour boiling, a pint of rich, clear, pale veal gravy on six fresh eggs,
which have been well beaten and strained: sprinkle in directly the
grated rind of a fine lemon, a little cayenne, some salt if needed, and a
quarter-teaspoonful of mace.   Put a paste border round a dish, pour in,
first two ounces of clarified butter, and then the other ingredients; bake
the Sefton in a very slow oven from twenty-five to thirty minutes, or
until it is quite firm in the middle, and send it to table with a little good
gravy.   Very highly flavoured game stock, in which a few mushrooms
have been stewed, may be used for this dish with great advantage in
lieu of veal gravy; and a sauce made of the smallest mushroom buttons,
may be served with it in either case.   The mixture can be baked in a
whole paste, if preferred so, or in well-buttered cups; then turned out
and covered with the sauce before it is sent to table.
Rich veal or game stock, 1 pint; fresh eggs, 6; rind, 1 lemon; little

salt and cayenne; pounded mace, ¼ teaspoonfu. , butter, 2 ozs.: baked,
25 to 30 minutes, *slow* oven.

APPLE CAKE, OR GERMAN TART.

Work together with the fingers ten ounces of butter and a pound of
flour, until they resemble fine crumbs of bread ; throw in a *small* pinch
of salt, and make them into a firm smooth paste with the yolks of twe
eggs and a spoonful or two of water.   Butter thickly a plain tin cake,
or pie mould (those which open at the sides are best adapted for the
purpose)'; roll out the paste thin, place the mould upon it, trim a bit to
its exact size, cover the bottum of the mould with this, then cut a band
the height of the sides, and press it smoothly round them, joining the
edge, which must be moistened with egg or wat. r, to the bottom crust;
and fasten upon them, to prevent their separation, a narrow and thin
band of paste, also moistened.   Next, fill the mould nearly from the
brim with the following marmalade, which must be quite cold when it
is put in.   Boil together, over a gentle fire at first, but more quickly
afterwards, three pounds of good apples with fourteen ounces of pounded
sugar, or of the finest Lisbon, the strained juice of a large lemon, three
ounces of the best butter, and a teaspoonful of pounded cinnamon, or
the lightly grated rind of a couple of lemons: when the whole is perfectly smooth and dry, turn it into a pan to cool, and let it be quite cold
before it is put into the paste.   In early autumn, a larger proportion of
sugar may be required, but this can be regulated by the taste.   When
the mould is filled, roll out the cover, lay it carefully over the marmalade that it may not touch it; and when the cake is securely closed,
trim off the superfluous paste, add a little pounded sugar to the parings,
spread them out very thin, and cut them into leaves to ornament the
top of the cake, round which they may be placed as a sort of wreath.*
Bake it for an hour in a moderately brisk oven; take it from the mould,
and should the sides not be sufficiently coloured, put it back for a few
minutes into the oven upon ʌ baking tin.   Lay a paper over the top,
when it is of a fine light brown, to prevent its being too deeply coloured.
This cake should be served hot.

Paste: flour, 1 lb.; butter, 10 ozs.; yolks of eggs, 2; little water.
Marmalade: apples, 3 lbs.; sugar, 14 ozs. (more if needed); juice of
lemon, 1; rinds of lemons, 2: butter, 3 ozs.: baked, 1 hour.

TOURTE MERINGUÉE, OR TART WITH ROYAL ICING.†

Lay a band of fine paste round the rim of a tart-dish, fill it with any
kind of fruit mixed with a moderate proportion of sugar, roll out the
cover very evenly, moisten the edges of the paste, press them together
carefully, and trim them off close to the dish; spread equally over the
top, to within rather more than an inch of the edge all round, the whites
of three fresh eggs beaten to a quite solid froth, and mixed quickly at
the moment of using them, with three tablespoonsful of dry sifted sugar.

* Or, instead of these, fasten on it with a little white of egg, after it is taken from
the oven, some ready-baked leaves of almond-paste (see page 263), either plain or coloured. ,

† The limits to which we are obliged to confine this volume, compel us to omit many
receipts which we would gladly insert: we have, therefore, rejected those which may
be found in almost every English cookery book, for such as are, we apprehend, less
known to the reader : this will account for the small number of receipts for pies and
fruit tarts to be found in the present chapter.

Put the tart into a moderately brisk oven, and when the crust has risen well, and the icing is set, either lay a sheet of writing-paper lightly over it, or draw it to a part of the oven where it will not take too much colour. This is now a fashionable mode of icing tarts, and greatly improves their appearance.

Bake half an hour.

A GOOD APPLE TART.

A pound and a quarter of apples, weighed after they are pared and cored, will be sufficient for a small tart, and four ounces more for one of moderate size. Lay a border of English puff-paste, or of cream-crust round the dish, just dip the apples into water, arrange them very compactly in it, higher in the centre than at the sides, and strew amongst them from three to four ounces of pounded sugar, or more should they be very acid: the grated rind, and the strained juice of half a lemon will much improve their flavour. Lay on the cover rolled thin, and ice it or not at pleasure. Send the tart to a moderately brisk oven for about half an hour. This may be converted into the old-fashioned *creamed* apple tart, by cutting out the cover while it is still quite hot, leaving only about an inch-wide border of paste round the edge, and pouring over the apples when they have become cold, from half to three quarters of a pint of rich boiled custard. The cover divided into triangular sippets, was formerly stuck round the inside of the tart, but ornamental leaves of pale puff-paste have a better effect. Well-drained whipped cream may be substituted for the custard, and piled high, and lightly over the fruit.

BARBERRY TART.

Barberries, with half their weight of fine brown sugar, when they are thoroughly ripe, and with two ounces more when they are not quite so, make an admirable tart. For one of moderate size, put into a dish bordered with paste, three quarters of a pound of barberries stripped from their stalks, and six ounces of sugar in alternate layers; pour over them three tablespoonsful of water, put on the cover, and bake the tart for half an hour. Another way of making it is, to line a shallow tin pan with very thin crust, to mix the fruit and sugar well together with a spoon, before they are laid in, and to put bars of paste across instead of a cover; or it may be baked without either.*

ALMOND PASTE.

For a single dish of pastry, blanch seven ounces of fine sweet almonds and one of bitter;† throw them into cold water as they are done, and let them remain in it for an hour or two; then wipe, and pound them to the finest paste, moistening them occasionally with a few drops of cold water, to prevent their oiling; next, add to, and mix thoroughly with them, seven ounces of highly-refined, dried, and sifted sugar; put them into a small preserving-pan, or enamelled stewpan, and stir them over a clear and very gentle fire until they are so dry as not to adhere

---

* The French make their fruit-tarts generally thus, in large shallow pans. Plums, split and stoned (or if small kinds, left entire), cherries and currants freed from the stalks, and various other fruits, all rolled in plenty of sugar, are baked in the uncovered crust; or this is baked by itself, and then filled afterwards with fruit previously stewed tender.

† When these are objected to, use half a pound of the sweet almonds.

to the finger when touched; turn the paste immediately into an earthen
pan or jar, and when cold it will be ready for use.   •

Sweet almonds, 7 ozs.; bitter almonds, 1 oz.; cold water, 1 tablespoonful; sugar, 7 ozs.

Obs.—The pan in which the paste is dried should by no means be
placed *upon* the fire, but high above it on a bar or trevet: should it be
allowed by accident to harden too much, it must be sprinkled plentifully
with water, broken up quite small, and worked, as it warms, with a
strong wooden spoon to a smooth paste again.   We have found this
method perfectly successful; but, if time will permit, it should be moistened some hours before it is again set over the fire.

TARTLETS OF ALMOND PASTE.

Butter slightly the smallest-sized patty-pans, and line them with the
almond-paste rolled as thin as possible; cut it with a sharp knife close
to their edges, and bake or rather *dry* the tartlets slowly at the mouth
of a very cool oven.   If at all coloured, they should be only of the
palest brown; but they will become perfectly crisp without losing their
whiteness if left for some hours in a very gently-heated stove or oven.
They should be taken from the pans when two thirds done, and laid,
reversed, upon a sheet of paper placed on a dish or board, before they
are put back into the oven.   At the instant of serving, fill them with
bright-coloured whipped cream, or with peach or apricot jam; if the
preserve be used, lay over it a small star or other ornament cut from
the same paste, and dried with the tartlets.   Sifted sugar, instead of
flour, must be dredged upon the board and roller in using almond paste.
Leaves and flowers formed of it, and dried gradually until perfectly
crisp, will keep for a long time in a tin box or canister, and they form
elegant decorations for pastry.   When a fluted cutter the size of the
patty-pans is at hand, it will be an improvement to cut out the paste
with it, and then to press it lightly into them, as it is rather apt to
break when pared off with a knife.   To colour it, prepared cochineal,
or spinach-green, must be added to it in the mortar.

MINCEMEAT; (*Author's Receipt.*)

To one pound of an unsalted ox-tongue, boiled tender and cut free
from the rind, add two pounds of fine stoned raisins, two of beef kidney-
suet, two pounds and a half of currants well cleaned and dried, two of
good apples, two and a half of fine Lisbon sugar, from half to a whole
pound of candied peel according to the taste, the grated rinds of two
large lemons, and two more boiled quite tender, and chopped up entirely, with the exception of the pips, two small nutmegs, half an ounce
of salt, a large teaspoonful of pounded mace, rather more of ginger in
powder, half a pint of brandy, and as much good sherry or Madeira.
Mince these ingredients separately, and mix the others all *well* before
the brandy and the wine are added; press the whole into a jar or jars,
and keep it closely covered.   It should be stored for a few days before
it is used, and will remain good for many weeks.   Some persons like a
slight flavouring of cloves in addition to the other spices; others add
the juice of two or three lemons, and a larger quantity of brandy.   The
inside of a tender and well-roasted sirloin of beef will answer quite as
well as the tongue.

Of a fresh-boiled ox-tongue, or inside of roasted sirloin, 1 lb.; stoned raisins and minced apples, each 2 lbs.; currants and fine Lisbon sugar, each 2½ lbs.; candied orange, lemon or citron rind, 8 to 16 ozs.; boiled lemons, 2 large; rinds of two others, grated; salt, ½ oz.; nutmegs, 2 small; pounded mace, 1 large teaspoonful, and rather more of ginger; good sherry or Madeira, ½ pint; brandy, ½ pint.

Obs.—The lemons will be sufficiently boiled in from one hour to one and a quarter.

SUPERLATIVE MINCEMEAT.

Take four large lemons, with their weight of golden pippins pared and cored, of jar-raisins, currants, candied citron and orange-rind, and the finest suet, and a fourth part more of pounded sugar. Boil the lemons tender, chop them small, but be careful first to extract all the pips; add them to the other ingredients, after all have been prepared with great nicety, and mix the whole *well* with from three to four glasses of good brandy. Apportion salt and spice by the preceding receipt. We think that the weight of one lemon, in meat, improves this mixture; or, in lieu of it, a small quantity of crushed macaroons added just before it is baked.

MINCE PIES. (ENTREMÈTS.)

Butter some tin pattypans well, and line them evenly with fine puff-paste rolled thin; fill them with mincemeat, moisten the edges of the covers, which should be nearly a quarter of an inch thick, close the pies carefully, trim off the superfluous paste, make a small aperture in the centre of the crust with a fork or the point of a knife, ice the pies with cold water and sifted sugar (see page 250), or not, at pleasure, and bake them half an hour in a well-heated but not fierce oven: lay a paper over them when they are partially done, should they appear likely to take too much colour.

½ hour.

MINCE PIES ROYAL. (ENTREMETS.)

Add to half a pound of good mincemeat an ounce and a half of pounded sugar, the grated rind and the strained juice of a large lemon, one ounce of clarified butter, and the yolks of four eggs; beat these well together, and half fill, or rather more, with the mixture, some pattypans lined with fine paste; put them into a moderate oven, and when the insides are just set, ice them thickly with the whites of the eggs beaten to snow, and mixed quickly at the moment with four heaped tablespoonsful of pounded sugar; set them immediately into the oven again, and bake them of a fine light brown.

Mincemeat, ½ lb.; sugar, 1½ oz.; rind and juice, 1 large lemon; butter, 1 oz.; yolks, 4 eggs. Icing: whites, 4 eggs; sugar, 4 tablespoonsful.

THE MONITOR'S TART, OR TOURTE A LA JUDD.

Put into a German enamelled stewpan, or into a delicately clean saucepan, three quarters of a pound of well-flavoured apples, weighed after they are pared and cored; add to them from three to four ounces of pounded sugar, an ounce and a half of fresh butter, cut small, and half a teaspoonful of pounded cinnamon, or the lightly grated rind of a small lemon. Let them stand over, or by the side of a gentle fire until

they begin to soften, and toss them now and then to mingle the whole
well, but do not stir them with a spoon; they should all remain unbroken and rather firm.   Turn them into a dish, and let them become
cold.   Divide three quarters of a pound of good light crust into two
equal portions; roll out one quite thin and round, flour an oven-leaf
and lay it on, as the tart cannot so well be moved after it is made;
place the apples upon it in the form of a dome, but leave a clear space
of an inch or more round the edge; moisten this with white of egg,
and press the remaining half of the paste (which should be rolled out
to the same size, and laid carefully over the apples) closely upon it:
they should be well secured, that the syrup from the fruit may not burst
through.   Whisk the white of an egg to a froth, brush it over the
tart with a small bunch of feathers, sift sugar thickly over, and then
strew upon it some almonds blanched and roughly chopped; bake the
tart in a moderate oven from thirty-five to forty-five minutes.   It may
be filled with peaches, or apricots, half-stewed, like the apples, or with
cherries merely rolled in fine sugar; or with the pastry cream of
page 267.

Light paste, ½ to ¾ lb.; apples 12 ozs.; butter, 1½ oz.; sugar, 4 ozs.;
glazing of egg and sugar; almonds, ½ oz.: 35 to 45 minutes.

PUDDING PIES.   (ENTREMETS.)

This form of pastry (or its name at least) is, we believe, peculiar to
the county of Kent, where it is made in abundance, and eaten by all
classes of people during Lent.   Boil for fifteen minutes three ounces of
ground rice* in a pint and a half of new milk, and when taken from
the fire stir into it three ounces of butter and four of sugar; add to these
six well-beaten eggs, a grain or two of salt, and a flavouring of nutmeg
or lemon-rind at pleasure.   When the mixture is nearly cold, line some
large pattypans or some saucers with thin puff paste, fill them with it
three parts full, strew the tops thickly with currants which have been
cleaned and dried, and bake the pudding-pies from fifteen to twenty
minutes in a gentle oven.

Milk, 1½ pint; ground rice, 3 ozs.: 15 minutes.   Butter, 3 ozs.; sugar,
¼ lb.; nutmeg or lemon-rind; eggs, 6; currants, 4 to 6 ozs.: 15 to 20
minutes.

PUDDING PIES; (a commoner kind.)

One quart of new milk, five ounces of ground rice, butter, one ounce
and a half (or more), four ounces of sugar, half a small nutmeg grated,
a pinch of salt, four large eggs, and three ounces of currants.

COCOA-NUT CHEESE-CAKES.   (ENTREMETS.)   (Jamaica Receipt.)

Break carefully the shell of the nut, that the liquid it contains may
not escape.†   Take out the kernel, wash it in cold water, pare thinly
off the dark skin, and grate the nut on a delicately clean bread-grater;
put it, with its weight of pounded sugar, and its own milk, if not sour,
or if it be, a couple of spoonsful or rather more of water, into a silver or
block-tin saucepan, or a very small copper stewpan perfectly tinned,
and keep it gently stirred over a quite clear fire until it is tender: it
will sometimes require an hour's stewing to make it so.   When a little
cooled, add to the nut, and beat well with it, some eggs properly whisked

Or rice-flour.   † This is best secured by boring the shell before it is broken.

and strained, and the grated rind of half a lemon. Line some pattypans with fine paste, put in the mixture, and bake the cheese-cakes from thirteen to fifteen minutes.

Grated cocoa-nut, 6 ozs.; sugar, 6 ozs.; the milk of the nut, or of water, 2 large tablespoonsful: ½ to 1 hour. Eggs, 5; lemon-rind, ½ of 1: 13 to 15 minutes.

Obs.—We have found the cheese-cakes made with these proportions very excellent indeed, but should the mixture be considered too sweet, another egg or two can be added, and a little brandy also.

LEMON CHEESE-CAKES. (ENTREMETS.) (*Christ-Church-College Receipt.*)

Rasp the rind of a large lemon with four ounces of fine sugar, then crush, and mix it with the yolks of three eggs, and half the quantity of whites, well whisked; beat these together thoroughly; add to them four tablespoonsful of cream, a quarter of a pound of oiled butter, the strained juice of the lemon,—which must be stirred quickly in by degrees,—and a little orange-flower brandy. Line some pattypans with thin puff-paste, half fill them with the mixture, and bake them thirty minutes in a moderate oven.

Sugar, 4 ozs.; rind and juice, 1 large lemon; butter, 4 ozs.; cream, 4 tablespoonsful; orange-flower brandy, 1 tablespoonful: bake ½ hour.

COMMON LEMON TARTLETS.

Beat four eggs until they are exceedingly light, add to them gradually four ounces of pounded sugar, and whisk these together for five minutes; strew lightly in, if it be at hand, a dessertspoonful of potato-flour, if not, of common flour well dried and sifted; then throw into the mixture, by slow degrees, three ounces of good butter, which should be dissolved, but only just luke-warm; beat the whole well, then stir briskly in the strained juice and the grated rind of one lemon and a half. Line some pattypans with fine puff-paste rolled very thin, fill them two thirds full, and bake the tartlets about twenty minutes, in a moderate oven.

Eggs, 4; sugar 4 ozs.; potato-flour, or common flour, 1 dessertspoonful; butter, 3 ozs.; juice and rind of 1½ full-sized lemon: baked 15 to 20 minutes.

CREME PATISSIERE, OR PASTRY CREAM.

To one ounce of fine flour add, very gradually, the beaten yolks of three fresh eggs; stir to them briskly, and in small portions at first, three-quarters of a pint of boiling cream, or of cream and new milk mixed; then turn the whole into a clean stewpan, and stir it over a very gentle fire until it is quite thick, take it off, and stir it well up and round; replace it over the fire, and let it just simmer from six to eight minutes; pour it into a basin, and add to it immediately a couple of ounces of pounded sugar, one and a half of fresh butter, cut small, or clarified, and a spoonful of the store-mixture of page 120, or a little sugar which has been rubbed on the rind of a lemon. The cream is rich enough for common use without further addition; but an ounce and a half of ratifias, crushed almost to powder with a paste-roller improves it much, and they should be mixed with it for the receipt which follows.

Flour, 1 oz.; yolks of eggs, 3; boiling cream, or milk and cream mixed, ¾ pint: just simmered, 6 to 8 minutes. Butter, 1½ oz.; sugar, 2 ozs.; little store-flavouring, or rasped lemon-rind; ratifias, 1½ oz.

Obs.—This is an excellent preparation, which may be used for tartlets, cannelons, and other forms of pastry, with extremely good effect.

SMALL VOLS-AU-VENTS, A LA HOWITT. (ENTREMETS.)

Make some small vols-au-vents by the directions of page 261, either in the usual way, or with the rings of paste placed upon the rounds. Ice the edges as soon as they are taken from the oven, by sifting fine sugar thickly on them, and then holding a salamander or heated shovel over them, until it melts and forms a sort of pale barley-sugar glaze. Have ready, and quite hot, some crême patissière, made as above; fill the vols-au-vents with it, and send them to table instantly.

PASTRY SANDWICHES.

Divide equally in two, and roll off square and as thin as possible, some rich puff-crust;* lay one half on a buttered tin, or copper oven-leaf, and spread it lightly with fine currant, strawberry, or raspberry jelly; lay the remaining half closely over, pressing it a little with the rolling-pin after the edges are well cemented together; then mark it into divisions, and bake it from fifteen to twenty minutes in a moderate oven.

FANCHONNETTES. (ENTREMETS.)

Roll out very thin and square some fine puff-paste, lay it on a tin or copper oven-leaf, and cover it equally to within something less than an inch of the edge with peach or apricot jam; roll a second bit of paste to the same size, and lay it carefully over the other, having first moistened the edges with beaten egg, or water; press them together securely, that the preserve may not escape; pass a paste-brush or small bunch of feathers dipped in water, over the top, sift sugar thickly on it, then with the back of a knife, mark the paste into divisions of uniform size, bake it in a well-heated but not fierce oven for twenty minutes, or rather more, and cut it while it is still hot, where it is marked. The fanchonnettes should be about three inches in length and two in width. In order to lay the second crust over the preserve without disturbing it, wind it lightly round the paste-roller, and in untwisting it, let it fall gently over the other part.

This is not the form of pasty called by the French *fanchonnettes.*

Fine puff-paste, 1 lb.; apricot or peach-jam, 4 to 6 ozs.: baked 20 to 25 minutes.

CURRANT-JELLY TARTLETS, OR CUSTARDS.

Put four tablespoonsful of the best currant-jelly into a basin, and stir to it gradually twelve spoonsful of beaten egg; if the preserve be rich and sweet, no sugar will be required. Line some pans with paste rolled very thin, fill them with the custard, and bake them for about ten minutes.†

RAMEKINS A L'UDE, OR SEFTON FANCIES.

Roll out, rather thin, from six to eight ounces of fine cream-crust, or *feuilletage* (see page 250); take nearly or quite half its weight of grated Parmesan, or something less of dry white cheese; sprinkle it equally over the paste, fold it together, roll it out very lightly twice, and

---

* Almond paste is sometimes substituted for this.

† Strawberry o raspberry jelly will answer admirably for these.

continue this until the cheese and crust are well mixed. Cut the rame-kins with a small paste-cutter; wash them with yolk of egg mixed with a little milk, and bake them about fifteen minutes. Serve them very hot.

Cream-crust, or feuilletage, 6 ozs.; Parmesan, 3 ozs.; or English cheese, 2½ ozs. : 15 minutes.

CHAPTER XVII.

BOILED PUDDINGS.

GENERAL DIRECTIONS.

ALL the ingredients for puddings should be fresh and of good quality. It is a false economy to use for them such as have been too long stored, as the slightest degree of mustiness or taint in any one of the articles of which they are composed will spoil all that are combined with it. Eggs should *always* be broken separately into a cup before they are thrown together in the same basin, as a single very bad one will occasion the loss of many when this precaution is neglected. They should also be cleared from the specks with scrupulous attention, either with the point of a small three-pronged fork, while they are in the cup, or by straining the whole through a fine hair-sieve after they are beaten. The perfect sweetness of suet and milk should be especially attended to, before they are mixed into a pudding, as nothing can be more offensive than the first when it is over-kept, nor worse in its effect than the curdling of the milk, which is the certain result of its being ever so slightly soured.

Currants should be cleaned, and raisins stoned with exceeding care; almonds and spices very finely pounded, and the rinds of oranges or lemons rasped or grated lightly off, that the bitter part of the skin may be avoided, when they are used for this, or for any other class of dishes; if pared, they should be cut as *thin* as possible.

Custard-puddings, to have a good appearance, must be *simmered* only, but without ceasing; for if boiled in a quick and careless manner, the surface, instead of being smooth and velvety, will be full of holes, or honey-combed, as it is called, and the whey will flow from it and mingle with the sauce. A thickly-buttered sheet of writing-paper should be laid between the custard-mixture and the cloth, before it is tied over, or the lid of the mould is closed upon it; and the mould itself, or the basin in which it is boiled, and which should always be quite full, must likewise be well buttered; and after it is lifted from the water the pudding should be left in it for quite five minutes before it is dished, to prevent its breaking or spreading about.

Batter is much lighter when boiled in a cloth, and allowed full room to swell, than when confined in a mould: it should be well beaten the instant before it is poured into it, and put into the water immediately after it is securely tied.   The cloth should be moist and thickly floured, and the pudding should be sent to table as expeditiously as possible after it is done, as it will quickly become heavy.   This applies equally to all puddings made with paste, which are rendered uneatable by any delay in serving them after they are ready: they should be opened a little at the top as soon as they are taken from the boiler or stewpan.

Plum-puddings, which it is now customary to boil in moulds, are both lighter and less dry, when closely tied in stout cloths well buttered and floured, especially when they are made in part with bread; but when this is done, care should be taken not to allow them to burn to the bottom of the pan in which they are cooked; and it is a good plan to lay a plate or dish under them, by way of precaution against this mischance: it will not then so much matter whether they be kept floating or not. It is thought better to mix these entirely (except the liquid portion of them) the day before they are boiled, and it is perhaps an advantage when they are of large size to do so, but it is not really necessary for small or common ones.

A *very* little salt improves all sweet puddings, by taking off the insipidity, and bringing out the full flavour of the other ingredients, but its presence should not be in the slightest degree *perceptible*.   When brandy, wine, or lemon-juice is added to them it should be stirred in briskly, and by degrees, quite at last, as it would be likely otherwise to curdle the milk or eggs.

Many persons prefer their puddings steamed; but when this is not done, they should be dropped into plenty of boiling water, and be kept well covered with it until they are ready to serve; and the boiling should never be allowed to cease for an instant, for they soon become heavy if it be interrupted.

Pudding and dumpling cloths should not only be laid into plenty of water as soon as they are taken off, and washed afterwards, as we shall direct, but it is essential to their perfect sweetness that they should be well and quickly dried (in the open air if possible), then folded and kept in a clean drawer.   We have known them left wet by a careless servant, until when brought forward for use, they were as offensive almost as meat that had been too long kept.   To prevent their ever imparting an unpleasant flavour when used, they should be washed in a ley made as follows; but when from any circumstance this cannot be done, and soap is used for them, they should be rinsed, and soaked in abundance of water, which should be changed several times.

A LIE, OR LEY, FOR WASHING PUDDING-CLOTHS.

To a pint of wood-ashes pour three quarts of boiling water, and either wash the cloths in the mixture without straining it, or give them two or three minutes boil in it first, then let the whole cool together; wash the cloths perfectly clean, and rinse them in abundance of water changing it several times: this both takes the grease off, and renders them very sweet.   Two ounces of soda dissolved in a gallon of water will answer almost as well, providing the rinsing afterwards be carefully attended to.

TO CLEAN CURRANTS FOR PUDDINGS OR CAKES.

Put them into a cullender, strew a handful of flour over them, and rub them with the hands to separate the lumps, and to detach the stalks;

work them round in the cullender, and shake it well, when the small stalks and stones will fall through it. Next pour plenty of cold water over the currants, drain, and spread them on a soft cloth, press it over them to absorb the moisture, and then lay them on a very clean oven-tin, or a large dish, and dry them *very gradually* (or they will become hard), either in a cool oven, or before the fire, taking care in the latter case that they are not placed sufficiently near it for the ashes to fall amongst them. When they are perfectly dry, clear them entirely from the remaining stalks, and from *every stone* that may be amongst them. The best mode of detecting these is to lay the fruit at the far end of a large white dish, or sheet of paper, and to pass it lightly, and in very small portions, with the fingers, towards oneself, examining it closely as this is done.

TO MIX BATTER FOR PUDDINGS.

Put the flour and salt into a bowl, and stir them together; whisk the eggs thoroughly, strain them through a fine hair-sieve, and add them *very gradually* to the flour; for if too much liquid be poured to it at once it will be full of lumps, and it is easy, with care, to keep the batter perfectly smooth. Beat it well and lightly, with the back of a strong wooden spoon, and after the eggs are added, thin it with milk to a proper consistency. The whites of the eggs beaten separately to a solid froth, and stirred gently into the mixture the instant before it is tied up for boiling, or before it is put into the oven to be baked, will render it remarkably light. When fruit is added to the batter, it must be made thicker than when it is served plain, or it will sink to the bottom of the pudding. Batter should never *stick to the knife* when it is sent to table; it will do this both when a sufficient number of eggs are not mixed with it, and when it is not enough cooked. About four eggs to the half-pound of flour will make it firm enough to cut smoothly.

SUET-CRUST, FOR MEAT OR FRUIT PUDDINGS.

Clear off the skin from some fresh beef kidney-suet, and with a sharp knife slice it thin, free it entirely from fibre, and mince it very fine: six ounces thus prepared will be found quite sufficient for a pound of flour. Mix them well together, add half a teaspoonful of salt for meat puddings, and a third as much for fruit ones, and sufficient cold water to make the whole into a very firm paste; work it smooth, and roll it out of equal thickness when it is used. The weight of suet should be taken after it is minced. This crust is so much lighter, and more wholesome than that which is made with butter, that we cannot refrain from recommending it in preference to our readers. Some cooks merely slice the suet in thin shavings, mix it with the flour, and beat the crust with a paste roller, until the flour and suet are perfectly incorporated.

Flour, 2 lbs.; suet, 12 ozs.; salt, 1 teaspoonful; water, 1 pint.

BUTTER CRUST FOR PUDDINGS.

When suet is disliked for crust, butter must supply its place, but there must be no intermixture of lard in paste which is to be boiled. Eight ounces to the pound of flour will render it sufficiently rich for most eaters, and less will generally be preferred; rich crust of this kind being more indigestible by far than that which is baked. The butter may be lightly broken into the flour before the water is added, or it may be laid on, and rolled into the paste as for puff-crust.   A small portion of salt must be added to it always, and for a meat pudding the same proportion as directed in the preceding receipt.   For kitchen, or for quite common family puddings, butter and clarified dripping are used sometimes in equal proportions.   From three to four ounces of each will be sufficient for the pound and quarter of flour.

Flour, 1 lb.; butter, 8 ozs.; salt, for fruit puddings, ½ saltspoonful; for meat puddings, ½ teaspoonful.

SMALL BEEF-STEAK PUDDING.

Make into a very firm, smooth paste, one pound of flour, six ounces of beef-suet, finely minced, half a teaspoonful of salt, and half a pint of cold water.   Line with this a basin which holds a pint and a half.   Season a pound of tender steak, free from bone and skin, with half an ounce of salt and half a teaspoonful of pepper well mixed together; lay it in the crust, pour in a quarter-pint of water, roll out the cover, close the pudding carefully, tie a floured cloth over, and boil it three hours and a half.   We give this receipt as an exact guide for the proportions of meat-puddings in general.

Flour, 1 lb.; suet, 6 ozs.; salt, ½ teaspoonful; water, ½ pint; rump-steak, 1 lb.; salt, ½ oz.; pepper, ½ teaspoonful; water, ¼ pint: 3½ hours

RUTH PINCH'S BEEF-STEAK PUDDING.

To make *Ruth Pinch's* celebrated pudding (known also as beef-steak pudding *à la Dickens*), substitute six ounces of butter for the suet in this receipt, and moisten the paste with the well-beaten yolks of four eggs, or with three whole ones, mixed with a little water; butter the basin very thickly before the crust is laid in, as the pudding is to be turned out of it for table.   In all else, proceed exactly as above.

SUPERLATIVE BEEF-PUDDING.

Take a fine woodcock (or half a dozen rice-birds) that is ready for the spit, and put it into the middle of a large beef-pudding, laying the meat under, over, and round it; finish it as usual, and boil it four hours or more: the fine flavour of the bird will pervade the whole contents of the pudding.

MUTTON PUDDING.

Mutton freed perfectly from fat, and mixed with two or three sliced kidneys, makes an excellent pudding.   The meat may be sprinkled with fine herbs as it is laid into the crust.   This will require rather less boiling than the preceding puddings, but it is made in precisely the same way.

PARTRIDGE PUDDING.

Skin a couple of well-kept partridges and cut them down into joints; line a deep basin with suet crust, observing the directions given in the preceding receipts; lay in the birds, which should be rather highly seasoned with pepper or cayenne, and moderately with salt; pour in water for the gravy, close the pudding with care, and boil it from three hours to three and a half.   The true flavour of the game is admirably preserved by this mode of cooking.   When mushrooms are plentiful, put a layer of buttons, or small flaps, cleaned as for pickling, alternately with a layer of partridge, in filling the pudding, which will then be most excellent eating: the crust may be left untouched, and merely emptied of its contents, where it is objected to; or its place may be supplied with a richer one made of butter. A seasoning of pounded mace or nutmeg can be used at discretion. Puddings of veal, chickens, and young rabbits, may all be made by this receipt, or with the addition of oysters, which we have already noticed.

COMMON BATTER PUDDING.

Beat four eggs thoroughly, mix with them half a pint of milk, and pass them through a sieve, add them by degrees to half a pound of flour, and when the batter is perfectly smooth, thin it with another half pint of milk. Shake out a wet pudding-cloth, flour it well, pour the batter in, leave it room to swell, tie it securely, and put it immediately into plenty of fast-boiling water. An hour and ten minutes will boil it. Send it to table the instant it is dished, with wine sauce, a hot compote of fruit, or raspberry vinegar: this last makes a delicious pudding sauce. Unless the liquid be added very gradually to the flour, and the mixture be well stirred and beaten as each portion is poured to it, the batter will not be smooth: to render it *very* light, a portion of the whites of the eggs, or the whole of them, should be whisked to a froth and stirred into it just before it is put into the cloth.

Flour, ½ lb.; eggs, 4; salt, ¼ teaspoonful; milk, 1 pint: 1 hour and 10 minutes.

Obs.—Modern taste is in favour of puddings boiled in moulds, but, as we have already stated, they are seldom or ever so light as those which are tied in cloths only. Where *appearance* is the first consideration, we would recommend the use of the moulds, of course.

ANOTHER BATTER PUDDING.

Mix the yolks of three eggs smoothly with three heaped tablespoonsful of flour, thin the batter with new milk until it is of the consistency of cream, whisk the whites of eggs apart, stir them into the batter, and boil the pudding in a floured cloth or buttered basin for an hour. Before it is served, cut the top quickly into large dice, half through the pudding, pour over it a small jarful of fine currant, raspberry, or strawberry jelly, and send it to table without delay.

Flour, 3 tablespoonsful; eggs, 3; salt, ½ teaspoonful; milk, from ½ to a whole pint: 1 hour.

Obs.—For a very large pudding, double the quantity of ingredients and the time of boiling will be required.

BATTER FRUIT PUDDING.

Butter thickly a basin which holds a pint and a half, and fill it nearly to the brim with *good* boiling apples pared, cored, and quartered; pour over them a batter made with four tablespoonsful of flour, two large or three small eggs, and half a pint of milk. Tie a buttered and floured cloth over the basin, which ought to be quite full, and boil the pudding for an hour and a quarter. Turn it into a hot dish when done, and strew sugar thickly over it: this, if added to the batter at first, renders it heavy. Morella cherries make a very superior pudding of this kind; and green gooseberries, damsons, and various other fruits, answer for it extremely well: the time of boiling it must be varied according to their quality and its size.

For a pint and a half mould or basin filled to the brim with apples or other fruit; flour, 4 tablespoonsful; eggs, 2 large or three small; milk, ½ pint: 1¼ hour.

Obs.—Apples cored, halved, and mixed with a good batter, make an excellent baked pudding, as well as red currants, cherries, and plums of different sorts.

ANOTHER SUET PUDDING.

Make into a somewhat lithe, but smooth paste, half a pound of fine stale bread-crumbs, three quarters of a pound of flour, from ten to twelve ounces of beef-suet, chopped extremely small, a large half-teaspoonful of salt, and rather less of pepper, with two eggs and a little milk. Boil it two hours and a quarter.

A CHEAP SUET PUDDING.

With a pound of flour mix well an equal weight of good potatoes boiled and grated (or prepared by Captain Kater's receipt, page 230), a quarter pound of suet, and a small teaspoonful of salt. Make these into a stiff batter, with milk, and boil the pudding one hour in a well-floured cloth.

APPLE, CURRANT, CHERRY, OR OTHER FRESH FRUIT PUDDING.

Make a paste as for a beaf-steak pudding, either with suet or butter; lay into a basin a well-floured cloth, which has been dipped into hot water, wrung dry, and shaken out; roll the paste thin, press it evenly into the basin upon the cloth, fill it with apples, pared, cored, and quartered, or with any other fruit; put on the cover, taking care to moisten the edges of the paste, to press them well together, and fold them over; gather up the ends of the cloth, and tie it firmly close to the pudding, which should then be dropped into plenty of fast boiling water. When it is done, lift it out by twisting a strong fork into the corner of the cloth, turn it gently into the dish in which it is to be served, and cut immediately a small round or square from the top, or the pudding will quickly become heavy; send it to table without the slightest delay, accompanied by pounded, and by good Lisbon sugar, as many persons prefer the latter, from its imparting a more mellowed flavour to the fruit. A small slice of fresh butter, and some finely grated nutmeg, are usually considered improvements to an apple pudding; the juice, and the grated rind of a lemon may be added with good effect, when the fruit is laid into the crust, especially in spring, when the apples generally will have become insipid in their flavour. When puddings are preferred boiled in moulds or basins, these must be thickly buttered before the paste is laid into them, and the puddings must be turned from them gently, that they may not burst.

Currant, gooseberry, or cherry pudding, 1 to 1¼ hour. Greengage, damson, mussel, or other plum, 1 to 1½ hour. Apple pudding, from 1 to 2 hours, according to its size, and the time of year.

Obs.—If made of mellow fruit, an apple pudding will require only so much boiling as may be needed for the crust.

A COMMON APPLE PUDDING.

Make a light crust with one pound of flour and six ounces of very finely minced beef-suet, roll it thin, and fill it with one pound and a quarter of good boiling apples; add the grated rind and strained juice

of a small lemon, tie it in a cloth, and boil it one hour and twenty minutes before Christmas, and from twenty to thirty minutes longer after
Christmas. A small slice of fresh butter, stirred into it when it is
sweetened, will, to many tastes, be an acceptable addition; grated nutmeg, or a little cinnamon in fine powder, may be substituted for the
lemon-rind when either is preferred. To convert this into a richer pudding, use half a pound of butter for the crust, and add to the apples a
spoonful or two of orange or quince marmalade.

Crust: flour, 1 lb.; suet, 6 ozs. Fruit, pared and cored, 1½ lb.;
juice and rind of 1 small lemon (or some nutmeg or cinnamon in
powder).

Richer pudding: flour, 1 lb.; butter, ½ lb.; in addition to fruit, 1 or
2 tablespoonsful of orange or quince marmalade.

THE PUBLISHER'S PUDDING.

This pudding can scarcely be made *too rich.* First blanch, and then
beat to the smoothest possible paste, six ounces of fresh sweet almonds,
and a dozen bitter ones; pour very gradually to them, in the mortar,
three quarters of a pint of boiling cream; then turn them into a cloth,
and wring it from them again with strong expression. Heat a full half
pint of it afresh, and pour it, as soon as it boils, upon four ounces of fine
bread-crumbs, set a plate over, and leave them to become nearly cold;
then mix thoroughly with them four ounces of macaroons, crushed tolerably small; five of finely-minced beef-suet, five of marrow, cleared
very carefully from fibre, and from the splinters of bone which are sometimes found in it, and shred, not very small, two ounces of flour, six of
pounded sugar, four of dried cherries, four of the best Muscatel raisins,
weighed after they are stoned, half a pound of candied citron, or of
citron and orange-rind mixed, a quarter saltspoonful of salt, half a nutmeg, the yolks only of seven full-sized eggs, the grated rind of a large
lemon, and last of all, a glass of the best Cognac brandy, which must be
stirred briskly in by slow degrees. Pour the mixture into a *thickly*
buttered mould or basin, which contains a full quart, fill it to the brim,
lay a sheet of buttered writing-paper over, then a well-floured cloth, tie
them securely, and boil the pudding for four hours and a quarter; let it
stand for a couple of minutes before it is turned out; dish it carefully,
and serve it with the German pudding sauce of page 112.

Jordan almonds, 6 ozs.; bitter almonds, 12; cream, ¾ pint; bread-
crumbs, 4 ozs.; cream wrung from almonds, ½ pint; crushed macaroons, 4 ozs.; flour, 2 ozs.; beef-suet, 5 ozs.; marrow, 5 ozs.; dried
cherries, 4 ozs.; stoned Muscatel raisins, 4 ozs.; pounded sugar, 6 ozs.;
candied citron (or citron and orange-rind mixed), ½ lb.; pinch of salt;
½ nutmeg; grated rind 1 lemon; yolks of eggs, 7; best cognac, 1 wineglassful: boiled in mould or basin, 4¼ hours.

Obs.—This pudding, which, if well made, is very light as well as
rich, will be sufficiently good for most tastes without the almonds.
when they are omitted, the boiling cream must be poured at once to
the bread-crumbs.

SMALL CUSTARD PUDDING; (*Aldeburgh White Lion Receipt.*)

Dissolve in half a pint of new milk a dessertspoonful of pounded sugar
and pour it to three well-beaten eggs; strain the mixture into a but

tered bas in, which should be *full;* lay a half sheet of buttered writing paper, and then a floured cloth over it, and tie them tightly on; boil the pudding gently for twenty-five minutes, and let it stand four or five more before it is turned out, that it may not spread in the dish. Serve it with wine sauce.

New milk, ½ pint; sugar, 1 dessertspoonful; fresh eggs, 3: 25 minutes.

COMMON CUSTARD PUDDING.

Whisk three eggs well, put them into a pint basin, and add to them sufficient milk to fill it; then strain, flavour, and sweeten it with fine sugar; boil the pudding very softly for an exact half hour, let it stand a few minutes, dish, and serve it with sugar sifted over, and sweet sauce in a tureen, or send stewed gooseberries, currants, or cherries to table with it. A small quantity of lemon-brandy, or of ratafia can be added, to give it flavour, when it is made, or the sugar with which it is sweetened may be rasped on a lemon or an orange, then crushed and dissolved in the milk; from an ounce and a half to two ounces will be sufficient for general taste.

OERMAN PUDDING, AND SAUCE.

Stew, until very tender and dry, three ounces of whole rice in a pint and a quarter of milk; when a little cooled, mix with it three ounces of beef-suet, finely chopped, two ounces and a half of sugar, an ounce of candied orange or lemon-rind, six ounces of sultana raisins, and three large eggs well beaten and strained. Boil the pudding in a buttered basin, or in a well-floured cloth, for two hours and a quarter, and serve it with the following sauce:—Dissolve an ounce and a half of sugar broken small in two glasses of sherry, or of any other white wine, and stir them, when quite hot, to the beaten yolks of three fresh eggs; then stir the sauce in a small saucepan held high above the fire until it resembles custard, but by no means allow it to boil, or it will instantly curdle; pour it over the pudding, or, if preferred, send it to table in a tureen. We think a full teaspoonful of lemon-juice added to the wine an improvement to this sauce, which is excellent; and we can recommend the pudding also to our readers.

Milk, 1¼ pint; rice, 3 ozs.: 1 hour, or more. Suet, 3 ozs.; sugar, 2½ ozs.; candied peel, 1 oz.; sultana raisins, 6 ozs.; eggs, 3 large: 2¼ hours. Sauce: sherry, 2 glasses; sugar, 1½ oz.; yolks of eggs, 3; little lemon-juice.

We have already, in a previous part of the volume, directed that the German sauce should be milled to a fine froth, and poured upon the pudding with which it is served: when this is not done, the quantity should be increased.

MISS BREMER'S PUDDINO.

Blanch, dry, and beat to the smoothest possible paste, half a pound of fresh Jordan almonds and five or six bitter ones; and moisten them as they are done with a few drops of water, or a little white of egg, to prevent their oiling. Add to them in *very* small portions at first, or they will be lumpy, the yolks of seven fresh eggs, and the whites of two well beaten; then throw in gradually four ounces of pounded and sifted sugar, and whisk the mixture thoroughly until it looks very light;

next, strew in, continuing the whisking, four ounces of fine bread-crumbs, and the grated rind of a lemon; and last of all, add four ounces of just-liquid butter, which must, by no means, be heated more than enough to dissolve it, and which must be poured in by slow degrees, and beaten thoroughly to the other ingredients, until there is no appearance of it left. Butter thickly a pint and a half mould, shake fine bread-crumbs thickly and equally over it, half fill it very gently with the pudding-mixture, and place lightly upon this a layer of apricot-jam; put the remainder of the pudding carefully upon it, lay a buttered paper over the mould, then close it, or should there be no cover, tie a cloth securely round it, and boil the pudding a full hour. Serve it with German, or common sweet wine sauce.

Jordan, or sweet almonds, ½ lb.; bitter ones, 5 or 6; yolks of 7 eggs, whites of 2; pounded sugar, 4 ozs.; bread-crumbs, 4 ozs.; lemon-rind, 1; butter, 4 ozs.; apricot-marmalade, 1 jarful: full hour.

VERY GOOD RAISIN PUDDING.

To three quarters of a pound of flour add four ounces of fine crumbs of bread, one pound of beef-suet, a pound and six ounces of raisins, weighed after they are stoned, a quarter-teaspoonful of salt, rather more of ginger, half a nutmeg, an ounce and a half of candied peel, and four large or five small eggs, beaten, strained, and mixed with a cupful of milk, or as much more as will make the whole of the consistency of a *very* thick batter. Pour the mixture into a well-floured cloth of close texture, which has previously been dipped into hot water, wrung, and shaken out. Boil the pudding in plenty of water for four hours and a half. It may be served with very sweet wine, or punch-sauce; but if made as we have directed, will be much lighter than if sugar be mixed with the other ingredients before it is boiled; and we have found it generally preferred to a richer plum-pudding.

Flour, ¾ lb.; bread crumbs, 4 ozs.; beef-suet, 1 lb.; stoned raisins, 1 lb. 6 ozs.; candied peel, 1½ oz.; ½ nutmeg; eggs, 4 large, or 5 small; little salt and ginger: 4½ hours.

THE ELEGANT ECONOMIST'S PUDDING.

Butter thickly a plain mould or basin, and line it entirely with slices of cold plum or raisin pudding, cut so as to join closely and neatly together; fill it quite with a good custard, lay, first a buttered paper, and then a floured cloth over it, tie them securely, and boil the pudding gently for an hour; let it stand for ten minutes after it is taken up before it is turned out of the mould. This is a more tasteful mode of serving the remains of a plum-pudding than the usual one of broiling them in slices, or converting them into fritters. The German sauce, well milled or frothed, is generally much relished with sweet boiled-puddings, and adds greatly to their good appearance; but common wine, or punch-sauce, may be sent to table with the above quite as appropriately.

Mould or basin holding 1½ pint, lined with thin slices of plum-pudding; ¾ pint new milk boiled gently 5 minutes with grain of salt; 5 bitter almonds, bruised; sugar in lumps, 2½ ozs.; thin rind of ½ lemon, strained and mixed directly with 4 large well-beaten eggs; poured into mould while just warm; boiled gently 1 hour.

PUDDING A LA SCOONES.

Take of apples finely minced, and of currants, six ounces each; of suet, chopped small, sultana raisins, picked from the stalks, and sugar, four ounces each, with three ounces of fine bread-crumbs, the grated rind, and the strained juice of a small lemon, three well-beaten eggs, and two spoonsful of brandy. Mix these ingredients perfectly, and boil the pudding for two hours in a buttered basin; sift sugar over it when it is sent to table, and serve wine or punch sauce apart.

Minced apples and currants, each, 6 ozs.; suet, sultana raisins, and sugar, each, 4 ozs.; bread-crumbs, 3 ozs.; lemon, 1; eggs, 3; brandy, 2 spoonsful: 2 hours.

COTTAGE CHRISTMAS PUDDING.

A pound and a quarter of flour, fourteen ounces of suet, a pound and a quarter of stoned raisins, four ounces of currants, five of sugar, a quarter-pound of potatoes smoothly mashed, half a nutmeg, a quarter-teaspoonful of ginger, the same of salt, and of cloves in powder: mix these ingredients thoroughly, add four well-beaten eggs with a quarter-pint of milk, tie the pudding in a well-floured cloth, and boil it for four hours.

Flour, 1¼ lb.; suet, 14 ozs.; raisins stoned, 20 ozs.; currants, 4 ozs.; sugar, 5 ozs.; potatoes, ¼ lb.; ½ nutmeg; ginger, salt, cloves, ¼ teaspoonful each; eggs, 4; milk, ½ pint: 4 hours.

SMALL LIGHT PLUM PUDDING.

Put half a pint of fine bread crumbs into a basin, and pour on them a quarter-pint of boiling milk; put a plate over, and let them soak for half an hour; then mix with them half a pint of suet chopped extremely small, rather more of stoned raisins, three teaspoonsful of sugar, one of flour, three eggs, a tiny pinch of salt, and sufficient grated lemon-peel or nutmeg to flavour it lightly. Tie the pudding in a well-floured cloth, and boil it for two hours.

Bread-crumbs, ½ pint; milk, ¼ pint; suet, ½ pint; raisins, nearly ¾ pint; sugar, 3 teaspoonful, and 1 of flour; eggs, 3; little salt nutmeg: 2 hours.

ANOTHER PUDDING, LIGHT AND WHOLESOME.*

With three ounces of the crumb of a stale loaf finely grated and soaked in a quarter-pint of boiling milk, mix six ounces of suet minced very small, one ounce of dry bread-crumbs, ten ounces of stoned raisins, a little salt, the grated rind of a china-orange, and three eggs, leaving out one white. Boil the pudding for two hours, and serve it with very sweet sauce; put no sugar in it.

VEGETABLE PLUM PUDDING. *(Cheap and good.)*

Mix well together one pound of smoothly-mashed potatoes, half a pound of carrots boiled quite tender, and beaten to a paste, one pound of flour, one of currants, and one of raisins (full weight after they are stoned), three quarters of a pound of sugar, eight ounces of suet, one nutmeg, and a quarter-teaspoonful of salt. Put the pudding into a well-floured cloth, tie it closely, and boil it for four hours. The correspond-

* Both this, and the preceding pudding, will be found very delicate, and well suited to invalids.

ent to whom we are indebted for this receipt says, that the cost of the ingredients does not exceed half a crown, and that the pudding is of sufficient size for a party of sixteen persons. We can vouch for its excellence, but as it is rather apt to break when turned out of the cloth, a couple of eggs would perhaps improve it. Sweetmeats, brandy, and spices, can be added at pleasure.

Mashed potatoes, 1 lb.; carrots, 8 ozs.; flour, 1 lb.; suet, ½ lb.; sugar, ¾ lb.; currants and raisins, 1 lb. each; nutmeg, 1; little salt: 4 hours.

AN EXCELLENT SMALL MINCEMEAT PUDDING.

Pour on an ounce of bread-crumbs, sufficient boiling milk to soak them well; when they are nearly cold drain as much of it from them as you can, and mix them thoroughly with half a pound of mincemeat, a dessertspoonful of brandy, and three eggs beaten and strained. Boil the pudding for two hours in a well-buttered basin, which should be full, and serve it with sauce made with a little melted butter, half a glass of white wine, a tablespoonful of brandy, half as much lemon-juice, and sufficient sugar to make it tolerably sweet.

Bread-crumbs, 1 oz.; mincemeat, ½ lb.; brandy, dessertspoonful; eggs, 3: 2 hours.

THE AUTHOR'S CHRISTMAS PUDDING.

To three ounces of flour, and the same weight of fine, lightly-grated bread-crumbs, add six of beef kidney-suet, chopped small, six of raisins weighed after they are stoned, six of well cleaned currants, four ounces of minced apples, five of sugar, two of candied orange-rind, half a tea-spoonful of nutmeg mixed with pounded mace, a very little salt, a small glass of brandy, and three whole eggs. Mix and beat these ingredients well together, tie them tightly in a thickly floured cloth, and boil them for three hours and a half. We can recommend this as a remarkably light small rich pudding: it may be served with German, wine, or punch sauce.

Flour, 3 ozs.; bread-crumbs, 3 ozs.; suet, stoned raisins, and currants, each, 6 ozs.; minced apples, 4 ozs.; sugar, 5 ozs.; candied peel, 2 ozs.; spice, ½ teaspoonful; salt, few grains; brandy, small wineglass-full; eggs, 3: 3½ hours.

ROLLED PUDDING.

Roll out thin a bit of light puff paste, or a good suet crust, and spread equally over it to within an inch of the edge, any kind of fruit jam. Orange marmalade and mincemeat make excellent varieties of this pudding, and a deep layer of fine brown sugar, flavoured with the grated rind and strained juice of one very large, or of two small lemons, answers for it extremely well. Roll it up carefully, pinch the paste together at the ends, fold a cloth round, secure it well at the ends, and boil the pudding from one to two hours, according to its size and the nature of the ingredients. Half a pound of flour made into a paste with suet or butter, and covered with preserve, will be quite sufficiently boiled in an hour and a quarter.

BREAD PUDDING.

Sweeten a pint of new milk with three ounces of fine sugar, throw in a few grains of salt, and pour it boiling on half a pound of fine, and lightly-grated bread-crumbs; add an ounce of fresh butter, and cover them with a plate; let them remain for half an hour or more, and then stir to them four large well-whisked eggs, and a flavouring of nutmeg, or of lemon-rind; pour the mixture into a thickly-buttered mould or basin, which holds a pint and a half, and which ought to be quite full; tie a paper and a cloth tightly over, and boil the pudding exactly an hour and ten minutes. This is quite a plain receipt, but by omitting two ounces of the bread, and adding more butter, one egg, a small glass of brandy, the grated rind of a lemon, and as much sugar as will sweeten the whole richly, a very excellent pudding will be obtained; candied orange-peel also has a good effect when sliced thinly into it; and half a pound of currants is generally considered a further improvement.

New milk, 1 pint; sugar, 3 ozs.; salt, few grains; bread-crumbs, ½ lb.; eggs, 4 (5, if very small); nutmeg or lemon-rind at pleasure: 1 hour and 10 minutes.

Or: milk, 1 pint; bread-crumbs, 6 ozs.; butter, 2 to 3 ozs.; sugar, 4 ozs.; eggs, 5; brandy, small glassful; rind, 1 lemon. Further additions at choice: candied peel, 1½ oz.; currants, ½ lb.

BROWN BREAD PUDDING.

To half a pound of stale brown bread, finely and lightly grated, add an equal weight of suet, chopped small, and of currants cleaned and dried, with half a saltspoonful of salt, three ounces of sugar, the third of a small nutmeg grated, two ounces of candied peel, five well-beaten eggs, and a glass of brandy. Mix these ingredients thoroughly, and boil the pudding in a cloth for three hours and a half. Send wine sauce to table with it. The grated rind of a large lemon may be added with good effect.

Brown bread, suet, and currants, each 8 ozs.; sugar, 3 ozs.; candied peel, 2 ozs.; salt, ½ saltspoonful; ½ of small nutmeg; eggs, 5; brandy, 1 wineglassful; 3½ hours.

A GOOD BOILED RICE PUDDING.

Swell gradually,* and boil until quite soft and thick, four ounces and a half of whole rice in a pint and a half of new milk; sweeten them with from three to four ounces of sugar, broken small, and stir to them, while they are still quite hot, the grated rind of half a large lemon, four or five bitter almonds, pounded to a paste, and four large well-whisked eggs; let the mixture cool, and then pour it into a thickly buttered basin, or mould, which should be quite full; tie a buttered paper and a floured cloth over it, and boil the pudding exactly an hour; let it stand for two or three minutes before it is turned out, and serve it with sweet sauce, fruit syrup, or a compote of fresh fruit. An ounce and a half of candied orange-rind will improve it much, and a couple of ounces of butter may be added to enrich it, when the receipt without is considered too simple. It is *excellent* when made with milk highly flavoured with cocoanut (see Chapter XX).

Whole rice, 4½ ozs.; new milk (or cocoa-nut-flavoured milk), 1½ pint; sugar, 3 to 4 ozs.; salt, a few grains; bitter almonds, 4 to 6; rind of ½ lemon; eggs, 4: boiled 1 hour.

* That is to say, put the rice into the milk while cold, heat it *slowly*, and let it simmer only until it is done.

CHEAP RICE PUDDING.

Wash six ounces of rice, mix it with three quarters of a pound of raisins, tie them in a well-floured cloth, giving them plenty of room to swell; boil them exactly an hour and three quarters, and serve the pudding with very sweet sauce: this is a nice dish for the nursery. A pound of apples pared, cored, and quartered, will also make a very wholesome pudding, mixed with the rice, and boiled from an hour and a quarter to an hour and a half.

Rice, 6 ozs.; raisins, ½ lb.: 2 hours.   Or, rice, 6 ozs.; apples, 1 lb.: 1¼ to 1½ hour.

TOMATA DUMPLINGS, OR PUDDINGS; (*an American Receipt.*)

" In the manner of composition, mode of cooking, and saucing, the good housewife must proceed in the same way as she would for an apple dumpling, with this exception, care must be taken in paring the tomata not to extract the seed, nor break the meat in the operation of skinning it. We have eaten tomatas raw without anything;—cut up with pepper, salt, vinegar, and mustard;—fried in butter and in lard;—broiled and basted with butter;—stewed with and without bread, with cream and with butter;—and, with a clear conscience, we can say, we like them in every way they have ever been *fixed for the palate;* but of all the modes of dressing them, known to us, we prefer them when cooked in dumplings, for, to us it appears that the steaming they receive in their dough-envelope increases in a very high degree that delicate spicy flavour which, even in their uncooked state, makes them such decided favourites with the epicure."

Obs.—It is possible that the tomata, which is, we know, abundantly grown and served in a great variety of forms in America, may there, either from a difference of climate, or from some advantages of culture, be produced in greater perfection than with us, and possess really " the delicate spicy flavour" attributed to it in our receipt, but which we cannot say we have ever yet discovered here; nor have we put its excellence for puddings to the proof, though some of our readers may like to do so.

FASHIONABLE APPLE DUMPLINGS.

These are boiled in small *knitted* or closely-netted cloths (the former have, we think, the prettiest effect), which give quite an ornamental appearance to an otherwise homely dish. Take out the cores without dividing the apples, which should be large, and of a good boiling sort, and fill the cavity with orange or lemon marmalade, enclose them in a good crust rolled thin, draw the cloths round them, tie them closely and boil them for three quarters of an hour. Lemon dumplings may be boiled in the same way.

¾ to 1 hour, if the apples be *not* of the best boiling kind.

ORANGE SNOW-BALLS.

Take out the unhusked grains, and wash well half a pound of rice; put it into plenty of water, and boil it rather quickly for ten minutes; drain and let it cool. Pare four large, or five small oranges, and clear from them entirely the thick white inner skin; spread the rice, in as many equal portions as there are oranges, upon some pudding or dumpling-cloths; tie the fruit separately in these, and boil the snow-balls for an hour and a half; turn them carefully on to a dish, and strew plenty of sifted sugar over them.

Rice, 8 ozs.; oranges, 5: 1½ hour.

APPLE SNOW-BALLS.

Pare and core some large pudding-apples, without dividing them, prepare the rice as in the foregoing receipt, enclose them in it, and boil them for an hour: ten minutes less will be sufficient should the fruit be but of moderate size. An agreeable addition to them is a slice of fresh butter, mixed with as much sugar as can be smoothly blended with it, and a flavouring of powdered cinnamon, or of nutmeg: this must be sent to table apart from them, not in the dish.

LIGHT CURRANT DUMPLINGS.

For each dumpling take three tablespoonsful of flour, two of finely-minced suet, and three of currants, a slight pinch of salt, and as much milk or water as will make a thick batter of the ingredients. Tie the dumplings in well-floured cloths, and boil them for a full hour: they may be served with very sweet wine-sauce.

LEMON DUMPLINGS.

Mix, with ten ounces of fine bread-crumbs, half a pound of beef-suet, chopped extremely small, one large tablespoonful of flour, the grated rinds of two small lemons, or of a very large one, four ounces of pounded sugar, three large, or four small eggs beaten and strained, and last of all the juice of the lemons, also strained. Divide these into four equal portions, tie them in well-floured cloths, and boil them an hour. The dumplings will be extremely light and delicate; if wished *very* sweet more sugar must be added to them.

SWEET BOILED PATTIES. (GOOD.)

Mix into a very smooth paste, three ounces of finely-minced suet, with eight of flour, and a slight pinch of salt; divide it into fourteen balls of equal size, roll them out quite thin and round, moisten the edges, put a little preserve into each, close the patties very securely to prevent its escape, throw them into a pan of boiling water, and in from ten to twelve minutes lift them out, and serve them instantly. Butter-crust may be used for them instead of suet, but it will not be so light.

Flour, 8 ozs.; suet, 3 ozs.; *little* salt; divided into fourteen portions: boil 10 to 12 minutes.

BOILED RICE TO BE SERVED WITH STEWED FRUITS, PRESERVES, OR RASPBERRY VINEGAR.

Take out the discoloured grains from half a pound of good rice; and wash it in several waters; tie it very loosely in a pudding-cloth and boil it for three-quarters of an hour; it will then be quite solid, and resemble a pudding in appearance. Sufficient room must be given to allow the grain to swell to its full size, or it will be hard; but too much space will render the whole watery. With a little experience the cook will easily ascertain the exact degree to be allowed for it. Four ounces of rice will require quite half an hour's boiling; a little more or less of time will sometimes be needed, from the difference of quality in the grain.

Carolina rice, ½ lb. boiled ¾ hour; 4 ozs. rice, ½ hour.

CHAPTER XVIII.

BAKED PUDDINGS.

INTRODUCTORY REMARKS.

WE have little to add here to the remarks which will be found at the commencement of the preceding Chapter, as they will apply equally to the preparation of these and of boiled puddings.

All of the custard kind, whether made of eggs and milk only, or of sago, arrow-root, rice, ground or in grain, vermicelli, &c., require a very gentle oven, and are spoiled by fast-baking. Those made of batter, on the contrary, should be put into one sufficiently brisk to raise them quickly, but without scorching them. Such as contain suet and raisins must have a well-heated, but not a fierce oven; for as they must remain long in it to be thoroughly done, unless carefully managed, they will either be much too highly coloured, or too dry.

By whisking to a solid froth the whites of the eggs used for any pudding, and stirring them softly into it at the instant of placing it in the oven, it will be rendered exceedingly light, and will rise very high in the dish; but as it will partake then of the nature of a *soufflé*, it must be despatched with great expedition to table from the oven, or it will become flat before it is served.

When a pudding is sufficiently browned on the surface (that is to say, of a fine equal amber-colour) before it is baked through, a sheet of writing paper should be laid over it, but not before it is *set:* when quite firm in the centre, it will be done.

Potato, batter, plum, and every other kind of pudding indeed, which is sufficiently solid to allow of it, should be turned reversed on to a clean hot dish from the one in which it is baked, and strewed with sifted sugar, before it is sent to table.

Minute directions for the preparation and management of each particular variety of pudding will be found in the receipt for it.

THE PRINTER'S PUDDING.

Grate very lightly six ounces of the crumb of a stale loaf, and put it into a deep dish. Dissolve in a quart of cold new milk four ounces of good Lisbon sugar; add it to five large, well-whisked eggs; strain, and mix them with the bread-crumbs; stir in two ounces of a fresh finely-grated cocoa-nut; add a flavouring of nutmeg or of lemon-rind, and the slightest pinch of salt; let the pudding stand for a couple of hours to soak the bread; and bake it in a gentle oven for three quarters of an hour: it is excellent if carefully made, and not too quickly baked. When the cocoa-nut is not at hand, an ounce of butter just dissolved, should be poured over the dish before the crumbs are put into it; and the rind of an entire lemon may be used to give it flavour; but the cocoa-nut imparts a peculiar richness when it is good and fresh.

Bread-crumbs, 6 ozs.; new milk, 1 quart; sugar, 4 ozs.; eggs, 5; cocoa-nut, 2 ozs.; (or rind, 1 large lemon, and 1 oz. butter) slightest pinch of salt: to stand 2 hours. Baked in gentle oven full ¾ hour.

Obs.—When a very sweet pudding is liked, the proportion of sugar may be increased.

ALMOND PUDDING.

On two ounces of fine white bread-crumbs pour a pint of boiling cream, and let them remain until nearly cold, then mix them very gradually with half a pound of sweet and six bitter almonds pounded to the smoothest paste, with a little orange-flower water, or, when this is not at hand, with a few drops of spring water, just to prevent their oiling; stir to them by degrees the well-beaten yolks of seven and the whites of three eggs, six ounces of sifted sugar, and four of clarified butter; turn the mixture into a very clean stewpan, and stir it without ceasing over a slow fire until it becomes thick, but on no account allow it to boil. When it is tolerably cool add a glass of brandy, or half a one of noyeau, pour the pudding into a dish lined with very thin puff paste, and bake it half an hour in a moderate oven.

Bread-crumbs, 2 ozs.; cream, 1 pint; pounded almonds, ½ lb.; bitter almonds, 6; yolks of 7, whites of 3 eggs; sugar, 6 ozs.; butter, 4 ozs.; brandy, 1 wineglassful, or ½ glass of noyeau: ½ hour, moderate oven.

AN EXCELLENT LEMON PUDDING.

Beat well together four ounces of fresh butter, creamed, and eight of sifted sugar; to these add gradually the yolks of six and the whites of two eggs, with the grated rind and the strained juice of one large lemon:—this last must be added by slow degrees, and stirred briskly to the other ingredients. Bake the pudding in a dish lined with very thin puff-paste for three-quarters of an hour, in a slow oven.

Butter, 4 ozs.; sugar, ½ lb.; yolks of 6, whites of 2 eggs; large lemon, 1: ¾ hour, slow oven.

ANOTHER LEMON PUDDING; (good.)

Stir over a slow fire until they boil, four ounces and a half of butter with seven ounces of pounded sugar, then pour them into a dish and let them remain until cold, or nearly so. Mix very smoothly a large dessertspoonful of flour with six eggs that have been whisked and strained; add these gradually to the sugar and butter, with the grated rinds and the juice of two moderate-sized lemons; put a border or a lining of puff-paste to the pudding, and bake it for an hour in a gentle oven.

Butter, 4½ ozs.; sugar, 7 ozs.; flour, 1 large dessertspoonful; eggs, 6; lemons, 2: 1 hour, gentle oven.

Obs.—The proportion of butter in these puddings is less than is commonly used for them, but a larger quantity renders them so unwholesomely rich that they are usually preferred with less. When a very powerful flavour of the fruit is liked, an additional lemon may be used in either of these receipts. The rinds may be rasped on part of the sugar, instead of being grated. A couple of sponge-biscuits soaked in cream, then pressed dry, and very finely bruised, can be substituted for the flour.

LEMON SUET-PUDDING.

To eight ounces of finely-grated bread-crumbs, add six of fresh beef kidney-suet, free from skin, and minced very small, three and a half of pounded sugar, six ounces of currants, the grated rind and the strained juice of a *large* lemon, and four full-sized or five small well-beaten eggs; pour these ingredients into a thickly-buttered pan, and bake the pudding for an hour in a brisk oven, but draw it towards the mouth when it is of a fine brown colour. Turn it from the dish before it is served, and strew sifted sugar over it or not, at pleasure: two ounces more of suet can be added when a larger proportion is liked. The pudding is very good without the currants.

Bread-crumbs, 8 ozs.; beef-suet, 6 ozs.; pounded sugar, 3½ ozs.; lemon, 1 *large*; currants, 6 ozs.; eggs, 4 large, or 5 small: 1 hour, brisk oven.

BAKEWELL PUDDING.

This pudding is famous not only in Derbyshire, but in several other English counties, where it is usually served on all holiday-occasions. Line a shallow tart-dish with quite an inch-deep layer of several kinds of good preserves mixed together, and intermingle with them from two to three ounces of candied citron or orange-rind. Beat well the yolks of ten eggs, and add to them gradually half a pound of sifted sugar; when they are well mixed, pour in by degrees half a pound of good clarified butter, and a little ratafia or any other flavour that may be preferred; fill the dish two-thirds full with this mixture, and bake the pudding for nearly an hour in a moderate oven. Half the quantity will be sufficient for a small dish.

Mixed preserves, 1½ to 2 lbs.; yolks of eggs, 10; sugar, ½ lb.; butter, ½ lb.; ratafia, lemon-brandy, or other flavouring to the taste: baked, moderate oven, ¾ to 1 hour.

Obs.—This is a rich and expensive, but not a very refined pudding. A variation of it, known in the south as an Alderman's Pudding, is, we think, superior to it. It is made without the candied peel, and with a layer of apricot-jam only, six ounces of butter, six of sugar, the yolks of six, and the whites of two eggs.

THE ELEGANT ECONOMIST'S PUDDING.

We have already given a receipt for an exceedingly good boiled pudding bearing this title, but we think the baked one answers even better, and it is made with rather more facility. Butter a deep tart-dish well, cut the slices of plum-pudding to join exactly in lining it, and press them against it lightly to make them adhere, as without this precaution they are apt to float off; pour in as much custard (previously thickened and left to become cold), or any other sweet pudding mixture as will fill the dish almost to the brim; cover the top with thin slices of the plum pudding, and bake it in a slow oven from thirty minutes to a full hour, according to the quantity and quality of the contents. One pint of new milk poured boiling on an ounce and a half of *tous les mois*, smoothly mixed with a quarter pint of cold milk, makes with the addition of four ounces of sugar, four small eggs, a little lemon-grate, and two or three bitter almonds, or a few drops of ratafia, an excellent pudding of this kind; it should be baked nearly three quarters of an hour in a quite slack oven. Two ounces and a half of arrow-root may be used in lieu of the *tous les mois*, when this last is not procurable. We would especially recommend for trial the ingredients of the lemon-pudding of page 284, (second receipt), with the plum-pudding crust, as likely to make a very superior variety of this dish; we have not had it tested, but think it could scarcely fail. It must be well, though slowly baked.

RICH BREAD AND BUTTER PUDDING.

Give a good flavour of lemon-rind and bitter almonds, or of cinna-mon, if preferred, to a pint of new milk, and when it has simmered a sufficient time for this, strain and mix it with a quarter-pint of rich cream; sweeten it with four ounces of sugar in lumps, and stir while still hot to five well-beaten eggs; throw in a few grains of salt, and move the mixture briskly with a spoon as a glass of brandy is added to it. Have ready in a thickly-buttered dish three layers of thin bread and butter cut from a half-quartern loaf, with four ounces of currants, and one and a half of finely shred candied peel, strewed between and over them; pour the eggs and milk on them by degrees, letting the bread absorb one portion before another is added: it should soak for a couple of hours before the pudding is taken to the oven, which should be a moderate one. Half an hour will bake it. It is very good when made with new milk only; and some persons use no more than a pint of liquid in all, but part of the whites of the eggs may then be omitted. Cream may be substituted for the entire quantity of milk at pleasure.

New milk, 1 pint; rind of small lemon, and 6 bitter almonds bruised (or ½ drachm of cinnamon): simmered 10 to 20 minutes. Cream, ¼ pint; sugar, 4 ozs.; eggs, 6; brandy, 1 wineglassful. Bread and but-ter, 3 layers; currants, 4 ozs.; candied orange or lemon-rind, 1½ oz.: to stand 2 hours, and to be baked 30 minutes in a moderate oven.

COMMON BREAD AND BUTTER PUDDING.

Sweeten a pint and a half of milk with four ounces of Lisbon sugar; stir it to four large well-beaten eggs, or to five small ones, grate half a nutmeg to them, and pour the mixture into a dish which holds nearly three pints, and which is filled almost to the brim with layers of bread and butter, between which three ounces of currants have been strewed. Lemon-grate, or orange-flower water can be added to this pudding in-stead of nutmeg, when preferred. From three quarters of an hour to an hour will bake it.

Milk, 1½ pint; Lisbon sugar, 4 ozs.; eggs, 4 large, or 5 small; ½ small nutmeg; currants, 3 ozs.: baked ¾ to 1 hour.

A GOOD BAKED BREAD PUDDING.

Pour, quite boiling, on six ounces (or three quarters of a pint) of fine bread-crumbs and one ounce of butter, a pint of new milk, cover them closely, and let them stand until the bread is well soaked; then stir to them three ounces of sugar, five eggs, leaving out two of the whites, two ounces of candied orange-rind, sliced thin, and a flavouring of nut-meg: when the mixture is nearly or quite cold pour it into a dish, and place lightly over the top the whites of three eggs beaten to a firm froth, and mixed at the instant with three large tablespoonsful of sifted sugar. Bake the pudding half an hour in a moderate oven. The icing may be omitted, and an ounce and a half of butter, just warmed, put into the dish before the pudding, and plenty of sugar, sifted over it just as it is sent to the oven.

Bread, 6 ozs.; butter, 1 oz.; milk, 1 pint; sugar, 3 ozs.; eggs, 5 yolks, 3 whites; candied orange-rind, 2 ozs.; little nutmeg. Icing, 3 whites of eggs; sugar, 3 tablespoonsful: baked, ½ hour.

ANOTHER BAKED BREAD PUDDING.

Add to a pint of new milk a quarter-pint of good cream, and pour them boiling on eight ounces of bread-crumbs, and three of fresh butter; when these have stood half an hour covered with a plate, stir to them four ounces of sugar, six ounces of currants, one and a half of candied orange or citron, and five eggs.

SUTHERLAND, OR CASTLE PUDDINGS.

Take an equal weight of eggs in the shell, of good butter, of fine dry flour, and of sifted sugar. First, whisk the eggs for ten minutes, or until they appear extremely light; then throw in the sugar by degrees, and continue the whisking for four or five minutes; next, strew in the flour, also gradually, and when it appears smoothly blended with the other ingredients, pour the butter to them in small portions, each of which should be beaten in until there is no appearance of it left. It should previously be just liquefied with the least possible degree of heat; this may be effected by putting it into a well-warmed saucepan, and shaking it round until it is dissolved. A grain or two of salt should be thrown in with the flour; and the rind of half a fine lemon rasped on sugar, or grated, if more convenient, or some pounded mace, or the store-flavouring of page 120, can be added at choice. Pour the mixture, directly it is ready, into well-buttered cups, and bake the puddings from twenty to twenty-five minutes. When cold, they resemble good pound-cakes, and may be served as such. Wine sauce should be sent to table with them.

Eggs, 4; their weight in flour, sugar, and butter; *little* salt; flavouring of pounded mace or lemon-rind.

Obs.—Three eggs are sufficient for a small dish of these puddings. They may be varied with an ounce or two of candied citron; or with a spoonful of brandy, or a little orange flower water. The mode we have given of making them will be found perfectly successful if our directions be followed with exactness. In a slack oven they will not be too much baked in half an hour.

MADELEINE PUDDINGS; (to be served cold.)

Take the same ingredients as for the Sutherland pudddings, but clarify an additional ounce of butter; skim, and then fill some round tin pattypans with it almost to the brim, pour it from one to the other until all have received a sufficient coating to prevent the puddings from adhering to them, and leave half a teaspoonful in each; mix the remainder with the eggs, sugar, and flour, beat the whole up very lightly, fill the pans about two thirds full, and put them directly into a rather brisk oven, but draw them towards the mouth of it when they are sufficiently coloured; from fifteen to eighteen minutes will bake them. Turn them out, and drain them on a sheet of paper. When they are quite cold, with the point of the knife take out a portion of the tops, hollow the puddings a little, and fill them with rich apricot-jam, well mixed with half its weight of pounded almonds, of which two in every ounce should be bitter ones.

A FRENCH RICE PUDDING, OR GATEAU DE RIZ.

Swell gently in a quart of new milk, or in equal parts of milk and cream, seven ounces of the best Carolina rice, which has been cleared of the discoloured grains, and washed and drained; when it is tolerably tender, add to it three ounces of fresh butter, and five of sugar roughly powdered, a *few* grains of salt, and the lightly grated rind of a fine lemon, and simmer the whole until the rice is swollen to the utmost; then take it from the fire, let it cool a little, and stir to it quickly, and by degrees, the well-beaten yolks of six full-sized eggs. Pour into a small copper stewpan * a couple of ounces of clarified butter, and incline it in such a manner that it may receive an equal coating in every part; then turn it upside down for an instant, to drain off the superfluous butter; next, throw in some exceedingly fine light crumbs of stale bread, and shake them entirely over it, turn out those which do not adhere, and with a small brush or feather sprinkle more clarified butter slightly on those which line the pan. Whisk quickly the whites of the eggs to snow, stir them gently to the rice, and pour the mixture softly into the stewpan, that the bread-crumbs may not be displaced; put it immediately into a *moderate* oven, and let it remain in a full hour. It will then, if properly baked, turn out from the mould or pan well browned, quite firm, and having the appearance of a cake; but a fierce heat will cause it to break, and present an altogether unsightly appearance. In a very slack oven, a longer time must be allowed for it.

New milk, or milk and cream, 1 quart; Carolina rice, 7 ozs.: ¾ hour. Fresh butter, 3 ozs.; sugar, in lumps, 5 ozs.; rind, 1 large lemon: ¾ to 1¼ hour. Eggs, 6: baked in a moderate oven, 1 hour.

Obs.—An admirable variety of this gâteau is made with cocoa-nut flavoured milk, or cream (see Chapter XX.), or with either of these poured boiling on six ounces of Jordan almonds, finely pounded, and mixed with a dozen of bitter ones, then expressed from them with strong pressure; it may likewise be flavoured with vanilla, or with candied orange-blossoms, and covered, at the instant it is dished, with strawberry, apple, or any other clear jelly.

A COMMON RICE PUDDING.

Throw six ounces of rice into plenty of cold water, and boil it gently from eight to ten minutes; drain it well in a sieve or strainer, and put it into a clean saucepan with a quart of milk; let it stew until tender, sweeten it with three ounces of sugar, stir to it, gradually, three large, or four small eggs, beaten and strained; add grated nutmeg, lemon-rind, or cinnamon, to give it flavour, and bake it one hour in a gentle oven.

Rice, 6 ozs.; in water, 8 to 10 minutes. Milk, 1 quart: ¾ to 1 hour. Sugar, 3 ozs.; eggs, 3 large, or 4 small; flavouring of nutmeg, lemon-rind, or cinnamon: bake 1 hour, gentle oven.

RICHER RICE PUDDING.

Pick and wash very clean four ounces of whole rice, pour on it a pint and a half of new milk, and stew it slowly till quite tender; before it is taken from the fire, stir in two ounces of good butter, and three of sugar; and when it has cooled a little, add four well-whisked eggs, and the grated rind of half a lemon. Bake the pudding in a gentle oven from thirty to forty minutes. As rice requires long boiling to render it soft in milk, it may be partially stewed in water, the quantity of

---

* One which holds about five pints is well adapted to the purpose. When this is not at hand, a copper cake mould may be substituted for it. The stewpan must not be covered while the gâteau is baking.

milk diminished to a pint, and a little thick sweet cream mixed with it, before the other ingredients are added.

Rice, 4 ozs.; new milk, 1½; butter, 2 ozs.; sugar, 3 ozs.; eggs, 4; rind of ½ lemon: 30 to 40 minutes, slow oven.

RICE-PUDDING MERINGUÉ.

Swell gently four ounces of Carolina rice in a pint and a quarter of milk or of thin cream; let it cool a little, and stir to it an ounce and a half of butter, three of pounded sugar, a grain or two of salt, the grated rind of a small lemon, and the yolks of four large, or of five small eggs. Pour the mixture into a well-buttered dish, and lay lightly and equally over the top the whites of four eggs, beaten as for sponge-cakes, and mixed at the instant with from four to five heaped tablespoonsful of sifted sugar. Bake the pudding half an hour in a moderate oven, but do not allow the meringué to be too deeply coloured; it should be of clear brown, and very crisp. Serve it directly it is taken from the oven.

Rice, 4 ozs.; milk, or cream, 1¼ pint; butter, 1½ oz.; sugar, 3 ozs.; rind, 1 lemon; yolks of eggs, 4 or 5; the whites beaten to snow, and mixed with as many tablespoonsful of sifted sugar: baked ½ hour, moderate oven.

Obs.—A couple of ounces of Jordan almonds, with six bitter ones, pounded quite to a paste, will improve this dish, whether mixed with the pudding itself, or with the meringué.

GOOD GROUND RICE PUDDING.

Mix very smoothly five ounces of flour of rice (or of *ground* rice, if preferred), with half a pint of milk, and pour it into a pint and a half more which is boiling fast; keep it stirred constantly over a gentle fire from ten to twelve minutes, and be particularly careful not to let it burn to the pan; add to it before it is taken from the fire, a quarter of a pound of good butter, from five to six ounces of sugar, roughly powdered, and a half-saltspoonful of salt; turn it into a pan, and stir it for a few minutes, to prevent its hardening at the top; then mix with it, by degrees, but quickly, the yolks of eight eggs, and the whites of only two, the grated or rasped rind of a fine lemon, and a glass of brandy. Lay a border of rich paste round a buttered dish, pour in the pudding, strain a little clarified butter over the top, moisten the paste with a brush, or small bunch of feathers dipped in cold water, and sift plenty of sugar on it, but less over the pudding itself. Send it to a *very* gentle oven to be baked for three-quarters of an hour.

Rice-flour (or ground rice), 5 ozs.; new milk, 1 quart: 10 to 12 minutes. Butter, 4 ozs.; sugar, 5 to 6 ozs.; salt, ½ saltspoonful; yolks, 8 eggs; whites, 2; rind, 1 large lemon; brandy, large wineglassful: ¾ hour, *slow* oven.

Obs.—These proportions are sufficient for a pudding of larger size than those served usually at elegant tables; they will make two small ones; or two-thirds of the quantity may be taken for one of moderate size. Lemon-brandy or ratafia, or a portion of each, may be used to give it flavour with good effect; and it may be enriched, if this be desired, by adding to the other ingredients from three to four ounces of Jordan almonds, finely pounded, and by substituting cream for half of the milk.

18

COMMON GROUND-RICE PUDDING.

One pint and a half of milk, three ounces and a half of rice, three of Lisbon sugar, one and a half of butter, some nutmeg, or lemon-grate, and four eggs, baked slowly for half an hour, or more, if not quite firm.

POTATO-PUDDING.

With a pound and a quarter of fine mealy potatoes, boiled very dry, and mashed perfectly smooth while hot, mix three ounces of butter, five and a half of sugar, five eggs, a few grains of salt, and the grated rind of a small lemon. Pour the mixture into a well-buttered dish, and bake it in a moderate oven for nearly three-quarters of an hour. It should be turned out and sent to table with fine sugar sifted over it; or for variety, red currant-jelly, or any other preserve may be spread on it as soon as it is dished.

Potatoes, 1¼ lb.; butter, 3 ozs.: sugar, 5½ ozs.; eggs, 5; lemon-rind, 1; salt, few grains: 40 to 45 minutes.

Obs.—When cold, this pudding eats like cake, and may be served as such, omitting, of course, the sugar or preserve when it is dished.

A RICHER POTATO PUDDING.

Beat well together fourteen ounces of mashed potatoes, four ounces of butter, four of fine sugar, five eggs, the grated rind of a small lemon, and a slight pinch of salt; add half a glass of brandy, and pour the pudding into a thickly-buttered dish, ornamented with slices of candied orange or lemon rind; pour a little clarified butter on the top, and then sift plenty of white sugar over it.

Potatoes, 14 ozs.; butter, 4 ozs.; sugar, 4 ozs.; eggs, 5; lemon-rind, 1; little salt; brandy, ½ glassful; candied peel, 1½ to 2 ozs.: 40 minutes.

Obs.—The potatoes for these receipts should be lightly and carefully mashed, but never pounded in a mortar, as that will convert them into a heavy paste. The better plan is to prepare them by Captain Kater's receipt (page 230), when they will fall to powder almost of themselves; or they may be grated while hot through a wire-sieve. From a quarter to a half pint of cream is, by many cooks, added to potato puddings.

AN EXCELLENT SPONGE CAKE PUDDING.

Slice into a well-buttered tart-dish three penny sponge cakes, and place on them a couple of ounces of candied orange or lemon-peel cut in strips. Whisk thoroughly six eggs, and stir to them boiling a pint and a quarter of new milk, in which three ounces of sugar have been dissolved; grate in the rind of a small lemon, and when they are some-what cooled, add half a wineglassful of brandy; while still warm, pour the mixture on to the cakes, and let it remain an hour; then strain an ounce and a half of clarified butter over the top, sift or strew pounded sugar rather thickly on it, and bake the pudding for half an hour in a moderate oven.

Sponge cakes, 3; candied peel, 2 ozs.; eggs, 6; new milk, 1¼ pint; sugar, 3 ozs.; lemon-rind, 1; brandy, ½ glass; butter, 1 oz.; sifted sugar, 1½ oz.: ½ hour.

THE DUCHESS'S PUDDING.

Mix with half a pound of potatoes very smoothly mashed, three quarters of a pound of mincer reat, the grated rind of half a lemon, a dessertspoonful of sugar, and four large, or five small eggs; pour the whole into a well-buttered dish, and put over the top clarified butter and sugar, as in the preceding receipt. Bake the pudding for a full hour, and twenty minutes.

Potatoes, ½ lb.; mincemeat, ¾ lb.; rind of lemon, ½; sugar, 1 dessertspoonful; eggs, 4 large, or 5 small: 1 hour 20 minutes.

BAKED APPLE PUDDING, OR CUSTARD.

Weigh a pound of good boiling apples after they are pared and cored, and stew them to a perfectly smooth marmalade, with six ounces of sugar, and a spoonful or two of water: stir them often that they may not stick to the pan. Mix with them while they are still quite hot, three ounces of butter, the grated rind and the strained juice of a lemon, and lastly, stir in by degrees the well-beaten yolks of five eggs, and a dessertspoonful of flour, or in lieu of the last, three or four Naples' biscuits, or macaroons crushed small. Bake the pudding for a full half hour in a moderate oven, or longer should it not be quite firm in the middle. A little clarified butter poured on the top, with sugar sifted over, improves all baked puddings.

Apples, 1 lb.; sugar, 6 ozs.; water, 1 cupful; butter, 3 ozs.; juice and rind, 1 lemon; 5 eggs: ½ hour, or more.

Obs.—Many cooks press the apples through a sieve after they are boiled, but this is not needful when they are of a good kind, and stewed, and beaten smooth.

A COMMON BAKED APPLE PUDDING.

Boil a pound and a quarter of apples with half a small cupful of water and six ounces of brown sugar; when they are reduced to a smooth pulp, stir to them two ounces of butter, a tablespoonful of flour, or a handful of fine bread-crumbs, and five well-beaten eggs; grate in half a nutmeg, or flavour the pudding with pounded cinnamon, and bake it nearly three quarters of an hour. More or less of sugar will be required for these puddings, according to the time of year, as the fruit is much more acid when first gathered than when it has been some months stored.

Apples, 1¼ lb.; water, ½ *small* cupful; sugar, 6 ozs.; butter, 2 ozs.; flour, 1 tablespoonful, or bread-crumbs, 1 handful; ½ nutmeg; eggs, 5: ¾ hour.

ESSEX PUDDING. (CHEAP AND GOOD.)

Mix with a quarter of a pound of mashed potatoes, half a pound of good boiling apples minced, four ounces of brown sugar, four small eggs well beaten and strained, and a little grated lemon-peel or nutmeg. Increase the ingredients one half, and add two ounces of butter, should a larger and better pudding be desired: about half an hour will bake it.

Potatoes mashed, 4 ozs.; apples, 8 ozs.; sugar, 4 ozs.; eggs, 4: ½ hour.

DUTCH CUSTARD, OR BAKED RASPBERRY PUDDING.

Lay into a tart-dish a border of puff-paste, and a pint and a half of freshly-gathered raspberries, well mixed with three ounces of sugar Whisk thoroughly six large eggs with three ounces more of sugar, and pour it over the fruit: bake the pudding from twenty-five to thirty minutes in a moderate oven.

Break the eggs one at a time into a cup, and with the point of a small three-pronged fork take off the specks or germs, before they are beaten, as we have directed in page 269.

Raspberries, 1½ pint; sugar, 6 ozs.; eggs, 6: 25 to 30 minutes.

VERMICELLI PUDDING.

Drop lightly into a pint and a half of boiling milk four ounces of fresh vermicelli, and keep it simmering and stirred gently for ten minutes, when it will have become very thick; then mix with it three ounces and a half of sugar, two ounces of butter, and a small pinch of salt. When the whole is well blended, pour it out; beat it for a couple of minutes to cool it a little; then add by degrees five well-whisked eggs, the grated rind of a lemon, and just before it is put into the dish, a small glass of brandy: bake it from half to three quarters of an hour. Vermicelli varies much in quality, and of some kinds three ounces will render the pudding quite firm enough.

Milk, 1½ pint; vermicelli, 4 ozs.; 10 minutes. Sugar, 3½ ozs.; butter, 2 ozs.; pinch of salt; eggs, 5; lemon-rind, 1; brandy, 1 wineglassful: ½ to ¾ hour.

Obs.—This pudding requires, more than many others, a little clarified butter poured on the top, and sugar sifted over. Candied peel may be added to it with good effect; and three or four bitter almonds, pounded, may be used to give it flavour instead of lemon-rind.

SMALL COCOA-NUT PUDDINGS.

Melt together over a slow fire two ounces of fresh butter cut small, and four of pounded sugar; pour them out when they have boiled for a couple of minutes, and let them cool; mix with them two ounces of finely-grated cocoa-nut, an ounce of citron shred small, the grated rind of half a large lemon, and four eggs: when these have been well beaten together, add the strained juice of the half lemon; put the mixture into buttered pattypans, or pudding-cups, sift sugar over, and bake them half an hour in a moderate oven. This is an excellent and a perfectly new receipt; but in making use of it care should be taken to ascertain that the nut be fresh and sweet flavoured, as the slightest degree of rancidity will spoil the puddings. They are better hot than cold, though very good either way.

Fresh butter, 2 ozs.; pounded sugar, ¼ lb.; cocoa-nut, 2 ozs.; candied citron, 1 oz.; rind and juice of ½ lemon; eggs, 4: ½ hour.

Obs.—The same ingredients may be made into one pudding only, and longer baked.

GOOD YORKSHIRE PUDDING.

To make a very good and light Yorkshire pudding, take an equal number of eggs and of heaped tablespoonsful of flour, with a teaspoonful of salt to six of these. Whisk the eggs *well*, strain, and mix them gradually with the flour, then pour in by degrees as much new milk as will reduce the batter to the consistency of rather thin cream. The tin which is to receive the pudding must have been placed for some time previously under a joint that has been put down to roast: one of beef is usually preferred. Beat the batter briskly and lightly, the in-

stant before it is poured into the pan, watch it carefully that it may not
burn, and let the edges have an equal share of the fire. When the
pudding is quite firm in every part, and well-coloured on the surface,
turn it to brown the under side. This is best accomplished by first
dividing it into quarters. In Yorkshire it is made much thinner than
in the south, roasted generally at an enormous fire, and *not* turned at
all: currants there are sometimes added to it.

Eggs, 6; flour, six heaped tablespoonsful, or from 7 to 8 ozs.; milk,
nearly or quite, 1 pint; salt, 1 teaspoonful: 2 hours.

Obs.—This pudding should be quite an inch thick when it is browned
on both sides, but only half the depth when roasted in the Yorkshire
mode. The cook must exercise her discretion a little in mixing the
batter, as from the variation of weight in flour, and in the size of eggs,
a little more or less of milk may be required: the whole should be rather
more liquid than for a boiled pudding.

COMMON YORKSHIRE PUDDING.

Half a pound of flour, three eggs (we would recommend a fourth),
rather more than a pint of milk, and a teaspoonful of salt.

NORMANDY PUDDING. (GOOD.)

Boil, until very soft and dry, eight ounces of rice in a pint and a half,
or rather more, of water,* stir to it two ounces of fresh butter, and three
of sugar, and simmer it for a few minutes after they are added; then
pour it out, and let it cool for use. Strip from the stalks as many red
currants, or morella cherries, as will fill a tart-dish of moderate size,
and for each pint of the fruit allow from three to four ounces of sugar.
Line the bottom and sides of a deep dish with part of the rice; next,
put in a thick layer of fruit and sugar; then one of rice and one of fruit
alternately until the dish is full. Sufficient of the rice should be reserved to form a rather thick layer at the top: smooth this equally with
a knife, and send the pudding to a moderate but not very slow oven, for
half an hour, and more, should it be large. When two thirds baked, it
may be glazed with yolk of egg, brushed over, and fine sugar sifted on
it. Morella cherries, with a little additional sugar, make an excellent
pudding of this kind.

DAMSON-AND-RICE PUDDING.

With five ounces of whole rice boiled soft and dry, mix an ounce of
butter, ten ounces of damson-jam, a teaspoonful of lemon-juice, and five
eggs. Beat the whole well together, and bake it about half an hour.

Rice, 5 ozs.; damson-jam, 10 ozs.; butter, 1 oz.; eggs, 5: ½ hour.

BARBERRY-AND-RICE PUDDING.

Mix ten ounces of barberries stripped from the stalks, with four ounces
of whole boiled rice, eight ounces of sugar, a small slice of butter, and
five large, or six small eggs.

APPLE-AND-RICE PUDDING.

Boil together one pound of good pudding-apples, and six ounces of
sugar, until they are reduced to a smooth pulp; stir them often to prevent their burning; mix with them four ounces of boiled rice, two ounces

---

* A quart of milk can be substituted for this; but with the fruit water perhaps answers better.

of butter, and five large eggs. Should the apples be very acid, increase
the quantity of sugar: add lemon rind or juice, at pleasure. These
puddings are better if mixed while the ingredients are still warm.

Apples, 1 lb.; sugar, 6 ozs.; boiled rice, 4 ozs.; butter, 2 ozs.; eggs,
5: 30 to 35 minutes.

COMMON RAISIN PUDDING.

Beat well together three quarters of a pound of flour, the same quantity of raisins, six ounces of beef-suet, finely chopped, a small pinch of
salt, some grated nutmeg, and three eggs which have been thoroughly
whisked, and mixed with about a quarter-pint of milk, or less than this,
should the eggs be large. Pour the whole into a buttered dish, and
bake it an hour and a quarter. For a large pudding, increase the quantities one half.

Flour and stoned raisins, each ¾ lb.; suet, 6 ozs.; salt, small pinch;
nutmeg, ½ teaspoonful; eggs, 3; milk, ¼ pint: 1¼ hour.

A RICHER RAISIN PUDDING.

Mix and whisk well, and lightly together, a pound of raisins weighed
after they are stoned, ten ounces of finely minced beef-suet, three quarters of a pound of flour, a little salt, half a small nutmeg, or the grated
rind of a lemon, four large eggs, and as much milk as may be needed
to make the whole into a *very* thick batter: bake the pudding a few
minutes longer than the preceding one. The addition of sugar will be
found no improvement, as it will render it much less light.

POOR AUTHOR'S PUDDING.

Flavour a quart of new milk by boiling in it for a few minutes half a
stick of well-bruised cinnamon, or the thin rind of a small lemon; add a
few grains of salt, and three ounces of sugar, and turn the whole into a
deep basin; when it is quite cold, stir to it three well-beaten eggs, and
strain the mixture into a pie-dish. Cover the top entirely with slices
of bread free from crust, and half an inch thick, cut so as to join neatly,
and buttered on both sides: bake the pudding in a moderate oven for
about half an hour, or in a Dutch oven before the fire.

New milk, 1 quart; cinnamon, or lemon-rind; sugar, 3 ozs.; little
salt; eggs, 3; buttered bread: baked ½ hour.

PUDDING A LA PAYSANNE; (*cheap and good.*)

Fill a deep tart-dish with alternate layers of well-sugared fruit, and
very thin slices of the crumb of a light stale loaf; let the upper layer be
of fruit, and should it be of a dry kind, sprinkle over it about a dessertspoonful of water, or a little lemon-juice: raspberries, currants, and cherries, will not require this. Send the pudding to a somewhat brisk oven
to be baked for about half an hour. The proportion of sugar used must
be regulated, of course, by the acidity of the fruit. For a quart of ripe
greengages, split and stoned, five ounces will be sufficient. Apricots,
peaches, and nectarines will scarcely require more; but damsons, bu'
laces, and various other plums will need a much larger quantity. A
superior pudding of this kind is made by substituting sponge cake for
the bread.

INDIAN PUDDING.

Put into a deep dish from six to eight ounces of rice which has been washed, and wiped in a dry cloth; just moisten it with milk, and set it into a gentle oven ; add milk to it at intervals, in small quantities, until the grain is swollen to its full size, and is tender, but very dry; then mix with it two dessertspoonsful of fine sugar, and if it should be at hand, four or five tablespoonsful of rich cream.   Fill a tart-dish almost to the brim with fruit properly sugared, heap the rice equally over it, leaving it rough, and bake it in a moderate oven for half an hour, unless the fruit should be of a kind to require a longer time; when very hard, it must be half stewed with the sugar before it is put into the dish.   The rice may be swelled over a very slow fire when more convenient; and the Dutch or American oven will serve quite well to bake the pudding.

BAKED HASTY PUDDING.

Take from a pint of new milk sufficient to mix into a thin batter two ounces of flour, put the remainder, with a *small* pinch of salt, into a clean saucepan, and when it boils quickly, stir the flour briskly to it; keep it stirred over a gentle fire for ten minutes, pour it out, and when it has become a little cool, mix with it two ounces of fresh butter, three of pounded sugar, the grated rind of a small lemon, four large, or five small eggs, and half a glass of brandy, or as much orange-flower water. To these half a dozen bitter almonds, pounded to a paste, are sometimes added.   Bake the pudding half an hour in a gentle oven.

New milk, 1 pint; flour, 2 ozs.: 10 minutes. Butter, 2 ozs.; sugar, 3 ozs.; eggs, 4 or 5; grated rind of lemon; brandy, or orange-flower water, ½ wineglassful.

CHAPTER XIX.

SOUFFLÉS, OMLETS, &c.

OBSERVATIONS ON OMLETS, FRITTERS, &C.

The composition and nature of a soufflé are altogether different, but there is no difficulty in making good omlets, pancakes, or fritters, and as they may be expeditiously prepared and served, they are often a very convenient resource when, on short notice, an addition is required to a dinner.   The eggs for all of them should be well and lightly whisked; the lard for frying batter should be extremely pure in flavour, and quite hot when the fritters are dropped in; the batter itself should be smooth as cream, and it should be briskly beaten the instant before it is used. All fried pastes should be perfectly drained from the fat before they are served, and sent to table promptly when they are ready.   Eggs may be dressed in a multiplicity of ways, but are seldom, in any form, more relished than in a well-made and expeditiously served omlet.   This may be plain, or seasoned with minced herbs, and a very little eschalot, when the last is liked, and is then called an " *Omlette aux fines herbes ;*" or it may be mixed with minced ham, or grated cheese; in any case, it should be light, thick, full-tasted, and *fried only on one side ;* if turned in the pan, as it frequently is, it will at once be flattened and rendered tough.   Should the slight rawness which is sometimes found in the

middle of the inside, when the omlet is made in the French way, he
objected to, a heated shovel, or a salamander, may be held over it for
an instant, before it is folded on the dish.   The pan for frying it should
be quite small ; for if it be composed of four or five eggs only, and then
put into a large one, it will necessarily spread over it and be thin, which
would render it more like a pancake than an omlet; the only partial
remedy for this, when a pan of proper size cannot be had, is to raise the
handle of it high, and to keep the opposite side close down to the fire,
which will confine the eggs into a smaller space.   No gravy should
ever be poured into the dish with it, and indeed, if properly made, it
will require none.   Lard is preferable to butter for frying batter, as it
renders it lighter ; but it must not be used for omlets.

A COMMON OMLET.

From four to eight very fresh eggs may be used for this, according to
the sized dish required.   Half a dozen will generally be sufficient.
Break them singly and carefully; clear them in the way we have
already pointed out in the introduction to boiled puddings, or when they
are sufficiently whisked. pour them through a sieve, and resume the
beating until they are very light.   Add to them from half to a whole
teaspoonful of salt, and a seasoning of pepper.   Dissolve in a small frying pan a couple of ounces of butter, pour in the eggs, and as soon as
the omlet is well risen and firm throughout, slide it on to a hot dish,
fold it together like a turnover, and serve it *immediately*; from five to
seven minutes will fry it.

For other varieties of the omlet, see the observations which precede
this.

AN OMLETTE SOUFFLÉE.

Separate, as they are broken, the whites from the yolks of six fine
fresh eggs; beat these last thoroughly, first by themselves and then with
four tablespoonsful of dry, white sifted sugar, and the rind of half a
lemon grated on a fine grater.*   Whisk the whites to a solid froth, and
just before the omlet is poured into the pan, mix them well, but lightly,
with the yolks.   Put four ounces of fresh butter into a very small delicately clean omlet, or frying-pan, and as soon as it is all dissolved, add
the eggs and stir them round, that they may absorb it entirely.   When
the under side is just set, turn the omlet into a well-buttered dish, and
send it to a tolerably brisk oven.   From five to ten minutes will bake
it; and it must be served the *instant* it is taken out; carried, indeed, as
quickly as possible to table from the oven.   It will have risen to a great
height, but will sink and become heavy in a very short space of time:
if sugar be sifted over it, let it be done with the utmost expedition.

Eggs, 6; sugar, 4 tablespoonsful; rind, ½ lemon; butter, 4 ozs.:
omlet baked, 5 to 10 minutes.

Obs. — A large common frying-pan will not answer for omlets: a
very small one should be kept for them, when there is no regular omlet-
pan.

SOUFFLÉS.

The admirable lightness and delicacy of a well-made soufflé render it
generally a very favourite dish, and it is now a fashionable one also.   It

---

* As we have before said, a much more delicate flavour is imparted by *rasping* the
lemon-rind on sugar.

may be greatly varied in its composition, but in all cases must be served the very instant it is taken from the oven; and even in passing to the dining-room it should, if possible, be prevented from sinking by a heated iron or salamander held above it.   A common soufflé-pan may be purchased for a dollar, in England, but those of silver or plated metal are of course expensive; the part in which the soufflé is baked is placed within the more ornamental dish when it is drawn from the oven.   A plain, round, shallow cake-mould, with a strip of writing-paper six inches high, placed inside the rim, will answer on an emergency to bake a soufflé in.   The following receipt will serve as a guide for the proper mode of making it: the process is always the same whether the principal ingredient be whole rice boiled very tender in milk and pressed through a sieve, bread-crumbs soaked as for a pudding and worked through a sieve also, arrow-root, potato-flour, or anything else of which light puddings in general are made.

Take from a pint and a half of new milk or of cream sufficient to mix four ounces of flour of rice to a perfectly smooth batter; put the remainder into a very clean, well-tinned saucepan, and when it boils, stir the rice briskly to it; let it simmer, keeping it stirred all the time, for ten minutes, or more should it not be very thick, then mix well with it two ounces of fresh butter, one and a half of pounded sugar, and the grated rind of a fine lemon (or let the sugar which is used for it be well rubbed on the lemon before it is crushed to powder); in two or three minutes take it from the fire, and beat quickly and carefully to it by degrees the yolks of six eggs; whisk the whites to a very firm solid froth, and when the pan is buttered, and all else quite ready for the oven, stir them gently to the other ingredients; pour the soufflé immediately into the pan and place it in a moderate oven, of which keep the door closed for a quarter of an hour at least.   When the soufflé has risen very high, is of a fine colour, and quite done in the centre, which it will be in from half to three quarters of an hour, send it instantly to table.   The exact time for baking it depends so much on the oven that it cannot be precisely specified.   We have known quite a small one not too much baked in forty-five minutes in an *iron* oven; but generally less time will suffice for them: the heat, however, should always be moderate.

New milk or cream, 1½ pint; flour of rice, 4 ozs.; fresh butter, 2 ozs.; pounded sugar, 1½ oz.; eggs, 6; grain of salt; rind, 1 lemon: 30 to 45 minutes.

Obs. 1.—The soufflé may be flavoured with vanilla, orange-flowers, or aught else that is liked.   Chocolate and coffee also may be used for it with soaked bread: a very strong infusion of the last, and an ounce or two of the other, melted with a little water, are to be added to the milk and bread.

Obs. 2.—A soufflé is commonly served in a dinner of ceremony as a remove of the roast, but the better plan for this, as for a fondu, is to have it quickly handed round, instead of being placed upon, the table.

A PONDU.

Mix to a smooth batter, with a quarter of a pint of new milk, two ounces of potato-flour, arrow-root, or *tous les mois:* pour boiling to them three quarters of a pint more of milk, or of cream in preference, stir *hem well together, and then throw in two ounces of butter cut small. When this is melted, and well-beaten into the mixture, add the well whisked yolks of four large or of five small eggs, half a teaspoonful of salt, something less of cayenne, and three ounces of lightly-grated cheese, Parmesan or rich old cheese, or equal parts of both. Whisk the whites of the eggs to a quite firm and solid froth; then proceed, as for a soufflé, to mix and bake the foudu.

20 minutes.

KENTISH FRITTERS.

Beat up the whites of three eggs and the yolks of six with half a pound of flour, a cupful of milk, and a large teaspoonful of yeast: put the mixture into a jug, cover it, and set it by the fire until the next day, then add to the batter two large apples finely chopped, and fry the fritters as usual.

Whites of eggs, 3; yolks, 6; flour, 8 ozs.; milk, 1 cupful; yeast, 1 teaspoonful: 24 hours.

PLAIN COMMON FRITTERS.

Mix with three well-beaten eggs a quarter-pint of milk, and strain them through a fine sieve: add them gradually to three large table-spoonsful of flour, and thin the batter with as much more milk as will bring it to the consistency of cream; beat it up thoroughly at the moment of using it, that the fritters may be light. Drop it in small portions from a spouted jug or basin into boiling lard; when lightly coloured on one side, turn them, drain them well from the lard as they are lifted out, and serve them very quickly. They are eaten generally with fine sugar, and orange or lemon juice: the first of these may be sifted thickly over them after they are dished, the oranges or lemons cut in two, and sent to table with them. The lard used for frying them should be fresh and pure-flavoured: it renders them more crisp and light than butter, and is, therefore, better suited to the purpose.

Eggs, 3; flour, 3 tablespoonsful; milk, ¼ to ½ pint.

PANCAKES.

These may be made with the same batter as fritters, if it be sufficiently thinned with an additional egg or two, or a little milk or cream, to spread quickly over the pan: to fry them well, this ought to be small. When the batter is ready, heat the pan over a clear fire and rub it with butter in every part, then pour in sufficient batter to spread over it entirely, and let the pancake be very thin: in this case it will require no turning, but otherwise it must be tossed over with a sudden jerk of the pan, in which the cook who is not somewhat expert will not always succeed; therefore the safer plan is to make them so thin that they will not require this. Keep them hot before the fire until a sufficient number are ready to send to table, then proceed with a second supply, as they should always be quickly served. Either roll them up and strew fine sugar over them, or spread them quickly with preserve, laying them one on the other. A richer kind of pancake may be made with a pint of cream, or of cream and new milk mixed, five eggs, or their yolks only, a couple of ounces of flour, a little pounded cinnamon or lemon-rind rasped on sugar and scraped into them, with two ounces more of pounded sugar, and two ounces of clarified butter.

From 4 to 5 minutes.

FRITTERS OF CAKE AND PUDDING.

Cut plain pound, or rice cake into small square slices half an inch thick; trim away the crust, fry them slowly a light brown, in a small quantity of fresh butter, and spread over them when done a layer of apricot-jam, or of any other preserve, and serve them immediately. These fritters are improved by being moistened with a little good cream before they are fried: they must then be slightly floured. Cold plum-pudding sliced down as thick as the cake, and divided into portions of equal size and good form, then dipped into batter, and gently fried, will also make an agreeable variety of fritter.

MINCEMEAT FRITTERS.

With half a pound of mincemeat mix two ounces of fine bread-crumbs (or a tablespoonful of flour), two eggs well beaten, and the strained juice of half a small lemon. Mix these well, and drop the fritters with a dessertspoon into plenty of very pure lard or fresh butter; fry them from seven to eight minutes, drain them on a napkin or on white blotting paper, and send them very hot to table: they should be quite small.

Mincemeat, ½ lb.; bread-crumbs, 2 ozs. (or flour, 1 tablespoonful); eggs, 2; juice of ½ lemon: 7 to 8 minutes.

VENETIAN FRITTERS. (*Very good.*)

Pick, wash, and drain three ounces of whole rice, put it into a full pint of cold milk, and bring it very slowly to boil; stir it often, and let it simmer gently until quite thick and dry. When about three parts done, add to it two ounces of pounded sugar, and one of fresh butter, a grain of salt, and the grated rind of half a small lemon. Let it cool in the saucepan, and when only just warm mix with it thoroughly three ounces of currants, four apples, chopped fine, a teaspoonful of flour, and three large or four small well-beaten eggs. Drop the mixture in small fritters, fry them in butter from five to seven minutes, and let them become quite firm on one side before they are turned: do this with a slice. Drain them as they are taken up, and sift white sugar over them after they are dished.

Whole rice, 3 ozs.; milk, 1 pint; sugar, 2 ozs.; butter, 1 oz.; grated rind of ½ lemon; currants, 3 ozs.; minced apples, 4 ozs.; flour, 1 teaspoonful; a little salt; eggs, 3 large or 4 small; 5 to 7 minutes.

FRITTERS OF SPRING FRUIT.

The rhubarb for these should be of a good sort, quickly grown, and tender. Pare, cut it into equal lengths, and throw it into the French batter of page 113; with a fork lift the stalks separately, and put them into a pan of boiling lard or butter: in from five to six minutes they will be done. Drain them well and dish them on a napkin, or pile them high without one, and strew sifted sugar plentifully over them: they should be of a very light brown, and quite dry and crisp. The young stalks look well when left in their entire length, and only slightly encrusted with the batter, through which they should be merely drawn.

5 to 6 minutes.

APPLE, PEACH, APRICOT, OR ORANGE FRITTERS.

Pare and core without dividing the apples, slice them in rounds the full size of the fruit, dip them into the same batter as that directed for the preceding fritters; fry them a pale brown, and et them be very dry. Serve them heaped high upon a folded napkin, and strew sifted sugar over them. After having stripped the outer rind from the oranges, remove carefully the white inner skin, and in slicing them take out .ne pips; then dip them into the batter and proceed as for the apple fritters. The peaches and apricots should be merely skinned, halved, and stoned before they are drawn through the batter, unless they should not be fully ripe, when they must first be stewed tender in a thin syrup 8 to 12 minutes.

POTATO FRITTERS. (ENTREMETS.)

See directions for potato puddings. The same mixture dropped in fritters into boiling butter, and fried until firm on both sides, will be found very good.

LEMON FRITTERS. (ENTREMETS.)

Mix with six ounces of very fine bread-crumbs four of beef suet, minced as small as possible, four ounces of pounded sugar, a small table-spoonful of flour, four whole eggs, well and lightly whisked, and the grated rind of one large or of two small lemons, with half or the whole of the juice, at choice; but before this last is stirred in, add a spoonful or two of milk or cream, if needed. Fry the mixture in small fritters for five or six minutes.

CANNELONS. (ENTREMETS.)

Roll out very thin and evenly some fine puff-paste into a long strip of from three to four inches wide, moisten the surface with a feather dipped in white of egg, and cut it into bands of nearly two inches wide; lay some apricot or peach marmalade equally along these, and fold the paste twice over it, close the ends carefully, and when all are ready slide them gently into a pan of boiling lard; * as soon as they begin to brown, raise the pan from the fire that they may not take too much colour before the paste is done quite through. Five minutes will fry them. Drain them well, and dry them on a soft cloth before the fire; dish them on a napkin, and place one layer crossing another, or merely pile them high in the centre. If well made, and served of a light brown and very dry, these cannelons are excellent: when lard is objected to butter may be used instead, but the paste will then be somewhat less light. Only lard of the purest quality will answer for the purpose. 5 minutes.

CROQUETTES OF RICE. (ENTREMETS.)

Wipe very clean, in a dry cloth, seven ounces of rice, put it into a clean stewpan, and pour on it a quart of new milk; let it swell gently by the side of the fire, and stir it often that it may not stick to the pan, nor burn; when it is about half done, stir to it five ounces of pounded sugar, and six bitter almonds beaten extremely fine: the thin rind of half a fresh lemon may be added in the first instance. The rice must be simmered until it is soft, and very thick and dry; it should then be spread on a dish, and left until cold, when it is to be rolled into small balls, which must be dipped into beaten egg, and then covered in every part with the finest bread-crumbs. When all are ready, fry them a

* Cannelons may be either baked or fried: if sen . to the oven, they may first be glazed with white of egg and sugar.

light brown in fresh butter, and dry them well before the fire, upon a sieve reversed and covered with a very soft cloth, or with a sheet of white blotting-paper. Pile them in a hot dish, and send them to table quickly.

Rice, 7 ozs.; milk, 1 quart; rind of lemon: ¼ hour. Sugar, 5 ozs.; bitter almonds, 6: 40 to 60 minutes, or more. Fried, 5 to 7 minutes.

FINER CROQUETTES OF RICE. (ENTREMETS.)

Swell the rice in thin cream, or in new milk strongly flavoured with cocoa-nut; then add the same ingredients as in the foregoing receipt, and when the rice is cold, form it into balls, and with the thumb of the right hand hollow them sufficiently to admit in the centre a small portion of peach jam, or of apricot marmalade; close the rice well over it; egg, crumb, and fry the croquettes as usual. As, from the difference of quality, the same proportions of rice and milk will not always produce the same effect, the cook must use her discretion in adding, should it be needed, sufficient liquid to soften the rice perfectly: but she must bear in mind that if not boiled extremely thick and dry, it will be difficult to make it into croquettes.

RISSOLES. (ENTRÉE.)

This is the French name for small fried pastry of various forms, filled with meat or fish previously cooked; they may be made with *brioche*, or with light puff-paste, either of which must be rolled extremely thin. Cut it with a small round cutter fluted or plain; put a little rich mince, or good pounded meat, in the centre, and moisten the edges, and press them securely together that they may not burst open in the frying. The rissoles may be formed like small patties, by laying a second round of paste over the meat; or like *cannelons;* they may, likewise, be brushed with egg, and sprinkled with vermicelli, broken small, or with fine crumbs. They are sometimes made in the form of *croquettes*, the paste being gathered round the meat, which must form a ball.

In frying them, adopt the same plan as for the croquettes, raising the pan as soon as the paste is lightly coloured. Serve all these fried dishes well drained, and on a napkin.

From 5 to 7 minutes, or less.

VERY SAVOURY RISSOLES. (ENTRÉE.)

Make the forcemeat No. 1, page 122, sufficiently firm with unbeaten yolk of egg, to roll rather thin on a well-floured board; cut it into very small rounds, put a little pounded chicken in the centre of one half, moistening the edges with water, or white of egg, lay the remaining rounds over these, close them securely, and fry them in butter a fine light brown; drain and dry them well, and heap them in the middle of a hot dish, upon a napkin folded flat: these rissoles may be egged and crumbed before they are fried.

RISSOLES OF FISH. (ENTRÉE.)

Take perfectly clear from bones and skin, the flesh of any cold fish that can be pounded to an exceedingly fine paste; add to it, when in the mortar, from one quarter to a third as much of good butter, and a high seasoning of cayenne, with a moderate one of mace and nutmeg. To these may be added, at pleasure, a few shrimps, or a little of any of

the finer fish sauces, or some lobster-coral. When the whole is well
beaten and blended together, roll out some good puff-paste extremely
thin, and with a small round tin shape, cut out the number of rissoles
required; put some of the fish into each of these, moisten the edges
with white of egg, fold and press them securely together, and when all
are ready, slip them gently into a pan of boiling lard or butter; fry them
a pale brown, drain them well, and dry them on white blotting-paper,
laid upon a sieve, reversed; but do not place them sufficiently near to
scorch or to colour them.

TO BOIL PIPE MACCARONI.

We have found always the continental mode of dressing maccaroni the
best. English cooks sometimes soak it in milk and water for an hour
or more, before it is boiled, that the pipes may be swollen to the utmost,
but this is apt to render it pulpy, though its appearance may be improved by it.   Drop it lightly, and by degrees, into a large pan of fast-
boiling water, into which a little salt, and a bit of butter the size of a
walnut, have previously been thrown, and of which the boiling should
not be stopped by the addition of the maccaroni.   In from three quarters of an hour to an hour this will be sufficiently tender; it should
always be perfectly so, as it is otherwise indigestible, though the pipes
should remain entire.   Pour it into a large cullender, and drain the
water well from it.   It should be very softly boiled after the first minute
or two.

¾ to 1 hour.

RIBBAND MACCARONI.

This is dressed in precisely the same manner as the pipe maccaroni,
but requires only from fourteen to sixteen minutes' boiling in water,
and twenty or more in broth or stock.

DRESSED MACCARONI.

Four ounces of pipe maccaroni is sufficient for a small dish, but from
six to eight should be prepared for a family party where it is liked.
The common English mode of dressing it is with grated cheese, butter,
and cream, or milk.   French cooks substitute generally a spoonful or
two of very strong rich jellied gravy for the cream; and the Italians,
amongst their many other modes of serving it, toss it in rich brown
gravy, with sufficient grated cheese to flavour the whole strongly; they
send it to table also simply laid into a good *Espagnole* or brown gravy
(that drawn from the stufato, for example), accompanied by a plate of
grated cheese.   Another, and an easy mode of dressing it is to boil and
drain it well, and to put it into a deep dish, strewing grated cheese on
every layer, and adding bits of fresh butter to it.   The top, in this case,
should be covered with a layer of fine bread-crumbs, mixed with grated
cheese· these should be moistened plentifully with clarified butter, and
colour given to them in the oven, or before the fire; the crumbs may be
omitted, and a layer of cheese substituted for them.   An excellent preparation of maccaroni may be made with any well-flavoured, dry white
cheese, which can be grated easily, at much less cost than with the Parmesan, which is expensive, and in the country not always procurable
even; we think that the rich brown gravy is also a great advantage *to*
the dish, which is further improved by a tolerably high seasoning of

cayenne. These, however, are innovations on the usual modes of serving it in England.

After it has been boiled quite tender, drain it well, dissolve from two
to three ounces of good butter in a clean stewpan, with a few spoonsful
of rich cream, or of white sauce, lay in part of the maccaroni, strew
part of the cheese upon it, add the remainder of the maccaroni and the
cheese, and toss the whole gently until the ingredients are well incorporated, and adhere to the maccaroni, leaving no liquid perceptible :
serve it immediately.

Maccaroni, 6 ozs.; butter, 3 ozs.; Parmesan cheese, 6 ozs.; cream,
4 tablespoonsful.

Obs.—If preferred so, cheese may be strewed thickly over the maccaroni after it is dished, and just melted and browned with a salamander.

MACCARONI A LA REINE.

This is a very excellent and delicate mode of dressing maccaroni.
Boil eight ounces in the usual way (see page 302), and by the time it is
sufficiently tender, dissolve gently ten ounces of any rich, well-flavoured
white cheese in full three quarters of a pint of good cream ; add a little
salt, a rather full seasoning of cayenne, from half to a whole saltspoonful of pounded mace, and a couple of ounces of sweet fresh butter.
The cheese should, in the first instance, be sliced very thin, and taken
quite free of the hard part adjoining the rind ; it should be stirred in the
cream without intermission until it is entirely dissolved, and the whole
is perfectly smooth : the maccaroni, previously well-drained, may then
be tossed gently in it, or after it is dished, the cheese may be poured
equally over the maccaroni. The whole, in either case, may be thickly
covered before it is sent to table, with fine crumbs of bread fried of a
pale gold colour, and dried perfectly, either before the fire or in an oven,
when such an addition is considered an improvement. As a matter of
precaution, it is better to boil the cream before the cheese is melted
in it; rich white sauce, or béchamel, made not very thick, with an
additional ounce or two of butter, may be used to vary and enrich this
preparation. If Parmesan cheese* be used for it, it must of course be
grated. Half the quantity may be served.

Maccaroni, ½ lb.; cheese, 10 ozs.; good cream, ¾ pint (or rich white
sauce); butter, 2 ozs. (or more); little salt, *fine* cayenne, and mace.

FORCED EGGS FOR SALAD.

Boil six fresh eggs for twelve minutes, and when they are perfectly
cold, halve them lengthwise, take out the yolks, pound them to a paste
with a third of their volume of fresh butter; then add a quarter teaspoonful of mace, and as much cayenne as will season the mixture well;
beat these together thoroughly, and fill the whites of egg neatly with
them. A morsel of garlic, not larger than a pea, perfectly blended with the
other ingredients, would to some tastes greatly improve this preparation.

Eggs, 6; butter, size of 2 yolks; mace, ¼ teaspoonful; cayenne, third
as much.

FORCED EGGS, OR EGGS EN SURPRISE. (ENTREMETS.)

Boil, and divide, as in the receipt above, half a dozen very fresh eggs,

---

* The Parmesan being apt to gather into lumps, instead of mingling smoothly with
the liquid, had better be avoided for this dish.

pound the yolks perfectly, first by themselves, then with three ounces of good butter, a seasoning of salt, cayenne, and nutmeg, or mace, a large teaspoonful or more of minced parsley, and the yolks of two raw eggs. Slice a small bit off the whites to make them stand flat, hollow the insides well, fill them smoothly with the yolks, form a small dome in the centre of the dish with the remainder of the mixture, and lean the eggs against it, placing them regularly round. Set them into a gentle oven for ten minutes,* and send them quickly to table.

CHAPTER XX.

SWEET DISHES, OR ENTREMETS.

TO PREPARE CALF'S FEET STOCK.†

THE feet are usually sent in from the butcher's ready to dress, but as a matter of economy‡ or of convenience it is sometimes desirable to have them altogether prepared by the cook. Dip them into cold water, lay them into a deep pan, and sprinkle equally over them on both sides some rosin in fine powder; pour in as much boiling water as will cover them well, and let them remain for a minute or two untouched; then scrape the hair clean from them with the edge of a knife. When this is done, wash them very thoroughly both in hot and in cold water; divide them at the joint, split the claws, and take away the fat that is between them. Should the feet be large, put a gallon of cold water to the four, but from a pint to a quart less if they be of moderate size or small. Boil them gently down until the flesh has parted entirely from the bones, and the liquor is reduced nearly or quite half; strain, and let it stand until cold; remove every particle of fat from the top before it is used, and be careful not to take the sediment.

Calf's feet, (large) 4; water, 1 gallon: 6 to 7 hours.

TO CLARIFY CALF'S FEET STOCK.

Break up a quart of the stock, put it into a clean stewpan with the whites of five large or of six small eggs, two ounces of sugar, and the strained juice of a small lemon; place it over a gentle fire, and do not stir it after the scum begins to form; when it has boiled five or six minutes, if the liquid part be clear, turn it into a jelly-bag, and pass it through a second time should it not be perfectly transparent the first. To consumptive patients, and others requiring restoratives, but forbidden to take stimulants, the jelly thus prepared is often very acceptable, and may be taken with impunity, when it would be highly injurious made with wine. More white of egg is required to clarify it than when sugar and acid are used in large quantities, as both of these assist the process. For blamange omit the lemon-juice, and mix with the clarified stock an

---

* Half of one of the raw egg-yolks may be omitted, and a spoonful of rich cream used instead; the eggs can also be steamed until the insides are firm, by placing them with a little good gravy, or white sauce, in a stewpan, and simmering them gently from fifteen to twenty minutes.

† For fuller and better directions for this, see page 160, Chapter IX.

‡ They are sold at a much lower price when not cleared from the hair.

equal proportion of cream (for an invalid new milk), with the usual
flavouring, and weight of sugar; or pour the boiling stock very gradually to some finely pounded almonds, and express it from them as
directed for Quince Blamange, allowing from six to eight ounces to the
pint.

Stock, 1 quart; whites of eggs, 5; sugar, 2 ozs.; juice, 1 small lemon:
5 to 8 minutes.

TO CLARIFY ISINGLASS.

The finely-cut purified isinglass, which is now in general use, requires no clarifying except for clear jellies: for all other dishes it is
sufficient to dissolve, skim, and pass it through a muslin strainer.
When two ounces are required for a dish, put two and a half into a
delicately clean pan, and pour on it a pint of spring water which has
been gradually mixed with a teaspoonful of beaten white of egg; stir
these thoroughly together, and let them heat slowly by the side of a
gentle fire, but do not allow the isinglass to stick to the pan. When
the scum is well risen, which it will be after two or three minutes' simmering, clear it off, and continue the skimming until no more appears,
then, should the quantity of liquid be more than is needed, reduce it by
quick boiling to the proper point, strain it through a thin muslin, and
set it by for use: it will be perfectly transparent, and may be mixed
lukewarm with the clear and ready sweetened juice of various fruits, or
used with the necessary proportion of syrup, for jellies flavoured with
choice liquors. As the clarifying reduces the strength of the isinglass,—
or rather as a portion of it is taken up by the white egg,—an additional
quarter to each ounce must be allowed for this: if the scum be laid to
drain on the back of a fine sieve which has been wetted with hot water,
a little very strong jelly will drip from it.

Isinglass, 2½ ozs.; water, 1 pint; beaten white of egg, 1 teaspoonful.

SPINACH GREEN, FOR COLOURING SWEET DISHES, CONFECTIONARY, OR SOUPS.

Pound quite to a pulp, in a marble or wedgewood mortar, a handful
or two of young freshly-gathered spinach, then throw it into u hair-
sieve, and press through all the juice that can be obtained from it; pour
this into a clean white jar, and place it in a pan of water that is at the
point of boiling, and which must be allowed to just simmer afterwards;
in three or four minutes the juice will be poached or *set;* take it then
gently with a spoon, and lay it upon the back of a fine sieve to drain.
If wanted for immediate use, merely mix it in the mortar with some
finely-powdered sugar;* but if to be kept as a store, pound it with as
much as will render the whole tolerably dry, boil it to candy-height
over a very clear fire, pour it out in cakes, and keep them in a tin
box or canister. For this last preparation consult the receipt for orange-
flower candy.

PREPARED APPLE, OR QUINCE JUICE.

Pour into a clean earthen pan two quarts of spring water, and throw
into it as quickly as they can be pared, cored, and weighed, four pounds
of nonsuches, pippins, or any other good boiling apples of fine flavour
When all are done stew them gently until they are well broken, but

* For soup, dilute it first with a little of the boiling stock, and stir it to the remainder

not reduced quite to pulp; turn them into a jelly-bag or strain the juice from them without pressure through a closely-woven cloth, which should be gathered over the fruit, and tied, and suspended above a deep pan until the juice ceases to drop from it: this, if not very clear, must be rendered so before it is used for syrup or jelly, but for all other purposes once straining it will be sufficient. Quinces are prepared in the same way, and with the same proportions of fruit and water, but they must not be too long boiled, or the juice will become red. We have found it answer well to have them simmered until they are perfectly tender, and then to leave them with their liquor in a bowl until the following day, when the juice will be rich and clear. They should be thrown into the water very quickly after they are pared and weighed, as the air will soon discolour them.

Water, 2 quarts; apples, or quinces, 4 lbs.

COCOA-NUT FLAVOURED MILK. (*For sweet dishes, &c.*)

Pare the dark outer rind from a very fresh nut, and grate it on a fine and exceedingly clean grater; to every three ounces pour a quart of new milk, and simmer them *very softly* for three quarters of an hour, or more, that a full flavour of the nut may be imparted to the milk without its being much reduced; strain it through a fine sieve, or cloth, with sufficient pressure to leave the nut almost dry: it may then be used for blamange, custards, rice, and other puddings, light cakes and bread.

To each quart new milk, 3 ozs. grated cocoa-nut: ¾ to 1 hour.

Obs.—The milk of the nut, when perfectly sweet and good, may be added to the other with advantage. To obtain it, bore one end of the shell with a gimlet, and catch the liquid in a cup; and to extricate the kernel, break the shell with a hammer: this is better than sawing it asunder.

COMPOTES OF FRUIT.

We would particularly invite the attention of the reader to these wholesome and agreeable preparations of fruit, which are much less served at English tables, generally, than they deserve to be. We have found them often peculiarly acceptable to persons of delicate habit who were forbidden to partake of pastry in any form; and accompanied by a dish of boiled rice, they are very preferable for children, as well as for invalids, to either tarts or puddings.

Compote of spring fruit.—(Rhubarb.) Take a pound of the stalks after they are pared, and cut them into short lengths, have ready a quarter-pint of water boiled gently for ten minutes with five ounces of sugar, or with six should the fruit be very acid; put it in, and simmer it for about ten minutes. Some kinds will be tender in rather less time, some will require more.

Obs.—Good sugar in lumps should be used generally for these dishes and when they are intended for dessert the syrup should be enriched with an additional ounce or two. Lisbon sugar will answer for them very well on ordinary occasions, but that which is refined will render them much more delicate.

Compote of green currants. — Spring water half pint; sugar five ounces; boiled together ten minutes. One pint of green currants stripped from the stalks; simmered three to five minutes.

Compote of green gooseberries.—This is an excellent compote if made

with fine sugar, and very good with any kind.   Break five ounces into
small lumps and pour on them half a pint of water ; boil these gently for
ten minutes, and clear off all the scum ; then add to them a pint of fresh
gooseberries freed from the tops and stalks, washed, and well drained.
Simmer them gently from eight to ten minutes, and serve them hot or
cold.   Increase the quantity for a large dish.

Compote of green apricots.—Wipe the down from a pound of quite
young apricots, and stew them *very* gently for nearly twenty minutes in
syrup made with eight ounces of sugar and three quarters of a pint of
water, boiled together the usual time.

Compote of red currants.—A quarter-pint of water and five ounces
of sugar : ten minutes.   One pint of ready picked currants to be just
simmered in the syrup from five to six minutes.   This receipt will serve
equally for raspberries, or for a compote of the two fruits mixed together.   Either of them will be found an admirable accompaniment to
batter, custard, bread, ground rice, and various other kinds of puddings,
as well as to whole rice plainly boiled.

Compote of cherries.—Simmer five ounces of sugar with half a pint
of water for ten minutes ; throw into the syrup a pound of cherries
weighed after they are stalked, and let them stew gently for twenty
minutes ; it is a great improvement to stone the fruit, but a larger
quantity will then be required for a dish.

Compote of Morella Cherries.—Boil together for fifteen minutes, five
ounces of sugar with half a pint of water ; add a pound and a quarter
of ripe Morella cherries, and simmer them *very* softly from five to seven
minutes ; this is a delicious compote.

Compote of Damsons. — Four ounces of sugar and half a pint of
water to be boiled for ten minutes ; one pound of damsons to be added,
and simmered gently from ten to twelve minutes.

Compote of the Magnum Bonum, or other large plums.—Boil six
ounces of sugar with half a pint of water the usual time ; take the
stalks from a pound of plums, and simmer them very softly for twenty
minutes.   Increase the proportion of sugar if needed, and regulate the
time as may be necessary for the different varieties of fruit.

Compote of bullaces.—The large, or shepherds' bullace, is very good
stewed, but will require a considerable quantity of sugar to render it
palatable, unless it be quite ripe.   Make a syrup with eight ounces, and
three-quarters of a pint of water, and boil in it gently from fifteen to
twenty minutes, a pint and a half of the bullaces freed from their stalks.

COMPOTE OF PEACHES.

Pare half a dozen ripe peaches, and stew them very softly from eighteen to twenty minutes, keeping them often turned in a light syrup,
made with five ounces of sugar, and half a pint of water boiled together
for ten minutes.   Dish the fruit ; reduce the syrup by quick boiling,
pour it over the peaches, and serve them hot for a second-course dish, or
cold for dessert.   They should be quite ripe, and will be found delicious
dressed thus.   A little lemon-juice may be added to the syrup, and the
blanched kernels of two or three peach or apricot stones.

Sugar, 5 ozs. ; water, ½ pint : 10 minutes.   Peaches, 6 : 18 to 20
minutes.

Obs.—Nectarines, without being pared, may be dressed in the same way, but will require to be stewed somewhat longer, unless they be perfectly ripe.

ANOTHER RECEIPT FOR STEWED PEACHES.

Should the fruit be not perfectly ripe, throw it into boiling water and keep it just simmering, until the skin can be easily stripped off. Have ready half a pound of fine sugar boiled to a light syrup with three quarters of a pint of water; throw in the peaches, let them stew softly until quite tender, and turn them often that they may be equally done; after they are dished, add a little strained lemon-juice to the syrup, and reduce it by a few minutes' very quick boiling. The fruit is sometimes pared, divided, and stoned, then gently stewed until it is tender.

Sugar, 8 ozs.; water, ¾ pint: 10 to 12 minutes. Peaches, 6 or 7; lemon-juice, 1 large teaspoonful.

STEWED BARBERRIES, OR COMPOTE D'EPINE-VINETTE.

Boil to a thin syrup half a pound of sugar and three quarters of a pint of water, skim it well, and throw into it three quarters of a pound of barberries stripped from the stalks; keep them pressed down into the syrup, and gently stirred: from five to seven minutes will boil them.

Sugar, 8 ozs.; water, ¾ pint: 12 to 15 minutes. Barberries, ¾ lb.: 5 to 7 minutes.

ANOTHER COMPOTE OF BARBERRIES FOR DESSERT.

When this fruit is first ripe it requires, from its excessive acidity, nearly its weight of sugar to render it palatable; but after hanging some time upon the trees it becomes much mellowed in flavour, and may be sufficiently sweetened with a smaller proportion. According to the state of the fruit then, take for each pound (leaving it in bunches) from twelve to sixteen ounces of sugar, and boil it with three quarters of a pint of water until it forms a syrup. Throw in the bunches of fruit, and simmer them for five or six minutes. If their weight of sugar be used, they will become in that time perfectly transparent. As all vessels of tin affect the colour of the barberries, they should be boiled in a copper stewpan, or in a German enamelled one, which would be far better.

Barberries, 1 lb.; sugar, 12 to 16 ozs.; water, ¾ pint: fruit simmered in syrup, 5 to 6 minutes.

GATEAU DE POMMES.

Boil together for fifteen minutes a pound of well-refined sugar and half a pint of water; then add a couple of pounds of nonsuches, or of any other finely-flavoured apples which can be boiled easily to a smooth pulp, and the juice of a couple of small, or of one very large lemon. Stew these gently until the mixture is perfectly free from lumps, then boil it quickly, keeping it stirred, without quitting it, until it forms a very thick and dry marmalade. A few minutes before it is done add the finely grated rinds of a couple of lemons; when it leaves the bottom of the preserving-pan visible and dry, press it into moulds of tasteful form; and either store it for winter use, or if wanted for table, serve it plain for dessert, or ornament it with spikes of blanched almonds, and pour a custard round it for a second-course dish.

Sugar, 1 lb.; water, ½ pint: 15 minutes. Nonsuches or other apples, 2 lbs.; juice, 1 large or 2 small lemons: 2 hours or more.

GATEAU OF MIXED FRUITS. (GOOD.)

Extract the juice from some fresh red currants by simmering them very gently for a few minutes over a slow fire; strain it through a folded muslin, and to one pound of it add a pound and a half of non-suches or of freshly gathered apples, pared, and rather deeply cored, that the fibrous part of the apple may be avoided. Boil these quite slowly until the mixture is perfectly smooth, then, to evaporate part of the moisture, let the boiling be quickened. In from twenty-five to thirty minutes draw the pan from the fire, and throw in gradually a pound and a quarter of sugar in fine powder; mix it well with the fruit, and when it is dissolved continue the boiling rapidly for twenty minutes longer, keeping the mixture constantly stirred; put it into a mould, and store it, when cold, for winter use, or serve it for dessert, or for the second course: in the latter case decorate it with spikes of almonds blanched, and heap solid whipped cream round it, or pour a custard into the dish. For dessert, it may be garnished with dice of the palest apple-jelly.

Juice of red currants, 1 lb.; apples (pared and cored), 1½ lb.: 25 to 30 minutes. Sugar, 1½ lb.: 20 minutes.

Obs.—A portion of raspberries, if still in season, may be mixed with the currants for this gâteau, should their flavour be liked.

JELLIES.

CALF'S FEET JELLY. (ENTREMETS.)

We hear inexperienced housekeepers frequently complain of the difficulty of rendering this jelly perfectly transparent; but, by mixing with the other ingredients, while quite cold, the whites, and the crushed *shells* of a sufficient number of eggs, and allowing the head of scum which gathers on the jelly to remain undisturbed after it once forms, they will scarcely fail to obtain it clear. It should be strained through a thick flannel-bag of a conical form (placed before the fire, should the weather be at all cold, or the mixture will jelly before it has run through), and if not perfectly clear it must be strained again and again until it becomes so; though we generally find that once suffices. Mix thoroughly in a large stewpan five half-pints of strong calf's-feet stock (see page 304,) a full pint of sherry, half a pound of sugar, roughly powdered, the juice of two fine lemons, the rind of one and a half, cut very thin, the whites and shells of four large eggs, and half an ounce of isinglass. Let these remain a few minutes off the fire, that the sugar may dissolve more easily; then let the jelly be brought to boil gradually, and do not stir it after it begins to heat. When it has boiled gently sixteen minutes, draw it from the fire, and let it stand a short time before it is poured into the jelly-bag, under which a bowl should be placed to receive it. When clear and cool, put it into the moulds which have been laid for some hours in water: these should always be of earthenware in preference to metal. If to be served in glasses, or *roughed*, the jelly will be sufficiently firm without the isinglass, of which, however, we recommend a small quantity to be thrown in always when the jelly begins to boil, as it facilitates the clearing.

Calf's feet stock, 2½ pints; sugar, ½ lb.; sherry, 1 pint; juice of lemons, 2 *large*; rind of 1½; whites and shells of eggs, 4 large, or 5 small: 16 minutes.

Obs. 1.—After all the jelly has dropped through the bag, an exceedingly agreeable beverage may be obtained by pouring in some boiling water; from one to three half-pints, according to the quantity of jelly which has been made. The same plan should be pursued in making orange or lemon jelly for an invalid.

Obs. 2.—As it is essential to the transparency of calf's-feet jelly of all kinds that the whole of the ingredients should be quite cold when they are mixed, and as the stock can only be measured in a liquid state, to which it must be reduced by heating, the better plan is, to measure it when it is first strained from the feet, and to put apart the exact quantity required for a receipt; but when this has not been done, and it is necessary to liquefy it, it must be left until quite cold again before it is used.

ANOTHER RECEIPT FOR CALF'S FEET JELLY.

To four calf's feet, well cleaned and divided, pour a gallon of water, and let them stew until it is reduced to rather less than two quarts; or if, after the flesh has quite fallen from the bones, the liquor on being strained off should exceed that quantity, reduce it by rapid boiling in a clean uncovered pan over a very clear fire. When it is perfectly firm and cold, take it, clear of fat and sediment, and add to it a bottle of sherry, which should be of good quality (for poor, thin wines are not well adapted to the purpose), three quarters of a pound of sugar broken small, the juice of five large or of six moderate-sized lemons, and the whites, with the shells finely crushed, of seven eggs, or of more, should they be very small. The rinds of three lemons, pared exceedingly thin, may be thrown into the jelly a few minutes before it is taken from the fire; or they may be put into the jelly-bag previously to its being poured through, when they will impart to it a slight and delicate flavour, without deepening its colour much. If it is to be moulded, something more than half an ounce of isinglass should be dropped lightly in where the liquid becomes visible through the head of scum, when the mixture begins to boil; for if not sufficiently firm, it will break when it is dished. It may be roughed, or served in glasses without this addition; and in a liquid state will be found an admirable ingredient for Oxford, or other punch.

Calf's feet, 4; water, 1 gallon; to be reduced more than half. Sherry, 1 bottle; sugar, ¾ lb. (more to taste); juice of 5 large lemons, or of six moderate-sized; whites and shells of 7 eggs, or more if small; rinds of lemons, 3 (for moulding, nearly ¾ oz. of isinglass): 15 to 20 minutes.

Obs.—An excellent and wholesome jelly for young people may be made with good orange or raisin wine, instead of sherry; to either of these the juice of three or four oranges, with a small portion of the rind, may be added instead of part of the lemons.

APPLE CALF'S FEET JELLY.

Pour a quart of prepared apple-juice (see page 305) on a pound of fresh apples pared and cored, and simmer them until they are well broken; strain the juice, and let it stand until cold; then measure, and put a pint and a half of it into a stewpan with a quart of calf's feet stock (see page 304), nine ounces of sugar broken small, or roughly pounded, the juice of two fine lemons, and the thin rinds of one and a half, with the whites and shells of eight eggs. Let it boil gently for ten minutes, then strain it through a flannel-bag, and when cool put it into moulds. It will be very clear, and firm, and of pleasant flavour. Apples of good quality should be used for it, and the quantity of sugar must be regulated by the time of year, as the fruit will have lost much of its acidity during the latter part of the season. This receipt, which is the result of our own experiment, and which we have found very successful, was first tried just after Christmas, with pippins. A little syrup of preserved ginger, or a small glass of fine white brandy, would perhaps, to some tastes, improve the jelly; but we give it simply as we have had it proved ourselves.

Prepared apple juice, 1 quart; fresh apples, 1 lb.: $\frac{1}{4}$ to $\frac{3}{4}$ hour. Strained juice, 1$\frac{1}{2}$ pint; calf's feet stock, 1 quart; sugar, 9 ozs.; juice of lemons, 2; rind of 1$\frac{1}{2}$; whites and shells of eggs, 8: 10 minutes.

Obs.—We would recommend the substitution of quinces for apples in this receipt as likely to afford a very agreeable variety of the jelly: or equal portions of the two fruits might answer well.

Unless the stock be very stiff, add isinglass to this, as to the calf's feet jelly, when it is to be moulded.

ORANGE CALF'S FEET JELLY.

To a pint and a half of firm calf's feet stock, put a pint of strained China orange-juice, mixed with that of one or two lemons; add to these six ounces of sugar, broken small, the *very* thin rinds of three oranges and of one lemon, and the whites of six eggs with half the shells crushed small. Stir these gently over a clear fire until the head of scum begins to form, but not at all afterwards. Simmer the jelly for ten minutes from the first *full* boil; take it from the fire, let it stand a little, then pour it through a jelly-bag until perfectly clear. This is an original, and entirely new receipt, which we can recommend to the reader, the jelly being very pale, beautifully transparent, and delicate in flavour: it would, we think, be peculiarly acceptable to such invalids as are forbidden to take wine in any form.

The proportions both of sugar and of lemon-juice must be somewhat varied according to the season in which the oranges are used.

Strong calf's feet stock, 1$\frac{1}{2}$ pint; strained orange-juice, mixed with a small portion of lemon-juice, 1 pint; sugar, 6 ozs.; rinds of oranges, 3; of lemon, 1: 10 minutes.

Obs.—A small pinch of isinglass thrown into the jelly when it begins to boil will much assist to clear it. When the flavour of Seville oranges is liked, two or three can be used with the sweet ones.

ORANGE ISINGLASS JELLY.

To render this perfectly transparent the juice of the fruit must be filtered, and the isinglass clarified; but it is not usual to take so much trouble for it. Strain as clear as possible, first through a sieve or muslin, then through a thick cloth or jelly-bag, one quart of orange-juice, mixed with as much lemon-juice as will give an agreeable degree of acidity. Dissolve two ounces and a half of isinglass in a pint of water, skim it well, throw in half a pound of sugar, and a few strips of the orange-rind, pour in the orange-juice, stir the whole well together, skim it clean without allowing it to boil, strain it through a cloth or through a muslin, many times folded, and when nearly cold put it into the moulds.* This jelly is sometimes made without any water, by dissolving the isinglass and sugar in the juice of the fruit.

Orange-juice, 1 quart; water, 1 pint; isinglass, 2½ ozs.; sugar, ½ lb.

ORANGES FILLED WITH JELLY.

This is one of the fanciful dishes which make a pretty appearance on a supper table, and are acceptable when much variety is desired. Take some very fine oranges, and with the point of a small knife cut out from the top of each a round about the size of a shilling; then with the small end of a tea or egg spoon, empty them entirely, taking great care not to break the rinds. Throw these into cold water, and make jelly of the juice, which must be well pressed from the pulp, and strained as clear as possible. Colour one half a fine rose colour with prepared cochineal, and leave the other very pale; when it is nearly cold, drain and wipe the orange rinds, and fill them with alternate stripes of the two jellies; when they are perfectly cold cut them in quarters, and dispose them tastefully in a dish with a few light branches of myrtle between them. Calf's feet or any other variety of jelly, or different blamanges, may be used at choice to fill the rinds: the colours, however, should contrast as much as possible.

LEMON CALF'S FEET JELLY.

Break up a quart of strong calf's feet stock, which should have been measured while in a liquid state; let it be quite clear of fat and sediment, for which a small additional quantity should be allowed; add to it a not very full half-pint of strained lemon-juice, and ten ounces of sugar, broken small (rather more or less according to the state of the fruit), the rind of one lemon pared as thin as possible, or from two to three when a full flavour of it is liked, and the whites, with part of the shells crushed small, of five large or of six small eggs. Proceed as for the preceding jellies, and when the mixture has boiled five minutes throw in a small pinch of isinglass; continue the boiling for five or six minutes longer, draw the pan from the fire, let it stand to settle; then turn it into the jelly-bag. We have found it always perfectly clear with once passing through; but should it not be so, pour it in a second time.

Strong calf's feet stock, 1 quart; strained lemon-juice, short ½ pint; sugar, 10 ozs. (more or less according to state of fruit); rind of from 1 to 3 large lemons; whites and part of shells of 5 large or 6 small eggs: 5 minutes. Pinch of isinglass: 5 minutes longer.

Obs.—About seven large lemons will produce the half pint of juice. This quantity is for one mould only. The jelly will be found almost colourless unless much of the rinds be used, and as perfectly transparent as clear spring water: it is also very agreeable in flavour. For variety,

* In France, orange-jelly is very commonly served in the halved rinds of the fruit, or in little baskets.

part of the juice of the fruit might be omitted, and its place supplied by maraschino, or any other rich white liquor of appropriate flavour.

CONSTANTIA JELLY.

Infuse in a pint of water for five minutes the rind of half a Seville orange, pared extremely thin; add an ounce of isinglass; and when this is dissolved throw in four ounces of good sugar in lumps; stir well, and simmer the whole for a few minutes, then mix with it four large wineglassesful of Constantia, and strain the jelly through a fine cloth of close texture; let it settle and cool, then pour it gently from any sediment there may be, into a mould which has been laid for an hour or two into water. We had this jelly made in the first instance, for an invalid who was forbidden to take acids, and it proved so agreeable in flavour that we can recommend it for the table. The isinglass, with an additional quarter ounce, might be clarified, and the sugar and orange-rind boiled with it afterwards.

Water, 1 pint; rind ½ Seville orange: 5 minutes. Isinglass, 1 oz.; sugar, 4 ozs.: 5 to 7 minutes. Constantia, 4 large wineglassesful.

STRAWBERRY ISINGLASS JELLY.

A great variety of equally elegant and excellent jellies for the table may be made with clarified isinglass, clear syrup, and the juice of almost any kind of fresh fruit; but as the process of making them is nearly the same for all, we shall limit our receipts to one or two, which will serve to direct the makers for the rest. Boil together quickly for fifteen minutes one pint of water and three quarters of a pound of very good sugar; measure a quart of ripe richly-flavoured strawberries without their stalks; the scarlet answer best from the colour which they give; on these pour the boiling syrup, and let them stand all night. The next day clarify two ounces and a half of isinglass in a pint of water, as directed at the beginning of this chapter; drain the syrup from the strawberries very closely, add to it two or three tablespoonsful of red currant juice, and the *clear* juice of one large or of two small lemons; and when the isinglass is nearly cold mix the whole, and put it into moulds. The French, who excel in these fruit-jellies, always mix the separate ingredients when they are almost cold; and they also place them over ice for an hour or so after they are moulded, which is a great advantage, as they then require less isinglass, and are in consequence much more delicate. When the fruit abounds, instead of throwing it into the syrup, bruise lightly from three to four pints, throw two tablespoonsful of sugar over it, and let the juice flow from it for an hour or two; then pour a little water over, and use the juice without boiling, which will give a jelly of finer flavour than the other.

Water, 1 pint; sugar, ¾ lb.: 15 minutes. Strawberries, 1 quart, isinglass, 2½ ozs.; water, 1 pint (white of egg 1 to 2 teaspoonsful)· juice, 1 large or 2 small lemons.

Obs.—The juice of any fruit mixed with sufficient sugar to sweeten, and of isinglass to stiffen it, with as much lemon-juice as will take off the insipidity of the flavour, will serve for this kind of jelly. Pine apples, peaches, and such other fruits as do not yield much juice, must ·be infused in a larger quantity of syrup, which must then be used in ieu of it. In this same manner jellies are made with various kinds of wine and liquors, and with the ingredients for punch as well; but we cannot further multiply our receipts for them.

To give greater transparency of appearance to jelly, it is often made in a mould with a cylindrical tube in the centre. The space left in the centre is sometimes filled with very light, whipped cream, flavoured and coloured so as to eat agreeably with it, and to please the eye as well: this may be tastefully garnished with preserved, or with fresh fruit. Italian jelly is made by half filling a mould of this, or any of more convenient shape, and laying round upon it in a chain, as soon as it is set, some blamange made rather firm, and cut of equal thickness and size with a small round cutter; the mould is then filled with the remainder of the jelly, which must be nearly cold, but not beginning to set. Brandied morella cherries, drained very dry, are sometimes dropped into moulds of pale jelly; and fruits, either fresh or preserved, are arranged in them with exceedingly good effect when skilfully managed; but this is best accomplished by having a mould for the purpose, with another of smaller size fixed in it by means of slight wires, which hook on to the edge of the outer one. By pouring water into this it may easily be detached from the jelly; the fruit is then to be placed in the space left by it, and the whole filled up with more jelly : to give the proper effect, it must be recollected that the dish will be *reversed* when sent to table.

QUEEN MAB'S PUDDING; (*an elegant summer dish.*)

Throw into a pint of new milk the thin rind of a small lemon, and six or eight bitter almonds, blanched and bruised; or substitute for these half a pod of vanilla, cut small, heat it slowly by the side of the fire, and keep it at the point of boiling until it is strongly flavoured, then add a small pinch of salt, and three quarters of an ounce of the finest isinglass, or a full ounce should the weather be extremely warm; when this is dissolved, strain the milk through a muslin, and put it into a clean saucepan, with four ounces and a half of sugar in lumps, and half a pint of rich cream; give the whole one boil, and then stir it briskly and by degrees to the well-beaten yolks of six fresh eggs; next, thicken the mixture as a custard, over a gentle fire, but do not hazard its curdling; when it is of tolerable consistency, pour it out, and continue the stirring until it is half cold, then mix with it an ounce and a half of candied citron, cut in small spikes, and a couple of ounces of dried cherries, and pour it into a mould rubbed with a drop of oil: when turned out it will have the appearance of a pudding. From two to three ounces of preserved ginger, well drained and sliced, may be substituted for the cherries, and an ounce of pistachio-nuts, blanched and split, for the citron; these will make an elegant variety of the dish, and the syrup of the ginger, poured round as sauce, will be a further improvement. Currants steamed until tender, and candied orange or lemon-rind, are often used instead of the cherries, and the well-sweetened juice of strawberries, raspberries (white or red), apricots, peaches, or syrup of pine-apple, will make an agreeable sauce; a small quantity of this last will also give a delicious flavour to the pudding itself, when mixed with the other ingredients. Cream may be substituted entirely for the milk, when its richness is considered desirable.

New milk, 1 pint; rind 1 small lemon; bitter almonds, 6 to 8 (or, vanilla, ½ pod); salt, few grains; isinglass, ¾ oz. (1 oz. in sultry wea-ther); sugar, 4½ oz.; cream, ½ pint; yolks, 6 eggs; dried cherries, 2 ozs.; candied citron, 1½ oz.; (or preserved ginger, 2 to 3 ozs., and the syrup as sauce, and 1 oz. of blanched pistachio-nuts; or 4 ozs. currants, steamed 20 minutes, and 2 ozs. candied orange-rind). For sauce, sweetened juice of strawberries, raspberries, or plums, or pine-apple syrup.

Obs.—The currants should be steamed in an earthen cullender, placed over a saucepan of boiling water, and covered with the lid. It will be a *great* improvement to place the pudding over ice for an hour before it is served.

NESSELRODE CREAM.

Shell and blanch twenty-four fine Spanish chestnuts, and put them with three quarters of a pint of water into a small and delicately clean saucepan. When they have simmered from six to eight minutes, add to them two ounces of fine sugar, and let them stew very gently until they are perfectly tender; then drain them from the water, pound them, while still warm, to a smooth paste, and press them through the back of a fine sieve. While this is being done, dissolve half an ounce of isinglass in two or three spoonsful of water, and put to it as much cream as will, with the small quantity of water used, make half a pint; two ounces of sugar, about the third of a pod of vanilla, cut small, and well bruised, and a strip or two of fresh lemon-rind, pared extremely thin. Give these a minute's boil, and then keep them quite hot by the side of the fire, until a strong flavour of the vanilla is obtained. Now, mix gradually with the chestnuts half a pint of rich, unboiled cream, strain the other half pint through a fine muslin, and work the whole well to-gether until it becomes *very* thick; then stir to it a couple of ounces of dried cherries, cut into quarters, and two of candied citron, divided into very small dice. Press the mixture into a mould which has been rubbed with a particle of the purest salad-oil, and in a few hours it will be ready for table. The cream should be sufficiently stiff, when the fruit is added, to prevent its sinking to the bottom, and both kinds should be *dry* when they are used.

Chestnuts, large, 24; water, ¾ pint; sugar, 2 ozs.; isinglass, ½ oz.; water, 3 to 4 tablespoonsful; cream, nearly ½ pint; vanilla, ⅓ of pod; lemon-rind, ¼ of 1 large: infuse 20 minutes or more. Unboiled cream, ½ pint; dried cherries, 2 ozs.; candied citron, 2 ozs.

Obs.—When vanilla cannot easily be obtained, a little noyeau may be substituted for it, but a *full* weight of isinglass must then be used. This receipt is entirely new, and our directions must be followed with *exactness*, should the reader wish to ensure its success.

AN EXCELLENT TRIFLE.

Take equal parts of wine and brandy, about a wineglassful of each, or two thirds of good sherry or Madeira, and one of spirit, and soak in the mixture four sponge-biscuits, and half a pound of macaroons; cover the bottom of the trifle-dish with part of these, and pour upon them a full pint of rich boiled custard made with three quarters of a pint, or rather more, of milk and cream taken in equal portions, and six eggs; and sweetened, flavoured and thickened by the receipt of page 522, lay the remainder of the soaked cakes upon it, and pile over the whole, to the depth of two or three inches, the whipped syllabuh of page 318, previously well drained; then sweeten and flavour slightly with wine only, less than half a pint of thin cream (or of cream and milk mixed); wash and wipe the whisk, and whip it to the lightest possible froth: take it off with a skimmer and heap it gently over the trifle.

Macaroons, ½ lb.; wine and brandy mixed, ¼ pint; rich boiled custard, 1 pint; whipped syllabub (see page 318); light froth to cover the whole, short ½ pint of cream and milk mixed; sugar, dessertspoonful; wine, ½ glassful.

SWISS CREAM, OR TRIFLE; (*very good.*)

Flavour pleasantly with lemon-rind and cinnamon a pint of rich cream, after having taken from it as much as will mix smoothly to a thin batter four teaspoonsful of the finest flour; sweeten it with six ounces of well-refined sugar, in lumps; place it over a clear fire in a delicately clean saucepan, and when it boils stir in the flour, and simmer it for four or five minutes, stirring it gently without ceasing; then pour it out, and when it is quite cold mix with it by degrees the strained juice of two moderate-sized and very fresh lemons. Take a quarter of a pound of macaroons, cover the bottom of a glass dish with a portion of them, pour in a part of the cream, lay the remainder of the macaroons upon it, add the rest of the cream, and ornament it with candied citron, sliced thin. It should be made the day before it is wanted for table. The requisite flavour may be given to this dish by infusing in the cream the very thin rind of a lemon, and part of a stick of cinnamon, slightly bruised, and then straining it before the flour is added; or, these and the sugar may be boiled together, with two or three spoonsful of water, to a strongly flavoured syrup, which, after having been passed through a muslin strainer, may be stirred into the cream. Some cooks boil the cinnamon and the *grated* rind of a lemon with all the other ingredients, but the cream has then to be pressed through a sieve after it is made, a process which it is always desirable to avoid.

Rich cream, 1 pint; sugar, 6 ozs.; rind, 1 lemon; cinnamon, 1 drachm; flour, 4 teaspoonsful; juice, 2 lemons; macaroons, 4 ozs. candied citron, 1 to 2 ozs.

Chantilly Basket,

FILLED WITH WHIPPED CREAM AND FRESH STRAWBERRIES.

Take a mould of any sort that will serve to form the basket on, just dip the edge of some macaroons in melted barley sugar, and fasten them

together with it; take it out of the mould, keep it in a dry place until
wanted, then fill it high with whipped strawberry cream which has been
trained on a sieve from the preceding day, and stick very fine ripe
s'rawberries over it. It should not be filled until just before it is
served.

CREME MERINGUÉE.

Infuse in a pint of new milk the very thin rind of a lemon, with four
or five bitter almonds bruised. As the quantity should not be reduced,
it should be kept by the side of the fire until strongly flavoured, and not
be allowed to boil for more than two or three minutes. Sweeten it with
three ounces of fine sugar in lumps, and when this is dissolved, strain,
and mix the milk with half a pint of cream; then stir the whole gradually to the well-beaten yolks of six fresh eggs, and thicken it like
boiled custard. Put it, when cold, into a deep dish, beat to a solid froth
the whites of six eggs, mix them with five tablespoonsful of pounded
and sifted sugar, and spread them evenly over the custard, which should
be set immediately into a moderate oven, baked half an hour, and
served directly it is taken out.

New milk, 1 pint; rind of one lemon; bitter almonds, 5; sugar, 3
ozs.; cream, ½ pint; yolks of eggs, 6; frothed whites of eggs, 6;
sifted sugar, 5 tablespoonsful: baked, ½ hour.

Obs. — A layer of apricot, peach, or magnum bonum, marmalade
placed in the dish before the custard-mixture is poured in will convert
this into the gentleman commoner's pudding.

LEMON CREAM, MADE WITHOUT CREAM.

Pour on the very thin rinds of two fresh lemons, and a pound of fine
sugar broken small, or roughly powdered, one pint of boiling water, and
let them remain an hour; then add the whites of six eggs and the yolks
of two, previously well beaten together, and the juice of six lemons;
mix them thoroughly, strain the whole into a deep jug, set this into a
pan of boiling water, and stir the cream without quitting it until it is
well thickened; pour it out, and continue the stirring at intervals until
it is nearly cold, when it may be put into the glasses. In cool weather
this cream will remain good for several days, and it should always be
made at least twenty-four hours before it is served.

Lemon-rinds, 2; sugar, 1 lb.; water, 1 pint: 1 hour. Whites of 6
eggs; yolks of 2; juice of 6 lemons.

VERY GOOD LEMON CREAMS.

Pour over the very thin rinds of two moderate-sized but perfectly
sound fresh lemons, and six ounces of sugar, half a pint of spring water,
and let them remain six hours; then add the strained juice of the
lemons, and five fresh eggs well beaten, and also strained; take out the
lemon-rind, and stir the mixture without ceasing over a gentle fire until
it has boiled softly from six to eight minutes: it will not curdle as it
would did milk supply the place of the water and lemon-juice. The
creams are, we think, more delicate, though not quite so thick, when
the yolks only of six eggs are used for them. They will keep well for
nearly a week in really cold weather.

Rinds of lemons, 2; sugar, 6 ozs. (or 8 when a *very* sweet dish is
preferred); cold water, ½ pint: 6 hours. Juice of lemons, 2; eggs, 5,
to be boiled softly 6 to 8 minutes.

Obs.—Lemon creams may, on occasion, be more expeditiously prepared, by rasping the rind of the fruit upon the sugar which is used for them; or, by paring it thin, and boiling it for a few minutes with the lemon-juice, sugar, and water, before they are stirred to the eggs.

FRUIT CREAMS, AND ITALIAN CREAMS.

These are very quickly and easily made, by mixing with good cream a sufficient proportion of the sweetened juice of fresh fruit, or of well-made fruit jelly or jam, to flavour it: a few drops of prepared cochineal may be added to deepen the colour when it is required for any particular purpose. A quarter-pint of strawberry or of raspberry jelly will fully flavour a pint of cream: a very little lemon-juice improves almost all compositions of this sort. When jam is used it must first be gradually mixed with the cream, and then worked through a sieve, to take out the seed or skin of the fruit. All fresh juice, for this purpose, must, of course, be cold; that of strawberries is best obtained by crushing the fruit and strewing sugar over it. Peaches, pine-apple, apricots, or nectarines, may be simmered for a few minutes in a little syrup, and this, drained well from them, will serve extremely well to mix with the cream when it has become thoroughly cold: the lemon-juice should be added to all of these. When the ingredients are well blended, lightly whisk or mill them to a froth; take this off with a skimmer as it rises, and lay it upon a fine sieve reversed, to drain, or if it is to be served in glasses, fill them with it at once.

Italian creams are either fruit-flavoured only, or mixed with wine like syllabubs, then whisked to a stiff froth and put into a perforated mould, into which a muslin is first laid: or into a small hair-sieve (which must also first be lined with the muslin), and left to drain until the following day, when the cream must be very gently turned out, and dished, and garnished as fancy may direct.

VERY SUPERIOR WHIPPED SYLLABUBS

Weigh seven ounces of fine sugar and rasp on it the rinds of two fresh sound lemons of good size, then pound or roll it to powder, and put it into a bowl with the strained juice of the lemons, two large glasses of sherry, and two of brandy; when the sugar is nearly or quite dissolved add a pint of rich cream, and whisk or mill the mixture well; take off the froth as it rises, and put it into glasses. These syllabubs will remain good for several days, and should always be made, if possible, four and twenty hours before they are wanted for table. The full flavour of the lemon-rind is obtained with less trouble than in rasping, by paring it very thin indeed, and infusing it for some hours in the juice of the fruit.

Sugar, 7 ozs.; rind and juice of lemons, 2; sherry, 2 large wineglassesful; brandy, 2 wineglassesful; cream, 1 pint.

Obs.—These proportions are sufficient for two dozens or more of syllabubs: they are often made with almost equal quantities of wine and cream, but are certainly neither so good nor so wholesome without a portion of brandy.

BLAMANGES.

GOOD COMMON BLAMANGE, OR BLANC MANGER. (*Author's Receipt.*)

Infuse for an hour in a pint and three quarters of new milk the very thin rind of one small, or of half a large lemon and eight bitter almonds, blanched and bruised; then add two ounces of sugar, or rather more for persons who like the blamange very sweet, and an ounce and a half of isinglass. Boil them gently over a clear fire, stir-

Modern blamange or cake mould.

ring them often until this last is dissolved, take off the scum, stir in half a pint of rich cream, and strain the blamange into a bowl: it should be moved gently with a spoon until nearly cold to prevent the cream from settling on the surface. Before it is moulded, mix with it by de-grees a wineglassful of brandy.

New milk, 1¾ pint; rind of lemon, ½ large or whole small 1; bitter almonds, 8; infuse 1 hour. Sugar, 2 to 3 ozs.; isinglass, 1½ oz.: 10 minutes. Cream, ½ pint; brandy, 1 wineglassful.

RICHER BLAMANGE.

A pint of good cream with a pint of new milk, sweetened and fla-voured as above, or with a little additional sugar, and the rind of one very fresh lemon with the same proportion of isinglass will make very good blamange. A couple of ounces of almonds may be pounded and mixed with it, but they are not needed with the cream.

JAUMANGE, OR JAUNE MANGER; SOMETIMES CALLED DUTCH FLUMMERY.

Pour on the very thin rind of a large lemon, and half a pound of sugar broken small, a pint of water, and keep them stirred over a gentle fire until they have simmered for three or four minutes, then leave the saucepan by the side of the stove, that the syrup may taste well of the lemon. In ten or fifteen minutes afterwards add two ounces of isin-glass, and stir the mixture often until this is dissolved, then throw in the strained juice of four sound, moderate-sized lemons, and a pint of sherry; mix the whole briskly with the beaten yolks of eight fresh eggs, and then pass it through a delicately clean hair-sieve: next thicken it in a jar or jug placed in a pan of boiling water, turn it into a bowl, and when it has become cool, and been allowed to settle for a minute or two, pour it into moulds which have been laid in water. Some persons add a small glass of brandy to it, and deduct so much from the quantity of water.

Rind of 1 lemon; sugar, 8 ozs.; water, 1 pint: 3 or 4 minutes. Isinglass, 2 ozs.; juice, 4 lemons; yolks of 8 eggs; wine, 1 pint; brandy (at pleasure), 1 wineglassful.

EXTREMELY GOOD STRAWBERRY BLAMANGE.

Crush slightly, with a silver or a wooden spoon, a quart, measured without their stalks, of fresh and richly-flavoured strawberries; strew over them eight ounces of pounded sugar, and let them stand three or four hours; then turn them on to a fine hair-sieve reversed, and press

them through it.   Melt over a gentle fire two ounces of the best isinglass
in a pint of new milk, and sweeten it with four ounces of sugar; strain it
through a muslin, and mix it with a pint and a quarter of sweet thick
cream; keep these stirred until they are nearly or quite cold, then pour
them gradually to the strawberries, whisking them briskly together;
and last of all throw in, by small portions the strained juice of a fine
sound lemon.   Mould the blamange, and set it in a very cool place for
twelve hours or more, before it is served.

Strawberries stalked, 1 quart; sugar, 8 ozs.; isinglass, 2 oz.; new
milk, 1 pint; sugar, 4 ozs.; cream, 1¼ pint; juice, 1 lemon.

QUINCE BLAMANGE.   (*Delicious.*)

This, if carefully made, and with ripe quinces, is one of the most
richly-flavoured preparations of fruit that we have ever tasted; and the
receipt, we may venture to say, will be altogether new to the reader.
Dissolve in a pint of prepared juice of quinces (see page 305), an ounce
of the best isinglass; next, add ten ounces of sugar, roughly pounded,
and stir these together gently over a clear fire, from twenty to thirty
minutes, or until the juice jellies in falling from the spoon.   Remove
the scum carefully, and pour the boiling jelly gradually to half a pint
of thick cream, stirring them briskly together as they are mixed: they
must be stirred until very nearly cold, and then poured into a mould
which has been rubbed in every part with the smallest possible quantity
of very pure salad oil, or, if more convenient, into one that has been
dipped into cold water.

Juice of quinces, 1 pint; isinglass, 1 oz.: 5 to 10 minutes.   Sugar,
10 ozs.; 20 to 30 minutes.   Cream, ½ pint.

QUINCE BLAMANGE, WITH ALMOND CREAM.

When cream is not procurable, which will sometimes happen in the
depth of winter, almonds, if plentifully used, will afford a very good substitute, though the finer blamange is made from the foregoing receipt.
On four ounces of almonds, blanched and beaten to the smoothest paste,
and moistened in the pounding with a few drops of water, to prevent
their oiling, pour a pint of boiling quince-juice; stir them together, and
turn them into a strong cloth, of which let the ends be held and twisted
different ways by two persons, to express the cream from the almonds,
put the juice again on the fire, with half a pound of sugar, and when it
boils, throw in nearly an ounce of fine isinglass; simmer the whole for
five minutes, take off the scum, stir the blamange until it is nearly cold,
then mould it for table.   Increase the quantity both of this and of the
preceding blamange, when a large dish of either is required.

Quince-juice, 1 pint; almonds, 4 ozs.; sugar, ½ lb.; isinglass, nearly
1 oz.: 5 minutes.

APRICOT BLAMANGE, OR CREME PARISIENNE.

Dissolve gently an ounce of fine isinglass in a pint of new milk or of
thin cream, and strain it through a folded muslin; put it into a clean
saucepan, with three ounces of sugar, broken into small lumps, and
when it boils, stir to it half a pint of rich cream; add it, at first, by
spoonsful only, to eight ounces of the finest apricot jam, mix them very
smoothly, and stir the whole until it is nearly cold, that the jam may
not sink to the bottom of the mould: a tablespoonful of lemon-juice will
improve the flavour.

When cream is scarce, use milk instead, with an additional quarter-ounce of isinglass, and enrich it by pouring it boiling on the same proportion of almonds as for the second quince blamange (see page 320). Cream can in all cases be substituted entirely for the milk, when a very rich preparation is desired. Peach jam will answer admirably for this receipt; but none of any kind should be used for it which has not been passed through a sieve when made.

Isinglass, 1 oz.; new milk, 1 pint; cream, ½ pint; sugar, 3 ozs., apricot jam, ½ lb.; lemon-juice, 1 tablespoonful. Or: peach jam, ½ lb.; cream, 1½ pint.

BLAMANGE RUBANÉ, OR, STRIPED BLAMANGE.

Make in the ordinary way, but a little firmer, one quart or two of blamange, according to the number of moulds that are to be filled; divide it into three or four equal portions; add to one, sufficient prepared spinach-juice (see page 305), to colour it a full or a pale green; to another, some liquid cochineal or carmine; to a third, should further variety be desired, a few drops of strong infusion of saffron, or if its peculiar flavour be objected to, stir quickly some of the blamange quite boiling to the well-beaten yolks of three or four fresh eggs, and thicken it a little over a gentle fire with an additional spoonful or two of milk, for unless the whole be nearly of the same consistency, it will be liable to separate in the unmoulding. Chocolate, first boiled very smooth in a small quantity of water, will give an additional colour; and some firm, clear isinglass, or calf's-foot jelly, may be used for an occasional stripe, where great variety is desired. The different kinds of blamange should be poured into the mould in half-inch depths, when so cool as to be only just liquid, and one colour must be perfectly cold before another is added, or they will run together, and spoil the appearance of the dish. When ice is not procurable, the moulds in warm weather may be set into water, mixed with plenty of salt and saltpetre: the insides should be rubbed with a drop of very pure salad oil, instead of being laid into fresh water, as usual.

AN APPLE HEDGE-HOG, OR, SUÉDOISE.

This dish is formed of apples, pared, cored without being divided, and stewed tolerably tender in a light syrup. These are placed in a dish,

after being well drained, and filled with apricot, or any other rich marmalade, and arranged in two or more layers, so as to give, when the whole is complete, the form shown in the engraving. The number required must depend on the size of the dish. From three to five pounds more must be stewed down into a smooth and dry marmalade, and with this all the spaces between them are to be filled up, and the whole are to be covered with it; an icing of two eggs, beaten to a very solid froth, and mixed with two heaped tablespoonsful of sugar, must then be spread evenly over the suédoise, fine sugar sifted on this, and spikes of blanched almonds, cut lengthwise, stuck over the entire surface; the dish is then to be placed in a moderate oven until

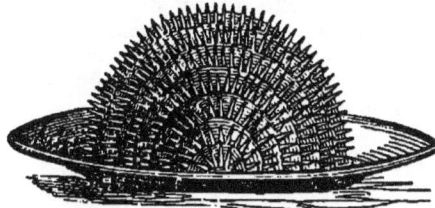

the almonds are browned, but not too deeply, and the apples are hot through. It is not easy to give the required form with less than fifteen apples; eight of these may first be simmered in a syrup made with half a pint of water and six ounces of sugar, and the remainder may be thrown in after these are lifted out. Care must be taken to keep them firm. The marmalade should be sweet, and pleasantly flavoured with lemon.

IMPERIAL GOOSEBERRY-FOOL.

Simmer a pound of green gooseberries which have been freed from the buds and stalks, in three-quarters of a pint of water, until they are well broken, then strain them, and to half a pound of the juice add half a pound of sugar, broken small: boil these together for fifteen minutes. Dissolve half an ounce of isinglass in a quarter-pint of rich cream, pour them into a basin, and stir them till only lukewarm, then mix them by degrees with the sugar and gooseberry-juice, which should also have been allowed to cool; add the strained juice of half a small lemon, and mould the mixture, which should stand at least twelve hours, in a cool place, before it is turned out.

These proportions are sufficient for a small mould only, and must be doubled for a large one. The dish is too sweet for our own taste, but as it has been highly approved by several persons who have tasted it, we give the receipt exactly as we had it tried in the first instance: it will be found extremely easy to vary it.

VERY GOOD OLD-FASHIONED BOILED CUSTARD.

Throw into a pint and a half of new milk, the very thin rind of a fresh lemon, and let it infuse for half an hour, then simmer them together for a few minutes, and add four ounces and a half of white sugar. Beat thoroughly the yolks of fourteen fresh eggs, mix with them another half-pint of new milk, stir the boiling milk quickly to them, take out the lemon-peel, and turn the custard into a deep jug; set this over the fire in a pan of boiling water, and keep the custard stirred gently, but without ceasing, until it begins to thicken; then move the spoon rather more quickly, making it always touch the bottom of the jug, until the mixture is brought to the point of boiling, when it must be instantly taken from the fire, or it will curdle in a moment. Pour it into a bowl, and keep it stirred until nearly cold, then add to it by degrees a wineglassful of good brandy, and two ounces of blanched almonds, cut into spikes; or omit these, at pleasure. A few bitter ones, bruised, can be boiled in the milk in lieu of lemon-peel, when their flavour is preferred.

New milk, 1 quart; rind of 1 lemon; sugar, 4½ ozs.; yolks of eggs, 14; salt, ¼ saltspoonful.

RICH BOILED CUSTARD.

Take a small cupful from a quart of fresh cream, and simmer the remainder for a few minutes with four ounces of sugar and the rind of a lemon, or give it any other flavour that may be preferred. Beat and strain the yolks of eight eggs, mix them with the cupful of cream, and stir the rest boiling to them: thicken the custard like the preceding one.

Cream, 1 quart; sugar, 4 ozs.; yolks of eggs, 8.

THE QUEEN'S CUSTARD.

On the beaten and strained yolks of twelve new-laid eggs pour a pint and a half of boiling cream which has been sweetened, with three ounces of sugar; add the smallest pinch of salt, and thicken the custard as usual. When nearly cold, flavour it with a glass and a half of no-yeau, maraschino, or cuirasseau; add the sliced almonds or not, at pleasure.

Yolks of eggs, 12; cream, 1½ pint; sugar, 3 ozs.; little salt; noyeau maraschino, or cuirasseau, 1½ wineglassful.

CURRANT CUSTARD.

Boil in a pint of clear currant-juice ten ounces of sugar for three minutes, take off the scum, and pour the boiling juice on eight well-beaten eggs, thicken the custard in a jug set into a pan of water, pour it out, stir it till nearly cold, then add to it carefully, and by degrees, half a pint of rich cream, and last of all two tablespoonsful of strained lemon-juice. When the currants are very ripe, omit one ounce of the sugar.

White currants and strawberries, cherries, red or white raspberries, or a mixture of any of these fruits, may be used for these custards with good effect: they are excellent.

Currant-juice, 1 pint; sugar, 10 ozs.: 3 minutes. Eggs, 8; cream, ½ pint; lemon-juice, 2 tablespoonsful.

QUINCE OR APPLE CUSTARDS.

Add to a pint of apple-juice prepared as for jelly, a tablespoonful of strained lemon-juice, and from four to six ounces of sugar according to the acidity of the fruit; stir these boiling, quickly, and in small portions, to eight well-beaten eggs, and thicken the custard in a jug placed in a pan of boiling water, in the usual manner. A large proportion of lemon-juice and a high flavouring of the rind can be given when approved. For quince custards, which if well made are excellent, observe the same directions as for the apple, but omit the lemon-juice. As we have before observed, all custards are much finer when made with the yolks only of the eggs, of which the number must be increased nearly half, when this is done.

Prepared apple-juice (see page 305), 1 pint; lemon-juice, 1 table-spoonful; sugar, 4 to 6 ozs.; eggs, 8. Quince custards, same proportions, but no lemon-juice.

Obs.—In making lemon-creams the apple-juice may be substituted very advantageously for water, without varying the receipt in other respects.

CHOCOLATE CUSTARDS.

Dissolve gently by the side of the fire an ounce and a half of the best chocolate in rather more than a wineglassful of water, and then boil it until it is perfectly smooth; mix with it a pint of milk well flavoured with lemon-peel or vanilla, add two ounces of fine sugar, and when the whole boils, stir it to five well-beaten eggs that have been strained. Put the custard into a jar or jug, set it into a pan of boiling water, and stir it without ceasing until it is thick. Do not put it into glasses or a dish till nearly or quite cold. These, as well as all other custards, are infinitely finer when made with the yolks only of the eggs,

of which the number must then be increased. Two ounces of chocolate, a pint of milk, half a pint of cream, two ounces and a half or three
ounces of sugar, and eight yolks of eggs, will make very superior custards of this kind.

Rasped chocolate, 1½ oz.; water, 1 *large* wineglassful: 5 to 8 minutes. New milk, 1 pint; eggs, 5; sugar, 2 ozs. Or, chocolate, 2
ozs.; water, ¼ pint; new milk, 1 pint: sugar, 2½ to 3 ozs.; cream, ½
pint; yolks of eggs, 8.

Obs.—Either of these may be moulded by dissolving from half to
three quarters of an ounce of isinglass in the milk. The proportion of
chocolate can be increased to the taste.

COMMON BAKED CUSTARD.

Mix a quart of new milk with eight well-beaten eggs, strain the
mixture through a fine sieve, and sweeten it with from five to eight
ounces of sugar, according to the taste; add a small pinch of salt, and
pour the custard into a deep dish with or without a lining or rim of
paste, grate nutmeg or lemon rind over the top, and bake it in a *very*
slow oven from twenty to thirty minutes, or longer, should it not be
firm in the centre. A custard, if well made, and properly baked, will
be quite smooth when cut, without the honey-combed appearance which
a hot oven gives; and there will be no whey in the dish.

New milk, 1 quart; eggs, 8; sugar, 5 to 8 ozs.; salt, ¼ salt-spoon-
ful; nutmeg or lemon-grate: baked, slow oven, 20 to 30 minutes, or
more.

A FINER BAKED CUSTARD.

Boil together gently, for five minutes, a pint and a half of new milk,
a few grains of salt, the very thin rind of a lemon, and six ounces of
loaf sugar; stir these boiling, but very gradually to the well-beaten
yolks of ten fresh eggs, and the whites of four; strain the mixture, and
add to it half a pint of good cream; let it cool, and then flavour it with
a few spoonsful of brandy, or a little ratafia; finish and bake it by the
directions given for the common custard above; or pour it into small
well-buttered cups, and bake it very slowly from ten to twelve minutes.

FRENCH CUSTARDS.

To a quart of new milk allow the yolks of twelve fresh eggs, but to
equal parts of milk and cream of ten only. From six to eight ounces
of sugar will sweeten the custard sufficiently for general taste, but more
can be added at will; boil this for a few minutes gently in the milk
with a grain or two of salt, and stir the mixture briskly to the eggs, as
soon as it is taken from the fire. Butter a round deep dish, pour in the
custard, and place it in a pan of water at the point of boiling, taking
care that it shall not reach to within an inch of the edge; let it *just
simmer*, and no more, from an hour to an hour and a half: when quite
firm in the middle, it will be done. A very few live embers should be
kept on the lid of the stewpan to prevent the steam falling from it into
the custard. When none is at hand of a form to allow of this, it is better to use a charcoal fire, and to lay an oven-leaf, or tin, over the pan,
and the embers in the centre. The small French furnace, shown in
Chapter XXL, is exceedingly convenient for preparations of this kind;
and there is always more or less of difficulty in keeping a coal fire en-

cirely free from smoke for any length of time.   Serve the custard cold, with chopped macaroons, or ratafias, laid thickly round the edge so as to form a border an inch deep.   A few petals of fresh orange-blossom infused in the milk, will give it a most agreeable flavour, very superior to that derived from the distilled water.   Half a pod of vanilla, cut in short lengths, and well bruised, may be used instead of either; but the milk should then stand some time by the fire before or after it boils, and it must be strained through a muslin before it is added to the eggs, as the small seed of the vanilla would probably pass through a sieve.

New milk, 1 quart; yolks of eggs, 12; sugar, 6 to 8 ozs.   Or, new milk, 1 pint; cream, 1 pint; yolks of eggs, 10; flavouring of orange-flowers or vanilla: simmered in water-bath, 1 to 1½ hour.

GERMAN PUFFS.

Pound to a perfectly smooth paste two ounces of sweet almonds and six bitter ones; mix with them, by slow degrees, the yolks of six, and the whites of three eggs.   Dissolve in half a pint of rich cream, four ounces of fresh butter, and two of fine sugar; pour these hot to the eggs, stirring them briskly together, and when the mixture has become cool, flavour it with half a glass of brandy, or of orange-flower water; or, in lieu of either, with a little lemon-brandy.   Butter some cups thickly, and strew into them a few slices of candied citron, or orange rind; pour in the mixture, and bake the puffs twenty minutes, in a slow oven.

Sweet almonds, 2 ozs.; bitter almonds, 6; eggs, whites, 3,—yolks, 6; cream, ½ pint; butter, 4 ozs.; sugar, 2 ozs.; brandy, cuirasseau, or orange-flower water, ½ wineglassful (or little lemon-brandy): 20 minutes, slow oven.

RASPBERRY PUFFS.

Roll out thin some fine puff-paste, cut it in rounds or squares of equal size, lay some raspberry jam into each, moisten the edges of the paste, fold and press them together, and bake the puffs from ten to fifteen minutes.   Strawberry, or any other jam will serve for them equally well.

CREAMED TARTLETS.

Line some pattypans with very fine paste, and put into each a layer of apricot jam; on this pour some thick-boiled custard, or the pastry cream of page 267.   Whisk the whites of a couple of eggs to a solid froth, mix a couple of tablespoonsful of sifted sugar with them, lay this icing lightly over the tartlets, and bake them in a gentle oven from twenty to thirty minutes, unless they should be very small, when less time must be allowed for them.

AN APPLE CHARLOTTE, OR CHARLOTTE DES POMMES.

Butter a plain mould (a round or square cake-tin will answer the purpose quite well), and line it entirely with thin slices of the crumb of a stale loaf, cut so as to fit into it with great exactness, and dipped into clarified butter.   When this is done, fill the mould to the brim with apple marmalade; cover the top with slices of bread dipped in butter, and on these place a dish, a large plate, or the cover of a stewpan with a weight upon it.   Send the charlotte to a brisk oven for three quarters of an hour should it be small, and for an hour if large.   Turn it out with

great care, and serve it hot. If baked in a slack oven it will not take
a proper degree of colour, and it will be liable to break in the dishing.
The strips of bread must of course join very perfectly, for if any spaces
were left between them the syrup of the fruit would escape, and destroy the good appearance of the dish: should there not have been sufficient marmalade prepared to fill the mould entirely, a jar of quince or
apricot jam, or of preserved cherries even, may be added to it with
advantage. The butter should be well drained from the charlotte before
it is taken from the mould; and sugar may be sifted thickly over it before it is served, or it may be covered with any kind of clear red jelly.

A more elegant, and we think an easier mode of forming the crust,
is to line the mould with small rounds of bread stamped out with a
plain cake, or paste-cutter, then dipped in butter, and placed with the
edges sufficiently one over the other to hold the fruit securely: the
strips of bread are sometimes arranged in the same way.

¾ to 1 hour, quick oven.

MARMALADE FOR THE CHARLOTTE.

Weigh three pounds of good boiling apples, after they have been
pared, cored, and quartered; put them into a stewpan with six ounces
of fresh butter, three quarters of a pound of sugar beaten to powder,
three quarters of a teaspoonful of pounded cinnamon, and the strained
juice of a lemon: let these stew over a gentle fire, until they form a
perfectly smooth and *dry* marmalade; keep them often stirred that they
may not burn, and let them cool before they are put into the crust. This
quantity is for a moderate-sized charlotte.

A CHARLOTTE A LA PARISIENNE.

This dish is sometimes called a Vienna cake; and it is known also,
we believe, as a *Gâteaux de Bordeaux.* Cut horizontally into half-inch
slices a sponge cake, and cover each slice with a different kind of preserve; replace them in their original form, and spread equally over the
cake an icing made with the whites of three eggs, and four ounces of
the finest pounded sugar; sift more sugar over it in every part, and put
it into a very slack oven to dry. The eggs should be whisked to snow
before they are used. One kind of preserve, instead of several, can be
used for this dish; and a rice or a pound cake may, on an emergency,
supply the place of the Savoy, or sponge biscuit.

A GERTRUDE A LA CREME.

Slice a plain pound or rice cake as for the *Charlotte à la Parisienne,*
and take a round out of the centre of each slice with a tin-cutter before
the preserve is laid on; replace the whole in its original form, ice the
outside with a green or rose-coloured icing at pleasure, and dry it in a
gentle oven; or decorate it instead with leaves of almond paste, fastening them to it with white of egg. Just before it is sent to table, fill it
with well-drained whipped cream, flavoured as for a trifle, or in any
other way to the taste.

POMMES AU BEURRE; (*buttered apples. Excellent.*)

Pare six or eight fine apples of a firm kind, but of a good cooking
sort, and core without piercing them through, or dividing them; fill the
cavities with fresh butter, put a quarter-pound more cut small into a

stewpan just large enough to contain the apples in a single layer, place
them closely together on it, and stew them as softly as *possible*, turning
them occasionally until they are almost sufficiently tender to serve; then
strew upon them as much sifted sugar as will sweeten the dish highly,
and a teaspoonful of pounded cinnamon; shake these well in and upon
the fruit, and stew it for a few minutes longer. Lift it out, arrange it
in a hot dish, put into each apple as much warm apricot jam as it will
contain, and lay a small quantity on the top; pour the syrup from the
pan round, but not on the fruit, and serve it immediately.

Apples, 6 to 8; fresh butter, 4 ozs., just simmered till tender. Sugar,
6 to 8 ozs.; cinnamon, 1 teaspoonful: 5 minutes. Apricot jam as
needed.

Obs.—Particular care must be taken to keep the apples entire; they
should rather steam in a gentle heat than boil. It is impossible to
specify the precise time which will render them sufficiently tender, as
this must depend greatly on the time of year and the sort of fruit. If
the stewpan were placed in a very slow oven, the more regular heat of
it would perhaps be better in its effect than the stewing.

SUÉDOISE OF PEACHES.

Pare and divide four fine, ripe peaches, and let them *just simmer*
from five to eight minutes in a syrup made with the third of a pint of
water and three ounces of very white sugar, boiled together for fifteen
minutes; lift them out carefully into a deep dish, and pour about half
the syrup over them, and into the remaining half throw a couple of
pounds more of quite ripe peaches, and boil them to a perfectly smooth,
dry pulp, or marmalade, with as much additional sugar, in fine powder,
as the nature of the fruit may require. Lift the other peaches from the
syrup, and reduce it by very quick boiling more than half. Spread a
deep layer of the marmalade in a dish, arrange the peaches symmetri-
cally round it, and fill all the spaces between them with the marmalade; place the half of a blanched peach-kernel in each, pour the reduced syrup equally over the surface, and border the dish with Italian
macaroons, or, in lieu of these, with candied citron, sliced very thin,
and cut into leaves with a small paste-cutter. A little lemon-juice
brings out the flavour of all preparations of peaches, and may be added
with good effect to this. When the fruit is scarce, the marmalade
(which ought to be very white) may be made in part or entirely with
nonsuches. The better to preserve their form, the peaches are sometimes merely wiped, and then boiled tolerably tender in the syrup before
they are pared or split. Half a pint of water, and from five to six
ounces of sugar must then be allowed for them. If any of those used
for the marmalade should not be quite ripe, it will be better to pass it
through a sieve, when partially done, to prevent its being lumpy.

Large ripe peaches, pared and halved, 4; simmered in syrup, 5 to 9
minutes. Marmalade: peaches (or nonsuches), 2 lbs.; sugar, ½ to ¾
lb.: ¾ to 1 hour, and more: strained lemon-juice, 1 tablespoonful. Cit
ron, or macaroons, as needed.

Peaches, if boiled whole in syrup, 15 to 18 minutes.

Obs.—The number of peaches can, at pleasure, be increased to six
and three or four of the halves can be piled above the others in the centre of the dish.

AROCE DOCE (OR SWEET RICE. A LA PORTUGAISE)

Wipe thoroughly, in a dry soft cloth, half a pound of the best Carolina rice, after it has been carefully picked; put to it three pints of new milk, and when it has stewed gently for half an hour, add eight ounces of sugar, broken into small lumps; let it boil until it is dry and tender, and when it is nearly so, stir to it two ounces of blanched and pounded almonds. Turn the rice, when done, into shallow dishes, or soup-plates, and shake it until the surface is smooth; then sift over it, rather thickly, through a muslin, some freshly-powdered cinnamon, which will give it the appearance of a baked pudding. Serve it cold. It will remain good for several days. This is quite the best sweet preparation of rice that we have ever eaten, and it is a very favourite dish in Portugal, whence the receipt was derived. One or two bitter almonds, pounded with the sweet ones, might a little improve its flavour, and a few spoonsful of rich cream could occasionally be substituted for a small portion of the milk, but it should not be added until the preparation is three parts done.

Rice, 8 ozs.; milk, 3 pints: 30 minutes. Sugar, 8 ozs.: 1 hour, or more. Pounded almonds, 2 ozs.; cinnamon, 1 teaspoonful.

Obs.—The rice must be frequently stirred while boiling, particularly after it begins to thicken; and it will be better not to add the entire quantity of milk at first, as from a quarter to half a pint less will sometimes prove sufficient. The grain should be thoroughly tender, but dry and unbroken.

BERMUDA WITCHES.

Slice equally some rice, pound, or sponge cake, not more than the sixth of an inch thick; take off the brown edges, and spread one half of it with Guava jelly, or, if more convenient, with fine strawberry, raspberry, or currant jelly of good quality (see Norman receipt, 338); on this strew thickly some fresh cocoanut grated small, and lightly; press over it the remainder of the cake, and trim the whole into good form; divide the slices if large, pile them slopingly in the centre of a dish upon a very white napkin folded flat, and garnish or intersperse them with small sprigs of myrtle. For very young people a French roll or two, and good currant jelly, red or white, will supply a wholesome and inexpensive dish.

STRENGTHENING BLAMANGE.

Dissolve in a pint of new milk, half an ounce of isinglass, strain it through a muslin, or a fine silk sieve, put it again on the fire with the rind of half a small lemon pared very thin, and two ounces of sugar, broken small; let it simmer gently till well flavoured, then take out the lemon-peel, and stir the milk to the beaten yolks of three fresh eggs; pour the mixture back into the saucepan, and hold it over the fire, keeping it stirred until it begins to thicken; put it into a deep basin, and keep it moved with a whisk or spoon, until it is nearly cold; pour it into moulds which have been laid in water, and set in a cool place till firm.

New milk, 1 pint; isinglass, ½ oz.; lemon-rind, ½ of 1: 10 to 15 minutes. Sugar, 2 ozs.; yolks of eggs, 3.

CHAPTER XXI.

PRESERVES.

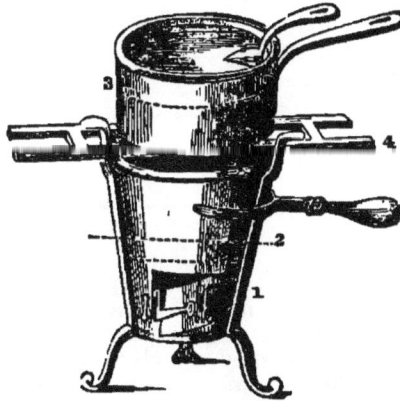

Portable French Furnace, with Stewpan and Trevet.

No. I. Portable French Furnace.—2. Depth at which the grating is placed.— 3. Stew pan.—4. Trevet.

INTRODUCTORY REMARKS.

FRUIT for preserving should always be gathered in perfectly dry weather; it should also be free both from the morning and evening dew, and as much so as possible from dust. When bottled, it must be steamed or baked during the day on which it is gathered, or there will he great loss from the bursting of the bottles; and for jams and jellies it cannot be too soon boiled down after it is taken from the trees.

The small portable French stove, or furnace,* shown above, with the trevet and stewpan adapted to it, is exceedingly convenient for all preparations which require either more than usual attention, or a fire entirely free from smoke; as it can be placed on a table in a clear light, and the heat can be regulated at pleasure. It has been used for all the preserves, of which the receipts are given in this chapter, as well as for various dishes contained in the body of the work. There should always be a free current of air in the room in which it stands when lighted, as charcoal or *braise* (that is to say, the little embers of large well-burned wood, drawn from an oven, and shut immediately into a closely-stopped iron or copper vessel to extinguish them) is the only fuel suited to it. To kindle either of these, two or three bits must be lighted in a common fire, and laid on the top of that in the furnace, which should be evenly placed between the grating and the brim, and then blown gently with the bellows until the whole is alight: the door

---

* Called in France, *Unforneau Economique.* A baking-tin should be placed on the table for the furnace to stand upon, to guard against danger from the ashes or embers falling. American stoves or furnaces may be made in a similar manner.

ot the furnace must in the meanwhile be open, and remain so, unless
the heat should at any time be too fierce for the preserves, when it must
be closed for a few minutes, to moderate it. To extinguish the fire

Closed Furnace and Cover.   Form of Trevet.

altogether, the cover must be pressed closely on, and the door be quite
shut: the embers which remain will serve to rekindle it easily, but
before it is again lighted the grating must be lifted out and all the ashes
cleared away.   It should be set by in a place which is not damp.
   The German enamelled stewpans, now coming into general use, are,
from the peculiar nicety of the composition with which they are lined,
better adapted than any others to pickling and preserving, as they may
be used without danger for acids; and red fruits, when boiled in them,
retain the brightness of their colour as well as if copper or bell-metal
were used for them,   The form of the old-fashioned preserving-pan,
made usually of one or the other of these, is shown above; but it has
not, we should say, even the advantage of being of convenient shape;
for the handles quickly become heated, and the pan, in consequence,
cannot always be instantaneously raised from the fire when the contents
threaten to over-boil, or to burn.
   It is desirable to have three or four wooden spoons or spatulas, one
fine hair-sieve, at the least, one or two large squares of common muslin, and a strainer, or more of closer texture, kept exclusively for preparations of fruit, for if used for other purposes, there is the hazard,
without great care, of their retaining some strong or coarse flavour,
which they would impart to the preserves.   A sieve, for example,
through which any preparation of onions has been poured, should never,
on any account, be brought into use for any kind of confectionary, nor
in making sweet dishes, nor for straining eggs or milk for puddings,
cakes, or bread.   Damp is the great enemy, not only of preserves and
pickles, but of numberless other household stores; yet, in many situations, it is extremely difficult to exclude it.   To keep them in a " dry
cool place" (words which occur so frequently both in this book, and in
most others on the same subject), is more easily directed than done.
They remain, we find, more entirely free from any danger of moulding,
when covered with a brandied paper only, and placed on the shelves of
a tolerably dry store-room; but they are rather liable to candy when
thus kept, and we fancy that the flavour of the fruit is somewhat less
perfectly preserved than when they are quite secured from the air by

skins stretched over the jars. If left uncovered, the inroads of mice upon them must be guarded against, as they will commit great havoc in a single night on these sweet stores. When the slightest fermentation is perceptible in syrup, it should immediately be boiled for some minutes, and well skimmed; the fruit taken from it should then be hrown in, and well scalded also, and the whole, when done, should be turned into a very clean dry jar: this kind of preserve should always be covered with one or two skins, or with parchment and thick paper.

A FEW GENERAL RULES AND DIRECTIONS FOR PRESERVING.

1. Let every thing used for the purpose be delicately clean and *dry;* bottles especially so.

2. Never place a preserving-pan *flat upon the fire*, as this will render the preserve liable to *burn to*, as it is called; that is to say, to adhere closely to the metal, and then to burn; it should rest always on a trevet, or on the lowered bar of the kitchen range.

3. After the sugar is added to them, stir the preserves gently at first, and more quickly towards the end, without quitting them until they are done; this precaution will always prevent the chance of their being spoiled.

4. All preserves should be perfectly cleared from the scum as it rises.

5. Fruit which is to be preserved in syrup must first be blanched or boiled gently, until it is sufficiently softened to absorb the sugar; and a thin syrup must be poured on it at first, or it will shrivel instead of remaining plump, and becoming clear. Thus, if its weight of sugar is to be allowed, and boiled to a syrup with a pint of water to the pound, only half the weight must be taken at first, and this must not be boiled with the water more than fifteen or twenty minutes at the commencement of the process; a part of the remaining sugar must be added every time the syrup is reboiled, unless it should be otherwise directed in the receipt.

6. To preserve both the true flavour and the colour of fruit in jams and jellies, boil them rapidly until they are well reduced, *before* the sugar is added, and quickly afterwards, but do not allow them to become so much thickened that the sugar will not dissolve in them easily, and throw up its scum. In some seasons, the juice is so much richer than in others, that this effect takes place almost before one is aware of it; but the drop which adheres to the skimmer, when it is held up, will show the state it has reached.

7. Never use tin, iron, or pewter spoons, or skimmers for preserves, as they will convert the colour of red fruit into a dingy purple, and impart, besides, a very unpleasant flavour.

8. When cheap jams or jellies are required, make them at once with loaf-sugar, but use that which is *well refined* always, for preserves in general; it is a false economy as we have elsewhere observed, to purchase an inferior kind, as there is great waste from it in the quantity of scum which it throws up. The *best* has been used for all the receipts given here.

TO EXTRACT THE JUICE OF PLUMS FOR JELLY.

Take the stalks from the fruit, and throw aside all that is not per-

fectly sound; put it into very clean, large stone jars, and give part of
the harder kinds, such as bullaces and damsons, a gash with a knife as
they are thrown in; do this especially in filling the upper part of the
jars. Tie one or two folds of thick paper over them, and set them for
the night into an oven from which the bread has been drawn four or
five hours; or cover them with bladder, instead of paper, place them
in deep pans of water, and boil them gently from two to three hours, or
until the fruit is quite soft, and has yielded all the juice it will afford:
this last is the safer and better mode for jellies of delicate colour.

TO WEIGH THE JUICE OF FRUIT.

Put a basin into one scale, and its weight into the other; add to this
last the weight which is required of the juice, and pour into the basin
as much as will balance the scales. It is always better to weigh than
to *measure* the juice for preserving, as it can generally be done with
more exactness.

GREEN GOOSEBERRY JELLY.

Wash some freshly-gathered gooseberries very clean, after having
taken off the tops and stalks, then to each pound, pour three-quarters of
a pint of spring water, and simmer them until they are well broken;
turn the whole into a jelly-bag or cloth, and let all the juice drain
through; weigh, and boil it rapidly for fifteen minutes. Draw it from
the fire, and stir into it until entirely dissolved an equal weight of good
sugar reduced to powder; boil the jelly from fifteen to twenty minutes
longer, or until it jellies strongly on the spoon or skimmer; clear it
perfectly from scum, and pour it into small jars, moulds, or glasses. It
ought to be very pale and transparent. Preserved fruits just dipped into
hot water to take off the syrup, then well drained and dried, may be
arranged with good effect in the centre of the gooseberry jelly if the
glasses be rather less than half filled before they are laid in, and the
jelly just set: the remainder must be kept liquid to fill them up. The
sugar may be added to the juice at first, and the preserve boiled from
twenty-five to thirty-five minutes, but the colour will not then be so
good. When the fruit abounds the juice may be drawn from it with
very little water, as directed for apples, page 350, when it will require
much less boiling.

Gooseberries, 6 lbs.; water, 4 pints: 20 to 30 minutes. Juice boiled
quickly, 15 minutes; to each pound, 1 lb. sugar: 15 to 20 minutes.

GREEN GOOSEBERRY-JAM; (*firm and of good colour.*)

Cut the stalks and tops from the fruit, weigh and bruise it slightly,
boil it for six or seven minutes, keeping it well turned during the time;
then to every three pounds of gooseberries add two and a half of sugar,
beaten to powder, and boil the preserve quickly for three-quarters of an
hour. It must be constantly stirred, and carefully cleared from scum.

Green gooseberries, 6 lbs.: 6 to 7 minutes. Sugar, 5 lbs.: ¾ hour.

TO DRY GREEN GOOSEBERRIES.

Take the finest green gooseberries, fully grown, and freshly gathered;
cut off the buds, split them across the tops half way down, and with the
small end of a tea or of an egg-spoon, scoop out the seeds. Boil together for fifteen minutes a pound and a half of the finest sugar, and a
pint of water; skim this syrup thoroughly and throw into it a pound of

the seeded gooseberries; simmer them from five to seven minutes, when they ought to be clear and tender; when they are so lift them out, and throw as many more into the syrup; drain them a little when done, spread them singly on dishes, and dry them *very* gradually in a quite cool stove or oven, or in a sunny window. They will keep well in the syrup, and may be potted in it, and dried when wanted for use.

Green gooseberries without the seeds, 2 lbs.; water, 1 pint; sugar, 1½ lb.: boiled 15 minutes. Gooseberries simmered, 5 to 7 minutes.

GREEN GOOSEBERRIES FOR TARTS.

Fill very clean, dry, wide-necked bottles with gooseberries gathered the same day, and before they have attained their full growth. Cork them lightly, wrap a little hay round each of them, and set them up to their necks in a copper of cold water, which should be brought very gradually to boil. Let the fruit be gently simmered until it appears shrunken and perfectly scalded; then take out the bottles, and with the contents of one or two fill up the remainder, and use great care not to break the fruit in doing this. When all are ready, pour *scalding* water into the bottles and cover the gooseberries entirely with it, or they will become mouldy at the top. Cork the bottles well immediately, and cover the necks with melted rosin; keep them in a cool place; and when they are used pour off the greater part of the water, and add sugar as for the fresh fruit, of which they will have quite the flavour and appearance; and they will be found much more wholesome prepared in this manner than if simply baked or steamed in the bottles.

GREEN GOOSEBERRY SOLID.

Bruise well, and boil six pounds of fresh green gooseberries for an hour and a quarter without sugar, and for half an hour after having stirred to them a couple of pounds of good quality, reduced quite to powder. Press the preserve into shallow pans or small shapes, and unmould it when it is wanted for table.

Green gooseberries, 6 lbs.: 1¼ hour. Sugar, 2 lbs.: ½ hour.

RED GOOSEBERRY JAM.

The small rough red gooseberry, when fully ripe, is the best for this preserve, which may, however, be made of the larger kinds. When the buds and stalks have been taken carefully from the fruit, weigh, and boil it quickly for three quarters of an hour, keeping it well stirred; then for six pounds of the gooseberries add two and a half of good roughly-powdered sugar (or three of fine Lisbon, if only a common preserve be wanted); boil these together briskly, from twenty to twenty-five minutes, and stir the jam well from the bottom of the pan, as it is liable to burn if this be neglected.

Small red gooseberries, 6 lbs.: ¾ hour. Pounded sugar, 2½ lbs, (for common jam Lisbon sugar 3 lbs.): 20 to 25 minutes.

GOOSEBERRIES DRIED WITHOUT SUGAR.

Choose them fine and ripe, spread them separately on large dishes, and dry them very gradually by the heat of a gentle oven, or in the sun where they will be well protected from dust. If flattened with the finger when partially done, they will preserve a better form, and be more quickly dried.

CHERRY JAM.

First stone, and then weigh some freshly gathered preserving cherries; boil them over a brisk fire for an hour, keeping them almost constantly stirred from the bottom of the pan, to which they will otherwise be liable to stick and burn. Add half a pound of good sugar roughly powdered for each pound of the fruit, and boil the preserve quickly for twenty minutes, taking off the scum as it rises. The blanched kernels of part of the cherries may be added to the jam five minutes before it is taken from the fire. We can recommend this receipt as producing a firm preserve of fine colour and flavour, and very far superior to any that can be made by the more common method of boiling the fruit and sugar together from the beginning.

Stoned cherries, 6 lbs.: 1 hour. Sugar, 3 lbs.: 20 minutes.

Obs.—Increase the proportion of sugar, when it is liked, to twelve or sixteen ounces, and diminish the boiling a quarter of an hour before it is added, and ten minutes after. We have found almost invariably, that preserves made by the receipts we have given have been preferred to richer ones.

TO DRY CHERRIES WITH SUGAR; (*a quick and easy method.*)

Stone some fine, sound cherries; weigh and put them into a preserving-pan, with six ounces of sugar reduced to powder to each pound of the fruit: set them over a moderate fire, and simmer them gently for nearly or quite twenty minutes; let them remain in the syrup until they are a little cooled, then turn them into a sieve, and before they are cold lay them singly on dishes, and dry them very gradually, as directed for other fruits. When the cherries are quite ripe the stones may generally be drawn out with the stalks, by pressing the fruit gently at the same time; but when this method fails, they must be extracted with a new quill, cut round at the end; those of the *very* short-stalked, turnip-shaped cherry, which abounds, and is remarkably fine in many parts of Normandy, and which we have occasionally met with here, though it is not, we believe, very abundant in our markets, are easily removed with a large pin, on the point of which the stone may be caught at the stalk end, just opposite the seam of the fruit, and drawn out at the top, leaving the cherry apparently entire.

DRIED CHERRIES; (*superior Receipt.*)

To each pound of cherries, weighed after they are stoned, add eight ounces of good sugar, and boil them very softly for ten minutes; pour them into a large bowl, or pan, and leave them two days in the syrup; then simmer them again for ten minutes, and set them by for two or three days; drain them slightly, and dry them very slowly, as directed in the previous receipts. Keep them in tin cases, or canisters, when done. These cherries are generally preferred to such as are dried with a larger proportion of sugar; but when the taste is in favour of the latter, three quarters or a full pound can be allowed to the pound of fruit, which may then be potted in the syrup and dried at any time, though we think the flavour of the cherries is better preserved when this is done within a fortnight of their being boiled.

Cherries, stoned, 8 lbs.; sugar, 4 lbs.: 10 minutes. Left 2 or 3 days. Boiled again, 10 minutes; left 2 days; drained and dried.

CHERRIES DRIED WITHOUT SUGAR.

These are often more pleasant and refreshing to invalids and travellers than a sweetened confection of the fruit, their flavour and agreeable acidity being well preserved when they are simply spread on dishes or hamper lids, and slowly dried.* Throw aside the bruised and decayed fruit, and arrange the remainder singly, and with the stalks uppermost on the dishes.

MORELLA CHERRIES.

Take off the stalks but do not stone the fruit; weigh and add to it an equal quantity of the best sugar reduced quite to powder, strew it over the cherries and let them stand for half an hour, then turn them gently into a preserving-pan, and simmer them softly from five to seven minutes.

COMMON CHERRY CHEESE.

Stone the fruit, or if this trouble be objected to, bruise and boil it without, until it is sufficiently tender to press through a sieve, which it will be in from twenty to thirty minutes. Weigh the pulp in this case, and boil it quickly to a dry paste, then stir to it six ounces of sugar for the pound of fruit, and when this is dissolved, place the pan again over, but not *upon*, a brisk fire, and stir the preserve without ceasing, until it is so dry as not to adhere to the finger when touched; then press it immediately into small moulds or pans, and turn it from them when wanted for table. When the cherries have been stoned, a good common preserve may be made of them without passing them through a sieve, with the addition of five ounces of sugar to the pound of fruit, which must be boiled very dry both before and after it is added.

Other cherries without stoning: 20 to 30 minutes. Passed through a sieve. To each pound of pulp (first boiled dry), 6 ozs. sugar. To each pound of cherries stoned and boiled to dry paste, 5 ozs. sugar.

CHERRY PASTE. (FRENCH.)

Stone the cherries, boil them gently in their own juice for thirty minutes; press the whole through a sieve; reduce it to a very dry paste; then take it from the fire, and weigh it; boil an equal proportion of sugar to the candying point, mix the fruit with it, and stir the paste, without intermission, over a moderate fire, until it is again so dry as to form a ball round the spoon, and to quit the preserving-pan entirely; press it quickly into small moulds, and when it is cold, paper, and store it like other preserves.

STRAWBERRY JAM.

Strip the stalks from some fine scarlet strawberries, weigh, and boil them for thirty-five minutes, keeping them very constantly stirred; throw in eight ounces of good sugar, beaten small, to the pound of fruit, mix them well off the fire, then boil the preserve again quickly for twenty-five minutes. One pound of white currant-juice added in the first instance to four of the strawberries, will greatly improve this preserve, which will be quite firm, and sufficiently, but not over sweet.

Strawberries, 6 lbs.: 35 minutes. Sugar, 3 lbs.: 25 minutes. Or:

* The dishes on which they are laid should be changed daily.

strawberries, 4 lbs.; currant-juice, 1 lb.: 30 to 35 minutes. Sugar, 2½ lbs.: 25 minutes.

Obs.—We do not think it needful to give directions with each sepa-rate receipt for skimming the preserve with care, and keeping it con-stantly stirred, but neither should in any case be neglected.

STRAWBERRY JELLY.

This, when made with fine, full-flavoured, scarlet strawberries, is a very delicious preserve, and is by many persons preferred to guava jelly, which it greatly resembles. Stalk the fruit, bruise it very slightly, and stir it for a few minutes over a gentle fire; strain it with-out pressure, weigh, and boil it quickly for twenty minutes in a Ger-man enamelled stewpan, or preserving-pan, if possible, that the colour may not be injured; take it from the fire, and stir into it twelve ounces of sugar to the pound of juice; when this is dissolved, boil it again quickly for twenty minutes, clear it perfectly from scum, and pour it into jars or glasses. The preserve will be firmer, and require less boil-ing, if one-fourth of red or white currant juice be mixed with that of the strawberries, but the flavour will not then be quite so perfect. A superior jelly to this is made by taking an equal weight of juice and sugar, and by boiling the latter to candy-height, before the juice (which should previously be boiled five minutes) is added to it; and when they have been stirred together off the fire until this is entirely dissolved, boiling the whole quickly from ten to twenty minutes; the time re-quired varying very much from the difference which is found in the quality of the fruit.

Fruit, simmered 4 to 5 minutes. Juice of strawberries, 4 lbs.: 20 minutes. Sugar, 3 lbs.: 20 minutes. Or, juice of strawberries, 4 lbs.: 5 minutes. Sugar, boiled to candy-height, 4 lbs.: 10 to 20 minutes.

ANOTHER VERY FINE STRAWBERRY JELLY.

Express the juice from the fruit through a cloth, strain it clear, weigh, and stir to it an equal proportion of the finest sugar, dried and reduced to powder; when this is dissolved, place the preserving-pan over a very clear fire, and stir the jelly often until it boils; clear it carefully from scum, and boil it quickly from fifteen to twenty-five minutes.

Equal weight of strawberry-juice and sugar: 15 to 25 minutes.

Obs.—This receipt is for a moderate quantity of the preserve: a very small portion will require much less time.

TO PRESERVE STRAWBERRIES OR RASPBERRIES, FOR CREAMS OR ICES, WITHOUT BOILING.

Let the fruit be gathered in the middle of a warm day, in very dry weather; strip it from the stalks directly, weigh it, turn it into a bowl or deep pan, and bruise it gently; mix with an equal weight of fine dry sifted sugar, and put it immediately into small, wide-necked bottles; cork these firmly without delay, and tie bladder over the tops. Keep them in a cool place, or the fruit will ferment. The mixture should be stirred softly, and only just sufficiently to blend the sugar and the fruit. The bottles must be perfectly dry, and the bladders, after having been cleaned in the usual way, and allowed to become nearly so, should be moistened with a little spirit on the side which is to be next to the cork.

Unless these precautions be observed, there will be some danger of the whole being spoiled.

Equal weight of fruit and sugar.

RASPBERRY JAM.

Bruise gently, with the back of a wooden spoon, six pounds of ripe and freshly-gathered raspberries, and boil them over a brisk fire for twenty-five minutes; stir to them half their weight of good sugar, roughly powdered, and when it is dissolved, boil the preserve quickly for ten minutes, keeping it well stirred and skimmed. When a richer jam is wished for, add to the fruit at first its full weight of sugar, and boil them together twenty minutes.

Raspberries, 6 lbs.: 25 minutes. Sugar, 3 lbs.: 10 minutes.

GOOD RED OR WHITE RASPBERRY JAM.

Boil quickly, for twenty minutes, four pounds of either red or white sound ripe raspberries in a pound and a half of currant-juice of the same colour; take the pan from the fire, stir in three pounds of sugar, and when it is dissolved, place the pan again over the fire, and continue the boiling for ten minutes longer: keep the preserve well skimmed and stirred from the beginning.

Raspberries, 4 lbs.; currant-juice, 1½ lb.: 20 minutes. Sugar, 3 lbs.; 10 minutes.

RASPBERRY JELLY FOR FLAVOURING CREAMS.

Take the stalks from some quite ripe, and freshly-gathered raspberries, stir them over the fire until they render their juice freely, then strain and weigh it; or press it from them through a cloth, and then strain it clear; in either case boil it for five minutes after it is weighed, and for each pound stir in a pound and a quarter of good sugar, reduced quite to powder, sifted, and made very hot; boil the preserve quickly for five minutes longer, and skim it clean. The jelly thus made will sufficiently sweeten the creams without any additional sugar.

Juice of raspberries, 4 lbs.: 5 minutes. Sugar, made hot, 5 lbs.: 5 minutes.

ANOTHER RASPBERRY JELLY. (*Very good.*)

Bruise the fruit a *little*, and draw the juice from it by four or five minutes gently simmering; strain and weigh it, boil it quickly for twenty minutes, draw it from the fire, add three-quarters of a pound of good sugar for each pound of juice, and when this is dissolved, place the pan again on the fire, and boil the preserve *fast* from twelve to fifteen minutes longer; skim it thoroughly, and keep it well stirred. This jelly is infinitely improved in colour and in firmness, though not perhaps in flavour, by mixing with the raspberry juice one-fourth, or even as much as a third of the juice of ripe white currants: the preserve will then require rather less boiling. When it jellies in falling from the spoon or skimmer, it is done. Nothing of tin or iron should be used in making it, as these metals will convert its fine red colour into a dingy purple.

Fruit, simmered 5 to 6 minutes. Juice of raspberries, 4 lbs.: 20 minutes. Sugar, 3 lbs.: 12 to 15 minutes. Or, juice of raspberries, 4 lbs.; juice of white currants, 2 lbs.: 20 minutes. Sugar, 4½ lbs.: 10 minutes, or less.

GREEN CURRANT JAM.

For each pound of currants take fourteen ounces of good sugar, in fine powder; bruise part of the fruit with a small portion of the sugar, and put it first into the preserving-pan, that the juice may flow from it sufficiently to prevent the remainder from being burned; it should be placed over a very gentle fire, and stirred constantly until it has yielded moisture enough for this. All the fruit and sugar may then be added, and the whole (well mixed and stirred) boiled from ten to fifteen minutes, or until it jellies strongly in falling from the skimmer. Some fruit will require less time, and some rather more.

To each pound of currants, stripped from stalks, 14 ozs. of sugar: 10 to 15 minutes.

RED CURRANT JELLY.

With three parts of fine ripe red currants freshly gathered, and stripped from the stalks, mix one of white currants; put them into a clean preserving-pan, and stir them gently over a clear fire until the juice flows from them freely; then turn them into a fine hair-sieve, and let them drain well, but without pressure. Pass the juice through a folded muslin, or a jelly-bag; weigh it, and then boil it *fast* for a quarter of an hour; add for each pound, eight ounces of sugar coarsely powdered, stir this to it off the fire until it is dissolved, give the jelly eight minutes more of quick boiling, and pour it out. It will be firm, and of excellent colour and flavour. Be sure to clear off the scum as it rises both before and after the sugar is put in, or the preserve will not be clear.

Juice of red currants, 3 lbs.; juice of white currants, 1 lb.: 15 minutes. Sugar, 2 lbs.: 8 minutes.

Obs.—An excellent jelly may be made with equal parts of the juice of red and of white currants, and of raspberries, with the same proportion of sugar and degree of boiling as in the foreguing receipt.

SUPERLATIVE RED CURRANT JELLY; (*Norman Receipt.*)

Strip carefully from the stems some quite-ripe currants of the finest quality, and mix with them an equal weight of *good* sugar reduced to powder; boil these together quickly for exactly eight minutes, keep them stirred all the time, and clear off the scum as it rises; then turn the preserve into a *very* clean sieve, and put into small jars the jelly which runs through it, and which will be delicious in flavour, and of the brightest colour. It should be carried immediately, when this is practicable, to an extremely cool but not a damp place, and left there till perfectly cold. The currants which remain in the sieve make an excellent jam, particularly if only part of the jelly be taken from them. In Normandy, where the fruit is of richer quality than in England, this preserve is boiled only one minute, and is both firm and beautifully transparent.

Currants, 3 lbs.; sugar, 3 lbs.: 8 minutes.

FRENCH CURRANT JELLY.

Mix one third of white currants with two of red, and stir them over a gentle fire until they render their juice freely, pour it from them, strain and weigh it; for every four pounds break three of fine sugar into large lumps, just dip them into cold water, and when they are nearly dissolved boil them to a thick syrup; stir this without ceasing until it falls in large thick white masses from the skimmer; then pour 'n the currant juice immediately, and when the sugar is again dissolved, boil the whole quickly for five minutes, clear off the scum perfectly, pour the jelly into jars or warm glasses, and set it in a cool place.

Red currants, two thirds; white currants, one third; juice, 4 lbs.; sugar boiled to candy height, 3 lbs.; jelly boiled: 5 minutes.

Obs.—A flavouring of raspberries is usually given to currant jelly in France, the preserve being there never served with any kind of joint, as it is with us.

DELICIOUS RED CURRANT JAM.

This, which is but an indifferent preserve when made in the usual way, will be found a very fine one if the following directions for it be observed; it will be extremely transparent and bright in colour, and will retain perfectly the flavour of the fruit. Take the currants at the height of their season, the finest that can be had, free from dust, but gathered on a dry day; strip them with great care from the stalks, weigh and put them into a preserving-pan with three pounds of the best sugar reduced to powder to four pounds of the fruit; stir them gently over a brisk clear fire, and boil them quickly for exactly eight minutes from the first full boil. As the jam is apt to rise over the top of the pan, it is better not to fill it more than two thirds, and if this precaution should not be sufficient to prevent it, it must be lifted from the fire and held away for an instant. To many tastes, a still finer jam than this (which we find sufficiently sweet) may be made with an equal weight of fruit and sugar boiled together for seven minutes. There should be great exactness with respect to the time, as both the flavour and the brilliant colour of the preserve will be injured by longer boiling.

Red currants (without stalks), 4 lbs.; fine sugar, 3 lbs.: boiled quickly, 8 minutes. Or, equal weight fruit and sugar: 7 minutes.

VERY FINE WHITE CURRANT JELLY.

The fruit for this jelly should be very white, perfectly free from dust, and picked carefully from the stalks. To every pound add eighteen ounces of double refined sifted sugar, and boil them together quickly for six minutes; throw in the strained juice of a sound fresh lemon, or of two, should the quantity of preserve be large; boil it two minutes longer; pour it into a delicately clean sieve, and finish it by the directions given for the Norman red currant jelly (page 338).

White currants, 6 lbs.; highly refined sugar, 6¾ lbs.: 6 minutes. Juice of 2 moderate-sized lemons: 2 minutes.

WHITE CURRANT JAM, A BEAUTIFUL PRESERVE.

Boil together quickly for seven minutes equal quantities of fine white currants, picked with the greatest nicety, and of the best sugar pounded and passed through a sieve. Stir the preserve gently the whole time, and be careful to skim it thoroughly. Just before it is taken from the fire, throw in the strained juice of one good lemon to four pounds of the fruit.

White currants, 4 lbs.; best sugar, 4 lbs.: 7 minutes. Juice, 1 lemon.

CURRANT PASTE.

Stalk and heat some red currants as for jelly, pour off three parts of the juice, which can be used for that preserve, and press the remainder, with the pulp of the fruit, closely through a hair-sieve reversed; boil it briskly, keeping it stirred the whole time, until it forms a dry paste; then for each pound (when first weighed) add seven ounces of pounded sugar, and boil the whole from twenty-five to thirty minutes longer, taking care that it shall not burn. This paste is remarkably pleasant and refreshing in cases of fever, and acceptable usually for winter-desserts.

Red currants boiled from 5 to 7 minutes, pressed with one-fourth of their juice through a sieve, boiled from 1½ to 2 hours. To each pound add 7 ozs. pounded sugar: 25 to 30 minutes.

Obs.—Confectioners add the pulp, after it is boiled dry, to an equal weight of sugar at the candy height: by making trial of the two methods, the reader can decide on the better one.

BLACK CURRANT JELLY.

After having extracted the juice of the fruit in the usual way, proceed exactly with regard to the time of boiling, and the proportion of sugar as in the first receipt for red currant jelly in the present chapter. This is a most refreshing and useful preserve in illness; and in many cases no other will supply its place: it may be made with Lisbon sugar on occasion.

NURSERY PRESERVE.

Take the stones from a couple of pounds of cherries, and boil them twenty minutes; then add to them a pound and a half of raspberries, and an equal quantity of red and of white currants, all weighed after they have been cleared from their stems. Boil these together briskly for twenty minutes; mix with them three pounds and a quarter of common sugar, and give the preserve fifteen minutes more of quick boiling. A pound and a half of blackberries may be substituted for the cherries; but they will not require any stewing before they are added to the other fruits. The jam must be well stirred from the beginning, or it will burn to the pan.

Cherries, 2 lbs.: 20 minutes. Raspberries, red currants, and white currants, of each 1½ lb.: 20 minutes. Sugar, 3¼ lbs.: 15 minutes.

ANOTHER GOOD COMMON PRESERVE.

Boil together, in equal or in unequal portions (for this is immaterial), any kinds of early fruit, till they can be pressed through a sieve; weigh, and then boil the pulp over a brisk fire for half an hour; add half a pound of sugar for each pound of fruit, and again boil the preserve quickly, keeping it well stirred and skimmed, from fifteen to twenty minutes. Cherries, unless they be morellas, must be first stewed tender apart, as they will require a much longer time to make them so than other of the first summer fruits.

A GOOD MÉLANGE, OR MIXED PRESERVE.

Boil for three quarters of an hour, in two pounds of clear red currant juice, one pound of very ripe greengages, weighed after they have been pared and stoned; then stir to them one pound and a half of good sugar and boil them quickly again for twenty minutes. If the quantity of preserve be much increased, the time of boiling it must be so likewise: this is always better done before the sugar is added.

Juice of ripe currants, 2 lbs.; greengages, pared and stoned, 1 lb.: ¾ hour.   Sugar, 1½ lb.: 20 minutes.

GREENGAGE JAM, OR MARMALADE.

When the plums are thoroughly ripe, take off the skins, weigh, and boil them quickly without sugar for fifty minutes, keeping them well stirred; then to every four pounds add three of good sugar reduced quite to powder, boil the preserve from five to eight minutes longer, and clear off the scum perfectly before it is poured into the jars.   When the flesh of the fruit will not separate easily from the stones, weigh and throw the plums whole into the preserving-pan, boil them to a pulp, pass them through a sieve, and deduct the weight of the stones from them when apportioning the sugar to the jam.   The Orleans plum may be substituted for greengages, in this receipt.

Greengages, stoned and skinned, 6 lbs.: 50 minutes.   Sugar, 4½ lbs.; 5 to 8 minutes.

PRESERVE OF THE MAGNUM BONUM, OR MOGUL PLUM.

Prepare, weigh, and boil the plums for forty minutes; stir to them half their weight of good sugar beaten fine, and when it is dissolved continue the boiling for ten additional minutes, and skim the preserve carefully during the time.   This is an excellent marmalade, but it may be rendered richer by increasing the proportion of sugar.   The blanched kernels of a portion of the fruit-stones will much improve its flavour, but they should be mixed with it only two or three minutes before it is taken from the fire.   When these plums are not entirely ripe, it is difficult to free them from the stones and skins: they should then be boiled down and pressed through a sieve, as directed for greengages, in the receipt above.

Mogul plums, skinned and stoned, 6 lbs: 40 minutes.   Sugar, 3 lbs.: 5 to 8 minutes.

TO DRY OR PRESERVE MOGUL PLUMS IN SYRUP.

Pare the plums, but do not remove the stalks nor stones; take their weight of dry sifted sugar, lay them in a deep dish or bowl, and strew it over them; let them remain thus for a night, then pour them gently into a preserving-pan, with all the sugar, heat them slowly, and let them just simmer for five minutes; in a couple of days repeat the process, and do so again and again at an interval of two or three days, until the fruit is tender and very clear; put it then into jars, and keep it in the syrup, or drain and dry the plums very gradually, as directed for other fruit.   When they are not sufficiently ripe for the skin to part from them easily, they must be covered with spring water, placed over a slow fire, and just scalded until it can be stripped off easily.

MUSSEL PLUM CHEESE AND JELLY.

Fill large stone jars with the fruit, which should be ripe, dry, and sound, set them into an oven from which the bread has been drawn several hours, and let them remain all night; or, if this cannot conveniently be done, place them in pans of water, and boil them gently until the plums are tender, and have yielded their juice to the utmost.   Pour this from them, strain it through a jelly-bag, weigh, and then boil it rapidly for twenty-five minutes.   Have ready, broken small, three pounds of sugar for four of the juice, stir them together until it is dissolved, and then continue the boiling quickly for ten minutes longer, and be careful to remove all the scum. Pour the preserve into small moulds or pans, and turn it out when it is wanted for table; it will be very fine, both in colour and in flavour.

Juice of plums, 4 lbs.: 25 minutes. Sugar, 3 lbs.: 10 minutes.

The cheese.—Skin and stone the plums from which the juice has been poured, and after having weighed, boil them an hour and a quarter over a brisk fire, and stir them constantly; then to three pounds of fruit add one of sugar, beaten to powder; boil the preserve for another half hour, and press it into shallow pans or moulds.

Plums, 3 lbs.: 1¼ hour. Sugar, 1 lb.: 30 minutes.

TO DRY APRICOTS; (a quick and easy method.)

Wipe gently, split, and stone some fine apricots, which are not over-ripe; weigh, and arrange them evenly in a deep dish or bowl, and strew in fourteen ounces of sugar, in fine powder, to each pound of fruit; on the following day turn the whole carefully into a preserving-pan, let the apricots heat slowly, and simmer them very softly for six minutes, or for an instant longer, should they not in that time be quite tender. Let them lay in the syrup for a day or two, then drain and spread them singly on dishes to dry.

To each pound apricots, 14 ozs. of sugar: to stand 1 night, to be simmered from 6 to 8 minutes, and left in syrup 2 or 3 days.

PEACH JAM, OR MARMALADE.

The fruit for this preserve, which is a very delicious one, should be finely flavoured, and quite ripe, though perfectly sound. Pare, stone, weigh, and boil it quickly for three quarters of an hour, and do not fail to stir it often during the time; draw it from the fire, and mix with it ten ounces of well-refined sugar, rolled or beaten to powder, for each pound of the peaches; clear it carefully from scum, and boil it briskly for five minutes; throw in the strained juice of one or two *good* lemons; continue the boiling for three minutes only, and pour out the marmalade. Two minutes after the sugar is stirred to the fruit, add the blanched kernels of part of the peaches.

Peaches, stoned and pared, 4 lbs.: ¾ hour. Sugar, 2½ lbs.: 2 minutes. Blanched peach-kernels: 3 minutes. Juice of 2 *small* lemons: 3 minutes.

Obs.—This jam, like most others, is improved by pressing the fruit through a sieve after it has been partially boiled. Nothing can be finer than its flavour, which would be injured by adding the sugar at first; and a larger proportion renders it cloyingly sweet. Nectarines and peaches mixed, make an admirable preserve.

TO PRESERVE, OR TO DRY PEACHES OR NECTARINES. (An easy and excellent Receipt.)

The fruit should be fine, freshly gathered, and *fully ripe*, but still in its perfection. Pare, halve, and weigh it after the stones are removed · lay it into a deep dish, and strew over it an equal weight of highly refined pounded sugar; let it remain until this is nearly dissolved, then lift the fruit gently into a preserving-pan, pour the juice and sugar to it and heat the whole over a very slow fire; let it just simmer for ten minutes, then turn it softly into a bowl, and let it remain a couple of days; repeat the slow-heating and simmering at intervals of two or three days, until the fruit is quite clear, when it may be potted in the syrup, or drained from it, and dried upon large clean slates or dishes, or upon wire-sieves. The flavour will be excellent. The strained juice of a lemon may be added to the syrup, with good effect, towards the end of the process, and an additional ounce or two of sugar allowed for it.

DAMSON JAM. (VERY GOOD.)

The fruit for this jam should be freshly gathered and quite ripe. Split, stone, weigh, and boil it quickly for forty minutes; then stir in half its weight of good sugar roughly powdered, and when it is dissolved, give the preserve fifteen minutes additional boiling, keeping it stirred, and thoroughly skimmed.

Damsons, stoned, 6 lbs.: 40 minutes. Sugar, 3 lbs.: 15 minutes.

Obs.—A more refined preserve is made by pressing the fruit through a sieve after it is boiled tender; but the jam is excellent without.

DAMSON JELLY.

Bake separately in a very slow oven, or boil in a water-bath (see page 332), any number of fine ripe damsons, and one third the quantity of bullaces, or of any other pale plums, as a portion of their juice will, to most tastes, improve, by softening the flavour of the preserve, and will render the colour brighter. Pour off the juice clear from the fruit, strain and weigh it; boil it quickly without sugar for twenty-five minutes, draw it from the fire, stir into it ten ounces of good sugar for each pound of juice, and boil it quickly from six to ten minutes longer, carefully clearing off all the scum. The jelly must be often stirred before the sugar is added, and constantly afterwards.

DAMSON SOLID. (GOOD.)

Pour the juice from some damsons which have stood for a night in a very cool oven, or been stewed in a jar placed in a pan of water; weigh and put it into a preserving-pan with a pound and four ounces of pearmains (or of any other fine boiling apples), pared, cored, and quartered, to each pound of the juice; boil these together, keeping them well stirred, from twenty-five to thirty minutes, then add the sugar, and when it is nearly dissolved, continue the boiling for ten minutes. This, if done with exactness, will give a perfectly smooth and firm preserve, which may be moulded in small shapes, and turned out for table.

To each pound clear damson-juice, 1¼ lb. pearmains (or other good apples), pared and cored: 25 to 30 minutes. Sugar, 14 ozs.: 10 minutes.

EXCELLENT DAMSON CHEESE.

When the fruit has been baked or stewed tender, as directed above, drain off the juice, skin and stone the damsons, pour back to them from a third to half their juice, weigh and then boil them over a clear brisk fire until they form a quite dry paste; add six ounces of pounded sugar for each pound of the plums; stir them off the fire until this is dissolved, and boil the preserve again without quitting or ceasing to stir it, until it leaves the pan quite dry, and adheres in a mass to the spoon. If it should not stick to the fingers when lightly touched, it will be sufficiently done to keep very long; press it quickly into pans or moulds; lay on it a paper dipped in spirit when it is perfectly cold; tie another fold over it, and store it in a dry place.

Bullace cheese is made in the same manner, and almost any kind of plum will make an agreeable preserve of the sort.

To each pound of fruit, pared, stoned, and mixed with the juice, and boiled quite dry, 6 ozs. of pounded sugar: boiled again to a dry paste.

GRAPE JELLY.

Strip from their stalks some fine ripe black-cluster grapes, and stir them with a wooden spoon over a gentle fire until all have burst, and the juice flows freely from them; strain it off without pressure, and pass it through a jelly-bag, or through a twice-folded muslin; weigh and then boil it rapidly for twenty minutes; draw it from the fire, stir in it till dissolved, fourteen ounces of good sugar, roughly powdered, to each pound of juice, and boil the jelly quickly for fifteen minutes longer, keeping it constantly stirred, and perfectly well skimmed. It will be very clear, and of a beautiful pale rose-colour.

Juice of black-cluster grapes: 20 minutes. To each pound of juice, 14 ozs. good sugar: 15 minutes.

Obs.—We have proved this jelly only with the kind of grape which we have named, but there is little doubt that fine purple grapes of any sort would answer for it well.

ENGLISH GUAVA.

Strip the stalks from a gallon or two of the large kind of bullaces called the shepherd's bullace; give part of them a cut, put them into stone jars, and throw into one of them a pound or two of imperatrice plums, if they can be obtained; put the jars into pans of water, and boil them as directed at page 332; then drain off the juice, pass it through a thick strainer or jelly-bag, and weigh it; boil it quickly from fifteen to twenty minutes; take it from the fire, and stir in it till dissolved, three-quarters of a pound of sugar to the pound of juice; remove the scum with care, and boil the preserve again quickly from eight to twelve minutes, or longer should it not then jelly firmly on the skimmer. When the fruit is very acid, an equal weight of juice and sugar may be mixed together in the first instance, and boiled briskly for about twenty minutes. It is impossible to indicate the *precise* time which the jelly will require, so much depends on the quality of the plums, and on the degree of boiling previously given to them in the water-bath When properly made, it is remarkably transparent and *very* firm. It should be poured into shallow pans or small moulds, and turned from them before it is served. When the imperatrice plum cannot be procured, any other that will give a pale red colour to the juice will answer. The bullaces alone make an admirable preserve; and even the commoner kind afford an excellent one.

Juice of the shepherd's bullace and imperatrice, or other red plum, 4 lbs.: 15 to 20 minutes. Sugar, 3 lbs.: 8 to 12 minutes. Or juice of bullaces and sugar, equal weight: 20 minutes.

Obs.—After the juice has been poured from the plums they may be stoned, pared, weighed, and boiled to a paste; then six ounces of sugar added to the pound, and the boiling continued until the preserve is again very dry: a small portion of the juice should be left with the fruit for this.

TO DRY PLUMS; (an easy method.)

Put them into jars, or wide-necked bottles, with half a pound of good sugar, rolled or pounded, to twice the weight of fruit; set them into a very cool oven for four and five hours; or if more convenient place them, with a little hay between them, in a pan of cold water, and boil them gently for rather more than three hours. Leave them in the syrup for a few days, and finish them as directed for the drying of other fruits. Tie a bladder over the necks of the jars or bottles before they are placed in the pan of water, and fasten two or three folds of paper over the former, or cork the bottles when the fruit is to be baked. The sugar should be put in after the fruit, without being shaken down; it will then dissolve gradually, and be absorbed by it equally.

To each pound of plums, 8 ounces pounded sugar: baked in cool oven 4 or 5 hours, or steamed 3 hours.

TO BOTTLE FRUIT FOR WINTER USE.

Gather the fruit in the middle of the day in very dry weather; strip off the stalks, and have in readiness some perfectly clean and dry wide-necked bottles; turn each of these the instant before it is filled, with the neck downwards, and hold in it two or three lighted matches; drop in the fruit before the vapour escapes, shake it gently down, press in some new corks, dip the necks of the bottles into melted rosin, set them at night into an oven from which the bread has been drawn six or seven hours at least, and let them remain until the morning: if the heat be too great the bottles will burst. Currants, cherries, damsons, green-gages, and various other kinds of plums will remain good for quite twelve months when bottled thus if stored in a dry place.

To steam the fruit, put the bottles into a copper or other vessel up to their necks in cold water, with a little hay between and under them; light the fire, let the water heat slowly, and keep it at the point of gentle simmering until the fruit is sufficiently scalded. Some kinds will of course require a much longer time than others. From half to three-quarters of an hour will be sufficient for gooseberries, currants, and raspberries; but the appearance of all will best denote their being done. When they have sunk almost half the depth of the bottles, and the skins are shrivelled, extinguish the fire, but leave them in the water until it is quite cold; then wipe and store the bottles in a dry place. A bit of moistened bladder tied over the corks is better than the rosin when the fruit is steamed.

APPLE JELLY.

Various kinds of apples may be used successfully to make this jelly, but the nonsuch is by many persons preferred to all others for the purpose. The Ripstone pippin, however, may be used for it with very good effect, either solely, or with a mixture of pearmains. It is necessary only that the fruit should be finely flavoured, and that it should boil easily to a marmalade. Pare, core, quarter, and weigh it quickly that it may not lose its colour, and to each pound pour a pint of cold water, and boil 't until it is well broken, without being reduced to a quite thick pulp, as it would then be difficult to rex ler the juice perfectly clear, which it ought to be. Drain this well from the apples, either through a fine sieve or a folded muslin strainer, and pass it afterwards through a jelly-bag, or turn the fruit at once into the last of these, and pour the liquid through a second time if needful. When it appears quite transparent, weigh, and reduce it by quick boiling for twenty minutes; draw it from the fire, add two pounds of sugar, broken very small, for three of the decoction, stir it till it is entirely dissolved, then place the preserving-pan again over a clear fire, and boil the preserve quickly for ten minutes, or until it jellies firmly upon the skimmer when poured from it; throw in the strained juice of a small lemon for every two pounds of jelly, a couple of minutes before it is taken from the fire.

Apples, 7 lbs.; water, 7 pints: ½ to full hour. Juice, 6 lbs.: 20 minutes *quick* boiling. Sugar, 4 lbs.: 10 to 15 minutes. Juice, 3 lemons.

EXCEEDINGLY FINE APPLE JELLY.

Pare quickly some highly flavoured juicy apples of any kind, or of various kinds together, for this is immaterial; slice, without dividing them; but first free them from the stalks and eyes, shake out some of the pips, and put the apples evenly into very clean large stone jars, just dipping an occasional layer into cold water as this is done, the better to preserve the colour of the whole. Set the jars into pans of water, and boil the fruit slowly until it is quite soft, then turn it into a jelly-bag or cloth, and let the juice all drop from it. The quantity which it will have yielded will be small, but it will be clear and rich. Weigh and boil it for ten minutes, then draw it from the fire, and stir into it, until it is entirely dissolved, twelve ounces of *good* sugar to the pound and quarter (or pint) of juice. Place the preserve again over the fire and stir it without intermission, except to clear off the scum, until it has boiled from eight to ten minutes longer, for otherwise it will jelly on the surface with the scum upon it, which it will then be difficult to remove, as when touched it will break and fall into the preserve. The strained juice of one small fresh lemon to the pint of jelly should be thrown into it two or three minutes before it is poured out, and the rind of one or two cut very thin may be simmered in the juice before the sugar is added; but the pale, delicate colour of the jelly will be injured by too much of it, and many persons would altogether prefer the pure flavour.

Juice of apples, 1 quart, or 2½ lbs.: 10 minutes. Sugar, 1½ lb.: 8 to 10 minutes. Juice, 2 small lemons; rind of 1 or more, at pleasure.

Obs. 1.—The quantity of apples required for it renders this a rather expensive preserve, where they are not abundant; but it is a remarkably fine jelly, and turns out from the moulds in perfect shape and *very* firm. It may be served in the second course, or for dessert. It is sometimes made without paring the apples, or dipping them into the water, and the colour is then a deep red: we have occasionally had a pint of water added to about a gallon and a half of apples, but the jelly was not then *quite* so fine in flavour.

Obs. 2.—The best time for making this apple-jelly is from the end of November to Christmas.

Obs. 3.—Quince-jelly would, without doubt, be very fine made by this receipt; but as the juice of that fruit is richer than that of the apple, a little water might be added. Alternate layers of apples and quinces would also answer well, we think.

QUINCE JELLY.

Pare, quarter, core, and weigh some ripe but quite sound quinces, as quickly as possible, and throw them as they are done into part of the water in which they are to be boiled, as directed at page 305; allow one pint of this to each pound of the fruit, and simmer it gently until it is a little broken, but not so long as to redden the juice, which ought to be very pale. Turn the whole into a jelly-bag, or strain the liquid through a fine cloth, and let it drain very closely from it, but without the slightest pressure. Weigh the juice, put it into a delicately clean preserving-pan, and boil it quickly for twenty minutes; take it from the fire and stir into it, until it is entirely dissolved, twelve ounces of sugar for each pound of juice, or fourteen ounces if the fruit should be very acid, which it will be in the earlier part of the season; keep it constantly stirred and thoroughly cleared from scum from ten to twenty minutes longer, or until it jellies strongly in falling from the skimmer; then pour it directly into glasses or moulds. If properly made, it will be sufficiently firm to turn out of the latter, and it will be beautifully transparent, and rich in flavour. It may be made with an equal weight of juice and sugar mixed together in the first instance, and boiled from twenty to thirty minutes. It is difficult to state the time precisely, because from different causes it will vary very much. It should be reduced rapidly to the proper point, as long boiling injures the colour: this is always more perfectly preserved by boiling the juice without the sugar first.

To each pound pared and cored quinces, 1 pint water: ¾ to 1½ hour. Juice, boiled 20 minutes. To each pound, 12 ozs. sugar: 10 to 20 minutes. Or, juice and sugar equal weight: 20 to 30 minutes.

QUINCE MARMALADE.

When to economize the fruit is not an object, pare, core, and quarter some of the inferior quinces, and boil them in as much water as will nearly cover them, until they begin to break; strain the juice from them, and for the marmalade put half a pint of it to each pound of fresh quinces: in preparing these, be careful to cut out the hard stony parts round the cores. Simmer them gently until they are perfectly tender then press them, with the juice, through a coarse sieve; put them into a perfectly clean pan, and boil them until they form almost a dry paste; add for each pound of quinces and the half pint of juice, three quarters of a pound of sugar, in fine powder, and boil the marmalade for half an hour, stirring it gently without ceasing: it will be very firm and bright in colour. If made shortly after the fruit is gathered, a little additional sugar will be required; and when a richer and less dry marmalade is better liked, it must be boiled a shorter time, and an equal weight of fruit and sugar must be used.

Quinces, pared and cored, 4 lbs.; prepared juice, 1 quart: 2 to 3 hours. Boiled fast to dry, 20 to 40 minutes. Sugar, 3 lbs.: 30 minutes.

Richer marmalade: quinces, 4 lbs.; juice, 1 quart; sugar, 4 lbs.

QUINCE AND APPLE MARMALADE.

Boil together, from three quarters of an hour to an our, two pounds of pearmains, or of any other well-flavoured apples, in an equal weight of prepared quince-juice (see page 305), then take them from the fire, and mix with them a pound and a half of sugar, in fine powder; when this is a little dissolved, set the pan again over a brisk fire, and boil the preserve for twenty minutes longer, keeping it stirred all the time.

Prepared quince-juice, 2 lbs.; apples, 2 lbs.: ¾ to 1 hour. Sugar, 1½ lb.: 20 minutes.

QUINCE PASTE.

If the full flavour of the quinces be desired, stew them sufficiently tender to press through a sieve in the prepared juice of page 305; otherwise, in just water enough to about three parts cover them; when they are soft quite through, lift them out, let them cool, and then pass them through a sieve; reduce them to a dry paste, over a very clear fire, and stir them constantly; then weigh the fruit, and mix it with an equal proportion of pounded sugar, or with sugar boiled to candy height (we find the effect nearly the same, whichever method be pursued), and stir the paste without intermission until it is again so dry as to quit the pan and adhere to the spoon in one large ball; press it into shallow pans or dishes; cut it, as soon as cold, into small squares, and, should they seem to require it, dry them with a very gentle degree of heat, and when they are again cold store them in tin cases with well-dried foolscap paper between them; the paste may be moulded, when more convenient, and kept until it is wanted for table in a very dry place. In France, where the fruit is admirably confected, the *pâte des coigns*, or quince paste, is somewhat less boiled than we have directed, and dried afterwards in the sun, or in an extremely gentle oven, in square rims of tin, about an inch and a half deep, placed upon clean plates.

JELLY OF SIBERIAN CRABS.

This fruit makes a jelly of beautiful colour, and of pleasant flavour also; it may be stored in small moulds of ornamental shape, and turned out for a dessert dish. Take off the stalks, weigh, and wash the crabs; then, to each pound and a half, add a pint of water, and boil them gently until they are broken, but do not allow them to fall to a pulp. Pour the whole into a jelly-bag, and when the juice is quite transparent, weigh it, put it into a clean preserving-pan, boil it quickly for ten minutes, take it from the fire, and stir in it, till dissolved, ten ounces of fine sugar, roughly powdered, to each pound of the juice; boil the jelly from twelve to fifteen minutes, skim it very clean, and pour it into the mould. Should the quantity be large, a few additional minutes boiling must be given to the juice before the sugar is added.

To each 1½ lb. of crabs; water, 1 pint: 12 to 18 minutes. Juice to be boiled fast 10 minutes; sugar, to each pound, 10 ozs.: 12 to 15 minutes.

TO PRESERVE BARBERRIES IN BUNCHES.

Take the finest barberries, without stones, that can be procured, tie them together in bunches of four or five sprigs, and for each half pound of the fruit (which is extremely light), boil one pound of very good sugar in a pint of water for twenty minutes, and clear it well from scum; throw in the fruit let it heat gently, and then boil from five to seven minutes, when it will be perfectly transparent. So long as any snapping noise is heard, the fruit is not at all done; it should be pressed equally down into the syrup until the whole of the berries have burst; it should then be turned into jars, which must be covered with skin, or with two or three folds of thick paper, as soon as the preserve is perfectly cold. The barberries thus prepared make a beautiful garnish for sweet dishes, or for custard puddings.

Barberries, tied in bunches, 1½ lb. Sugar, 3 lbs.; water, 1½ pint: 20 minutes. Barberries boiled in syrup, 5 to 7 minutes.

BARBERRY JELLY.

To each pound of barberries, stripped from the stalks, put a pint and a half of cold water, and boil them for fifteen minutes; bruise them with the back of a wooden spoon, pour them into a hair-sieve or muslin strainer, and pass the juice afterwards through a jelly-bag. When it appears perfectly clear, weigh and then boil it fast for ten minutes; take it from the fire, and stir into it as many pounds of sugar in fine powder as there were pounds of juice; when this is dissolved, boil the jelly again for ten minutes, skim it carefully, and pour it into jars or glasses: if into the latter, warm them previously, or the boiling jelly may cause them to break.

Barberries, 3 lbs.; water, 4½ pints: 15 minutes. Juice alone: 10 minutes. To each pound of juice 1 lb. of sugar: 10 minutes.

BARBERRY JAM. (*A good Receipt.*)

The barberries for this preserve should be quite ripe, though they should not be allowed to hang until they begin to decay. Strip them from the stalks, throw aside such as are spotted, and for each pound of the fruit allow eighteen ounces of well-refined sugar; boil this, with one pint of water to every four pounds, until it becomes white, and falls in thick masses from the spoon; then throw in the fruit, and keep it stirred over a brisk fire for six minutes only; take off the scum, and pour it into jars or glasses.

Sugar, 4½ lbs.; water, 1¼ pint, boiled to candy height. Barberries, 4 lbs.: 6 minutes.

BARBERRY JAM. (*Second Receipt.*)

The preceeding is an excellent receipt, but the preserve will be *very* good if eighteen ounces of pounded sugar be mixed and boiled with the fruit for ten minutes; and this is done at a small expense of time and trouble.

Sugar pounded, 2¼ lbs.; fruit, 2 lbs.: boiled 10 minutes.

VERY COMMON BARBERRY JAM.

Weigh the fruit after it has been stripped from the stalks, and boil it for ten minutes over a moderate fire, keeping it stirred all the time; then add to it an equal weight of good Lisbon sugar, and boil the preserve for five minutes.

Barberries, 3 lbs.: 10 minutes. Lisbon sugar, 3 lbs.: 5 minutes.

Obs.—The small barberry, without stones, must be used for the foregoing receipts, but for those which follow either sort will answer.

SUPEI.IOR BARBERRY JELLY, AND MARMALADE.

Strip the fruit from the stems, wash it in spring-water, drain, bruise it slightly, and put it into a clean stone jar, with no more liquid than the drops which hang about it. Place the jar in a pan of water, and steam the fruit until is quite tender: this will be in from thirty minutes to an hour. Pour off the clear juice, strain, weigh, and boil it fast from five to seven minutes, with eighteen ounces of sugar to every pound. For the marmalade, press the barberries through a sieve with a wooden spoon, and boil them quickly for the same time, and with the same proportion of sugar as the jelly.

Barberries boiled in water-bath until tender; to each pound of juice, 1 lb. 2 ozs. sugar: 5 minutes. Pulp of fruit, to each pound, 18 ozs. sugar: 5 minutes.

Obs.—We have always had these preserves made with very ripe fruit, and have found them extremely good; but more sugar may be needed to sweeten them sufficiently when the barberries have hung less time upon the trees.

ORANGE MARMALADE.

Rasp very slightly on a fine and delicately clean grater the rinds of some sound Seville oranges; cut them in quarters, and separate the flesh from the rinds; then with the small end of a tea, or egg spoon, clear it entirely from the pips, and from the loose inner skin and film. Put the rinds into a large quantity of cold water, and change it when they have boiled about twenty minutes. As soon as they are perfectly tender lift them out, and drain them on a sieve; slice them thin, and add eight ounces of them to each pound of the pulp and juice, with a pound and a half of highly-refined sugar in fine powder; boil the marmalade quickly for half an hour, skim it well, and turn it into the jars. This marmalade has not a very powerful flavour of the orange-rind. When more of this is liked, either leave a portion of the fruit unrasped, or mix with the preserve some of the zest which has been grated off, allowing for it its weight of sugar. Or proceed thus: allow to a dozen Seville oranges two fine juicy lemons, and take the weight of the whole in sifted sugar, of excellent quality. With a sharp knife cut through the rinds just deep enough to allow them to be stripped off in quarters with the end of a spoon, and throw them for a night into plenty of cold spring-water; on the following morning boil them sufficiently tender to allow the head of a pin to pierce them easily; then drain them well, let them cool, and scrape out the white part of the rind, and cut the remainder into thin chips. In the mean time have the pulp of the fruit quite cleared from the pips and film; put it with the sugar and chips into a preserving-pan, heat it slowly, then boil it from twenty to thirty minutes: it will be very rich, good marmalade. The sugar, first broken into large lumps, is sometimes made into a very thick syrup, with so much water only as will just dissolve it; the pulp and juice are in that case boiled in it quickly for ten minutes before the chips are added; and a part of these are pounded and stirred into the preserve with the others. March is the proper month for making this preserve, the Seville orange being then in perfection. For lemon marmalade proceed exactly in the same manner as for this. The whole of the rinds of either fruit are pounded to a paste, and then boiled with the pulp, to make what is called transparent marmalade.

Rinds of Seville oranges, lightly rasped and boiled tender, 2 lbs., pulp and juice, 4 lbs.; sugar, 6 lbs.: ½ hour. Or, weight of oranges, first taken in sugar, and added, with all the rinds, to the pulp after the whole has been properly prepared.

GENUINE SCOTCH MARMALADE.

"Take some bitter oranges, and double their weight of sugar; cut the rind of the fruit into quarters and peel it off, and if the marmalade be not wanted very thick, take off some of the spongy white skin inside the rind. Cut the chips as thin as possible, and about half an inch long, and divide the pulp into small bits, removing carefully the seeds, which may be steeped in part of the water that is to make the marmalade, and which must be in the proportion of a quart to a pound of fruit. Put the chips and pulp into a deep earthen dish, and pour the water boiling over them; let them remain for twelve or fourteen hours, and then turn the whole into the preserving-pan, and boil it until the chips are perfectly tender. When they are so, add by degrees the sugar (which should be previously pounded), and boil the marmalade until it jellies. The water in which the seeds have been steeped, and which must be taken from the quantity apportioned to the whole of the preserve, should be poured into a hair-sieve, and the seeds well worked in it with the back of a spoon; a strong clear jelly will be obtained by this means, which must be washed off them by pouring their own liquor through the sieve in small portions over them. This must be added to the fruit when it is first set on the fire.

Oranges, 3 lbs.; water, 3 quarts; sugar, 6 lbs.

Obs.—This receipt, which we have not tried ourselves, is guarantied as an excellent one by the Scotch lady from whom it was procured.

ORANGE CONSERVE FOR PUDDINGS.

Wash and then soak in plenty of spring-water for three days, changing it night and morning, half a dozen Seville oranges; then boil them till they are sufficiently tender for the head of a pin to pierce them easily; drain and weigh them, and for each pound take and reduce to fine powder two pounds of good sugar. Cut the oranges asunder, and remove the pips and the coarse loose skin of the cores; then beat them, with the sugar, in a large mortar, and pick out as this is done any pits of fibre or coarse inner skin which cannot be reduced to a paste. When the whole forms a smooth conserve, put it into small jars for use, as it requires no boiling after the fruit and sugar are mixed: if stored in a dry place, it will remain good for two years. Each orange should be tied in a thin small cloth or a bit of muslin when it is boiled, and the water should be changed once (or even twice when the fine aromatic bitter of the rind is altogether objected to), or the fruit may be lifted from the water and thrown immediately into another pan containing more which is ready boiling. Two tablespoonsful of this conserve, with the yolks of five or six eggs, a couple of ounces of sugar, and as much clarified butter smoothly mixed and well beaten together, will make good cheesecakes, or an excellent but not large pudding: the same proportion will be found an agreeable addition to a plum-pudding also.

Seville oranges, boiled tender, 2 lbs.; sugar, 4 lbs.; beaten together, not boiled.

CHAPTER XXII.

PICKLES.

OBSERVATIONS ON PICKLES.

THE first requisite in making pickles is to have unadulterated vinegar, for all the expense and trouble bestowed upon them is often
entirely lost in consequence of ingredients being mixed with this which
soften, and sometimes even partially decompose, the substances immersed in it. That which is home-made is generally found for all purposes to answer best, and it may be prepared of almost any degree of
strength by increasing the ordinary proportion of fruit and sugar, or
whatever else may be used for it. The refuse of raisin-wine, and
green gooseberries, may both be converted into excellent vinegar: but
unless the pickles be quite covered with their liquor, and well protected
from the air, and from the influence of damp, which is more than anything destructive of them, the purity of the vinegar will not preserve
them eatable. We can confidently recommend to the reader the
rather limited number of receipts which follow, and which might
easily be multiplied did the size of our volume permit. Pickling is so
easy a process, however, that when in any degree properly acquired, it
may be extended to almost every kind of fruit and vegetable successfully. A few of the choicer kinds will nevertheless be found generally
more acceptable than a greater variety of inferior preparations. Mushrooms, gherkins, walnuts, lemons, eschalots, and peaches, for all of
which we have given minute directions, will furnish as much choice as
is commonly required.

TO PICKLE CHERRIES.

Leave about an inch of their stalks on some fine, sound cherries, that
are not over-ripe; put them into a jar, cover them with cold vinegar,
and let them stand for three weeks; pour off two-thirds of the liquor
and replace it with fresh vinegar; then, after having drained it
from the fruit, boil the whole with an ounce of coriander seed, a small
blade of mace, a few grains of cayenne, or a teaspoonful of white peppercorns, and four bruised cochineals to every quart, all tied loosely in a
fold of muslin. Let the pickle become quite cold before it is added to
the cherries: in a month they will be fit for use. The vinegar which
is poured from the fruit makes a good syrup of itself when boiled with
a pound of sugar to the pint, but it is improved by having some fresh
raspberries, cherries, or currants previously infused in it for three or
four days.

TO PICKLE GHERKINS,* OR CUCUMBERS.

Let the gherkins be gathered on a dry day, before the frost has
touched them; take off the blossoms, put them into a stone jar, and pour
over them sufficient boiling brine to cover them well. The following
day take them out, wipe them singly, lay them into a clean stone jar,

---

* Small cucumbers. All cucumbers may be pickled in the same way.

with a dozen bay-leaves over them, and pour upon them the following pickle, when it is boiling fast: as much vinegar as will more than cover the gherkins by an inch or two, with an ounce and a quarter of salt, a quarter-ounce of black peppercorns, an ounce and a half of ginger sliced, or slightly bruised, and two small blades of mace to every quart; put a plate over the jar, and leave it for two days, then drain off the vinegar, and heat it afresh: when it boils, throw in the gherkins, and keep them just on the point of simmering for two or three minutes; pour the whole back into the jar, put the plate again upon it, and let it remain until the pickle is quite cold, when a skin, or two separate folds of thick brown paper, must be tied closely over it. The gherkins thus pickled are very crisp, and excellent in flavour, and the colour is sufficiently good to satisfy the prudent housekeeper, to whom the brilliant and *poisonous* green produced by boiling the vinegar in a brass skillet (a process constantly recommended in books of cookery) is anything but attractive. To satisfy ourselves of the effect produced by the action of the acid on the metal, we had a few gherkins thrown into some vinegar which was boiling in a brass pan, and nothing could be more beautiful than the colour which they almost immediately exhibited. We fear this dangerous method is too often resorted to in preparing pickles for sale.

Brine to pour on gherkins;—6 ozs. salt to each quart water: 24 hours. Pickle:—to each quart vinegar, salt, 1¼ oz.; black peppercorns, ¼ oz.; ginger, sliced or bruised, 1½ oz.; mace, 2 small blades; bay-leaves; 24 to 100 gherkins, more when the flavour is liked: 2 days. Gherkins simmered in vinegar, 2 to 3 minutes.

PICKLES.

Obs.—The quantity of vinegar required to cover the gherkins will be shown by that of the brine: so much depends upon their size, that it is impossible to direct the measure exactly. A larger proportion of spice can be added at pleasure.

TO PICKLE NASTURTIUMS.

These should be gathered quite young, and a portion of the buds, when very small, should be mixed with them. Prepare a pickle by dissolving an ounce and a half of salt in a quart of pale vinegar, and throw in the berries as they become fit, from day to day. They are used instead of capers for sauce, and by some persons are preferred to them. When purchased for pickling, put them at once into a jar, and cover them well with the vinegar.

TO PICKLE PEACHES.

Take, at their full growth, just before they begin to ripen, six large or eight moderate-sized peaches; wipe the down from them, and put them into brine that will float an egg. In three days let them be taken out, and drained on a sieve reversed for several hours. Boil in a quart of vinegar for ten minutes two ounces of whole white pepper, two of ginger slightly bruised, a teaspoonful of salt, two blades of mace, half a pound of mustard-seed, and a half-teaspoonful of cayenne tied in a bit of muslin. Lay the peaches into a jar, and pour the boiling pickle on them: in two months they will be fit for use.

Peaches, 6 or 8: in brine 3 days. Vinegar, 1 quart; whole white
22

pepper, 2 ozs.; bruised ginger, 2 ozs.; salt, 1 teaspoonful; mace, 2 blades; mustard-seed, ½ lb.: 10 minutes.

Obs.—The peaches may be converted into excellent mangoes by cutting out from the stalk-end of each a round of sufficient size to allow the stone to be extracted: this should be done after they are taken from the brine. They may be filled with *very fresh* mustard-seed, previously washed in a little vinegar; to this a small portion of garlic, or bruised eschalots, cayenne, horse-radish, chilies (the most appropriate of any), or spice of any kind may be added, to the taste. The part cut out must be replaced, and secured with a packthread crossed over the fruit.

TO PICKLE MUSHROOMS.

Select for this purpose, if they can be procured, the smallest buttons of the wild or *meadow* mushrooms, in preference to those which are artificially raised, and let them be as freshly gathered as possible. Cut the stems off quite close, and clean them with a bit of new flannel slightly moistened, and dipped in fine salt; throw them as they are done into plenty of spring-water, mixed with a large spoonful of salt, but drain them from it quickly afterwards, and lay them into a soft cloth to dry, or the moisture which hangs about them will too much weaken the pickle. For each quart of the mushrooms thus prepared, take *nearly* a quart of the palest white wine vinegar (this is far superior to the distilled vinegar generally used for the purpose, and the variation in the colour of the mushrooms will be very slight), and add to it a heaped teaspoonful of salt, half an ounce of whole white pepper, an ounce of ginger, sliced or lightly bruised, about-the fourth of a saltspoonful of cayenne, tied in a small bit of muslin, and two large blades of mace; to these may be added half a small nutmeg, sliced; but too much spice will entirely overpower the fine natural flavour of the mushrooms. When the pickle boils, throw them in, and boil them in it over a clear fire moderately fast from six to nine minutes, or somewhat longer, should they *not* be very small. When they are much disproportioned in size, the larger ones should have two minutes boil before the others are thrown into the vinegar. As soon as they are tolerably tender, put them at once into small stone jars, or into *warm* wide-necked bottles, and divide the spice equally amongst them. The following day, or as soon as they are perfectly cold, secure them from the air with large corks, or tie skins and paper over them. They should be stored in a dry place, and guarded from severe frost. When the colour of the mushrooms is more considered than the excellence of the pickle, the distilled vinegar can be used for it. The reader may rely upon this receipt as a really good one; we have had it many times proved, and it is altogether our own.

Mushroom-buttons (without the stems), 2 quarts; palest white wine vinegar, short ½ gallon; salt, *large* dessertspoonful, or 1½ oz.; white peppercorns, 1 oz.; whole ginger, 2 ozs.; cayenne, small ½ saltspoonful; 1 small nutmeg.

MUSHROOMS IN BRINE; (*for winter use.*) (*Very good.*)

We have had small mushroom-buttons excellently preserved through the winter prepared as follows, and we therefore give the exact proportions which we had used for them, though the same quantity of brine would possibly allow of rather more mushrooms in it. Prepare them exactly as for-the preceding pickle, and measure them after the stems

are taken off. For each quart, boil together for five minutes two quarts
of water, with half a pound of common white salt, a small dessertspoon
ful of white peppercorns, a couple of blades of mace, and a race of ginger; take off the scum thoroughly, and throw in the mushrooms; boil
them gently for about five minutes, then put them into well-warmed,
wide-necked bottles, and let them become perfectly cold, pour a little
good salad oil on the top, cork them with new corks, and tie bladder
over, or cover them with two separate bladders. When wanted for
use, soak the mushrooms in warm water till the brine is sufficiently
extracted.

Mushrooms, 1 quart; water, ½ gallon; salt, ½ lb.; peppercorns, 1
small dessertspoonful; mace, 2 blades; ginger, 1 race: 5 minutes.
Mushrooms, in brine, 5 minutes.

TO PICKLE WALNUTS.

The walnuts for this pickle must be gathered while a pin can pierce
them easily, for when once the shell can be felt, they have ceased to be
in a proper state for it. Make sufficient brine to cover them well, with
six ounces of salt to the gallon of water; take off the scum, which will
rise to the surface as the salt dissolves, throw in the walnuts, and stir
them night and morning; change the brine every three days, and if
they are wanted for immediate eating, leave them in it for twelve days;
otherwise, drain them from it in nine, spread them on dishes, and let
them remain exposed to the air until they become black; this will be in
twelve hours, or less. Make a pickle for them with something more
than half a gallon of vinegar to the hundred, a teaspoonful of salt, two
ounces of black pepper, three of bruised ginger, a drachm of mace, and
from a quarter to half an ounce of cloves (of which some may be stuck
into three or four small onions), and four ounces of mustard-seed. Boil
the whole of these together for about five minutes; have the walnuts
ready in a stone jar, or jars, and pour it on them as it is taken from the
fire. When the pickle is quite cold, cover the jar securely, and store it
in a dry place. Keep the walnuts always well covered with the vinegar, and boil that which is added to them.

Walnuts, 100; in brine made with 12 ozs. salt to 2 quarts water, and
changed twice or more, 9 or 12 days. Vinegar, *full* ½ gallon; salt, 1
teaspoonful; whole black pepper, 2 ozs.; ginger, 3 ozs.; mace, 1
drachm; cloves, ¼ to ½ oz.; small onions, 4 to 6; mustard-seed, 4 ozs.:
5 minutes.

TO PICKLE BEET-ROOT.

Boil the beet-root tender by the directions of page 247, and when it
is quite cold, pare and slice it; put it into a jar, and cover it with common vinegar previously boiled and allowed to become again perfectly
cold: it will soon be ready for use. It is excellent when merely covered
with vinegar. A few small onions may be boiled in the pickle for it
when their flavour is liked.

To each quart vinegar, salt, 1 teaspoonful; cayenne tied in muslin,
½ saltspoonful, or white peppercorns, ½ to whole oz.

PICKLED ESCHALOTS.

For a quart of ready-peeled eschalots, add to the same quantity of the
best pale white-wine vinegar, a dessertspoonful of salt, and an ounce of

whole white pepper; bring these quickly to a boil, take off the scum, throw in the eschalots, simmer them for two minutes only; turn them into a clean stone jar, and when they are quite cold, tie a skin, or two folds of thick paper over it.

Eschalots, 1 quart; vinegar, 1 quart; salt, 1 dessertspoonful; whole white pepper, 1 oz.

Obs.—The sooner the eschalots are pickled after they are ripe and dry, the better they will be.

PICKLED ONIONS.

Take the smallest onions that can be procured, just after they are harvested, for they are never in so good a state for the purpose as then; proceed, after having peeled them, exactly as for the eschalots, and when they begin to look clear, which will be in three or four minutes, put them into jars, and pour the pickle on them. The vinegar should be very pale, and their colour will then be exceedingly well preserved Any favourite spices can be added to it.

TO PICKLE LEMONS AND LIMES; (*excellent.*)

Wipe eight fine sound lemons very clean, and make, at equal distances, four deep incisions in each, from the stalk to the blossom end, but without dividing the fruit; stuff them with as much salt as they will contain, lay them into a deep dish, and place them in a sunny window, or in some warm place for a week or ten days, keeping them often turned and basted with their own liquor; then rub them with some good pale turmeric, and put them with their juice, into a stone jar with a small head of garlic, divided into cloves and peeled, and a dozen small onions stuck with twice as many cloves. Boil in two quarts of white-wine vinegar, half a pound of ginger lightly bruised, two ounces of whole black pepper, and half a pound of mustard-seed; take them from the fire and pour them directly on the lemons; cover the jar with a plate, and let them remain till the following day, then add to the pickle half a dozen capsicums (red peppers), and tie a skin and a fold of thick paper over the jar.

Large lemons stuffed with salt, 8: 8 to 10 days. Turmeric, 1 to 2 ozs.; ginger, ½ lb.; mustard-seed, ½ lb.; capsicums, 6 ozs.

Obs.—The turmeric and garlic may, we think, be omitted from this pickle with advantage. It will remain good for seven years if the lemons be kept well covered with vinegar; that which is added to them should be boiled and then left till cold before it is poured into the jar. The lemons will not be fit for table in less than twelve months; but if wanted for more immediate use, set them for one night into a cool oven after the bread is drawn; they may then be eaten almost directly.

Limes must have but slight incisions made in the rinds; and they will be sufficiently softened in four or five days. Two ounces of salt only will be required for half a dozen; and all which remains unmelted must, with their juice, be put into the jar with them before the vinegar is poured on: this should be mixed with spice and mustard-seed, and be boiling when it is added to the limes.

TO PICKLE BARBERRIES AND SIBERIAN CRABS.

When wanted for garnishing only, take the fruit before it is very ripe, cut half the length of their stalks from the crabs, and free the barberries from the leaves, and from any discoloured berries that may be amongst them.   Put them into stone jars, and cover them well with brine, which has been boiled and left to become perfectly cold.   Look at them occasionally during the winter, and should any scum or mould have gathered on the surface, clear it well off, drain the brine closely from the fruit, and fill the jars with some that is freshly made.   Six ounces of salt, and a morsel of alum half the size of a bean to the quart of water should be boiled together for ten minutes, and well skimmed, both for the first brine, and for any that may be required afterwards.

To pickle these fruits in vinegar, add the alum to a sufficient quantity to cover them, and boil it with a few white peppercorns, which must be strained out before it is poured into the jars: it must be quite cold when added to the barberries or crabs; these last should not be ripe when they are used, or they will burst in the pickle; they should have attained their growth and full colour, but be still hard.

CHAPTER XXIII.

CAKES.

Modern Cake Mould.

GENERAL REMARKS ON CAKES.

THE ingredients for cakes, as well as for puddings, should all be fresh and good, as well as free from damp; the lightness of many kinds depends entirely on that given to the eggs by whisking, and by the manner in which the whole is mixed.   A *small* portion of carbonate of soda, which will not be in the slightest degree perceptible to the taste after the cake is baked, if thrown in just before the mixture is put into the oven, will ensure its rising well.

To guard against the bitterness so often imparted by yeast when it is used for cakes or biscuits, it should be *sparingly* added, and the sponge should be left twice the usual time to rise.   This method will be found to answer equally with bread. For example: should a couple of spoonsful of yeast be ordered in a receipt, when it is bitter, use but one, and let it stand two hours instead of half the time: the fermentation, though slow, will be quite as perfect as if it were more quickly effected, and the cake or loaf thus made will not become dry by any means so soon as if a large portion of yeast were mixed with it.

All light cakes require a rather brisk oven to raise and set them; very large rich ones a well-sustained degree of heat sufficient to bake them through; and small sugar-cakes a very slow oven, to prevent their taking a deep colour before they are half done: gingerbread too should be gently baked, unless it be of the light thick kind. Meringues, macaroons, and ratafias, will bear a slight degree more of heat than these.

For sponge and savoy cakes the French butter their moulds thickly, and shake fine sugar in them until they are equally covered with it: the loose sugar must be turned out before they are used.

To ascertain whether a cake be done, thrust a knife into the centre, and should this come out clean draw it from the oven directly; but should the paste adhere to it, continue the baking. Several sheets of paper are placed usually under large plum-cakes.

TO BLANCH ALMONDS.

Put them into a saucepan with plenty of cold water, and heat it slowly; when it is just scalding, turn the almonds into a basin, peel, and throw them into cold water as they are done: dry them well in a soft cloth before they are used. If the water be too hot, it will turn them yellow.

TO POUND ALMONDS.

Almonds are more easily pounded, and less liable to become oily, if dried a little in a very gentle degree of heat after they are blanched; left for example, in a warm room for two or three days, lightly spread on a large dish or tin. They should be sprinkled during the beating with a few drops of cold water, or white of egg, or lemon-juice, and pounded to a smooth paste: this is more easily done, we believe, when they are first roughly chopped, but we prefer to have them thrown at once into the mortar.

TO REDUCE ALMONDS TO A PASTE. (*The quickest and easiest way.*)

Chop them a little on a large and very clean trencher, then with a paste-roller (rolling-pin), which ought to be thicker in the middle than at the ends, roll them well until no small bits are perceptible amongst them. We have found this method answer admirably; but as some of the oil is expressed from the almonds by it, and absorbed by the board, we would recommend a marble slab for them in preference, when it is at hand; and should they be intended for a sweet dish, that some pounded sugar should be strewed under them. When a board or strong trencher is used, it should be rather higher in the middle than at the sides.

TO COLOUR ALMONDS FOR CAKES, OR PASTRY.

Blanch, dry, and chop them rather coarsely; pour a little prepared cochineal into the hands, and roll the almonds between them until they are equally coloured; then spread them on a sheet of paper, and place them in a *very* gentle degree of heat to dry. Use spinach-juice (see page 233) to colour them green, and a strong infusion of saffron to give them a yellow tint. They have a pretty effect when strewed over the icing of tarts or cakes, especially the rose-coloured ones, which should be rather pale.

TO PREPARE BUTTER FOR RICH CAKES.

For all large and very rich cakes the usual directions are, *to beat the butter to a cream;* but we find that they are quite as light, if not more so, when it is cut small and gently melted with just so much heat as will dissolve it, and no more. If it be shaken round in a saucepan previously warmed, and held near the fire for a short time, it will soon be liquefied, which is all that is required: it must on no account be *hot* when it is added to the other ingredients, to which it must be poured in small portions after they are all mixed, in the way which we have minutely described in the receipt for a Madeira cake, and that of the Sutherland puddings (Chapter XVIII.) To *cream* it, drain the water well from it, after it is cut, soften it a little before the fire should it be very hard, and then with the back of a large strong wooden spoon beat it until it resembles thick cream. When prepared thus, the sugar is added to it first, and then the other ingredients in succession.

TO WHISK EGGS FOR LIGHT RICH CAKES.

Break them one by one, and separate the yolks from the whites: this is done easily by pouring the yolk from one half of the shell to the other, and letting the white drop from it into a basin beneath. With a small three-pronged fork take out the specks from each egg as it is broken, that none may accidentally escape notice. Whisk the yolks until they appear light, and the whites until they are a quite solid froth; while any liquid remains at the bottom of the bowl they are not sufficiently beaten: when a portion of them, taken up with the whisk, and dropped from it, remains standing in points, they are in the proper state for use, and should be mixed into the cake directly.

ORANGE-FLOWER MACAROONS. (DELICIOUS.)

Have ready two pounds of very dry white sifted sugar. Weigh two ounces of the petals of freshly-gathered orange-blossoms after they have been picked from the stems; and cut them very small with a pair of scissors *into* the sugar, as they will become discoloured if not mixed with it quickly after they are cut. When all are done, add the whites of seven eggs, and beat the whole well together till it looks like snow; then drop the mixture upon paper without delay, and send the cakes to a very cool oven.

Pounded sugar, 2 lbs.; orange-blossoms, 2 ozs.; whites of eggs, 7: 20 minutes, or more.

Obs.—It is almost impossible to state with accuracy the precise time required for these cakes, so much depends on the oven: they should be very delicately coloured, and yet dried through.

ALMOND MACAROONS.

Blanch a pound of fresh Jordan almonds, wipe them dry, and set them into a very cool oven to render them perfectly so; pound them to an exceedingly smooth paste, with a little white of egg; then whisk to

a firm solid froth the whites of seven eggs, or of eight, should they be
small; mix with them a pound and a half of the finest sugar; add
these by degrees to the almonds, whisk the whole up well together,
and drop the mixture upon wafer-paper, which may be procured at the
confectioner's: bake them in a moderate oven a very pale brown. It is
an improvement to the flavour of these cakes to substitute an ounce of
bitter almonds for one of the sweet: they are sometimes made with an
equal weight of each; and another variety of them is obtained by
gently browning the almonds in a slow oven before they are pounded.

Jordan almonds blanched, 1 lb.; sugar, 1½ lb.; whites of 7 or 8 eggs:
15 to 20 minutes.

IMPERIALS. (NOT VERY RICH.)

Work into a pound of flour six ounces of butter, and mix well with
them half a pound of sifted sugar, six ounces of currants, two ounces
of candied orange-peel, the grated rind of a lemon, and four well-beaten
eggs. Flour a tin lightly, and with a couple of forks place the paste
upon it in small rough heaps quite two inches apart. Bake them in a
very gentle oven, from a quarter of an hour to twenty minutes, or until
they are equally coloured to a pale brown.

Flour, 1 lb.; butter, 6 ozs.; sugar, 8 ozs.; currants, 6 ozs.; candied
peel, 2 ozs.; rind of 1 lemon; eggs, 4: 15 to 20 minutes.

VERY GOOD SMALL RICH CAKES.

Beat and mix well together four eggs properly whisked, and half a
pound of fine sifted sugar; pour to them by degrees a quarter pound of
clarified butter, as little warmed as possible; stir lightly in with these
four ounces of dry sifted flour, beat the mixture for about ten minutes,
put it into small buttered patty-pans, and bake the cakes a quarter of an
hour in a moderate oven. They should be flavoured with the rasped or
grated rind of a small lemon, or with pounded mace or cinnamon.

Eggs, 4; sugar, ½ lb.; butter, 4 ozs.; flour, 4 ozs.; lemon-rind, mace,
or cinnamon: baked, 15 minutes.

ALMOND ROCHER.

Chop very fine together eight ounces of almonds, blanched, and
dried, six of candied orange-rind, or of orange and lemon-rind mixed,
and one ounce of citron; then add to them two ounces of flour, three
quarters of a pound of sugar, a small teaspoonful of mace and cinnamon mixed, and the whites of three large eggs; roll the mixture into
balls about the size of a large marble, and bake them on wafer-paper
twenty minutes in a moderate oven: they should be quite crisp, but not
deeply coloured.

Almonds, 8 ozs.; candied orange-rind, 6 ozs.; citron, 1 oz.; flour, 2
ozs.; sugar, ¾ lb.; mace and cinnamon mixed, 1 teaspoonful; whites
of eggs, 3 large: baked, moderate oven, 20 minutes.

Obs.—When the flavour is not disliked, it will be found an improvement to substitute an ounce of bitter almonds for one of the sweet; and
we prefer the whole of the almonds and candied peel also cut into
spikes instead of being chopped: the ingredients must then be made
into a lighter paste, and placed in small heaps on the paper.

BITTER ALMOND BISCUITS.

Blanch, and then chop as fine as possible, two ounces of bitter almonds, and add them to half a pound of flour, half a pound of sifted sugar, and two ounces of butter, previously well mixed together. Whisk the whites of a couple of eggs to a strong froth, beat them lightly to the other ingredients, drop the cakes on a buttered tin, or copper oven-leaf, and bake them rather slowly from ten to twelve minutes: they should be very small. Should the proportion of bitter almonds be considered unhealthful, use half as many, and substitute sweet ones for the remainder.

Flour, ½ lb.; sugar, ½ lb.; butter, 2 ozs.; bitter almonds, 2 ozs.; whites of eggs, 2: slow oven, 10 to 12 minutes.

FINE ALMOND CAKE.

Blanch, dry, and pound to the finest possible paste, eight ounces of fresh Jordan almonds, and one ounce of bitter, moisten them with a few drops of cold water or white of egg, to prevent their oiling; then mix with them *very* gradually twelve fresh eggs which have been whisked until they are *exceedingly* light; throw in by degrees one pound of fine, dry, sifted sugar, and *keep* the mixture light by constant beating, with a large wooden spoon, as the separate ingredients are added. Mix in by degrees three quarters of a pound of dried and sifted flour of the best quality; then pour gently from the sediment a pound of butter which has been just melted, but not allowed to become hot, and beat it very gradually, but very thoroughly, into the cake, letting one portion entirely disappear before another is thrown in: add the rasped or finely-grated rinds of two sound fresh lemons, fill a thickly-buttered mould rather more than half full with the mixture, and bake the cake from an hour and a half to two hours in a well-heated oven. Lay paper over the top when it is sufficiently coloured, and guard carefully against it being burned.

Sweet almonds, ½ lb.; bitter almonds, 1 oz.; eggs, 12; sugar, 1 lb., flour, ¾ lb.; butter, 1 lb.; rinds lemons, 2: 1½ to 2 hours.

Obs.—Three quarters of a pound of almonds may be mixed with this cake when so large a portion of them is liked, but an additional ounce or two of sugar, and one egg or more, will then be required.

POUND CAKE.

Mix, as directed in the foregoing receipt, ten eggs (some cooks take a pound in weight of these), one pound of sugar, one of flour, and as much of butter. A glass of brandy and a pound of currants may be added very gradually just before the cake is put into the oven, with any spice that is liked; and two or three ounces of candied orange or lemon-rind, sliced thin, or an ounce of caraway-seeds, may supply the place of all. A cake made with half the quantity of the ingredients must be baked one hour.

RICE CAKE.

Take six eggs, with their weight in fine sugar, and in butter also, and half their weight of flour of rice, and half of wheaten flour; make the cake as directed for the Madeira or almond cake, but throw in the rice after the flour: then add the butter in the usual way, and bake the cake about an hour and ten minutes. Give any flavour that is liked. The butter may be altogether omitted. This is a moderate-sized cake.

Eggs, in the shell, 6; their weight in butter and in sugar; half as much flour of rice, and the same of wheaten flour: 1 hour, 10 minutes.

WHITE CAKE.

Beat half a pound of fresh butter to a cream, add to it an equal weight of dried and sifted sugar, the yolks and whites of eight eggs, separately whisked, two ounces of candied orange-peel, half a teaspoonful of mace, a glass of brandy, one pound of flour strewed in by degrees, and last of all a pound and a quarter of currants. Directly it is mixed send the cake to a well-heated oven, and bake it for a couple of hours. Four ounces of beaten almonds are sometimes added to it.

Butter, ½ lb.; sugar, ½ lb.; eggs, 8; mace, ½ teaspoonful; brandy, 1 wineglassful; flour, 1 lb.; candied peel, 2 ozs.; currants, 1¼ lb.: 2 hours.

A GOOD SPONGE CAKE.

Rasp on some lumps of well-refined sugar the rind of a fine sound lemon, and scrape off the part which has imbibed the essence, or crush the plums to powder, and add them to as much more as will make up the weight of eight or ten fresh eggs in the shell; break these one by one, and separate the whites from the yolks; beat the latter in a large bowl for ten minutes, then strew in the sugar gradually, and beat them well together. In the mean time let the whites be whisked to a quite solid froth, add them tn the yolks, and when they are well blended sift and *stir* the flour gently to them, but do not beat it into the mixture; pour the cake into a well-buttered mould, and bake it an hour and a quarter in a moderate oven.

Rasped rind, 1 large lemon; fresh eggs, 8 or 10; their weight of dry, sifted sugar; and half their weight of flour: baked, 1¼ hour, moderate oven.

A SMALLER SPONGE CAKE. (*Very good.*)

Five full-sized eggs, the weight of four in sugar, and of nearly three in flour, will make an exceedingly good cake: it may be flavoured, like the preceding one, with lemon-rind, or with bitter almonds, vanilla, or confected orange-blossoms reduced to powder. An hour will bake it thoroughly. All the ingredients for sponge cakes should be of good quality, and the sugar and flour should be dry; they should also be passed through a fine sieve kept expressly for such purposes. The excellence of the whole depends much on the manner in which the eggs are whisked; this should be done as lightly as possible; but it is a mistake to suppose that they cannot be too long beaten, as after they are brought to a state of perfect firmness they are injured by a continuation of the whisking, and will at times curdle, or render a cake heavy from this cause.

A SPONGE CAKE. (*Good and quickly made.*)

Beat together for between twenty and thirty minutes the yolks of nine and the whites of five fresh eggs; then by degrees add three-quarters of a pound of sugar, and six and a half of flour. Flavour it or not, at choice, with the grated rind of a lemon, and bake it an hour, or rather more, in a brisk oven.

A GOOD MADEIRA CAKE.

Whisk four fresh eggs until they are as light as possible, then, continuing still to whisk them, throw in by *slow* degrees the following ingredients in the order in which they are written: six ounces of dry, pounded, and sifted sugar; six of flour, also dried and sifted; four ounces of butter just dissolved, but not heated; the rind of a fresh lemon; and the instant before the cake is moulded, beat well in the third of a teaspoonful of carbonate of soda: bake it an hour in a moderate oven. In this, as in all compositions of the same nature, observe particularly that each portion of butter must be beaten into the mixture until no appearance of it remains before the next is added; and if this be done, and the preparation be kept light by constant and light whisking, the cake will be as good, if not better, than if the butter were creamed. Candied citron can be added to the paste, but it is not needed.

Eggs, 4; sugar, 6 ozs.; flour, 6 ozs.; butter, 4 ozs.; rind of 1 lemon, carbonate of soda, ⅓ of teaspoonful: 1 hour, moderate oven.

BANBURY CAKES.

First, mix well together a pound of currants, cleaned with great nicety and dried, a quarter-pound of beef-suet, finely minced, three ounces each of candied orange and lemon-rind, shred small, a few grains of salt, a full quarter-ounce of pounded cinnamon and nutmeg mixed, and four ounces of macaroons or ratafias rolled to powder. Next, make a light paste with fourteen ounces of butter to the pound of flour; give it an extra turn or two to prevent its rising too much in the oven; roll out one half in a very thin square, and spread the mixed fruit and spice equally upon it; moisten the edges, lay on the remaining half of the paste, rolled equally thin, press the edges securely together, mark the whole with the back of a knife in regular divisions of two inches wide and three in length; bake the pastry in a well-heated oven from twenty-five to thirty minutes, and divide it into cakes while it is still warm. They may be served as a second-course dish either hot or cold, and may be glazed at pleasure.

Currants, 1 lb.; beef-suet, 4 ozs.; candied orange and lemon-rind each, 3 ozs.; salt, small pinch; mixed spices, ¼ oz.; macaroons or ratafias, 4 ozs.: baked 25 to 30 minutes.

MERINGUES.

Beat to a very solid froth the whites of six fresh eggs, and have ready to mix with them half a pound of the best sugar, well dried and sifted. Lay some squares or long strips of writing-paper closely upon a board, which ought to be an inch thick to prevent the meringues from receiving any colour from the bottom of the oven. When all is ready for them, stir the sugar to the beaten eggs, and with a table or dessert-spoon lay the mixture on the paper in the form of a half egg; sift sugar quickly over, blow off all that does not adhere, and set the meringues immediately into a moderate oven: the process must be expeditious, or the sugar melting will cause the meringues to spread, instead of retaining their shape. When they are coloured a light brown, and are firm to the touch, draw them out, raise them from the paper, and press back the insides with a teaspoon, or scoop them out so as to leave space enough to admit some whipped cream or preserve, with which they are to be filled, when cold, before they are served. Put them again into the oven to dry gently, and when they are ready for table fasten them together in the shape of a whole egg, and pile them lightly on a napkin for the second course.

Whites of *fresh* eggs, 6; sifted sugar, ½ lb.

Obs.—Four ounces of pounded almonds may be mixed with the eggs and sugar for these cakes, and any flavour added to them at pleasure. If well made, they are remarkably good and elegant in appearance. They must be fastened together with a little white of egg.

THICK, LIGHT GINGERBREAD.

Crumble down very small eight ounces of butter into a couple of pounds of flour, then add to, and mix thoroughly with them, half a pound of good brown sugar, two ounces of powdered ginger, and half an ounce of good caraway-seeds; beat gradually to these, first two pounds of treacle (molasses), next three well-whisked eggs, and last of all half an ounce of carbonate of soda, dissolved in a very small cupful of warm water; stir the whole briskly together, pour the mixture into very shallow tins, put it immediately into a moderate oven, and bake it for an hour and a half. The gingerbread made thus will be remark-ably light and good. For children, part of the spice and butter may be omitted.

Flour, 2 lbs.; butter, 8 ozs.; sugar, ½ lb.; powdered ginger, 2 lbs.; eggs, 3; carbonate of soda, ½ oz.; water, *very small* cupful: baked 1½ hour.

Obs.—We think that something less than the half ounce of soda would be sufficient for this gingerbread, for with the whole quantity it rises in the oven to three times its height, and is apt to run over the tops of the tins even when they are but half filled with it at first.

GOOD COMMON GINGERBREAD.

Work very smoothly six ounces of fresh butter (or some that has been well washed from the salt, and wrung dry in a cloth) into one pound of flour, and mix with them thoroughly an ounce of ginger in fine powder, four ounces of brown sugar, and half a teaspoonful of beaten cloves and mace. Wet these with three-quarters of a pound, or rather more, if needful, of cold treacle; roll out the paste, cut the cakes with a round tin cutter, lay them on a floured or buttered baking tin, and put them into a very slow oven. Lemon-grate or candied peel can be added, when it is liked.

Flour, 1 lb.; butter, 6 ozs.; sugar, ¼ lb.; ginger, 1 oz.; cloves and mace, ½ teaspoonful; treacle, ¾ lb.: ½ to ¾ hour.

RICHER GINGERBREAD.

Melt together three-quarters of a pound of treacle and half a pound of fresh butter, pour these hot on a pound of flour mixed with half a pound of sugar and three quarters of an ounce of ginger. When the paste is quite cold, roll it out with as much flour as will prevent its ad-hering to the board: bake the cakes in a very gentle oven.

COCOA-NUT GINGERBREAD.

Mix well together ten ounces of fine wheaten flour, and six of flour of rice (or rice ground to powder), the grated rind of a lemon, and three-quarters of an ounce of ginger; pour nearly boiling upon these a pound of treacle, five ounces of fresh butter and five of sugar melted together in a saucepan; beat the mixture, which will be almost a butter, with a wooden spoon, and when quite smooth leave it till it is perfectly cold, then add to it five ounces of grated cocoa-nut, and when it is thoroughly blended with the other ingredients, lay the paste in small heaps upon a buttered tin, and bake them in a very slack oven from half to three-quarters of an hour.

Flour, 10 ozs.; ground rice, 6 ozs.; rind of one lemon; ginger, ¾ oz.; treacle, 1 lb.; sugar, 5 ozs.; butter, 5 ozs.; cocoa-nut, 5 ozs.: ½ to ¾ hour.

CHEAP GINGER BISCUITS.

Work into quite small crumbs three ounces of good butter, with two pounds of flour, then add three ounces of pounded sugar and two of ginger, in fine powder, and knead them into a stiff paste, with new milk. Roll it thin, cut out the biscuits with a cutter, and bake them in a slow oven until they are crisp quite through, but keep them of a pale colour. A couple of eggs are sometimes mixed with the milk for them, but are no material improvement; an additional ounce of sugar may be used when a sweeter biscuit is liked. To make good ginger *cakes*, increase the butter to six ounces, and the sugar to eight, for each pound of flour, and wet the ingredients into a paste with eggs: a little lemon-grate will give it an agreeable flavour.

Biscuits: flour, 2 lbs.; butter, 3 ozs.; pounded sugar, 3 ozs.; ginger, 2 ozs.

Cakes: flour, 1 lb.; butter, 6 ozs.; sugar, 8 ozs.; ginger, 1 oz.; 3 to 4 eggs; rind of ½ lemon.

A GOOD SODA CAKE.

Rub half a pound of good butter into a pound of fine dry flour, and work it very small; mix well with these half a pound of sifted sugar, and pour to them first a quarter of a pint of boiling milk, and next three well-whisked eggs; add some grated nutmeg, or fresh lemon-rind, and eight ounces of currants; beat the whole well and lightly together, and the instant before the cake is moulded and set into the oven, stir to it a teaspoonful of carbonate of soda in the finest powder. Bake it from an hour to an hour and a quarter, or divide it in two, and allow from half to three quarters of an hour for each cake.

Flour, 1 lb.; butter, 3 ozs.; sugar, 8 ozs.; milk, full quarter-pint; eggs, 3; currants, ½ lb.; carbonate of soda, 1 teaspoonful; 1 to 1½ hour. Or, divided, ½ to ¾ hour, moderate oven.

Obs.—This, if well made, resembles a pound-cake, but is much more wholesome. It is very good with two ounces less of butter, and with caraway-seeds or candied orange or citron substituted for the currants.

CINNAMON, OR LEMON CAKES.

Rub six ounces of good butter into a pound of fine dry flour, and work it lightly into crumbs, then add three quarters of a pound of sifted sugar, a dessertspoonful of pounded cinnamon (or half as much when only a slight flavour is liked), and make these ingredients into a firm paste with three eggs, or four, if needed. Roll it, not very thin, and cut out the cakes with a tin shape. Bake them in a very gentle oven from fifteen to twenty minutes, or longer, should they not be done quite through. As soon as they are cold, put them into a clean and dry tin canister, a precaution which should be observed with all small sugar cakes, which ought also to be loosened from the oven-tins while they are still warm.

Flour, 1 lb.; butter, 6 ozs.; sugar, ¾ lb.; cinnamon, 1 dessertspoonful (more or less, to the taste); eggs, 3 to 4.

Obs.—Lemon cakes can be made by this receipt by substituting for the cinnamon the rasped or grated rinds of two lemons, and the strained juice of one, when its acidity is not objected to. More butter, and more or less of sugar, can be used at will, both for these and for the cinnamon cakes.

QUEEN CAKES.

To make these, proceed exactly as for Sutherland puddings (see Chapter XVII.), but allow ten eggs for the pound of sugar, butter, and flour, and when these are all well mixed, throw in half a teaspoonful of mace, and a pound of clean dry currants. Bake the cakes in small well-buttered tin pans (heart-shaped ones are usual), in a somewhat brisk oven, for about twenty minutes.

A GOOD LIGHT BUN.

Break quite small three ounces of good butter into a pound and a quarter of flour, stir into the middle of these a spoonful and a quarter of solid, well-purified yeast, mixed with something more than a quarter-pint of warm milk, and leave it to rise before, but not close to the fire, for an hour, or longer, should it not then appear extremely light. Add to three eggs, properly whisked, a few spoonsful of warm milk, strain and beat them to the bun; next, mix with it six ounces of pale brown sugar, six of well-cleaned currants, and the grated rind of a small lemon, or some nutmeg, if preferred; or, in lieu of either, slice into it an ounce and a half of candied orange-rind. Let it again rise for an hour, then beat it up lightly with a wooden spoon, put it into a buttered pan, and bake it in a brisk oven for nearly or quite an hour. An additional ounce of butter will improve it.

Flour, 1¼ lb.; yeast, 1¼ tablespoonful: 1 hour, or more. Eggs, 3; milk, in all not ½ pint; sugar, 6 ozs.; currants, 6 ozs.; lemon-grate, nutmeg, or candied orange-rind, at pleasure: 1 hour. Baked nearly or quite an hour; brisk oven.

COCOA-NUT BISCUIT; (*excellent.*)

With a pound of flour mix three ounces of a sound fresh cocoa-nut, rasped on a fine grater; make a leaven as for the bun in the foregoing receipt, with a large tablespoonful of good yeast, and about the third of a pint of warm new milk; let it stand for an hour, then strew over and mix well up with it four ounces of pounded sugar; next, dissolve two ounces of butter in a very little milk, cool it down with a few spoonsful of cold milk if needful, and pour it to a couple of well-whisked eggs; with these wet the other ingredients into a very light dough, let it stand from three quarters of an hour to an hour, and bake it about the same time in a rather quick oven. Two ounces more of sugar, one of butter, and two of candied orange-rind, sliced thin, will convert this into a good *cake*, the cocoa-nut imparting great richness as well as flavour to the mixture: the proportion of this can also be regulated by the taste, after the first trial.

Flour, 1 lb.; grated cocoa-nut, 3 ozs.; yeast, 1 *large* tablespoonful;

milk, ⅓ of pint: 1 hour.   Pounded sugar, 4 ozs.; butter, 2 ozs.; eggs,. 2; little milk: ¾ to 1 hour.   Or: sugar, 6 ozs.; butter, 3 ozs.; canoied orange-rind, 2 ozs.; baked nearly or quite an hour.

THREADNEEDLE STREET BISCUITS.

Mix with a couple of pounds of sifted flour of the very best quality, three ounces of good butter, and work it into the smallest possible crumbs; add four ounces of fine, dry, sifted sugar, and make them into a firm paste with new milk; beat this forcibly for some minutes with the rolling-pin, and when it is extremely smooth roll it the third of an inch thick, cut it with a small square cutter, and bake the biscuits in a very slow oven until they are crisp to the centre: no part of them should remain soft.   Half a teaspoonful of carbonate of soda is said to improve them, but we have not put it to the test.   Caraway-seeds can be added when liked.

Flour, 2 lbs.; butter, 3 ozs.; sugar, 4 ozs.; new milk, 1 pint, or more: biscuits *slowly* baked till crisp.

A GALETTE.

The galette is a favourite cake in France, and may be made rich, and comparatively delicate, or quite common, by using more or less butter for it, and by augmenting or diminishing the size.   Work lightly three quarters of a pound of good butter into a pound of flour, add a large saltspoonful of salt, and make these into a paste with the yolks of a couple of eggs mixed with a small cup of good cream, should it be at hand; if not, with water; roll this into a complete round, three quarters of an inch thick; score it in small diamonds, brush yolk of egg over the top, and bake the galette for about half an hour in a tolerably brisk oven; it is usually eaten hot, but is served cold also.   An ounce of sifted sugar is sometimes added to it.

A good galette: flour, 1 lb.; butter, ¾ lb.; salt, 1 saltspoonful; yolks of eggs, 2; cream, small cupful: baked ½ hour.   Common galette: flour, 2 lbs.; butter, ¾ to 1 lb.; no eggs.

CORNISH HEAVY CAKE.

Mix with a pound and a half of flour, ten ounces of well-cleaned currants, and a *small* teaspoonful of salt; make these into a smooth paste with clotted cream (any which is *very* thick will do), roll the cake till it is an inch and a quarter in depth, and bake it thoroughly in a quick oven, after having scored the top.

Flour, 1½ lb.; currants, 10 ozs.; salt, small teaspoonful; clotted, or *very thick* cream, ¾ to full pint: 35 to 45 minutes, brisk oven.

FLEED OR FLEAD CAKES.

These are very much served as a tea-cake at the tables of the superior order of Kentish farmers.   For the mode of making them, proceed as for flead-crust (see Chapter XVI.); cut the cakes small with a round cutter, and leave them more than half an inch thick; if well made, they will rise much in the oven.   Bake them in a moderate but not slow oven.

Flour, 2 lbs.; flead, 1¼ lb.; butter, 6 ozs.: baked 10 to 15 minutes.

GOOD CAPTAIN'S BISCUITS.

Make some fine white flour into a smooth paste with new milk. divide it into small balls; roll, and afterwards pull them with the fin

gers as *thin as possible;* prick them all over, and bake them in a somewhat brisk oven from ten to twelve minutes.

THE COLONEL'S BISCUITS.

Mix a slight pinch of salt with some fine sifted flour; make it into a
very smooth paste with good cream, and bake the biscuits gently, after
having prepared them for the oven like those which precede. Store
them as soon as they are cold in a dry canister, to preserve them crisp:
they are excellent.

AUNT CHARLOTTE'S BISCUITS.

These biscuits, which are very simple and wholesome, may be made
with the same dough as good white bread, with the addition of from
half to a whole ounce of butter to the pound kneaded into it after it has
risen. Break the butter small, spread out the dough a little, knead it
in well and equally, and leave it for about half an hour; then roll it a
quarter of an inch thick; prick it well all over; cut out the biscuits;
and bake them in a moderate oven from ten to fifteen minutes: they
should be crisp quite through, but not deeply coloured.

White-bread dough, 2 lbs.; butter, 1 to 2 ozs.: to rise ½ hour. Baked
in moderate oven 10 to 15 minutes.

Obs.—To make the biscuits by themselves, proceed as for Bordyke
bread; but use new milk for them, and work three ounces of butter
into two pounds of flour before the yeast is added.

CHAPTER XXIV.

CONFECTIONARY.

TO CLARIFY SUGAR.

It is an economy to use at once the very best sugar for confectionary
in general, for when highly refined it needs little or no clarifying, even
for the most delicate purposes; and the coarser kinds lose considerable
weight in the process. Break it into large lumps, and put it into a very
clean preserving-pan; measure for each pound a pint of spring water if
it be intended for syrup, but less than half that quantity for candying
or making barley-sugar. Beat first apart (but not to a strong froth),
and afterwards with the water, about half the white of an egg for
six pounds of sugar, unless it should be *very* common, when twice as
much may be used. When they are well mixed, pour them over the
sugar, and let it stand until it is nearly dissolved; then stir the whole
thoroughly, and place it over a gentle fire, but do not disturb it after the
scum begins to gather on the top; let it boil for five minutes, then take
the pan from the fire, and when it has stood a couple of minutes clear
off the scum entirely, with a skimmer; set the pan again over the fire,
and when the sugar begins to boil throw in a little cold water, which
has been reserved for the purpose from the quantity first measured, and
repeat the skimming until the syrup is very clear; it may then be
strained through a muslin, or a thin cloth, and put into a clean pan for
further boiling.

For syrup: sugar, 6 lbs.; water, 3 quarts; ½ white of 1 egg. For candying, &c.: sugar, 6 lbs.; water, 2½ pints: 5 to 10 minutes.

TO BOIL SUGAR FROM SYRUP TO CANDY, OR TO CARAMEL.

The technicalities by which confectioners distinguish the different degrees of sugar-boiling, seem to us calculated rather to puzzle than to assist the reader; and we shall, therefore, confine ourselves to such plain English terms as may suffice, we hope, to explain them. After having boiled a certain time, the length of which will in a measure depend upon the quality of the sugar as well as the quantity of water added, it becomes a thin syrup, and it will scarcely form a short thread if a drop be pressed between the thumb and finger and they are then drawn apart; from five to ten minutes more of rapid boiling will bring it to a *thick* syrup, and when this degree is reached the thread may be drawn from one hand to the other at some length without breaking; but its appearance in dropping from the skimmer will perhaps best denote its being at this point, as it hangs in a sort of string as it falls. After this the sugar will soon begin to whiten, and to form large bubbles in the pan, when, if it be intended for barley-sugar, or caramel, some lemon-juice or other acid must be added to it, to prevent its *graining* or *becoming sugar again*; but if wanted to candy, it must be stirred without ceasing, until it rises almost to the top of the pan, in one large white mass, when it must be used immediately or ladled out into paper cases or on to dishes, with the utmost expedition, as it passes in an instant almost from this state to one in which it forms a sort of powder, which will render it necessary to add water, to stir it until dissolved, and to reboil it to the proper point. For barley-sugar likewise it must be constantly stirred, and carefully watched after the lemon-juice is added. A small quantity should be dropped from time to time into a large basin of cold water by those who are inexperienced in the process; when in falling into this it makes a bubbling noise, and if taken out immediately after it snaps clean between the teeth without sticking to them, it must be poured out *instantly:* if wanted for sugar-spinning, the pan must be plunged as quickly as possible into a vessel of cold water.

BARLEY-SUGAR.

Add to three pounds of highly-refined sugar one pint and a quarter of spring water, with sufficient white of egg to clarify it in the manner directed in the last receipt but one: pour to it, when it begins to whiten and to be very thick, a dessertspoonful of the strained juice of a fresh lemon; and boil it quickly till it is at the point which we have indicated above. A few drops of essence of lemon may be added to it, just as it is taken from the fire. Pour it on to a marble slab, or on to a shallow dish which has been slightly oiled, or rubbed with a *morsel* of fresh butter; and when it begins to harden at the edges, form it into sticks, lozenges, balls, or any other shapes at pleasure. While it is still liquid it may be used for various purposes, such as Chantilly baskets, palace bonbons, *des croques-en-bouches,** cerises au caramel,* &c.: for these the vessel containing it must be set into a pan of water, and it

---

* These are formed of small cakes, roasted chestnuts, and various other things, just dipped singly into the barley-sugar, and then arranged in good form and joined in a mould, from which they are turned out for table.

must again be liquefied with a very gentle degree of heat should it cool too quickly. As it soon dissolves if exposed to damp, it should be put into very dry canisters as soon as it is cold, and these should be kept in a dry place.

Best sugar, 3 lbs.; water, 1¼ pint; white of egg, ¼ of 1; lemon-juice, 1 dessertspoonful.

GINGER CANDY.

Break a pound of highly-refined sugar into lumps, put it into a preserving-pan, and pour over it about the third of a pint of spring water: let it stand until the sugar is nearly dissolved, then set it over a perfectly clear fire, and boil it until it becomes a thin syrup. Have ready in a large cup a teaspoonful of the very best ginger in powder, mix it smoothly and gradually with two or three spoonsful of the syrup, and then stir it well into the whole. Watch the mixture carefully, keep it stirred, and drop it often from a spoon to ascertain the exact point of boiling it has reached. When it begins to fall in *flakes*, throw in the freshly-grated rind of a very large lemon, or of two small ones, and work the sugar round quickly as it is added. The candy must now be stirred constantly until it is done: this will be when it falls in a mass from the spoon, and does not *sink* when placed in a small heap on a dish. It must be poured, or *laded* out, as expeditiously as possible when ready, or it will fall quite into powder. If this should happen, a little water must be added to it, and it must be reboiled to the proper point. The candy, if dropped in cakes upon cold dishes, may be moved off without difficulty before it is thoroughly cold, but must not be touched while quite hot or it will break.

Sugar, highly refined, 1 lb.; water, ¼ of a pint; ginger, 1 teaspoonful; rind of 1 large lemon.

ORANGE-FLOWER CANDY.

Beat in three quarters of a pint, or rather more, of water, about the fourth part of the white of an egg; and pour it on two pounds of the best sugar broken into lumps. When it has stood a little time, place it over a very clear fire, and let it boil for a few minutes, then set it on one side, until the scum has subsided; clear it off, and boil the sugar till it is very thick, then strew in by degrees three ounces of the *petals* of the orange-blossom, weighed after they are picked from their stems. Continue to stir the candy until it rises in one white mass in the pan, then pour it into small paper cases, or on to dishes, and follow for it precisely the same directions as are given for the ginger-candy in the preceding receipt. The orange-flowers will turn brown if thrown too soon into the syrup: it should be more than three parts boiled when they are added. They must be gathered on the day they are wanted for use, as they become soon discoloured from keeping.

Sugar, 2 lbs.; water, ¾ pint; ¼ white of egg; orange-blossoms, 3 ozs.

ORANGE-FLOWER CANDY; (*another Receipt.*)

The French, who are very fond of the delicious flavour of the orange-blossom, leave the petals in the candy; but a more delicate confection, to English taste, is made as follows:—Throw the orange-flowers into the syrup when it has boiled about ten minutes, and after they have simmered in it for five more, pour the whole out, and leave them to infuse until the following day, or even longer, if more convenient; then bring the syrup to the point of boiling, strain it from the blossoms through a muslin, and finish it by the foregoing receipt.

PALACE-BONBONS.

Take some fine fresh candied orange or lemon-peel, take off the sugar that adheres to it, cut it into inch-squares, stick these singly on the prong of a silver fork, or on osier-twigs, dip them into liquid barley-sugar, and place them on a dish rubbed with the smallest possible quantity of very pure salad oil. When cold, put them into tin boxes or canisters well dried, with paper between each layer.

EVERTON TOFFIE.

Put into a brass skillet, if at hand, three ounces of very fresh butter, and as soon as it is just melted add a pound of brown sugar of moderate quality; keep these stirred gently over a very clear fire for about fifteen minutes, or until a little of the mixture, dropped into a basin of cold water, breaks clean between the teeth without sticking to them: when it is boiled to this point, it must be poured out immediately, or it will burn. The grated rind of a lemon, added when the toffie is half done, improves it much; or a small teaspoonful of powdered ginger, moistened with a little of the other ingredients, as soon as the sugar is dissolved, and then stirred to the whole, will vary it pleasantly to many tastes. The real Everton toffie is made, we apprehend, with a much larger proportion of butter, but it is the less wholesome on that very account. If dropped upon dishes first rubbed with a buttered paper, the toffie when cold can be raised from them easily.

Butter, 3 ozs.; sugar, 1 lb.: 15 to 18 minutes.

TOFFIE. (ANOTHER WAY.)

Boil together a pound of sugar and five ounces of butter for twenty minutes; then stir in two ounces of almonds blanched, divided, and thoroughly dried in a slow oven, or before the fire. Let the toffie boil after they are added, till it crackles when dropped into cold water, and snaps between the teeth without sticking.

Sugar, 1 lb.; butter, 5 ozs.; almonds, 2 ozs.: 20 to 30 minutes.

CHAPTER XXV.

DESSERT DISHES.

MÉLANGE OF FRUIT.

HEAP a dessert-dish quite high with alternate layers of fine fresh strawberries stripped from the stalks, white and red currants, and white or red raspberries; strew each layer plentifully with sifted sugar, and just before the dish is sent to table, pour equally over the top a glass and a half of brandy, or, if preferred, the same quantity or rather more of white wine, mixed with the strained juice of one small, or of half a large lemon. Currants by themselves are excellent prepared in this

way, and strawberries also. The fruit should be gently stirred with a
spoon when it is served. Each variety must be picked with great
nicety from the stalks. The brandy would, we think, be less to the
general taste in this country than the wine.

FRUIT EN CHEMISE, OR PERLÉ.

Select for this dish very fine bunches of red and white currants, large
ripe cherries, and gooseberries of different colours, and strawberries or
raspberries very freshly gathered. Beat up the white of an egg with
about half as much cold water, dip the fruit into this mixture, drain it
on a sieve for an instant, and then roll it in fine sifted sugar until it is
covered in every part; give it a gentle shake, and lay it on sheets of
white paper to dry. In England, thin gum-water is sometimes used,
we believe, for this dish, instead of the white of egg; we give, however, the French method of preparing it. It will dry gradually in a
warm room, or a sunny window, in the course of three or four hours.

PEACH SALAD.

Pare and slice half a dozen fine ripe peaches, arrange them in a dish,
strew them with pounded sugar, and pour over them two or three glasses
of champagne: other wine may be used, but this is best. Persons who
prefer brandy can substitute it for wine. The quantity of sugar must
be proportioned to the sweetness of the fruit.

ORANGE SALAD.

Take off the outer rinds, and then strip away entirely the white
inside skin from some fine China oranges; slice them thin, and remove
the pips as this is done; strew over them plenty of white sifted sugar,
and pour on them a glass or more of brandy: when the sugar is dissolved, serve the oranges. In France, ripe pears of superior quality are
sometimes sliced in with the oranges. Powdered sugar-candy used instead of sugar, is an improvement in this salad; and the substitution of
port, sherry, or Madeira for the brandy is often considered so. The first
may be used without being pared, and a little cuirasseau or any other
liquor may be added to the brandy; or this last, when unmixed, may
be burned after it is poured on the oranges.

COMPÔTE OF ORANGES; (a Hebrew dish.)

After having pared and stripped the white inner rind from some fine
oranges, pull them into quarters, arrange them neatly in a dish, and
just before they are sent to table pour over them some rich syrup, and
garnish the whole tastefully with preserved citron cut in thin slices.
Half a pint of syrup will be sufficient for a large number of oranges; it
would be improved, we think, if the rind of one pared very thin were
infused in it for an hour before it is used. This is one of the receipts
which we have not considered it needful to prove.

ORANGES WARMED.

Place them in a Dutch oven at a considerable distance from the fire,
and keep them constantly turned: they should only be just warmed
through. Fold them in a napkin when done, and send them immediately to table. This mode of treating them is said to improve greatly
the flavour of the oranges.

NORMANDY PIPPINS.

To one pound of the apples, put one quart of water and six ounces of sugar; let them simmer gently for three hours, or more should they not be perfectly tender. A few strips of fresh lemon-peel and a very few cloves are by some persons considered agreeable additions to the syrup.

Dried Normandy pippins, 1 lb.; water, 1 quart; sugar, 6 ozs.: 3 tr 4 hours.

Obs.—These pippins, if stewed with care, will be converted into a rich confection: they may be served hot in a border of rice, as a second course dish.

STEWED PRUNEAUX DE TOURS, OR TOURS DRIED PLUMS.

These plums, which resemble in form small dried Norfolk biffins, make a delicious compôte: they are also excellent served dry. In France they are stewed till tender in equal parts of water, and of the light red wine of the country, with about four ounces of sugar to the pound of fruit: when port wine is used for them a smaller proportion of it will suffice. The sugar should not be added in stewing any dried fruits until they are at least half-done, as they will not soften by any means so easily in syrup as in unsweetened liquid.

Dried plums, 1 lb.; water, ½ pint, and light claret, ½ pint, or water, ¾ pint, and port wine, ¼ pint: 1½ hour. Sugar, 4 ozs.: 1 hour, or more.

Obs.—Common French plums are stewed in the same way with or without wine. A little experience will teach the cook the exact quantity of liquid and of sugar which they require.

BAKED COMPÔTE OF APPLES. (*Our little lady's receipt.*)

Put into a wide jar, with a cover, two quarts of golden pippins, or any small apple which resembles them in appearance, pared and cored, but without being divided; strew amongst them some small strips of very thin fresh lemon-rind, and throw on them, nearly at the top, half a pound of very good sugar, and set the jar, with the cover tied on, for some hours, or for a night, into a very slow oven. The apples will be extremely good, if not too quickly baked: they should remain entire, but be perfectly tender and clear in appearance. Add a little lemon-juice when the season is far advanced.

Apples, 2 quarts; rind, quite small lemon; sugar, ½ lb.: 1 night in slow oven; or some hours baking in a *very* gentle one.

Obs.—These apples may be served hot or cold for a second course dish; or they will answer admirably to fill *Gabrielle's pudding*.

TO BAKE PEARS.

Wipe some large sound iron pears, arrange them on a dish with the stalk end upwards, put them into the oven after the bread is drawn, and let them remain all night. If well baked, they will be excellent, very sweet, and juicy, and much finer in flavour than those which are stewed or baked with sugar: the *bon chrétien* pear also is delicious baked thus.

STEWED PEARS.

Pare, cut in halves, and core a dozen fine iron pears, put them into a close-shutting stewpan with some thin strips of lemon-rind, half a pound of sugar, in lumps, as much water as will nearly cover them, and should a very bright colour be desired, a dozen grains of cochineal, bruised, and tied in a muslin; stew the fruit as gently as possible, from four to six hours, or longer, should it not be very tender. The Chaumontel pear, which sometimes falls in large quantities before it is ripe, is excellent, if first baked until tolerably tender, and then stewed in a thin syrup.

BOILED CHESTNUTS.

Make a slight incision in the outer skin only of each chestnut, to prevent its bursting, and when all are done, throw them into plenty of boiling water, with about a dessertspoonful of salt to the half gallon. Some chestnuts will require to be boiled nearly or quite an hour, others little more than half the time; the cook should try them occasionally, and as soon as they are soft through, drain them, wipe them in a coarse cloth, and send them to table quickly in a hot napkin.

ROASTED CHESTNUTS.

The best mode of preparing these is to roast them, as in Spain, in a coffee-roaster, after having first boiled them from five to seven minutes, and wiped them dry. They should not be allowed to cool, and will require but from ten to fifteen minutes roasting. They may, when more convenient, be finished over the fire as usual, or in a Dutch or common oven, but in all cases the previous boiling will be found an improvement.

Never omit to cut the rind of each nut slightly before it is cooked. Serve the chestnuts very hot in a napkin, and send salt to table with them.

CHAPTER XXVI.

SYRUPS, LIQUEURS, &c.

STRAWBERRY VINEGAR, OF DELICIOUS FLAVOUR.

TAKE the stalks from the fruit, which should be of a highly flavoured sort, quite ripe, fresh from the beds, and gathered in dry weather; weigh and put it into large glass jars, or wide-necked bottles, and to each pound pour about a pint and a half of fine pale white wine vinegar, which will answer the purpose better than the entirely colourless kind sold under the name of *distilled vinegar*, but which is, we believe, the pyroligneous acid greatly diluted. Tie a thick paper over them, and let the strawberries remain from three to four days; then pour off the vinegar and empty them into a jelly-bag, or suspend them in a cloth that all the liquid may drop from them without pressure; replace them with an equal weight of fresh fruit, pour the vinegar upon it, and three days afterwards repeat the same process, diminishing a little the proportion of strawberries, of which the flavour ought ultimately to overpower that of the vinegar. In from two to four days drain off the liquid very closely, and after having strained it through a linen or a flannel bag, weigh it, and mix with it an equal quantity of highly-refined sugar roughly powdered; when this is nearly dissolved, stir the syrup over a

very clear fire until it has boiled five minutes, and skim it *thoroughly* ;
pour it into a delicately clean stone pitcher, or into large china jugs,
throw a folded cloth over and let it remain until the morrow; put it
into pint or half-pint bottles, and cork them lightly with new velvet
corks ; for if these be pressed in tightly at first, the bottles would be
liable to burst: in four or five days they may be closely corked, and
stored in a dry and cool place. Damp destroys the colour and injures
the flavour of these fine fruit-vinegars ; of which a spoonful or two in
a glass of water affords so agreeable a summer beverage, and one
which, in many cases of illness, is so acceptable to invalids. They
make also most admirable sauces for common custard, batter, and various
other simple and sweet light puddings.

Strawberries (stalked), 4 lbs. ; vinegar, 3 quarts : 3 to 4 days. Vinegar drained and poured on fresh strawberries, 4 lbs. : 3 days. Drained
again on to fresh fruit, 3 to 4 lbs. : 2 to 4 days. To each pound of the
vinegar, 1 lb. of highly-refined sugar : boiled 5 minutes. *Lightly*
corked, 4 or 5 days.

Obs.—Where there is a garden the fruit may be thrown into the
vinegar as it ripens, within an interval of forty-eight hours, instead of
being all put to infuse at once, and it must then remain in it a proportionate time : one or two days in addition to that specified will make
no difference to the preparation. The enamelled German stewpans are
the best possible vessels to boil it in ; but it may be simmered in a stone
jar set into a pan of boiling water when there is nothing more appropriate at hand ; though the syrup does not usually keep so well when
this last method is adopted.

Raspberries and strawberries mixed will make a vinegar of very
pleasant flavour ; black currants also will afford an exceedingly useful
syrup of the same kind.

STRAWBERRY ACID ROYAL.

Dissolve in a quart of spring water two ounces of citric acid, and
pour it on as many quite ripe and richly-flavoured strawberries, stripped
from their stalks, as it will just cover ; in twenty-four hours drain the
liquid closely from the fruit, and pour on it as much more; keep it in a
cool place, and the next day drain it again entirely from the fruit, and
boil it gently for three or four minutes, with its weight of very fine
sugar, which should be dissolved in it before it is placed over the fire.
It should be boiled, if possible, in an enamelled stewpan. When perfectly cold put it into small dry bottles for use, and store it in a cool
but not damp place. It is one of the most delicate and deliciously
flavoured preparations possible, and of beautiful colour. If allowed to
remain longer than the eight-and-forty hours before it is boiled, a brisk
fermentation will commence. It must be well secured from the air
when stored.

Water, 1 quart ; citric acid, 2 ozs. ; strawberries, 2 to 3 lbs. : 24
hours. Same quantity of fruit : 24 hours. Equal weight of sugar and
this liquid : 3 to 4 minutes *at the utmost.*

VERY FINE RASPBERRY VINEGAR.

Fill glass jars, or large wide-necked bottles, with very ripe but perfectly sound, freshly gathered raspberries, freed from their stalks, and
cover them with pale white wine vinegar : they may be left to infuse

from a week to ten days without injury, or the vinegar may be poured
from them in four and five, when more convenient. After it is drained
off, turn the fruit into a sieve placed over a deep dish or bowl, as the
juice will flow slowly from it for many hours; put fresh raspberries into
the bottles, and pour the vinegar back upon them; two or three days
later change the fruit again, and when it has stood the same space of
time, drain the whole of the vinegar from it, pass it through a jelly-bag,
or thick linen cloth, and boil it gently for four or five minutes with its
weight of good sugar roughly powdered, or a pound and a quarter to
the exact pint, and be very careful to remove the scum entirely, as it
rises. On the following day bottle the syrup, observing the directions
which we have given for the strawberry vinegar. When the fruit is
scarce, it may be changed twice only, and left a few days longer in the
vinegar.

Raspberries, 6 lbs.; vinegar, 9 pints: 7 to 10 days. Vinegar drained
on to fresh raspberries (6 lbs. of): 3 to 5 days. Poured again on fresh
raspberries, 6 lbs.: 3 to 5 days. Boiled 5 minutes with its weight of
sugar.

Obs.—When the process of sugar-boiling is well understood, it will
be found an improvement to boil that which is used for raspberry or
strawberry vinegar to candy height before the liquid is mixed with it;
all the scum may then be removed with a couple of minutes simmering,
and the flavour of the fruit will be more perfectly preserved. For more
particular directions as to the mode of proceeding, the chapter on confectionary may be consulted.

OXFORD PUNCH.

Extract the essence from the rinds of three lemons by rubbing them
with sugar in lumps; put these into a large jug with the peel of two
Seville oranges and of two lemons cut extremely thin, the juice of four
Seville oranges and of ten lemons, and six glasses of calf's feet jelly in
a liquid state. Stir these well together, pour to them two quarts of
boiling water, cover the jug closely, and set it near the fire for a quarter of an hour, then strain the mixture through a sieve into a punch
bowl or jug, sweeten it with a bottle of capillaire, add half a pint of
white wine, a pint of French brandy, a pint of Jamaica rum, and a bottle of orange shrub; stir the punch as the spirits are poured in. If not
sufficiently sweet, add sugar in small quantities, or a spoonful or two of
capillaire.

Rinds of lemons rubbed with sugar, 3; thin peel of lemons, 2; of
Seville oranges, 2; juice of 4 Seville oranges, and 10 lemons; calf's
feet jelly, 6 glasses; water, 2 quarts: ¼ hour. Capillaire, 1 bottle;
white wine, ½ pint; French brandy and Jamaica rum, each 1 pint;
orange shrub, 1 bottle.

OXFORD RECEIPT FOR BISHOP.

"Make several incisions in the rind of a lemon,* stick cloves in
these, and roast the lemon by a slow fire. Put small but equal quantities of cinnamon, cloves, mace, and allspice, with a race of ginger, into
a saucepan with half a pint of water: let it boil until it is reduced one
half. Boil one bottle of port wine, burn a portion of the spirit out of it

---

* A Seville orange stuck with cloves, in many tastes imparts a finer flavour than
the lemon.

by applying a lighted paper to the saucepan. Put the roasted lemons and spice into the wine; stir it up well, and let it stand near the fire ten minutes. Rub a few knobs of sugar on the rind of a lemon, put the sugar into a bowl or jug, with the juice of half a lemon (not roasted), pour the wine into it, grate in some nutmeg, sweeten it to your taste, and serve it up with the lemon and spice floating in it."

TO MULL WINE. (*An excellent French receipt.*)

Boil in a wineglassful and a half of water a quarter of an ounce of spice (cinnamon, ginger slightly bruised, and cloves), with three ounces of fine sugar, until they form a thick syrup, which must not on any account be allowed to burn. Pour in a pint of port wine, and stir it gently until it is on the *point* of boiling only: it should then be served immediately. The addition of a strip or two of orange-rind cut ex-tremely thin, gives to this beverage the flavour of bishop. In France light claret takes the place of port wine in making it, and the better kinds of *vin du pays* are very palatable thus prepared.

Water, 1½ wineglassful; spice, ¼ oz., of which fine cloves, 24, and of remainder, rather more ginger than cinnamon; sugar, 3 ozs.: 15 to 20 minutes. Port wine or claret, 1 pint; orange-rind, if used, to be boiled with the spice.

Obs.—Sherry, or very fine raisin or ginger wine, prepared as above, and stirred hot to the yolks of four fresh eggs, will be found excellent.

A BIRTHDAY SYLLABUB.

Put into a large bowl half a pound of sugar broken small, and pour on it the strained juice of a couple of fresh lemons, stir these well together, and add to them a pint of port wine, a pint of sherry, and half a pint of brandy; grate in a fine nutmeg, place the bowl under the cow, and milk it full. In serving it put a portion of the curd into each glass, fill it up with whey, and pour a little rich cream on the top. The rind of a lemon may be rasped with part of the sugar when the flavour is approved, but it is not usually added.

Juice of lemons, 2; sugar, ½ lb. or more; port wine, 1 pint; sherry, 1 pint; brandy ½ pint; nutmeg, 1; milk from the cow, 2 quarts.

Obs.—We can testify to the excellence of this receipt.

CUIRASSEAU, OR CURAÇOA. (*An excellent and wholesome liqueur.*)

Stick into the rind of a very fine China orange of rich flavour from three to four cloves; put it into a glass jar, and shower over it half a pound of good West Indian sugar, not very brown; pour in a quart of French brandy; tie a couple of bladders over the jar, or stop it with a cork fitted to its size, and place it in a sunny window, or any other warm place, for a month; shake it gently round every day to dissolve the sugar, or stir it, if needful; then strain it off, and bottle it. It is sometimes filtered; but the long exposure to the air which this occasions is better avoided. It is an admirable household stomachic liqueur, of which we obtained the receipt abroad, from a friend who had it made yearly in considerable quantity.

1 very fine richly-flavoured China orange, left whole (or two small ones), stuck with 3 or 4 cloves; good pale brown sugar, ½ lb.; French brandy, 1 quart: infuse, 1 month.

MINT JULEP. (An American Receipt.)

" Strip the tender leaves of mint into a tumbler, and add to them as much wine, brandy, or any other spirit, as you wish to take. Put some pounded ice into a second tumbler; pour this on the mint and brandy, and continue to pour the mixture from one tumbler to the other until the whole is sufficiently impregnated with the flavour of the mint, which is extracted by the particles of the ice coming into brisk contact when changed from one vessel to the other. Now place the glass in a larger one, containing pounded ice: on taking it out of which it will be covered with frost-work."

DELICIOUS MILK LEMONADE.

Dissolve six ounces of loaf sugar in a pint of boiling water, and mix with them a quarter-pint of lemon-juice, and the same quantity of sherry; then add three quarters of a pint of cold milk, stir the whole well together, and pass it through a jelly-bag till clear.

EXCELLENT PORTABLE LEMONADE.

Rasp, with a quarter-pound of sugar, the rind of a very fine juicy lemon, reduce it to powder, and pour on it the strained juice of the fruit. Press the mixture into a jar, and when wanted for use dissolve a tablespoonful of it in a glass of water. It will keep a considerable time. If too sweet for the taste of the drinker, a very small portion of citric acid may be added when it is taken.

EXCELLENT BARLEY WATER. (Poor Xury's Receipt.)

Wipe very clean, by rolling it in a soft cloth, two tablespoonsful of pearl barley; put it into a quart jug, with a lump or two of sugar, a grain or two of salt, and a strip of lemon-peel, cut thin; fill up the jug with boiling water and keep the mixture gently stirred for some minutes; then cover it down, and let it stand till perfectly cold. In twelve hours, or less, it will be fit for use; but it is better when made overnight. If these directions be followed, the barley-water will be comparatively clear, and very soft and pleasant to drink. A glass of calf's feet jelly added to the barley is an infinite improvement; but as lemon-rind is often extremely unpalatable to invalids, their taste should be consulted before that ingredient is added, as it should be also for the degree of sweetness that is desired. After the barley-water has been poured off once, the jug may be filled a second time with boiling water, and even a third time with advantage.

RAISIN WINE; (which, if long kept, really resembles foreign.)

First boil the water which is to be used for the wine, and let it again become perfectly cold; then put into a sound sweet cask eight pounds of fine Malaga raisins for each gallon that is to be used, taking out only the quite large stalks; the fruit and water may be put in alternately until the cask is *full*, the raisins being well pressed down in it; lay the bung lightly over, stir the wine every day or two, and keep it full by the addition of water that has, like the first, been boiled, but which must always be quite cold when it is used. So soon as the fermentation has entirely ceased, which may be in from six to seven weeks, press in the bung, and leave the wine untouched for twelve months; draw it off then into a clean cask, and fine it, if necessary, with isinglass, tied in a muslin and suspended in it. We have not ourselves had this receipt tried; but we have tasted wine made by it which had been five years kept, and which so much resembled a rich foreign wine, that we could with difficulty believe it was home made.

To each gallon of water (boiled and left till cold) 8 lbs. of fine Malaga raisins; to stand twelve months; then to be drawn off and fined.

Obs.—The refuse raisins make admirable vinegar if fresh water be poured to them, and the cask placed in the sun. March is the best time for making this wine.

EXCELLENT ELDERBERRY WINE.

Strip the berries, which should be fresh, and gathered on a dry day, clean from the stalks, and measure them into a tub or large earthen pan. Pour boiling water on them, in the proportion of two gallons to three of berries, press them down into the liquor, cover them closely, and let them remain until the following day; then strain the juice from the fruit through a sieve or cloth, and, when this is done, squeeze from the berries the greater part of the remaining juice, mix it with that which was first poured off, measure the whole, add to it three pounds of sugar, three quarters of an ounce of cloves, and one ounce of ginger, for every gallon, and boil it twenty minutes, keeping it thoroughly skimmed. Put it, when something more than milk-warm, into a perfectly dry and sweet cask (or if but a *very* small quantity of wine be made, into large stone bottles, which answer the purpose quite well), fill this entirely, and set the wine directly, with a large spoonful of new yeast dropped into the bung-hole, and just stirred round in the liquor, or with a small toasted crust thickly spread with yeast.*

VERY GOOD GINGER WINE.

Boil together, for half an hour, fourteen quarts of water, twelve pounds of sugar, a quarter of a pound of the best ginger bruised, and the thin rinds of six large lemons. Put the whole, when milk-warm, into a clean dry cask, with the juice of the lemons, and half a pound of sun raisins; add one large spoonful of thick yeast; and stir the wine every day for ten days. When it has ceased to ferment, add an ounce of isinglass, and a pint of brandy; bung the wine close, and in two months it will be fit to bottle, but must remain longer in the cask should it be too sweet. When it can be obtained, substitute for the water in this receipt cider fresh from the press, which will give a very superior wine.

Water, 14 quarts; sugar, 12 pounds; lemon-rinds, 6; ginger, ¼ lb.; ½ hour. Juice of lemons, 6; raisins, ½ lb.; yeast, 1 spoonful; isinglass, 1 oz.; brandy, 1 pint.

EXCELLENT ORANGE WINE.

Take half a chest of Seville oranges, pare off the rinds as thin as possible, put two thirds of them into six gallons of water, and let them remain for twenty-four hours. Squeeze the oranges (which ought to yield seven or eight quarts of juice) through a sieve into a pan, and as they are done throw them into six gallons more of water; let them

---

* In from fourteen to twenty days this wine will have fermented sufficiently: in three months it will be ready to drink.

be washed well in it with the hands, and then put into another six gallons of water and left till the following day. For each gallon of wine, put into the cask three pounds and a quarter of loaf sugar, and the liquor strained clear from the rinds and pulp. Wash these again and again, should more liquor be required to fill the cask; but do not at any time add raw water. Stir the wine daily until the sugar is perfectly dissolved, and let it ferment from four to five weeks; add to it two bottles of brandy, stop it down, and in twelve months it will be fit to bottle.

Obs.—The excellence of all wine depends so much upon the fermentation being properly conducted, that unless the mode of regulating this be understood by the maker, there will always be great danger of failure in the operation. There is, we believe, an excellent work upon the subject by Dr. McCulloch, which the reader who needs information upon it will do well to consult: our own experience is too slight to enable us to multiply our receipts.

CURRANT WINE.

Gather the currants when dry, extract the juice, either by mashing and pressing the fruit, or putting it in a jar, placed in boiling water; strain the juice, and for every gallon allow one gallon of water and three pounds of sugar Dissolve the sugar in the water, and take off the scum; let it cool, add it to the currant-juice, and put the mixture in a keg, but do not close it tightly till it has ceased fermenting, which will not be under a week. In three or four weeks it may be bottled. The white of an egg beaten, mixed with a teaspoonful of cream of tartar, and stirred into the liquid, makes the wine look clear and bright.

TO CLEAN BOTTLES IN LARGE NUMBERS.

To do this in the best and quickest maner, rinse such amongst them as may particularly require it; put a little hay or a coarse cloth into a copper, and arrange them in it as compactly as possible; cover them with cold water, light the fire, and boil them gently for half an hour; take them out, let them cool, rinse them well, and when dry they will be ready for use. One or two may be broken in the process, but it is considered the most advantageous method of proceeding where they are very extensively used.

CHAPTER XXVII.

COFFEE, CHOCOLATE, &c.

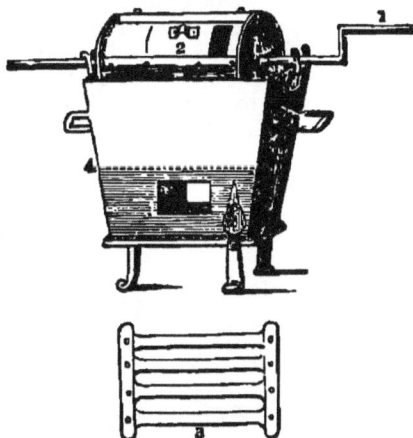

TO ROAST COFFEE.

Persons who drink coffee habitually, and who are particular about its flavour and quality, should purchase the best kind in a raw state, and have it roasted at home. This can be done in very small quantities by means of the inexpensive apparatus shown above; and the supply of charcoal needed for it being very trifling indeed. The cylinder which contains the coffee should be only half filled, and it should be turned rather slowly over the fire, which should never be fierce, until a strong aromatic smell is emitted; the movement should then be quickened, as the grain is in that case quite heated, and it will become too highly coloured before it is roasted through, if slowly finished. When it is of a fine, light, equal brown, which must be ascertained, until some little experience has been acquired, by sliding back the door of the cylinder, and looking at it occasionally towards the end of the process, spread it quickly upon a large dish, and throw a folded cloth over it. Let it remain thus until it is quite cold, then put it into canisters or bottles, and exclude the air carefully from it. Mr. Webster, in his admirable Encyclopædia of Domestic Economy,* says, "Mr. Donovan recommends that, instead of roasting the coffee in an atmosphere of its own steam, it should first be dried in an iron pan, over a very gentle fire, being constantly stirred until the colour becomes yellow; it is then to be pounded into coarse fragments, by no means too fine, each grain being divided into four or five parts only: it is then to be transferred to the roaster, and scorched to the proper degree." This plan we have not tried, because we have found the other to answer

* This work contains much useful and valuable information on an infinity of subjects connected with Domestic economy.

quite well· though Mr. Donovan's might nevertheless prove a very superior one.

TO MAKE COFFEE.

It is more usual at the present day to filter than to boil coffee, but
many persons still prefer the lattor mode.   The degree of strength
which is to be given must of course depend on the taste of 'those for
whom it is prepared; but it should always be *good* when served to
strangers, as a preference for weak coffee is very rare, and in a vast
many instances it would be peculiarly disagreeable to the drinkers,
more especially so to those who have resided much abroad, where this
beverage is in general much better prepared than it is here.

An ounce of the berries, if recently roasted, and ground at the instant of using them, will make, with the addition of a pint of water,
two breakfast-cupsful of suffi-
ciently good coffee for common family use.   It will be
stronger if slowly filtered in
what is called a percolator, or
coffee-biggin, than if it be
boiled. Press the powder closely down, measure the proper
quantity of water into a common coffee-pot, or small kettle, pour in sufficient to just
wet the coffee in the first instance, and then add the remainder slowly, keeping the
water boiling all the time.
Let it run quite through before the top of the percolator
is lifted off, and serve it very

Patent Percolator with Spirit-Lamp.

hot with boiling milk or cream, or with both, or with boiling milk and
cold cream.   The proportion of coffee, after the first trial, can easily be
increased or diminished at will.   To make French breakfast-coffee,
pour only a third as much of water on the powder, fill. the cups two-
thirds with good new boiling milk, then add the coffee, which should be
very strong.   For the *café noir* served after dinner in all French families put less water still (this is the very essence of coffee, of which,
however, not more than a small cup about two-thirds filled, and highly
sweetened with sugar in lumps, is generally taken by each person), and
serve it without cream or milk, or any accompaniment, except white
sugar-candy in powder, or highly refined sugar in lumps.   This is drunk
immediately after the dinner, in families of moderate rank, generally
before they leave the table; in more refined life, it is served in the
drawing-room the instant dinner is ended; sometimes with liquors after
it, but not invariably.

To boil coffee and refine it: put the necessary quantity of water into
a pot which it will not fill by some inches; when it boils, stir in the
coffee; for unless this is at once moistened, it remains on the top and
is liable to fly over.   Give it one or two strong boils, then raise it from
the fire, and simmer it for ten minutes only; pour out a large cupful
twice, hold it high over the coffee-pot and pour it in again, then set it

on the hob for ten minutes longer. It will be perfectly clear, unless mismanaged, without any other fining. Should more, however, be deemed necessary, a *very* small pinch of isinglass, or a clean egg-shell, with a little of the white adhering to it, is the best that can be used. (We cannot recommend the skin of *any* fish.) If tried, with the same proportions by both the methods we have given, the reader will easily ascertain that which answers best. *Never* use mustard to fine coffee with. It is a barbarous custom of which we have heard foreigners who have been in England vehemently complain !

Coffee, 2 ozs.; water, 1 quart. Filtered; or boiled 10 minutes; left to clear 10 minutes.

BURNT COFFEE; (*in France vulgarly called Gloria.*)

Make some coffee as strong and clear as possible, sweeten it in the cup with white sugar almost to syrup, then pour brandy on the top gently over a spoon, set fire to it with a lighted paper, and when the spirit is in part consumed, blow out the flame and drink the gloria quite hot.

TO MAKE CHOCOLATE; (*French Receipt.*)

An ounce of chocolate, if good, will be suffi- cient for one person. Rasp, and then boil it from five to ten minutes with about four table- spoonsful of water; when it is extremely smooth add nearly a pint of new milk, give it another boil, stir it well, or mill it, and serve it directly. For water-chocolate use three quarters of a pint of water instead of the milk, and send rich hot cream to table with it. The taste must decide whether it shall be made thicker or thinner.

Chocolate, 2 ozs.; water, quarter-pint, or ra- ther more; milk, 1¾ pint: ½ minute.

Obs.—The general reader will understand the use of the chocolate-mill shown in the engraving with the pot; but to the uninitiated it may be as well to observe, that it is worked quickly round between both hands to give a fine froth to the chocolate. It also serves in lieu of a whisk for working creams, or jellies, to a froth or *whip.*

TO MAKE TEA.

Scald the teapot with boiling water; then put in the tea, allowing three teaspoonsful to a pint of water—or for every two persons. Pour on the water. It must be boiling hot, and let the tea steep about ten minutes.

Black tea is healthier than green. Hyson and Souchong mixed to- gether, half and half, is a pleasanter beverage than either alone, and safer for those who drink *strong* tea, than to trust themselves wholly with green.

CHAPTER XXVIII.

BREAD.

TO PURIFY YEAST FOR BREAD OR CAKES.

THE yeast procured from a public brewery is often so extremely bitter that it can only be rendered fit for use by frequent washings, and after these even it should be cautiously employed. Mix it, when first brought in, with a large quantity of cold water, and set it by until the following morning in a cool place; then drain off the water, and stir the yeast up well with as much more of fresh; it must again stand several hours before the water can be poured clear from it. By changing this daily in winter, and both night and morning in very hot weather, the yeast may be preserved fit for use much longer than it would otherwise be; and should it ferment rather less freely after a time, a *small* portion of brown sugar stirred to it before the bread is made will quite restore its strength.

German yeast, imported in a solid state, is now much sold in London, and answers, we are told, remarkably well; but we have not ourselves had an opportunity of proving it.

THE OVEN.

A brick oven, heated with wood, is far superior to any other for baking bread, as well as for most other purposes, the heat of an iron one being much less easy to regulate; but those attached to the kitchen ranges are convenient, for the facility they afford at all times of baking in a small way. They are, however, we should say, far from economical as regards the proportion of fuel required to heat them; and the same objection may be made to the American oven also; the strong smell, too, emitted from the iron ones, and diffused often entirely through a house, is peculiarly unpleasant. A brick oven should be well heated with faggot wood, or with a faggot, and two or three solid logs; and after it is cleared, the door should be closely shut for quite half an hour before the baking commences; the heat will then be well sustained for a succession of bread, pies, cakes, and small pastry. The servant who habitually attends at an oven will soon become acquainted with the precise quantity of fuel which it requires, and all other peculiarities which may be connected with it. In general more time must be allowed to bake any thing in an iron than in a brick oven.

TO MAKE BREAD.

Every cook, and we might almost say, *every woman*, ought to be perfectly acquainted with the mode of making good household bread; and skill in preparing other articles of food is poor compensation for ignorance upon this one essential point. A very slight degree of attention, moreover, will enable any person to succeed in it, and there is, consequently, small excuse for those who neglect to render themselves properly acquainted with the process.

The best flour will generally be found the cheapest in the end; it should be purchased if possible from a miller who can be depended on for supplying it good and unadulterated. Let it be stored always in a dry place, as damp is very injurious to it; if kept habitually in a chest, this should be entirely emptied at intervals, cleaned with great nicety, and not filled again until it is perfectly dry. The kneading trough tub, or pan, with every thing else indeed used for the bread, or for the oven, should at all times be kept scrupulously clean.

The yeast of mild home-brewed beer is the best that can be procured, and requires no purifying; but it should be strained through a hair-sieve after it is mixed with a portion of warm milk, or water, before it is added to the flour.

Very rapid fermentation, which is produced by using more than the necessary quantity of yeast, is by no means advantageous to the bread, which not only becomes dry and stale from it, but is of less sweet and pleasant flavour than that which is more slowly fermented. In winter it should always be placed near the fire, but never sufficiently so to become hot; nor should it ever be allowed to become perfectly cold. Put half a bushel (more or less, according to the consumption of the family) of flour into the kneading tub or trough, and hollow it well in the middle; dilute a pint of yeast as it is brought from the brewery, or half the quantity if it has been washed and rendered solid, with four quarts or more of lukewarm milk or water, or a mixture of the two; stir into it, from the surrounding part, with a wooden spoon, as much flour as will make a thick batter; throw a little over it, and leave this, which is called the leaven, to rise before proceeding further. In about an hour it will have swollen considerably, and have burst through the coating of flour on the top; then pour in as much more warm liquid as will convert the whole, with *good kneading*, and this should not be spared into a firm dough, of which the surface should be entirely free from lumps or crumbs. Throw a cloth over, and let it remain until it has risen very much a second time, which will be in an hour, or something more, if the batch be large. Then work it lightly up, and mould it into loaves of from two to three pounds weight; send them directly to a well-heated oven, and bake them from an hour and a half to an hour and three quarters.

Flour, ½ bushel; salt (when it is liked), 4 to 6 ozs.; yeast, 1 pint unwashed, or ½ pint if purified; milk, or water, 2 quarts: 1 to 1½ hour. Additional liquid as needed.

BORDYKE BREAD. *(Author's Receipt.)*

Mix with a gallon of flour a large teaspoonful of fine salt, make a hollow in the centre, and pour in two tablespoonsful of solid, well-purified yeast, gradually diluted with about two pints and a half of milk, and work it into a thick batter with the surrounding flour; dust a little on the top, and leave it to rise from an hour to an hour and a half; then knead it up with as much more warm skimmed milk as will render it quite firm and smooth without being very stiff; let it rise another hour, and divide it into three loaves; put them into square tins slightly buttered, or into round baking pans, and bake them about an hour and a quarter in a well-heated oven. The dough can be formed into household loaves if preferred, and sent to the oven in the usual way. When a finer and more spongy kind of bread is required for immediate eating, substitute new milk for skimmed, dissolve in it about an ounce of butter, leave it more liquid when the sponge is set, and let

24

the whole be lightly kneaded into a lithe dough; the bread thus made
will be excellent when new, and for a day or so after it is baked, but it
will become dry sooner than the other.

Flour, 1 gallon; salt, 1 teaspoonful; skimmed milk, 2½ pints: to rise
from 1 to 1½ hour. Additional milk, 1 to 2 pints: to rise 1 hour. 3
loaves, baked 1¼ hour.

Obs. 1.—A few spoonsful of cream will wonderfully improve either
of the above receipts, and sweet butter-milk substituted for the other
will give to the bread the shortness of a cake; we would particularly
recommend it for trial when it can be procured.

Obs. 2.—For an invalid, especially when the digestion is impaired,
butter should be altogether omitted from the bread; and eggs, which
are often added to the finer sorts of rolls, are better avoided also.

Obs. 3.—We must repeat our caution against milk or water of a
scalding heat being ever mixed with the yeast: it should be warm,
rather more so than when taken from the cow, but not much.

BROWN BREAD.

Make this by any of the foregoing receipts, with meal, as it is called
(that is to say, the wheat just as it is ground, either separated from the
coarse bran or not, according to the quality of the bread required),
instead of flour. It ferments easily, and does not, therefore, require a
very full proportion of yeast; and it absorbs more moisture than the
flour; it also retains it longer, if properly baked. The loaves should be
well soaked in the oven, but not over-dried.

Obs.—The best bread we ever tasted was made in great part with
rye-flour: this was in a provincial town in France.

POTATO BREAD.

One pound of good mealy potatoes, steamed or boiled very dry, in the
ordinary way, or prepared by Captain Kater's receipt (see Chapter
XV.), and rubbed quite hot, through a coarse sieve, into a couple of
pounds of flour, with which they should be well mixed, will produce
excellent bread, which will remain moist much longer than wheaten
bread made as usual. The yeast should be added immediately after the
potatoes. An ounce or two of butter, an egg, and some new milk, will
convert this bread into very superior rolls.

DYSPEPSIA BREAD.

This bread is now best known as "Graham bread"—not that Doctor
Graham invented or discovered the manner of its preparation, but that
he has been unwearied and successful in recommending it to the public.
It is an excellent article of diet for the dyspeptic and the costive; and
for most persons of sedentary habits would be beneficial. It agrees
well with children; and, in short, I think it should be used in every
family, though not to the exclusion of fine bread. The most difficult
point in manufacturing this bread, is to obtain good pure meal. It is
said that much of the bread commonly sold as *dyspepsia*, is made of the
bran or *middlings*, from which the fine flour has been separated; and
that *saw-dust* is sometimes mixed with the meal. To be certain that it
is good, send good, clean wheat to the mill, have it ground rather
coarsely, and keep the meal in a dry, cool place. Before using it, sift

it through a common hair-sieve; this will separate the very coarse and harsh particles.

Take six quarts of this wheat meal, one tea-cup of good yeast, and a half a tea-cup of molasses, mix these with a pint of milk-warm water and tea-spoonful of pearlash or saleeratus. Make a hole in the flour, and stir this mixture in the middle of the meal till it is like batter. Then proceed as with fine flour bread. Make the dough when sufficiently light into four loaves, which will weigh two pounds per loaf when baked. It requires a hotter oven than fine flour bread, and must bake about an hour and a half.

RYE AND INDIAN BREAD.

This is a sweet and nourishing diet, and generally acceptable to children.

It is economical, and when wheat is scarce, is a pretty good substitute for dyspepsia bread.

There are many different proportions of mixing it—some put one-third Indian meal with two of rye; others like one-third rye and two of Indian; others prefer it half and half.

If you use the largest proportion of rye meal, make your dough stiff, so that it will mould into loaves;—when it is two-thirds Indian, it should be softer and baked in deep earthen or tin pans after the following rules.

Take *four quarts* of sifted Indian meal; put it into a glazed earthen pan, sprinkle over it a tablespoonful of fine salt; pour over it about two quarts of boiling water, stir and work it till every part of the meal is thoroughly wet; indian meal absorbs a great quantity of water. When it is about milk-warm, work in *two quarts of rye meal, half a pint* of lively yeast, mixed with a pint of warm water; add more warm water if needed. Work the mixture well with your hands: it should be stiff, but not firm as flour dough. Have ready a large, deep, well-buttered pan; put in the dough, and smooth the top by putting your hand in warm water, and then patting down the loaf. Set this to rise in a warm place in the winter; in the summer it should not be put by the fire. When it begins to crack on the top, which will usually be in about an hour or an hour and a half, put it into a well-heated oven, and bake it three or four hours. It is better to let it stand in the oven all night, unless the weather is warm. Indian meal requires to be well cooked. The loaf will weigh between seven and eight pounds. Pan-bread keeps best in large loaves.

Many use milk in mixing bread;—in the country, where milk is plentiful, it is a good practice, as bread is certainly richer wet with sweet milk than with water; but it will not keep so long in warm weather.

Baking can very well be done in a stove; during the winter this is an economical way of cooking—but the stove must be carefully watched, or there is danger of scorching the bread.

GENEVA ROLLS.

Break down very small three ounces of butter into a couple of pounds of flour; add a little salt, and set the sponge with a large tablespoonful of solid yeast, mixed with a pint of new milk, and a tablespoonful or more of strong saffron water; let it rise for a full hour, then stir to a couple of well-beaten eggs, as much hot milk as will render them luke-warm, and wet the rolls with them to a light, lithe dough; leave it from half to three quarters of an hour longer, mould it into small rolls, brush them with beaten yolk of egg, and bake them from twenty minutes to half an hour. The addition of six ounces of good sugar, three of butter, half a pound or more of currants, the grated rind of a large lemon, and a couple of ounces of candied orange-rind, will convert these into excellent buns. When the flavour of the saffron is not liked, omit it altogether. Only so much should be used at any time as will give a rich colour to the bread.

Flour, 2 lbs.; butter, 3 ozs.; solid yeast 1 large tablespoonful (saffron, 1 teaspoonful; water, less than a quarter-pint); new milk, 1 pint: 1 hour, or more. 2 eggs, more milk: ¾ hour: baked 20 to 30 minutes.

RUSKS.

Break very small, six ounces of butter into a couple of pounds of fine dry flour, and mix them into a lithe paste, with two tablespoonsful of mild beer-yeast, three well-beaten eggs, and nearly half a pint of warm new milk. When it has risen to its full height knead it smooth, and make it into very small loaves or thick cakes, cut with a round cake-cutter; place them on a floured tin, and let them stand in a warm place, to *prove*, from ten to twenty minutes before they are set into the oven. Bake them about a quarter of an hour; divide them while they are still warm, and put them into a very slow oven to dry. When they are crisp quite through, they are done. Four teaspoonsful of sifted sugar must be added when sweetened rusks are preferred.

Flour, 2 lbs.; butter, 6 ozs.; yeast, 2 tablespoonsful; eggs, 3; new milk, nearly half a pint; baked ½ hour.

CRUSTS TO SERVE WITH CHEESE.

Take a half-baked loaf from the oven, and tear it into small rough bits with a couple of forks; lay these on a tin, and put them back into the oven for ten minutes. If a light loaf be made for the purpose, with a couple of ounces of butter and new milk, they will quite resemble rusks.

GOOD CAPTAINS' BISCUITS.

Make some fine white flour into a smooth paste with new milk; divide it into small balls; roll, and afterwards pull them with the fingers as *thin as possible*; prick them all over, and bake them in a somewhat brisk oven from eight to twelve minutes. Thin cream may be used for them on occasion, instead of milk, or a *morsel* of butter may be worked into the flour; but they are very good without this last.

BREAKFAST BATTER-CAKES.

Take one pint of milk, three eggs, a piece of butter as large as an egg, two spoonsful of yeast, and flour enough to make a stiff batter; bake them in tin hoops or on a griddle, let them stand and rise all night, but not in a very warm place.

TEA CAKES.

Rub into a pound of flour, an ounce of butter, a beaten egg, and half a teaspoonful of salt; wet it with warmed milk; make the paste rather stiff, and let it remain before the fire, where it will be kept warm for an hour or two; then roll it thin and cut it with the top of a tumbler; bake it quick.

MUFFINS.

Muffins are baked on a hot iron plate, and not in an oven. To a quarter of a peck of flour add three-quarters of a pint of yeast, four ounces of salt, and as much water (or milk) slightly warmed, as is sufficient to form a dough of rather a soft consistency. Small portions of the dough are then put into holes, previously made in a layer of flour about two inches thick, placed on a board, and the whole is covered up in a blanket, and suffered to stand near a fire, to cause the dough to rise; when this is effected, they will each exhibit a semi-globular shape; they are then placed on a heated iron plate, and baked; when the bottoms of the muffins begin to acquire a brownish colour, they are turned, and baked on the opposite side.

WHEAT MUFFINS.

Melt a small piece of butter into a quart of milk, and set it aside until cold—beat four eggs very light, and make a batter by adding alternately and very gradually a little milk and a little flour, until the batter is of the proper consistence, which is quite thin—then add a large spoonful of yeast, if you do not use the powders. Bake them in muffin-rings on a griddle, and butter them before serving—they must be torn asunder to butter, as cutting them open renders them heavy.

RICE MUFFINS.

Rice muffins are made in the same manner exactly as rice cakes, except that the batter of the former is thinner—that is, to a quart of milk and three eggs, you put less rice and less flour.

RICE CAKES.

Boil half a pint of rice until quite soft, setting it aside until perfectly cool; beat three eggs very light and put them with a pint of wheat flour to the rice, making it into a batter with a quart of milk; beat it well, and set it to rise with a spoonful of yeast, or use the yeast powders as directed in a note at the foot of this page. Bake on a griddle, and butter them before sending them to table.

BUCKWHEAT CAKES.

To a quart of buckwheat meal put a little Indian meal (say a tablespoonful) and a little salt; make them into a batter with cold water, taking care to beat it *very* well, as the excellence of buckwheat cakes depends very much on their being well beaten; then put in a large spoonful of good yeast,* and set to rise; when sufficiently risen, bake them a clear brown on a griddle. They are usually buttered before being sent to table.

FLANNEL CAKES.

Melt a table-spoonful of butter in a quart of milk, and after stirring it

---

* Many persons now make use of the yeast powders, and give them a decided preference. They certainly possess the advantage of requiring less time, and thereby enabling you to make muffins, buckwheat cakes, &c.—which, set with yeast, require some hours in the preparation—at a quarter of an hour's notice. The ingredients are the super-carbonate of soda and tartaric acid, to be used in the following manner:— spoonful of soda, and a spoon *two thirds* full of tartaric acid, are to be dissolved *separately* in a little water. The soda is to be put into the batter when it is partly beaten, taking care that it is *perfectly* dissolved; and the acid is to be added when the cook is *ready* to begin baking, as they must not be allowed to stand after the effervescence takes place.

well, set it away to cool; then heat four eggs very light, and stir them into the milk in turn with half a pound of sifted flour; put in a spoonful of yeast, and set it aside. These are baked on a griddle like buckwheat cakes, and are always buttered before being sent to table.

YEAST.

It is impossible to have good light bread, unless you have lively, sweet *yeast*. When common family beer is well brewed and kept in a clean cask, the settlings are the best of yeast. If you do not keep beer, then make common yeast by the following method.

Take two quarts of water, one handful of hops, two of wheat bran; boil these together twenty minutes; strain off the water, and while it is boiling hot, stir in either wheat or rye flour, till it becomes a thick batter; let it stand till it is about blood warm; then add a half pint of good smart yeast and a large spoonful of molasses, if you have it, and stir the whole well. Set it in a cool place in summer and a warm one in winter. When it becomes perfectly light, it is fit for use. If not needed immediately, it should, when it becomes cold, be put in a clean jug or bottle; do not fill the vessel, and the cork must be left loose till the next morning, when the yeast will have done working. Then cork it tightly, and set in a cool place in the cellar. It will keep ten or twelve days.

MILK YEAST.

Take one pint of new milk; one teaspoonful of fine salt, and a large spoon of flour—stir these well together; set the mixture by the fire, and keep it just lukewarm; it will be fit for use in an hour. Twice the quantity of common yeast is necessary; it will not keep long. Bread made of this yeast dries very soon; but in the summer it is sometimes convenient to make this kind when yeast is needed suddenly.

Never keep yeast in a tin vessel. If you find the old yeast *sour*, and have not time to prepare new, put in saleratus, a teaspoonful to a pint of yeast, when ready to use it. If it foams up lively, it will raise the bread; if it does not, never use it.

HARD YEAST.

Boil three ounces of hops in six quarts of water, till only two quarts remain. Strain it, and stir in while it is boiling hot, wheat or rye meal till it is thick as batter. When it is about milk-warm add half a pint of good yeast, and let it stand till it is very light, which will probably be about three hours. Then work in sifted Indian meal till it is stiff dough. Roll it out on a board; cut it in oblong cakes about three inches by two. They should be about half an inch thick. Lay these cakes on a smooth board, over which a little flour has been dusted; prick them with a fork, and set the board in a dry clean chamber or store-room, where the sun and air may be freely admitted. Turn them every day. They will dry in a fortnight unless the weather is damp. When the cakes are fully dry, put them into a coarse cotton bag; hang it up in a cool, dry place. If rightly prepared these cakes will keep a year, and save the trouble of making new yeast every week.

Two cakes will make yeast sufficient for a peck of flour. Break them into a pint of lukewarm water and stir in a large spoonful of flour, the evening before you bake. Set the mixture where it can be kept moderately warm. In the morning it will be fit for use.

POTATOE YEAST

Is made of mealy potatoes boiled thoroughly soft—they are then skinned and mashed as smooth as possible, when as much hot water should be put on them as will make a mash of the consistency of good beer yeast. Add to every pound of potatoes two ounces of treacle, and when just warm stir in for every pound of potatoes two large spoonsful of yeast. Keep it warm till it has done fermenting, and in twenty-four hours it will be fit for use. A pound of potatoes will make nearly a quart of yeast, and it is said to be equally as good as brewers' yeast.

The following is Dr. Lettsom's directions for making another Prepared Yeast.

Thicken two quarts of water with four ounces of flour, boil it for half an hour, then sweeten it with three of brown sugar; when almost cold, pour it along with four spoonsful of bakers' yeast into an earthen jug, deep enough for the fermentation to go on without running over; place it for a day near the fire; then pour off the thin liquor from the top, shake the remainder, and close it up for use, first straining it through a sieve. To preserve it sweet, set it in a cool cellar, or hang it some depth in a well. Always keep some of this yeast to make the next quantity that is wanted.]

CHAPTER XXIX.

AMERICAN MODE OF COOKING INDIAN CORN, PUMP-KINS, &c.

MAIZE or Indian corn has never been extensively used in Great Britain, and the editor has every reason to believe that this has arisen from the almost total ignorance of the English people as to the mode of preparing it for human food. It is, perhaps, the most productive crop that can be grown, and its nutritious qualities, when properly prepared, are equal to its productiveness. We are satisfied that it may be grown in that country, or, at any rate, in the south and eastern parts of it, with great advantage; indeed, the experiment has been tried, and with decided success. The late Mr. Cobbett grew an average crop of the dwarf kind on Barn Elms farm, Surrey, for three or four years.

INDIAN CAKE, OR BANNOCK.

This, as prepared in our own country, is cheap and very nice food. Take one quart of Indian meal, dressed or sifted, two tablespoonsful of treacle or molasses, two teaspoonsful of salt, a bit of "shortening" (butter or lard) half as big as a hen's egg, stirred together; make it pretty moist with scalding water, put it into a well-greased pan, smooth over the surface with a spoon, and bake it brown on both sides before a quick fire. A little stewed pumpkin, scalded with the meal, improves the cake. Bannock split and dipped in butter makes very nice toast.

GREEN INDIAN CORN.

This is a most delicious vegetable. When used as a vegetable, the cobs, or ears, are plucked about the time that the corn has arrived at a milky state, or just before it assumes a solid substance. A part of the leaves or filaments by which the cob, or ear is surrounded, is taken away, and the cobs boiled from twenty to forty minutes, "according to its age." When it is done, it is served with cold or melted butter, and eaten (after being stripped of its remaining leaves) by taking the two ends of the cob in the hands, and biting off the corn. The editor can bear testimony to its delicious quality.

INDIAN CORN, OR MAIZE PUDDING, BAKED.

Scald a quart of milk (skimmed milk will do), and stir in seven table-spoonsful of sifted Indian meal, a teaspoonful of salt, a teacupful of mo-lasses or treacle, or coarse moist sugar, and a tablespoonful of powdered ginger or sifted cinnamon: bake three or four hours. If whey is wanted, pour in a little cold milk after it is all mixed.

BOILED MAIZE PUDDING.

Stir Indian meal and warm milk together "pretty stiff;" a little salt and two or three "great spoonsful" of molasses added; also a spoonful of ginger, or any other spice that may be preferred. Boil it in a tight-covered pan, or in a very thick cloth; if the water gets in, it will ruin it. Leave plenty of room, for Indian meal swells very much. The milk with which it is mixed should be merely warmed; if it be scalding hot, the pudding will break to pieces. Some chop suet very fine, and warm in the milk; others warm thin slices of apple to be stirred into the pudding. Water will answer instead of milk.

PUMPKIN AND SQUASH PIE.

The usual way of dressing pumpkins in England in a pie is to cut them into slices, mixed with apples, and bake them with a top crust like ordinary pies. A quite different process is pursued in America, and the editor can testify to the immense superiority of the Yankee method. In England, the pumpkin is grown for show rather than for use; nevertheless, when properly dressed, it is a very delicious vege-table, and a universal favourite with our New England neighbours.

The following is the American method of making a pumpkin pie:—Take out the seeds, and pare the pumpkin or squash; but in taking out the seeds do not scrape the inside of the pumpkin; the part nearest the seed is the sweetest; then stew the pumpkin, and strain it through a sieve or colander. To a quart of milk, for a family pie, three eggs are sufficient. Stir in the stewed pumpkin with your milk and beaten-up eggs till it is as thick as you can stir round rapidly and easily. If the pie is wanted richer make it thinner, and add another egg or two; but even one egg to a quart of milk makes "very decent pies." Sweeten with molasses or sugar; add two teaspoonsful of salt, two tablespoonsful of sifted cinnamon, and one of powdered ginger; but allspice may be used, or any other spice that may be preferred. The peel of a lemon grated in gives it a pleasant flavour. The more eggs, says our Ame-rican authority, the better the pie. Some put one egg to a gill of milk. Bake about an hour in deep plates, or shallow dishes, without an upper crust, in a warm oven.

There is another method of making this pie, which we know from experience, produces an excellent dish: Take out the seeds, and grate the pumpkin till you come to the outside skin. Sweeten the pulp: add a little ground allspice, lemon-peel, and lemon-juice; in short, flavour it to your taste. Bake without an upper crust.

CARROT PIES.

These pies are made like pumpkin pies. The carrots should be boiled very tender, skinned, and sifted.

AMERICAN CUSTARD PUDDINGS,

Sufficiently good for common use, may be made by taking five eggs beaten up and mixed with a quart of milk, sweetened with sugar and spiced with cinnamon, allspice, or nutmeg. It is well to boil your milk first, and let it get cold before using it. "Boiling milk enriches it so much, that boiled skim milk is about as good as new." (We doubt this assertion; at any rate, it can only be improved by the evaporation of the water.) Bake fifteen or twenty minutes.

AMERICAN PLUM PUDDING.

Pound six hard fine biscuits (crackers), soak them for some hours in milk sufficient to cover the mass; add three pints of milk, beat up six eggs, and mix; flavour with lemon-brandy, and a whole nutmeg grated: add three-quarters of a pound of stoned raisins, rubbed in flour. Bake not quite two hours.

AMERICAN APPLE PUDDINGS.

Take your apples, and bore out the core without cutting them in two. Fill up the holes with washed rice. Tie up each apple very tight, and separately in the corners of a pudding-bag. Boil an hour, or an hour and a half.

BIRD'S NEST PUDDING.

If you wish to make what is called a bird's nest pudding, prepare your custard; take eight or ten pleasant apples, prepare them and take out the core, but leave them whole; set them in a pudding-dish, pour your custard over them, and bake about thirty minutes.

HASTY PUDDING.

Boil water, a quart, three pints, or two quarts, according to the size of your family; sift your meal, stir five or six spoonsful of it thoroughly into a bowl of water; when the water in the kettle boils, pour into it the contents of the bowl; stir it well, and let it boil up thick; put in salt to suit your own taste, then stand over the kettle, and sprinkle in meal, handful after handful, stirring it very thoroughly all the time, and letting it boil between whiles. When it is so thick that you stir it with great difficulty, it is about right. It takes half an hour's cooking. Eat it with milk or molasses. Either Indian meal or rye meal may be used. If the system is in a restricted state, nothing can be better than *rye* hasty pudding and *West India* molasses. This diet would save many a one the horrors of dyspepsia.

DRY BREAD.

As far as possible, have bits of bread eaten up before they become hard. Spread those that are not eaten, and let them dry, to be pounded for puddings, or soaked for brewis. *Brewis* is made of crusts and dry pieces of bread, soaked a good while in hot milk, mashed up and salted, and buttered like toast.

ANOTHER SORT OF BREWIS.

The author of Domestic Cookery observes, that a very good meal may be bestowed on poor people in a thing called *brewis*, which is thus made: Cut a very thick upper crust of bread, and put it into the pot where salt beef is boiling, and nearly ready; it will attach some of the fat, and when swelled out, will be no unpalatable dish to those who rarely taste meat.

TO PRESERVE CHEESE.

Cover the cheese carefully with paper, fastened on with paste, so as totally to exclude the air. In this way cheese may be kept for years.

AMERICAN MINCE MEAT.

Take the good bits of vegetables, and the cold meat left after dinner. Mash your vegetables fine, and chop your meat very fine. Warm it with what remains of gravy, or roast-meat dripping. Two or three apples, sliced and fried to mix with it, are considered an improvement. Some like a little sifted sage sprinkled in it. After it is warmed, lay it upon a large slice of toasted bread. Potatoes should not be used in the preparation of American mince meat.

AMERICAN SOUSE.

Take pigs' feet, ears, &c. well cleaned, and boil or rather simmer them for four or five hours, until they are too tender to be taken out with a fork. When taken from the boiling water, it should be put into cold water. After it is packed down tight, boil the jelly-like liquor in which it was cooked with an equal quantity of vinegar; salt as you think fit, and add cloves, allspice, and cinnamon.

PORK AND BEANS

Is an economical dish; but it does not agree with weak stomachs. Put a quart of beans into two quarts of cold water, and hang them all night over the fire, to swell. In the morning pour off the water, rinse them well with two or three waters poured over them in a colander. Take a pound of pork, that is not very fat, score the rind, then again place the beans just covered with water in the kettle and keep them hot over the fire for an hour or two; then drain off the water, sprinkle a little pepper and a teaspoonful of salt over the beans; place them in a well-glazed earthen pot, not very wide at the top, put the pork down in the beans, till the rind only appears; fill the pot with water till it just reaches the top of the beans, put it in a brisk oven and bake three or four hours.

Stewed beans and pork are prepared in the same way, only they are kept over the fire, and the pork in them three or four hours instead of being in the oven. The beans will not be white or pleasant to the taste unless they are well soaked and washed—nor are they healthy without this process.

CHAPTER XXX.

DIRECTIONS FOR CARVING.

GARNISHING, AND SETTING OUT A TABLE.

IN preparing meat for the table, and in laying out the table, refer
ence ought to be had to the carving department—a very onerous one
to all, and to many a very disagreeable one. The carving-knife of
course ought to be sharp, and if to be used by a lady, in particular, light
and handy; dexterity and address in the manner of using it being more
required than strength, either in the knife or the carver. When a
lady presides, a seat sufficiently high for her to have a complete command over the joints should be provided, and the dish should be sufficiently deep and capacious, so as not to endanger the splashing of the
gravy. It should also be placed as near to the carver as possible, leaving room for his or her plate. A knife with a long blade is required for
a large fleshy joint; for ham or bacon a middling sized, sharp-pointed
one is preferable, and for poultry or game a short knife and sharp-
pointed is best. Some like this knife a little curved. We do not pre-
sume to give any directions as respects the serving of the guests; no
one it is presumed would take the head of the table not acquainted with
the common rules of politeness, which principally consist in endeavour-
ing to please everybody.

FISH.

As fish is the first thing to be carved, or served, we shall first speak
of it. In helping fish, take care not to break the flakes, which in cod
and fine fresh salmon, and some other sorts, are large. A fish trowel
is necessary, not to say indispensable, in serving many kinds of fish, particularly the larger sort.

TURBOT, &c.

The trowel is to be carried flatways from the middle of the fish, and
the carver should bring out as much meat as will lie upon it. The
thick part is the best, and of course most esteemed. When one side is
cleared, the bones ought to be taken away—which done, serve the
under part. The meat on the fins is considered by some a great
delicacy. Halibuts, plaice, and other large fish, are served in a similar way.

A COD'S HEAD AND SHOULDERS.

These, perhaps, require more attention in serving than any other. It
is, too, considered a handsome dish. In carving, introduce the trowel
along the back, and take off a piece quite down to the bone, taking care
not to break the flakes. Put in a spoon and take out the sound, a jelly-
like substance, which lies inside the back-bone. A part of this should
be served with every slice of fish. The bones and glutinous parts of a
cod's head are much liked by most people, and are very nourishing.

SALMON.

Cut slices along the back-bone, and also along the flank. The flank
or thin part is the best and richest, and is preferred by all accomplisned
gourmands. The back is the most solid and thick. The tail of salmon

is not so fine as the other parts. The head is seldom used. The liver, melt, and roe, are generally served, but seldom eaten.

SOLES.

These are easily carved. You have only to cut through the middle part of the fish, bone and all, and subdivide and serve according to the size of fish. The thick parts are best; the roes when well done are very nice.

MACKEREL.

The trowel should be carried under the meat, horizontally over the back-bone, so as to raise one side of the meat from the bone. Remove the bone, and serve the other side of the fish. When fresh, well cleaned, and well done, the upper end is considered the best. The roes are much liked.

EELS, WHITING JACK, &c.

These when intended to be fried, are previously cut in pieces of a suitable size for serving. When they are boiled, cut through them in the same way as soles. Large jacks will admit of slices being taken off with a trowel without the bones. Small fish are served whole.

AITCH BONE OF BEEF.

Cut a slice an inch thick all through. Put this by, and serve in slices from the remainder. Some persons, however, like outside, and others take off a thinner slice before serving, for the sake of economy. The rich, delicious, soft fat, which resembles marrow, lies at the back of the bone: the firm fat is cut in horizontal slices at the edge of the meat. Some prefer one and some the other. The skewer used to keep the meat together when boiling, should be taken out before coming to the table, and, if necessary, be replaced by a silver one.

A ROUND, OR BUTTOCK, AND THICK FLANK OF BEEF.

These are carved in horizontal slices, that is, in slices from the top. Pare and neatly cut all round. Some prefer the silver side.

A BRISKET OF BEEF.

This is cut lengthways, right down to the bone. The soft mellow fat is found underneath. The upper part is firm, but gristly; if well done, they are equally good to our taste.

SIRLOIN OF BEEF,

The glory of the dinner-table, may be commenced carving, either by beginning at the end, and cutting slices along the bones, or across the middle; but this latter mode will drain the gravy from the remainder. The inside is very juicy and tender, but the outside is frequently preferred. The inside fat is rich and marrowy, and is considered too much so by many. The inside of a sirloin is frequently dressed (in various ways) separately.

FILLET OF VEAL

Is the corresponding part to the round in an ox, and is cut in the same way. If the outside brown be not desired, serve the next slice. Cut deep into the stuffing, and help a thin slice, as likewise of fat. A fillet of veal should be cut very smooth and thin.

BREAST OF VEAL

Answers to the brisket of an ox. It should be cracked lengthways, across the middle of the bones, to divide the thick gristly part from the ribs. There is a great difference in these parts; and as some prefer the one, and some the other, the best way is to ask to which the preference is to be given. The burr, or sweetmeat, is much liked, and a part should be served with each slice.

NECKS AND LOINS

Of all sorts of meat, if properly jointed by the butcher, require only to be cut through; but when the joints are too thick for one, cut a slice between each, that is, cut one slice without bone, and another with. Some prefer one, and some the other.

CALF'S HEAD

Affords a great variety of excellent meat, differing in texture and flavour, and therefore requires a judicious and skilful carver properly to divide it. Cut slices loogways under the eye, taking care that the knife goes close to the bone. The throat sweetbread or kernel, lies in the fleshy part, at the neck end, which you should help a slice of with the other part. The eyes are considered great delicacies by some. They should be taken out with the point of your knife, and each cut into two. A piece of the palate (which lies under the head), a slice of the tongue, with a portion of the brains, should be given to each guest. On drawing out the jaw-bone, some delicious lean will be found. The heads of oxen, sheep, lambs, &c., are cut in the same way as those of calves. '

A LEG OF MUTTON, &C.

Begin to cut in the midway, between the knuckle and farther end. The slices should be thin and deep. If the outside is not fat enough, cut some from the fat on the broad end, in slices. Many prefer the knuckle, or venison bit, to the middle part; the latter is the most juicy, the former, in good, well-done mutton, is gelatinous, and delicately tender. There is some good meat on the back of the leg, or aitch bone; this should be cut lengthways. It is, however, seldom carved when hot. To cut out the cramp bone, take hold of the shank in your left hand, and steadily cut down to the thigh bone; then pass the knife under the cramp bone. Legs of lamb and pork are cut in the same way.

A SADDLE OR COLLAR OF MUTTON,

Sometimes called the chine, should be cut lengthways, in long slices, beginning close to the backbone, and thus leaving the ribs bare. The fat is taken from the outer ends. The inside of the loin is very tender, and in the opinion of some gourmands, is preferred to the upper part. It is best, perhaps, to cut the inside lengthways.

SHOULDER OF MUTTON.

To carve this joint (which when properly dressed is very fine eating) economically for a very small family, the best way is to cut away the underneath part when hot, and if any more is required, to take it from the knuckle. This plan leaves all the gravy in the upper part, which is very nice when cold. The usual way, however, of carving a shoulder of mutton, is to cut slices deep to the bone, in the hollow part. The prime part of the fat lies on the outer edge, and is to be cut in thin slices. Some good delicate slices of lean may be taken from each side of the ridge of the blade-bone. No slices can be cut across the edge of the blade-bone.

HAUNCH OF VENISON OR MUTTON.

Cut down to the bone in circular slices at the narrow end, to let out the gravy. You may then turn the broad end of the haunch towards you; insert the knife in the middle of the cut, and cut thin deep slices lengthways to the broad end of the haunch. The fat of venison is much esteemed; those who help should take care properly to apportion both the fat and gravy.

FORE-QUARTER OF LAMB.

Separate the shoulder from the scovel, or breast and ribs, by passing the knife under it (the shoulder). The shoulder of grass lamb, which is generally pretty large, should have a little lemon or Seville orange-juice squeezed over it, and be sprinkled with a little pepper and salt, and then placed upon another dish. If the lamb be small, it is usual to replace the shoulder. The breast and ribs should be cracked across by the butcher, and be divided. Help either from that, the ribs, or shoulder, according to choice.

HAM.

The most economical way of cutting a ham, which is seldom or never eaten at one meal, is to begin to cut at the knuckle end, and proceed onwards. The usual way, however, is to begin at the middle, and cut in long slices through the thick fat. By this means you come at once to the prime, but you let out the gravy. Another plan is to cut a small hole on the top of the ham, and with a very sharp knife enlarge the hole, by cutting thin circular slices. In this latter way you preserve the gravy, and of course keep the meat moist to be eaten when cold.

TONGUE.

This much-esteemed relish, which often supplies the place of ham, should be cut in thin slices across, beginning at the thick middle part. Serve slices of fat and kernel from the root.

A SUCKING PIG

Is generally slit down the middle in the kitchen, and the cook garnishes the dish with the jaws and ears. Separate a shoulder from the carcase on one side, and then do the same thing with the leg. Divide the ribs, which are frequently considered the most choice part, into two or three helpings, presenting an ear or jaw with them as far as they will go, and plenty of sauce. Some persons prefer the leg, because not so rich and luscious as the ribs. The neck end between the shoulders is also sometimes preferred. The joints may be divided into two each, or pieces may be cut from them.

A FOWL.

The legs of a boiled fowl are always bent inwards, and tucked into the belly, but before it is put upon the table, the skewers by which they are secured ought to be removed. The fowl should be laid on the carver's plate, and the joints as they are cut off placed on

the dish.   In taking off the wing, the joint only must be divided with
the knife, for, by lifting up the pinion of the wing with the fork, and
then drawing it towards the legs, the muscles will separate in a much
better form than you can effect by cutting with a knife.   Next place
the knife between the leg and body, and cut to the bone; turn the leg
back with the fork, and the joint will give way, if the fowl be young
and well done.   The merrythought is taken out when the legs and
wings are all removed; the neck bones are taken off by putting in the
knife, and pressing it under the long broad part of the bone, then lift
the neck-bone up and break it off from the part that sticks to the breast.
The breast itself has now to be divided from the carcase, by cutting
through the tender ribs close to the breast, quite down to the tail; then
lay the back upwards, put your knife into the bone half-way from the
neck to the rump, and on raising the lower end it will readily separate.
The last thing to be done is to turn the rump from you, and neatly to
take off the two sidesmen.   Each part should be neatly arranged on the
dish, but it is almost impossible to give effectual written descriptions
for carving fowls; the best plan is to observe carefully a good carver,
and then, by a little practice, you will become perfect.   The breast and
the wings are considered the best parts.

A PHEASANT.

Take out the skewers; fix your fork in the centre of the breast, slice
it down; remove the leg by cutting in the sideway direction, then take
off the wing, taking care to miss the neck-bone.   When the legs and
wings are all taken off, cut off slices of the breast.   The merrythought
is separated by passing the knife under it towards the neck; the other
parts are cut as before directed in a fowl.   The breast, wings, and
merrythought, are the favourites, particularly the former, but the leg
has a higher flavour.

PARTRIDGES AND PIGEONS.

Partridges are carved like fowls, but the breast and wings are not
often divided, the bird being small.   The wing is the prime bit, particularly the tip; the other choice parts are the breast and merrythought.   *Pigeons* may be cut in two, either from one end to the other
of the bird, or across.

GOOSE OR DUCK.

Cut off the apron of the goose and pour into the body a large spoonful of gravy, which should be mixed with the stuffing.   Some persons
put, instead of the gravy, a glass of port-wine, in which a large teaspoonful of mustard has been previously stirred.   Cut as many slices
from the breast as possible, and serve with a portion of the apron to
each plate.   When the breast is all served, and not till then, cut off
the joints; but observe, the joints of water-fowl are wider spread and
go farther back than those of land-fowl.

A TURKEY

Should not be divided till the breast is disposed of; but if it be
thought proper to divide, the same process must be followed as directed
in a fowl.   The following is the best mode of serving this delicious
bird: Begin cutting close to the breast-bone, scooping round so as to
leave the mere pinions.   Each slice should carry with it a portion of
the pudding, or force meat, with which the craw is stuffed.

HARE.

Put the point of the knife under the shoulder, and cut all the way down to the rump, on the side of the back-bone. By doing the same on the other side, the hare will be divided into three parts. The back should be cut into four parts: the shoulder must be taken off in a circular line. The pieces as they are cut should be neatly placed on the dish; in helping, some pudding and gravy should be given to each person. The above mode of carving is only applicable to a young hare; when the hare is old, it is not practicable to divide it down, but put the knife between the leg and back, and give it a little turn inwards at the joints, which you must endeavour to hit, and then cut, and with the fork turn it completely back. When both legs are taken off, you will find a fine collop on each side of the back, which back you may divide into as many pieces as are necessary. Take off the shoulders, which some persons are very fond of, and which are called the sportsman's pieces; but the legs and back are considered the prime. When all the guests are served, it is usual to take off the head, and by putting the knife between the upper and lower jaw, you may divide them; then lay the upper flat upon your plate, put the point of the knife into the centre, and cut the head into two; you will thus get at the brains, which may be served with the ears and tail to those who like them. Some persons direct the carver to serve with slices, as much as possible, off the sides of the back-bone, from the shoulder to the rump.

RABBITS

Are generally cut up in the same way as hares. The back and legs are considered the best parts. The back should be cut into two pieces.

GARNISHES.

Parsley is the most universal garnish to all kinds of cold meat, poultry, fish, butter, cheese, and so forth. Horse-radish is the garnish for roast beef, and for fish in general; for the latter, slices of lemon are sometimes laid alternately with heaps of horse-radish.

Slices of lemon for boiled fowl, turkey, and fish, and for roast veal and calf's head.

Carrot in slices for boiled beef, hot or cold.

Barberries fresh or preserved for game.

Red beet-root sliced for cold meat, boiled beef, and salt fish.

Fried smelts as garnish for turbot.

Fried sausages or force meat-balls round roast turkey, capon, or fowl.

Lobster coral and parsley round boiled fish.

Fennel for mackerel and salmon, either fresh or pickled.

Currant jelly for game, also for custard or bread pudding.

Seville orange in slices for wild ducks, widgeons, teal and so forth.

Mint, either with or without parsley, for roast lamb, either hot or cold.

Pickled gherkins, capers, or onions, for some kinds of boiled meat and stews.

SETTING OUT A TABLE.

A prudent housekeeper, in providing for a family, or for company, will endeavour to secure variety, and avoid extravagance, taking care not to have two dishes alike, or nearly alike, such as ducks and pork, veal and fowls; and avoiding, when several sorts are required, to have such things as cannot be eaten cold, or cannot be warmed or re-cooked. There is a great waste occasioned if these principles are overlooked in providing for a party. When a table is to be set out, it is usual to place nearly the whole provisions at once; but if comfort is the object, it is better to have each dish and its accompanying sauces and vegetables sent in separately, hot from the kitchen.

For plain family dinners, soup or pudding is placed at the head of the table, and meat at the lower end; vegetables on each side of the middle, and sauce boats in the middle. Boiled meat at the top; roast meat at bottom; soup in the middle; then the vegetables and sauce boats at cross corners of the middle dish. Poultry or mutton at bottom; boiled poultry at top; roast poultry, or game, at bottom; vegetables and sauces so disposed as to give the appearance of the whole table being covered without being crowded.

When there are several courses, the first consists of soups, stews, boiled fish, fricassees; poultry with ham, bacon, tongue, or chine; and roast or boiled meat.

For second course, birds and game of all sorts, fish fried, pickled, or potted; pigeon pies, patties, brawn, omelets, oysters stewed or scolloped, and lobsters or crabs. Tarts, cheesecakes, and sweet dishes of all kinds, are sometimes placed with the second course, but more frequently form separate courses by themselves.

The dessert is usually served in another room, which is a great accommodation both to the servants, who can prepare it at leisure, and to the guests in quitting the smell of a hot dinner. A d'oyley, a finger-glass, two wine-glasses, a China dessert plate, and silver knife and fork, and spoon, to each person. Every variety of fruit, fresh and preserved, is admissible; and biscuits, and pound-cake, with an epergne or stand of jellies in the middle. Varieties of wine are generally placed at each end.

The modern practice of dining late has added importance to the luncheon, and almost annihilated the supper meal. The following are suitable for either: soups, sandwiches of ham, tongue, dried sausage, or beef; anchovy, toast or husks; potted beef, lobster, or cheese; dried salmon, lobsters, crayfish, or oysters, poached eggs; patties; pigeon-pies; sausages; toast with marrow (served on a water-plate), cheesecakes; puffs, mashed or scolloped potatoes, brocoli; asparagus, sea-kale with toast, creams, jellies, preserved or dried fruits, salad, radishes, &c. If a more substantial supper is required, it may consist of fish, poultry, game; slices of cold meat, pies of chickens, pigeons, or game; lamb or mutton chops, cold poultry, broiled with high seasoning, or fricasseed; rations or toasted cheese.

25

APPENDIX

RELATIVE DUTIES OF MISTRESS AND MAID.

COOKING is neither a mean, nor a simple art. To make the *best* and the *most* of everything connected with the sustenance of a family, requires not only industry and experience, but also considerable mental capacity, or at any rate, an aptness to learn.

One of the principal, if not the principal, requisite in a cook, is order —that faculty by which a person is enabled to keep all things in their proper places. Without order there can be no cleanliness, another indispensable requisite in a cook: to be always cleaning, is not to be clean. There are some foolish, fussy women, who, with all the disposition on earth to be clean, not having order, dirty one thing as fast as they clean another. Nor is order an essential requisite, as regards the cleanliness of a kitchen, and of kitchen utensils only; in dressing food, without order there can be no good cooking.

We have said, that the mistress will take a part in a small family in the business of cooking. We, perhaps, should have rather said, ought to take a part; for we are sorry to say, that there is too much reason to believe, that good housewifery is much neglected in the educating of young ladies now-a-days. If a mistress be really not acquainted with the general principles of cooking, she ought to do one of two things— either to make herself acquainted with them as an humble learner, or to keep out of the kitchen altogether; for her ignorant interference with a good cook-maid will do no good, but may do a great deal of harm. And while on this subject we must give a word of friendly advice to the unfortunate cook, who may happen to fall in with an ignorant, irritable mistress. Let her take care to refrain from going into a passion with her: if the mistress scolds, let the maid be mild; and above all, let her not scold again, or answer in an angry or insulting manner. This is a hard thing to do, we are aware, particularly where a servant feels herself injured; but if she can do it, she will not only gain the victory over her mistress, but she will also feel a consciousness, a happy consciousness, of having left undone those things which she ought not to have done, and of having done those things which she ought to have done. But if the tempers and habits of the mistress and maid are incompatible to that good understanding which ought always to subsist between the employer and the employed, the best course for the servant to do is, to give notice and leave. Let not this, however, be done in anger: before giving warning, let her consult her pillow.

It has been well observed, that it behoves every person to be extremely careful whom she takes into her service; to be very minute in investigating the character she receives, and equally cautious and scrupulously just in giving one to others. Were this attended to, many bad people would be incapacitated for doing mischief, by abusing the trust reposed in them. It may be fairly asserted, that the robbery, or waste, which is but a milder epithet for the unfaithfulness of a servant, will be laid to the charge of that master or mistress, who knowing, or having well-founded suspicions, of such faults, is prevailed upon by false pity, or entreaty, to slide him, or her, into another place. There are, however, some who are unfortunately capricious, and often refuse to give a character, because they are displeased that a servant leaves their service; but this is unpardonable, and an absolute robbery; servants having no inheritance, and depending on their fair name for employment. To refuse countenance to the evil, and to encourage the good servant, are actions due to society at large; and such as are honest, frugal and attentive to their duties, should be liberally rewarded, which would encourage merit, and inspire servants with zeal to acquit themselves well.

Servants should always recollect that everything is provided for them, without care and anxiety on their part. They run no risks, are subject to no losses, and under these circumstances, honesty, industry, civility, and perseverance, are in the end sure to meet with their reward. Servants possessing these qualifications, by the blessing of God, must succeed. Servants should be kind and obliging to their fellow-servants; but if they are honest themselves, they will not connive at dishonesty in others. They who see crimes committed and do not discover them, are themselves legally and morally guilty. At the same time, however, well recollect, that tittle-tattling and tale-bearing, for the sake of getting in your mistress's good graces, at the expense of your fellow-servants, is, to the last degree, detestable. A sensible mistress will always discourage such practices.

We have known servants imagine, that because their employers are kind to them, that because they do not *command* them to do this or that, but rather *solicit* them, that, therefore, they cannot do without them, and instead of repaying their good-nature and humanity by gratitude and extra attention, give themselves airs, and become idle and neglectful. Such conduct cannot be too much condemned, and those servants who practise it may depend upon it, that, sooner or later, they will have cause to repent. Let it be remembered, that vice as well as virtue has its reward, though of a very different character.

We shall conclude this our friendly advice to young cooks, by an extract from the "*Cook's Best Friend*," by the late Dr. Kitchener. Nothing can be done in perfection, which must be done in a hurry, (except catching of fleas),—"Therefore," says the Doctor, "if you wish the dinner to be sent up to please your master and mistress, and do credit to yourself, be punctual; take care, that as soon as the clock strikes, the dinner-bell rings. This shows the establishment is orderly is extremely gratifying to the master and his guests, and is most praise-worthy in the attendants. But remember you cannot obtain this desirable reputation without good management in every respect; if you wish to ensure ease and independence in the latter part of your life, you must not be unwilling to pay the price for which only they can be obtained, and earn them by a diligent and faithful performance of the duties of your station in your young days, in which if you steadily persevere, you may depend upon ultimately receiving the reward your services deserve."

All duties are reciprocal; and if you hope to receive favour, endeavour to deserve it by showing yourself fond of obliging, and grateful when obliged. Such behaviour will win regard, and maintain it; enforce what is right, and excuse what is wrong.

Quiet, steady perseverance, is the only spring which you can safely depend upon infallibly to promote your progress on the road to independence.

If your employers do not immediately appear to be sensible of your endeavours to contribute your utmost to their comfort and interests, be not easily discouraged; *persevere*, and do all in your power to MAKE YOURSELF USEFUL.

Endeavour to promote the comfort of every individual in the family; let it be manifest that you are desirous to do rather more than is required of you, than less than your duty; they merit little who perform nothing more than what would be exacted. If you are desired to help in any business that may not strictly belong to your department, undertake it *cheerfully*, *patiently* and *conscientiously*.

The foregoing advice has been written with an honest desire to augment the comfort of those in the kitchen, who will soon find, that the ever-cheering reflection of having done their duty to the utmost of their ability, is in itself, with a Christian spirit, a never-failing source of comfort in all circumstances and situations, and that

" Virtue is its own reward."

WHAT MUST ALWAYS BE DONE, AND WHAT MUST NEVER BE DONE.

1. Keep yourself clean and tidy; let your hands, in particular, be always clean whenever it is practicable. After a dirty job, always wash them. A cleanly cook must wash her hands many times in the course of the day, and will require three or four aprons appropriated to the work upon which she is employed. Your hair must never be blowsy, nor your cap dirty.

2. Keep apart things that would injure each other, or destroy their flavour.

3. Keep every cloth, saucepan and all other utensils to their proper use, and when done with, put them in their proper places.

4. Keep every copper stewpan and saucepan bright without, and perfectly clean within, and take care that they are always well tinned. Keep all your dish-covers well dried, and polished; and to

effect this, it will be necessary to wash them in scalding water as soon as removed from the table, and when these things are done let them be hung up in their proper places.

5. The gridiron, frying-pan, spit, dripping-pan, &c., must be perfectly cleaned of grease and dried before they are put in their proper places.

6. Attention should be paid to things that do not meet the sight in the way that tins and copper vessels do. Let, for instance, the pudding-cloth, the dish-cloth, and the dish-tub, be always kept perfectly clean. To these may be added, the sieve, the cullender, the jelly-bag, &c., which ought always to be washed as soon after they are used as may be practicable.

7. Scour your rolling-pin and paste-board as soon after using as possible, but without soap, or any gritty substance, such as sand or brick-dust; put them away perfectly dry.

8. Scour your pickle and preserve-jars after they are emptied; dry them and put them away in a dry place.

9. Wipe your bread and cheese-pan out daily with a dry cloth, and scald them once a week. Scald your salt-pan when out of use, and dry it thoroughly. Scour the lid well by which it is covered when in use.

10. Mind and put all things in their proper places, and then you will easily find them when they are wanted.

11. You must not poke things out of sight instead of cleaning them, and such things as onions, garlic, &c., must not be cut with the same knife as is used in cutting meat, bread, butter, &c. Milk must not be put in a vessel used for greasy purposes, nor must clear liquids, such as water, &c., be put into vessels, which have been used for milk, and not washed; in short, no vessel must be used for any purpose for which it is not appropriated.

12. You must not suffer any kind of food to become cold in any metal vessel, not even in well-tinned iron saucepans, &c., for they will impart a more or less unpleasant flavour to it. Above all things you must not let liquid food, or indeed any other, remain in brass or copper vessels after it is cooked. The rust of copper or brass is absolutely poisonous, and this will be always produced by moisture and exposure to the air. The deaths of many persons have been occasioned by the cook not attending to this rule.

13. You must not throw away the fat which, when cold, accumulates on the top of liquors in which fresh or salt meat has been boiled; in short, you ought not to waste fat of any description, or any thing else, that may be turned to account; such as marrow-bones, or any other clean bones from which food may be extracted in the way of soup, broth, or stock, or in any other way: for if such food will not suit your table, it will suit the table of the poor. Remember, "Wilful waste makes woful want."

14. A very essential requisite in a cook is punctuality: therefore rise early; and get your orders from your mistress as early as possible, and make your arrangements accordingly. What can be prepared before the business of roasting and boiling commences should always bo prepared.

15. Do not do your dirty work at a dresser set apart for cleanly pre

parations. Take care to have plenty of kitchen cloths, and mark them so as a duster may not be mistaken for a pudding-cloth, or a knife-cloth for a towel.

16. Keep your spit, if you use one, always free from rust and dust, and your vertical jack clean. Never draw up your jack with a weight upon it.

17. Never employ, even if permitted to do so, any knives, spoons, dishes, cups, or any other articles in the kitchen, which are used in the dining room. Spoons are sure to get scratched, and a knife used for preparing an onion, takes up its flavour, which two or three cleanings will not entirely take away.

18. Take great care to prevent all preparations which are delicate in their nature, such as custards, blancmange, dressed milks, &c., &c., from burning, to which they are very liable. The surest way to effectually hinder this is to boil them as the carpenter heats his glue, that is, by having an outside vessel filled with water.

19. You ought not to do any thing by halves. What you do, do well. If you clean, clean thoroughly, having nothing to do with the "slut's wipe," and the "lick and a promise."

20. And *last*, though *not least*, be teachable: be always desirous to learn—never be ashamed to ask for information, lest you should appear to be ignorant; for be assured, the most ignorant are too frequently the most self-opinionated and most conceited; while those who are really well informed, think humbly of themselves, and regret that they know so little.

INDEX.

THE END.

LIST OF NEW PUBLICATIONS.

MAILING NOTICE.—Single copies of any of these Books will be sent to any address, post-paid, on receipt of price. This very convenient mode may be adopted where your neighboring bookseller is not supplied with the work.　　Address,

JOHN E. POTTER & CO., Publishers,
No. 617 Sansom Street, Philadelphia.

LIFE AND PUBLIC SERVICES OF ABRAHAM LINCOLN. Containing his early History and Political Career. By Frank Crosby, of the Philadelphia Bar. With Portrait on steel. 12mo., cloth. Price $1 75.

THE SAME TRANSLATED INTO THE GERMAN LANGUAGE. By Professor Carl Theodor Eben. 12mo., cloth. Price $1 75.

LIFE AND PUBLIC SERVICES OF STEPHEN A. DOUGLAS. To which are added his Speeches and Reports. By H. M. Flint. With Portrait on steel. 12mo., cloth. Price $1 75.

LIFE OF DANIEL BOONE, the Great Western Hunter and Pioneer. By Cecil B. Hartley. With illustrations. 12mo., cloth. Price $1 75.

LIFE OF KIT CARSON, the Great Western Hunter and Guide. By Charles Burdett. With illustrations. 12mo., cloth. Price $1 75.

LIFE OF DAVID CROCKETT, the Original Humorist and Irrepressible Backwoodsman. With illustrations. 12mo., cloth. Price $1 75.

LIFE AND ADVENTURES OF MISS MAJOR PAULINE CUSHMAN, the Celebrated Union Spy and Scout. By F. L. Sarmiento, Esq., of the Philadelphia Bar. With Portrait and illustrations. 12mo., cloth. Price $1 75.

THRILLING STORIES OF THE GREAT REBELLION.
Including an Account of the Death of President Lincoln, and Capture of
the Assassins. By Lieutenant-Colonel Charles S. Greene, late of the
United States Army. With illustrations. 12mo., cloth. Price $1 75.

THRILLING ADVENTURES AMONG THE EARLY
SETTLERS. Embracing Desperate Encounters with Indians, Refugees,
Gamblers, Desperadoes, etc. etc. By Warren Wildwood, Esq. Illus-
trated by 200 engravings. 12mo., cloth. Price $1 75.

THRILLING INCIDENTS IN THE WARS OF THE
UNITED STATES. Embracing all the Wars previous to the Rebellion.
With 300 engravings. 12mo., cloth. Price $1 75.

OUR BOYS. The rich and racy scenes of Army and Camp
Life, as seen and participated in by one of the Rank and File. By A.
F. Hill, of the Eighth Pa. Reserves. With illustrations. 12mo., cloth.
Price $1 75.

OUR CAMPAIGNS; or, a Three Years' Term of Service in
the War. By E. M. Woodward, Adjutant Second Pennsylvania Reserves.
12mo., cloth. Price $1 75.

THE BEAUTIFUL SPY. An exciting story of Army and
High Life in New York in 1776. By Charles Burdett. 12mo., cloth.
Price $1 75.

THE ROYALIST'S DAUGHTER AND THE REBELS.
A tale of the Revolution of unusual power and interest. By Rev. David
Murdoch, D. D. 12mo., cloth. Price $1 75.

THE HERO GIRL, and how she became a Captain in the
Army. By Thrace Talmon. With illustrations. 12mo., cloth. Price
$1 75.

HUNTING ADVENTURES IN THE NORTHERN
WILDS. By S. H. Hammond. Illustrated. Cloth. Price $1 75.

WILD NORTHERN SCENES. By S. H. Hammond, au-
thor of "Hunting Adventures in the Northern Wilds." Illustrated.
Cloth. Price $1 75.

FANNY HUNTER'S WESTERN ADVENTURES. Illustrated. 12mo., cloth. Price $1 75.

WONDERFUL ADVENTURES BY LAND AND SEA of the Seven Queer Travellers who met at an Inn. By Josiah Barnes. 12mo., cloth. Price $1 75.

THE EARLY DAYS OF CALIFORNIA. By Col. J. T. Farnham. 12mo., illustrated, cloth. Price $1 75.

NICARAGUA, PAST, PRESENT, AND FUTURE. By Peter F. Stout, Esq., late United States Vice-Consul. With a Map. 12mo., cloth. Price $1 75.

FEMALE LIFE AMONG THE MORMONS. By Maria Ward, the Wife of a Mormon Elder. Illustrated. 12mo., cloth. Price $1 75.

MALE LIFE AMONG THE MORMONS. By Austin N. Ward. Illustrated. 12mo., cloth. Price $1 75.

THE WHITE ROCKS; or, the Robber's Den. A Tragedy of the Mountains of thrilling interest. By A. F. Hill, author of "Our Boys," etc. 12mo., cloth. Price $1 75.

TUPPER'S COMPLETE POETICAL WORKS. With Portrait on steel. 12mo., cloth. Price $1 75.

THE YOUNG LADY'S OWN BOOK. An offering of Love and Sympathy. By Emily Thornwell. 12mo., cloth. Price $1 75.

SUNLIGHT AND SHADOW; or, the Poetry of Home. By Harry Penciller. 12mo., cloth. Price $1 75.

GREAT EXPECTATIONS. By Charles Dickens. With steel engravings. 12mo., cloth. Price $1 75.

THE SOLDIER AND THE SORCERESS; or, the Adventures of Jane Seton. 12mo., cloth. Price $1 75.

THE ORPHAN BOY; or, Lights and Shadows of Humble Life. By Jeremy Loud. 12mo., cloth. Price $1 75.

THE ORPHAN GIRLS. A Tale of Southern Life. By James S. Peacocke, M. D., of Mississippi. 12mo., cloth. Price $1 75

BOOK OF ANECDOTES AND JOKER'S KNAPSACK.
Including Witticisms of the late President Lincoln, and Humors, Incidents, and Absurdities of the War. 12mo., cloth. . Price $1 75.

WAY DOWN EAST; or, Portraitures of Yankee Life. By Seba Smith, the original Major Jack Downing. Illustrated. 12mo., cloth. Price $1 75.

THE LADIES' MEDICAL GUIDE AND MARRIAGE FRIEND. By S. Pancoast, M. D., Professor of Physiology in Penn Medical University, Philadelphia. With upwards of 100 illustrations. 12mo., cloth. Price $1 75.

BOYHOOD'S PERILS AND MANHOOD'S CURSE. An earnest appeal to the young men of America. By S. Pancoast, M. D. With numerous illustrations. 12mo., cloth. Price $1 75.

THE CURABILITY OF CONSUMPTION by Medicated Inhalation and Adjunct Remedies. By S. Pancoast, M. D. With illustrations. Cloth. Price $1 50.

THE AMERICAN TEXT-BOOK. Containing the Constitution of the United States, the Declaration of Independence, and Washington's Farewell Address. 24mo., cloth. Price 25 cents.

HORSE TRAINING MADE EASY. A New and Practical System of Teaching and Educating the Horse. By Robert Jennings, V. S. of the Veterinary College of Philadelphia, author of "The Horse and his Diseases," etc. etc. With illustrations. 16mo., cloth. Price $1 25.

THE HORSE AND HIS DISEASES. By Robert Jennings, V. S., author of "Horse Training Made Easy," etc. etc. With numerous illustrations. 12mo., cloth. Price $1 75.

CATTLE AND THEIR DISEASES. By Robert Jennings, V. S. With numerous illustrations. 12mo., cloth. Price $1 75. (Uniform with the above.)

SHEEP, SWINE, AND POULTRY. By Robert Jennings, V. S. With numerous illustrations. 12mo., cloth. Price $1 75. (Uniform with the above.)

EVERYBODY'S LAWYER AND COUNSELLOR IN BUSINESS. By Frank Crosby, Esq., of the Philadelphia Bar. 12mo. Price $1 75.

THE FAMILY DOCTOR; containing, in Plain Language, free from Medical Terms, the Causes, Symptoms, and Cure of Disease in all forms. By Henry S. Taylor, M. D. With illustrations. Cloth. Price $1 50.

MODERN COOKERY in all its Branches. By Miss Eliza Acton. Carefully revised by Mrs. S. J. Hale. With numerous illustrations. 12mo., cloth. Price $1 75.

THE EARLY MORN. An Address to the Young on the Importance of Religion. By John Foster. 24mo., cloth. Price 25 cts.

FAMILY PRAYERS. Adapted to every day in the week. By the late Rev. William Wilberforce. Cloth. Price 37 cents.

THE HISTORY OF PALESTINE from the Patriarchal Ages to the Present Time. By John Kitto. With illustrations. Cloth. Price $1 50.

THE WREATH OF GEMS. A gift book for the young of both sexes. By Emily Percival. Cloth. Price $1 50.

THE RAINBOW AROUND THE TOMB; or, Rays of Hope for those who Mourn. By Emily Thornwell. Cloth. Price $1 50.

THE LIFE OF OUR LORD AND SAVIOUR JESUS CHRIST, from his Incarnation to his Ascension into Heaven. By Rev. John Fleetwood, D. D. With steel and colored plates. Crown 8vo., library style. Price $4.

THE RELIGIOUS DENOMINATIONS IN THE UNITED STATES. Their History, Doctrine, Government, and Statistics. By Rev. Joseph Belcher, D. D., author of "William Carey, a Biography," and editor of the "Complete Works of Andrew Fuller," "Works of Robert Hall," etc. With nearly 200 engravings. Crown 8vo., library style. Price $4 50.

THE GOOD CHILD'S ILLUSTRATED INSTRUCTION BOOK. With more than sixty illustrations. Quarto, bound in cloth. Plain pictures, $1. Illuminated, $1 25.

THE LITTLE FOLKS' OWN BOOK. With sixty illustrations. Quarto, cloth. Plain pictures, $1. Illuminated, $1 25.

UNCLE JOHN'S OWN BOOK OF MORAL AND IN-
STRUCTIVE STORIES. With more than fifty illustrations. Crown
quarto, cloth. Plain pictures, $1 50. Illuminated, $2.

GRANDFATHER'S STORIES. With sixty illustrations.
Crown quarto. Plain pictures, $1 50. Illuminated, $2.

NATIONAL NURSERY TALES. With sixty illustrations.
Folio, bound in cloth. Plain pictures, $1 50. Illuminated, $2.

NATIONAL FAIRY TALES. With more than seventy
illustrations. Folio, cloth. Plain pictures, $1 50. Illuminated, $2.

THE LITTLE KITTEN STORIES. With fifty beautiful
illustrations. Folio, oloth. Plain pictures, $1 50. Illuminated, $2.

THE FUNNY ANIMALS. With more than sixty illustrations. Folio, cloth. Plain pictures, $1 50. Illuminated, $2.

OUR NINA'S PET STORIES. With fifty beautiful illustrations. Folio, cloth. Plain pictures, $1 50. Illuminated, $2.

FAMILY AND PULPIT BIBLES. Nearly sixty different
styles; with Family Record and with and without Photograph Record.
With clasps or otherwise, and ranging in price from $5 to $30.

JUVENILE AND TOY BOOKS. Embracing 150 varieties,
beautifully illustrated and adapted to the tastes of the little ones everywhere; at prices ranging from 10 cents to $2.

PHOTOGRAPH ALBUMS in every size and variety, hold-
ing from twelve to two hundred pictures, and ranging in price from 75
cents to $20.

Persons wishing a full catalogue of all our Books, Albums, and
Bibles, will please send two red stamps to pay return postage.

The trade everywhere supplied on favorable terms.

Address,   **JOHN E. POTTER & CO., Publishers,**
617 Sansom Street, Philadelphia.

www.ingramcontent.com/pod-product-compliance
Lightning Source LLC
Chambersburg PA
CBHW032337280326
41935CB00008B/366